BRAIN CHILD

Peggy Napear

BRAIN CHILD

A MOTHER'S DIARY

HARPER & ROW, PUBLISHERS

NEW YORK
EVANSTON
SAN FRANCISCO
LONDON

1817

BRAIN CHILD: A MOTHER'S DIARY. Copyright © 1974 by Peggy Wood Napear. All rights reserved. Printed in the United States of America. No part of this book may be used or reproduced in any manner whatsoever without written permission except in the case of brief quotations embodied in critical articles and reviews. For information address Harper & Row, Publishers, Inc., 10 East 53rd Street, New York, N.Y. 10022. Published simultaneously in Canada by Fitzhenry & Whiteside Limited, Toronto.

FIRST EDITION

INTERNATIONAL STANDARD BOOK NUMBER: 0-06-013156-X

LIBRARY OF CONGRESS CATALOG CARD NUMBER: 72-9141

Designed by Sidney Feinberg

TO MARY
who was unafraid
in the dark

AND TO JANE
who went along
like a dream

Contents

Acknowledgments

To Nat LaMar and Barbara Ellwood, who started me on this project; and to Abigail Angell and Frances McCullough, my editors at Harper & Row, who helped me finish it. Most of all, to my husband, Bert, who always said, "Go ahead, write. We'll manage it somehow." *He* was the one who managed, the one who shopped and cooked and did the laundry and took care of the family for hundreds of weekends during the five years it took to write this book.

And to the nearly two hundred other people who helped to get Jane well, whose contribution is priceless:

Lucy Aker, Louise Ames, Arel Anderson, Penny Anderson, Debbie Annabel, Sue Azer, Bonnie Baraban, Bob Barasch, Charlie Barasch, Barbara Barnhart, Marie Basius, Chris Beck (deceased), Donna Biddinger, Priscilla Boos, Mary Brower, Lori Brown, Kathy Burke, Patti Burke, Reenie Burke, Deane Butler, Gregg Butler, Jean Butler, Stan Butler, Brenda Castignola, Michael Castignola, Pat Chapman, Marion Charatan, Jill Cleary, Mary Cleary, Debbie Collins, Melanie Connors, Ruth Cooper, Sue Cytryn, Stella Dackowski, Robin Danziger, Barbara Davis, Isabelle Davis, Chris Dawson, Laurie Dawson, Muriel Dawson, Grace DeJose, Valerie DeJose, Kay Dewey, Emily Dobyns, Elaine Dominy, Anne Donovan, Diane Donovan, Joan Donovan, Robin Donovan, Pat Eastment, Ken Elligers, Muriel Emery, Claudia Figlia, Mae Fischer, Eudy Fishman, Janice Foley, Mildred Frohnhoefer, Barbara Geyer, Lewis ("Lou") Geyer, Beth Goldstein, Debbi Goldstein, Mimi Goldstein, Audrey Goodell, Debby Grant, Netta Grant, Eileen Green, Carol Greenbaum, Alice Gromisch, Barbara Groome.

Judy Haight, Sally Hansen, Fran Harris, Muriel Hartley, Kay Hendrickson, Edna Heyman, Virginia Hildebrandt, Mildred Hoover, Anita Hulley, Ruth Iffinger, Blanche Johansson, Helen Keith, Renie Kelman, Bob Klang, Fred Klang, Jane Klang, Miriam Klang, Moe ("Red") Klang, Janice Klein, Betsy Knortz, Lorraine Knortz, Stephen Knortz, Phil Kotik, Susan Kowalski, Nancy Kudder, Amy Kunstler, Richard Lalanne, Elma Lamont, Faith

Lamont, Suzy Lavery, C. C. Lee, Jo Leff, Alice Leuteman (deceased), Chris Leuteman, Lisa Leuteman, Tory Leuteman, Cathy Lovelock, Ruth Lovelock, Helen MacGregor, Liz McCormack, Maureen McManus, Marge McMillan, Fran Moschitto, Alice Mittelstaedt, Diana Molod, Nancy Morrison, Harriet ("Hat") Munro, Lucille Napear, Grant Napear, Stuart Napear, Virginia Nattrass, Amy Nelson, Cathy Nelson, Madeline Nettere, Vicki Noble.

Jane O'Connor, Margaret Pedersen, Jane Perlstein, Justin ("Jim") Perlstein, John Perlstein, Tom Perlstein, June Perlstein, Lisa Perrin, Maidli Perrin, Jane Pettigrew, Ellen Pitt, Nancy Popper, Dottie Reid, Elsie Reilly, Karin Reiner, Philippa Robin, Lisa Roebuck, Roberta Ross, Janet Roundy, Nancy Roundy, Beryl Russell, Carolyn Salemi, Bob Sancetta, Susan Schmidt, Ruth Schondelmeier, Jean Schwartz, Lorraine Schwartz, Martha Schwartz, Betsy Sheedy, Mary Sheedy, Sally Sheedy, Stuart Sheedy, Jessica Siegel, Chris Sleeper, Liz Sleeper, Louise Sleeper, Anna Stabler, Jim Steinert, Ebie Sturges, Gloria Suspenski, Marilyn Suspenski, Meryl Sutherland, Thelma Sutherland, Ken Taormina, Pat Terrosi, Mary Unruh, Kathy Voorhest, Bruce Wallace, Don Wallace, Gordon Wallace, Peggy Wallace, Tom Wallace, Laurie Watson, Claire Waugh, Joan Weber, Nancy Weber, Buddy Wechsler, Debby Wiggins, Mia Winter, Nita Winter, Tanja Winter, Myra Wood, Betty Woodruff, Holly Wynne, Betty Young, Sue Young, Cary Zissman.

Preface

This is the question they always ask and the one I want to answer right now: "When did you find out she's—," which meant, I learned, "Tell me what it's like to find out."

It was exactly as this diary has it. Nowhere is there a big moment when the family finds out. So don't look for it.

Three weeks too early—on January 22, 1962—we named her Jane Emerson after (of all people) Ralph Waldo Emerson, a favorite of ours. A little girl—premature, induced birth, and born with respiratory distress: hyaline membrane disease. But as the pediatric resident said, as I waited babyless on the rooming-in floor, they had had nine others that month and they all had lived. So did Janey. She got home about the same time she would have anyway—Valentine's Day.

Two and a half years before, the afternoon of baby Grant's arrival home, I had found three-year-old Stuart sitting in the screened crib, telling the sleeping form at his knees a story, a picture book opened on his lap.

With Jane there really weren't any cute stories. Most of the time Grant, now a big brother himself, waited for her to wake up. As we all did. I, especially, since I had kept my milk going the three weeks she was in the hospital nursery. I figured the least she could do was wake up and thank me, at least twice a day.

Three months later I stopped fighting with the family doctor about whether she was "getting enough" and weaned her to the bottle. We weighed her often at the doctor's office, and at home I charted the dribbles of milk forced in every two hours. An ounce of milk was cause for celebration once, I remember. Bert was telling everyone how girls were a heck of a lot more trouble than boys. Privately he and I lay awake at night wondering if she were blind or not. Something was wrong with her look. And finally, giggling nervously, I asked the doctor if he might have missed that in his evaluations, possible blindness. He said no, and don't look for trouble everywhere. Go on home and enjoy her.

A month later the doctor suggested we take her back to the hospital. Have them check her over. Give them the chart of the slight weight gain. Well, no wonder the little devil was a bundle of problems. She was hypothyroid. Actually she probably didn't have a thyroid gland at all! The "weight gain" was all edema—swelling of her hands and feet. Poor little thing. Four and a half months old and *still* a "preemie." The admitting doctor said it was a good thing the condition was caught before she was six months old; she would have *at least* average intelligence like other children.

It was the June fourth weekend, 1962, when I left her there and went home. Lifting an eighty-pound bag of fertilizer out of the station wagon, I tore the world right off its axis. Through the thunder and lightning I inched my way to the doctor's office for a slipped-disc diagnosis ("I could tell the minute you walked in!"), a shot of cortisone, a later appointment, and I was on my way again. I did give the doctor the results of the baby's hospital admission. Hm-m. A-thyroidism. Cretinism. Extremely rare. Apologized for not having detected it himself. Hadn't seen a case in twenty years. Hospitals see that sort of thing. We don't. Chat, about how one-fourth of a general practice these days is obesity. I know. My father was a G.P.

The baby picked up and began to grow, to eat, to see on the thyroid hormone, which was to be administered daily for the rest of her life. By mid-July she was home, for good this time. Well—for better or worse. I agreed with Bert. Girls *were* a lot different from boys. Not as bright-eyed and bushy-tailed. This one was so sweet and nice, I wanted to scream, *"Do* something. So I can do something. With you." Bert kept saying all that year and the next, it didn't seem right, her playing in the crib all day. Don't tell me what's right. The doctor told me not to pick her up from a playpen. Remember? To lift her as little as possible. Unless you want to see me back in the hospital traction-bit again. Anyway, she would cry or let us know with a whine or a whimper if she weren't happy in the crib, wouldn't she? And have you ever seen any baby so full of smiles?

Christmas of 1963 I had sprayed the old playpen a lovely off-white, lowered her into it, and showered her with rubber and plastic toys and all the kitchen utensils babies adore. One thing, she had a mind of her own. It was the key chain of plastic keys, Stu's Christmas present to her, she played with by the hour.

Grandmother returned to Chattanooga, leaving the baby a birthday gift—a walker, a new fancy one with a sling back she could sit up in without a prop. Those next six months she was busy getting cute as a button, so sociable, never still, pushing her walker to just anywhere she wished.

Bert and I were telling everyone we weren't finished with hospitals yet. Our medical bills were so high, even the Internal Revenue Service couldn't believe it. Sure enough. My three-week bout with nephritis and The New York Hospital's Internal Medicine Man (following a winter of strep throat) and the strep-prevention undertaken at home "in case," were only the prelude to all-three-down with chicken pox that spring of 1964.

One thing was better, the baby having a local pediatrician. The hospital's Pediatric Out-Patient Clinic had suggested it in 1963. Wouldn't we like to save the wear-and-tear of the trip all those miles to the hospital each month? Actually we were supposed to transfer to the Metabolic Clinic that day. Now they were suggesting we needn't come back again at all! A year of hospital waiting rooms (for monthly checkups) after her thyroid summer there, no, sir, we wouldn't miss it, and thank you.

The new pediatrician was nearby, with partner and back-ups, which was a great relief for all her colds and congestions too. Soon enough they suggested an eye exam and exercises for her legs. Walking was indeed past due. "She could either go to a cerebral palsy center or to a hospital for the exercises," the pediatrician said. "Why a cerebral palsy center?" I asked. "Because they have a physical therapy department there," he replied. It was up to me. So there we were, back at The New York Hospital, another department, after all. All Bert and I could think about was that she would see us in the poorhouse yet.

We moved through these first years with Jane, humming this sort of tune, laughing about it all.

We should have been crying. The crying was there, going on inside all the time, no doubt. ("I don't care if it's a boy or a girl. Just so it's healthy.")

One thing I learned later, when you're hurt, you protest.

There are a lot of ways to protest. At first, you can protest you aren't even hurt, because it's not even happening; this sort of thing simply wouldn't be happening to us. You can find "differences" in a child downright winsome, if you tend to sleepwalk that way. And if that isn't enough, you can attempt to straighten out the whole school district. There's always the White House needing a cleaning. And look at the shape the United Nations is in. It was the "family of man" that occupied most of our attention those days, as I remember. What could possibly (ever) be wrong in our family?

Be positive and take pride in whatever is promising. That's always a nice sleepy nook to wander around in. We found promise wherever we looked. We became expert lookers and finders, Bert and I. (Maybe the doctors too?) We simply looked over Jane's head (legs, eyes, you name it) and expected her to get on the ball. Watch it, young lady, we can just take so much. Don't rock the boat. Not now. (We are helping to organize a Human Rights group.)

Ah, the irony of that! It was weird how it worked out. To hold tight to Jane's normalcy, to find and confirm "smartness" over "slowness"—to The

New York Hospital (to myself?)—I noted all her "new" stuff. I inadvertently provided the first such notes recorded in the literature. And, too, the documentation for this story.

By sharing it, I hope that for once it will be possible to exclaim over the child and what he might become, to be awed by the human brain and what it may become.

And I hope too that perhaps the quality of literature about the so-called handicapped child, as well as the neurologically superior one, will increase. Perhaps it will from now on seem obsolete to publish a book about a *child* that at its best can offer only sympathy for and praise to the *parents*.

P.N.

PART I

The In-Between Time

1

From July 1964 to January 1965

JULY 23, 1964. Big Day. How to tell Bert tonight? That woman today at the hospital, Mrs. Lawrence. Was it a coincidence or was she looking for us?

Tell Bert about the baby first, then mention Stuart, what she said about Stuart. Now that we've got the baby out of the woods, we'll just have to think about our other child headed for trouble. Yes, Stuart. His speech. His *development*.

"You're making a mountain out of a molehill." That would be Bert's first reply. And about the baby, probably this: "Just like a girl! Don't try to figure 'em out, just enjoy 'em. Right, Girlus?" He'd be zooming the baby up to the sky, rafter-height, oh my, and back down again, swish. A few bounces on his arm as he stretches again for the full reach.

I'd be saying, "That's enough, Bert. She's hysterical, can't you see?"

"She loves it. All kids do. Remember the boys?"

"She seems scared to me— Anyway, it makes her hiccup. Trying to cry and breathe like that."

"She's not crying, she's laughing. Aren't you, Miss Hysterical?"

"Well, laughing makes her hiccup too. That's enough, don't you think? Anyway, supper's ready."

Or a different conversation with the same pattern.

And she'll hurry the walker after him to the bedroom with her legs in that X-push. "Scissored" the doctor last week called them. If she doesn't walk soon, every bit of paint will be banged off that hall corner. "Grant, help her. Push the walker around that— That's it. And give her something else to bang with. Give Daddy's keys back——"

Always that start-and-stop squealing, something back there thrilling the daylights out of her. Daddy's home. My biggest thrill too. Six-foot-four second team to keep up with Miss Perpetual-Motion-Machine through the highchair and bedtime routine.

But tonight *will be different*.

Set Bert the scene today, how The New York Hospital-Cornell Medical Center is a good place to feel lucky. Mention first my running into an old "friend"—one of the mothers Bert and I had heart-to-heart talks with that summer our babies were roommates-in-trouble. She still comes from the South with her child. Still keeps a watchful eye for anything that might cause a cut, cause him to bleed to death. I told her I'd collected for hemophilia each year, and thought of him. Should have bitten my tongue off first. My do-gooding was like some grain in her sandbox, I sensed.

Both of us today were exchanging luckies, compared to some. My baby growing so well now on thyroid. Just got into the habit, put the pills into her dessert each night. Never skip a day. You get used to it. Same with her. Watches him all the time without thinking about it. Had she seen any of the other parents? I hadn't either. Reminisced. Those two mothers whose babies were born brain-damaged, how they brought *toys* to theirs too, all summer like that. Talked to them as they fed them, played with them after. How that day when mine was getting a blood transfusion (some low red-blood thing all of a sudden), I didn't want them to see my crying, they were so cheerful all the time. Remembering today the one whose baby had the horrible lopsided head, how she cradled and cuddled it just the same. And the illegitimate baby with *no* mother to visit. Brain-damaged also. What would they do with it? Not adoptable, of course. No one to claim him. And one of "those" mothers coming over to cradle him, saying, "He really has a personality, this one!" Bert and I were feeling guilty and small; we couldn't even bear to look at him! Hemophilia-mom was saying today, "Let's face it; I couldn't either."

Bert should see what other people go through on this floor. Physical Medicine and Rehabilitation. How dependent the life is here. Old stroke patients, waiting their turn on tables. And a girl, undeveloped or something, who could have been eight or eighteen, hard to tell. So thin, so pale, her legs were like white sticks above heavy high-top shoes. Just half-human, sitting in that oversized strollerlike chair, with a thing to hold her head up. Her mother was thin and pale too, her life drained into the care and feeding of this one child.

Waiting rooms are all the same though, too small. I pushed the baby in a little circle, watching all the feet retreat. Motion is the best medicine. How she hates the hospital. How I could too, but I don't. I'll tell you someday, how it saved your life, more than once. How babies were dying those years of hyaline membrane respiratory distress, even the Kennedys' Patrick. But they pulled you through.

How first you were blue. And that French nurse in the delivery room got angry, red-hot, and yelled, "This time I want a doctor to stay, right here, and watch this with me." And "Don't leave this room until you see what I'm seeing on and off." And I was thinking something silly about pink and blue, baby colors. Or pink *or* blue. But never pink *then* blue, pink, blue. And they were whisking you off to pediatrics.

And then you were yellow. "Jaundiced," they called it. And then, "hypotonic, no muscle tone." One night when Daddy and I came to the glass, you were back in the isolet, the oxygen thing for preemies. A lifeless chicken-look to you. We both said soft things to each other, trying to make it all real. Trying to grab you back, to come live with us. Trying to send little messages. Through our glass, your glass, through that tube down your mouth, here to there, to a slight breathing down there. Letting you know we *wanted* you. A little girl. Daddy and I whispering how we now had a little girl. Turning around and going back somewhere, before we'd even had a chance to hold her and help her. Standing there at that glass pulling your breathing into ours. Still breathing. Still breathing. I kept thinking, "still breathing" all the way to the hotel where I was waiting for you. And in the morning you moved. "There she was—moving and kicking a little— when we saw her this morning on rounds," the resident called to tell me. Today look at you, one of the lucky ones, pink and soft in your rosebud smocking.

Tell Bert it was a good choice to go back to the same hospital for the exercises the pediatrician suggested. That woman today was very interested in the baby and Stuart both.

Not like the quick visit here last week to have the doctor of physical medicine and rehabilitation (physiatrist, he's called) check the baby over and order the leg exercises. Said you had other tightness too—tight knees, tight elbows, neck not tight enough I gathered, hip adductors too-some-thing—and those ankles that haven't even learned to move yet! How long before she could walk? It was hard to tell. How long does it usually take, approximately—weeks, months—the general time is usually what? Would depend on how well she reacted to the treatments, my exercising her at home. And he was out the door with that Germanic stride of his, leaving the student physical therapist to teach me. To be done three times a day. And I asked to come back today, to check *me,* before we left for Maine and tried to do exercises I never even heard of before.

But today was quite different. This woman was in no hurry. Stood there in the doorway, just looking at the baby. White starched uniform. No hat. Completely ignored the PT student and me, lifting the baby's leg up from the table a bit to stretch the tight tendon back of the knee. Hamstrings tight. Gastroc (calf) muscle too short, too tight, and I don't know-what-all. Then the other leg. Baby still crying. Keep stretching. A little more each time. Go just beyond the "point of resistance," feel that rubber-bandlike resistance, and go just into it and leave off. Ten this week, three times a day like the other. More next week. And so on. Baby's reaction not what they expected, I guess. Cries the whole time here too. Resistance is more than any little old rubber band.

Say something, before I cry myself. "I'll get her used to it. Singing, you know. Don't worry. We'll learn it. I just can't stand to see her frightened like this." Singing into her ear, hugging her head in my hands. "She hates all of it—even the easier exercises, opening her arm out at the elbow or pulling her up from the bed at the neck to get her sitting started—all of it. Hates to lie down, you see. Bed just as bad as a table. A real phobia about lying down on *any* of it." I looked up. The woman in white was still watching.

Started the heel-cord exercise. Trying to stretch the Achilles tendon so the ankle could learn to move. "I bet *this* will take awhile." No one answered. Lady in white moving over to our table without a word. Head down. Holding a chart: JANE NAPEAR. Head down staring at the—baby's face? More interested in the way she was acting than her legs, I was thinking. Apologizing, wiping the baby's tears, I began outlining the baby's "case" against this place—against the doctors, the halls, even the tables. "She's been on so many here." Made a nervous remark about the passive exercises (their name!) not "passivefying" her at all, with no one laughing and the baby still bawling.

The lady in white suddenly moved down to my end of the table, *"Let* her cry." And as an afterthought almost, "I'm Mrs. Lawrence." Seemed more interested in the baby's mouth than in the legs I'm moving in "bicycles"— "reciprocal motion."

She asked if Jane sits up yet, and I told her not yet, grateful for the "yet." Added the baby is now starting to walk, however, holding onto the sofa or crib. It looks like a circus act, so funny. Cute, though, the way she tries: way *up* on her toes, way *down* otherwise, fanny in back where her knees are out front! Looks like a Z. And her legs are an X. But she manages beautifully—all the way down the sofa and back.

She asked if Jane talks and I said again, not yet. A lot of children don't talk at two and a half, and the doctors don't expect her to catch up until about four. She'll be slower for awhile. Premature, you know. "Kept moving her from table to table for all sorts of things, bone age, spinal tap, blood transfusion—I think that's when this table phobia started."

Mrs. Lawrence was saying something about "maybe visual" (or "may be visual"?), then asked about Jane's floor activities as a baby. Whether Jane ever did any crawling or creeping. Stopped looking at the baby, and turned to me.

"I bet I know why you're asking that."

"You do?" (Knew that would surprise her.)

"I think I do. I read an article in *Life* last year about crawling and creeping—about that place in Philadelphia."

"What did you think of it?" That's when she invited me into her office. "I'm Supervisor of Therapy Services here and with it comes the office!" Told the PT student to find a toy for Jane.

A rattle, something with noise, I suggested. Or maybe someone could stroll her around. "She's fine if she's moving."

"Don't worry. Jane will get undivided attention. We're all little-girl crazy up here. Most of our patients are adults."

"I noticed." (Maybe that's why the big interest in Jane?)

Mrs. Lawrence really wanted to know. What did I think about that article? Most of it was about brain-damaged children, but I thought the part about stuttering was very interesting.

"Stuttering? You were most interested in the stuttering?" She turned around, bringing file folders to her desk. "May I ask why?"

I told her about Stuart. Stammers, I guess you'd call it. Has for five years, since he was three, almost since he started talking. On and off. For weeks maybe not at all. Then in a stammering "period," some *days* not at all. It's the weirdest thing. Very interesting the adults in that article—was it *fifty* people from the same company?—stopped stuttering after all those years, after changing their brains or whatever they did. "I almost wrote for an appointment for him!"

"Why didn't you?"

I told her the truth. Changing your brain is pretty weird—And as a physician's daughter, I'd been raised to avoid advice over the back fence and from magazine articles. Never know, might be some magic-pill quack-approach.

She didn't say anything. (Acts interested in everything I say, but not chatty.) I explained Stuart was on the waiting list to see the school psychologist. Teachers say since his stuttering does not affect his school work—he's grade-level—the other kids come first.

What did *she* think about that place, what's its name? And what does stuttering have to do with the brains you've got?

I don't remember everything that was said in the next two hours. But tell Bert how she thinks the brain is very interesting—that's all she talks about. How she's on the waiting list herself. To get trained there! Didn't get in the last class for professionals. Maybe September. She's been down there quite a bit though, and she's interested in their approach to child development.

"What are you? A psychologist?"

No—a physical therapist! Arms and legs. Interested in this new approach to the brain, that works the arms and legs. Twice she said the same phrase, "whole child, not the bits and pieces." Does she mean the arms and legs are pieces?

Very interested in Jane *and* Stuart. I talked about my not picking the baby up from a low place that year and a half. How she was very happy, though, to stay in the crib. I only put her out in the living room when grandparents were there. So they could see what she was doing, you know.

My father-in-law mentioned her legs didn't seem to be developing right that first Christmas. Kept on and on about it. Made me mad. She'd been through so much, stop pushing. Bert told him to mind his own business. The best doctors see her every month at the hospital's Well-Baby Clinic; she's *got* "specialists," so stop making a mountain out of a molehill. Give her a chance, forchrissakes!

"But you say she did a little crawling?" Asked me to "get down here" and show her. "Just do it like Jane did it." I was bunny-hopping all around her office, and not too embarrassed either. Then she told me, "Actually that's not crawling. That's *creeping*. You're on hands and knees. Homologous creeping." Spelled it for me even. Means two arms move forward (step) together, then two legs move forward (step) together. (If Jane had done it on her stomach—can't remember—it would be homologous crawling.)

I was panting and laughing, "I've been calling it 'bunny-hopping.' "

Both of us laughing. Mrs. Lawrence said, "Can't you just see it. One mother turning to another on the block, 'My baby creeps homologously now.' "

She was watching me, saying something about, "One of these days mothers may take great pride in the kinds of crawls and creeps they are seeing at home."

"You mean there are kinds of creeps?"

She just smiled. During all that time of a baby's life, he's organizing all the kinds of movement there are—homologous, homolateral, cross-pattern. (Cross-pattern is really what we call "follow-through" in tennis.) And he's actually organizing his brain! His whole central nervous system has a step-by-step organization to it.

It's not a haphazard kind of organization, The Philadelphians discovered. There's a certain sequencing of movement—of crawls and creeps. A baby gets coordinated *before* he walks. Or not. Because many children don't get all the steps finished. With blotchy sequencing, you get a blotchy bunch of systems going for you. The first year of life is the most important because more happens brain-wise than in the next five to six years.

And I always thought the first year of life was pretty much a drag. Me and everybody else apparently. So the baby gets a drag year, and gets a lousy foundation for all the stuff to come later.

"Like what?"

"Like walking, talking, reading, writing—" Other things about seeing sharply, hearing—"listening" she changed it to—and all about getting the five senses "used" in their sequences. Lot of stuff about the baby needing to "use" his old brains. Mentioned the amphibian life of a baby, then the reptile life, crawling then creeping the way movement evolved long, long ago. Evolution, for heaven's sakes—toddlers beginning to walk, following along the ape-to-man look of arms and legs.

She wants Jane to get all that development she's missed. Think about walking *after* she can do the things that come before.

Remind Bert: You're not born walking and talking. Some preparatory stuff comes first. That's what those people in Philadelphia started taking a look at twenty years ago. What does come before walking in babies? One thing is reciprocal motion—"bicycles," moving one leg, then the other. Jane can only move both legs at the same time. Try to get the separation, left then right, from creeping instead of that passive exercise.

Get other things too if we can. Use arms, hips, trunk, neck, eyes—everything—together, the way a baby does it.

Then drop the flare, and hope Bert doesn't laugh. Leave her on the floor all day! Only pick her up to diaper her, feed her, or love her!

"She wouldn't be able to do that, Mrs. Lawrence."

"There's any number of clever devices to help keep her down and on course." That's exactly what she said. Telling about an "outrigger" to keep her on her front side, "So she can't roll over on her back *or stand up*——"

"You don't understand. This baby wouldn't do any of that. She loves the walker all day, pushing from room to room. Very busy banging around after me. She's very sociable! And she can't bear to be on her stomach. She'd just cry!"

"Yes, but then soon she'd get tired of crying and might move off to explore . . . under the beds . . . places she's never really seen before . . . things she hasn't heard before. Gradually she would find more and more to explore. You might try it outdoors the first day or two, where it's cooler. You could make knee pads, have her just wear shorts for the summer." She was quite serious.

"Tell me about stuttering——"

Stuttering, the research in Philadelphia shows, is a little war going on in the brain, a competition between the two halves, the hemispheres, of the brain. *Every* child stutters early in his childhood, but only for a little while. Then about the age of three one hemisphere starts getting more dominant than the other, one hand is used more than the other, the foot on that side is used more to kick a ball or to step off with, the eye on that side naturally is used more with that hand, that foot. When he begins to get a dominant side, he begins to get a dominant hemisphere (the opposite hemisphere actually). And he stops stuttering. From three to six his preferred side is increasingly established. That is the final stage, the finish, to the whole birth-to-six child brain-wise. It's the icing on the cake, neurologically speaking.

This final stage of brain organization does not always happen automatically. A lot of things can go wrong, activities mostly. The environment (for the brain) a child gets. Such as, limited floor activities for the baby. Maybe the present bike culture, where a little fellow is constantly using both sides of his body. (Girls fortunately get more eye-hand opportunities: stirring on the play stove, drawing, bean-bag games, hopscotch with that pretty piece of glass. But boys are busy gymnasts, tacklers and blockers, king of the mountain. Who can run the fastest? Who can climb the highest?) It's quite easy for a boy to miss this final step. He remains more the two-year-old, two-sided (bilateral) child he was. Doesn't come out to be the six-year-old, smoothly one-sided (unilateral) one. Neurologically he isn't six. Socially, of course, he may be a prince. A prince who stutters.

All this was making more sense out of Stuart. Would teachers agree? They were all so reluctant to send him to the psychologist anyway. Bright, interesting, enthusiastic student. Well liked. Last Wednesday the ophthal-mologist called him a "mature lad" with "good social presence for his age." I laughed that day. I was just getting him lined up to see a psycholo-gist about his stuttering. The eye doctor said why not sit down and discuss it with *him?* "He's that kind." Why a psychologist? And then I mentioned it might be something else, and the *Life* article. The doctor had read it too, said "I gave a shout for joy. It confirms what I have observed in fifteen years of clinical experience. There is, I have always thought, a correlation between the eyes and the clumsy child, the incoordinate ones. I see it all the time." Something like that. All this came up twice in the same week!

Very important to tell Bert this: stuttering is not in the lips, or tongue, or vocal chords. Or the mother! It's speech. And speech is in the brain. Stresses *can* affect the brain, Mrs. Lawrence was saying, can affect speech; notice people stuttering on the telephone when they're not sure how they're "going over." But a person who is neurologically well organized has a stronger bunch of systems going for him, and can take more stress before *his* speech gets shaky.

Mrs. Lawrence says there is an eighteen-month waiting list at Phila-delphia for the more seriously involved child. They would probably see Stu's case a lot sooner. Might at the same time ask for an appointment for the baby too.

Jane's coordination? Stuart's brain? Tell Bert about Jane first. And just keep on talking about coordination. How the line in football—listen to this—is a bilateral sport. How the backfield is a unilateral sport. Some sports have components of both. And did he realize Stu is best in the bilateral ones? I know, he makes "outstanding" in Physical Education, but Mrs. Lawrence says most gym is bilateral. And try to think of one thing Stu is even interested in that has eye-hand going for a target. You can't. We should have given him a gun all those years, backyard-brainwashing-for-peace notwithstanding.

Stuart and Grant will squawk and throw a body-block or two about the Maine vacation delay. Should Bert be the one to tell them that we have to get the baby squared away in her new floor life? Here first, then try it in Maine. Promise the boys Jones Beach Sunday.

JULY 24, 1964. So humiliating the way Jane acts in a strange place. That man even thought she was *unhealthy*. I didn't even bother to explain her beginnings to him. He meant no harm, but it's her business if she hates hospitals! This one is the Hospital for Special Surgery. Special surgery? Wasn't it all? Better than the historical name still chiseled there: THE SOCIETY FOR THE RELIEF OF THE RUPTURED AND THE CRIPPLED.

Mrs. Lawrence was explaining our problem at the window to the brace shop. Would one of the men figure it out with this mother?

Yesterday's phone call to get an outrigger from The Institutes in Philadelphia was just one long wait. Got a director finally. No, The Institutes gave out no information unless they had seen the child. And, no, he couldn't tell me where to get one. It was simple to make one if I gave the idea—the functional idea—to a craftsman. Red tape. He'd send me an application for my child to be seen there. Make it two, please. Waiting for thirty minutes, talking for one.

At noon to the window man again, this time louder and bolder. He went into the workroom. All of them shook their heads. The baby was bawling and banging herself left and right against the stroller sides. Then a man came out.

I explained: to help her to creep before she walked, you see. Would have to be lightweight, yes. Some inch-wide hollow aluminum stuff. Fine. Bend angles into it to come down off the back and out for the tail. A piece across the waist and down and out for the sides. Together a T. That's it.

Holding her in my arms, I watched him working over the flame. Gently, gently, now bending, gently. He was proud and relieved too.

"What do you call this?" and he looked up for the first time.

"An outrigger, I think that's what they call it at The Institutes for the Achievement of Human Potential."

"You lost me there. What's that name?"

"The Institutes for the Achievement of Human Potential—in Philadelphia."

"Never heard of it." Smiling and turning his head, slowly side to side. "Well, I wish you all the— Well, I hope it goes well for the little girl there. I'll have this ready for you Monday."

First child to ever get an outrigger there? First child Mrs. Lawrence suggested the floor for—to get legs to separate left-right? Was the baby different somehow?

And now Stuart, please.

Mrs. Lawrence was very reluctant to take a look at him. She could determine his handedness and footedness, but not eyedness. Says she's very insecure in that area, and also doesn't know anything about stuttering. A mysterious phenomenon. She's often wondered about people who work in that area and the results they get.

According to The Institutes his symptoms indicate he does not have dominance. Someone needs to determine whether he is bilateral *enough* before giving him a program to "encourage his natural unilaterality." She's not trained to do that. Yet . . .

I'm talking fast. Begging, but who cares? "You just couldn't imagine how crucial it's becoming—he's getting older—his friends are older." Playmates had noticed his speech. That day in the sandbox, I quieted them with, "Stuart is learning so many new questions to ask and is learning to put it all into words!" That was three or four years ago. Soon they would murder him with mocking.

Finally she agreed to give him some things to do in Maine to brush up his bilateral activities, his two-sidedness. It certainly could do no harm.

JULY 27, 1964. Took the children to the hospital to meet Mrs. Lawrence. Stuart liked her: those hazel eyes always tell it honestly. Mrs. Lawrence was talking to him as if he were older. He does seem older than eight.

She said she'd like to see him creep, get down on hands and knees and move around like a baby. His mom and she were not sure whether he'd gotten enough of it as a baby.

Stuart was smiling, slowly, surely.

Then she hit the target square on. He had a hesitation in his speech—a stutter. Had he ever noticed? Well, he did. And to have smooth speech and smooth ability on the ball field, a person needed (for one thing) to have smooth cross-pattern ability. Had he ever heard of "follow-through?" The leg steps out and the opposite hand follows through at the exact same time. Yes, like in pitching. He would tell her all about it. Whitey Ford was his closest friend, it seemed.

Mrs. Lawrence demonstrated precisely how to practice creeping in cross-pattern. Wrote all the components down, so he could check himself as he practiced. How the hand and knee will "step" together, exactly together, and make a habit eventually. A reflex. Why not do an hour a day of it while he was in Maine? Maybe three sessions, twenty minutes each. Also filled him in on the rest of a program to achieve strong bilaterality in case he didn't have two good sides. Use two arms, two legs, also two ears, two eyes—so everything works together. Something like that. Perhaps when The IAHP in Philadelphia saw him he would be ready for a program to get one-sided . . . smooth . . . dominance.

As for the baby, in three days I had made a white duck romper suit that looked awful but fit beautifully down to the snap-fastener crotch. And four pairs of knee pads out of padded pot holders and wide elastic. And purchased the clothesline cord to run from the heel of one shoe to the other shoe through the ring on the baby suit's derriere.

I even had the large back zipper in and the three three-inch zippers sewed on to hold the outrigger to the baby's back. The brace-shop man had charged me only fifteen dollars, including the insertion of the steel loops in the heels of the shoes I had just bought her—the orthopedic ones the doctor of physical medicine (physiatrist, I'm getting it) had prescribed last week. All this—romper suit, outrigger and harness line—to keep her down, prone, and on course.

JULY 28, 1964. Notes to show Mrs. Lawrence (Baby doing it already?).
Yesterday, 4:00 to 7:00 P.M.:
Indoors: Baby struggled at first, kneeled, arched on head and looked under legs a lot. (Intrigued by the outrigger tail trailing behind?) Crawled (or crept, which is which?) arms together first, legs scooting together second most of time. Pulled with arms to knee position onto furniture. (Mrs. Lawrence, isn't this supposed to keep her completely down?)
Outdoors: Baby cross-creeping over grass. A few times. (Three times for sure.) Once in a while separates legs a little, inch or two, moves one then the other. Doing it already? Bet it's harder to slide knees together over the grass in bunny hops (homologous ~~creep,~~ ~~crawl,~~ creep)! Lying prone most of the time. Resting? Hard work? And crying and crying. Weak and tired.

At seven we were both crying, and I brought her in and sat on the sofa loving her. More than ever before. I, her mother, rescuer in uneasy situations. Was she looking at me strangely? Hard to tell in her eyes. If tomorrow wasn't better, I vowed we wouldn't do it anymore, but go on to Maine.
Today, on and off all day:
Whiney but no crying. Mostly the two arms, two legs crawl (creep?). Cross-pattern occasionally, especially when she has to go over raised doorsill or outdoors on grass.

Pulled up on knees on walls and furniture. Outrigger thing doesn't keep her down completely; probably lousy romper suit. If it weren't for the harness line, just long enough to allow one knee to move ahead in crosspattern, I bet she'd be up on furniture all the time. Rested prone a lot. Also went from room to room and seemed to enjoy it. No other activity, but I took it off to feed her, change her, and love her, like Mrs. Lawrence said. Took my time about it, to break her in gradually.

Leaving for Maine tomorrow, and we're all champing at the bit.

Asked Bert about going with us now instead of last weeks. Can't, too much office mess. Doris W. and son coming later—good. Originally I had said, "in case of snakebite." Someone to go for help in that wilderness. Now the need is companionship. Or compassion. Have to tell Doris and David W. the truth—that Stuart and the baby are learning to creep in cross-pattern. It's clued in somehow to the midbrain, the reptile brain still in us. Give Doris a drink first.

JULY 30, 1964. Maine. Such beauty here. Such buoyance in us all. Pancakes? Of course. And the mess? Strange. Messes in Maine are called fun. How we've needed Maine these past two years.

Notes for Mrs. Lawrence:

Baby: No crying, having fun on large, bare cabin floor. Cross-pattern creeping a lot of the time. Stops to play with metal wastebaskets, rolls them around. Noise is deafening. Loves noise, this girl.

Very excited when she gets on knees and pulls herself up to a standing position at walls and furniture. Notice she uses right hand for objects in her path.

No other activity today—just the floor. Mrs. Lawrence would be impressed.

Stuart: Worked out a schedule for *his* "special activities," and posted them on the kitchen door camp-style.

Perrin children here early today on their bikes. Loved the trampoline! Telling Stu and Grant, "You're lucky!"

Janet came over later to gather her brood. Sitting on back steps with coffee, watching the trampoline fun, we got into and stayed on subject of crawling and creeping. Talked about Billy, the do-everything child. Remembered three summers ago when Janet and I were pregnant together. How much Bert and I had been through since, getting Jane out of the woods. Bert rented the Maine house for the whole month this time, as "our reward." When you get through a bad time, you're allowed to double-treat yourselves.

Billy only four months older than Jane. But Billy *is* amazing for his age, riding bikes and all. Even Janet said so.

AUGUST 1, 1964. Baby outdoors, out of reach of furniture. Good idea. Cross-pattern creeping (whenever I looked) for three hours in the morning. Into the blueberry bushes and laughing!

Afternoon indoors. Able to raise torso up despite outrigger occasionally, big deal to look at reflection in French-door glass. Would cross-creep to move to another area. I wonder if Mrs. Lawrence expected J. so quickly to learn to creep in cross-pattern, to start immediately to separate hands and knees.

Never moves on her stomach (crawling). Moves forward only on hands and knees (creeping). But she does rest on her stomach when tired, head to one side like Mrs. Lawrence said babies do. True, the bottom eye is against the floor, so she must be using the top eye to see with. Forgot to watch if this is done alternately so each eye gets *equal* workout. Check tomorrow.

At 4:00 P.M. put J. on the trampoline for diversion when some whineyness started while the boys and I played ball. She was on her stomach at first, but then learned to bounce on her knees (a little) holding onto the frame . . . two happy hours, content with that constant motion.

Spent one hour at lake without outrigger. When moving she used crosspattern creep over the sand a couple of times (I think) but mostly sat on her knees putting stone-filled fists into her mouth, then plunking rocks into water. So wary of the water but interested, I think. I expect she'll try moving into it soon.

Grant's freckles are so run together now, his face is just that much more orange below the hair. Peaceful with his sailboat, shy and cautious, he always seems as if he's in a corner, even in the wide expanse of lake and beach.

Stuart is kicking and noisy without rest. Glad Mrs. Lawrence's program says swim a lot.

AUGUST 2, 1964. Doris and David made it over all the dirt roads to find this place, in a taxi from Conway, New Hampshire!

I gave up trying to explain to Doris about the old brainstem, the amphibian and reptile "brains" we have, and gave her the *Life* article describing crawling and creeping movements of those animals. We talked and talked about babies missing these evolutionary movements—some, no doubt, because of playpen, carriage, stroller, car seat and infant seats and holders of all kinds. All in hysterics trying to say, "ontogeny recapitulates phylogeny."

Stuart surprised us by asking what does "ontogeny" mean? I said, "The way a baby grows." Fortunately he didn't ask about phylogeny. Describing the evolution of the species is something I'd rather not ruin a sunny day with.

AUGUST 5, 1964. Today Doris, the sport, got down to creep with Stuart. Made flattering remarks about his guts and stamina to do this three times a day. Told me afterward she didn't know which was worse, the creeping or that record, "It's a Small, Small World." (Mrs. Lawrence said ten minutes listening to music for binaural activity [both ears stuff], but Stu insists on its going the whole twenty minutes, over and over. Times three sessions, ugh.)

AUGUST 9, 1964. Bert and Lucille arrived at noon. Bert came crashing through the woods, calling to the boys, "Well, hi. How's the gang? Just passed Chris Perrin headed this way. On his bike. Think I scared him a little. Close shave——"

"Chris is *here!* That was probably Billy."

"Hey, Dad. Bring anything? Hi, Aunt Lu!"

Bert taking the back porch steps in one, "Hey, everybody." Shaking his head, "If that was Billy Perrin, he looks exactly like Chris did. Wasn't he born the year Jane was?"

"That kid is unbelievable, Bert. He's only four months older. I can't get over it myself."

Lu saying, "That kid on the bike is Jane's age? His mother must be ready for the funny farm——"

"Oh, he's great, Lu. Very self-sufficient. Interesting. Happy. Just very advanced in what he can do."

I took Lu in the canoe through the narrow passageway from our lake. Saw the girls from Blazing Trail Camp learning to sail, and counselors getting more pursed-lipped by the moment. Last week they had passed our beach, all staring at the child down on all fours with some steely contraption on her back.

Back on the pier, Lu pointed out that for two hours we hadn't mentioned creeping—cross-pattern or otherwise. She didn't know it, but I'd been thinking all the time about the baby, back in our suburban neighborhood, creeping around on the ground with the outrigger on her back for all to see. Did it look cruel? Well, it wasn't. Wish I could hang a sign on it: DON'T WORRY. WEIGHS ONLY A POUND AND A HALF.

We sat at the fire till all hours talking about crawling and creeping and playpens and brain, outlining Stu's bi-everything programs. Binaural . . . me reading. Stu listening without looking at the book . . . and just how could you possibly listen *without* using two ears? Stuart begged me to read from *Wind in the Willows* "for Aunt Lucille." So I read it aloud and let the boys stay up extra late for hot chocolate. We ignored the baby's banging away, as she scooted the crib almost across the bedroom. Bert wedged the crib between the wall and the table, and with another bottle she finally went to sleep.

AUGUST 11, 1964. Picked nine quarts on "Blueberry Mountain" yesterday. Coming down the steep part, Stu insisted on carrying berries. He's always been a climber—loves to show it, picking his way over rocks and crevices. Grant picking his way too—literally. *Ate* everything in sight, up and back to the ski lift. This year Grant complained less about the hiking part. Five is much older than four, thank goodness.

Left J. at cabin with Sue, the oldest Roundy girl. Before we left, I explained very matter-of-factly, not once looking into her eyes, that J. was to stay on the floor or ground outdoors wearing outrigger, etc. Showed her how to zip it on and off. Knee pads would keep falling down. Just let them. Her knees were getting calloused. That was good . . . exercise for her legs and it was good for her . . . keep her face wiped off, if it bothers you . . . pick her up for lunch and diapering only . . . ignore her and let her find her interests of the day . . . don't entertain her. The floor and ground would do that. It sounded good and I ran out, not daring to look back or think.

It worked! It really worked. Sue said J. had so much fun, spent a lot of time banging a spoon against metal wastebaskets. She was amazed at how J. loved crawling—I corrected, "creeping"—outside on the pine needles and into the bushes "in that thing"—I corrected, "outrigger." As if we had owned one all our lives. She'd be glad to sit again. Hallelujah!

Later on we took Lu to Portland Airport. Jane was awful in Bert's arms, so he put her down on the floor. Bunny-hopped all around, so took her outside to the concrete, figuring without knee pads she'd stay still. Don't predict with this little one! Bunny-hopped—Mrs. Lawrence would say "crept homologously"—into everyone's path. Bert picked her up again and tried to interest her in the airplane taxiing toward us. She never looked at it, even though Grant, crushed, kept saying, "See the airplane, a big airplane, Janey." Bert said he didn't think she could see that far. I said she wasn't interested in airplanes, and she was active and always liked to be moving.

AUGUST 16, 1964. Stuart's stuttering is worse, much worse. He's gagging, it seems. Just a humming sound comes out before the sentence.

Every day now, and it hasn't been this bad since he was four—at nursery school. Yes, it was worse at four than at three. And now it's worse at eight!

But it doesn't seem to bother him. Is he aware at all that he does it? Keeps right on talking, and he certainly likes to talk.

Nighttimes I find myself lying awake pulling for this sweet boy. Same way, same feeling, as when the baby was in trouble. Is this prayer? When you promise your right arm? As if *that* would help any.

Daytimes I do what Bev Howe, his nursery school teacher, said to do four years ago. Put down what I am doing, look him in the eyes and listen, for as long as it takes. Do not help him in any way. It's a habit after all these years. Why do I go through all that freeze-and-listen stuff? He truly seems unaware and just "gags" it out. After he's finished talking (stuttering), he never lowers his eyes or looks embarrassed or says anything like, "Boy, am I having trouble talking!" He would, too, if he were aware of it. Other times he seems interested in "the subject" of his speech difficulty.

The truth is that stuttering is not on his priority list. Playing with the gang is. Knowing the answer to the question is. And in these two areas he's O.K. So I come to two conclusions: (1) I don't think he hears himself stutter. (2) He doesn't know yet it is an unacceptable characteristic.

If the two hemispheres of his brain are in competition with each other, then this month they are, for some reason, warring more than ever. But why?

AUGUST 21, 1964. Bert is supervising Stuart's creeping now after lunch and supper. I still play the toll-booth game during the after-breakfast creep session. (When Stuart and Grant are not at golf with Bert.) I sit under the drop-leaf table in the corner and say encouraging things to the "driver" as he creeps through the "gate" each round trip. Ask where he's been, which "city" he's going to—usually Chattanooga, or Tokyo or Yankee Stadium. I change myself to gas-station attendant: tap him on the thigh and squirt five gallons in or wipe his forehead-windshield. It's so unusually hot here that I took to wiping his windshield with a cool washcloth.

We change Stu's creeping road each day, using wicker chairs in an off-beat manner. Decided against curves since his creeping is better and feet drag behind him more consistently if he doesn't have to think about turning. He's progressed from using any knee pads at all to only blue jeans.

We hardly have to remind him of the specifics anymore: his knee base is always good, about eight to twelve inches apart. His fingers are flat and together, but the thumb is not close to hand yet without a reminder. Does focus his eyes on his forward hand, as it precedes him. And I can see the head-neck gently moving on the trunk in a slight left-to-right manner. This tells me that his eyes are shifting smoothly left to right and back to left, and so on. Does better if I only talk to him at the toll booth. He's certainly moving as Mrs. Lawrence showed us. It looks pretty, a sort of streamlined movement, all the appendages gliding together that way. Serialized, Mrs. Lawrence calls it.

The baby has a long way to go to creep this well, but obviously no problem in the long run. Already she's moving right hand with left knee. And vice versa. But, of course, not exactly together the way Stu does it. Lower legs and feet aren't yet beginning to trail. Still up in the air and scissored above her when she's creeping. And her knees are too far apart and she wobbles. Fingers are curved, not yet flat to the ground. But she is definitely moving in cross-pattern, left knee with opposite hand, etc. That is, with the outrigger. Without it—at the beach—she is still a bunny-hopper.

AUGUST 25, 1964. Finished *Wind in the Willows*. Stuart had tears in his eyes as he had when I read him the part about Otter waiting and watching every night by the river bank for Portly, who maybe had not drowned and who *might* come wandering back. Started another book, but Stuart wasn't interested. Asked me for *Wind in the Willows* again. Sure, kid. If any more *Wind in the Willows,* or any other binaural activity, can help toward stopping this awful gagging-stuttering—it's so bad all the time now, I could cry. I would call Mrs. Lawrence long distance but it's only a few days more till we go home.

Still somehow I *cannot* believe it's emotional. Stu is so happy here, has such fun. Seems to like *himself.* He can do so many things that his peers deem important: he's a good swimmer and trampoline jumper and bike rider and climber, and is asked to join in all activities of the lake kids. Yesterday they chose him to go first again up the giant pine on the island.

I dread him entering school like this next week. The children will surely mimic him. His teacher last year mentioned that, said third-graders are more discriminating than second-graders.

Thank goodness he has discussed freely and openly with the Perrin children his program to stop stuttering. But is that sort of "practice" for five weeks enough to face a class of more than twenty cruelly honest classmates?

SEPTEMBER 1, 1964. Home. Back in the swing of things. High and low. "Return" was abrupt and abrasive. Called Mrs. Lawrence about Stuart's speech falling apart.

"Stop the program. O.K.? Right now." Then she asked how Stuart was taking it. Funny thing, he still, I'm sure, doesn't hear himself stutter. Mrs. Lawrence started laughing. Could it be possible we had actually made things worse with too much bilaterality? Good grief. Could stuttering get worse just because a little boy did all that for a few weeks? She said don't do any more till we get him to Philadelphia.

After every report of the baby's creeping, she said, "Good, good, good."

Told her I'd received a form letter from The Institutes (IAHP) requesting a doctor's letter of referral. For each child. Even before the application could be sent!

She suggested I ask the children's pediatrician for a referral letter and send it along with a covering letter asking for an early appointment. Jotted down her suggested phrases: "We're making feeble attempts . . . bilateral activities . . . floor activities . . . refer for evaluation . . . M. Lawrence's title, Supervisor of Therapy Services, Department of Physical Medicine and Rehabilitation."

Mrs. Lawrence didn't make the September training class at IAHP. They have a long waiting list. Maybe January class. I couldn't think of anything to say. So. You'd think somebody with her title wouldn't have to wait.

SEPTEMBER 4, 1964. Called Mrs. Lawrence. She sensed right away I was having trouble.

"It's O.K. I've got lots of time."

I had asked the doctor for a referral letter. He didn't know what I was talking about. Never heard of this program. Never heard of The Institutes in Philadelphia, but would look into it. "I suggested he call *you*. Told him your title and all that. And he didn't even call *you*." Told me he had called two doctors in New York. (Mrs. Lawrence says they are big names in rehabilitation.) Both had been very discouraging about all this. Doctor said it would be a bad idea to mess around with Stuart's stuttering and his handedness . . . everybody knows you shouldn't . . . could get into a lot of trouble tampering with a child's handedness . . . might make stuttering a lot worse . . . he talked more about Stuart than Jane. All in kindness, but his voice had a firm warning ring to it.

Bert agrees. He keeps telling me, "There's nothing wrong with Stuart." I think he blames me for his stuttering, you know, the attachment to mother, the home, since I'm with him so much of the time and Bert isn't. Bert thinks it's O.K. for the baby though to go to The Institutes.

Begged Mrs. Lawrence to please call Bert and explain it to him—neurologically. After Maine he's really confused about all this. Then would she call the doctor and explain it to *him?*

No, she wouldn't explain it to the doctor. Just ask him for the referral letter anyway, telling him I've decided to go ahead and do it. "I rather expected this." Then she said I should realize that the doctors he had called were experts in their field. This program would be foreign to their approaches. "In our business we have a saying: So-and-so likes what So-and-so does. That is true with both these men. They have worked hard to do the best they know how in operative and supportive methods." Told me "supportive" means "bracing."

I felt better after I told her, and said she needn't call Bert either. I would brainwash him with her words. But I would hope he could meet her sometime.

"Mrs. Napear, I think I should tell you. Your husband did contact me. He didn't seem to mind asking for an appointment there for Jane, but he did for Stuart. I think you should know what I told him. I told him I thought he had it reversed. I feel quite strongly they can clean up Stuart's problem, if it is as I think—lack of a dominant hemisphere. But with Jane, I am not sure about anything. I really do not know what they can do for Jane. Jane's problems are much more complex . . ." Almost word for word.

SEPTEMBER 11, 1964. With the boys in school, the place is sweetly quiet. Noticed again the new sounds (no words yet) the baby is making. No longer just the "wo" and "ow" sounds. Moving on ground from tree shadow to tree shadow, from bush light to bush light, she is constantly "exclaiming" over something or other. J. seems even happier creeping here and there than when she bumped around in the walker. Less confined, for sure.

I wonder what her voice will sound like. Are little girls' voices like little boys' voices when they start talking? Will she sound like me, copying the Southern accent? The boys were late talkers too.

Grant's coming in from kindergarten now with four-letter words—top-level stuff. Found I don't really care too much. Second children do have a different environment. Mothers are into second motherings, and not as easily shocked. Hardly anything shocks me anymore. If little sister copies Grant's new vocabulary—well—I wouldn't care; glad to hear her say just anything. Funny, how different, how worn through you are by the time you're in third mothering.

SEPTEMBER 17, 1964. Had Jane's hair cut off. Necessary. Creeping with the head down and around is supposed to be some important step in vision and hearing. Two eyes fusing, ears also working in concert, and all that. That is, if your hair isn't in your face. Buster Brown haircut is harsh-looking, as if all her glow has gone. All you can see are those kooky eyes. No softness anywhere. And that lousy woman, doing the lousy cut. Kept trying to make her stop crying with, "See in the mirror?" Even after I told her Jane wasn't interested in the mirror, screaming and crying the whole time, clutching at the arms of the chair on that awful half-seat thing. Lollipop juice and hair all over.

Why didn't she look in the mirror like the boys loved to do? She is so stubborn sometimes, won't stop crying long enough to listen. I get so embarrassed.

SEPTEMBER 23, 1964. Appointment at The New York Hospital today. Another day to remember with this Mrs. Lawrence. Baby's sitting balance has improved. Head more erect; shoulders not so slumped. I too had noticed the sitting. Watched her in the rear-view mirror during the ride back from Maine. She doesn't need a car seat anymore, we learned, but I still have to encircle her with my arms as I lower her into a seat. Clutching, hanging on for dear life till she's altogether sat-down. But now she keeps her hips to the back of the chair and supports herself by holding on to the chair arms. In the car she places her hands beside her for balance. Mrs. Lawrence says creeping is supposed to be great for torso-neck-hip function. I have the feeling Mrs. Lawrence is learning from *Jane*. Very pleased over notes about Janey on floor and ground. Did she have a lot of children doing this? No, there are mostly adults in her department.

Mrs. Lawrence mentioned again that the insecurity with seating her or lying her down is understandable—probably visual.

Told Mrs. Lawrence that Janey seems less afraid generally; she gets onto and off a sofa or bed now.

MRS. LAWRENCE: Really?

ME: Yes, is that important?

MRS. LAWRENCE: Well, it is, if she never did it before, isn't it?

She's always seemed far behind in everything, so I expect her to be slower. But all those things come naturally, don't they? I mean, the doctors told me she won't catch up till she's about four.

Mrs. Lawrence said, "In the meantime it certainly can't hurt if we speed up the process a bit. Right?"

God knows, that's what I want to do, speed it up. But when I asked before about sitting and talking and walking, the doctors cautioned me against pushing the baby and comparing her to my other children. Because she had such a slow start. But even with a "late talker" I find waiting is hard on the nerves. I am dying to hear her voice.

Lately J. has been making all sorts of sounds, and I keep trying to catch her "real" voice in it.

MRS. LAWRENCE: She's been making sounds lately?

ME: Yes, not just "wo" and "mah" and "dah" but a lot of other sounds, like "wah," "ah," "ya," "yo," and "nam-nam."

MRS. LAWRENCE: Good.

She worked Jane's legs and feet and saw her stand. She winces, she says, every time she sees this child stand. On tippest tips of toes, as if she could break them. It *is* scarey-looking but Janey doesn't seem to mind the acrobatics. Heels are a bit looser—and maybe knees—when Mrs. Lawrence works them.

Mrs. Lawrence also saw Janey creep with and without the outrigger. Also several therapists were gathering to see the outrigger arrangement.

It reminded me of that day the baby was readmitted to the hospital at four months, all the doctors gathering to see the case of hypothyroidism. Then I learned it was cretinism and got out my old psychology text book to see the horrible picture I had remembered of a cretin. An untreated case of a two-year-old. Right then thanked God and The New York Hospital.

And there she was at four months plus, center stage for all to learn from, interns and residents. Some waited around, hoping to hear her funny cry. They all felt her scalp first thing. Then pulled her diapers down to see the umbilical hernia. Me neatly explaining to each that her doctor had said we would operate on that when she was older. Little did I know that doses of thyroid administered daily would cancel all her symptoms.

Five symptoms. She had them all. Five questions. The doctor, a woman, picking up the phone in the admitting office the day before, had asked them all. I thought, golly, how smart she is, because I was answering, "Why, yes" to everything. She interrupted all my protestations about not really caring to have a fat baby, it's just that this baby doesn't seem to be gaining much weight *at all*. Even after I weaned her from the breast to the bottle as our doctor suggested——

"Does your baby have an umbilical hernia?" (*Why, yes.*)

"Does your baby have a dry scalp?" (*Why, yes.*)

"Does your baby have a sand-paper cry? Or loud snorting?" (*Why, yes.*)

"Does your baby have constipation?" (*Why, yes. I give her suppositories our doctor prescribed.*)

"Does your baby have swelling of the back of the hands and feet?"

To the last one I practically burst, "Why, yes! Her doctor keeps mentioning she must be lying on her hands at night. But I told him she sleeps on her back."

She seemed "to know" our baby right over the phone. Told her, "I'm certainly glad you answered the telephone. You know the perfect questions to ask!"

She laughed and said, "I'm glad too. I don't usually answer the telephone." And something about her specialty being endocrinology—glands, you know. "If you'd like, you can bring her in tomorrow morning for admittance."

And I did. Across her chart they already had written, "Check for hypothyroidism." Saw several doctors who had literally kept her alive through hyaline membrane disease the winter before. Like old times again.

And today, the same scene. Our baby was center stage again, some sort of learning situation for these therapists. Mrs. Lawrence was pointing out the homologous hop and then the reciprocal motion of the legs in cross-pattern creeping, which the baby was doing all over the place.

I have the feeling Mrs. Lawrence does not think Janey will be naturally caught up at four.

SEPTEMBER 24, 1964. Well, well. Went to PTA night to meet Stuart's teacher, Mrs. Hefner. Sitting next to her at the third grade table I barely mentioned, please, to wait awhile on that referral to the school psychologist for his stuttering problem. Told her it had been suggested that he go to Philadelphia for evaluation, new approach to stuttering, something to do with the way the brain organizes itself in a child. She smiled and whispered—the speaker was starting—"I agree with you. I know about that. And I think that is a good idea." Also said his stuttering comes and goes. To reassure me?

In the classroom Mrs. Hefner described the goals of the year and explained the ungraded philosophy based on reading level, for the benefit of new parents. Afterwards drew me aside to deliver what seemed like another boost. She expected Stuart would move into the top reading group before the year is out. "He's sure got the mind for it . . . quick intelligence . . . enthusiastic . . . such a nice fellow. He still has trouble reading fluently and with expression, but we are working on that."

SEPTEMBER 26, 1964. Bert and I went to a dinner party where we met a biologist.

"Tell us, please, Peggy, all about crawling and creeping and how that redoes evolution in the baby."

Well—I tried. Went through the bi-ocularity bit. One eye doing the seeing when the baby is a *crawler* on the stomach. Bottom eye occluded against the floor surface; top eye "looking." Then the other eye getting used when the baby turns his head.

Then I went through the bi*n*ocularity bit. The use of two eyes in concert, fusion—when baby gets up on his knees, a *creeper* now. His first focusings with eyes looking down and around.

Then on to stereopsis of vision, the three-dimensional seeing of the upright *walker,* when eyes do not look down and around, but out and around. Where binocularity is perfected on its earlier-established base, born out of creeping.

I quickly mentioned that the same sort of sequential development goes with the ears. Kids who missed this day-to-day workout of brain pathways grow up to have visual or auditory problems, seen even years later in reading or phonetics.

And that wasn't all. Went into The Institutes' believing that the human brain has a *final* stage, which a lot of children never get to. One hemisphere of the brain should become dominant by age six to eight. And the sharpest, smoothest, best-coordinated second-graders are the ones whose preferred hand, foot, eye, and ear are all on the same side!

Somehow I felt I'd done a lousy job of it. I stumbled and bumbled. Finally the biologist asked something about what-this-has-to-do-with evolution and I hurried to clear it up.

The crawler is the amphibian, the creeper the reptile. And the way the baby comes to the upright position is like the years through ape-man, primitive man. Finally I got on the floor and moved in cross-pattern to show how it was a higher, more complicated mixture of arms and legs than homolateral one-sided movement. Eventually wound up doing a few bunny hops and could hardly breathe to say, "This homologous movement is an even *lower* function." I caught Bert's face and tried to return to my chair as gracefully as possible. Everyone was kind. The subject was concluded with a remark or two, including mine, about interesting . . .

October 1, 1964

The Institutes for the Achievement of Human Potential
8801 Stenton Avenue
Philadelphia 18, Pennsylvania

Dear Sirs:

I hopefully request an early appointment for Stuart, age eight years, and Jane, age thirty-two months. With the help of Mrs. Mary Lawrence, RPT, Supervisor of Therapy Services, New York Hospital Department of Physical Medicine and Rehabilitation, we have since July 28, 1964 made feeble attempts as outlined below at the Doman-Delacato method. We do not know where to go from here as regards motor development. And not wishing to break the routines we have set up with the children nor their interest, as well as ours, we therefore urge that you see us as soon as possible.

STUART—born 4/27/56
    Problem: Stuttering.
    Activities (daily) since 7/28/64:
        Cross-pattern creeping (one hour).
        Bimanual, binocular, bipedal, binaural:
            Visual pursuit (vertical, horizontal, circular) of an object held in both hands (ten minutes).
            Music with rhythmic beat (one hour).
            Listening to reading without watching reader or book.
            Games requiring sounds or memory of sounds.
            Trampoline (thirty minutes).
            Beachball.
            Swimming.
    Results: Stuttering *more* pronounced, *more* frequent, and *more* times in same sentence. Has not stuttered this much since four years old. Program discontinued 9/1/64.
    Family History: Rarely allowed on the floor as a baby. Moved from crib to feeding table, to bounce chair, to car seat, to playpen, to stroller. I am not sure about his crawling and creeping as a baby. He walked at fifteen months. Excellent student but needs improvement in reading fluency and handwriting. Speech therapy (forty minutes weekly) last year at school. School reluctant to refer him to school psychologist at our suggestion because "his stuttering does not affect his school work." Very vocal and outgoing and perseveres in his speech to the end. Has not as yet learned that stuttering is "bad" or "wrong." The school feels that this attitude may reach him soon because children in the third grade are bolder and may start teasing him. Very athletic and always received "outstanding" in Physical Education. We have always considered him well coordinated, but perhaps his enthusiasm and general fearlessness carry him along in sports.

JANE—born 1/22/62

Problems: Inability to walk. Inability to talk. Inability to focus eyes correctly. Retarded in motor functions. Appears alert, sociable, and intelligent and has a wonderful sense of humor. (Giggles and laughs most of the time.) Difficult to assess whether mentally retarded because motor functions so limit her opportunities to "tell us" or "show us." Speech is limited to consonant sounds, "mama," "wo-wo," etc., and "nam-nam" when anticipating a meal; but vocalization is mostly squeals and yells.

Activities since 7/28/64: On the floor except when fed, diapered, loved, or put to bed. Wears homemade romper suit with outrigger and harness line attached, constructed by Orthopedic Equipment Department of the Hospital for Special Surgery, New York City, at the request of Mrs. Lawrence, RPT. (We copied it from your picture.) It prevents her from turning over to her back and from standing up. Has worn daily since 7/28/64.

Results: Has learned to cross-pattern creep, more and more each day now. She prefers homologous creeping, her only means of locomotion before treatment started 7/28. Very investigatory; has learned to creep or get into everything near the floor. Can pull herself up to anything, outrigger and all, by the strength of her arms, but soon falls back to floor, and moves on to something else. Stands (on tiptoes, with legs crossed, and with knees and hips flexed) at every opportunity in crib or car; can cruise alongside crib bars. Has learned to "scoot," using hips, from one end to the other of sofa or seat of car since July. Has learned to back off a bed or chair onto floor, legs first. More vocalization; making more sounds daily. Has learned to squeeze a squeaky toy with hands to hear it squeak.

Family History: Was never on the floor very much. I, her mother, had a chronic lower back problem from the time Jane was four months old. Coincidentally, at four and a half months old, Jane was diagnosed a "congenital hypothyroid (cretin)" and hospitalized for a summer. My doctor told me not to pick Jane up from a playpen or from the floor, in fact, to lift her as little as possible in order to give my back a rest. This situation lasted till she was two years old. Consequently, she was moved from crib to bounce chair, to car seat, to feeding table, and eventually to a walker. *Therefore, Jane's problems may not be due to her lack of a thyroid gland but to her lack of opportunity to move about.*

We are in receipt of your letter of July 31, 1964. Enclosed you will find referrals and history by our pediatrician, who is also connected with New York Hospital. Stuart received help through an informal arrangement with Mrs. Lawrence while she was assisting Jane. Perhaps we could take advantage of a cancellation, since we, my husband and I and children, would be willing to come immediately at any time.

Very sincerely,
Mrs. Bertram Napear

OCTOBER 13, 1964. Finally I settled down to the history questionnaire from The Institutes in Philadelphia regarding Stuart. (Jane's due later, another department or institute.)

The questions concern everything a body can do or not do. I'm fast realizing, though, they are talking about the *brain,* not the body.

Got out the huge leather scrapbook I made during my first-child-syndrome years, and with the help of all those nauseating phrases and photographs, pieced Stuart's babyhood together.

So many questions I'd always wondered about too: the one eye that always had a problem of tear duct or sty or itching, and looked smaller in pictures; the inability to whisper.

The question about "monotone singer" intrigued me. I'd already figured out from the IAHP research notes from Mrs. Lawrence that Stuart fell into the 10 percent category of stutterers:

Stuttering is too much hemispheric balance . . . 90 percent of those without cortical hemispheric dominance perform above mean in music. . . . Remaining 10 percent usually extremely poor on tonal performance, monotones . . .

True, also, that Stuart does *not* stutter when he sings or reads or is in a school play. Interesting too that stutterers often make careers of music or drama. If not careers, then avocations, large record libraries, etc. The stage—safeground for stutterers?

OCTOBER 14, 1964. New issue of *Look* has an article about IAHP program and a brain-injured boy who had been hit by a car. A *revisit* article, after one on him two years ago, apparently. Seems he's "patterned" to crawl and creep and walk correctly, since his brain (he's brain-damaged) can't move his arms and legs the right way.

Bert says it sounds like the way golf pros teach arm swings, so you can get the feel of it. People come in to help the family move the arms and legs so the brain can get the message.

The brain-injured kids in last year's *Life* article are going through the same thing. Not allowed to walk, even with crutches or braces. In fact, not allowed to walk at all. Just stayed on the floor to get arms and legs to develop through crawls and creeps. *Then* walk!

Now I can see what a big difference in treatment this program is. Will the men in the brace shops be out of a job someday, after all those special years of training? Looks like a case of reverse automation, from machines to people. Wouldn't that be something! One doctor, I bet, would really have loved this natural, developmental approach—Dad.

OCTOBER 21, 1964. Sat down to read *Newsday* today, and there it was: "Community Comes to Aid of Bobby," all about a thirteen-year-old doing

The Institutes' program. He had to wait a year for his appointment. Also the article mentions they expect the therapy to take "a few years." Mrs. Lawrence told me there are a lot of mistakes in articles about this program.

When I asked the doctor, the physiatrist in Mrs. Lawrence's department, how long I would probably do the leg exercises, he was noncommittal. Must ask Mrs. Lawrence if she thinks Jane's legs will take as long as the brain-injured children's.

Article also says it takes a minimum of 180 people to do "patterning." Probably another mistake.

OCTOBER 22, 1964. Started calling Stuart's classmates to see if we could get five to form a 4-H boys' club. They could meet here in the playroom and use that door to come and go. Out of the eleven I called, eleven called back before night and said yes. Horrors! We are now looking for a leader.

OCTOBER 23, 1964. Fall conference with Stu's teacher today. Tuesday I'd sent her a whole pile to read. When she returned the reading material, she returned my letter and underlined certain words as her comment.

Dear Mrs. Hefner,

Before I see you Friday, I would appreciate your reading the articles outlined below and enclosed. I hesitate to ask you to do this because I know you have no extra time. And yet, for Stuart's sake, I must. As his teacher I would want you to be aware of this information now and throughout the school year. And as a teacher in general, I'm sure you will find it all very exciting.

Perhaps you are aware of the enclosures—at least you seemed to know exactly what I was talking about at the September PTA meeting. I was so happy to have such a response from you, because there are still those in medicine, reading and speech therapy who are not aware of these new developments, or, if aware, cannot believe! . . .

Very sincerely,

Well, today she and I discussed the Philadelphia approach to the way the child has developed, as opposed to the way the teacher teaches or the books she uses teach. Mrs. Hefner told me she could pick out the children right now in her class who have "perceptual" problems, either visual or auditory. She could put the names in her desk drawer today. Have The Institutes in Philadelphia evaluate each child in the class, she would bet the ones who were perceptually deficient would be on the list in the drawer! She is certainly delighted someone is finally taking a look at the child. *Teachers* understand what Doman and Delacato and the whole Philadelphia group are saying. We went through the problems of telling *parents* this, especially if the word *brain* were ever used. I proposed using expressions like "development not organized as it should have been."

"Oh, no," she said, "then the parents would think I was blaming them. You see, they think it's the teacher's fault, or they blame the ungraded program, or the child sitting next to theirs. Interesting, this distractibility symptom. Parents ought to observe more. There are those who get all the same interference and who are not distracted. I think Carl Delacato down there in Philadelphia is right. Distractibility has something to do with one's auditory system. The child is poorly developed brain-wise for listening and not listening."

Mrs. Hefner mentioned 4-H. Stuart and the boys in class were all excited when she told them she had a twenty-five-year 4-H pin. She showed me samples of Stuart's compositions, and we looked at his uneven print—chicken scratch I called it—and saw that he crosses the same word out three or four times even if it's correct in the first place. According to The Institutes' research, *stutterers also stutter or hesitate in vision and mobility.* Stuart does that false-start business, left-right-left-right, before he kicks a ball. It's now apparent that he actually stutters in handwriting too. Does this account for his fluency problem in reading too?

How is Stu doing socially? Were the kids giving him a rough time about his speech? It is beginning, but Mrs. Hefner is talking generally to the class about "difficulties" everyone has. Stu is not the only one by any means. "A lot of children are laughed at, for one reason or another. Outdoors they are incoordinate and 'ruinin'' the team. Indoors they are 'not finished yet.' My desk-drawer group."

Anyway, apparently Stuart doesn't stutter *at all* some days.

NOVEMBER 6, 1964. Letter from Grant's kindergarten teacher today. "Fall Conference Guide" enclosed. She had to cancel my appointment, home sick, but wrote:

. . . Grant could not be a better boy in school and he is learning every day. He is a fine helper. Holds the school door frequently for us to go out and sits at a table with five very nice boys. What more could we ask? All keep well. . . .

The guide with this and that checked with "Good, good, good . . ." And a final paragraph:

Grant adjusted very nicely and quickly to his kindergarten class.
He participates in all kindergarten activities—floor play, blocks, cars, table work, clay, puzzles etc.
Grant's social behavior is very good. He is happy in school. . . .

In fact, I missed it the first time among all the "goods":

Clarity of speech _____Fair_____

Well, it's true, he talks like he doesn't enunciate or something. And he's so "reserved," she calls it.

NOVEMBER 18, 1964. Moving dreamlike all day. That place in Philadelphia. What kind of place is it, to have kids like this waiting all over the land? What's so special about Stu he's got to wait till April 12, 1965, before they can even see him? The letter today was so cordial, so professional, so disappointing. A five-month wait! Fellows, that could be the straw to break him wide open, if his peers decide to flail more than a few gut-honest comments. Are you so busy as all that down there? So he's got an appointment. Just hope we can hold it all together till then. Keep lips tight, and the calendar moving. One thing, for some unholy reason, his stuttering hasn't again hit the skids the way it did doing their program. On some days it is really noticeable though. Days when he's often the happiest, I swear.

Let him read the letter today, all about the two sessions: 10:00 A.M. for evaluation and 12:30 P.M. for evaluation and programing. And bring along reports and evaluations done "on your child." And a lot more, all for seventy-five dollars. Wow.

"Hey, Mom, must have a lot of people who stutter coming there, wouldn't you think?"

"Oh, yes. You're not stuttering much anyway, it seems to me, these days. What do you think? More or less?"

"I do it sometimes in school, I think."

"At home sometimes too. I hear it once in awhile."

So he'll stutter for five months. Don't mention it unless he does. Still not sure he knows when he's doing it—that he's doing it. Weird. Or maybe after five years of it, it's an old hat he runs around with, on his way to the ball game, to the class, to the big things of life.

DECEMBER 3, 1964. It came! It came just like any other letter today. Saw the date in capitals before I had the letter out of the envelope "WEDNESDAY, OCTOBER 27, 1965 . . ." October 27? Next year? She'll be almost four years old!

At 8:20 A.M. . . . Confirm appointment by January 1, 1965. . . . Enclosed history form. Bring it with you . . . evaluation and orientation . . . rigorous three days in store for you. If . . . live beyond fifty miles, plan to arrive Tuesday evening . . . separated part of time. Make notes to nurses . . . special feeding, medication, toileting, playing . . . diapers . . . both parents *must* attend.

First day . . . families scheduled . . . later . . . afternoon . . . finished by 3:00 to 4:00 A.M. next day . . . fifty dollars. . . . Second day . . . 8:30 A.M. Child taken from you and cared . . . by trained staff . . . parents . . . detailed orientation . . . brain function and our program . . . fifty dollars. . . . Third day . . .

I read it again, but I knew there was no mistake. What to do with her for a year? She can't stay another whole year in the outrigger. Just . . . waiting in the outrigger?

The boys came home from school, and could tell I'd been crying. They got very quiet and kind of tiptoed around. Went in and told them that I'd gotten the letter. No, I didn't know what we would do. It was a popular place. There were a lot of children with difficulties like Jane's. Stuart said maybe she could go when he did, next April. I said they were in different departments, that's why it was called "The Institutes."

Grant said it seemed stupid to go for "free" days. I looked at him. Pal, you've got "the problem" too? And if your upside-down, back-side-up ABC's don't get better soon, I'm going to either get you an evaluation or a mirror, or I'm going to scream. I pasted his manila paper on the refrigerator. How in the world can someone actually write backwards and not know it?

I went to my room, till I remembered Mrs. Lawrence and called her. I half-laughed, half-cried about the three of them. She did too and said, "Well, now with Grant's visual perception and articulation problems, you've got in your family the full range of symptoms of neurological disorganization—except ambidexterity."

I said, "Oh, you forgot Bert. He's left-handed, you know, for eating and writing, but throws and plays golf and tennis and I-don't-know-what-all with his right hand."

"Really?" she said.

"Cut it out, Mrs. Lawrence."

Mrs. Lawrence said there's a good chance she might make January class at The Institutes, and if so, she would ask them to take Jane earlier.

DECEMBER 4, 1964. Again I read over the history questionnaire for Janey today from IAHP. Eleven legal-size pages. At one page a month, I'll have the thing licked by next October!

Janey needs someone to check her over this thoroughly. She still isn't doing much of anything naturally. That "age of four" is only a year from now. She's so far behind.

Like Stuart's much shorter questionnaire, this one asks good questions, things I never thought of, and so much I've wondered about since she was tiny: sensitivity to sunlight, fears, crib-scooting and other needs for motion, sleeplessness, medication I took during pregnancy, including appetite-depressant mood-stimulant pills the doctor prescribed for my weight gain. A New York Hospital pediatrician had dismissed that as not important history when J. was admitted for thyroid problem. This place seems to dismiss nothing. It's a good thing. Most of this stuff has never been asked me in a checkup of Jane.

I had no notes on Janey until July's outrigger days. Hated the baby book; it only had places for first smile, first step, first words, etc. Even the weight-gain page was blank. There was no weight gain until she was five months old, just the swelling of her hands and feet, and how could you put that in a baby book. So I put the pretty book back in the closet and called Mrs. Lawrence for help.

She said she'd try to get permission to help. Locate in Jane's hospital chart dates of developmental landmarks, psychological tests, bone ages, etc.

DECEMBER 5, 1964. Had children's silhouettes done for Christmas gifts to grandmothers. Janey sat on a folding chair without arms! Sat quietly several minutes till the lady had finished! I loved the silhouette of J. No crossed eyes, funny face, to give you that harsh look. Good thing silhouettes don't get down to legs either. Janey looks like any other little girl in a silhouette. Just adorable.

DECEMBER 7, 1964. Mary Lawrence called with little bits of developmental info on J.

"So glad you called. I got a copy of the hospital's birth history from her original doctor. And, Mrs. Lawrence, this is wrong—they don't have her recorded as a premature birth. 'Induced, full-term delivery' they have. That's wrong! When the obstetrician sent me to the hospital, that day I was in for a check—for low back pain, it was—he said we must have miscalculated the month. He explained that I was already into dilation—convinced me I probably had 'spotting' that first month, even though I told him I didn't see how any of this was possible, trying to think back. But wouldn't he have known after the birth, her being small—five pounds, fourteen ounces they have here—not as he prophesied in the office an eight-pounder at all. And born with hyaline membrane disease and all. When she was readmitted to the hospital at four and one half months, they took a bone age, said it showed she was only an eighth-month term baby, ungrown, still with the broken clavicle bone she was born with! She *was* premature. And The Institutes' questionnaire asks about that.

"Mrs. Lawrence, is inducing three weeks prematurely—But Grant was induced by the same doctor. We lived an hour away from the city—I just made an appointment to have Grant on June eighteenth, instead of the thirtieth. I remember, my dad was here at the time and made some remark about babies getting ripe, which I thought was crude and said so."

Mrs. Lawrence thinks I should tell The Institutes what I know about it; they're very interested in what parents have to offer about these things.

That part about birth reflexes just means she was missing some at birth: ankle jerk, biceps, triceps, chvostek (no contraction of facial muscles when you tap on face in front of ear). On her readmission to the hospital at age four and a half-months (really age zero!) the deep tendon reflexes were "depressed to absent." "Do you think at this late date, all this birth stuff is really that necessary? This questionnaire seems a bit too much."

Mrs. Lawrence thinks a lot of this is for research purposes. They use these histories for prenatal, natal, and postnatal research. They would get to know Jane more from her *functions* than from this anyway. I murmured, "You mean her dysfunctions."

"I mean, Mrs. Napear, I think you should seriously consider everything about Jane, give them as much information as you possibly can."

"I can't even remember turning, rolling, pivoting, much less describe how she did any of it."

Mrs. Lawrence was able to supply this so I could add it to what I already have: several notes in her chart regarding "eye-following" and "object-passing," but no mention of mobility except "no sitting" and "no sitting" and "no sit."

"That was me! *I* kept telling them that."

The psychological tests were a little more helpful:

13 months—not sitting; rolls over; primitive vocalizations; no crawl [crawl? or creep? did they know diff.?]; thumb in palm.

[That was the I.Q. 63 day.]

20 months—no talking; "ma-ma" without meaning; repeats simple syllables; laughed but not at anything in particular; very social.

[That was her I.Q. 43 day.]

Mrs. Lawrence also found a note from when Jane was fifteen months— when the Pediatric Out-Patient Department recommended she go to Metabolic Department in a month—that I reported she was starting to crawl (creep?); no sitting.

Other tests: no record of EEG, or arteriogram, or x-ray study, or ventriculogram, so I wrote *no* in beside those questions. Added "Many lab tests relating to thyroid, icteric, and respiratory problems."

No bone ages that first hospitalization. One was ordered about ten days after she was born. No record of results.

"Oh, yeah, they mentioned something about bone-testing, and later I asked one of the new residents—it was the last day of January and the new group came onto the floor for the next six months—how were her bones, and he said, 'Fine.' I bet that's what happened: they were going to give her a bone-age test that day, and they probably didn't because of the old group leaving. Oh, well, one thing they would have known if they had: they were dealing with a premature baby. At least, they found it out four and a half months later."

DECEMBER 9, 1964. Today's psychological exam was like all the others: I.Q. 40. Very hard to get Jane to do much to measure. She sat in a chair at the table, not on my lap this time. Kept leaning over—to get on the floor, I suppose. In all cup tests she held the cup out for water. Finally gave her some. Cup tests O.K. after that. The psychologist heard J.'s jargon and commented on its improvement. It now goes up and down a little like *our* voices. *Inflection,* psychologist said.

Suggested I talk to J. and turn on TV all day to help speech along. I talk to her all the time—we all do—because she is so sociable, but we'd never thought about keeping the TV on. J. hates to stop at one place very long, keeps moving, a real busybody. Could keep it on in the room with her though. Since J. is supposed to creep on a textured surface—rug areas, etc.—we'll have to move the TV out of the tiled playroom. Boys'll hate that. So will Bert. So will I. But it's a good idea.

Took J. in stroller up the elevator to see Mrs. Lawrence. J.'s eyes get kookier with the elevator whiz.

Mrs. Lawrence had J. creep all through the rooms and hall. *Without* the outrigger, J. is now doing an occasional cross-pattern movement interspersed with bunny hops. She suggested asking the brace man to add twelve inches to the outrigger. When J. attempts to pull up to counters and tables, a longer tail will stop her before she can start. Good idea.

DECEMBER 16, 1964. Went to Grant's Christmas program at his school. Noticed again his speech and lack of "th" sound: "Back and forf dey scamper, busy as can be. Now dey chop and trim Santa's Christmas tree."

The speech teacher had sent the form letter for his enrollment in speech therapy. After the program she showed me a mirror and the techniques she would use to teach him to say all the blends he's missing. Thought: someone has been teaching him ABC's with a mirror too!

Mentioned the IAHP program just incidentally to see if she'd heard of it. She had, somewhere, but couldn't understand putting a child through all those baby exercises when it was only a matter of "cleaning up the blends."

I would clear it up for her: "It's a symptom of neurological disorganization—poor sequencing—poor development——"

"We see this in the immature child. Maturation is slower in some. Those ABC's will probably clear up with time too."

I left, figuring we were talking about the same thing, but calling it different names.

Maybe what is new under the sun is that the people at The Institutes started asking "Why?" and "How come?"

DECEMBER 22, 1964. I got out the long poem I had written about a baby's (Stuart's) Christmas and read it to them. Sure enough they got the idea and started giving Janey a piece of everything they worked with. Pretty soon the floor was littered, and there she was, creeping around with ribbons and wrapping-paper pieces caught up in the tail and side bars of the outrigger. Swishing and turning, she tried to set them free. Grant said she was giggling and hiccuping too hard to do it. I said she needed her hands to creep on. Stuart said don't help her and see what she will do. Soon enough she managed to balance on one hand and two knees and picked off a ribbon caught on her aluminum side bar. Stu ran in. "She did it, Mom!"

Took the kids out in the car to see the lighted menorahs and Christmas trees. They were so disgusted with Janey—she never looks at anything you want her to. Just giggles as the car starts, and screams when it stops.

JANUARY 4, 1965. Telegram to Philadelphia: WE CONFIRM APPOINT-MENT MADE FOR JANE NAPEAR, OCTOBER 27, 1965. BECAUSE OF PROGRAM ALREADY BEGUN BY THE NEW YORK HOSPITAL, WE HOPED APPOINTMENT COULD BE SOONER. MUCH PROGRESS SINCE JULY THROUGH USE OF OUT-RIGGER AND FLOOR ACTIVITIES, BUT SURE PROGRESS COULD BE GREATER. PLEASE ADVISE IF CANCELLATION APPEARS IN YOUR CALENDAR . . . MR. AND MRS. BERTRAM NAPEAR

JANUARY 18, 1965. Talked on the phone with Lydia about that day three years ago and how Lydia came to visit me at the hospital, but the rooming-in plan allowed for only two visitors and Bert and a friend were already there. How she left so disappointed and furious and worked herself into labor pains, she says. Robin was born that night. Bert always said it was a good thing she hadn't come up to find Jane in the pediatric nursery in respiratory distress.

And how I was moved to the second floor to wait for Jane, using the electric breast pump. I couldn't stand it anymore one night, and when the babies were brought in to my roommates for feeding, I slipped out and called Lydia to tell her how depressed I was. All she could talk about was Robin, and how marvelous her hospital was, and how marvelous breast feeding . . . and I hung up quickly, about to cry, because she didn't care. Nobody cared. How then I demanded to go up to my baby and nurse her . . . and I practically screamed that I could save her, I knew it. She might not vomit breast milk . . . and I quoted studies to them, ending with the one about a rabbit needing a furry mother to snuggle up to, to survive . . . and I was a doctor's daughter and could "scrub up" and put on surgical clothes!

Then Lydia reminding me I'd gone back to my bed sobbing, and, by mistake, knocked over the water pitcher and was worried that they might think I had thrown it! And again I reminded Lydia it had all been her damn fault. That night, even though it was Sunday, Bert had driven in to

New York to visit and brought a cake. He had baked it and the boys had iced it. The icing was dark gray because they had mixed all the food colors, being unable to decide on one. Each of the nurses came in to see how I was feeling "now," and Bert asked each of them to have a piece of the gray cake. I told him it was a good thing he came and to be sure to drop in tomorrow before he went home . . . that other people had their own babies and really no one else especially cared about Jane.

Lydia and I today, three years later, both laughing.

JANUARY 21, 1965. I finally finished the new light blue denim romper suit with all the zippers in and on somehow. Only took three weeks of working every night! What this program needs is a central ordering place— for the paraphernalia one has to make and doesn't have time to. Maybe someday I'll set up something like that. Outriggers in all different colors. Romper suits with adjustable, growing power. Shoes with metal loops in the heels, so I won't have to send to the brace man to have loops inserted for harness-line hooks, just because of a new pair of shoes. (These are red oxfords. New pair of orthopedic shoes pretty stupid with this "knee" program.) How about harness lines out of nylon so mothers won't drive themselves batty finding out that cotton breaks too frequently? Maybe harness lines to match outriggers? You're kidding . . .

JANUARY 22, 1965. The boys and I were blowing balloons when Mrs. Lawrence called. Back from Philadelphia, exhausted. Every day from 8:00 A.M. to 1:00 or 2:00 A.M. the next. It was a fascinating, mixed group of therapists, psychologists, doctors, and school people of all kinds— remedial, classroom, and administrative. Mixed geographically, too, on purpose.

Doman and Delacato were apparently quite a pair. They met each other while working with Dr. Temple Fay, the maverick Philadelphia neurosurgeon. He did odd things like working on human refrigeration thirty years ago, a technique now used widely in operations. It was his theory also that basic patterns of movement were somehow related to evolutionary development. She said they started looking at normal babies, even took movies and tapes of them. One time they spent eighteen months looking at creeping, and were amazed at how much development occurs right on the floor. It was a gentle sequencing, breathtaking to behold. One pattern actually built on another. Unless. Unless interfered with. And daily, in how many homes, that was truly and tragically the case.

Hm-m. Modern mother in her affluent madness had penned her baby in an ivory tower?

Mrs. Lawrence says Glenn Doman, the physical therapist, his brother

Robert, the M.D. in physical medicine and rehabilitation (physiatrist!) and Carl Delacato, the psychologist-teacher, are an interesting combination of medicine and education coming together—finally—to take a look at the "whole child." She thinks their work will influence the future of both fields.

Glenn Doman is one of the most enthusiastic lecturers she's ever heard. He seems terribly pleased with what The Institutes have learned already about the brain's organizing itself birth-to-six. So much so, a person would either love or hate him. No neutral reaction possible. Mrs. Lawrence's description makes him sound exactly like he writes in the Preface to his book, *How to Teach Your Baby to Read.*

Now Mrs. Lawrence wants to start a more intensive program with Jane, to make her days more meaningful. So J. will not be put off completely to "hack it herself" the next eleven months. Does this mean patterning? Mrs. Lawrence says yes, and some other things—to increase J.'s seeing, listening, and something-else abilities.

Will only check out J.'s *functions*. Not a neurological work-up. The Institutes will do that and get into diagnosis and etiology with us. Etiology means the causes, contributing factors, to Jane's slowness. She doesn't need to know that anyway to set up a functional program. Mentioned something about masking . . . carbon dioxide . . . diet program . . . would prefer to have IAHP prescribe all that. Gathered she is leaving out some stuff.

Wants Bert and me to bring Jane to the hospital Monday for evaluation according to the same Doman-Delacato Developmental Profile used in Philadelphia.

So excited, I forgot to tell her it's Janey's birthday.

Professional Evaluation

January 25, 1965. New York Hospital. Mrs. Lawrence telling Bert and me about the IAHP program. Or was she talking about us?

"No guarantees . . . I don't know whether this program will work or not. But I do know what will *not* work with these kids. This program is directed to the brain, not the limbs, so this program has higher possibilities. At least we are thinking "brain" with Jane. I believe it is possible to influence the brain. What we do in a sensory sense out here—in the child's immediate physical environment—makes some change in there . . . influences what comes out of that brain. That's the way any child learns to do anything. You will provide for Jane an environment, which, for some reason or other, she cannot provide for herself. Remember, the important thing is . . . 500 percent more of it."

Hard work ahead. Every day. For how long a time? We don't know how long. Intense, tedious when you don't know what you're going to get at the end. No guarantees.

I didn't look at Bert the whole time, and I don't think he ever looked over at me either.

Mrs. Lawrence checked out these six functional areas (according to the Doman-Delacato Developmental Profile, see. p. 504):

1. *Mobility.* Cannot or does not crawl on stomach. Creeps homologously with infrequent cross-pattern step or two. (With the harness line to her heels she creeps only in a cross pattern, and that creep is looking smoother, more serialized.) She cruises on her toes with poor balance and two-hand support.

2. *Language.* Makes many repetitive throat sounds, but no sounds involving lips or tongue. Never noticed before, but Mrs. Lawrence is right.

3. *Manual Competence.* Has prehensile grasp (baby fist-clutch). Cannot pick up a penny using forefinger and thumb. With either hand. Mrs. Lawrence says J. beginning to use thumb in "crude cortical efforts," whatever that means.

4. *Visual Competence.* J. has light-reflex and even higher abilities: outline perception, and some ability to see detail within a configuration (light switch or doorknob), but this is poor. Cannot differentiate similar but unlike simple objects or pictures (for example, an apple from a ball). Well, that's no news. Also has an alternating strabismus (both eyes turn in, but alternately),* which she can control on attention to convergence of two inches. Mrs. Lawrence will explain later.

5. *Auditory Competence.* Really lousy. J. only differentiates sounds, like sweet talk from scolding. Responds to our voices. Does not understand our words or follow directions. True.

6. *Tactile Competence.* J. responds to pain stimulus and gnostic (pleasant) sensation in all limbs except right leg. This really shocked us. Also, still has a Babinski reflex in one foot. (Saw the big toe go up when Mrs. Lawrence stroked the foot bottom.) She "understands" by feeling with her hands that there is a third dimension to objects which appear to be flat, but she is quite poor at this with both hands.

* In July 1964 the diagnosis by an ophthalmologist was "Slight left esotropia (left convergent strabismus)" and he suggested an operation for the muscle imbalance when she was older. An earlier ophthalmologist (September 1963) said she had no strabismus (crossed eye); the wide bridge of her nose made it look that way to us (her family and pediatrician).

Going to teach J. to crawl, since she did little or none as a baby. We'll "pattern" her to show her body (really her brain) how it "feels." Sensory input, Mrs. Lawrence said, like the entire Doman-Delacato program. Four patterning sessions each day. Five minutes each. We need two people, one for each side of J.'s body, plus someone to move J.'s head left and right, like babies do it. (Me the head part?)

Might ask friends and neighbors to help us for *one* five-minute session during the week.

Mrs. Lawrence is coming here Monday night to teach them and us. We need some "patients," little kids we can practice on.

On the way home Bert and I multiplied the two other people (me do all the weekday sessions, Bert the weekend ones) times four patternings a day. Times seven days. Wow. How could we get fifty-six friends in one week? We couldn't use the Human Rights' mailing list for this. The few women I knew in PTA or Women Strike activities are same ones mostly. That's what comes of keeping church affiliation and extracurriculars centered in New York City.

Mrs. Lawrence says they can swap among themselves on days they can't make it. Sounds like the old coop nursery school routine. She suggested I not ask people myself; it's too emotionally draining. They can say no easier to a coordinator, and we want only those who are yes through and through.

Bert was betting Barbara Barnhart would do it; she is so diplomatic and charming. Said I knew he really meant "good-looking," and to keep his mind on the driving and try to think of someone else. I wouldn't have the guts to ask her. (Bert said *he* would.) Guidance counseling at the high school has so much paper work, and she brings it home every night. Bert figured it out. Ask Barbara to ask seven "captains," one for each day, and let them report back who they got to volunteer. O.K. Insurance brokers are so clearheaded.

Here we are, just like the people in the magazine articles. Finally it's here. Is it as good as it sounds? Is it as bad, as difficult as it sounds? What is it really? Is this stupid, to start all this when we don't even know it will work? I wonder what made other parents—the ones in the articles—say yes to this. Maybe they weren't as busy as we are? Maybe their kids weren't as cute as Janey is? Or maybe they were actually brain-damaged and not cute at all.

Mrs. Lawrence notices the funniest things about Jane. This morning she said J. is "more directed" now in her activities. J. was into everything in the steel cabinet there. Mrs. Lawrence, watching, said not to stop her. It's a big difference, she thinks. I mentioned J. is interested in cabinets and closets at home now too. Bert thought Mrs. Lawrence was more impressed with this than anything else. Strange . . .

2

JANUARY 26, 1965. Bev Howe, nursery school director: "Outdoor time is becoming a veritable ed course for me" on gross-motor differences in coordination. She's beginning to be able to tell the smoothly coordinated kid from the not so sharp—at a glance. Inside she can hardly keep her eyes off their eyes, their eye-hands, their fine-finger differences, deft or clumsy. Fascinating, this picture of the neurological child. It's getting increasingly harder to listen to parents' anxieties over "his" this and that: "Shy . . . only likes his bike . . . won't sit still . . . could do it but won't try . . . lazy like his daddy was at his age . . . so different from his older brother and sister that way. . . ." What a natural, crawling and creeping time in a nursery school, she just might do it.

JANUARY 29, 1965. Peggy Wallace called. She got twenty-four patterners at last night's choir practice at her church. And she's not even a captain. How did she know? Her husband called her from his office after Bert mentioned it in commuter rush to New York that morning. Plus themselves and sons!

FEBRUARY 1, 1965. Finished Carl Delacato's new book, *The Diagnosis and Treatment of Speech and Reading Problems.* Hm-m. Mirror-writing, mirror-reading, late speech, late articulation problems—*all* symptoms of poor neurological organization. Baby making weak pathway systems on the inside while glowing and giggling and gurgling on the outside? But Grant was so content to stay in the playpen or bounce chair. How were we to know?

I think Grant should be evaluated at least, to see how well organized he is. No starch from Bert this time.

FEBRUARY 2, 1965. Mrs. Lawrence called to ask me to call a woman who was in the same class last month in Philly. To help Mrs. Lawrence teach patterning here Monday night. She's a reading consultant in a school district somewhere near here. *Privately* evaluates and programs kids in addition to those in her school district. Certified to do IAHP program with this type kid. Edith Alfred is her name. Mrs. Alfred is speaking at a meeting of school psychologists. Could I observe? Also Beverly Howe?

The meeting for school psychologists, it turned out, was to me shocking in its stumblebum search, and touching in its sincerity.

"Special classes" for "exceptional" children are the new experiment. The chairman explaining today's meeting would get away from testing, etc., and have teachers of these experimental classes speak from "the practical field." "We are very excited over this new knowledge." Solving lots of problems in these special classes "we've never solved before." "These children" should have private help, but it's hard to get parents to pay for it.

A panel of teachers was introduced as people "here to help the kids." From my notes, words used to describe "these children":

aggressive—withdrawn—extroverted—too active—emotionally disturbed—is a learning problem—has a learning problem—learning block here—borderline I.Q.'s—hyperactive—has above-average I.Q.!—has brain damage—brain-damaged—perceptual difficulties (mentioned by only one teacher)—distractibility—troublemakers—functionally retarded—mentally retarded

Not only was this "exceptional" mix under one teacher, but now having gotten to "know" them, each teacher was happily sharing in a hushed room the new knowledge—ways and means—the chairman referred to:

small number
get away from academic pressure till behavior improves
emphasis on praise
more play and food breaks
spend lunch time with other (normal) children
educational games
start children playing separately (to allow them to "let loose," let them do what they want in gym, etc.), then bring together in groups, eventually
give children with visual problems other clues, tactile or kinesthetic ones (that one teacher again)
give love and mothering in play groups

Edith Alfred, the last panelist to speak, very softly explained she was a bit different: no "special class," children programed individually. For years the goal was a reading consultant in every school. Remember those days? *Still* there are problems. The last two years, using a "developmental approach" to both evaluation and program, finally she sees great improvement.

She's seen children on a sensory-motor program for only two months attain an increase in reading level of one year. Even some in two months travel one and a half years in reading. A flutter in the room at this point, a general gasp and whispers. A man stood up, the psychologist in charge of special pupil services in her district. He said it was only right that he stand up to confirm what Mrs. Alfred had just said.

She went on to describe the visual perceptual "symptoms" one can see even in the copying of geometric figures, ones which a five-year-old should be able to do with ease.

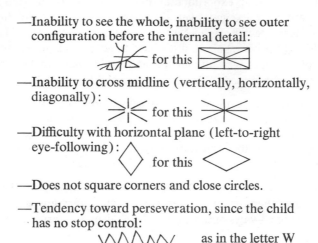

—Inability to see the whole, inability to see outer configuration before the internal detail:

for this

—Inability to cross midline (vertically, horizontally, diagonally):

for this

—Difficulty with horizontal plane (left-to-right eye-following):

for this

—Does not square corners and close circles.

—Tendency toward perseveration, since the child has no stop control:

as in the letter W

And many more besides the common flaws of poor spacing and not "sitting on the line."

She then listed some of the perceptual problems like letter-reversing (we've always taken that one for granted), which grow into a reading problem like word-reversing.

All these are only *symptoms* though. Results, not causes.

Here Edith's voice got a bit stronger. "They are symptoms of poor neurological organization in the child's past." Other perceptions—auditory and tactile—could be sharpened, as well as the visual, toward better differentiation. And permanently.

When this child sees sharply, hears sharply, the world then is no longer a "buzz" to him. And the child no longer shuts it out, in withdrawal or hyperactivity. Then there's no need to teach him with special techniques.

Proper evaluation is the key to the kindergartener who will surely be into remedial reading soon enough. This program can easily be incorporated in the young child's school day (the junior and senior high schoolers' day too) for approximately thirty minutes a day. It's the child's *neurological organization* a school must take a look at, The Whole Child—and early.

Me wondering who had originally cut the child into pieces anyway? The gym teacher sees his poor coordination, the speech therapist his poor speech, the nurse checks to see if he has 20/20 vision (acuity, that is), and the art teacher gets his long-and-tall, everything-vertical drawings. But *who* is putting it all together? The class teacher? And she's sending him to the school psychologist. And what is the psychologist doing? At the moment he is sitting in an all-day meeting, looking like anybody's dad or mom, probably going home at night complaining about his work load. How much work load would he have left, how many truly psychological challenges would he have left, if each learning problem got rid of its learning problem?

FEBRUARY 7, 1965. Emergency team in case of snow? Neighbors standing by? Mary Lawrence impatient with my attitude, she's so serious about never missing a patterning session.

Anita, just a backyard away, is best for this eighth team captain.

"Peggy, are you saying that Jane is the way she is because she never did any crawling or creeping? Is that what you're saying?"

"That's what I said. She was never allowed on the floor." Describing the rationale, how the patterners are part of this new program— "When we get to Philadelphia we will find out more about her, why she is coming along so slowly——"

"You mean to say you don't *know* yet?"

What does she think is wrong with Janey? She thinks Janey is dumb or something?

FEBRUARY 9, 1965. Someone gave me the lift I needed, a spirit to last the evening. She walked in without knocking, ahead of a whole bunch of people I'd never seen, and said, "You'll never remember our names. We're here to help with the patterning. That's all you need to know!"

Mary Lawrence explained to everyone quite seriously what we're about. Simple. We want a developing little girl. We have to go the normal way, the way other children do it, the evolution thing. Starting with the fish—the fishlike movements of baby in the womb and the few weeks after. Those early undulating movements, resulting in *accidental* pivoting, rolling over, moving backwards and forwards in place. A worm has only a spinal cord, and its central nervous system only one function: propulsion forward. Mobility, therefore, is our oldest function in phylogeny and our earliest function in ontogeny.

Smell-brain, see-brain, etc., came later, and it may well be that these functions—smelling, seeing, etc.—are dependent upon pathways earlier created and used by a baby's early movement. Remember, movement-brain is the *first brain*.

We're not starting back at the worm undulations with Jane since she can already do that level. A little higher. The amphibian. Salamander, moving in a belly-down position. Neat little pattern to its arms and legs. Baby in belly-down life we call crawling. At first, a random schlunking, you might say. Then he starts to move arms and legs in some sort of repetitive pattern. Maybe he pulls two arms and pushes two legs, somewhat froglike, in homologous crawling. Looks like an undulating scoot, top half and bottom half telling the brain all about—what else—the top half and the bottom half! J. has homologous movement on hands and knees; we're not going back to get it belly down. Babies spend little time at this, if they ever do it at all. Why? They get their heads to one side for a higher "fun"—the homolateral crawl—a one-side-then-the-other-side amphibian. Homolateral means "one-sided." As the baby works first one side, then the other, the brain finds out it has two sides down there. Two halves the other way. Left side works, pause, head turns to right, right side works, pause, head turns to left, and we're home again. Arm-job is still pull, leg-job is still push, but the lefties are becoming a team to *equal* the righties over there. Flexing and extending arms and legs as a pull-push is begun and completed, "headquarters" is learning a lot about its own teamwork down there. How a neck feels turning, how a top eye sights, how a top ear hears (and listens some more?). How the bottom eye and ear against the floor are getting their turn next.

We'll pattern homolateral movement into Jane first. Tell the old amphibian brain—the pons, just above the spinal cord—what we want it to know about its business. Till it gets on the ball.

If J. "gets it" and crawls homolaterally on her own long enough, it should trigger automatically the highest form of crawling: cross-pattern— right hand synchronizing with left leg and vice versa. If J. has mistakes in that, we'll pattern correct cross-pattern movement into her.

About this time babies get their knees up under them, fall back to belly down, get up on knees, fall down, get up. Maybe it's the picture "up there," the new depth picture he finds off the floor, that entices him to take all this punishment. And so he stays a little longer each time.

And into creeping on hands and knees he goes, like the reptile, off his belly to work, to move; back to belly-down amphibian to rest. Using wobbly arms and legs in "steppings" after a rocking and random period. Then off to a homologous bunny hop perhaps. Or a taste of homolateral, one side steps forward and he falls over on his side! The other side steps forward. Oops. There must be a better way. There is: four-point cross-pattern creeping for straight-line, long-distance, speedy runs. He is now a full-blown reptile, "higher" in evolution, "smoother" in coordination, and "brainier" in what he knows about arms and legs on opposite sides, head down and around, eyes focusing, ears hearing together, and what's in that cabinet over there. Brainier because he's using his reptile brain—the midbrain—higher yet in the head than pons and spinal cord below. By the time he has his first birthday, he has learned to use his three "old" brains, and mastered all the normal patterns of movement he need ever know about: random—if you want to count—homologous, homolateral, and cross-pattern. He has led four lives: fish, worm, amphibian, reptile. He will now stand on whatever he just built for himself.

Our job is to build Janey a good beginning. Underneath walking. Under the remarkable human cortex whose business it is to walk her in cross-pattern, the way we walk, someday. When J.'s lower functional levels of crawl and creep look normal, we can allow her to leave animal-baby and move on to human-child.* That is our goal in mobility. Patterners will be directly associated with this one area the brain works.

Other human-child goals for Jane too: good sharp senses, seeing, hearing, and feeling. And good sharp "doings" which follow: speaking and writing the language, and all that. Each area of human function has levels, little steps too, the way mobility builds a well-coordinated body. All the "brains"—spinal cord and medulla, pons and midbrain, the cortex—all come into use *visually* too, for example. There's a fantastic hierarchy of functions in human growth that recapitulates evolution every time a baby takes to the floor!

Mary asked me to bring Jane in. I did, in my arms in her blue clown pajamas with the feet. Better the patterners not see her legs all at once. Also carried her on my hip so her legs wouldn't be scissored. Patterners all sort of sighed, smiled, and someone said, "Isn't she adorable?" J. was smiling, trembling with the excitement of being picked up, dimples could be seen from the back row I bet. Even with the crossed eyes on and off, she always "gets by" because of the auburn hair and beautiful skin, a kind of glow about her.

"How old is she?" someone asked. I told them she was three last month. Saw a few purses open and a few tissues.

Quickly said, "I hope you'll be able to stand her. She's got her mother's looks and her father's disposition." They laughed and I said, "Goodnight and thank you from Janey."

Tucking her in, I could hear Mary telling patterners how busy I'd be. The four five-minute patternings all together took only twenty minutes a day, but the rest of the day was to Jane's advantage also. The senses . . . a program of sensory stimulation . . . more even than from the floor and from movement . . . intense . . . through J.'s eyes, ears, body, hands . . . to the brain . . . bits of data to a computer! Didn't hear anyone laugh.

Mary read the following list of suggestions she'd composed:

1. May arrive early, sit-read, never late, because of program which follows. No socializing. Leave immediately.
2. For swapping, call "preference" list first, then try people on "available-except" list.
3. Never call Mrs. Napear. Phone will be turned off till 8:00 P.M. anyway.
4. Don't get into situations that may delay you, such as traffic or phone calls.

* Final creeping perfection is attained in the normal child after he begins walking. Final crawling perfection is, likewise, attained after the onset of creeping. His preferred locomotion will be the lower level while he struggles with the new one.

5. You may bring a responsible older child in mornings (either 9:00 or 11:00 patternings) and at 3:30 to play with Grant, age five, so patterning will not be broken or distracted. (Grant at kindergarten during 1:30 patterning session.)
6. If you do not come and do not send an alternate, then automatically you are off the list.
7. If you have to resign, please, get someone to take your place. The Napears will train everyone.
8. Make phone conversations brief when trying to find alternate. Yes or no only, so caller can continue looking.

After that the fun began. Mary Lawrence, Edith Alfred, and "the other mother" showed us patterning. The patient: Little Kimmie McMillan, who had worn a party dress, had to peel to panties for this. This homolateral movement wasn't at all cloddish. Nonstop perfect rhythm of move, pause, move, pause again where nothing moves for one second. Left-side and right-side "engineers" watching the head movement for signal to "go." Head-engineer neither looking nor listening, except to a rhythm somewhere? Someone figured it's all done in 2/4 time.

Mary cautioned patterners that it was a central nervous system movement we were after. And, please, not to think of it as an "arm this or a leg that." Strive for smooth, rhythmic serialization. All four appendages moving exactly together, whether they are being flexed or extended. As the left side extends, the right side flexes. *Exactly together*. Watch the head. "Get it" before you leave tonight, please. We'll come and cheer you on.

Then off to the living room, storage room, bedrooms, and playroom, each group to pattern "a patient." Bert and I floated from group to group, so impressed with the mixture: old and young, men and women, the shy and the outgoing, the smooth and the clumsy. Whole families. Also couples, women to do weekdays, men weekends. Chatted with Chris Beck, the young man who volunteered "to give a little back"—just out of the hospital and glad to be alive, you can tell, head bandage the least of his worries.

People looking at Jane's new crib-cage. A fantastic job; could win a design award anyday for function—or construction. Never for beauty. We stood over it, just looking down at the rough slats and rabbit wire. Well, wait till I put the mattress and yellow rosebud sheets in it. And Janey. With the top anchored she would be able to get up on all fours. Or lie down. Period. All standing opportunities would be prevented from now on. All day. All night.

Mary hastily explained the two tactile programs to me in the kitchen. First, the "salt-glo procedure" and a list of every part of the body I was to rub in the tub, in what order, and toward midline of body or away from it, stay off spine area, O.K. What is midline? The line down the middle, of course. Well, it *could* be the waist . . .

Then the "other" program. Nameless. Can see why. Send a variety of sensations to J.'s brain: rough, smooth, cold, hot, etc. And a tuning fork to say hello to "headquarters" via bone vibrations from all those bony prominences—wrist, elbows, and I-don't-know-what-all. Mary not batting an eyelash. Buy a flower holder? Those round things with needlelike spines? All J.'s body should be touched with it—chest, tummy, the works! Every day? Yes. Mentioned psychological aspects of mother hurting child. Mary countered: if J. could *feel* all that on her right leg someday, "We'll have succeeded in what I would call one of her primary needs, telling headquarters all about that right leg down there!" Then as she was leaving she gave me her phone number at home, and added, "Hey, I did some fancy Nancy Drew footwork in Philly. Solved last summer's Maine mystery."

"What mystery?"

"The case of the stutterer's small, small world."

"What?"

"Get Edith to tell you how I loused up Stuart last summer. That's her field, and she's great at it."

"Mary, tell me!"

"Not me. I no longer deal in stutterers. From now on I am strictly an arm and leg man."

I was laughing again, doubling over in the doorway. With Mary it's like that. Serious professional, intense in her work, deeply committed to getting J. going. But not one to take herself seriously. Here we are about to start all this for Jane. And Grant? And Stuart? And me not crying. *Laughing.*

Decided to introduce the tactile, visual, and auditory programs gradually this week. Start patterning a week from today, Valentine's Day, which happens to be the day Jane was due three years ago. Sentimental slob.

FEBRUARY 12, 1965. I asked Edith Alfred about Stuart and what Mary Lawrence meant by "loused Stuart up last summer." What "mystery"?

Edith chuckled. The big mistake was music, as well as too much bilateral activity.

"Music?"

"Yes, all stutterers on this program should have music removed from their environment."

"All music?"

"Yes, until cortical hemispheric dominance is firmly established. I say 'firmly,' because it can be a difficult feat. These stutterers are strongly bilateral people and they love the bilateral activities they do so well. Right now both of his hemispheres are in competition, since neither is dominant. Both are sub-dominant, you see."

"A little mistake like music during the day makes such a difference?"

Edith thought that funny. Said music for a stutterer is not a "little mistake," but the trigger that turns it on! Then something that bordered on "don't knock it till you've tried it."

When one of the two hemispheres becomes dominant, it controls the skills of language—the words themselves.

The other hemisphere, the sub-dominant one, will control the sound— the tonal qualities of speech, the music our voices make when we talk, the sounds you can find somewhere along a piano keyboard.

So, it's the tonality from out here feeding the *two sub*-dominant hemispheres in there that's making the competition rough for Stu's language? So that's the war. Neither side can win—with language. Because neither side's been given the ball to carry?

I'd better let The Philadelphians explain it to him—and Bert.

FEBRUARY 20, 1965. Stuart very sensitive. Jane not enough.

"You're not *really* laughing. You're just making believe, right?"

"Right. I feel more like the opposite. Actually."

"Crying, you mean? *I* wouldn't do it then."

"In a moment, Stu— Not now." (Flower holder prick-prick down the arm, the outside . . . now the sticky wicket, J. pulling her arm against herself, me trying to open it out to get "under" . . . Prick-prick-prick down this side, just the same, Punkin' . . . So strong—how she's always kept her elbows glued to her sides that way . . .)

"I think that whole thing is really stupid!"

"Not now, Honey— Zippadee-doo-dah, zippadee-a-a-a— My, oh, my, what a beautiful day-ay-ay—" (Down the leg, outside first . . . *does* feel it on this one, bothers her . . . now the other one, Mary's right, big difference . . .)

"You can't sing good enough. It still bothers her, I bet. She's got a lot more tender skin than you do! It wouldn't bother me— But— Why do you have to do it there? (Front torso now.) That is *really* stupid!"

"Stuart, out, please. I'll explain why as soon as I'm finished."

(I get a cold can from the freezer compartment.) "Don't tell me she's got to have that . . . now!"

"Yes. All over. Like the other stuff. So— Look— This does bother her, so just go out and wait for me— Camptown races sing this song, doo-dah, doo-dah——"

"I know, but why now? That is the stupidest thing I ever heard of!"

"Out! Now! I'm busy."

"O.K. But——"

Then an honest heart-to-heart talk with Stuart. How *I* hate it too. But I don't want Jane to think of it as a "crying thing." And how it really bothers *anybody* who's got enough sense to figure out it's a pretty unusual thing to be doing to a child. But J. has not had enough "experience" yet to figure that out. Actually you notice *she's* not crying. Never whines with any of it. In fact, she laughs when I laugh, giggles with the songs. I don't know what it is to her. A special music game maybe. The important thing: what is it to Stuart?

Tiny lecture on "tactile." Stuart wide-eyed, asking for more. How it's the brain that feels. And the body that sends the stuff to feel. All the tactile stuff—rough, smooth, cold, hot—from out here goes there. And Janey needs a lot more than she gets by herself on the floor. So I come in. To send it.

Stu still calling it "stupid." Natch.

FEBRUARY 21, 1965. One whole week done. She still cries every pattern-ing session, have to stop many times before the timer rings to wipe tears. And the table's so messy with mucus. Such a long five minutes; J. looking so vulnerable, so frightened, lying on her stomach in a diaper only, on that hard (cold?) white plastic. Singing is the only thing that pacifies her, but I can't remember all the words of anything, even a nursery rhyme.

Patterners are so great, and don't look across at me. Seriously, intently, they just start again; arm and leg up, pause, arm and leg down, pause, over and over. Nobody's got rhythm, what with my groping for lyrics and J.'s pitiful cry on and off.

Explained pauses again to each patterning group. *I* must begin head before *they* begin arm and leg. Told them it was part of the old TNR (tonic neck reflex): infants keep their faces turned toward the hand of their flexed arm, with the fingers near the mouth and the other arm in extension. A baby moves his head to change position or to find the light, and auto-matically, reflexively, the arm and leg on that side flex up while the other side extends down, but the head always starts the switch. Watch any baby.

FEBRUARY 23, 1965. Tactile program for body sensitivity: salt-glo bath. Bitter fun. Each day at 4:00 P.M. till forever. Hate it all the time I'm rubbing that coarse stuff in, singing. I don't look at her face. Don't want to lock eyes, I *would* cry.

Bending over her, half in the tub myself, I say out loud, "Wake up little right leg. Get good at feeling like your little left pal over there." Brain does the feeling, but I'd rather talk to the right leg. Try to disentangle one from under her, encircle her slippery body with all of mine. Both of us are frightened by this feat; J. can't sit that way. Singing louder now till the leg is rubbed with the salt paste, all its parts: foot (back, toes), sole (toes), shank (front and inner), thigh (front and inner). Years later I finish all that, turn her over to do shanks, thighs, hips, buttocks, and so on, carefully avoiding the spine. And so on and so over the whole body. She's taking it all, better than I am. Who ever thought this up? Someone in Philly, Mary says.

When I spray the water, cold-warm-cold, I laugh like crazy. She's not sure, but now it's over, you see. Upsy-daisy to the bed and rub-a-dub-dub. Rub so hard my hands hurt through the towel. Red now. That's it. Then the alcohol all over. Now let's go! Down on the carpet and let's see—no, let's feel what you can feel. Little Glowworm.

FEBRUARY 24, 1965. Have found three songs that fit the patterning best: "Jingle Bells," "London Bridge," and "This Is the Way We Wash Our Clothes."

Grant still upset somehow about my wearing slacks! Said today again, "You look like a man." All attempts to ease him are failing: "Other mothers wear slacks, see?" "It's too cold for shorts." "I can't move on the floor with J. if I'm in a skirt." "Or creep with you either—" It must be rather like a two-and-a-half-year old's fright about masks. His mother isn't the same with one on. His mother went away?

MARCH 1, 1965. One patterner brought the current issue of *McCalls:* "Train Your Baby to Be a Genius" by Glenn Doman and Carl Delacato. Thank goodness, the magazines have picked up this program for its *preventive* value. I'm surprised the magazine risked the ire of baby equipment advertisers to let this one through.

The article simply tells mothers of newborns to get off the pastel-and-quiet-house kick and move out of bland and placid babies into the business of the human person in their care. So many good easy-to-do suggestions for waking them up to sights and sounds and touchings. Mary said in Philadelphia they say convert the garage to a crawling room if you're afraid of your precious things and electrical outlets. Leave the car outdoors. Which do you want, a rusty car or a rusty child?

Bert read it. Said, "Almost makes you want to have another one, to do it right this time, doesn't it?"

"No. No such urgings. And you can just cut that out!"

It was the shot in the arm I needed, though. Got in all of Jane's program today. Schedules on the wall are a good idea. Also changing J.'s patterning table cover to oilcloth over foam rubber and using powder to eliminate friction, and a shirt.

All patterners pretty smooth now. And so nice. Several ask about evaluation for their children who have good I.Q.'s but who are "under-achievers." Difficult not to chitchat as they leave. Gotta stop all that, but the subject's so interesting.

MARCH 6, 1965. Almost broke down in the shoe store today. It wasn't what I said to the salesman as he measured J.'s foot . . . that was simple enough . . . I wanted black patent-leather Mary Janes . . . Did he have the cute ones that buttoned? . . . The cheapest, because she couldn't walk yet and would just be wearing them for outings. He didn't have any small enough for her thin little feet, but we took the smallest he had and said it really didn't matter anyway.

It was because one of the Saturday patterners was there. Hardly know each other. But I had the feeling she was feeling sorry for me. Something like that. A rough moment for *her,* about the shoes, I suppose. A minor detail to me. She left, quite eager to be gone? I suppose all this *would* look pathetic to someone else, shopping for shoes that don't matter. To others, do Jane and I make a pathetic picture? It jarred me somehow.

MARCH 12, 1965. Took Jane to local doctor-group today. Another upper respiratory infection, third one since the new year, no different so far from the old year.

Gave the doctor a copy of her daily schedule, so he could see what this program is all about. Something was wrong? Thought he glanced at his partner in a kind of knowing way. He only scanned the sheet and put it down. Would put it in her file. Did not ask a single question! Thought surely he would ask, "What is a salt-glo bath?" Maybe it was all *my* stuff, bed-making, laundry pickup, etc. As if I were showing I was a wonderful parent to do all this . . . I had so much else to do . . . I could hardly get her program in . . . even had to make up a schedule. Should have made a proper list of *her* program only.

Anyhow, I asked him if he were finished with Delacato's book. I'd given it to him for a kind of fast one-shot information-guide about this program's rationale. He pulled it from the papers on his desk. About halfway through it, said I could have it back. I was in no hurry, he could keep it. Said he really didn't think he wanted to finish it. But what did he think of the child development outlined therein, how a baby's brain organizes itself even in those first days? Maybe he could keep it to understand the rationale behind the remedial help some children need. Didn't it pique his interest about his *own* kids? He said his kids were O.K. whether they had done all that crawling and creeping or not. And the author had made mistakes about the brain. What? Attributes Parkinson's disease to the midbrain, when anyone knows it is frontal lobe. (Or something like that.) Since I certainly did not know, I took the book and left.

Mary says Parkinson's *treatment* has been frontal lobe. But etiology is midbrain. Delacato is always more interested in causes than symptoms, she says. Also, he has plenty of doctors down there to read his manuscript. Mary was disappointed. I said it was O.K.; I don't have time to educate the guy anyway. And he's a good pediatrician for whatever else ails her.

Two choices, according to Mary: change to another doctor-bunch, or go with the nit-pickers. It just might be harder from now on though.

The world is full of professional jealousies, Mary says. I know. Dad clued me in long ago about that and the in-groupness of medicine.

The world is full of Janes too. That Dad *didn't* tell me about. But neither did any other doctor. Only Mary, to share this nightmare.

MARCH 15, 1965. Forget the phone. Ignore click-clicking. The schedule's too tight before the 1:30 P.M. patterning. Patterners were waiting today while I finished J.'s visual program in the dark. Hot-water heater closet's a lousy place. J. can't follow the flashlight very long. Horizontal very poor. Is it too hot in there to keep her interest? Make window shades to darken room somewhere; our all-white house is bad for this program, but the radiant-heat floor is good.

Telephone a nuisance. A doctor's wife called today about her son. What did I suggest? I suggested she take a look at him. Couldn't tell her I'd noticed him already, his writings in the school hallway; he stands out with his incoordination and hyperactivity. Just hinted, just listened. Do I have anything for her husband to read? Professional studies?

Lunch was a mess. Schedule a mess. Their kid is a mess. J. is a mess. Got to get on the ball. Stop the world. Not to get off, just to get set, get everything scheduled.

MARCH 17, 1965. A heck of a telephone conversation with Stuart's principal, after we settled the form for requesting Stu's tests, reports for Philadelphia. A plea on my part—plaintive and long-winded—about Sports Night at the school. What good did it do to ask a child to turn a simple somersault when he couldn't, not even on the third try, all his pals and parents standing by while he finished and failed? Wasn't it just like the world to applaud the loudest for the lowest? It would take more than heavy applause to conquer the inadequacies of simple hopping on one foot. Could he *see* that some don't know their left from their right? They *look* disorganized.

He *had* seen. Already knew which ones. Spends a lot of time observing in gym these days. But it's a heart-breaker not to allow all to participate.

Yes, and the world would get tougher. There comes a time when no one claps for the clumsy. There comes a time when it isn't cute anymore.

He mentioned the *Scholastic Teacher* article, "You Have to Crawl Before You Can Read." Read well, that is. Why not crawl-and-creep breaks instead of get-up-and-stretch breaks for class "breathers?" We discussed the possibility of including this in gym, as schools are beginning to do. Or just send the reading consultant to Philly for their postgraduate course.

He's sighing at my asking for the big jump. Right now he's busy interesting the teachers to get interested in perceptual problems. And could I get together with the gym teacher, give him stuff to read? Promised I would.

Great guy, the gym teacher. He and his wife are weekend patterners here. Must tell him about last month's track meet at Madison Square Garden, with Mary discovering a lot more than walk, run, and jump. Our

husbands were in stitches over Mary's rundown on the runners. What a
high hurdler needs a pole vaulter doesn't—brain-wise. And who on a track
team might get reading medals as well. And who *never* could, Mary was
betting. All this from a physical therapist lady in the end-arena section.
Coaches also know which fellow can do what. They just don't know why.

I bet most school gym programs are 90-something percent bilateral too.
Rhythms, gymnastics, team ball, to meet the energy pounding into the gym
in herds. No encouragement here for children in kindergarten and first-
grade who are moving into preferred-side dominance. Wondering if the
whole USA backyard-equipment culture, the front-yard bike culture, and
the indoor stereo culture hasn't (on top of the playpen culture) given a
bilateral herd to the gym teachers in the first place? A gym program
planned for neurological needs, reading needs—will that be the future of
phys ed?

Tongue in cheek, I challenged the principal to make a list of incoordinate
students in gym, then compare it with the remedial readers list. So a few
don't add up. Then how about those who may be outstanding athletes in
the two-arms, two-legs gym program, but have a heck of a time with *fine*-
finger coordination or eye-hand games? Wouldn't hurt to take a look.

He says the problem is to get others to see it, especially the parents. The
reading-technique-controversy (look-say versus phonics) is still news to
some. He says you can't say "incoordinate" or "neurological" or even
"baby development" to a parent. Alternatives are limited: reading clinic,
psychologist, family doctor. Certainly you could never intimate that the poor
reading has anything to do with the child's brain. He would hope the family
doctor would do that.

I said he might, if he knew anything about it, but med schools don't
teach that course yet. From doctors I had talked with about this, they also
refer the parent. To the reading clinic, or the psychologist, or the *school
principal.*

It was all understandable—terribly. But I told him about Edith Alfred,
School Reading Consultant, anyway.

MARCH 19, 1965. Stu's "school history" is here before me, the kindergarten application showing how bilateral this child was at five. "What
Activities Does Your Child Seem to Enjoy Most?"

Activities using the body—climbing, trampoline, ball playing, dancing and
marching, relay races.

When he wasn't on his bike! My extra paragraph about it:

In general, Stuart is one of the most fearless children I've seen and because of
his coordination has been allowed to climb trees, jump into water and float, and
do rather advanced gymnastics on jungle gym since he was much younger. This
energy may be a problem inside, especially during long winter months, and

results in a "heavy approach"—wrestling, running, etc.—where other children are concerned . . .

And the report cards over the years saying the fuzzy part:

. . . a light speech impediment, but it shows improvement. Does not faze him at all. Seldom does it.
. . . needs to develop more fluency and expression in reading.
. . . on occasions Stuart reads haltingly but is working toward developing more fluency and expression. . . . His comprehension is excellent . . . word-attack skills are good.
. . . continues to stammer. However, the problem has occurred less frequently and with not as much severity. Mr. S——— [speech therapist] has observed Stuart during formal speech instruction.

I remembered Mr. S. Awfully nice. Wanted to discuss Stuart's home situation. What could I tell him? It had everything in it. We screamed. We were silent. We loved. And we hated. More often than not, we enjoyed each other. The only thing I could think of that might be too much stimulation for Stuart was the high enthusiasm, the general exuberant tone of the home. We simply commented a lot about each other's goings-on. Did he think that could be it? No, he liked enthusiastic families.

The following year (each Friday), another speech therapist. Young, pretty, explaining she had been playing cards with him to establish rapport and put him at ease. It was spring, and so far that year she had never heard him stutter. As I left, she said, "He's about the smartest, sharpest card player I've ever played with."

That he was. In the pile of papers from the principal was his California Short Form Test (last year). Total Data brought it out to a neat 136! I knew what that meant. And last year's Stanford Achievement Test in the second grade slotted him neatly into the fourth grade, with Average Reading running 4.6!

With all this plus "excellent comprehension" why was he a middle reading group student? *Who* is in the top group? Visually the kid has been "stuttering" as well, K through 3, and only his smart mother knows for sure?

MARCH 23, 1965. Janey and I doing reflexive crawls after patterning (four times a day): J.'s legs getting stronger, or am I imagining? Left push *is* better since last month. While digging my thumb into her arch and pulling the toes down to make her knee flex, I am saying, "Push off, little weak right leg!" More and more I catch myself in these little meditations.

During our break on the kitchen floor, just before we turn and start back down our course to the playroom again, J. is a scream in front of the refrigerator. She uses the chrome strip on the bottom like a mirror. Eyes stay put, but head moves up and down. (Copying the vertical eye-following exercise we do in the closet?)

At outrigger-creeping time I often find her doing "other" eye exercises. Head lowered, but eyes do the moving, up and down and almost out of sight.

The boys really get a kick out of this one: J. practices left-right head turns, but leaves eyes front and center, staring forward. So funny. Could be mom's horizontal light-in-the-dark-sky is making her aware of all this. Or is it the head-turns in patterning?

Sometimes we find her with her head going left and right and her eyes moving *all* around. Screeching halt, stop, stare. Again. Make it all happen again. Swish, swish. Dizzy-busy, stop, stare.

Then back to the "other" one, head moves but eyes fix, slowly, quietly, don't move my eyes! Alternates these two "crazies" with some secret planning board of her own. Is she trying to tell the difference between smooth and dizzy? Or between head and eye? The brain is getting a few new signals, I guess.

Stu says we shouldn't laugh, because she's not doing it for us. Yes, it's a private thing. Entertaining herself with today's new floor show.

MARCH 26, 1965. "Thirty, thirty-one, thirty-two, thirty-three——"

I heard it from the kitchen, Grant counting his stars on his "My Program" chart. "Thirty-sev-ven——"

Tiptoed up behind him, wiping my hands as I went. Not only the "th's" but every single syllable enunciated beautifully.

"Forty-fi*v*e, Mom. You owe me for-ty-fi*v*e cents for my program this week."

I shook his hand and said, "Good deal, MacNeal! Did you really get forty-five stars in one week?"

"Sure, Mom, see?" And he started counting each one again, touching fingers to the brilliant reds, blues, greens and then on to the thirty's—ironically with the new gold stars.

I held my breath. He said the "thirty-three" like a pro. For the first time in his life that I knew of, he had left behind the blurred "firty's" and arrived at the sharp "thirty's." And all the rest of it too, "-se*v*-*v*en." And all without the benefit of his school's speech therapy.

Edith Alfred had explained it to me. Grant would have to hear "th" first before he said it. An improved auditory system would "clean up the blends." Speech to babies is unbroken noise to start with. Later they distinguish noise into inflections (sweet talk from scolding—Jane in January). And later the brain becomes more perceptive, more "distinguishing," catches the pauses between sounds (words). Sounds-to-words are clearer now. Finally words are clear. The child's speech reflects these increases in auditory perception. Grant hears "firty," he will say "firty"; when he hears it clearer, his speech will reflect that too.

MARCH 31, 1965. Collected all notes and came up with the following new doings of Jane tactilely:

1. Feels rug, then feels wood, then feels slate. What a look afterwards! Then does it all again. Grant in hysterics.
2. When she's playing on the floor she rubs her body, arms, legs over the hot water bottle I just did her tactile program with. Also tuning fork, actually pinging it against bony prominences of knees and ankles. (Doesn't do shoulder or elbow bones.) Avoids the sharp spiny flower holder like the plague.
3. Loves cornstarch play on patterning table. Helps me spread it around in circles. Later, on floor, does circles too. Making believe? Or just likes the circling feel.
4. Washes patterning table in a haphazard hand swab when I'm cleaning it. (What goes under tactile notes and what under manual?)
5. After salt-glo, turns her arms over and over, rubbing them on the carpet. That skin-tingling sensation really lasts. Takes awhile for *my* hands and forearms to get back to normal.

APRIL 5, 1965. Think J. now knows outdoors from indoors; shows delight the minute the breeze hits her face. (Knows night from day too, I think, from reaction to lights when I take her in car.)

Outdoors she has a ball swishing low pine branches. So much light and dark there and so much full vision workout. (Tell Mary.) Found her extricating herself out of the rose hedge precisely. She knows the outrigger as well as her body. (Same "sense" I have driving the car through narrow spaces?) Heads for the rose bushes repeatedly. (Not much "sense" there.) Showed her the thorns, touched her finger to them, and said, "Danger, thorns," with a sound of the ominous. She just laughed. Her general attitude. The all-yard-creep smile.

Indoors she's an altogether different Reptile Lady. Not the same indoor-child we had last summer in Maine. Doesn't bluster and bang around, knock over things or grab. Those silent, hard, glassy objects on the low tables, once examined, now have no interest for her. Her floor life since July has gone from a kind of creeping-for-creeping's sake to more selective adventurings. Does she see and get with more planning? More precision? Her reach?

Here's some of it—a plan of some sort. Yesterday I found J. in the hall, prone, slowly brushing her leg against the brick wall. Scooted sideways a little to the opposite sheetrock wall and rubbed her right leg against it with a few back-and-forth brushes. Scooting that way from sheetrock to brick, finally a summary of sorts, brushing *arms* the same way. Very quiet. No squealing or jargon-making.

What area is this, Mary? Tactile? Mobility?

APRIL 7, 1965. Something interesting is going on in J.'s hearing, I think. Some time ago I wrote:

J. covering her ears with her arms, inside upper part, first left then right. Does it lying on floor *all* the time. Also lies down on me and rubs her ears over my hair. Then rubs her arms (only inner area) over my hair. Got something going with tender part of arm; this is not "cuddling." Also ears. A connection here? One looks like tactile experimentation; the other, ears against hair, a muffling practice of each ear as in patterning!

Then I wrote (date?):

Think J. is starting to listen. Very keen for "z-z-z" sounds in "Fuzzy Wuzzy Wuz a Bear" and "woof-woof" in "Old MacDonald." *Fee, fie, fo, fum,* etc.— much laughter and pleasure. Also turns and listens to opening of front door. Also beginning to know when I substitute a word (a sound to Janey?) in songs. Doing more of this, to encourage her "listening" during patterning. Good equal practice to top-listening ear, one then the other? I hope. Patterners are mentioning all this since they were here last week.

This week:

J. is listening for *language*—I *think.* Looks at my mouth when my hands are holding objects behind my back. (Auditory program three times a day.) Also "thinks" before she reaches for the one I name. If she chooses the wrong one (shoe instead of ball with my "ball"), I do it again, but sometimes switch hands. Gets to play with object if correct. Also getting idea of function of these: Puts hat on her head, or mine, brushes her bangs or mine, extends foot for shoe or sock. Knows that a pencil marks paper, eye glasses go over eyes, things go *in* a purse (not just for openings and closings).

Mary says all UNDERSTANDING, all COMPREHENSION equals AUDITORY SYSTEM, even if you are talking about reading!

APRIL 9, 1965. Noticed J. in the bedroom, rubbing arms and legs against pegboard walls. More like nestling one side of her body into wall. Then she squirms a few times to get an arm and leg full of pegboard. Has to turn completely to rub the other side because bed is in the way. Looks back over her shoulder to watch her body turn. Gradually and gloriously! Must tell Mary. Using vision out of the corner of her eye for all this, so why do I have to do it four minutes more each day with my frantic flashlight? Is this what Mary means by "lateral fields?" I can tell ahead of time, Mary will say the normal amount of floor stimulation isn't enough for J. Send lots more—Mary usually says 500 percent—visual data to J.'s brain-computer.

APRIL 11, 1965. Yesterday: took me awhile to realize the sound of crystal glasses . . . *tink-tink-tink*. Janey was in the foyer cabinet. Tapping, so carefully, wine glasses, goblets, etc. against one another. Just playing with the sounds—highs and lows. Tapped the wooden shelf too. Touched the carpet—no sound. Wheeled around and touched one to the slate floor. Brought them all over to the slate, one by one. Accidentally touched a smaller slate the second time. Then the fun began. She "checked out" a half-dozen slates in the foyer, finally using wine glasses only. I stood ready to rush in if one broke.

Today: went back to crystal-slate sound-makings the minute I put her on the floor for free creep. Then she took an iron bolt and started crystal and iron comparisons on the slate. Lying prone, braced on elbows, both hands going. Such eyebrow expression, such surprise. I will always remember her joy.

So the brain heard something it never heard before—a lot of somethings? Bits of data *tink-tink-tinking* their way up to headquarters?

APRIL 13, 1965. Yesterday's trip to Philadelphia. Carl Delacato is impressive with children. Direct honesty, loving bluntness, as if one's manner is the surest way to pay respect to a child, even those with a learning or speech problem.

After the morning's evaluation: "Hello, Stuart. You're some reader, aren't you? I see here you went over the top of our reading test. You don't need our program. . . . Stand up over there. . . . Now point your finger at this pencil. . . . O.K. . . . Do it again. . . . O.K. Now go out of the room—get lost for a few minutes—while I talk to your mom and dad."

Told us Stu's neurological organization had come along "quite well," except for far-point vision . . . neither left nor right . . . fluctuates when sighting at far point . . . as the ball comes toward him, for example, sights left, then right, continually alternating . . . "result rather than cause. Hear me, Napears? Result rather than cause."

The brain needs help in reaching final right-sidedness, a dominant left hemisphere, that is. Do two things: (a) take music out of his life for about six months; and (b) spend spring and summer in right-handed *outdoor* (away from echo chambers) activities. As right arm comes around for throwing, hitting, etc., his right eye will be brought into use more than left one. That's it.

Delacato expects the stuttering to disappear within six months. If not, "Call us. Collect. Anytime, day or night." Obviously he doesn't expect to hear from us again! In fact, we can leave right now.

Like going to the dentist the day the tooth doesn't ache—of course there was no stuttering today. Staff member taking history while Stu took tests said, "Stuart did not have music in the car on the ride down, I would wager." Touché. The radio's broken.

APRIL 16, 1965. J. is now using her hands in crawling. (Used her forearms to pull with before.) Sure enough, she's pulling with her fists. Gotta bend down and look under her; all this is happening under her chest, like a secret waterwheel under *The Mississippi Queen!*

Down on the waxed tile, kitchen to playroom and back again, we go, pushing the fire engine ahead—or blue and yellow detergent box, or balls, or whatever comes to mind. Let her play with the incentives as soon as she catches up to them, so she will always trust me. And to rest my own legs—this takes knees mostly. Knees and anticipation. She is bringing her knee up by herself, but I have to figure where that will leave the foot next time. Sock my hand in there, in case someone just might be ready to push-off against it. In fact she often does these days! And it is at these four daily crawling times, after the patternings, that I learn so much about what Janey sees and looks back to, hears and listens for, feels and pushes after, to enjoy it one more time.

Someone pulled a chain up there somewhere? Sounds. Shut in for so long, now falling all over the place. The blitherings continue—on fingers, backs of hands, arms. Raspberry sounds, Indian war whoops on fingertips or whatever is handy.

A few good moments like these can make you forget the drudgery of the rest. Today's Bert's birthday. No cake. No present. Will suggest "celebrating" tomorrow, Quick Thinker. How can it be April 16 already?

APRIL 20, 1965. I called Mary tonight.

"You sound tired. Of course, you *should,* doing what I am trying to imagine you did today."

"I am." Bert and I finished the crawl box, all disgusting eight feet of it. As tunnels go, the Holland couldn't have presented more problems. This item will head the list of my paraphernalia-for-parents-of-this-program store someday. Bert and I creeping around, crisscrossing clothesline rope to make the top, in and out of eyebolts as Mary suggested, but we forgot the part about the distance above J.'s head. So we did the whole "top" again, lower. All this the night after I "laid" eighty eggs for a 4-H Easter-egg hunt in the yard. A rough week all around. Two calls from parents. One boy had brain surgery at two but no follow-up as to function throughout childhood. How I hate the hinting routine. He "may" have a perceptual difficulty—when I've had my eye on the kid all along. All so depressing. Tried Janey in the crawl box twice. What a drag that is. Haven't had time since. So, what the hell——

"I always wondered when you would stop the dance and admit it's a grind——"

"What dance?"

"Oh, the one about I'm-on-top-of-everything, including the community, that rose-covered cottage you manage out there. Beautifully, I must say. It's just good to hear you're human and find it all a grind. That's all. How're the boys?"

"Fine. Each needs a social secretary."

"How's Jane?"

"So cute. Brushes the back of her hair all the time now."

"Really? Reaches in back to brush her own hair?"

"Yeah, why? Other than it's a new thing?"

"Arm extension. Full range of movement. 'ROM,' we say."

"Another PT term! Please, don't teach me anymore. I can't remember the other stuff. Is that important?"

"For someone who always kept her elbows clutched to her sides? I'd say. Remember that exercise they gave you for opening her arm out? The week before I met Jane?"

"Yes."

"She just hit the jackpot if she's reaching behind her head."

"That's good to hear, because I rarely get one hundred percent of the program in."

"I figure you do about eighty percent of it. That's probably a high average. Wish my other parents did as well."

"You mean, I don't have to do all the program each day?"

"I did *not* say that."

"But that's what you mean."

"I believe The Philadelphians are right. Do it all. Each day. That's the goal."

"But a little less wouldn't hurt, would it?"

"The question is, would a little more help? Peggy, do not *ever* ask me what *not* to do for Jane."

"I'm sorry. . . . By the way, she's really moving—so many ways, I can hardly keep notes."

"I'm not surprised. There's usually a tremendous surge with these kids the first few months of the program. In a baby, all this is so explosive that first big year of life, you wouldn't believe how fast——"

"It's just that I'm tired of all the managing and manipulation——"

"I don't wonder."

"What's that arm thing again? Something babies do naturally?"

"Yes. Or with patterning."

"With patterning?"

"Yes. Peggy, how many times have you extended those arms since I saw you last?"

"I wouldn't care to count, thank you."

"That may have something to do with it."

APRIL 23, 1965. Patterners call it the Watusi or "Luci-Baines-J" when Janey anticipates patterning. As they walk toward the table, she lies down and "patterns herself" from waist up! Laughing and hiccuping as they gather round. Moves head and arms exactly right. Nothing with the legs. Still scissored at the ankles and off the table from the knees down. We still cannot involve the lower legs (shanks) in the patterning "brush" against the table surface; only the thighs get in contact. Some days patterners seem to get shanks lower, closer to the powdered oilcloth. Or is J. "looser" some days? "Less spasticity," Mary wants to see, so the whole leg can "lie down" eventually. What is "spasticity" exactly? Dictionary says "hypertonic muscles"; too tense, I take it. So we have to loosen them up? But Mary says these are not "exercises for the legs" and tell everybody not to call them that. She's so funny.

APRIL 27, 1965. This morning, Betty Young was standing on tiptoes to peer out the window, half listening to my explanation about moving the patterning table to the living room, her back to me——

"Eh-o" again. Barely.

She turned. Looking at Janey, over to me——

"Eh-o" stronger, not so whispery, a voice? Third time. Janey on elbows, head lifted out to Betty, as long as I live the clearest, dearest picture I'll wrap in memory.

"Hello, hel-LO, Janey!" Betty walking to her. "She did say 'hello,' didn't she?"

"I think so. Three times. She was trying to get your attention. You were looking out the window, you know? You didn't say anything to her, always everybody does, you didn't, you were wondering about picking Elaine up or something——"

"I'm sorry——"

"No, no, you don't understand— It's the first thing she's ever said. It's the first thing she's ever said, the first *real* word. You just heard Janey say her first word. You were here to hear it, with me; we heard it together. She actually did, because you turned around and answered her, it sounded so like 'hello.' And she did it three times, so she must know 'hello,' I mean, you would think she really did say it, wouldn't you?"

"Oh, definitely. She kind of whispered it, so I didn't notice her at first. Sorry———"

I rushed toward Elaine before the door closed behind her. "Quick. Go stand by the window, look up and out, as if you're looking for someone. Don't say a thing. Don't look at us— No, don't take off your sweater— Quick."

Didn't work. So I'm still not—still really haven't heard her voice yet.

APRIL 29, 1965. Now Janey has found wool to rub against. Lying between the Moroccan bedspreads on the twin beds, she brushes the right bed with the right side, then scoots left to do left side on left bed again and again. All with the outrigger on!

I hope Mary will see some of this stuff Saturday when she re-evaluates Janey here. During crawling time (as we rest) she checks out everything, as if she had a list from Mary's lecture. Turning (pivoting), balancing on a side (like the sidestroke), sitting against the walls and rubbing her back, sitting with back to wall and feeling the wall behind her head with her palm, then the back of her hand. None of that is worm or frog or reptile, but she is a pretty cute animal these days.

I'm so eager seeing all this, we're off schedule with each crawling time. She should be in the crawl box, but J. doesn't use her right leg there for *anything,* not even bending it at the knee to fake a push. I have a devil of a time assisting it through those stupid ropes across the top. Why the crawl tunnel, Mary, when she gets less use of right leg there? Mary must be mistaken.

This schedule still is too tight. I hope Mary will drop some things, now that J.'s doing so well.

Regarding J.'s hands (manual competence): Look fine to me. No longer that fist-grasp anymore? Littered floor, as suggested, with things to handle. All this is new stuff, Mary:

1. Fills containers with small objects.
2. Flips checkers, marbles, and wheels, and watches them roll across floor. (Great eye-following exercise, heh, heh, since usually she has her head resting on one eye while she does this.) Flips dominoes and watches them come to a screeching halt, and never picks up dominoes again!
3. Uses pencil to make marks for the *sound,* I think; also scratches paper with her fingernails.
4. Index-finger pointing, but not at anything, more like finger-experiment if you ask me.
5. Brushes hands on floor (rug) as in patterning (can you believe?). Also brushes toys the same way (head to hip) while lying on side slightly. Watches this. Then does it again without watching. Then

watches again. "The toy is here by my eyes, going-going-gone, to my knees; I feel it stop there. Swish."

6. Controls patterning, clenches fists, won't let hand be brushed flat. Just started this, the little devil. Isn't that what you would call Jane's new awareness of her own hand?

7. Awareness and "practice" of thumbs: pushing against inside ridge of highchair top, pushing around the inside rims of cups and baby-feeding dish.

She's so fascinated with her fingers, it's almost embarrassing. Every combination—first with second, first and third, and so on. Also, wild inspection of separate fingers; pinches the back of each from first to fifth. Slow grin as she does this. If anyone saw this, he'd think she is stupid or something.

What *is* all this? Tactile? Manual competence? Or is it first *tactile* (input) then *manual* ability (output)? I bet Mary will say forget fingers and think floor or reptile or something. What does cortical opposition of thumb to finger mean? Said J. didn't have it. Sure looks to me like she's doing thumb-finger pickup, Mary.

Professional Evaluation

May 1, 1965. When Mary Lawrence walked in this morning, I thrust the "big news sheet" at her: "Hello real fast, Mary, and read this!"

Evolution of Human Speech as Recorded by Hysterically Happy Mom

1. Raspberry and Indian war whoop sounds on back of hand.
2. Lips, tongue, jaws—two months such practice.
3. Chopping motions—jaws and teeth.
4. With mirror (one of the things I littered the floor with), she plays with Indian war whoop and finger blitherings on lips.
5. Picked up ball 4/22/65, threw it, and said "ba." Wasn't sure then. But has several times since! Color it FIRST WORD.
6. Said "eh-o ("hello," natch) three times to get patterner's attention 4/27, and has many times since to patterners.
7. Says "bye-bye" to people (after front door is closed, so they never hear her). *Very* quiet, like double-*b* sound.
8. Says "mo ha" ("more water," natch); "mo" or "mo ma" for food.
9. Says "ow-ah" with line *"How I* wonder what you are" of "Twinkle, Twinkle, Little Star."
10. Says "deedle-deedle" with line from "My Son John."

11. Has repeated "ba-a" for *bath* four times. Yesterday said it spontaneously when she heard the water running in the bath. Was taking
off her shirt (by herself!) when I returned, looked at me and said
"ba-a" as a request.
12. Making "putchie-putchie" sounds a lot.
13. Might also have said "light," "tongue." Tongue is extended in tasks;
very aware of it. Looks at it move in mirror.
14. Moments between idea and speech, thinking?
15. Jargon all day long otherwise now.

Jane is talking . . . in English!

Mary is moving her head side to side, *Wow,* as she reads. Smiling, looking up——

"That's not all, Mary. Janey is really intelligent, I know it. I've just got to
tell you *all* this—I mean, how I know it is——"

"Is it O.K. if I take my coat off?" she deadpanned.

Both giggling. "I've been watching her and writing it down [see Appendix]
as she does each new thing—Now listen to this:

"One. Jane looks through a red cellophane fire hat at light and sun. She
puts her fingers behind all sorts of clear and opaque things to see what
they look like that way—clear plastic windows of fire engine, opaque table
top of highchair, an old door-screen in backyard. The psychologist at New
York Hospital always puts a glass between Jane and an object, and——"

Mary interrupted, "That's visual——"

"Two. And she puts a penny in a purse, but first she always feels inside
to see if it is empty."

"That's tactile differentiation of the third dimension——"

"Three. Oh, this too then? Stirring spoon in cup or pan; bouncing balls
in containers.

"Four. Get this: She is *controlling* situations. In patterning, also during
the 'visual program'——she turns her head and won't look, all with a pixie
look. Also during the 'auditory two-objects program,' does the same thing,
laughing, looking all around, won't choose for a teasing second, then does
it."

"Good!" Mary said.

"Five. But she is *really* smart at crawling times. Asks for water ('mo ha')
so I will leave the room and she can get off her belly *out of* crawling up
into creeping and run away—giggling and hiccuping and looking back
so much she can barely get going! She knows right from wrong, and she
teases!"

Mary chuckles.

"Six. Knows door opening at night is 'Daddy.' "

"That's auditory——"

"Seven. But this is really something, Mary. She has prolonged attention now. She looks at my lips when I talk and gives me, for the first time, a sense of *communication* between her and me.

"Eight. *And get this:* she shows extreme sensitivity—feelings—to arguments, especially between the boys. Cries if anyone cries. She knows, Mary, she knows.

"Nine. She is very sociable, Mary. Everyone says this, and I think her fearfulness has decreased tremendously. Why, she plays on the patterning table now like it's a jungle gym! Hangs her body down one side, holding onto the opposite edge, arms outstretched to reach across and over for a handlock. Goes just so far; feels when it's enough. Now that takes brains to figure out. She's smart, I know it."

Mary said, "Good, good. A lot of what you describe is visual, auditory, and tactile increases of differentiation. And that's what we want. She's got to see it, hear it, feel it, smell it, taste it. Then draw on all that information, make distinctions and choices out of all those bits of data. That's what intelligence is. Then, for other people to see it, Jane must talk it, or write it, or communicate it in some culturally accepted way." Mary says J. seems to be doing a lot of midbrain association from what I describe.

"What kind of *what?*" I asked.

"Association. She's beginning to organize some of that raw data—associating this sound with that action, et cetera. It's something babies do before they walk—you know, extend their foot when they see the sock, all that.

"Look, we've got all day. Let's go out into the yard and talk while we take a look at her creeping."

Mary was naming all the flowers for Jane, from iris to baby's breath to lilacs, still in bud. J. crept along, stopping to do a kind of sniff-out at each one. Now Mary got down on the grass blowing the puffballs, but Jane wasn't interested. Was Mary up too close, and J. sees better away?

Inside Mary wanted to observe Jane eating. What she observed was J.'s waiting-for-lunch antics: hips scooting the highchair to the counter from half a room away, and the wiggle up and out to this new formica floor. Mary was quite delighted by this, neurologically, that is.

I watched from the doorway during the tests for hand function. Over and over, Mary had J. pick up one penny with each hand, simultaneously. Afterwards, I remarked how well Janey did it.

"She's lousy," Mary said. "We want a deft, quick, thumb-to-index-finger pickup—tip to tip, not flat—with both hands simultaneously." No delay in one, even for a second.

Me, defensively: "I wonder if I can do that." I tried and could.

"That's what you need to hold a pencil well and without fatigue. It forms a circle, see?" Mary says a baby's grasp changes from prehensile fist-grasp, because the thumb gradually moves up the index finger, month by month, till he can pick up with thumb and first finger. But the baby doesn't get tip to tip until he's over a year old, about the time he starts walking. And he can't pick up simultaneously with both hands like that until he's about two. Kids in school right now are holding pencils flat, not tip to tip, just a symptom to her. They didn't finish their development sharply and finally.

"Mary, I've been wanting to talk to you about Janey's hands. The more I read—well, I kept coming across the word *athetoid.* I looked it up in my father's medical dictionary. It's out of date, but it has this picture of 'athetosis,' fingers that look all rubbery, like they each have an arch in them going the other way, uncontrollable-like. Well, kids that have brain damage have that, you know. And Jane's hands aren't like that."

"I'm listening."

"That's all. Her hands would be like that picture, if she had brain damage anywhere, wouldn't they?

"You're asking could Jane have some brain damage, even though her hands have no athetosis. The answer to that question, Peg, is yes. I didn't go into all that with you because the program is the same, whether she does or not. The Institutes will give you a very definite answer after their work-up. When you leave there, you will know as much about Jane as they do, believe me. But if they are right, if it is possible to start new pathways from the beginning the way babies start them—through the good live stuff never before 'used,' even in detour networks around cells without life— well, then, does it really make a whole lot of difference about what caused 'the slowness,' the symptoms, the dysfunctions? I mean, it's the same pro- gram, whether some cells are dead or not, the same supersouped-up all- day sensory stimulation idea."

Mary says it all so cleverly. Then this: Jane's new score, per the Doman- Delacato Developmental Profile (see Appendix): her *neurological* age*— twenty-one months.

"Oh, my God. Only twenty-one months? Now? What was her score then when we started patterning?"

"Nine months."

I'd never asked, never thought to.

"But this is excellent progress," Mary says. J. *had* been traveling func- tionally at one-fourth the rate of her age group. So she has doubled her neurological rate of growth in these nine weeks.

I told Bert the scoring as soon as he walked in. He went over to Janey on the table, and said, "Good work, Miss Girlus."

"Something for *me* maybe?"

---

* The neurological ages of Jane mentioned here reflect time-frame ages on the Doman-Delacato Developmental Profile before 1970. (See also p. 88.)

"You and Mary have a nice day?"

"Oh, you bet. We talked a lot and she taught Grant 'crazy-eights' when he came home from school."

"What's 'crazy-eights?' "

"Card game. I mentioned to Mary what Stuart asked me last week. About Jane."

"What's that?"

"Oh, one day he asked me if Janey were mentally retarded."

"What did you say?"

"For heaven's sakes, that's exactly the first thing Mary said to me, 'What did you tell him?'—like that. Well, I told him the truth. That Janey was certainly retarded, slow, behind a lot of three-year-olds in what she should be doing at this age. But it would not be true to say she is *mentally* retarded. Then Mary said, 'So—what did Stuart say?' "

"He just wanted to know. Somebody asked him if Janey was 'mentally retarded,' some boyfriend, I suppose. I tried to explain it. Simply. How some children might be permanently slow . . . on the same level of development . . . not developing at all . . . just not getting smarter and sharper, the way children usually do. But Janey is getting smarter every day, doesn't miss a trick, curious about everything she finds in her path. You can tell she isn't standing still, and I started telling him some of the stuff I had kept notes on, but he got impatient and said all he wanted to know was whether she was mentally retarded or not! And I said no. 'I think she's very curious and very smart.' We were doing the program to *prevent* her standing still, to speed her on to catch up with what she's *been* slow in. And now she's going lickety-split, I thought.

"Anyhow, I asked Mary what *she* would have said. What was the definition of 'mentally retarded,' actually? And you know how funny she is, she said, 'Write me that question last year. This year it's a big fuzzy thing with me. I'm beginning to think it's a progressive thing rather than a static something, could go *either* way, I would think. By next year I hope to figure it out. Ask me again after I know. O.K.?'

"That's the same seed I planted in Stu, as he ran out to play—we could take a look at it any time. Next month. Next year. You know. To keep it an open question, if he wanted to come back to it——

"But Mary did say this, 'Peg, the way she just went from nine to twenty-one months neurologically in these last two months is, to me, a surer label-ing, a safer ground for Jane's sake, than any other discussion we might have about her. When you cut through the mist of 'smart' or 'dull,' where do you go?'

"I said, 'To all that stuff you interrupted me with this morning—visual, auditory, tactile, association, recalling past experience to put with today's to get comparisons, choices, two-and-two. That?'

"That."

"Well, where does the 'mental' come in?"

"I think it has something to do with her brain. And yours."

That Mary is a scream, I'm telling Bert. "Anyway, Bert, there's something else we chitchatted about——"

"O.K., but I promised a catch to Grant."

"Don't you think *this* is a lot more important?"

"I don't see it makes any difference, Peggy."

"What's that supposed to mean?"

"It's interesting. But it's——" (shoulder shrug)

"It's *what?*"

"Pretty useless. Talking about it. Whether she's mentally retarded or not. Mary's right. Janey is a lot different now. Who knows why? Who will ever really know? Who cares why? She was doing hardly anything at all, and all of a sudden she seems to be going along as if she never really should have been called 'slow.' I don't know why you'd bother to label her. Or score her. Or anything. I think sometimes she's like 'a case' to you. You sound like she's a report to be charted. It's O.K. if you want to learn all the terms. I know it's interesting to you. But I'd just as soon think of her as a little girl who needs all the help we can give her, so she can catch up with her age group and get out to play with them. Hanging a label or a score on her is completely useless as far as *she* is concerned."

"Well put. I agree. So does Mary. The scoring bothers her actually. Scoring children— She said that. It's just an idiosyncrasy of mine that I work better at something—even a little girl—if I know *why* as I go. The notes and the terms, just consider them my crutch to get up and shake a leg at this stuff every day. It helps me to know where 'yesterday' was. With Janey. Before I start on 'today.' That's all."

3

From May 1965 to October 1965

MAY 4, 1965. Mary sent me a copy of the report she wrote for Jane's file. New program looks far too advanced for Janey. New schedule looks far too simple.

Good-bye forever to salt-glo, which left us with a half-case of coarse salt and seven bottles of alcohol.

Brought some iris in from the yard to show the boys what the flower holder is *really* for, so they wouldn't feel the urge to "correct" someone someday, "My mother used that on my sister."

No telling what friends and teachers have heard already.

At supper I mentioned Janey's depth perception. Grant stopped chewing on his steak bone long enough to ask, "What's she got?"

I explained. J. reached for a white button on Mary's blouse Saturday. Mary said, "What about that! Passing two "tests" before we even get started!": (1) detail within a configuration (small white circle *in* white background of blouse); and (2) depth (button *on* a blouse).

At the hospital in January Janey didn't notice the brown cookie on the brown table. Last month—no, March, I think—she started reaching for doorknobs and light switches. I remember, she bugged the patterners so, taking their eye glasses off. She used to see glasses as circles on a face, not a separate thing, you see. Oh, and all that skirt-lifting when the patterners arrived at the table to begin patterning was the same thing, Mary said. She's getting depth perception. Getting it. She has to focus eyes together more than 50 percent of the time to get any credit for that eye function.

Grant interrupted, "Do you think she'll ever get that?"

"If her eyes continue to get good as they have been doing, she will. She's doing creeping, you know, when she's not busy otherwise, uses her eyes all the time down there. Also has a new eye exercise this week. She's real cute with it, follows an object from her nose out. Show you sometime."

What does Grant get from these reports at supper? Depth perception will probably go around the kindergarten till it becomes "death session."

MAY 13, 1965. To think I bristled at Mary's book suggestion for Janey. I was so sure she's not interested in pictures at all, maybe in a year. The only thing Janey sees in a book is the banging possibilities, or ripping the metal spiral off that holds it together and banging with that. Mary said try, all the time writing, "Start visual symbols [pictures]—same size as object, outline only" on the program list and not bothering to discuss it with me. No wonder!

Meant to give Janey just one today—the yellow banana picture. She took to it so well, I gave her two others: ball and hat. Used Stu's Yankee baseball hat with team insignia. His idea. Because of the colors, and because she could feel it too; the insignia make "bumps" on it. Then he closed *his* eyes, and put *my* hand on it and said, "See?"

Home from school, Stu *saw* J. positioning the hat over the same size picture as Mary suggested. Then off she went, almost running in that fast cross-pattern creep of hers, hat on head, tossing her head this way and that, and body laughing with pride and pleasure.

Stu giggled and, hands in pockets, followed her to the bedroom. I peeked in. Yes, he was on the floor again playing with her, letting her get on top of him, outrigger and all, ingeniously ducking the side bars that poke out. (Must ask the brace man to cut these shorter; such length was really never needed and the walls are getting ruined from the scarring.)

Stu is playing with J. more and more. Now we don't have to say, "Don't get her too excited," because she's stopped hiccuping with laughing. That's some kind of progress. Mary will probably have some neurological explanation for it!

MAY 27, 1965. Nursery school make-believe time. Janey sitting in the straight-back chair at the boys' play table. First, the bag game, using the first-grade word bag I made for Stuart, then used with Grant. Who would ever have thought the old word bag would be involved now in the making of human stereognosis!

J. throws, bangs, bursts into yells then giggles, and occasionally really concentrates on what's in the bag—feels without trying to look. Still cannot distinguish an orange from a ball. Spoon from fork—maybe—fifty-fifty chance. She really "feels" for the pencil flashlight or the pencil, and gets a chance after to shine or scribble. Must think of some similar, familiar things that give doing-value. If she ever gets that orange, I swear I'll cut it for her, mess or no mess.

Getting restless; should have stopped before. Impossible to know "when." On to the wooden puzzles Bev Howe loaned me from the nursery school. I name each fruit as she fits it in. She stares so long at the orange, keeps turning it and feeling the edge with her fingers. Hide it till last. Then the shapes form-board.

I stopped hammer and pegs; J. just throws the hammer across the room. Mary doesn't know J. like I do. She is certainly not ready for one-hand-holding, one-hand-working stuff.

Anyway she won't sit long enough to do other stuff. In about twenty minutes she's ready to blow. Back on the floor for her favorite fun, O.K., O.K.

MAY 30, 1965. Philadelphia. Visit to The Institutes for the Achievement of Human Potential, of all places. Mary got permission to bring me along on another of her watch 'n' learn days. An experience and a half.

Such time, such patience, to look at and figure out programs to get a child to just move. The waiting room was full of families back for revisits, and no one rushing. To anybody who complains, "O.K. we'll catch up on our schedule when your child gets in here!"

Saw one staff woman watch, sit on the floor with, try this and that—all to determine a child's mobility. Age four years and motionless on his back since birth, till now. You could see him crawling now, but still random, they said. Neither homologous nor homolateral as yet, and a long long time till cross-pattern movement, if he ever gets that far at all. Mary and I thought his mother would be a problem. Apathetic, seemed to have given up over the years. Wanted him to walk, but didn't want to go through slight movement to movement forward to crawling and creeping to get it. The father was pacifying their new baby with one thing after another, while four-year-old "big" brother was turning his head feebly to one side and inching forward down on the floor. Mary whispered about the baby belonging on the floor, the greatest pacifier of all. Had they applied nothing learned here to their new baby? Turns out they've only been at the program three months. "Remarkable progress, this little fellow." After four years, I'd say.

We followed this family through every functional "area" all day. Programs to get functions, then to get them *perfect,* were indeed bizarre. Peanut butter on the roof of the mouth during crawling to get the tongue to be used at the same time. And bright lights to make eyes move. Eyes and tongue were muscles too. And if you want a muscle to work, you must first tell the brain you've got one.

Went down to the basement to the huge creeping floor. A place where adults and young people give themselves this program, mostly victims of stroke. Mary said she was planning to use this with some of her adult neurological patients, ones who could or would be willing to try. Marveled at some of them on the floor here, who had limited use of a limb. Mary describing how the poor body mechanics were cleverly dealt with by providing the necessary basis of support at a hand or a knee. A four-point creep stance was attained, from which movement retraining could begin. A kind of different "crutch." Mary, as usual, making the comparison under a perfect dead-pan.

On the way home she told me that the physical therapy rationale behind retraining methods for stroke patients had *talked* about making new pathways "to overcome the deficits." That's what everyone had always *said.* The talk was correct but the methods were inadequate. Rehabilitation methods up to now had tried to heal the patient through cortical "thinking" and "trying" ways. Not enough. You need to incorporate brain stem functions too—for optimum results on talking-and-walking cortical level.

JUNE 1, 1965. Whole family to the 6:30 Little League game to cheer for Stu (and Bert, the coach). Janey frightened of bleachers, even with my arm supporting her back. Bert was great, said let her creep around on the ground. Nobody minds. Everybody's watching his own out on the field.

What *do* others see in this picture of the three and a half year old Napear daughter creeping all around? Not walking yet and nobody doing anything about it?

I see 100 percent cross-pattern creeping without the outrigger on! No homologous hop anymore. So that took one year of every day doing. Her creep looks more like a baby's (the goal and the irony); feet beginning to drag on the ground behind. The left is dirtier than the right one, but right foot is down too.

I hold my breath through the whole scene, as Janey creep-runs down the hill and over to the first bleacher row to take a safe seat, hoping she won't go into crossing her eyes on purpose, her new "interest." Embarrassing. I have no idea what this is all about, but tell everyone J. is looking at her new-found nose. Even when they don't ask.

JUNE 2, 1965. J. seems to understand so much now. It's beautiful to watch her listen. Sparkles with excitement. Really gets what I'm saying in sentences. (I talk a bit louder, slower, use more emphasis with Jane. Must ask Mary; I notice she doesn't.) Janey listening, like the lights went on all over the world for her. A slight shake with delight, arms back to hugging her sides, hands near chest—an earlier baby reflex J. hasn't grown out of yet, Mary says.

I listed words J. "understands." I am leaving out a few; she seems to understand all objects and toys she plays with. Also several parts of her body. Now I can teach her "toes." She never let me do "This Little Piggy" with her before, squirmed as if in pain. Now she lets me. Maybe she likes the song. Or the lyrics? So difficult to tell *what* she understands, but I do know when she understands.

JUNE 14, 1965. For three years and four months those feet have been just chicken-skinny extensions of the leg. God, they're moving. This I will remember!

Yesterday, Sunday: Everyone gone to New York. J. not a crawling amphibian. Or creeping reptile. She's a do-nothing fly. Just lies there, touching feet together in back like a fly. Over and over. So still, head up, almost as if she's listening to the feeling. Rubbing heels together, then inner sides together, then big toes.

Then this: On patterning table, waiting for lunch, lying supine, knees up, right foot going tap, tap, tap—heel staying in contact with the table. I got down to try it. Yes, you do have to move your ankles to do that. Involuntary? Seems she's not looking at it or "planning" it.

And today: Janey did foot tap-tap on floor, prone, while resting in between crawls. Kind of an "I'm-doing-it-'cause-I-feel-it" expression all over her face. She's discovering her *feet*.

JUNE 16, 1965. A big four-column story about our Janey was in Sunday's *Daily Oklahoman*. By Edyth Thomas Wallace. There it was. She had only spent a couple of hours here visiting, but she had done a job, better than other reporters, about this program. Usually they describe patterning and barely mention the rest of the day. Even what they write is pointed to miracle aspects and tear-jerker praise of the "fantastic" family and "phenomenal" friends. Mary says every time she goes to The Institutes, they are chasing out reporters, tired of having their program butchered in the press. Mrs. Wallace used the material from IAHP expertly. I gave her Jane's entire day, stressing the program's real core—sensory stimulation.

Mrs. Wallace, syndicated columnist for years, was the author of the popular *Points for Parents*. I remember when I was a kid those not-that-way-but-this-way pictures. She wrote:

When I asked her [me!] what message I might give the mothers who read the column, she said:
"Tell them to take their babies out of playpens and put them on the floor to move about and develop both through movement and through their senses. This early development helps not only brain-damaged children but also stimulates the brain cells of well children, so that more brain cells are used and more average children can become members of the genius group."

You didn't get "more brain cells used" and "genius" from me, Mrs. Wallace. It's probably phrases like "more brain cells used" that drive Doman and Delacato right up the wall. It's not "how many" brain cells, Mrs. Wallace, it's how well traveled are the *pathways*. All green lights and "go?" Or traffic jams all up and down the line?

And it's words like "genius" that drive mothers up the walls. Just this: kids with good equipment, where learning is at ease, where all systems are "go."

JUNE 18, 1965. Grant got a birthday gift from Jane—a slap! I explained she's learning to extend her arms up and out in "full range of motion," Mary Lawrence calls it. Slaps walls, floor—and, yes, people. He went through this stage too. Grant's interest piqued, he switched the subject to himself, and how did he get "borned?" I switched the subject to the living room, showing him his baby pictures, telling him in fits and starts how darling he was getting born.

Stuart was across the room scanning *his* baby book.

Then it came to me. For the first time. We didn't have a single picture of Jane. Until she was two. Just those proofs at two. Bert, furious, wouldn't order a one. It was her eyes. And her slump, chest down on her stomach. And she had absolutely no neck. Stuart stood next to her, but his arm-prop around her waist just put his tie closer for clutching. The three of them were holding on for dear life in color.

How will I ever explain "none" to Janey? So busy with you those days? You were such a problem? Nothing darling about any of it?

JUNE 22, 1965. Jane's re-evaluation day. Mary arrived during patterning. Stood at the legs-end of table with that serious half-frown. After awhile she caught my eye, and shook her head slowly from side to side, eyebrows raised. "I can't believe it. They're almost down, the leg extension is five hundred percent better. When was I here last?"

"Seven weeks ago," I said. "Mary do you really mean it? You wouldn't kid me."

"I'd never kid about the kinks in Jane's legs. I'm impressed, that's all." Mary studying. "Tell me, have you all noticed her gaze?"

"What gaze?"

"Her gaze. The look on her face."

"Yes!" the five of us said at once.

"Mary, *everybody's* mentioning it. She looks different! What is it exactly?"

"I don't know. She just looks so much more 'directed.' " And Mary said again, softly, "She sure looks different, Peggy."

Later, while J. was waiting for lunch in the highchair, Mary noticed J. turning hands in and out toward each other.

I said, "Oh, that's some wrist motion she started."

"That is pronation and supination. When did that start?"

"This week, what's that?"

Mary showed me. "This is pronation (hands down); this is supination (hands up). Only humans do it."

"Oh, yeah, I know, I had all that stuff in school— And we also beat the apes out with cortical opposition of thumb to forefinger, right?"

"Marvelous! Jane is now ready to go to work on it. To perfect it, do pouring. Give her opportunities during the day for pouring objects from cup to cup, like this, see how the hands alternately pronate and supinate? Actually an activity kids naturally take to. Like all the 'tea-making' in the sandbox."

"How did she learn it?"

"Well, you've been doing it in patterning four times a day since February."

"We have?"

"Sure, pronation is brushing down, and supination is the hand turning over on the buttocks. Babies do it crawling on their little baby tummies. The hand pronates under the body and supinates at the end of the pull, coming to rest at the baby's side, like this. That's after they clump along on their forearms for awhile, of course. All that is sensory feed-in. Now you're seeing the motor, the output. She's doing it herself just sitting there, doing it her ever-lovin' self!"

"Well, wadduya know. Must tell the patterners."

"O.K., but remind them it's the total homolateral movement we want; we're giving sensory stimulation to the brain, Peggy. Don't think of arms and legs. One thing, I do think they should brush that hand-pull even stronger. We *never* want thumbs under the palm. Got to open those fingers to perfect flatness and get away from curvedness, even slight curvedness. There is a whole lot about flexors and extensors in the hand that I won't go into, but we want to tell the brain all about its *flat* hand. And strong brushing is the way—so say the people at The Institutes. From the improvement I've seen in those hands, I'm beginning to believe they are right."

Sometimes Mary gets silent and walks away. I know she's thinking how to let me have it. Tight-lipped disgust today when I said naming all the shapes in the wooden form-board would be "too confusing just now to Janey."

Walked away, came back. Just how did I think a brain could *get* sharp if it isn't used?

Well——

Just how was Jane's brain going to know "circle" from "square" if we don't tell it?

Well— I thought later——

Hadn't she told me the brain was an almost empty computer at birth? Till baby sees, till baby hears, till baby feels, till baby——

Yes, but——

You could not confuse the brain. The *more* information you give to a computer, the better *choice* it can make.

You mean——

I take that back. There is one way you can confuse a brain. You can give it *too little* information.

Stop thinking about Jane. Jane is not the patient you are treating. Just treat the environment.

JULY 5, 1965. Maine. A kind of Walden life. Functional recreation: lake play to wash self and clothes, denims and diapers rough-drying on the beach while we swim, walking to visit or borrow, and hip-slimming gymnastics to find kindling or to pump water (or to stack wood). Other games—how functional can you get? Darts, ring-toss, ad nauseam. Everything unilateral under the sun. Literally under the sun—and pines. Was it

	STUART	GRANT	JANE
8:30	breakfast		
9:00	chores*	his program	creep indoors
9:30	more chores*	"	"
	Roundy girls arrive:		
10:00	dress for swim	dress for swim	pattern
10:15	swim	swim	crawl outdoors
10:45	"	"	tactile and auditory
11:30	"	"	pattern
11:45	"	"	crawl outdoors
12:00	darts	ring-toss	creep outdoors
	horseshoes	Mother Hen	
		target game	
1:00	"	"	pattern
			crawl outdoors
1:15	Lunch		
1:30	ring-toss	darts	visual and manual
	Mother Hen	dart-gun	
	target game	target game	
1:55	collect games	chores†	pattern
	Roundy girls leave:		
2:00	free time	free time	crawl outdoors
2:30	"	"	swim or creep
			outdoors
6:00	supper		
7:30	story time		to bed
8:00	bedtime		

* Stack wood, bunkhouse, "spur-of-the-moment."
† Papers, beach, other.

only a year ago we were throwing our weight around in Stu's bilateral program? Maine life: close to the earth and every little movement has a meaning.

Janet and Nancy Roundy—what lovely kids. Janet, the all-American long-look, light brown hair and serious, questioning teen-ager. Nancy, the blonde beauty, two years younger, and quieter. Neither fearing work or the children. Acting as if they had seen outriggers and patternings for years. And even cortical hemispheric dominance is of interest. I half expected to see them split their sides laughing or go screaming off into the woods. But they didn't. They continue to come, *seven* days a week.

Thank heaven for little favors. Both boys are now on the same dominance program, and the right-hand, right-eye target games would appear a logical play-way to achieve it. Yet I wonder how it looks—our boys with "free time" only at 2:00 P.M.! That Napear family over there in the woods doing darts and ring toss when everyone else is out on the lake or just vacationing! One boon. The boys love the stuff, keeping a record of scores (hits) and racing to the challenge each day so far.

JULY 9, 1965. Janey going thigh-deep into water, *outrigger attached*. Knows to turn around when water gets to her chest. Not very eager to pour from container to container (wants to drink). Can do it though, but often misses the mark; doesn't supinate left hand enough (or is it pronate?). She'd much rather play with Grant's sailboat. If he gives permission, yes; otherwise, no. Janey doesn't understand, but Grant does; usually yes.

JULY 17, 1965. These two dear Roundy girls. Opening my eyes they are!

Best patterning J. has ever had. Janet has *all* J.'s toes (left foot) touching the table all the time. Nancy's got the right foot almost down. And J., so relaxed, so cooperative and content, eager to lie down into the speed-smooth serialization of it all. This patterning with the same three people every day is the best.

These girls really care; they set little goals for Janey, like encouraging her to attempt the three steps down from the porch, as soon as they had succeeded in getting her to go up.

Their girl friend is often here, exchanging stories with us about this program. Works at it herself in a cerebral palsy center, where the director was recently trained at The Institutes. Some of "her" kids hardly move, others tremble and shake constantly. But all are patterned and are given a full day's program when they come. Why aren't they programed at home? And why not every day? She, in turn, asking why I don't do all of J.'s program on the floor? Their kids aren't allowed to be in chairs at all. Me climbing high-horse to "Mrs. Lawrence says. . . ."

"Why do you pattern Janey for homolateral movement when she is crawling in cross-pattern?"

"What do you mean? Jane crawls in a homolateral pattern."

"Sure looks cross-pattern to me."

And to anyone, who's got sense enough to look. The little monkey! Sometime, somewhere, she slipped into a crawl pulling and pushing with *opposite* arm and leg! It's faster. (Thinking back to when I noticed the speed and thought, "She's sure crawling lickety-split.") How she flies. How time flies.

JULY 20, 1965. As expected, all schedules and systems fell apart with Bert's arrival. I'm half happy and half furious about it. Tired of fighting to get Grant's program squeezed in between trips to golf course and first attempts at fishing. *And* the new tennis court up the road.

Nobody leaves for tennis without my voice tearing through the woods: "Be sure to stack a log on your way back" or "Go right back up that path this minute—you forgot something."

One thing though. Everybody's now on vacation. Daddy is here. Bert, a real sparkle to the scene, breaking the back of mom's schedule and putting the light in all our eyes.

Teaching me to play tennis, again, mostly laughing at me. Jane's on the court too in her outrigger for all the neighbors to see, laughing at both of us. Her knees are so calloused she creep-runs over the asphalt.

Yesterday I had enough. Stomped off the court. That's exactly the way I feel about the program myself—*everybody's* programs.

Then I know. I can curse it, and I will continue. Because today just as the 2:00 P.M. patterning ended, Janey said "cawl."

JULY 23, 1965. A letter from Mary:

Dear Peggy,

Your letter is *very* exciting and must answer immediately—pencil and all. Maybe the air pollution index in N.Y. has been holding J. back. Or maybe she has some kind of pine needle intoxication that is making her such a swinger! Sounds great!! (This is a letter of many exclamation points!!!)

Absolutely start cross-patterning. This has all been cleared (not since your letter 3 min. ago but yesterday, because I've had it on my mind a great deal; and you have just described the situation when the switch occurs—when *crawling* becomes cross-pattern.) . . .

I'm *so* pleased to hear the legs are going down. That has concerned me very much, with my orthopedic hangover and joints and things like that. Do you *feel* less resistance in knees and ankles?

. . . The patterning should be a passive not a motor function—remember, you're programing the brain and you should try to avoid aberrations [Janet

Perrin says this means "mistakes"], so theoretically we don't want J. to do so much of the patterning that she programs abnormalities. . . . That crawl up the table is O.K. if it's done *after* the five minutes, but allow her to do none while you are patterning her.

The vocalization bit (talking in English!) is marvelous. . . . Have you tried any reading? You may really surprise yourself with that. I'm enclosing the magazine article [*Ladies' Home Journal,* March 1963, re: "How to Teach Your Baby to Read," Glenn Doman's book] to give you a format for the reading.

. . . Use your good old brain (from which I'm learning a lot). It doesn't have to be lights, Peg. You understand that I am not 100% sure of myself in the visual area, and it's something I hope to get cleared up on next Philly trip (next week I hope). We are *not* doing anything *wrong;* I hope we are complete enough, that's all.

New score: from 21 months to 29 months [average *neurological* age* of all six functional areas], which sounds considerable in two months' time, but I am still very leery of new score system. Also hope to get that cleared on next trip. (I didn't include this intentionally to you, when I sent you the paragraph I put into her file.) . . . The new one may be very valid, but I still would like some discussion with them.

Cattel Intelligence Scale is included. Not sure I'm glad I suggested giving it to you. If I thought you were going to use this as an I.Q. test, I wouldn't send it, because there are many subtleties in administering it. We use it as a PROGRESSION OF ACTIVITIES because it offers good guidelines. I've tried to make some notes for you. These go from examiner giving word, followed by child selecting object, to child giving word without examiner having said it; on from pointing to saying to pictures to identifying to commands to knowing use of object. Keep using reference list on side to see what they're talking about.

I think patterning instructions are clear enough (see IAHP sheet enclosed). It's like playing an accordion—arm and leg together, then arm and leg apart. Same serialization.

Must go. Your setting sounds lovely and do wish we could visit. Let me know how everything goes.

                                                                        Mary

Before me I have the Cattel Intelligence Scale and the *Journal* article by Glenn Doman, etc. Introduction says, "Few articles ever written can actually change the world. This is one . . ."

Exciting question: Does a high I.Q. produce an early reader, or does early reading produce a high I.Q.? If the latter *is* it, now won't that turn things around a bit in education?

Mary says to think of reading as visual therapy for J. (Distinguishing a word-symbol from a word-symbol is much more use of the visual pathways

* The neurological ages of Jane mentioned here reflect time-frame ages on the Doman-Delacato Developmental Profile before 1970. (See also p. 88.)

than, say, shapes—circle from square—or picture-symbols—dog from cat. Much more refined differentiation. Also, soon you'd run out of shapes. You never run out of words.)

And now IAHP is including reading for *speech*. Found out (accidentally) kids talk words they have read sooner than ones they have only heard. Double stimulation. The whole thing seems fantastically impossible for Jane, but will try. Feed in a word to her ears, then feed it into her eyes at the same time. No pressure. Game-play, Doman says. Kids love it, especially if they are leading the game, asking for it, so stop before the child is ready to stop. One boost, I do remember my nephew at two and a half reading "stop" and Coca-Cola signs—shapes, yes, but Mary says that's all this is, word-shapes (*ball* does not look like *doll,* that outside curve on the outline makes the difference?).

Hm-m. The *Journal's* "exclusive offering of Doman's Reading Exposure Materials" is probably no longer available. My luck. Mary says make words myself—three-inch red letters on white poster paper. Just teach Jane to read in my spare time. (Remember to add reading cards ready-made to my store for parents. How about a shingle outside: "Potential's Paraphernalia.")

Might start J.'s reading when we get back home. Anyway, I don't have time to do *my* reading. Also, Mary doesn't realize Jane really is talking now—nineteen new words since we got here.

JULY 27, 1965. I wouldn't have dreamed any of this two months ago.

I sit down with Janey now as Mary suggested. Doesn't try to get out of chair. Responds to all discipline. No throwing. Very attentive.

I darken the bedroom for eye-following pencil flashlight stuff (or tie objects to old-fashioned light cord and swing it for her to follow). Then turn on the light and have a school.

1. Works puzzles easily: fruits, shapes, animals, large jigsaw girl-puzzle. (Thank goodness she's stopped holding pieces on their edges at tip of her nose staring cross-eyed at them!)
2. Chooses puzzle pieces on command, including body parts of girl. (Remind myself to see Cattel Scale.)
3. Reaches for correct picture on command—homemade book (new "outline" page each day now). No need to show object with new page after one or two times. (See Cattel Scale.)
4. Loves cat, dog, how-big books. Role-plays with pictures: feeds Stuart's photo, cats and kittens, dogs and puppies; pats them too, giggling the whole time.
5. Twisting (open, not close) and nesting (needs help) Kitten-in-the-Kegs.
6. Nests blocks (doesn't understand size differences though?).

7. Tower of fourteen wooden ABC blocks: (Straightens, makes edges *exactly* flush as she goes along.) Bored with this now. Makes choo-choo blocks (line across table) on command. (See Cattel Scale.)
8. Hammers, hits pegs, holds with left hand (assist). Mary is right, she *is* ready for this.
9. Holds paper with left hand, scribbles with right. Very light marks though.
10. Can turn on and off pencil flashlights with thumb.
11. New interest in knocking, using closed fist.
12. Does "cortical opposition" practice in air—hilarious! (Thumb and finger together, open, together, open; well, it's something to do if you never did it before, Ma.)
13. Differentiates tactilely (bag): an ABC block from a large wooden die from a wooden domino—100 percent of time.

Janey loves an hour or an hour and a half of this stuff. Such increase in attention I can't believe. Then she says, "li" (Let's turn off the light) and "cawl."

JULY 29, 1965. Collected these scattered notes while packing:

Janey's getting expressions! Makes faces, moves eyes around, plays peekaboo. Boys love peekaboo, hang around to see if she'll start it, then play it with her. I don't say anything. The three of them in a three-part privacy, too delicate to expose with comment.

Lots of mirror-play on floor, examining inside of mouth and eye movements.

More of that body discovery stuff? Spanks right leg with right hand. Looks back over right shoulder. Then moves right leg.

Turns to other side, spanks left, thinks (left?), looks left, moves left leg. Mostly outdoors. Probably sharp blueberry bushes start it?

Felt mosquito bite on right leg and scratched it. Mary, is that leg completely equal to other one in sensation now?

Lifts hips up when I pull pants on. (J. lying on back, anticipates, and lifts pelvis.) Know *this* is important (hips), tell Mary.

Lots of toe movement.

Pats foot up and down, knees up, lying on her back.

How J. loves this floor! And how we will all miss it. And Maine. The best vacation ever. J. getting to be a show-off though. Without outrigger, no homologous bunny-hopping, but lots of walking on knees, right arm swinging back and forth. Head up and laughing.

AUGUST 8, 1965. Home. Chris Beck and Chris Leuteman are coming every day for all four patternings at a dollar a day, as smooth as the Roundy twosome in Maine. I thought two Chrises would be confusing to J., so we call him Chris and her Leuie. During the twenty-five minute breaks between patternings Chris is getting smooth rhythmic guitar strums from Leuie. Also, she's adding to the patterning repertoire her silly songs from camp counseling.

For Chris we do "Ramblin' Wreck from Georgia Tech" at least once each morning; it's J.'s favorite too, I think.

Chris never mentions his operations, that is, seriously, but the head bandage never lets us forget. An ear and that part of his head clearly gone. But the face is so awake with the knowledge of this day, this moment, that all I see is the life of him—a student, a cut-up, a depth and a maturity at nineteen that is more constant than mine at thirty-five. From Chris I am learning about the immediacy and innocence of childhood in a man, in each of us. And from the nineteen-year-old woman in Leuie, I am learning how to appreciate this day, this patterning and guitar session, as if Chris Beck will live forever.

In the days that cancer is leaving to him, he is busy, his life each morning moving into Jane's.

AUGUST 13, 1965. Asked the pediatrician what he thought of the quality of her speech; does she have a spastic tongue? Mary thinks not, but while we are here anyway, just thought I'd ask.

(I'm trying to remember this exactly as it happened.)

I held up a toy car, then a block, so he could hear J.'s words. She more interested in the tongue depressor he had given her, but if you listened closely you could hear "cah" and "lock." "Actually that is not as good as she can say——"

Then this: ". . . typical of the speech . . . children with cerebral palsy . . ." And something else about "these children" . . . something about "at the cerebral palsy center" . . . car and block had fallen on the floor, I was under the treatment table, plunking them into my purse, missing the last of the sentence . . . thinking call Mary, what is he talking about . . . Jane is like a child with cerebral palsy? But she doesn't shake; I know what palsy is. Cerebral palsy poster children with braces on, the crippled ones. Something incurable. What is it exactly? Aren't you born that way? Jane was born without a thyroid gland, not with cerebral palsy, the doctor knows that. Did he mean her speech is affected like a cerebral palsy child? It won't get any better? He turned around (remember), and looked at me when I said—asked—she doesn't have cerebral palsy? Didn't go into it. I was angry, saying she is talking now, even clearer than he had heard it. Probably he isn't sure what J.'s future will be so professionally didn't want to guess?

SEPTEMBER 7, 1965. Letter from Mary today, with the paragraph she put into Jane's file:

Child re-evaluated a few days ago (her third re-evaluation). Her progress continues. She has learned to crawl *and* creep in a very well-serialized fashion. There is *no* demonstrable spasticity in her arms and considerably *less* in her legs. While patterning, the legs are now completely flat on the table. She is not allowed to stand, as it still forces her on her toes. Manually she puts nursery school age puzzles together; identifies by tactile only; and enjoys all forms of activity. She has 25 words of meaningful speech and would seem to understand almost everything that is said to her. Her eyes seem to focus together over 50% of the time, and I hope the problem is one of left internal strabismus and that there is no suppression of vision in that eye. Her attention span increases constantly. She asks for what she wants with much less erratic hyperactivity. I am encouraged with her gains.

"I am encouraged with her gains": good old Mary keep-it-quiet. Why doesn't someone holler?

OCTOBER 2, 1965. I know my secret. I get past those early minutes of each day with the same set of dialogue—with myself.

PEGGY: Oh, I'll call the nine-thirty patterning off. Jane could use the sleep too. Wake her at ten-thirty for the eleven o'clock patterning. Maybe we could just take the whole day off. And tomorrow I will work hard again.
PEGGY: You do that, and it will probably be just your luck that this would be one of those days. Today may be the day she's going to do something— something for the first time. By tonight you will probably have seen——
PEGGY: Yeah. It might be one of those days.

And at night the usual: it was *not* one of those days. Tomorrow I will lie there and talk to myself again. But I will get up. Just to see how she looks.

OCTOBER 26, 1965. Tonight's weird world. I'm the only mother in it *wishing* her child *has* brain injury so they'll take her as a patient in Philadelphia tomorrow, and she'll have the help I know now she needs.

A year ago I was wishing she might just be "slow." The world messed up the words. To be kind? Please, don't do us any more favors, specialists. "Slow" does sound less frightening than "brain-injured." But next time, please, think of the little girls, not their mothers. Janey wasted three years that way.

Professional Evaluation

October 27, 1965. Philadelphia. Arrived 9:00 p.m. last night.

Exactly *no* sleep. None of us. Both Bert and I were ineffectual with Janey. A terrible feeling, to have no control of a child. (Does this mean we can never spend the night away with J. again? What everyone has been calling "sociable" all these years is actually "hyperactivity"—one of the things learned about her here.)

All night, bouncing on the bed. On the floor, walking around on her knees from room to room, never pausing. Thump, thump, thump for all "the neighbors" to hear. I tried spanking, to make her cry and release into sleep. Then I cried, to get Bert to watch her for awhile. I couldn't stand to watch his helplessness, so I took over again. I am more used to it than he is. All the time we knew she was ruining her chances for the performance tests tomorrow. Hated her for messing up this opportunity, this big day in her life. And hated Bert for mentioning all the noise we were making and all his other useless comments.

At 4:00 a.m. we were all in a bed, with Jane between us. Holding her down, our arms across her stomach. That didn't work. And I spanked her again, again, again—several stiff whacks. Calling Bert to come back, it couldn't hurt her through three diapers. Then I admitted *I* didn't know what to do either. And soon we were all in the bed again, giggling at the songs I was digging up to lull J. to sleep. Giggles muffled into pillows, we started on a "pretend sleep" attack. I knew the awful truth, that neither of us, nor Janey, would be any condition for our 8:20 a.m. appointment. Cancelling was out of the question. And I lay awake thinking of the irony of it all— the day we had waited and waited for.

At breakfast I did nothing right. Neither did Bert. Again the pressure of a public place, Bert never able to stand any of J.'s squeals or screams when people are around. Even though other kids do it in restaurants all the time, I would always remind him. Bert's saying, "Let's get the hell out of here," and rushing her outdoors in his arms.

"For God's sake, at least let me get her coat on."

We were the second of fifteen families to arrive. Plopped Jane into a folding chair and quickly headed for the coffee urn. I looked around: this, the huge double greenhouse, now converted neatly into paneled, carpeted rooms, one of the accessory buildings to the main estate where Stu had been evaluated.

Other families were gradually arriving on a scheduled basis, each bringing a child, each different from the others, but all part of an experience we could never have imagined. An awful educational nightmare. One child lying in some sort of homemade basket, motionless, supine, with tongue hanging out onto his cheek. Four years old. They had waited over a year also. His mother said it took two to three *hours* to feed him one meal. Another little boy about three, rocking backward and forward without rest, in the middle of the floor. Every now and then his parents would dash from the room with him. Later we learned he had convulsions around the clock, sometimes several an hour. Another little boy banging himself full against the walls, as he circled round and round the room, stopping only to get an animal cracker. His father with several boxes of the things. His mother with nothing, sat, as if there was nothing even to think about, but she was trying to remember it anyway. She never looked at the boy-machine, throwing himself at the paneling, at this spot and that. There was one long continuous sound, an animal monotone hum from an eight-year-old girl, waifish-pale and hardly bigger than Janey. A haunting horrible refrain which, I supposed, went on like this through every waking moment at home. And then there were the silent several, who never had made a sound at all.

Under, around, and beyond all this, Janey looked up at me and said, "Gum." I gave her a Chiclet and heard the woman behind me say, a husky whisper, "Your little girl is adorable. If he could ever sit in a chair like that and I could hear him say 'gum'—you're very lucky."

Bert stumbled out of the room, tripping over the little boy in the middle. I found him in the hall crying.

"Bert?"

"Did you hear what that woman said?"

"Yes. She does look good compared to the others——"

"God, those children— I never saw anything like—would you ever have thought someone would wish their child to be like Janey?"

"No," and we wiped our eyes on his handkerchief and discussed for a second or two how a year ago she could neither sit in a chair like that nor say anything. Maybe in a year they would look altogether different too.

After that it was easier. The others looked so dull-eyed next to Jane. She was only one of two to look at a book all day. The others moved crazily, banging about, or some lay in a corner without much movement at all.

Six tedious hours were spent on "history" questions. Jane moved about the room having her freedom without the outrigger. I was holding the eleven-page, legal-size document they had mailed a year ago, laughing about "needing that year to fill this thing out," notes, New York Hospital papers, a few photographs taken at the piano last Christmas along with the three of them that Christmas before. And odds and ends of info which could throw light on my pregnancy, her birth, her mobility development such as it was, from the first day on. But it wasn't enough. We stretched out to remember this and that. The detail was unbelievable. Bert remembered things I had forgotten: the number of shots of pitocin (?) to accelerate delivery, my hemorrhaging in the hospital, how the supervisor chewed out the nurses for not checking me during that first night. Every time another page of questions was begun, we would look at each other. Jane wouldn't hold out much longer. She would exhaust herself before they looked at what she could do.

The woman taking the history interrupted at one point to say, "How long has she been doing that?"

"Doing what?" we said together.

"Walking on her knees that way?"

"Oh, she started that a couple of months ago, why?"

"It's quite remarkable."

"Really? I always thought it was show-off stuff, swinging her arms that way. We call it the 'struts.' "

Continued past lunch time putting together the days-in-detail of her babyhood. All of this hitting dead center at the target of questions I had built up around her. Over the years this and that had been dismissed as "slowness" or "all children are different, so don't compare." From the history itself I was learning more about Jane than I ever knew about the boys. Bert wasn't so intrigued. He was edgy, his eye on Janey, waiting for her to go into one of her shrieks.

Again a pause in the history. The woman watching Janey again.

"What's the matter?" Bert leaned forward.

"Nothing, I am just enjoying watching her. Only about two months, you say?"

"Yes, but she's only done it a little because she's in an outrigger all the time. Down, you know."

"She's knee-walking in cross-pattern. See her arms swing with her opposite knees? The trunk balance is excellent. It looks to me as if you have done a heap of cross-pattern creeping, Janey. If these records are true from The New York Hospital—You say this Mrs. Lawrence is coming Friday, your last day here? She's the one who witnessed all that tightness as it disappeared—except for the spasticity remaining in her knees and ankles?"

"Yes, they took measurements of everything that was tight in the joints and all at the hospital when Jane first was seen in that department. They've been following Jane, learning about this program from her. She'll tell you. Her department is impressed too."

"I would like to meet her when she joins you."

Toward 1:30 the three students "observing" in the room asked to see my notes. (Literally read every page.) All adults, all spending several months at The Institutes, all leaving their orthodox approaches, to begin this program in some capacity. A speech therapist, soon to be director of a cerebral palsy center, and two reading teachers from the Midwest. (We had already learned that the nuns—teachers—were students too.)

The speech man was interested in Stuart. In return, I asked what possessed him to leave speech therapy for this program. Noticing the correlation between poor speech and poor coordination over the years, he too began to wonder how a child gets that way. He thinks they are right that all speech problems could be put along one continuum—from aphasia, to delayed talking, to articulation development, and so on. He had been treating kids as if these "different" speech problems were unrelated, always called it slow maturation. Even if he had thought to look at "no speech" or "poor speech" as a symptom, he never really thought much about correcting the poor development behind it. Very enthusiastic over-fortyish guy. He said we looked like the type who would give Jane good programing. We wished *him* well.

In every room during the day, we saw more of these students—all on sabbaticals from education or medicine. And one father (teacher)—his child had graduated from this program, and he had entered it, a new career!

We met Dr. Evan Thomas, who looks just like Norman Thomas, his brother, gracefully tall, marvelously handsome, with a deep resonant voice, who said very little while examining Jane. But after I explained Mary's putting Jane on the floor all day until she could find out what else to do, he said, "That's a smart physical therapist. Wish we had more like her in this business."

Jane was in that arm-swinging, knee-walking gait back and forth over the carpet. None of us were any the worse for wear for the night before. From what we saw of everyone else, including a couple who had flown in from India and another who had flown in from Canada this morning with their children, we all had similar stories about "last night." Performance wasn't dependent upon behavior or psychological considerations anyway. Neurological functions were the business here. The staff believes it is possible to separate the psychotic child (behavior is bizarre; functions are O.K.) from the brain-injured child (behavior is bizarre; functions are not O.K.). They don't accept psychotic children for this program, since it wouldn't help them any. But they think a truly psychotic child is a very rare thing; most of them are mislabeled—are actually brain-injured. Behavior is the blanket that wraps them into one bed.

Psychological testing is the net that traps them there. The evaluations of Jane seemed to be done easily and effortlessly, often without her knowledge or ours of what was being examined. But if you asked, the staff was happy to tell you. All sorts of things were checked that I never knew the brain did. Everything but eye-blinks. Bert was saying wryly, "I think I saw them doing that too!" We learned that Jane has no gag reflex in her throat (the ability to gag, I take it). And a startle reflex is still persisting. A Babinski reflex is still in her right foot but not in the left.* It would be necessary to establish reflexes that are missing, and then continue the development that would see them *disappear.* That's the way the normal baby's central nervous system does it.

Their evaluation (according to their Profile, p. 504) coincided with Mary's exactly, except three functions received less credit: (a) depth perception was not good enough—not enough inches of fusion from nose outward— to get *any* credit at all; (b) "cortical opposition of thumb to forefinger, bilaterally and simultaneously" was non-functional also (one of Jane's hands was a bit slower—could have shot her!); and (c) her bimanual function—one-hand work, one-hand assist—is not functionally perfect.

Jane's neurological age is twenty-six-months.† Mobility is the big drag in the average (six areas they check). Her rate of neurological growth at present is five-ninths. (When Mary first evaluated her it was one-fourth; since January, Jane has doubled that rate.)

A good part of the time Bert and I mingled with other parents waiting for Jane's name to be called for the next evaluation. By nightfall we knew the long story of each child there and had turned to laughter and a kind of playfulness about the day. It was nineteen hours later when Janey finally finished her last functional evaluation. Some would not finish till dawn.

So at three o'clock in the morning, in the clear starry coldness, we carried Janey to another building, up stone steps past ivy and latticed win-

---

* Jane's birth history records "Babinski Positive" but does not specify if the Babinski reflex was observed in both feet or only one. Mary Lawrence's evaluation of Jane on January 25, 1965 records a Babinski reflex still persisting in the left foot but not in the right. It may be the case here that Jane was misssing a Babinski reflex in the right foot at birth, three years later as well, but has established one in the past months; further, that the Babinski existing in the left foot at Mary's evaluation, has now disappeared.

† In 1970 IAHP changed its calculation of neurological age from a comparison with the "slow normal child" to that of the "normal child," resulting in a change in the time-frame ages as recorded on the Doman-Delacato Development Profile, as well as a higher level of performance required to elicit scoring increases. Any reference to Jane's neurological age or to scoring increases in this diary are on the old basis, and, therefore, *incorrect*. The up and up picture functionally is, of course, correct, as are the Profile Levels recorded in the Appendix, except as otherwise re-scored and noted. Parents and staff alike talk in terms of function, not figures, but the statistical improvement is kept for internal purposes of check, comparison, and the publishing of results, as was originally intended. By comparing a patient's neurological age to that of his normal peer, it is possible to arrive at the neurological *rate of growth* which is occurring with IAHP programing and eliminates the guesswork about developmental increases which might be ascribed to normal maturation. Even so, and the reader will need to make his own judgment about it, it may be noteworthy to see a brain-injured child maintain the *same* neurological rate of growth as his normal peer at any point in his life.

dows, into Glenn Doman's study, to hear officially that Jane is indeed
brain injured.

The official diagnosis: "Moderate-to-mild* diffuse, bilateral midbrain-
cortex injury."

Glenn Doman was explaining all the words as he went, and how theirs
is a functional evaluation and a functional diagnosis.† Then this: "We
listed all of what we call possible contributing factors to Jane's brain injury.
She could win the prize. In her case, the list is so long it covers a page
and a half. She has them all—prenatal, natal, and postnatal reasons to be
brain-injured." It has nothing to do with Bert's grandparents or mine,
so we can stop blaming the other side of the family.

This morning he would tell us a lot more about the potential of her
brain, a "magnificent computer system." Must be on time at eight o'clock.
If he could make it after he sees the parents after us, then we certainly
could make it too.

I was getting chatty, mentioning all the difficulties with medical people
I had talked to accepting this program in New York. Teachers seem to
understand all this a lot easier. That was the end of that. We had only
one business: to "get your kid fixed up." We would have time to think
about only one thing—*this* kid's program.

Janey, knee-walking all around his study, oblivious to the adults discussing the New York world of medicine, the brain, the child. He had
hardly taken his eyes off her the whole time, commented several times on
her trunkal balance. Bert asked him about his "studying" her, and he said

---

* "Severe"—unable to move or make sounds; "moderate"—able to move and make
sounds; "mild"—walks and talks, but poorly.

† For the professional reader who may have questions regarding the intent and
background of this statement, the following is submitted as further explanation, and
is quoted from *Brain-Injured Children* by Evan W. Thomas, M.D. (the Dr. Thomas
of this diary entry), his book published in 1969 by Charles C. Thomas, Springfield,
Illinois:

"It should be made clear that the concept of neurological organization, as presented
by the Domans and Delacato, does not depend on any theory about how the neuronal
systems are organized. . . . They believe that brain-injured children can be helped
because, in the words of Walshe (1965): 'There exists in the organism a capacity for
spontaneous adaptive reorganization by the nervous system and thus a measure of
equipotentiality is a primordial quality of all nervous systems' (p. 130).

"The word 'equipotentiality' originated with Lashley (1929, 1933), who found that
learning in rats did not depend on any specific cortical areas but on the amount of
cortex removed at operation. The amount of learning lost was proportional to the
amount of cortex removed. Equipotentiality, therefore, implies that all cortical structures have a potential for more than a specific function. . . .

"Without entering into controversy over the interpretation and validity of Lashley's
theory of equipotentiality, the implication that function can dominate structure and
use it for advantageous aims is, to a great extent, what Glenn Doman means when he
teaches that function determines structure phylogenetically and ontogenetically. Neurological organization can only be understood in terms of function." (pp. 102–103)

each was unlike any other, and each taught him more, and parents were his greatest teachers.

Jane was now at his desk.

Bert and I got up, halfway to the desk, both of us bumping into each other, and he said, "Stay where you are. She needs you running after her like a hole in the head." We were never to leave here till we understood perfectly what we were doing and why, ask all the questions that come to mind and to tell "us anything that might help us to help your child." A lot of their program-ideas had come from parents, who were often ingenious with ideas, once they understood what it was "we want to tell the brain about next." And "Jane here will teach us a lot more." And he was looking at her again.

"Perhaps she could sit here on the sofa with me—she's very tired. Shall I have her sit here with me?"

"That is up to you."

(Pause)

(Jane had never stopped, on knees, opening and closing, pushing and pulling, touching and trying, eyes like darts, zing goes the hand—there. Here. Everywhere. Back to there. Again. Knee-walk over, knee-walk back, find, reach, pick it up. Now put it down. Open, close. Pick up—she was in the middle of lifting the receiver off his phone—)

I started up after her.

She looked away, planting the receiver down, without so much as a glance its way, his or ours. And knee-walked over to the wall of books. Now she was stealing a glance sideways. Bert was chuckling, then stopped dead. I was looking at my rings. Doman was looking at both of us.

Finally: "Your kid is extremely hyperactive. She has more energy than all of us put together at this hour of the morning. She is smarter than both of you. Get busy with this kid. And, Mother, the New York doctors don't need you at all. I want you talking—to Jane. You get this kid well, that's all they need to know. And, Dad, you're in this too. All the way. Get serious about this kid. Or get out. Now. Put this kid first. Morning, noon, and night. This staff is spending seven days a week finding answers for your child. The least you can give is the same seven days." Something like that.

On the way out, I was apologizing, looking at his desk, hoping "everything is there, where you had it——"

"That desk is a piece of furniture." And "Did you understand me?"

"Oh, yes——"

"She is the business we are in."

October 28, 1965. Somehow we got back there at 8:00 a.m., to an ice-cold auditorium. "To keep you awake," Glenn Doman explained. (Last night—this morning—we'd all gone to sleep immediately, all in the same bed, waking exhausted but with an uncertain excitement. Jane went to another building for more intensive medical work-up.)

"Ask us any question, tell us anything that might help your child"— except one thing. The stuff we were *not* to discuss on trips back to Philly—suggestions we were not to offer—were in the realm of the so-called "psychological problems." Ours or the kid's:

1. Parents of brain-injured kids will have psychological problems as long as they have a brain-injured kid. "If you want to get rid of your psychological problems, make your child well."
2. Doman was adamant: he had never seen a young brain-injured child with a psychological problem. To have a psychological problem a child has to be able to make the abstract distinction that he is different from his peers.

   In the normal child this differentiation ability does not occur before age of about six. Too abstract a concept. In the first grade they begin to make concrete comparisons that are followed by abstract judgments about inadequacy: like Jimmy-finishes-the-workbook-before-I-do, or Manny-can-kick-the-ball-better-than-I-can. Then they get a psychological problem about being lousy in that, just *that,* not generally about everything. When they can do as well as the Jimmys and the Mannys, then they don't have a psychological problem about *that* anymore. Kids want to do as well as their peers. Adults are on edge about "beings," but it's really the "doings" that bother the kids.

   The ability to differentiate performance—make comparisons in the abstract—all this requires a six-year-old auditory (understanding) competence. That is higher than any of our kids have at present— in this group.
3. "So don't tell us your kid (or you) has a psychological problem. Just get his 'doings' going. We will be delighted to help you to do that, as much as we know, as much as we are learning, and as much as we will learn next year and the next. That is the business we are in."
4. The Institutes does not use words like *mentally retarded, exceptional, handicapped, trainable, educable,* or *underachiever.* Most of these were invented to be kind to parents, replacing words like *moron* and *idiot.*

   Terms other than "brain injury" are beforehand labeling and therefore ridiculous, if not criminally limiting. You don't know what's possible with the brain till you try it, use it.

   "Cerebral palsy" is an incorrect diagnosis. Most of these kids are injured in the midbrain. They can't pass the tests of mid-brain functions. True, the cerebral functions are affected—he can't walk and talk—but those are *results* you're looking at, not causes.

We have found parents prefer the truth. We learned a lot of this from them. We used to call everything in sight "cerebral palsy" too. It seemed a lot better than *imbecile,* for some reason. Now we talk about the brain. It seemed high time someone did.

You may call your child whatever. But his label will get him no-where. This program might. If you goof off, we will know it. If you don't work at what we program for your child, we will ease you out, kick you out. There are plenty of kids waiting for your child's spot.

That took about five minutes.

The other sixteen hours and fifteen minutes we learned about brain func-tion, what *they* had learned—the doctors, the educators, and the thera-pists who gathered at The Institutes. There were so many accidental insights along with the hard research and treatment of those twenty years.

The *what* of it sounded pretty simple. Bypassing dead cells that would forever and always remain dead. Stimulate the cells lying nearby that weren't dead, that had oxygen and a cell life, but were not, and had never been, part of a pathway system either. (Do those feathery dendritic exten-sions of the nerve cell reach out and multiply in their branchings—more and more imperceptibly—becoming highly activated from stimulation "out here," so synapse can occur over to them? Is this what all stimulation is about in all children? Is this how all pathways are started? Thinking about it, it's like a river you need help to cross, and you've got to holler louder for someone over there to hear you or see you or feel you—with a brain-injured kid you've got to holler 500 percent louder, and I missed some of the notes I wanted to get down from Doman.)*

But the *how* of it was downright delirious. It took them twenty years to even dream it. The ingredients were three: *intensity, frequency,* and *dura-tion.* You must send a message strong enough, frequently enough, and long enough to activate brain cells. You are in the all-day, everyday, for-years-maybe world of this program. Nothing less will do it. That's been tried.

It doesn't matter how many dead cells the kid's got. What matters is stimulating the live ones. They told us of the hemispherectomies (half a

---

* For a discussion of structural increases which accompany brain use, such as den-dritic branching, myelination of nerve fibers, multiplication of glial cells, etc., see books by Drs. Thomas and Le Winn (Recommended Reading List, page 433). For example, the normal baby does not see well until the optic nerve is myelinated; nerves within the central nervous system must be myelinated before full function can occur. (Myelin is a fatty layer of cells which surrounds the neurons and insulates them, thereby accelerating the speed of the nerve impulse.) Since function and structure are so closely integrated, each working to enhance the other, early mobility (crawling, creeping) can work to accelerate myelination.

brain removed except for the hypothalamus and something else) done in Philadelphia and the retraining done with the half that was left.

Close the input-output circuits wherever they are broken by damaged cells. Program the kid's brain exactly like a computer program. We were in the business of cybernetics, whether we liked it or not.

When the staff uses the word *well,* they mean what parents mean. Well. All symptoms of brain injury gone. No poor walk, no poor talk, no poor vision, no poor hands—the whole kit and caboodle!

Doman patiently answered all our questions. Later, he asked, didn't we want to ask the Big Question: What are the chances? They had projected that 30 percent might make it all the way. Another 30 percent they would project to be "failures" (including those who dropped out) and 40 percent "improved" (including those whose parents were pleased and dropped out but IAHP had not considered well.) "I know. It looks bad. You're not impressed. Before we got some of these answers to these kids, no one here who's previously been in the therapy business had ever seen a one get well, only 'improved,' and not enough of those to brag about." (Mary agrees.)

No, he did not want to hear what Dr. So-and-so said back home. We were here to learn what The Institutes had to say on the subject. Not many questions after that. All of us were stunned, oriented, and revved up. Bert, motionless, might have been watching the Philadelphia Eagles. It was midnight now.

The staff would go over our child's particular program tomorrow. Do it well. And then we would know if The Institutes knew what they were talking about or not.

Two families had left. Don't know why, maybe their kids weren't brain injured. Maybe they needed brain surgery and would begin this program later. Maybe the parents felt they could not do this program. One of the thirteen children left would be entering the next highest institute, the one that gave programs to kids which allowed schooling because they were neurologically "old" enough. His mother told me she had read enough to know to keep him on the floor during the long wait to get here and he had gotten too good for this group.

All day Jane had been examined. She had had an echogram, yes. She had been given *no* electroencephalogram. I was disappointed. "But I always thought brain-injured children were given EEG's if nothing else." Not here. "We know more about her than any EEG could show."

One o'clock in the morning: I settled under the only light at the end of the hotel bar and glanced at the pile of paper napkins that were scribbled over with blue ball-pen scratches. Fortunately I had numbered the crazy-quilt of notes from Doman's orientation as I flew through inner and outer folds of the huge napkins. It was impossible to tell the inside from the outside of a napkin once you had folded and refolded the thing. Ah, "page" 1-A. Sipping my drink, letting it all sink in.

Could I put off everything else and give J. such an enriched new world . . . always doing with children what I liked to do in the first place, no good at the other stuff . . . no martyr . . . selfish . . . let's face it, children *had* been secondary. Janey too, though she's more fun to be with now. I know her better or something, this last year. So cute. But the program's so dreary, so lonely when the morning patterners leave. Except the "school" time after lunch, such surprises there, and now that's out. They want J. on the floor all the day.

How could I put Jane first? I had tried in new starts a dozen times and always wound up not getting this or that program done during the day. Will *have* to. There's nobody else to lead it. I'm it. That thing running through me night and day, she *might not* catch up by herself. Janey's so cute, and smart; so keen, so curious. Nobody ever will think so unless she can walk and talk well. Probably think her an idiot, no matter what nice name they called it.

Doman was saying if a child does not move forward each day, he moves backward, the gap widens, because his peer group *did* move ahead that day. She's got to get to kindergarten with them—fall 1967. Oh, God, she's got to grow up to be dated and *danced* . . . to get married . . . to have her own little children. Some never move out. I remember Dad telling me long ago about the "crippled" personality. Doman mentioned it's easy for cripples to become con artists because they learn early to be masters of manipulation; families design it into them. . . . And me, oh, God. I don't have the guts to take care of Jane all my life. . . . And this Janey too good too cute too adorable too smart to be some sort of sister-act with a mother taking care of her like a child. Got to show everybody who she is. If she could talk, everybody would know it. Like Mary knows Janey. Mary coming this morning. *She* knows.

October 29, 1965. Great and funny day with Mary here.

The program sheets for each functional area were piling up. It looked like an all-day program all right.

No music from now on. For speech. Simple? At that very moment we were surrounded by background music. (What restaurant in the metropolitan area is sans music?) It wouldn't matter; we weren't going to any restaurants. We'd be lucky to get to bed each night. The other program for speech: reading! Mary said you could hardly expect the speech therapists to be overly wild about IAHP's entrance onto the speech scene. All of us were trying to imagine Janey's expression when mom begins back-to-finger-feeding all of a sudden. (Mary was too soon with the spoon.) J.'s last supper with a spoon. We drank a glass of wine on it. Her ice cream and dessert days would go too in conjunction with the fluid-restriction program. How was a child to grow up in the USA without sweets?

And I had a first. I was the first person to ever tell them their outrigger picture was wrong. The gal went running down the hall to tell the others. The artist had left off the second crossbar to keep the shoulders down. No wonder J has been pulling up on furniture all year!

We were all releasing our sleeplessness, our tension, in a kind of free-for-all hooray for The Institutes. Hope all around us. A great burst of yearning to get in there and start the game, anew. It was a matter of getting revved up. Glenn Doman had seen to that. Doman, who on first glance, first ear seemed all cockiness, was, on further reflection, a man of deep calm—heartbeat to heartbeat with a kid, eyeball to eyeball with a parent, and toe to toe with an awesome responsibility. You felt it in everything he said about "answers." Some answers they had already. Some answers they would get next year. And others in the years to come. I found myself wishing, for him and for us, we might all run out into the day and squeeze it to death, to hold time checked, just a little while, just until all the puzzle pieces were in place. Was Glenn Doman holding his breath too? No feigned modesty about the past. In a moment he would tell you about Brazil awarding him their Medal of Honor for work on brain-injured people there, about his book on the best-seller list in England. The past was a fact, so say it. The future's where it's at. No promises. Only that awe, that humility, that deep calm when he speaks of the human brain. A respect. And a reverence for "kid here."

It was this mixture of reverence and rev-up, silences between animated surges of conversation, we three (Bert, Mary, and I) wrapped ourselves in around this table somewhere in Chestnut Hill, Pennsylvania. The reverence for "kid there," the fourth we needed. The secret to doing all they suggested lay in her cooperation and in our ingenuity to get it, lay in her progress day after day. And year after year? We now knew so much about her. About this child tomorrow we knew nothing. Only one thing you really could trust, and that was yourself. To do it every single day. It was only a matter of getting revved up again and again.

You would have to raid the tool drawer, the jewelry box, the kitchen cabinets for medium-size objects, and to spend at least five minutes a day exposing her to them, talking to her about them and having her feel them (with both hands), then to test in a bag or box once a week, so she would draw conclusions from sensation alone. And that wasn't all for tactile competence. To eternally encourage differentiation of textures, sizes, and shapes. To talk *naturally* about everything we do with her and to strive constantly to increase complexity of vocabulary about everything within this environment. To listen to talking records. To do the visual pursuits twice a day for one minute each time in a darkened room, holding her head still so only her eyes follow the pencil flashlight, yellow cellophane over its white bulb. Oh, yes, remember to stand eighteen inches away. To do peripheral vision twice a day for one minute each time. To do convergence practice twice a day for one minute each time, and remember to stop when the reflection of the light is no longer in the very center of the pupils of both eyes at the same time. And encourage this function over and over for the full minute. To present the reading word for the day six or seven times for only thirty to forty-five seconds each time; and after a couple of days or so—test (she choosing the word rather than talking it). Provide an opportunity for the child to pick up pennies and other small objects. Give *crumbs* instead of bite-size pieces. That's what they said. Provide an opportunity to unscrew tops and pour from one glass to another.

To keep Jane on the floor for a minimum of "all hours" of the day. That's what they said. To pattern four times a day with new foot-brushing motion. To go to floor for crawling after each pattern, on a textured surface (gravel and flagstone on their list!). To keep the child shoeless, sockless, and in short sleeves and short pants. No knee pads allowed. Use tincture of benzoin to help toughen the skin and prevent abrasions. Plus powder on top. To keep stains off the rug? Something for the parents. How did that slip in there? To tighten tabs on her romper suit and get shoulder cross-bar riveted to outrigger.

The trick was to be ingenious and have fun with your child, all at the same time. Bert promised to take me to a movie when I finished—in February. Mary had inside information about our four-month wait for a revisit. IAHP just doubled the number of kids admitted to the program—crushed over the waiting list, people writing from all over the world, papers and magazines they never heard of writing about their program as some magical cure. Got in just under the wire. Appointments are already filled for the next three years. Imagine waiting three years. One year without Mary's help would have been unbearable. She was now looking at us across the table, as serious as I'd ever seen her, saying she had made up her mind that week of July 23 last year that the next child referred to her department would not get the old therapy approach. She would at least *try* this program. That child was Jane Napear.

Driving home Bert was asking Mary about Jane's label under the "old" symptomatic diagnoses—"athetoid, spastic, flaccid," etc. How would a doctor who did not know about "moderate-to-mild diffuse, bilateral mid-brain-cortex injury" diagnose Jane?

"Spastic. Jane is spastic. Certainly not 'flaccid,' floppy. As to 'athetoid,' that label is such a fuzzy, overlapping thing—I'm glad I don't have to use it anymore! You might have a doctor label some of Janey's symptoms as 'athetoid components' along with the spastic category. Another doctor would see the spasticity in the muscles and just write 'spastic' in that space on the chart. Her speech, for example, might be termed 'athetoid' and her muscles 'spastic.' "

Bert seemed relieved. Doman had spoken of "the athetoid" many times yesterday, coming back to the midbrain picture there. He dwelled on it: the awful-looking creature coming down the street, the guy you crossed the street to avoid, so you wouldn't have to look at him, shaking all over, mouth drawn to one side, eyes jerking too, bouncing and weaving along in an uncontrollable gait, talking in this state to everyone in a flow of un-ending, unintelligible speech, arms flailing not in gesture but to balance his body. All adult athetoids look alike. But there is no such thing as an athetoid-looking baby. Athetoid babies look like other babies. At three take a look again; he's taken on a little of the athetoid look. At seven he's worse. At twenty they all look exactly alike. Athetoids do not get better. They get worse. Structurally their bodies *follow* their dysfunctions. *Function deter-mines structure.* Don't forget it.

It was this worsening that Bert was groping to get settled here. I hoped he and Mary would go on all night. I was trying not to scream. *Spastic.* Say it again. *Jane is a spastic.* My God, it was one of the dirtiest words in the English language. More used than *athetoid* will ever be. Broadway stage, comedy sketches on TV, in conversation and jokes, The Spastic was The Village Idiot. Remembering the Duke University med students that night back in 1950 discussing the dum-dum of the class, always end-ing an escapade with, "That guy is really spastic!" Bert had no idea what Mary had just told us. Labels. How I wanted to hang one on too, wherever she went, "Moderate-to-mild diffuse, bilateral midbrain-cortex injury." Please, everybody, respect her brain, what it might become, even if you put *her* down. Give *it* a chance, at least.

Dropped Mary off in New York, all of us sleepy and irritable, except hyperactive Jane. Bouncing and banging herself from door to door in the back seat, on her knees, laughing and squealing every time we laughed. We "finally figured out" she must have some kind of terrible brain damage or something, the way she acts.

How would we ever pattern her without music? How could Janey live without it? How could we seal off the piano from her? How would I pacify her without song during the other programs?

And imagine, getting the habit to mask her with that plastic mask over her nose and mouth *every* hour—twelve times a day! To stimulate deep breathing and get more oxygen to the brain (from the effect of carbon dioxide exhaled into the mask), they explained. Bert was saying something about catching her first, explanations for *how* not *why* we could use. And to keep fluids to twenty ounces a day—in bottles or what? It was after midnight, three days later, and a thousand years after, when we turned off the expressway to home. I figured J. had literally knee-walked her way there and back without a moment's deep rest.

We'd start her new programs Monday when we returned from our football weekend—and gradually change her daily routine, till all new stuff was in and the old out. We were beginning to think anything was possible if ever you made up your mind to accept change. Over the last hours, I had been making up my mind.

Bert's mother called me aside while Bert was carrying J. in. Bert's friend had been killed in an automobile accident that evening. Bob was dead. But we were to meet Bob in Williamstown, Massachusetts, *tomorrow noon* for the game. Now Selma would not have to stay tomorrow. That was the only thing I could think of. Tomorrow is not as we planned. All these years, most of it had not been as we planned. Bert and I had been through so much. Still here. Still here. A numbness here. Stop the numbness. Go run. Maybe fall down. But do something. Wake up. Get busy. Help Bert. Help Janey. Oh, God, Help *me.*

PART II

Talking to the Brain

From Bert's letter to his sister in Tokyo, following Jane's initial evaluation at The Institutes:

November 5, 1965
Our visit to Philadelphia was most encouraging, and the prognosis for Jane is excellent. She was diagnosed as having mild to moderate diffuse midbrain and cortex damage. They feel the damage to the cortex is functional, and will clear up when the midbrain functions properly. We are optimistic, and hope that she will be able to enter the first grade, and be able to do what any well six-year-old does. There is a great deal more to write about, but I'm just not up to it now . . .

". . . the prognosis for Jane is excellent": *There was no prognosis.* We even signed a statement to that effect. No prognosis, no promises. But you enter with a heavy dose of the Puritan ethic, drilled into all of us schooled in the thirties and forties: if you work hard enough, eventually you will get what you are working (asking) for.

Doman's orientation emphasis was on "working," true. If you didn't work (use) the brain, there was no hope. To get response from the surviving (functionally depressed or untapped) cells in the brain, you would have to work like you never worked before. Jane's only hope was a suprasensory program, 500 percent more intensity, frequency, and duration of input than the world ever thought to give these kids. Work, work, work; it was there in everything he said.

We would give her brain the most enriched daily neurological environment they knew (to date) to give. Patterning gives sensory stimulation to all the body at once. Crawling does the same for babies. Anything less with brain-injured kids is impoverishment, so, yes, pattern your child every day, as many times as programed. We would utilize the nights too, by positioning her body in the sleep pattern of the young "organized" child —head, arms and legs "talking to" the ages-old homolateral "sleep brain," the pons. Work, work, work, if you want to get your child well.

We would provide the best environment for her brain chemically we knew (to date) to give, the best nutrition to keep the brain active, to receive the input. That meant extra oxygen to those live cells, thus the masking minute of each hour. That also meant not overloading the brain tissue with fluids. The brain is contained within the skull, which is a relatively fixed size after the fontanells have closed. Thus, an increase in the amount of fluid within the cells (injured cells tend to retain fluid) causes a decrease in the blood supply. A decrease in the blood supply decreases brain activity. Keeping the brain at its top performance in fluid balance was known to reduce spasticity in the muscles and hyperactivity in the child. Studies were cited for both, including the correlation seen in the thirsty hyperactive school child. And this little gem:

$$\begin{matrix} \text{hyperactivity} \\ \downarrow \\ \uparrow \\ \text{lethargy} \end{matrix} = \text{attention span (somewhere in between)}$$

We wouldn't tell Jane to do anything. That would be asking for output, the motor side of things. And anyone who's tried that with the brain-injured, *all* those who've tried that route, have fallen back in the same trap, murmuring to parents: there is no hope, nothing to be done about brain damage. They are right: there is nothing one can do, or should be trying to do, about brain *damage.*

It was to the brain *life* we would talk—or rather shout. We would talk to her brain through her eyes (vision), her ears (hearing, understanding, abstract concepts eventually), her hands (tactile), her body (tactile). First, to let the brain know that it had all those interesting parts to work. Secondly, to show the brain all the new and wonderful ways those parts *could* work. That was our job as parents: the input.

Doman said almost nothing about output—walking, talking and writing the language. Those were the *results* of a brain's knowing. You couldn't make a brain *do* what it didn't *know.* (So don't ask it.)

One very important thing, which I did not grasp fully until later: we would talk to the brain specifically. (I would even learn to think of toys as talk.) We would talk to the brain on the level on which it was *now* functioning or "just entering": visually, auditorially, and tactilely.

The secret was to perfect—to use to the hilt—the now-function. Its perfection would automatically trigger the next higher functional "breakthrough." Then we'd work to perfect *that* function. And so on, up the hierarchy. All brains evolved this way. All brains organized themselves this way. All children—even the Janeys—had neurological ages. Just trying to imagine such a system was, in itself, almost a religious experience. Just knowing nature hadn't left the Janeys out was the thing that touched you, and revived you.

And you could sit there, glowing in your new-found respect for the human brain—hurt or not—and picture Janey's crooked legs, crossed-looking eyes, all the cards she had been dealt, gradually falling into place, and walking right into the first grade. You could go further and wonder about the technicalities of whether to tell them she even had brain damage!

I have often wondered if there was a single parent who left Philadelphia, after such an introduction to the magnificence of "that littlest computer," who did not envision his child this way someday. I doubt it. Two things stand against it. One, you couldn't bear to look the other way. And, again, you intended to work, work, work. To Bert it all added up to an "excellent prognosis." It was a letter I wish I had seen at the time.

One thing Bert and I saw together and clearly was the need to reorder our priorities, to put off the old emphases, to center down *harder* on J.'s program. I would make the arrangements. He would explain it to the boys. She was brain-injured. It would take a lot of work to get all her doings going, the same things they could do quite easily. To Stuart's question, "It's the same as before, just more, right?" Bert had answered, "That's a good way to put it; we are simply putting her program first."

Before our trip to Philly, and for months after, I aimed at shedding this and that. At the time, I thought it was an honest effort.

I put off everyone who wanted to visit, to observe the program, to discuss the rationale. I had heard all the stories I wanted to hear, including those from parent-superintendents of school districts and a half-dozen from doctor-wife parents whose own children had been through the remedial-tutor-psychology route, smart parents who were now wondering if the child's hyperactive-incoordinate-poor learner picture was, in fact, neurologically based. I learned to give the name and address quickly of IAHP or Edith Alfred, depending upon whether the child was in a normal school class or not. No, I did not want to hear anything about the child, just "regular school class or not." Yes, I did care. Otherwise, I would never send them to do this program.

Before Philadelphia I had requested Stuart's principal to excuse him for six months from Music and Phys. Ed. (if in Phys. Ed. the activities were to be mostly bilateral in nature, as Stuart thought: rope climbing, tumbling, gymnastics) in exchange for a face-saving job in the library or with the custodian (Stuart helping with these "plans"). The principal found it no problem; in fact, he was interested in following something besides the speech outcome—Stuart's reading level. In five months (from the end of January to the end of June 1965) it had leapt from 3.1 (grade level) to 4.5 (a year and a half beyond).

After Philadelphia I stuck to my promise to stop hobnobbing with the school district. Parents were forming pressure groups to push for "special classes" within the district (stop transporting them out). These kids they referred to as "dyslexic" (Specific Learning Disability often the explanation, kids who don't know their left from their right, you see, as well as the usual can't-read-can't-write symptoms, a special group altogether to hear them talk). One thing they didn't know, the school administrators were way ahead of them. The child's neurological development was being investigated. I kept to my promise to let the school district find its way through "learning disabilities," "dyslexia," and "the handicapped" labels into special classes, reading clinics, or whatever. Somewhere teachers would run smack up against the child's brain, surely.

I took a look at the day itself. The crowding would have to go. Meetings, chauffeuring, telephoning, cupcakes and the like for school affairs—I would learn to say, "I can't. I have a fulltime job." And if necessary, "I work at home at my daughter's therapy program."

The number of patterners I would reduce to only those who could stay for all four patternings one morning a week. That would involve four women now (plus me), as we moved into the new team of five in order to turn the foot over to tell the brain about its underside for "crawl pushes." Saying good-bye to any of them would be rough. I would get tough and tougher, that's what I would do.

We ordered a beige carpeting to be cemented to our floor, wall to wall. And what better time to have the walls repainted. Why not set up a therapy room in J.'s bedroom, and have toy cabinets here and there to keep her creeping wall to wall?

It was good planning. And in *that* reorganization, the only thing neglected was Jane. After the four morning patternings, she stayed on her patterning table most days.

I learned. Just start the program. Better a dirty oily rug than no floor at all. And paint won't pep you up. Not when your Janey doesn't talk, doesn't say anything for all of November, December, and January. Three long months. About thirty years if you have to live through it.

And that's when you get to work. When you get scared. When you don't think "the prognosis is excellent." You realize that the worst thing to be without is not vision, as you once thought, but communication: to grow up and up, never having the words to tell them what you want, what you are thinking, what you are feeling.

When you do get going, you lose all pride about asking for help for your child. You reach out, and others reach back. And you find it is not true that not everybody could do this program. The truth is: everybody could if everybody helps.

4

Meetings and Maneuvers

Edith Alfred's speech at the nursery school had been gay, often funny, and well received by the parents there.

On our seats each of us found two comic-strips from *Peanuts:* Charlie Brown getting the heavy diagnosis from Linus about his reading difficulty. Rather than needing glasses he probably has "mixed brain dominance," and C. Brown replies, "That's the nicest thing anyone has ever said to me!" And later, explaining to Charlie Brown all about "mixed brain dominance," how "if this is true, we can rule out poor vision as the cause of your slow reading," and the inevitable Lucy saying, "Have you ruled out stupidity?"

Gradually the giggling and exchanges of info about "dominance" subsided and Edith started. She could not in one night do much more than give some symptoms of the slightly neurologically impaired child. Most of her emphasis to these parents concerned prevention. Her preventive pointers could well be the best child-development lesson they would ever have: "Developing Unilaterality (Dominance) in the Young Child." My notes:

A. When baby is tiny
   1. Shift him from one arm to other for feedings, cuddling, so eye, ear, hand, and foot on both sides get opportunity for seeing, hearing, moving.
   2. Place crib with headboard against wall, so both sides will be exposed to light and sound and mother.
   3. Keep the floor littered with sensory surprises.
B. Until the child shows preference for rightness or leftness
   1. Give both hands and feet equal opportunity for play (bilateral toys, tricycles, gross-motor opportunities such as jungle gyms, swings, etc.).
   2. Allow finger feeding till the child shows preference for one hand. (If you *have* to be more civilized, put fork or spoon above the plate, centered.)
   3. Do not seat children opposite each other (during this bilateral period) for meals or table work where one hand will be selected for task. (The

end of a table for your two-year-old would be best.) Handedness should come about internally, not from copying others.

C. When a choice appears naturally over a period of time, every effort should be made to help the child to keep that side as exclusively unilateral as possible (from about age three on).

1. Hand the child articles into his preferred hand. Feeding implements to right of the plate, or to the left for lefties.
2. Encourage the child to play with his toys with the dominant hand.
3. Encourage the use of one hand by the kinds of toys you get for a child, e.g., a tricycle is not a preferred-hand toy; try it and see. (One hand may assist, but the preferred hand will do the fine work.)
4. Teach games where the sighting eye is used as the dominant eye (ring-toss, archery, etc.).
5. When dressing the child, put on dominant side of clothing first.
6. During ages five and six, keep tonal activity (music) at a minimum. Use rhythmic instead.
7. Postpone piano and swimming lessons until dominance is established.

When Edith finished, a father stood up. He soon had us roaring with laughter about his struggle to get through school and into college and into a job. He said he was one of those kids where they tried everything, and still he would struggle all his life. In college he could read, if he had enough hours (all night) to do it; no one could read his writing (he couldn't either), so he learned to type. He couldn't make any of the teams—he needed the time to do homework anyway—and still doesn't know his left from his right. He turned to engineering and got a job via pull, so he didn't have to go through the application bit before he was hired. He was very attractive and quite intelligent, and said he got by with bluffing and a great gift for gab. Well, we could see that, he was a born actor. At least a developed one. He said it may seem funny to us; he had never once laughed about it.

I took another busman's holiday. Went to a meeting sponsored by parents of brain-injured children to hear a particular visiting speaker, a doctor who spoke to parent groups and medical societies, putting down the IAHP program. Mary was eager for me to go and bring back notes to her. She had heard him. She was anxious to know how the parents received him.

This was not a gay or funny meeting; it bordered on the criminal.

He opened his remarks, "There is nothing new in the treatment of brain injury." He never mentioned The Institutes, but it seemed to me he was referring to them all the time. My notes:

1. Slight brain-injured child—maturation is slow.
2. Brain after stroke injury will get well—after about six months.
3. Hyperactivity after age of twenty is gone anyway.

4. Did you ever see anyone reverse *b*'s and *d*'s after twenty?
5. Reversal of *b*'s and *d*'s is from repetition (from doing it so much).
6. Brain loses plasticity (at about twenty), and feedback is lost.
7. We stress at ———— (a medical center) *personality* and *socialization* of these youngsters.
8. We find ways for a brain-damaged boy to use other postural ways (his tonic neck reflex) to open a door. We have him attain balance by crooking his other arm whenever he has to open a door. (The doctor described what resembled the *en garde* stance in fencing.)
9. No formal teaching—just let them go. ("—at their own speed" may have been added here.)
10. Use drugs (tranquilizers) if situation warrants it; helps you to live with him, but you have to weigh risks and toxicity.
11. Technique is not it. There are no programs today better than any other, no news in the field of brain injury—he would tell us if there were. It is the person doing it.
12. I tell therapist not to set goals too high, let them go at their own speed. What you are doing tonight in setting up recreation centers and special Scout groups is what these children need. The child's acceptance of himself as he is, his social opportunities with his peers—this is our emphasis.

Then he wished the group luck. Knew they would have it; were wise in forming a parents' group this way.

First question: "What do you think of The Institutes for the Achievement of Human Potential in Philadelphia?" Apparently the lady did not know she was stepping back into the hole he had just covered up.

Answer: The doctor described his day at The Institutes, and mentioned *a physical therapist* who lectured all day about the brain. When the lecture was finished he (the doctor) had said, "Show me the children!" But the staff couldn't! There weren't any; it wasn't the day for them, or something. But they did have one child they could show him. They took him into an office and he saw one child crawling around a desk on the floor "like an animal." The doctor glanced over the audience, shook his head and exclaimed, "The staff there was very *proud* of this!" Some of the audience laughed. Some did not, I noticed. Maybe they were the parents of the "vegetables."

He said mothers who pattern are insecure. It gives them a twenty-four-hour-a-day job. And that's where the success lies.

I underlined the word *success* in my notes.

Then he went on to describe placebos—sugar pills—given in place of medicine (sometimes for years) to patients to "cure" this or that. It was always effective.

Second question: A mother telling about her twelve-year-old on the IAHP program for more than a year now. After two months of treatment, his coordination was markedly improved (all the teachers said so), more sure of himself (all the teachers said so), and had no more colds, had only missed three days of school this year. He used to be *out* more than *in* school. Had he (the doctor) not seen this type of improvement from this program?

Answer: Yes, he had seen four or five children at his rehabilitation center who had been helped. They had shown improvement, but he couldn't say the program had done it; he thought it was the time the mother had spent with the child. These mothers were emotionally insecure; they needed someone to tell them what to do. So out of their guilt they spent the entire day with their child. No matter what it was doing to the other children in the family.

Everything he said was true. It just didn't make sense.

Third question: I stood up. Everyone else was sitting like zombies. No one else was going to ask a question?

I explained I had all three of my children on the program, so no one was getting neglected. Then I said this was a highly complex rationale. He couldn't know much about the program if he had only been there one day. For instance, crawling *was* an animal——

He interrupted, "Oh, yes, nothing simple about this program. They have an answer for everything. And you are quite emotional about it, I can see that, young mother——"

I interrupted, "Why do you use the word *emotional* as a bad word? Anyone with a brain-injured child is emotional about *that;* you would be too. Otherwise I would be a zombie and my children's progress wouldn't be the talk of the school district." I sat down.

He looked not at me but out over the audience and smiled. He had stated what he thought of those people in Philadelphia. Were there any other questions?

There were none.

As I was walking out, three people approached me at once: the mother of the cold-less child, to whom I said I thought she was right, all that moving about on the floor must have changed my Janey's disposition to upper respiratory problems also; a special ed teacher who asked if I belonged to the group (No); and a man who walked out to my car with me who wanted the name of the director of the Training Institute at The Institutes! He wanted to go for their post-grad course, but couldn't get a sabbatical anytime soon. He wondered if they might have some kind of "short course." He was head of Special Services (reading, psychology, speech, etc.) in his school district. I told him of *all* people, he should get there somehow.

My "speech" to our school district's reading consultants and psychologists was somewhere out in left field. I explained, as an apology to Janey I guess, that I should really be home getting her afternoon program in. After I finished at 5:30, I'm sure they agreed.

I had decided after the orientation at IAHP to give them more rationale than Jane's program (as invited by Assistant Superintendent of Schools). These reading people needed to know that the kids coming from out the many homes were indeed related to one another. They needed to know how the brain organizes itself. Or doesn't. They should see that potential was a growing thing. Isn't it actually *made* as the brain is used? Is one's genetic potential ever realized? How can teachers talk about "evaluating Johnny's potential?" Wouldn't it be better just to evaluate Johnny?

But I couldn't say it that way. They were all so committed; otherwise, why would they specialize in remedial reading? So I tried to show them "the great continuum."

Doman had said they had now seen children go from the bottom range (what the world calls "the vegetables") to the superior level, up the route that all development travels. An aging person—you and I—will someday travel *down* it. Why then couldn't an "average" child, working on grade level, go that route? I put the "children" on the blackboard, straight from my notes taken in October at The Institutes:

NEUROLOGICAL ORGANIZATON*

11. **Ideal**—Could be. Should be. The child who says, "This library doesn't have enough on steam turbines that I want to know about!"
10. **Superior**—Both physically and intellectually. (Pete Dawkins of Army.)
 9. **Above Average**—With reading problem or not. Some of them can't read! (If passing is 70, he makes 85, but has a good I.Q. You can find this out by giving him a tape-recorder I.Q. test, i.e., nonvisual.)
 8. **Average**—Still a continuum.
 7. **Delacato's Syndrome**—Unable to read, hyperactive, incoordinate. The incoordination may be in *fine*-motor activities.
 6. **Strauss' Syndrome**—Hyperactive and incoordinate and a learning and behavior problem to teachers. Educators split this into three classifications: The home child (has frank brain injury),† the educable child (frank brain injury not observable), and the trainable child (somewhere in between).
 5. **Mildly Brain-Injured**—Walks and talks, but poorly.
 4. **Moderately Brain-Injured**—Able to move and make sounds.
 3. **Severely Brain-Injured**—Unable to move or make sounds.
 2. **Coma** ⎰ These lines are being crossed both ways now.
 1. **Death** ⎱

* Reproduced (with modifications) courtesy of Glenn J. Doman, Carl H. Delacato, Ed.D., and Robert J. Doman, M.D. copyright 1962, Glenn J. Doman.

† The child has been diagnosed to have actual brain damage, principally from the traditional test of EEG (electroencephalogram) measurement of brain waves of the cortex. In other words there is evidence that there are structural pathological reasons for his inabilities, behavior, etc.

Then I told them this is how the continuum goes:

The bottom level (death) has *no* neurological organization.

Levels 2 through 6 equal neurological *dis*organization (pathology, frank brain injury).

Levels 6 through 9 equal *poor* neurological organization (level 6 can contain children with and without frank brain injury; those without have brain injury in its "developmental" connotation. First you have to believe, or at least wonder, if there is such a thing as "developmental brain injury." If harm has been done to the brain's organization through developmental lacks, then you are on their side).

Top levels 9, 10, and 11 reflect *complete* neurological organization; level 9 people have a less enriched first year of life than level 10 people— neurologically.

Jane had started on level 4. Our goal was level 5, then 6, then 7, and so on.

By the time I got well into all that, it was five o'clock. One teacher asked if a great part of the tactile program were not Montessori's. I was so dumb, I didn't even know. I did say that if anyone were doing anything to influence the brain, the people in Philadelphia would be delighted to know about it.* One teacher asked me if The Institutes had made any studies to determine whether most neurologically disorganized children were from urban or rural areas. I didn't know. But I knew this town was full of them. Some of the most sensorily unenriched kids come from the "best" homes.

Bert had been working for J. too. Didn't tell me till we were seated in a posh restaurant in the city, having our drinks. He had decided to make out a will and wanted to include in it our wish for her continued care and IAHP program. Without asking me who I would choose to ask this of, he knew, and had asked Lydia and Warren, whose anniversary we were celebrating. Deep consideration to all that this would imply for Jane, for them, and for Robin, her two-day-younger best buddy. Lydia telling us what and how they had thought about it. And they said yes. Together with Mary Lawrence and Bert's college lawyer-friend, they would see that even without us her days would be filled with this corrective program.

A soft and weepy moment.

Happy Birthday

Oh, Janey, how you can tease. Four years old today, and your present to us the best of the lot. You finally talked again. You spied the cake on the counter in the afternoon and said, with a struggle, "Ahp Bir ay."

* IAHP tactile program is not Montessori. All programs are IAHP-conceived to meet the specific needs of specific children.

I know you can talk. Why haven't you? Stuart heard it too; he knew right away it was a new moment. Through November and December—till now—you have said *nothing* spontaneously. You forgot how to use all the beautiful words? All those sounds, just the first two sounds of a word to everyone else, but words to me. All those beginnings of naming objects in your day. Then you just stopped. The Potential People will call it a plateau, I suppose. But it is hell. It is cold fear. You said "bye-bye car" one day—a two-word couplet. Or were you repeating it as a one-word? Why didn't you ever say it again? November and December—your nothing period—I wandered in the wilderness of busy-work, silently hoping each day to hear your sounds. And finally you started again when December was closing, but into jargon again. But jargon with new inflection practice. Are your new ups and downs, your new inflections in "bye-bye," an increase of some sort, a higher function? Or is it some plain on the long plateau?

I got so excited when you saw the towel last week and said "ba" for bath. Why don't you do that again? Why do you come out this week with something as sophisticated as "Happy Birthday?" The last birthday was in September, mine. Did you remember that? Is it motivation that you need?

The boys loved the sound-effects records that they gave you today, every kind of indoor and outdoor sound used on the stage and on TV. It's a great idea. Now you can distinguish walks from runs, openings and closings, bells, motors, and machines. You should have had these long ago.

One gift I will give, I promise. Got to start reading with you. Tonight. Tonight I will make a card with HAPPY BIRTHDAY and let you take it to bed with you. And tomorrow we start with those cards we got at the Potential place. And it's time for a promise I *promise* to keep: I promise I won't spend three months like that again. And you promise you won't either.

Philadelphia Revisited

(February 8) I had said quite sharply, "Do *not* touch that door," as we started. So it was Sarah Heartburn the first five miles to Philly. (Dramatic sniffling, no tears.) Until I remembered the greatest pacifier of them all, a book. She checked out a dozen or so, page by page, from front to back, in that precise and gentle manner of hers. This child could be hypnotized by pictures. Then Bert, Stuart, and I discussed the headlines—the track meet scene, the Knickerbocker life in the cellar, and did the Bruins play last night?

Saw no one from our "October group" back at The Institutes today. Me watching, thinking. Another round here, some for their third revisit, some in the third *year* of the program. Glad Stuart could see and hear the stories of long struggles, as we compared notes back and forth. It was all at once a glance back where we had been and the possibilities of continued improvement that may lie ahead. (Couldn't take my eyes off kids "ahead" of J. Talked the full talk with those parents. Others, not too interested in. But those parents talking to Bert about Janey!) One family from Texas had *two* severely hurt children on the program. They were doing the program with the six-year-old when the second child was born. The staff had recognized the lack of development within the first two months and had prescribed a program of sensory stimulation right away, including patterning. For three years they had lived thus. It seemed both children might make it; the three-year-old was reading. A primer, with short sentences, I noticed. Weird. Doing better than us, actually. Terribly good about schedules, simplifications, priorities. Among the happier faces there. And Janey's knee-walking, up and down a flight of steps, the talk of the waiting room. For those just starting out, it was not a bad scene to observe.

The procedure always begins with history. Again? Yes, and again. Whatever is news since last time. Bert and I eyeing J. She's winding up and she's going to wear herself completely out, folks, and then there won't be any more history. Other notes I had taken were listened to but not recorded; apparently things they want to see for themselves, O.K., O.K.

Later—in the room where they checked tactile ability—I reported she was now turning pages without looking.

"Yes, I noted that already." The woman had been watching Jane the whole time. It was like that all day. Whatever J. was doing, mostly knee-walking or picture-reading, they were checking out eye movement, head movement, eye-head, eye-hand trunkal details, and fingers and toes!

Jane's "evaluation" at manual tasks and the like, requiring her at a desk, were mostly howls to get back and "cawl." We left the rooms, we stayed in the rooms, we ignored her, we pacified her, we yelled at her. She did not want any part of it. But the staff seemed to have seen worse. They found out what they wanted to know. They simply went ahead—with their bright lights, startle noises, and pick-up stuff. I learned something. If you shine a large red lantern in a child's eyes, he will stop screaming.

I wound up giving Jane the tests for stereognosis myself. "No crawl now. When you finish. Now cut that out. See? A little barrel. Feel it. Go get it," and I dropped it into the bag with an empty spool and a celluloid egg. The barrel was the small green one from the Kitten-in-the-Kegs set. Everything was the same size, Jane to get all three of them correctly to "pass." They wanted it done with the left hand too. It was scream and struggle from then on. I was angry. And she did it. "Good *girl*. Crawl? O.K. On the floor."

"Is this your usual way of speaking to Jane?"

"Oh, yes. She knows praise all right."

"I was referring to your 'sentences,' not the praise. But since you mentioned it, so does a dog know sweet talk from scolding. That's level III on our Profile. Jane is now into level VI in auditory competence. She can understand regular sentences, you know. If she has some to understand. She understands the concept of "making a deal," bargaining. When we saw her for the first time—let's see, in October—she was already on level V. Didn't we program that you should talk to her in full sentences?"

"I thought I did. It's hard to know just how simple to keep it—what *level* of sentence to say——"

"The same level you talk to your other children, your husband."

Bert: "God forbid."

Janey had scoring increases in every functional area except in mobility (but "qualitative improvement seen in crawling and creeping") and language (but "more tonality in speech").

For the first time she got some credit for "convergence of vision resulting in simple depth perception." She at last has entered that "block" on their Profile. And to ever get *full* credit for level IV in visual competence, the kid has got to have a perfect gaze—no crossed eyes at all—full fusion, full depth perception.

Jane has a long way to go before they will even concede that she is right-handed. They just noted what they are observing now, saying it could still fluctuate. I kept telling them, "She *is* right-handed; I know it." And they kept saying, we'll see. Apparently they are more interested that she have two good skilled hands right now. Everyone should, they said, a person just *prefers* one over the other. Well, now.

> *Dominance:*
> Foot—"not observable."
> Ear—"not observable."
> Eye—"midline to right."
> Hand—"tending to right."
> Tactile—"tending to right" (bilateral improvement seen in stereognosis).
> *Other Results:* "Affect—more aware of her environment."
> *Program Recommendations:* "Review and continue as before with minor revisions due to improved function. Re-evaluation in four months."

Bert and I looking like the original happily-ever-after couple, sitting on the steps to prevent J.'s ascent, waiting for Stuart to finish two floors above. We began to discuss seriously the "minor revisions" in the program.

   1. Tactile identification of coins (bag game).
        quarter and penny
        nickel and quarter
        penny and nickel
        all three
        introduce dime with each one
        all four

But then we moved quickly into a hysterical state of overaction: "I'll need extra money each week. There's bound to be losses, under the table, the chair cushions. But I don't always *have* those coins. You know, lately I've been paying the paper boy too."

2. Fabric identification: wool, satin, cotton, velvet, etc.

> Test: Put two swatches out in front. Then let her feel another swatch behind her back, like one of the two she's seen in front. Then ask her to pick up the one in front that feels like the one she felt in back. (They are out of their minds.)

Flashing back to what I said to them earlier: "You mean, like 'ouch' and 'ooh?' " The woman said, "No, more refined adjectives than 'ouch' and 'ooh.' " And me: "Like 'pretty?' " No, that's visual. You want to use tactile adjectives." "Like what?" "Feel the fabrics yourself. The right words will come." Bert and I had finally thought of two: "scratchy" and "smooth."

3. "Continue to delete music from the environment." And buy some talking records. (They gave us a list of five.)

4. Sound effects and other (talking) records intermittent with silent periods for contrast to arouse "listening." Program this during entire day.

Now where were we going to get silence?

5. Christmas tree blinking lights on wall with nothing else. Have Jane watch them for two to three minutes, five times a day.

6. Red and yellow 25-watt bulbs in lamp without shade; turn on and off.

7. Horizontal, vertical, and circular visual pursuit for treatment; no testing.

8. Convergence, divergence alternately with pencil flashlight. Each twice a day.

9. Miller High Life beer sign.

10. Reading: Introduce battery of six words, one each day. Introduce ones from before. On the seventh day, test all by "choice" method. Next week do another six, dropping old ones, one each day. End of second week, test all twelve, etc. *Note:* Show new word four or five times that first day. Show rest of words in battery twice each day. On the seventh day, don't present a new word. Review six words and test. (They are clearly mad.)

11. Pattern same as before on a rug-covered table. (As in wool, cotton, or nylon twist, whatever we wished to try first and gradually increase to rougher texture.)

12. Crawling box: Put slats on top instead of rope, to keep her head down, and they mean it. One hour a day. Use Rubatex as flooring

(texture). Put a two-by-four underneath to make an incline. Can also use in see-saw fashion.

13. Make incline (ramp) with push-off rungs from half-round molding. Hold J.'s foot in place at toe region as she pushes.

14. J. must wear harness line front and back to keep her down during the day. Ask a shoe man to make leather foot "holders" to attach line to, leaving toe and heel regions bare. (The doctor was right in his put-down of this program; they *do* have an answer for everything.)

15. In crawl box use handcuffs to restrict use of hands, to get more foot action. Five minutes.

Some parents (the kind you could get to hate) had made long crawling boxes over sand in the backyard and got good results, increased foot action. Another idea one of them had was for an outdoor contraption: make a series of "crawling boxes" inclining up to a regular slide. Take away ladder and attach ramps to slide. Child gets slide-ride for reward. For dads who prefer wood-working to the New York Giants, it's probably nothing.

16. Continue picking up small objects simultaneously. Two minutes a day. Continue finger feeding.

17. Practice screwing and unscrewing and pouring.

18. Pre-writing: twice, five minutes a day. I draw a large circle first, then let her do it. Use twenty-four by twenty-four inch paper on the floor. Also finger-paints are good.

For language, there was no program again. Just put in the input, and forget it. O.K. to ask her to name pictures, but only if she goes along without pressure. Speech comes naturally with the reading program. I promised myself again to really start the reading.

Well, we've got one good reader in the family. Stuart as a fourth-grader, reaching up and pulling down 7.2 grade speed, 8.2 grade vocabulary, and 6.6 grade comprehension, swung through their Gates Reading Test, Form I.

And his far-point vision no longer fluctuates; it's now right consistently.

And someone in the family finally had cortical hemispheric dominance. Nothing you'd want to shout about (or mention?).

He didn't have any sort of hesitation in his speech. Now. In the fall he did occasionally—with the excitement of competition, his teachers thought. "Might it return in the spring with baseball?"

Stuart would have to check it out himself, just what makes his stresses; he might examine the goals he sets for himself, look into desiring and winning.

Stuart smiled, "I know what you mean. I shouldn't want to win so badly."

"If I said that, forget it," the man said. "I've got this speech problem, saying what I mean. Play to win, of course. You're going to do that anyway. Just look into what getting excited has to do with it." And don't go joining any choral groups or playing any instruments for awhile, hey, Stu?"

Stuart said he wouldn't and asked again if it were now O.K. to go to music and gym. Then he asked where Dr. Delacato was.

He was at a reading conference, telling them how guys like Stu got "organized." Stuart laughed. "Well, tell him 'Hi,' " and lifted his hand a little.

Cancelled patterning to let Janey sleep. Arrived home a little before midnight. We wouldn't go again till June 1, their schedule was so full. And I promised this would be the best four months for her. Come hell or high water.

When J. awoke I took her to the village to gather in the new program materials.

"Christmas tree lights?" The man knew me, but I thought I saw him changing his mind about that.

"The kind that blink on and off. I know it's February, but——"

He laughed. "We've packed all that away. Long ago."

At the fabric center, I would have to buy one-eighth yard of each— Yes, it was understandable, but, no, thank you.

There were no three-inch stencils of lower-case letters in the village. I would have to make my own. I could eventually use the twenty-dollars' worth in the reading kit I bought, when J. got to two-inch red and on down to 1-inch anything.

Of course, the stores had never heard of "The Talking Record for Girls" or the Golden Records I named.

The hardware man said they *used* to have the 25-watt red and yellow bulbs, but no one called for them anymore. He had a large yellow "bug" light——

Talking to the poor toy lady about handcuffs with a chain. "Yes, it has to be quite strong."

"Well, they just play with them. It's all make-believe——"

"No, you see, I need them for my little girl— I mean, it's for a special program she is on. I know somebody makes them— If I could order them——"

A woman ran in the store, calling, "Does anyone know whose child this is? There's a little girl out here and she's going to get hurt——"

I ran. For God's sake. It *was* Jane. Creeping on all fours in the parking lot, laughing and squealing in the melting snow.

The tears were in my eyes so much I could hardly find the door handle, no one helping, just huddled in whispers a few feet away. One man saying, "Lady, she could have been run over. A child like that. She really shouldn't be left alone like that——"

I threw myself in after Jane and backed out in a skidding turn. I turned on the windshield wipers and drove two blocks or three before I realized I couldn't see because I was crying. Pulled over to the curb to let the hot humiliation pass.

Jane motionless in the back seat, staring at me. I said, gasping but in a gentle voice, "Danger, Jane, danger. Mommy will always open the door. Jane does *not* open car doors. *Do not ever* open that car door!"

Stopped the car in the drive, then remembered the "tactile bag" I hadn't gotten. For the coin game I had decided to change the bag, get the same purple one they used at The Institutes.

Drove back to the village and parked the car by the liquor store. I would teach Jane right now. And, boy, she'd better listen. I looked around to see if any of that huddle-crowd was left. Firmly and presidential-like, I said, "Mommy is going into the store. Mommy will be back. *Do not touch* these doors. If you touch these doors, Mommy will spank. (Now there's a deal for you.) I will be right back."

As soon as I had the liquor store door open, I asked for the "liquor that has a purple bag on it." Crown Royal, it is.

"So you like this purple bag, do you, young lady?"

"Yes."

I rushed out with it half out of the bag. Jane had not stirred, or blinked, I supposed. I smiled her a huge eye-glistening smile. And she smiled back, so glad to see me . . . smiling.

"Good girl! What a good girl to wait for Mommy!" And I leaned over the seat and kissed her.

My thoughts all over the place. Good to have a bottle of liquor in the house for a change. We'd have to get those children's door locks on the wagon. I envied the parents who were there in December, whose children were given the Christmas tree lights program. They probably just went right out and bought them. In fact, I bet the idea started one December, Doman driving home, thinking what else could you do to make eyes move, ah ha, that's it . . .

Bert found me in feathers again, preparing for tomorrow's 4-H bout, when he came home late. He didn't say a word. Just pitched a paper in front of me to read.

I turned. "Bert, this is the first time all week I've worked on Indian lore. I must do this tonight, they meet here tomorrow. I have to get things ready for them. You know, I do the program all day in the daytime!"

"Well, Peggy, I'm not sure you're doing any of it."

I jumped sideways on the chair, screamed, "You're not what? How

would you know? You're never here to see what the day is like! How do
you think Jane is— Just who do you think— Just how did her neurological
age go up twelve months in three months this time? I *might* have had
something to do with it, you know. And you could say, 'Good girl' or
something! Instead of just taking it all for granted. Just look at her hands.
Just look at what she can do with her hands now! Just look. She opened the
car door today. And she's talking again. Some. And I like Indian lore.
There's nothing wrong with that. This has meant more to Stuart than
anything he has ever done. Including sports. And if your mother had
ever——"

"Just leave my mother out of this— Just watch it——"

"Well, it's true——"

"What's true?"

"Nothing. Just nothing."

The bedroom door slammed and I picked up the paper he had thrown on
top of all the colored feathers. It was a letter to the president of the Miller
Brewing Corporation in Milwaukee, Wisconsin:

Dear Sir:

Yesterday, while at The Institutes for the Achievement of Human
Potential in Philadelphia, it was suggested to us that we write you about the
possibility of obtaining one of your wall lamps for our four-year-old daughter,
who is on a program of visual therapy. If you could advise us how we could
obtain one, or arrange for such a lamp to be sent to us, we would be most ap-
preciative. If a bill is enclosed, we would pay it by return mail.

Thank you for your cooperation.

Cordially yours,
BERTRAM J. NAPEAR

I went in to Bert and said, "That's a very good letter, Bert." And
thanked him for writing so quickly. And could he look for the "Talking
Record for Girls" in New York tomorrow? And also the Christmas tree
lights? And the red and yellow 25-watt bulbs? Maybe he had an insured in
the electrical business?

Took J. to shoe shop. Man was just plain good and kind about it all. The
pigskin from the 4-H'ers leather supply would do fine. Sure enough, with
moving back and forth between the sewing machine and Janey, he con-
toured the leather to just fit around her mid-foot, leaving the heels and toes
bare, and arranging a buckle-band around her ankle. Feet so small and
underdeveloped, he kept having to make the girth smaller and smaller, till
he had achieved a molded effect to represent her "last." To the ankle band
at the back, he then inserted the steel rings to which the harness line could
attach.

What did I owe him? He didn't know. He had never made anything like that before. He had spent one and a half hours, his other work had backed up. Would five dollars be too little? I'd be willing to pay anything. He said five dollars would be too much, it was enough to know it might help her. His brother (or cousin?) said, "Let us help anytime, anything you need like this———"

How long? I said I didn't know. But he meant how long had she been "doing all this?" A year and a half of "ground" work. (Strange someone should ask today. It had been *one year exactly* for the patterners. One year today—Valentine's Day.)

Left the bill on the counter, bundling J. into my arms, remarking how we may just start a new style for summer, a kind of sandal without a sole!

I was wondering about the kinship of hopes and omens, which comes first, about starting the full program on Valentine's Day (her would-be birthdate), about starting a new sandal style, about starting a new category of child: brain-injured, but. Whatever you called it, she was a different Janey, this one-year-after child. The patterners had been looking back, had said so. And didn't they respect us both enough not to say what they didn't see?

All Kinds of Friends

J. distinguishing the patterners! Wednesday she turned Kay around, just pushed her around and looked at her hair, wondering where the pink curlers were; it was obvious.

Patterners in distress over J.'s red, raw abrasions, where her feet bottoms and inner knee-areas are rubbing the patterning table carpeting. All my kidding about "good tactile stimulation" and "just goes to show who's brushing her foot like I taught them" isn't funny anymore. Several times we have had blood. Now we are on lookout for her fidgeting during the patterning in order to stop *before*. Will try awhile longer to continue the toughening, thankful for tincture of benzoin and an absence of calls from the family court.

(Last November) Girl Scouts? Maybe. Or would they be using us? Some merit badge to them? Janey filling somebody's "service" needs? What would a toe-push in crawling be to them as goals go? What would Janey be to them? College students would be fine, but eighth-graders! Joan Weber, so nice to offer her girls, but—

Grace DeJose, Village Chairman, offering Girl Scout help from the little ones—in the elementary schools. Make books, materials, whatever J. needs. Yes, yes. That we need. Added some more stuff to her list (no time to ask The Institutes what):

1. Make Jane a "feel-it box" (one she can't see into) for tactile input.

a. Suggested shapes—three dimensional: ball, square, block, rectangular block, cylinders, triangular block, pencil shape, etc.; two dimensional: same as above, but flat one-fourth inch plywood covered with texture.

b. Suggested textures—all grades sandpaper, felt, velvet, silk, satin, corduroy, nubby wool, carpet, bark, sponge, leather, cotton, fur, feathers, etc. Box should be about one-foot high, enclosed, with a window high enough for her not to see what she's getting (i.e., give her a chance to feel it first) and large enough to get everything out easily. (She will use this during floor play, prone.) Box can be three-sided triangular plus back and bottom.

2. Make Jane twelve- and eight-inch styrofoam shapes (color the styrofoam, if possible, with bright colors): two sizes each of circle, square, rectangle, triangle, at least one-inch thick. Do not cover styrofoam, leave rough.

3. Make pictures that can be used on walls around the floor of the house: twelve inches high; cut-out colored oaktag (poster paper) and pasted on white paper. Outer configuration only. Can use pictures listed below, but no texture. Also shapes plus glitter—twelve inches high.

4. Make "textured" picture book for Jane. One picture to a page (a page an eight-inch oaktag square), front and back, using little internal configuration and covering picture with appropriate texture (see suggestions above). Possibilities here for "sand painting." Do not leave anything sticking out that may allow her to pull it off. Also don't have any texture too thick, so as to make a messy book when pages are together. The purpose here is to attract her visually more than tactilely. Pictures should be large, but not all of them the same size, so as to keep interest throughout book.

Animals—solid color, have detail on the face only—dog, cat, rabbit, fish, bird, squirrel, elephant, cow, horse, lamb, duck, giraffe, teddy bear.
Fruit—apple, pear, orange, banana, grapes.
Body—eyes, hand, foot with toes, legs, face, mouth open (lips, teeth).
Transportation—car, choo-choo, fire engine, ship.
Furniture—chair, sofa, table, bathtub, piano, TV.
Clothes—coat, bonnet, mittens, long-sleeve shirt, red pajamas with feet, blue jumper dress with white blouse, short-sleeved.
Other—dish (plate), pan (with handle), telephone (wall), hammer, back of our house, comb, penny (two on same page, showing both sides), diaper pin, boy, girl, mother, father, watch.

(Mid-January) You have a new bunch of friends all right, J. The Girl Scouts are super. Current impasse (J. stops to look back, watch girls, as they attempt to hold her toes down in crawling for better foot-pushes) they solved. One of them suggested bringing in a cat or dog, some moving incentive. We did. Cats *and* dogs. What the girls don't know is that their dogs and cats, and their free-wheeling, try-anything attitude has made me look up again. I'm not depressed anymore.

(March) Jane not crying (and screaming) anymore. Girls all pretty proud. They should be. She was never unhappy about the program, anything *they* were doing. I know her cries, to the last sighing whimper. She just couldn't bear to move so slowly up the new ramp. Same thing with the Rubatex floor in the crawl box. Both are supposed to slow her down, make her push with her feet more. Disliking the slowness, the change, doesn't mean disliking them or disliking 4:30-to-5:30-on-a-program, believe me. Make it as pleasant as possible, but do it. Another thing. Act as if you do this wherever you go. Don't let her know it's new to *you*.

Now, moving along in a stronger more deliberate push, she spends most of the hour laughing at their antics. Are they good! In the silence and secrecy behind the door where they work, away from me, each group has devised its own set of distractions. Girls, for the most part, terribly uninhibited in their devices. Very free, wanting so much to make it a noncrying hour. Can hear their encouragements, "Hey, Janey, that was great. Now, let's do it again, and I will turn on the lights for you," or "Say, Jane, that was a good push, do another one just like that," or "Wow, Buddy, your right leg is going to town, that's the way!"

One girl stands at the patterning table—top of the ramp. The other sends J. up the ramp, placing and holding her toe against the half-round molding, waiting for her to push forward. And now this toe again. The girl at the top has a job, verbally using praise, physically using distraction— dancing dolls or jiggly things they bring in themselves, anything new, or balls she can throw off the table when she finally lands there for "a breather," before being carried back to the bottom of the incline. Most daily groups do up to twenty ramp trips with her.

Food rewards with the crawl box are now given after each *round trip*. (There's an improvement!) Hard to find something not sweet or salty, so usually it's fruit.

Each day someone mentions how frustrating it must be not to be able to talk; but "you can figure out a lot, even without her saying it." Girls thrilled with each new "word" along with the rest of us. This week, for the first time: "La-la" for *doll* (sometimes it is "da"), "te be" for *teddy bear,* "ap" for *apple,* and "juz" for *juice.* Tries to say *banana* also, just a bunch of "*n*'s!" Except for *teddy bear,* these are all reading words.

A day to remember, for the sweet *and* sour: Janey sitting at the teacher's desk in the ———— School. And about thirty girls of the G.S. troop presenting her with the book they made with this sweet song:

> Make new friends,
> But keep the old.
> One is silver,
> And the other is gold.

Some had made more than one picture, we were told, each covered lovingly in some "appropriate texture." (They took me at my word!) I turned the pages:

The car of royal blue *aluminum* foil.

A squirrel with a *real mink* tail.

The duck in yellow *duck* fabric.

One girl had *knitted* a miniature light blue dress, exactly like the one Bert's mother had knitted for Janey, then pasted it right onto the page. Another girl had painted the bathtub with real porcelain paint. And there was a sofa shaped in brown and black worsted like ours.

Jane had spied the blue car and said, "cah," and I gave her the book. (Perfect Kid.) Then she said, "cawl." I explained to the room—all hushed and staring with the smiles not quite gone—how Jane "loves to move around in the freedom of the floor"; and I let her "crawl"—fast knee-walk and running creep—out of their room and through the corridor to the main door. As I picked J. off the floor at the exit, heartrending screams shattered the hallway silence. Several people standing in the doors, watching the mother bending over the child, spanking the child, now in total temper-tantrum hysterics, and hearing the mother call above it all, "You may do this when you get home!" The stop-this-this-minute tactics ended with my hand over her mouth, as Beth helped me on with her coat.

We went along home in the car, my trying to correct what I had said. She couldn't crawl immediately. She couldn't crawl the moment we got home. But later. Before supper.

Spring Breakthroughs

Something is happening to Jane's sitting posture. She just changed it (sometime recently). From sitting on her knees to this: one leg in front, one leg in back. This *must* have happened this week, sits in the new-sit on her table all the time now. Wonder if *sitting* has progressions of development too?

Another thing, bet this is important. J. sits with both legs over the edge of the table now (no hand assist). Newcomers run over to stand near her, dart glances her way, till I say, "Don't worry; she won't fall."

A first this morning: "Peggy, I think I felt her ankle move!"

"What do you mean?"

"Yep, there, it did it again. I can feel some movement in this ankle."

"I thought she could move her ankles——"

"Sh-h. Go ahead. What does it feel like?"

"It's resisting a bit—when I turn her foot over to brush the bottom. Shall I keep on brushing hard, or sort of let her move it if she can?"

"No. Keep on. Patterning must be passive. And perfect. You will send mistakes to the brain if you do that."

"Heaven forbid that I should send a mistake to 'headquarters.' "

That broke patterning right up, with Jane joining in the whooping and hollering. The five minutes was almost over anyway, we figured.

Red-letter day. For the left ankle.

Called Mary Lawrence tonight. Great free-for-all about this "stupid program," how it makes so much sense.

Mary telling me why it's the best *so far*. Someday the chemical research people might save us all this wear and tear to get a pathway started and then make it solid all up and down the line.

"Not to mention the obstetrical people!" And those magazines in the doctors' waiting rooms—articles about baby's layette! Why not one or two on oxygenation of the baby's brain? (Really quite interesting.) How the heaviest newborn has the best chance to be the healthiest. Mom's crucial nutrition, mom's smoking, mom's sluggish fat were just not nice to picture in the fuzzy-wuzzy pages of pink snuggies and perfect playpens.

Mary knew it was one of my good times. No more plateauing. Every area—even language and mobility—clicking along on the steam of little breakthroughs, subtle changes that would forever be permanent.

Then I ran down my notes:

> J. now repeating nouns we say to her, never fails to try. Find boys doing this with her. They name something, she "says" it (some sound in it usually), and they go on for three or four more, then dash away.
>
> All the new sounds J. has never used before: "ser" for *cereal,* "pe" for *peaches* (the baby-food dessert she gets each night to sink the thyroid pills into), "sa" for *sweater,* "yen" for *pants,* "ka" for *kitty cat.*
>
> How reading had picked up when I threw out the eight words we had originally struggled with before February. Just started on a new bunch entirely, the new battery of one a day.
>
> How cute her dealings are with patterners and afternoon Scouts.

Mary thinks there is a good chance they could visit us in Maine for a few days this August. I *needed* her to observe the program, tell me what she thinks about everything, watch and make suggestions. And we will need a leg patterner.

May: Bouquets and Awards

A moment in the 4-H meeting here today:

Today's Leader was explaining what goes where in their record books. She was hilarious. She got all twisted up, paused, whistled, and started over again. We all were laughing at her antics, when one of the boys said, "Yeah, Stuart used to do that a lot. Like this: 'Da — duh — did you——'"

Another boy: "Yeah, I remember that."

"Hey, Stu, you don't do that anymore. You used to. Remember?"

"I remember when he used to. 'Da — duh — did you see—' like that."

"I remember it. Last year."

Stuart, gluing, head down, the smile beginning over his face. Looked sideways at me, and I winked and quickly glanced back to the news clippings I was clipping.

Mary here and enthusiastic over Janey's new "toys," compliments of Girl Scout ingenuity. The gorgeous varnished wood triangle-of-tactile-treasures (that phrase came in somewhere), made by one of the G.S. fathers, was so appealing, Mary sat down in front of it, reaching into its darkness to feel the shapes and their coverings.

"I wish Janey could be so intrigued. When she gets on the floor, she wants to either move or look at a book."

"Well, Peg, I am sure you can think of some game-way to get this over to her."

Touché.

Mary wants all these Girl Scout offerings for her department at the hospital when we are finished with them. Especially delighted with the see-through rattles made out of plastic lids and filled with bright, shiny or sparkling shapes and charms. Mary rattled each one and said, "There's a lot of difference in sound in these things too." The G.S. leader even went through drawers at home and came up with all sorts of prickly, spongy, and smooth-feeling things I had never thought of (like the wiry yellow-orange scouring thing). Mary said if only moms would pitch the same sort of clutter onto their floors across this country!

A nursery school teacher made the large outline pictures now hugging the walls along the baseboard strip. And bored Jane won't even look at them.

Mary: "When a child is beyond 'outline perception' and lapping up the *details* in all those books, why would she want to waste her time on those, for heavens' sakes?"

Touché.

"You're doing something right though. In all my years with these kids, let me tell you, she's got the best pair of hips and the best trunkal balance I have ever seen!"

"You've seen a lot, I take it?"

"I've seen too much, Peg."

"What's that mean?"

"I used to work with children *only.* That's why I took this job at the hospital, not many kids. They are sent across the street, all the quote cerebral palsied unquote ones."

"Why did you want to stop working with kids? You're such a natural with a child."

"I couldn't stand what we were doing—or not doing—for them. For awhile there, we did try some of Dr. Temple Fay's earlier patterning ideas, but we did it all wrong. You don't know how exciting this is for me after giving up on the Fay techniques, when I *knew* the idea made sense: man was first an animal, his movement patterns are all animal, established before a baby stands up."

"As you say, if it works, I'm all for it!"

Touché, my card.

April showers brought the May flowers all right. Our yard is in color everywhere; the blossoms seem bigger and brighter this year. Janey enjoying the Cinerama too.

Something else bigger and brighter: her hearing. She never lets an airplane pass without looking up. Didn't notice them before. She still shakes her head from side to side when trucks pass. Strange, I wonder if it sounds like the vacuum cleaner to her? Certain sounds like that bug her—no, attract her actually, always moves to the vacuum cleaner, hovers over it, her head going side to side in its booming face. One thing, she's distinguishing more and reacting. Associates sounds outside with driving away. (Me.) So I tell her when I am leaving now and "I'll be back later."

What if I didn't? Must not think about it. But I do. Often on the Expressway to the city. When it isn't the longest parking lot in the world, it is the meanest menace to life. At those times I think of her. Everybody weaving in and out, it can happen and it isn't even your fault. No one could care as deeply as I that she get well. No one else could possibly make it their Number One. I even have trouble with that myself some days.

Lydia, who would be her mother in case I didn't come back, or anyone else would soon know, as I do, how smart, how winsome, how winning her little ways, once they lived with her a little while. She surprises *me.* For example, her understanding is getting higher and higher. I don't repeat *anything* anymore. And she joins in arguments or crying going on in the next room. (She seems awfully involved, frightened perhaps, and I am trying to have us all verbalize our distresses—instead of "biting and fighting"—because, if it's the loud burst kind, it makes her cry too.)

I am getting smarter too. Enlarging my vocabulary for her, like "lunch" and "supper" instead of "eat." And having J. point to doll-parts such as chin, belly, fingers, tongue, teeth, etc.

Out here in the yard I wonder why J. does not do all that humming to herself like the first line of "Ring Around the Rosy?" Probably too much to listen to?

And this: today is Mother's Day. Ugh. Just as if the day before and the day after aren't. Feeling in the air lately though. The way everything's going O.K.

Professional Evaluation

June 1, 1966. Philadelphia. Jane's re-evaluation and new program: I was bursting with all the notes I had jotted down about Janey and quickly launched into the reading and speech thing, "Hi. I painted a huge outline of a girl's body on the door in Janey's room—we call her Shoulders because I started there and they are bigger than everything else—and I did a reading battery of body words, using the outline for reinforcement, you know, midbrain association with the picture. And now Janey says "no" for *nose,* "arm" exactly, "tee" for *teeth,* "eye," and "yin-yin" for *chinny-chin-chin.* I think you really have something, I mean, the reinforcement of visual pathways for speech therapy!"

"Well, Mrs. Napear, if it worked, it's good. I notice *your* vocabulary is bigger——"

All laughing and settling down. To the history, me practically delirious, the woman cool as a cucumber. Janey was doing *forty* ramps a day, pushes stronger and stronger, uses hands very little up that incline. No, I stopped the crawl box because of the time on the ramp, both mornings and afternoons now. Is that all right? Almost forgot, this was history—I tell her, the dull part.

But Bert and I are most often on pins and needles for the rest of it.

"Look right here, Jane. Put your hands down. *Put your hands down.*"

I looked at Bert. He was pinching his nose, looking at Janey, slumped down in the chair, peeking over the backs of her hands, now dropping them to her lap.

I said, "Do you want me to——"

"Mom, I am getting what I want." The woman said this looking straight at Jane. And later, "Jane, I will stop only when I am finished. I *am not finished.* Right here. Good. Excellent. That's it." Throughout she had not taken her eyes off J. But now she turned and wrote a lot into the chart, head down, but addressing us, "You understand, of course, this child knows everything that is going on here. . . . I'm talking to you, Mom, and to you too, Dad."

I said, "Well, I think she is very smart. She just doesn't understand why she can't crawl around when she's being evalua——"

"She understands it all. *You* don't know it. She has no way to show you. Don't underestimate this child."

"I try——"

"I was checking several things there. That's the reason I wanted it that way."

"Oh."

Bert let out a long slow laugh, "Well, you certainly had me fooled. I was beginning to think you'd better not tangle with me like that!"

She winked. "You thought we had had a rough day before you got here, I know. Well, we did. We always do. It's where I'd rather be though than anywhere else. This kid is great." An afterthought: "She's *way* ahead of you."

"You mean the Sarah Heartburn act?"

She laughed, and crossed the room to the door, "Yes, the Sarah Heartburn act and some other things." Someone would cover all that, as Bert was asking, "Like what?" And thanking us, and into the hall. Bert and I followed, out to the waiting room again, doing all sorts of things with *our* eyes and shoulders.

The report, Jane on paper, which is mailed to the referring pediatrician, showed Jane's scoring (Doman-Delacato Developmental Profile) increased in two areas:

Visual: Convergence continues to improve, as does visual attention and appreciation. Reading—progressing well.
Manual: Cortical opposition [thumb to forefinger] bilaterally and simultaneously, now normal.

No more crumbs!
Other remarks were very encouraging:

Mobility: Crawling—improved knee flexion and push with legs.
    Creeping—qualitative improvements.

Creeps we still had.

Language: More sounds. Better tonality. Obvious attempts to communicate vocally.
Auditory: Continues to increase. Poor time concept. Mild startle reflex persists.
Tactile: Stereognosis—identification faster, although not more refined.

Dominance: [About the same. Foot—not observable. Hand tending to right. Eye—
   right today. Ear—not observable. Tactile—right.]
Seizures: None. [They still ask about that even though she has *never* had any.]
Other: Jane has made significant and encouraging progress during this interval.

Looking back on it, I bet Bert that the dramatics elicited the "mild
startle reflex," as well as the Sarah Heartburn bit.

And the lights, the objects, the hand, the eye, the word cards, all added
up to a twelve-month increase in visual competence, all since February.

For her reading program we were to make a long tape to play on a tape
recorder, consisting of about three hundred nouns I would eventually
cover during the program. Each word to be said five times. With a five-second interval between each, little silences to arouse listening. Play this for
three hours, two times a day.

We discussed who should make the tape. Who would we most want to
hear six hours a day? Bert or me? I wondered if he might write one of
those pretty letters, like the one to the president of the Miller Brewing
Company, asking Gregory Peck to make the tape, for "my daughter's reading therapy, which is actually her speech therapy."

Bert opting for Doris Day.

No, they wanted the sounds to be the same Jane would hear in the
reading program. That left me. Why not write to Miller Brewing for a
couple cases of *beer,* of all things, for "my wife's auditory therapy during
the coming summer?"

5

From June 1966 to October 1966

JULY 4, 1966. Fireworks all right. Stu has the measles—temperature
105 degrees. First case here in a long time, the doctor says. Records
breaking outdoors too—107 degrees in the shade. Poor Stuart is burning
up. Physically. I'm burning up with anger. Grant and Stu's records were
never transferred to the new doctor as requested. This doctor gave Jane
Sabin vaccine, so we know she's O.K. I am mad. And I am scared.
Encephalitis the terror.

I talk merrily about camp while I'm bathing Stu in alcohol, so he won't
suspect my fears.

Made of steel these days. Bert too. He knows the danger. We both have
seen the children afterwards—those who started with a simple case of the

measles, to come out of the fire of fever and pressure later as someone else.

AUGUST 2, 1966. Maine. Way to Maine with the children and mother's helper, Dizzy Klang, trying to find some togetherness over a packed car and a wide generation gap. Diz wears a 007 shirt, likes only hamburgers and Coke, hates lobsters, no breakfast, never had blueberry pancakes, and cannot believe I never saw a James Bond movie. "What has my mom gotten me into?" *Very* good with the boys, two brothers herself.

Took a driver's break at Howard Johnson's, our usual halfway stop. Diz commented on how good Janey was, waiting like the rest of us for a hamburger. I explained it was the music. Dizzy hadn't noticed it. That half-glaze, head-tilted position, as she swayed left and right in the highchair, looked "sweet and good" to everyone else. To me—I was trying to put my finger on it—it provoked a pacification in her that was somehow a negative thing, an unhealthy something. I tried to describe it, telling Dizzy about brain injury and tonality and subdominant hemispheres, much too much I felt, but she kept asking me more and more.

She said she knew what I meant. When she baby-sat that day last November, she hadn't known what to do with Jane exactly, she was so rambunctious, just moving, moving—I said "hyperactive"—and so annoyed whenever she had to get off the floor. So Diz had played the piano each of those times. It was the only time J. seemed to be calm the whole day. She told her mother that night that the saying "Music soothes the savage beast" must be true, because "this little animal was soothed by it." Then she added, "I didn't mean that Jane really was like an animal——"

"That's O.K., Dizzy. You aren't the first to say that. All these hyperactive children look that way till you get to know them. That's what keeps me going. I want everyone—even strangers—to know the Janey I know. And she'll have to be a talker and a walker before they look at her and not think 'animal.' "

We picked up the boys who had long ago run out to walk the wall. Just before the Maine Turnpike I pulled into a shopping center parking lot. "I'll only be a minute. I have to buy some warm pajamas and stuff for myself." It was more than a minute.

Dizzy had Jane sitting on the hood of the car, trying to quiet her screams. J. was shaking with sobs and fright, which gradually subsided as I picked her up. I thanked Dizzy for all the bad moments she had endured. It wasn't the handling. It was the sitting. Jane needed a back to lean against in a new spot, till she got used to it. In fact, the only place she will sit without it is her patterning table. She's so used to that, she even sits with her legs over the side of it now. If she's lying on her stomach she's fine. Or sitting back on her haunches, you know, knee-sitting, she's O.K.

Dizzy thought she had missed me. No. She isn't that aware of absence yet. Then I added, "As we go along, you will learn all her idiosyncracies. Whatever you don't understand, just ask. I want you to know as much as I know."

Maine: midnight. The first moment inside the cabin, Jane began, "E-o-ooh" in an eerie hollow continuum. "Oh-ooh-e-e-i."

Diz glanced from Jane to me, paused, and said, "Uh, know any ghost stories?"

I laughed, "Miss Weirdo here is checking out the echo."

"What echo?"

"This room apparently has a slight echo. You know, large bare floor and cathedral ceiling. She has a fascination with echoes, hollow places."

Jane rocked herself in the wicker rocker, content to make lulling echo-like sounds while we set the crib-cage up.

DAILY SCHEDULE

	GIRLS	BOYS
8:00	wake up	wake up
8:30	breakfast and today's word	breakfast
(turn on tape recorder)		
9:00	pattern	Stuart—pattern and chores
	crawl	Grant—darts (his far-point program)
	pre-writing (guide her hand)	
	today's word and yesterday's word	
9:30	same as 9:00 except no writing	
10:00	same as 9:00	
10:30	same as 9:00 except no writing	
11:00	creep (outrigger, etc.)	swim (Diz or Mom lifeguard)
12:30	lunch	lunch
	today's word and yesterday's	
1:00	tactile programs	free time
	flash week's battery of words	
	visual pursuits	
(turn on tape recorder)		
2:30	creep (outrigger, etc.)	
4:30	ramp (Dizzy)	Stuart—ramp
	Grant's program (Mom)	Grant—his program
	today's word and yesterday's	
	pre-writing on table, two times	
	during ramp breaks	
6:30	supper	supper
	today's word and yesterday's	
7:30	Jane's bedtime and reading run-	Grant—flash J.'s reading battery
	through (all words)	evening fun
	sleep pattern	
8:30		bedtime

Note: Present no new word on Sundays. Test week's battery of words.

AUGUST 7. Fell over Jane's ramp in the dark. Sprained ankle. We patterned today somehow, my knee resting on a stump under the table. Hospital suggested crutches, till I explained the problems of carrying J. around. Trying wet heat, exercise, and elevation instead. Diz taking advantage of my bed-ridden state. She is so much fun, engaging in philosophical discussions at night, and retort-artistry by day. All truths coming now in jests.

ME (*from living room bed*): Don't forget to turn the tape on when they've finished breakfast.

DIZZY (*from the kitchen*): Ugh, do I have to listen to that while I do dishes and sweeping and psychiatry and——

ME: Hold your tongue, lass. You're getting ten dollars a week for mother's helper, remember?

DIZZY: Oh, joy. (*Beats the backs of her hands together like a seal.*) (*Mumbling*) If this is mother's helper, who is the mother?

ME: The more you listen to the tape, the more you get used to it.

DIZZY: I'll never get used to "chay-er, chay-er, chay-er, chay-er, chay-er."

ME: Ah, the charm of a Southern accent.

DIZZY: More like the low first grade. And "lay-g, lay-g——" and "hay-er, hay-er——"

ME: Don't forget to comb the child's auburn hay-er when you dress her. Oh, yes, and show the juice reading card with o.j. We forgot to do that yesterday.

DIZZY (*banging dishes around*): And the one that makes you want to throw up: "ay-g, ay-g——" How can you put two syllables in *egg?*

ME: Same way I put them in *leg*. Some have it. Some don't.

DIZZY (*to Jane*): O.K., kid, I'm turning on the tape recorder. It's torture time. (*Then something about a wildcat strike.*) (*Janey giggles.*)

ME: Also, Diz, will you bring me another cup of coffee?

DIZZY (*throwing her rag down at the doorway*): No. I'll just have to help you out to the "washhouse" later and I'll get behind in my overburdened schedule.

ME: Please, Diz, I'm so bored, just lying here. So frustrated, not able to do anything——

DIZZY: As long as I can stand up and sweat, you can depend on me, Stepmother. Where do you want it? On your foot?

ME: That's what's killing me. All the guff I have to take from a whimpering, simpering teen-ager. Get back into the ashes.

DIZZY: (*Stiffened salute and goes back into kitchen, returning to ask if I still want coffee.*)

ME: No, I can't stand to creep out there on the pine needles. It kills my hands.

DIZZY: Yeah, if you'd creep all day, you could toughen 'em up like Girlus here.

ME: Get back to the kitchen, Cinder. You're not paid to give advice.

AUGUST 9. Our neighbors are hosting two high school boys from England. Today they arrived. They saw Jane at her creeping time, moving noisily over the floor with Dizzy's loafers on her hands, releasing a steady flow of "e-i-o" jargon with high and low sounds. I saw it all through their eyes. An animal sort of a child, allowed to grow wild on the floor, in and out the banging screen door to the porch and back again, happy into herself with giggles and eerie noises. While the rest of us were making ▢ window ▢ cards (five) on the front porch, kidding ourselves we were going to teach her to read or something.

Dizzy felt it too, I think. She started right in explaining how able J. was—you should see her tactile ability. How we were really doing reading for visual reinforcement of words she heard on the tape. For speech. Not for status or anything.

They were great. Before they left, Dizzy had signed one of them to help her do the forty ramp trips, from four to six o'clock. Date-making in Maine on vacation, with an inclined ramp the vehicle and a four-year-old imp the chaperone. It was a superb touch to this lovely day.

AUGUST 10. Couplet! Finally! J. said "Bye-bye-cah-eat—" as we left the laundromat. She was asking to go back to the snack bar? After leaving the clothes to wash, we had eaten hamburgers there for lunch. This time with the clothes stacked into the back seat, I rushed headlong for the same place and ordered ice cream cones for all. Yes, Jane too. Thus, it became First Ice Cream Cone Day too. Couldn't have cared less about the mess a child can make with a cone on a hot summer day. Pure pleasure. Pure promise. Jane can "combine two units of speech meaningfully." We'll go for three.

Today's ramp scene. Dizzy and Stuart, bless them, were up to their eyeballs in a bored child. They could find nothing gay or funny for J. to go after, at least nothing worth all that effort up to the table. They were on "trip" number eighteen. No, we wouldn't give in. I would lie on my bed— finally—and give nursery rhymes for rewards. It was too abstract. Or that stuff belongs to the mornings? She didn't buy it. How about a half grape each time? No, she was tired of those. What else do we have? Nothing. Then tell her to do it anyway. That's a joke. Who wants to listen to crying to prove who's boss.

Just then nine-year-old Lisa Perrin came in and Janey brightened. Lisa hopped right up and sat down, cross-legged, at the top, squarely in the middle of the patterning table. "Hey, Janey, look at me!"

Janey did and pushed up to see, one strong labored thrust forward, then the other side. Stuart was ready there to hold that toe in place on the half-round, then Diz on the other side, ready. Janey pushed up the incline. There is somebody sitting on *my* table! And Janey Bear pushed Goldilocks off. The game was on. It lasted for the other twenty-one trips.

AUGUST 11. Dreary day. Ground too wet for J.'s after-pattern crawl. Diz did indoor crawling efforts, I did clean-up, including new shelving paper. Sometimes I need to be in the soap and water rather than in the mothering mire.

Jane said "Bye-bye-cah-eat———" I popped them all into the car and drove to Denmark for fresh corn and beans, first getting the "—em—" (ice cream) Jane requested. Jane is communicating. Diet is deteriorating. For maximum brain activity she must have adequate fluid intake (twenty-six ounces in the summer) and no more and no thirst-makers, like ice cream. But for maximum motivation she must be heard and responded to. This is one of the tightropes we're on. And the wind is from all directions. Glad Mary is coming Saturday.

AUGUST 12. At the lake. Diz settled Jane down on the sand. I started the tape recorder despite all the "ughs." Dizzy noticed the [**water**] card had fallen again; it was floating in the lake. She got the stencils and poster paper and made another one. And two [**Mary**] cards, one for her front and one for her back, when she gets here.

How to get a [**dog**] card on the Perrins' Gus?

"Hold it, everybody," and I put my hand up.

Jane had crept over to the tape recorder and was copying the word "Stuart!"

"Two-it."

Again the tape paused.

"Two-it."

"Hey, Stuart, come here quick!" Maidli Perrin called. "She just said your name!"

Stuart swam in and listened. Now it was on "Grandmother," and the moment was lost.

He belly-skimmed over to Janey at the edge, blowing bubbles in a smile on top of the water. "Hey, Janey, what's my name? Jane, my name is *Stuart.*"

"Two-it."

Grant leaped over the end of the pier. "Hey, Janey, what's *my* name? *Grant.* My name is *Grant.*"

Jane looked up at him and poured her pail of water over his feet.

"Grant, how would you like to wear your name card like Stuart's been doing?"

"Yeah? What other words?"

"Only your name."

"O.K. But I don't want to wear any other words."

They all bounded away, headed for the Perrins with our Tom Lehrer record. To copy all the verses for memorization, and to fill an afternoon.

AUGUST 13. Mary's here. This morning we were all standing around laughing at Gus, who was lying on the bed with ⃞ **dog** ⃞ attached to him. Grant had gotten on the table to test if Janey could see it from there.

MARY: Pardon me, folks, but are you doing that wacky Philadelphia program I've heard about?

DIZZY: Whatever gave you that— We are animal trainers—dogs, seals, amphibians, reptiles— Here is your name. Wear it in good health.

MARY: This seems to call for a ceremony, head-sprinkling or full immersion or something.

DIZZY: No, we thought we'd let you do the ramp this afternoon!

And she did. With a blueberry as the reward for each trip. Why hadn't we thought of that?

This morning Mary had discovered during outdoor crawls with Jane that a body could be made to move up a path in a straight line after a blueberry!

She also noticed J. still does not crawl with legs rotating inward. Said we must emphasize the correct way in patterning; brush stronger as we extend and rotate each. See what she means. The Marines' zigzag motion is what we're after.

After the children were in bed Dizzy and Mary had a discussion. Pitched to me. Something about the need to clarify relationships. Mother duck and her ducklings, especially the middlest, the freckled one. It seems some mother ducks threaten punishment a lot, but never give any. How people play games. How patterns get started in relationships. How big brother duck fills the void. How mother ducks need to go in a straight line instead of swimming around.

Everything they said was true. Would they like to take over?

After the high-horse act, new resolves were made and a few plans were constructed.

In all the fun and frolic of working with Jane, in all the wondering and worrying, in all the groupness, we would still be watchful of the other ducks. Each child needed the one-to-one private time. Not just sometimes. But every day.

AUGUST 14. (Tell Bert.) Today the tape recorder went on the blink. It continued to run, but slowly, slowly, changing the sound of my voice to a drawling, scratchy baritone. We had it out on the back steps so J. could hear it. About midway through the tape, it went several octaves lower.

Jane paused on the path, head up, looked all around and said, "Dada."

Everyone loves the change!

Tonight Mary watched us go through J.'s before-bed routine and exclaimed over this and that. Jane's finger ability now, zipping her own pajama-snuggy and saying something that sounds like "zipper." Grant doing the reading run-through just before J. is tucked in—so emphatic with each word card, so smart to wait till her eyes have glanced at the word before he names it, so sweet in the process even though he has done the same review each night before.

Tonight, as a bonus break from the boredom of it all, Grant then showed her the new review book Dizzy had made, page by page, covering the picture on each until the word was called, Grant whispering out of the side of his mouth. "She's looking, Mom!"

Mary was deeply impressed that Jane gets into her sleep pattern now by herself. From waist up. She doesn't involve her legs yet, but the arms flick into the normal position. One flexed—with its hand near the mouth in the old baby-thumb-sucking position. One extended behind her. Again, Mary said we must brush her legs stronger in patterning, to teach the brain its "bottom" body too.

This caused Dizzy to ask Mary how physical therapy, before this program came along, taught the brain about all this. Mary smiled and said no one mentioned the brain before. Legs and arms, yes. Dozens of ideas how to stimulate the arms and legs. No ideas how to stimulate the brain that works the arms and legs.

"Why did you do it then?"

Mary answered, "Oh, we were very busy. So busy massaging, and stretching, and electrifying the muscles. Then the patient would put his braces back on, put all those appendages back into a state where no movement was possible. And we'd say, 'See you Thursday.' All the time we were devising new techniques for all the next Thursdays. None of us ever sat down and said, 'You know, none of this is getting anybody well.' Can you see how painful that would be? To us? Everyone likes to think they are helping.

"But in Philly, they did. One week about twenty years ago. They admitted it. Why move a part, then immobilize it the rest of the day? They say it was a very painful gathering. Doctors and therapists had to explain what each was doing for brain-injured children. And each had to admit they had never gotten anyone well that way.

"So they decided to research how nature 'walks' the *normal* kids. They would start with the earliest movements. They would look at talking and other stuff too. But they just happened to start with 'walking' first. That was the lucky part. For years they bumped into the strangest things: babyhood was a subtle organizing system of movements. The baby goes through a neurological organization. A bunch of things happen before walking. And they happen the same way in all normal babies who are allowed movement. They found that kids sleep in a certain position. And disorganized kids sleep in a lot of other tangled ways. Because they watched hundreds of them.

"We didn't know anything about nature and kids. We were too busy with the arms and legs. And the neurologists, the brain surgeons, were too busy with the organic condition of the brain. Was there a tumor? That kind of question. They couldn't very well be looking at the well children. Their offices were too filled with the hurt ones. Their medical training concerned the hurt, not the well. Their evaluations usually ended with, 'You have a brain-damaged child.' That has meant 'period' and 'forever.' Until now. In Philadelphia they watched the neurosurgeon Temple Fay, M.D. operate in the mornings; he taught them all he knew about the structure of the brain. In the afternoons they watched the well children operate, in their cribs, on their floors, in their yards. The kids taught them function. Together they learned a lot about babies and the brain. From brain-injured children they have learned even more."

We refilled our hot chocolate mugs and Mary told us about other new developments in physical therapy, how she wished desperately all the mavericks could get together. But it was the same old story. Everyone likes what he is doing. Including The Institutes down in Philly.

"But, Mary, I thought you thought the program we're doing is the latest word," I said, weak and frightened.

"Peggy, they are the latest word. They are on the right track finally. But this business of influencing the brain from out here is a brand-new business. Doman and Delacato would be the first to agree. They are extremely humble about what they *don't* know. They want others to drop the old techniques and join in the search, the research, up *this* path.

"Path, pathways. Funny, isn't it. They want to know all the ways you can make a pathway through the brain. In and out. All those networks to get around dead cells. They want normal functioning from a ten-billion-celled computer. And it racks them up to hear about a new technique for massage. This is 1966. Time to switch to brain talk when you're talking about a brain-injured kid. That's all. They've got a communicating problem worse than Jane's: nobody is listening."

AUGUST 17. The Klang family here to take Dizzy home. Red Klang was a *fireman,* now retired, and his alternate had been a Lieutenant Bell!

Yesterday, for Red Klang's benefit, we allowed them to watch Jane in a reading test, although it wasn't the seventh day. She went along with the game, much faster now that she can point to the word I name. They heard her say a few too, including her clearest word *window*.

Miriam Klang was beaming. They gasped when she knew [**boat**] from [**book**], no matter how the cards were shuffled. I explained there is a different word-shape for each, although slight. But she does get [**ear**] and [**car**] mixed up, also [**nose**] and [**house**]. Miriam whispered to Red that Jane does all this without knowing anything about the ABC's yet.

After every response, I picked J. off the patterning table with glowing remarks and twirled her in my arms around the floor. Soon I was doing two or three words before the "dance." It was all joyous, like Doman had begged in his book, *How to Teach Your Baby to Read,* but I wasn't sure it was the right way. Jane didn't seem to get any inner satisfaction that I could tell. That's why I always gave her a dance or a bounce. Once a week—testing and twirling. At least it was working. And at least J.'s vocabulary was showing 90 percent reading influence.

Today I invited them to sit in on our little after-lunch, one-room school-house, the rustic unfinished wood bedroom-retreat I had come to love so much. Here everyday I caught J.'s gradual building of new abilities. Most days we spent a marvelous hour and a half here off the floor. I rationalized that Jane had a longer day on the floor than IAHP kids who nap after lunch. She spent five hours in crawling and creeping and two hours pushing up the ramp. Anyway I needed it. While everyone else was at the beach or out fishing, it was the silence and the progress that filled up my cup again.

Miriam and Red didn't move a muscle, and J. went along undistracted by their presence. She was intent on feeling in the bag for the jack (ball 'n' jack set), so I would spin it when she found it. The competition in the bag had gotten stiff. There were two other almost identical sharpish things, all no bigger than the jack: a tiny baby charm with sharp arms and legs and a small celluloid flower, whose petals on all sides resembled the jack prongs. Grouping the other little charms the dentist had given to me, I put Jane through several stereognosis tests, until she was choosing one out of four quite similar flat or round or sharp items.

(By the way, Stuart and Grant sit around after supper sometimes giving each other the "bag" test! Grant still has trouble with the skillet-clock-record charms, because that series is awfully small in its detail. Maidli and Lisa think Jane is better than they. Though Grant constantly reminds us all that "She practices every day!")

Next I did the coin-differentiation in the Crown Royal bag, but Jane is so bored with it. I tried spinning the quarter or the penny, but their spin is anticlimactic after the jack spinnings.

Then the eye-following stuff with the pencil flashlight, asking Miriam to hold J.'s head still. Then a few seconds of pouring ball or block from one container into another for pronation-supination. Then on to twisting the graduated kegs open, then twisting them closed.

For the fun of it, I let J. do four or five puzzles, large jigsaw wooden ones of eleven to thirteen pieces. She turned the pieces around in varying attempts without cues from me. Red liked that. It's one of those sure things that shows smartness, we agreed. I laughed. It's really a combination of visual and tactile ability. Later, children get even better. They position pieces tactilely after they figure out visually where it goes. Janey wanted to do them all again, but I said no. Better to stop before she's ready to. I suggested, "You may crawl now" instead, and she burst into squeals of delight. It was really creep time, but J. says, "Ah cawl (I crawl)," so we do too. Like everyone else, the kid doesn't know crawling from creeping.

AUGUST 19. Surprise—Bert, two days early and loaded with rackets, clubs, and fifty dollars' worth of groceries. Everyone but me had known he was coming early. Jane was lying on her table, a half-smile starting and stopping, as she watched the hushed scene. Then we all started talking at once, as the boys bounded in the room, fishing rods dangling dangerously.

"Leave them on the porch. Look, just put them in the corner——"

"Hey, Dad, did you bring my new reel?"

"Hi, Dad."

And Grant saying, mockishly, quickly, "Hi, Son." And then, "Pop, the hop, the big fat plop——"

"Hello, there, Grant the ant, the big fat— How ya doing, Stu?"

"Fine. I finished my golf lessons——"

"Hey, Dad! Mary taught me tennis! Want to play——"

"So I hear. Guess what I did? I sprained my ankle yesterday and can't do any of it for a couple of days——"

None of us had noticed, but Bert was noticably favoring the hurt foot. Grant started hopping around, hand on forehead in pained expression. "Oh, no, not that again!" Then he stopped, hands down at diagonals in stiffened disgust, "Mom just had all that——"

Eleven of us and four Perrin kids for supper, Bert feeling generous with hot dogs *and* hamburgers off the grill. We all perched on the porch steps and watched the sun fade over the lake. Before any of us had quite got started, Bert had stepped over to Jane's highchair. "Girlus, you look terrific!"

We turned. Just then she extended her plate, and with mouth filled said, "Mo ham-mer-mer."

Everyone saying at once, "She just asked for more hamburger!"

Dizzy said, "Thanks to a certain teen-ager with a unilateral taste!"

Diz left this morning amid a lot of kidding about what a dumb kid she is to leave all this for the Beatles Concert in Shea Stadium. It was that or weep. She left her loafers for Janey. Also left a bag of sugar-free gum for Jane. Gum-giving to Jane after patterning had been one of her simple sweetnesses. She was teaching Jane what "after" meant at first, then it got to be just plain love. Other times she would let J. ping the rubber bands attached to her braces, mouth opened, patiently letting J. check it all out. I suppose she would have left one of her arms if she felt it could help Jane.

Jane Elizabeth Klang, whom we nicknamed Liz then Diz for "communication" reasons, was leaving. We had laughed a lot. I would miss her philosophies and her fun. But as she was leaving, I was wondering most about who else would be so kind to my Jane ever again.

AUGUST 23. Janet Perrin told me about a doctor-friend who is researching or writing a paper about startle reflex. Something about some people had more of the reflex than others. I wound up explaining it to her, how it dies out as a baby becomes neurologically organized. It stays in people who are neurologically disorganized. After the initial reaction, it can persist *severely*—whole body jumps with a loud noise; *moderately*—arms or legs jump; or *mildly*—eyes blink. It should die out to nothing, even after the first loud noise. Jane still has a startle reflex, but it is mild. Babies who don't recapitulate the evolution of the species very well never get rid of it altogether. So the doctor is looking at degrees of neurological organization, that's all. Should we tell him? Too bad professionals don't have a common journal about such things—though The Institutes is supposed to be starting one.

AUGUST 29. A wild scramble today to get the reading cards in from the paths and beach when rain started. All | **tree** | and | **rock** | cards ruined again. Maidli thrashing around in back, looking for | **blueberries** | under the bushes. Stu left | **water** | and | **sand** | at the beach; they were smeared anyway. We forgot the | **johnny** | card on the side of the washhouse altogether.

Grant's suggestion: make a new | **water** | card and nail it to a pole stuck in lake bottom. Lisa's suggestion: cover cards with cellophane wrap and leave 'em there.

Three guesses what we did all afternoon.

AUGUST 30. Bert and I off to golf with the boys.

While we were away, Maidli thought Jane might have drunk charcoal-lighter fluid. But it was an empty can, left from last night's grilling. She told me how her mother had run over. They had called the hospital for an antidote. I knew J. hadn't. Something about Jane I can't quite put my finger on. She's not a baby. She's smarter than that. She would have noticed by now how Daddy uses that for fire-making. For some reason, she wouldn't drink out of such a container. She's older than that, I guess. Funny, she knows everything in a kitchen cupboard; takes it all out, puts it all back. But never has she spilled or drunk any of it. It would be more like her to take the can to the cupboard where it belongs. She's fastidious, a perfectionist, in a way I can't figure.

AUGUST 31. To New Hampshire this evening for family cookout. Bert and I realized in twelve years of marriage, this was the first time for our family to cook out away from home. And, indeed, we picked the dampest spot in the White Mountains. Two hours after bending and blowing, Stu's 4-H camp experiences notwithstanding, we still had been unable to start a fire. We had two matches left. Bert, who had been back and forth to Jane in the car till we got some warmth, sat down beside us.

"Maybe I can get it," he said.

"Look, Dad, it's not going to work. It's too wet."

"Sure, it will," he said, settling his huge frame in a little closer. "I know how."

"Where did you learn anything about this stuff, Bert? At *your* camp?" I asked, so Stuart would not be hurt.

"You've got to love it," Bert said.

"What?"

"You've got to love it." And he quietly bent his head down, struck the match to the fresh paper, sat back and stared at it.

"Dad, as soon as the paper stops, it stops, you'll see."

"Sh-h. Don't say anything. Just look at it. Sh-h. Just love it. Sh-h. Sit down. Steady now."

Grant's eyes were as big as saucers. It was as good as a ghost story. It was uncanny. For the first time another little flame, another color, licked out from under nowhere. A piece of wood was on fire. Stuart looked as if he had broken a hundred in golf, hand on head, flattening his crew cut cautiously, over and over.

"Now just sit here and love it," Bert said. We did. And it did. And Daddy went all the way to seven feet right before our eyes.

The blueberry pancakes were the best we had ever had, thanks to Grant. The bacon too, thanks to Stuart.

The love too, thanks to Bert.

From now on when nothing new is happening with Janey, I'm going to remember this, to tell the boys. To tell me. So I won't give up on the "rainy days."

Professional Evaluation

October 18, 1966. Philadelphia. Mary Lawrence with us for IAHP's evaluation of Jane.

Jane Napear has parents who are underestimating her. If she can understand the "deal" concept, involving "after" and "later" concepts, she can certainly understand "discipline." Use it. Discipline is "to teach." What is this business about letting her wear my high heels on her hands? These are Mommy's shoes, those are yours, hands off. What do we mean she "won't" do this and that? Make requirements of her.

But each pair of my shoes makes a different sound on the slate; you can see her listening to the difference. I did not win that round. Seems Jane is ready for higher auditory feed-in, like understanding concepts. O.K.

Mary agreed with the pediatrician who was dishing out all this. Have we really been that lousy, Mary? Yes. And we are lucky they told us, she added. As auditory organization increases, so should a parent's discipline. Once a child understands the "bargain" concept, he is ready for higher requirements. "I have seen a lot of parents with their brain-injured children. Believe me, listen to the doctor. Or you'll go the pampering, overcompensating sickly business of letting the child run you to death. Here they don't care about you and your problems as much as they care about Jane's wellness. Jane's level of understanding is their business. They are not being personal, so get off your high horse."

Some things we are doing right:

Jane reads seventy words for sure. Eight more maybe.

Startle reflex normal today, for the first time.

Stereognosis (tactile ability) is improved. She was given credit for entering the final tactile competence block, Level VII, on their Profile.

Language is nine months (neurologically) higher, thanks to the onset of word combinations, notably "Don't want it" and "Don't want nite-nite."

Her more than fifty new words, used spontaneously and with meaning, are all from reading. The lady just smiled, no one here ever hollers.

Jane has zippering and buttoning ability now. Bimanual function. Good. Now we will perfect it. Oh?

J.'s crawl shows a "marked improvement" (that's how they holler) in its hand-use. Remember the zipper bit? Her new interest in buttons? The ability to twist? All that is dependent upon a strong, well-developed hand and finger system. Her brain has learned a lot about the hand, as it crawls over everything. Conversely, the hand has heard the brain better. The message system works both ways. Look at J.'s crawl. See the way the crawl-pull is depending upon fingers now. Babies use forearm-pulls, then hand-pulls, and finally finger-pulls, if they crawl long enough. The man was right, she *is* using her fingers more than the palms now. Keep looking, keep crawling. That will progress to finer and finer pulls, till she ends her pull on her little finger, under her chest. See, she pronates in the pull and supinates slightly under her. When will she be finished? We'll see. The man literally means we will have to see it.

So with a stronger palm system and tip-to-tip finger ability, Jane is now ready for buttons. She has already started, by herself. And snaps. And laces we can begin.

How about shoes then? No. But the leg flexion is better this time. No toe-dig out to the side in crawling though. Shall we surgically operate on her heel cords? No. We will put all crawl efforts into the crawl box. Thanks a lot.

And the cute school bit we can cut out, except one-half hour in a chair during the day, if I want. Throw the puzzles on the floor. Get down there with her for the other stuff too.

And make a new tape. With three voices on it. To arouse listening. No, no sentences, except a very few to arouse listening, like, "Jane, are you listening to me?" All nouns. Most of them beyond her present understanding. To arouse listening through the five times they are said. How is she going to listen to three hundred new words when she doesn't understand what they mean? Just watch. Hm-m.

On the way home at midnight again, with Miss Bounce touring the back seat, Bert offered to make the tape, with the help of Stu and Grant. I would build the new crawl box, this time two eight-foot ones for double length. The old one was too narrow for her now. Mary wondered which of us had gotten the better deal. I said anything was better than listening to myself all day.

Then Bert said, with new resolve, "Jane, sit down on the seat. Now."

I had a few resolves of my own: after the Indian pageants at 4-H father-son weekend and the school's Thanksgiving program next month, I would say no to any more Indian lore projects. The problem was that we had had such fun with it all, and now Grant was getting interested. And the tightrope was unraveling again. What a child will accept about his busy mother intellectually is not what he will accept emotionally.

While the principal was discussing the Thanksgiving Indian program with me, he mentioned The Institutes. Our school district administrators were turned down for last April's weekend for educators that was held there . They are on the list for the November one. I told Mary about it.

She looked at me, "You still involved in all that?"

"No, others are carrying the ball, I hear. They're looking into it. That's all I ever really wanted. The program sells itself. If not today, it will, after they've tried teaching a child his left from his right and other little structures and props to learn around. They'll get tired of the struggle one of these days."

"Teachers never get tired. They like all the new techniques. It perks up each new year."

So true. It was the minor revisions in Janey's program that I was looking forward to, mulling over, thinking how to introduce them, how to schedule them, resolving to let nothing interfere with her next three-month input, to breeze through the winter's length, as we had the summer's "party." Also promising myself (again) to mask The Littlest Computer twelve times a day for purposes of "deep breathing." To do all the program every day. For *my* deep breathing.

PART III

Battling the Giants

There was "an attack" beginning. The children, the crippled, and the dumb, were huddled together in the trenches. Some of us were with them, busy at a new work called "organizing a child's brain." We could hear warnings from time to time, warnings to parents who were about to try new techniques, warnings to pediatricians who advise "already burdened and confused parents." The Goliaths were striking out with executive board statements which were quick to remind readers that theirs were the "established methods," the "accepted methods."*

The cerebral palsy giant, you might say, had had its "cerebral" banner torn away. If it's true that 90 percent of the "cerebral palsied" are actually injured lower in the midbrain, then the name "cerebral anything" is wrong. Walking and talking and all the beautiful human toys are up on the sixth floor in the Brain Department Store, yes, but the elevator shaft is clogged up on the third floor. That's where the repairmen ought to be. Changes in names had occurred before. A kid in 1940 had had "spastic paralysis"; before that he was "feeble-minded"; in biblical times he was "lame from his mother's womb."

And if "mentally retarded" is a result of harm done to the brain (either frank damage or developmental steps missing, or both, in the same disorganized child), there was no need to have it listed under "causes" at all.

And what about "rehabilitation," a world tall from years of surgical and bracing techniques? What effect does achievement of human potential thinking have on this?

Spotted among the tried and the true and their official spokesmen were assorted therapists, tired from years of working up on the sixth floor: physical (moving arms and legs) and speech (a) articulation problems: confusion, substitution, omission, distortion or addition of consonants,

---

* See "Official Statement: The Doman-Delacato Treatment of Neurologically Handicapped Children," approved by the American Academy for Cerebral Palsy, American Academy of Physical Medicine and Rehabilitation, American Congress of Rehabilitation Medicine, Canadian Association for Children with Learning Disabilities, Canadian Association for Retarded Children, Canadian Rehabilitation Council for the Disabled, National Association for Retarded Children, published in the *Archives of Physical Medicine and Rehabilitation* (April 1968, Vol. 49, No. 4) of the American Congress of Rehabilitation Medicine. (The statement's bibliography makes reference to the executive board statements which preceded it from 1965 on.)

vowels, diphthongs (b) voice problems: inadequate volume, defects of quality—especially nasality and denasality, breathiness, huskiness, too high or too low pitch range, inappropriate rate (c) hard-of-hearing problems (d) delayed speech (e) aphasia, etc. There were also vocational counselors (trainability) and social workers and psychologists (the child's "feelings" and the feelings of the "already burdened and confused parents"). Not to mention all the pediatricians who still referred the slow child at age three, or thereabouts, to these "services."

Why were some kids labeled "cerebral-palsied" and others "mentally retarded" and others "cerebral-palsied and mentally retarded?"

I couldn't figure that out. I'd seen a lot of crippled kids, dumb kids, and crippled and dumb kids. Some of the crippled ones were at a CP center; some of them were at a place for the mentally retarded. Some of the dumb ones were at a CP center; others were at a center for the mentally retarded. The kids who wore both labels were at either the cerebral palsy center or the center for the mentally retarded. Some of the centers were called "rehabilitation"; and there too were all kinds. And there were "softer" labels, used even by professional staff—"the retarded," "the handicapped," "the physically disabled" (from birth and from brain).

The mongoloid child, who it was thought had a poorly formed brain from conception (a different brain cell under the microscope), labeled "retarded" and leaving it at that, you could understand; that is, until a peculiar place in Pennsylvania decided to try its program on those who applied after all and began to get substantial results.

Previously, like the rest of the world, IAHP had thought the mongoloid a "deficient child"—irregularity of brain tissue. The traditional diagnosis of mongoloid—a chromosomal test—is now open to debate on two scores: (1) some "mongoloids" have a perfectly normal chromosome count; and (2) some "well" people have abnormal or "mongoloid-type" chromosomes.

Out in a new field stood The Institutes—a little "David"—with what appeared to some to be half-mast statements and childlike charts. They learned by studying cybernetics and watching babies! How simple. They had made a Developmental Profile, showing the up-and-up organization of neurological function from birth and put their name to it: Doman-Delacato. This they held aloft for all to see.

To the viewer who bothered to question such an oversimplification, it would be explained that the chosen brain levels are not exact, but selected to emphasize the hierarchical development of the brain which roughly corresponds to functional capabilities. That is, each stage emerges imperceptibly into the one above it. The "brains" so noted are each held to be *chiefly* responsible for the mobility level they accompany.

Mothers and teachers (I always had the feeling they were in the trenches) would ask, "You mean the 'gray matter' [the only part that makes you smart, everybody assumes] isn't even used until the baby starts walking? What's it doing, just sitting there?" Yes, just waiting to be used. Waiting for the action. It's got oxygen and a cell life, but the cells—the neurons—aren't hooked up into pathways yet, no circuits. Some never will be. We've got more than we'll ever use. (Most estimates put our use at 10 to 12 percent of total brain cells; Einstein's at 15 to 18 percent.)

The theory, so simple any one of us might have figured it out, would remain a theory. Unless someone could find a way to open the brain, down to its core, take some quick pictures and seal it closed again, before the volunteer died. There was no scientific proof, as they said, unless you counted function (does) or dysfunction (does not) as scientific. Just because normal babies do a universal crawl-and-creep sequencing, if you let them, that isn't scientific enough to send the brain-injured, the "cerebral-palsied," and the "mentally retarded" kids (and their parents!) through all that. Let's face it, crawl and creep is just not scientific. Nothing you would want to write out on a prescription blank. Stuart and Grant would be the first to tell you, it's babyish and humiliating (it's so simple).

And who knows what the midbrain "headquarters" control anyway? (*World Book Encyclopedia* allots it about an inch in a five-page spread on the brain.) The old brainstem (pons and midbrain) was like the appendix, used once upon a time, long ago, wasn't it? The Institutes had a lot of ideas about that. It was in charge of "Early Everything!" David was one of those outspoken, precocious Why-kids we'd all decided to hate over the years. He preferred to be called a "cybernetic developmentalist." (The rest of the class was named "doctor" or "therapist.") And you had to overlook him, sitting there with his hand up all the time, just to let the class know who's boss here.

Looking out, I could see David walking like a giant himself, but I had the feeling he was trembling too, not because he might lose his job, but with what he had come upon with his twenty-five years of testy questions. Bert and I before too long were going to realize there was a whole lot The Institutes didn't know about the brain. They knew it themselves.

Just the fact that The Institutes' eyes were on the trenches wasn't enough. You wanted everybody to look. Stop the silly moon-probe. Stop the wars. Stop the cars. Stop the fur coats. Stop worrying about killing the animals. Stop putting everything else first. Everybody figure out what David *and* Goliath don't know yet about Janey. Battle that, not them.

Out there were Doman and Doman, Delacato, and some doctors too. And in 1967 the new "D" came to join them: Raymond Dart, M.D., anatomist and anthropologist, discoverer of *Australopithecus.* Looking back on this battle today, I think Dart's entrance onto the scene will someday prove to be the slingshot David was without at the time. He would, this "discoverer of the missing link," with his knowledge of man-ape to ape-man, set a new stage for all the Janes.

Just before and during 1967, about the time Dart arrived to chair the Institute of Man at IAHP, Philadelphia, Bert and I ventured out of the trenches several times and saw "the established methods," "the accepted methods" up close and full-face. And fiercely began to be afraid for J.'s future.

It was a depressing time. Soon after the new year, Jane suffered burns on her upper arm and abdomen. A three-month bed and bandaging night-mare. Mary Lawrence moved away; she transferred because of her husband's new job. All Jane's peers were moving on, moving fast. Time moving on, twenty-four hours a day nothing like enough. And sometimes twenty-four hours too much to drag through, listening for a new word, any word at all.

And no sweet summertime in Maine to follow. Just the rain, a record they said, and the plague of earwigs with it. And three pets in the house, Christmas gifts to the children and speech stimulator—maybe—to Jane. (She did say 'kee-kawt" to Puff, her white kitten, a few times, but nothing to Grant's dog Smokey or to Stuart's myna bird.) And people calling, coming, desperate, announced and unannounced, what to do for child after child.

And all this with no music in the house. (That "restricted activity" ap-peared in the executive board statements!) Music was not only the Great Pacifier for hyperactivity, food to a poor auditory competence, but it had always been my mainstay too.

Nursery rhymes we had. And anything else that could be talked in 2/4 time! ("The Raven" could last an entire patterning session.)

One thing we had to hold us to Jane's program these months: laughter. Just about every morning, with the "pat-party" of sorts, Janey and I got a chance to laugh. Since those starch-stiff Patterning Rules of 1965 à la Mary Lawrence, we had all developed a crazy camaraderie about crawl-'n'-creep, The Institutes for the Achievement of Human *Parents,* and what-ever came over the radio early that morning or home with husband the night before. Each day's patterning group was different. So each day was. Jane was.

And the shots straight *into* the arm would come, now and then, when something was different about her since last time. If I kept mum and waited, they'd tell me.

Janey's need for socialization was getting fed by the diverse shenanigans and the thousands of words spoken to her by some twenty-odd patterners a week. And the need for "personality development?" I remember remark-ing to Mary I was beginning to see everything in terms of input-output, a neurological daftness I'd acquired. What is personality anyway? And Mary saying, "Boy, wouldn't you love to ask Jane that. Tell me, kid, how are you getting that personality? One thing, it *couldn't* be from her peer group down at the recreation program for handicapped youngsters!"

If there is a miracle to this story, it started with the afternoon teens in the fall of 1966. The Four: Cathy and Marilyn, Laurie and Holly. If this book were about Jane's "people," they would appear on most of its pages. Even when they are not on the pages, watch them anyway in the background, there in the living room. The Four, from the years of Girl Scouts until they went to college, will work Jane from now on, covering the weekday afternoons—for an hour at first, then for two, and eventually three—and patterning sometimes on weekends. They and Chris and Kay who made it the Six in later days, gave Janey miles of belly trips in a succession of crawl boxes, thousands of "Strumpels," which we were yet to learn about, and dozens of other "programs." In 1966, as ninth-graders, the Four started a snowball rolling.

6

OCTOBER 31, 1966. When we took J. out of the crawl box for the fourth pattern, Eudy and I noticed that the bottom of one of her big toes was bleeding. "First degree" they always say! We called "left leg" Jane Perlstein in to see how too-hard she had toe-brushed, all standing around laughing as her face went blank.

Quickly regaining her composure, she said, "Sure, I missed all those years of nursing, and— We'll fix this patient right up— I'll need sutures, boiling water— No, I think I'll just leave it this way, open. Good tactile stimulation!"

We Band-Aided instead of patterned. They drifted away to "finish cookies—why not?" I asked Eudy if she would like to see Jane read, and something about never shirking a challenge. We'd find out if she could read *all* this week's words. (I've got to stop this. The staff in Philly cautioned us not to get the show-off syndrome.)

We found out. She named pumpkin , football , mask , leaf , and jack-o'-lantern . Saying the last was a breathless struggle all the way, but she persevered, and it sounded a lot like it. Good ole girl, Janey must have known the spot we were in. Eudy sat on the sofa, oohing and ahing. I ran to get a stack of old ones. J. was in marvelous mood. Only a few did she fail to recognize out of more than thirty. And, bless her, she was *naming* them. Talking. As well as pointing to the correct one. Speech plus reading equals happiness.

Eudy said that before today, she had thought it an interesting idea, a wonderful try. That's all. Now she believed me. Jane *can* read.

I went over to Janey and grabbed her up for a dance-twirl through the living room and into the playroom to see the Halloween cookies, wrapped in orange cellophane, two basketfuls for tonight.

I would have to keep my feet on the ground. Tonight the four-year-olds would walk up our path and yell, "Trick or treat!" This year Jane would not. At this rate, she wouldn't next year either.

I would work harder. Maybe Jane could do more than one word a day. The fours were talking a mile a minute now. *And* running. Patterning would definitely be done seven days a week. Teens were the answer to the weekends. Dizzy had said last Saturday she would come both mornings. Holly and Laurie will do Friday crawl boxes and Saturday patternings. Chums from childhood, Cathy and Marilyn volunteered almost in unison. They will ask Cathy's sister Ruth for Sundays too. Was it our distress they were running to meet? Or was it because they saw Jane position her left toe out to the side—finally—in the crawl box twice last week? With Grant as an "arm" now, we only need a fifth for Sunday. Sometimes I catch myself looking up.

NOVEMBER 2, 1966. Last night Jane fell off the patterning table. On her head. Concussion. Slight unconsciousness. My heart stood still for five hours, till she began to come out of it. The doctor stood ready on call in case she didn't. His examination had been thorough. She might have some vomiting. Give her full rest for twenty-four hours.

I held her in my arms on the sofa, just talking to her—praying that the dazed eyes would clear—and searching for a smile, just a little one to come. They had said at The Institutes some damage can occur, some brain cells can die with a hit on the head—but it's not how many cells you have, it's how sharp, how used, are the network systems. How many cells could a person lose without loss of function? A lot, I soothed. There were all those billions up there. God, what if she—Kids fall out of trees all the time. And don't they sometimes fall on their heads?

At about eleven the train came in, finally. Jane didn't respond as usual to the far-off whistle. I was so glad to see Bert. He saw us sitting there and came over. Jane only whimpered to see her daddy. I knew then it was serious. He did too. He walked around with her. We sat together. Then I held her. All the time trying to keep her awake with our uneasy laughter and talk. At about two, she was looking different, and gradually managed a sort of smile, looking up at him.

We put her in her bed. I would stay up. What did he mean careless? She knee-walked right off the thing, her knee slipped near the edge. No, we would not make a bigger table. We would teach her she's not allowed to get on her knees there. And he could stay up with her. I was exhausted, not having sat in a meeting all night.

NOVEMBER 9, 1966. I got wounded today. Again. In the same old place. This is my protest. Just get rid of it, the whole messy experience. Put it onto paper. There is really no one to tell.

The psychologist is sweetly, slowly, silently letting the child Jane "feel at home" before beginning the evaluation. J. is all over the floor of her office, checking out the furniture, the toys, what's in the bag mom brought. The mom is eager to begin, before the child gets too entertained by the floor activity. But the psychologist announces with a knowing look born of years of experience in this sort of thing: we will wait. The problem is to find out "how smart she is," and I am as eager as Jane's pediatrician is—who has asked for the test—and glad the psychologist knows what to do. Somewhere I feel Mary Lawrence is in the wings, applauding already the upsurge in I.Q. score J. will show. There is then a struggle to get the child into the chair after a too-long floor show.

It starts because the mother suggests a bribe and takes out the Thermos of orange juice. The first mistake. It becomes the center of the stage in the child's "mind."

"What is this, Jane?" the woman intones, as she shows a black-and-white drawing of a house.

Jane looks across the table over the Lady's head, up to the ceiling and speaks, "Oh-ooh-e-i-o-ooh."

I, sitting at the table beside Jane, "She knows that. I don't know if she'll say it, but she knows pictures very well."

"Jane, what is this?" she asks, as she presents the next picture. It is a shoe.

Jane is looking all around for the Thermos bottle. The woman taps her forefinger on the picture. Getting no response, flips the next card in front of Jane, "Jane what is this?" Softly, gently, she asks again. And again.

Jane, it seems to me, is not really with us, has never "come to the table." "She knows all these, except maybe the last two." They were flag and star, as I remember. "I don't know if she is going to say them, but she knows them. She even reads most of their names."

The woman takes another group of cards and proceeds to do the same thing, asking Jane to tell her what she knows. So far Jane knows nothing. She looks at each of them in turn, "Oh-ooh-i-e—," and seems to be far off some place. Far off some place— That's it. She was aware of the blower in the room.

"Would you mind turning off your air conditioner. This may sound strange, but I think she's *listening* to *it*."

Without a word, the psychologist walks over, turns it off, and sits back down again.

The pictures are taken up again and the child is asked to name them— one by one. Nothing.

"Excuse me for interrupting again, but is it necessary for her to talk out the answers? She talks very little, as I told you on the phone. I don't know if she will today at all. Do you want to know if she knows these pictures, is that it?"

"I would like to hear her speech— The quality of it— Does she ever say these words?"

"Why, yes, I could give you a list— I don't think she will, unless she has some reason to. I mean— Why don't I send you a list of the sounds and words she makes——"

And the Lady smiles, and says gently, looking at Jane, "Well, let's go on with this a little, maybe she'll say a few." She turned the pages of a book with bright-colored photography of such simple items as an orange, a ball, Oreo cookies, etc. Jane said not a word. I wanted to shake her——

"Excuse me, may I try? I can *make* her do it——"

"Well, we don't want to——"

"Jane! Sit up here. Sit up now. What is this?" And I pointed to the orange.

Jane squirmed half-round in her chair again, leaning past me, looking at the bag with the Thermos and said, "Juz——"

To the Lady I whispered, "She just said j-u-i-c-e."

"Yes, I heard that. Maybe we should let her have it to get that out of the way."

I poured a couple of swallows in a cup. "All right now. What are these? Now just stop that. Look at the book." The picture was Oreo cookies.

"Deedle-deedle."

"Good girl!" And to the Lady, "That's her word for it. It's a long story. But anything else here, she'll have the right word for——"

"Well, I think that is enough anyway just now—" Then the Lady put an old-fashioned black engine on the table. "What's this, Jane?"

"Oh, goodness, she's never seen that kind. Do you have a diesel type? That she calls 'choo-choo.' " I mouthed it without saying the word.

"No, I'm sorry. I really should. I should get one of those, I suppose. But it doesn't matter. Here, let's see about this," and she put a small china figurine of a cat—or was it a rabbit—on the table.

"Jane! What is that?" After a few seconds I mouthed quietly, "She says that word, but I don't have any figurines——"

Then the Lady asked her again to tell what it was. Nothing.

When she put a key down on the table I said, "She's never said that. I'm sure. Does she have to say these too, before she gets credit for knowing them?"

The Lady had turned around and returned with a form board. I was shocked. It was the babyish kind—just a circle, square, and triangle. Jane reluctantly put them in. Then the board was turned upside down and Jane put them in again.

"Do you have some tests a little more advanced than this? I mean, she's quite beyond simple form boards——"

The Lady produced a shape-sorting mailbox. "Let's see about this. Has she had any experience with this sort of thing?"

"Oh, sure. She did all that last year."

With prodding, Jane put the shapes in, I think all of them correctly, but I was so disgusted with her, I couldn't have cared less. Again she asked for juice.

"You can have juice when you're finished. You're *not* finished. Go on, drop them in. Now. Good girl!"

Without a word, the Lady removed the mailbox and brought out an outline of a doll. Tapping the arm, she said, "What is this, Jane?"

Nothing.

"What is this, Jane?" as she went over the parts of the body.

Nothing. And nothing.

"Please, couldn't she point to them? So she doesn't have to talk?"

"Well, I thought we might get language response from her from this——"

"You call off the answers, and let her point to the part. Couldn't she do that?"

And she did. And Jane did. One hundred percent. She knew all five. As the lady started to put it up, I said, "Oh, she knows a lot more than that, like e-l-b-o-w and f-i-n-g-e-r. Don't you want to do the little things?"

"All right, if you would like for her to show me that."

"Well, I mean— You stopped so soon—" I could see her busy, checking off on the score sheet. Maybe it was the five-parts-of-a-body test. Yes, I remembered now. She was giving Jane the Cattel Intelligence Scale test. On the two-year-old level! It all came back to me. I hadn't seen the test in a year, Mary had the copy back. Almost everything on that test was "identifies objects by name," "naming objects"—I remember my confusion over those two categories—and "picture vocabulary." She had dropped back to a lower level when she produced the form board. Oh, golly, you had to talk on this test. I remember discussing that with Mary——

"If you'd like to hear her language, I could do it with her reading——"

"Yes, later, I would like to— If you think she's ready for that——"

"Oh, I can get her to do it all right. I'll just require it of her. She minds."

"Perhaps you should give her the juice now, we promised it to her when she finished, remember?"

"Oh, I meant at the end of the whole thing."

"Well, I think that's all for today. It has taken quite a lot out of her. She's been here an hour. That's about the right time."

"You mean, I should bring her back for the rest of it later? I mean you have higher and higher levels to attempt, don't you?"

"I think I have a pretty good idea of her——"

"You mean, that's all? I mean, a lot of this, I think, has been kind of boring— I mean, there is so much more she can do. She can draw a vertical line, start and stop it; I don't know why she just scribbled today. We're working on circle now. She knows almost all those pictures and a lot more difficult ones. She likes Sears catalogues now, the little black-and-white pages the most now. She likes very tiny stuff, not just the outline ones. Wouldn't you like to see her read?"

"Yes, I meant for you to do that before you go. Maybe she could play on the floor— Since that's what she's been wanting— While you and I talk for a few minutes."

So while Jane bounced around on her knees, swishing and swaying, to feel the dress brushing her legs, I told the Lady about how J. loves fabrics. About her tactile programs. I had brought the tactile bag with me, as she suggested I might on the phone, and showed her the charms J. can get by touch alone. How Jane is busy all her waking hours with programs of sensory stimulation. How enriched her environment was made. How much the world is learning now about influencing the brain.

Later with J. still on the floor, I held up a card: [**ice cream**]. Jane said "—em—."

"Good girl!" To the Lady I said, "She said 'em,' her word for it." With the next three— [**umbrella**] , [**window**] , and [**velvet**] —Jane stared right through me, her face a mask, a slack-jawed nothing. So I started pulling out only food or drink cards.

She said "mo wa" for [**water**] , "deedle-deedle" for [**cookie**] , and "juz" for [**juice**] , and "ap" for [**apple**] . For some stupid reason, she wouldn't even look at [**hamburger**] , so I stopped.

It had been a real struggle, and I could have killed her. In between cards I was "requiring" with a sergeant's firmness. I hated myself, what I was doing to Jane, proving a point like this. It was everything a reading session should not be.

I poured another half inch of juice and explained it was a lousy session. She can and does run through them quickly usually. And I was giving her one at a time to hear language. Actually it's better to have her choose the one, out of three, on a table, where she is sitting. Her voice is so thin and quiet, that's why it's hard to understand her. But, of course, I wouldn't say she answered them correctly if she hadn't. I mean, I wouldn't do *that* to Jane. She's putting endings on words now. These are mostly last year's vocabulary. And these she says like she first learned them——

"Do you think she understands them?"

"What do you mean 'understands them'?"

"I mean their function. Does she know the object they stand for?"

"Well, sure. You don't think I would just teach her words—I mean, sure, she can match them all to the object. I mean, that's how she's given the word in the first place——"

"Or she could have memorized them. But if you think she knows what they stand for——"

"Well, of course she memorized them. By their word-shape. I mean, that's what it's all about. *Doll* is slightly different from *ball,* but it *is* different. I mean, this whole thing is for visual differentiation—to make a sharper brain. Sure, she knows what *ice cream* and *cookie* are. And *umbrella*. And *velvet*. Why, Janey is very smart. I mean, don't go by what she did here today. She knows a lot more than any of this. I would like to bring her back sometime. When she is in a better mood or something."

"Yes, do that. In a year or so, if you think you see any significant change in Jane, we'll take a look at her again——"

"In a year?"

"Yes, at her age, that's what we generally do. That is, if she's made a lot of progress."

"Oh, she'll make a lot in a year. I'm sure."

All the time, putting her coat on, rushing her out in my arms, dragging the bag after me, I hated the little Pill. I could have spanked her good. What a lousy bit that was. My face and neck were burning. With disgust, with anger, with embarrassment.

I hated the Lady too. She had given the two-year-old part. I knew the test. It was those words I had put into Jane's reading program from the start, except *star* and *flag* and *keys*. It was that test I used last summer in Maine, to do the extra "manual" stuff Mary suggested. I wondered why she did not ask Jane to do any of the stuff above the two-year-old level. Jane was not cooperative enough to go on today? She didn't think Jane could do it? But it was all so infantile. And so verbal. Isn't there some way to test without speaking? Sure there is. Point to the correct answer. Or lay the cards out in a certain order. Or throw them all down, and see what Jane does with them. That's what I would do. Just throw the cards on the table. Then ask J. to hand me *knife, tree, glasses,* etc. At least it would give her something to do. And she might say them, as she does when she's picture-reading, just lazying through a book.

I hated the whole world. That's what I told Mary tonight. It's only a test, but the world is like that. People who can't talk are stupid. The world treats them stupid. If you're treated stupid, you will be stupid. I know I see her clearly. She's so keen. She's not dull. I would never exaggerate what she can do. And, oh, what a sense of humor. Don't you have to be smart to have a sense of humor?

NOVEMBER 21, 1966. About the psych test.

Edith Alfred got the picture right away, said The Institutes certainly didn't suggest that, did they? It is one of the ongoing myths: language equals intelligence. Language is only an expression of intelligence, she emphasized. So why was Jane tested verbally? Because first, the psychologist in question was probably trained according to methods developed thirty years ago. Secondly, the Lady most likely doesn't know any other way to do it. And Edith saying something about part of it sounds like the Stanford-Binet Intelligence Test and part the Cattel one and both are no good for Jane.

Then I told her the rest, stumbling along, half-crying, then angry, then breaking down again. The Lady had *counted* it, I was practically screaming. She had mailed a report to the pediatrician. She found no change in Jane. Her I.Q. remains at 40. Did Edith hear me? Forty! She thinks Jane's I.Q. is 40. Says she is traveling at one-eighth the rate of a normal child. She means it, Edith. She *counted* the test!

That will always be on Jane's record. In the doctor's office. What if someone gets hold of that? She would be labeled and stymied forever in the labeling process. And I can't even have a copy.

Then the doctor told me—all this on the phone—that the Lady noted that this program might be too much for Jane; it could produce trauma, psychologically, that sort of thing. You know, pressure. And suggested seriously for the parents to consider removing her from the program she was doing——

"Well, Peggy, he was doing his follow-up job——"

"I know. And that's why I made him listen to the rest. I told him about the test, gave him examples, said I was shocked she ever considered it a real test. I kept repeating that Jane was tested for speech. And that's Jane's problem!"

I paid her fifteen dollars. Why did she have to do anything but throw the whole thing in the wastebasket. I told her Jane was not herself. What's the big urge to get it scored and sent to the doctor? He isn't paying for it. *We* paid for it. And we can't even see it! Do they really think parents should be kept out of these things, they all are so muddled-headed about their own child, they want them to be raving intelligent beauties when they have an I.Q. of 40? Poor, poor parents of brain-injured children. They are so emotional. So confused. You have to watch them. Just be sure you don't tell them anything. You have to even be careful about telling them their child *is* brain-injured.

The doctor and I parted on the promise that it would be good to have another test done by someone else. Offhand he had not heard of anyone who did special testing of nontalkers. But he would find out.

Edith knows. Maimonides Hospital in Brooklyn is doing some very interesting work in that field. Gave me a name to call.

DECEMBER 7, 1966. Stuart and Jane to ophthalmologist today for checkups. Jane to find out if she's getting near-sighted, since myopia runs in the family.

Since Jane does not know ABC's for eye-chart test, I brought along some reading cards. She would have none of it. She was much more interested in all the lens trays and paraphernalia spread on the table next to her. Finally, through picture-reading at a distance, the doctor assessed that Jane had at least 20/60, using both eyes. It wasn't possible to check her eyes individually.

As Jane then looked at the doctor's pictures for further testing, the doctor said, "I'm very impressed with this young lady."

I took this as a go-ahead of some sort, and said IAHP was pleased with her progress too. She loves books. Especially the little stuff in catalogues. She was reading three new words a day now—had about one hundred altogether, nouns only—in three-inch red letters. And puzzles, she is definitely on her grade level with that stuff. And did the doctor ever get to Philly for post-graduate training? I had called in the training director's name and address here two years ago as requested.

I could have bitten my tongue. It seems the doctor is no longer interested in "that place." Had learned about "that program—all I needed to know." Without going there? Without working there? It seemed there were people in the eye business who shouldn't be. It was all negative. What had happened in the meantime to change the doctor's enthusiasm of two years ago?

I said something about realizing their approaches would conflict since The Institutes suggests creeping for crossed eyes, instead of operating on the muscles—and we both changed the subject.

When Stuart came out with his prescription, there was some remark about there being a small change, something about "right-eye," that was all.

I leapt up. "You're talking about far-point. It used to fluctuate."

"Yes, that's right," the doctor looked at the card.

"And now it's right."

"Yes," the doctor murmured.

"Well, it's good to hear you say that. He did a program for that. He did The Institutes' dominance program for stuttering, remember? We corrected that too."

"Yes, well, there are quite a lot of different views on that subject——"

"I know. But it's good to hear you confirm the change——"

JANUARY 4, 1967. I called Mary about Jane's re-evaluation in Philly yesterday.

She didn't get any score increases at all this time. Only qualitative improvements. But one of the directors there, a physical therapist thinks J.'s tight knee-and-ankle problems are "peripheral" now, not "central." That Jane's brain is walking her, albeit on knees. (Everyone was agape at her running knee-walk and trunkal balance, with arms swinging in cross pattern.) That if (a) knees were straight and (b) ankles were loose, she would have a beautiful gait. It was a big if. The biggest.

Mary thinks he's right. She doesn't have the hips and trunk of a "spastic" anymore. And her knees and ankles are less spastic.

Yes, the ankles are looser. I asked Mary again, for the hundredth time, "If you ever get something started, you can improve on it, can't you?"

"It would seem so," was her usual reply. This time she added, "The reason we don't know for sure, Peggy, is that this has never been tried before. To get full ankle movement and straight legs naturally—without operations followed by orthopedic devices to hold them that way—this has just never been done. It looks great so far. I certainly wouldn't give up at this point."

She asked me if they had ever mentioned at what age a baby should start on the floor, in order to get a finished crawl, how early do you start it? I had heard "three weeks." She had heard "within the first month," while involuntary arm and leg movements might accidentally start some propulsion forward. Remember what they said about a baby on its back, twitching arms and legs: it's like a Cadillac on its back with wheels spinning!

Then I told her their remarks about the intelligence testing of Jane. "Yes, that's a test to test Jane's ability to take a test." (Mary giggled.) "It tests output, not input." They reminded me there is no correlation between brain injury and intelligence, but certainly there is between brain injury and the ability to *express* intelligence. And then, "If you're sure of what Jane knows, why do you have to have her 'tested' anyway?"

And then I told the people at The Institutes what the ophthalmologist in New York had said. Jane would never get beyond "first fusion" and "something is missing at birth." Their answer was, "Tell the doctor to stick around!" (Mary giggled again.)

Mary wanted to know what did the ophthalmologist mean, you know, about babies.

I think the doctor meant that mid-range ability was "first fusion." But Jane would never be able to keep both eyes fused on an object real close or at a distance. As the baby becomes a child, his near-point fusion gets so refined, he can fuse (see one image from two eyes) within two inches of his nose. And his far-point fusion gets more refined too—outward and outward. I think the doctor thinks the very near and the very far are "out" for the Janeys.

But IAHP must not think so. They are constantly testing her for that. Also that accommodation test they are always doing—you know, range-finding. They observe the movements of her eyes, the light in her pupils as she looks at different points in the room, near and far. Something about the thickness of the lenses, that thickness alters as a person sharpens focus. I mean, they must think this function comes in the neural hierarchy too. You know, the eye is a muscle and the brain works the muscles. They don't agree that everything is or isn't at birth anyway. I mean, use it, or lose it.

And if you want to get it good, you have to use it all the more. I know they give a kid some credit for this if both eyes can stay on the target between the six-inch range and the eighteen-inch range. Jane can do that. To get full credit, she has to converge at two inches and continue that out to two or three feet. Full depth-perception and, of course, that means no crossed eyes at all.

Maybe the ophthalmologist is correct. But I certainly don't see why you'd never try for it!

Then Mary asked me if they still disagree among themselves about the baby crawling with his head down, turning it side to side. Every baby she had seen had his head up. In crawling. Yes, me too, but watching Lydia's new baby, Amy, I could see that she gets tired thrashing around on her stomach and *rests* that way a lot, head sometimes left, sometimes right. And the bottom eye, whichever, is occluded against the crawling surface. Guess that is why they think kids should start stomach life early, before the neck holds the head up too well.

Then we talked about slippery surfaces you could put a tiny baby down on, so it wouldn't hurt itself, and for how long a time you might do this at first, and then it began to dawn on me. . . .

"Mary! Are you— Mary, you are going to have a baby!"

Yep. Baby coming in July. Boy, what a ball this will be. Mary raising a baby neurologically correct! She laughed. Really, she expected to have fun with it, and would probably not start reading till it was at least a year old!

JANUARY 7, 1967. While the boys and I were planting the Christmas tree they had given her, Jane—without her harness-line on today because the "shoe" is lost—pulled herself up on the stove. Got second degree burns on her arm and her abdomen, right through the romper suit. So depressing I can't bear to think about it. No program for next seven days, then back to doctor for a look-see.

JANUARY 11, 1967. Took her back to get a better bandage. Infected. Third degree now. Doctor gently chewing his colleague out and explaining how to anchor bandage to shoulder and which ointment to use in the future. How difficult it is to treat the inside of an upper arm. Colleague apologizing, asking me again how it happened, and how it didn't look that bad that first day and it must be an electric burn, and I am explaining that the stove is gas and how I don't expect doctors to be perfect (anymore), all I want to know is what about tomorrow and the next day, because I'm looking down into Janey's arm at the gray muscle lying exposed there, and she's right-handed, and it's just that Janey can't afford to have anything else bad happen to her, you see.

FEBRUARY 28, 1967. I went to the doctor today. My doctor. I had gained twenty pounds. I weighed almost what I did when I was pregnant. And then I started crying. I don't know what happened. I just burst into tears. I must be cracking up, I said. I had never cried in a doctor's office before.

I thought maybe I had just been through a neurotic depression. What was that exactly? I heard it mentioned before by women friends. For the last two months, I just stayed in bed most of the time. Or ate. And then I would go back to bed again. And I gained twenty pounds in two months!

And then I told him about Jane's being burned. She had been in bed these two months. She was in one bed, and I was in the other.

The doctor was very sweet about it all. Yes, Jane was going to be all right. She would need plastic surgery for the scars to her arm someday. It was me who just couldn't take it. I must lose weight so I don't hurt my back. I took her every second or third day to get the dressings changed. I was carrying her a lot. I can hardly carry her now. She is growing so fast. I don't want to see anybody. I look awful. Part of the day I am up. I'm not in bed all the time. Stuart has been in bed for three weeks with bronchial pneumonia. He literally ran himself down, playing basketball. I've had to nurse him along. So I've been up more lately.

I couldn't stop crying, I was so embarrassed.

So I told him the real reason. When I was in the pediatrician's treatment room with Jane one day, her chart was lying open, and I saw the report by the psychologist who had counted that test—that 1940 Cattel Intelligence Scale I think it was. Did he know that test—well, it's a speech and manual test mainly. And Jane doesn't talk very much—she's beginning to talk—but she's very smart.

And the psychologist was reporting that Jane was only a trainable child, but her mother was treating her as if she were educable. This program was too much for a child like Jane. And, oh, so many unbelievable things. They are in Jane's "record" forever. And it just floored me, that this was on paper somewhere. Whoever decided to label some children "trainable" and some "educable?" Jane has dead cells in her brain, but her *brain* isn't dead. I had told this doctor about Jane before. Wasn't he impressed with her progress? The psychologist didn't even *ask* me about her progress, or her program for progress. Just figures the "trainables" make 40 on an I.Q. test. And schools actually use those records, those terms, to separate the ones who stay home and the ones who go to school. And parents accept it, thinking the psychologists know more than they. And I wouldn't have even known her label if I hadn't seen that report. Can you imagine giving a child a label like that and not even telling the parents you did?

In my intellectualizing I had stopped crying. I apologized for going on like this. I hadn't told anybody. I guess it was an outburst I had stored up for too long. Most of the time I tried not to think of the report—just went under the covers and hid. At other times I got real busy. With the new dog and the myna bird; they're nothing but mess to care for. And Jane's new cat; even the cat needs her box emptied daily and has to be fed. If it weren't for *National Geographic* magazine I would have probably withdrawn completely and never come back.

"The *National Geographic* magazine?" For the first time the doctor smiled.

Yes, pretending sleep, I kept watching Jane in the bed next to me. Something wonderful was happening. By the end of January she had picture-read every children's book in the house, in my sons' library too. And all the magazines. And all the third-class mail folders and catalogues. Friends of mine even brought books for her. Finally, in desperation, I gave her two *Geographics* one afternoon.

With any book, she turns *each* page and looks at everything, really studies it. Just like a sponge lapping up water. Well, with the *Geographics,* she found a whole new world. It became her hobby. Some of them became her favorites—she didn't want me to take them away—but others I could. She knew when she opened the first few pages whether she'd seen it or not. And something was happening with her fingers too. Her page-turning. She turns the pages at the upper corner in an adult way, and never skips a page.

So I started leaving a stack of *Geographics* by her bed after breakfast. All through February she has been looking at *Geographics,* eight hours a day! Whenever I tried to shift to puzzles or toys, she asked for "—zine." And that's what kept me alive. Anyone with visual interest that high . . . anyone who turns pages that deftly . . . anyone who smiles and laughs and thinks as they picture-read— She gets so involved. Anyone with that span of attention . . . well, it's a *crime* to label them anything. Maybe it sounds like compensation, but I think Jane is getting visually superior.

And now I have this other problem. I am fat. I feel dreadful this way. I must lose weight fast. Also, do you think I should see a psychiatrist? Crying this way, and talking on and on, and staying in bed.

Finally the doctor had a chance to say something. I had had plenty of cause to be depressed certainly. He laughed a little—it takes a lot less for some people. And I had come through it. I had figured it out by myself, didn't I think? He didn't see why I should need a psychiatrist now.

Then he talked to me about willpower and pushing the plate away and about an interesting group that gets together to discuss eating habits. He gave me a limited supply of mood-stimulating, appetite-depressing pills.

I asked him not to tell Bert I was like this. Bert is terribly worried about Jane being off her program so long. And he knows how strange I've been.

He knows I will be O.K. when the doctor lets Jane get out of bed. And we can get moving again. Maybe in a few weeks.

APRIL 15, 1967. Mary and I were talking about babies. How to plan a nursery that is bright and changing instead of pastel and dull, and all the things you could do for eyes and ears and skin awakenings from the very beginning. And an area in her dining room for the kid's floor show. Where the dining room table would be, if she had one. Down the middle, so she can get on both sides for whatever she's going to present at playtime.

I was complaining about it taking months to make callouses. And Jane is making faces now, trying different ones out I think. But it looks so strange to others; so much what they expect of the brain-injured. And often she is "lost in space," just vocalizing to herself. Such a weirdo when she does that.

Mary was laughing about her shopping trips. No one had any such thing as a large slippery pad for the floor. This pregnant lady, she supposed, was one of the first to look at the carry-around-sit-it-on-a-counter things with disgust, when everyone knows that's a must these days.

I said Doman was right. A baby's neurological environment should not be an accident, but on purpose. A *poor* environment was the more common accident.

Most mothers-to-be were so busy shopping for their newborn for things that *prevent* him from learning, things that repress his feeling, hearing, seeing, tasting, and smelling. She was talking about the light-blue-plastic-rattle moms. Who lovingly but quickly tend to baby, pinned up on his back somewhere. So they can get back to their business.

I kidded her. She sounded like "Mother C" already. And I told her about the three mythical mothers Doman drew for us, all living on the same mythical block. He was talking about newborns getting started up the visual ladder. Eye-use. Brain-use. All just-born babies get some use of their light reflex—the dilation and contraction of the pupils—which they are born with. Because the sun comes up and the sun goes down. Thank goodness for that. He gets a little more use of it, dark and light stimulus, when the lights are turned on and off in the nursery.

Mothers can do even more. Along comes Mother A. She paints large black squares on the white wall and shines a light on and off the black for eye contrast when she's in for diaperings. Baby A uses his light reflex even more. Also he's getting an outline to look at.

Down the block lives Mother B: She paints black squares on the nursery wall, but adds a large red circle to the middle of each. She too pops the light on and off when she's in and out. Baby B gets a better opportunity for outline perception—a variety. Interest of stimulus, you might say.

And there's Mother C around the corner. She paints a blue triangle inside a red circle inside a black square—all large configurations. Mother C's baby will sooner move into that higher visual ability—outline perception. It takes a certain number of times of use to trip the process—the evolutionary process?—from light reflex ability to outline perception ability. Higher and higher levels of function are triggered this way.

When the baby has outline perception he can see the circle of Mom's face, the outline of it leaning down to him.

Which reminded me—Jane is doing circles now. Wouldn't Mary like to have several drawing pads of circles to paper the nursery?

We talked of the playpen generation, better at science and math than the verbal arts, going the route with a transistorized rock-beat in their ear. Was that early rock 'n' roll, which ushered in this era, the result of a culture of babies without brain dominance? Delacato had said that the final phase of evolution was brain laterality, one hemisphere clearly at the controls. How many children were lacking Mother Nature's most uniquely human step? How many were neurologically back in the two's and three's when music is king and all are "born dancers?" When tonality is the stuff that feeds two very strong hemispheres at "headquarters?" How much of a home's background had been music, music, music? Who was influencing the brain more, the parents or the stereo manufacturers?

We were wondering if Delacato had ever spoken about this—this present rock culture. Or had we come up with some original questions from observing the teen-agers we each knew, which ones seem to need music all the time, which ones didn't.

We were getting silly, going over the music *we* favor.

Jane, of course, favors anything she can find. Which is anywhere—everywhere—outside the home: the supermarket, Bert's office elevator, the shoe store, the doctor's office.

APRIL 29, 1967. Another patterning first for Mimi.

Voice rising, she said, "Don't anybody look now, but Miss Someone is not (pant) letting (pant) me (pant) turn her ankle (pant). She is actually holding her foot (pant) on its side and——"

"In dorsi-flexion?" I asked.

"And will (pant) not release it (pant) when I try to brush the bottom of the big toe. And if you don't (pant) believe me, come on over here and try it (pant) yourself."

Jane giggled.

"And she knows everything you're saying" Louise said.

"And—she'd—very well better—cut it out," Mimi gritted.

Finally it dawned on me. "Are you saying Jane is everting her foot?"

"No, I said she's driving me crazy."

Trying to remember what Mary said about ankles. "If she's not letting you do it, she would then use her everting muscles. But she couldn't—Mary said—"

"Oh, yes she can. Now look, see that?"

Jane giggled again.

"You know, she *is* everting her foot!" I yelled. And stopped.

"What does this mean?"

"We've been saying, 'Look, brain, this is how you lift your foot—feel that—that's right-angled dorsi-flexion. At the same time you dig your toe for a crawl-push.' And the brain is saying, 'I will not. I will go the other way.' That's eversion."

"Sounds more like aversion——"

"So what?"

"We've got the foot going! Mary Lawrence showed me—I had a sprained ankle. This is ankle inversion, this is ankle eversion back to midline. Babies do it in crawling, the toe-dig and the recovery. Don't you see?" I was practically screaming. "We've got a pathway. Cripes, we've got a thing we never had before."

"Sounds like a song title."

Jane was laughing, up on her knees.

Wait till I tell Mary.

Janey-Pill, we love you.

MAY 6, 1967. Yesterday's homecoming from a trip to Denver. When I was on the plane, I was looking back. Thinking back to the Rockies, the peace and pleasure there, where for miles and miles a house could not be found. The timberline and beyond was a breathless place, where one life stopped and another life started, each with its changing circumstance. I was crossing something like that in my mind as I flew eastward. I was trying to get it into my head what I would be doing tomorrow. Next week. Trying to picture donning slacks again, to make those trips alongside the crawl box, working over the dozens of schedule changes to get J.'s full program in, and still meet the chauffeuring and activity needs of the others.

I would begin the new flashlight program, for reinforcement of her right eye. I also wasn't doing the fabric "testing" once a week. It was habit. I just had to set a—pattern? Changing habits had never been my good side. The reading was an example. Now, I was presenting three new words a day. I had known she could do more than one, and it wasn't difficult at all. I was wrapped up in the reading game. I needed to get wrapped up in the fabric game. Stupid pieces of raw data, giving a good workout to "headquarters." What would they think of next?

I was getting depressed, looking ahead to all the hours, always filled. To all the interruptions, to all the mistakes I would probably make in making decisions. With my second Manhattan I was beginning to cry! It was so difficult to come back.

So I took out all the bracelets I had bought, and began to arrange them in groups of four on the airplane table. A set to each patterner who had arrived an hour early to release Bert to his train, to Martha and Miriam who had stayed until the teens arrived at three, and to Louise who had cleaned and patterned and I can't wait to find out what else last Tuesday and Friday. To other sitters, Dizzy and Marilyn and Holly, who did double duty at program. I decided I'd better make a list. I arranged the paperlike circlets into families of pinks and greens and golds, each slightly different in shade, and sat back to admire them. They might pass for fancy. At least they had meaning. In celebration of circling—Jane's *and* mine. I had dug them out of a barrel for fifty cents a dozen.

Then I was home. What a welcome. Everyone was dancing around, mostly about did-you-bring-anything.

Yes, from the top of the Rockies a paperweight for Daddy's desk. It had looked so pink in the stream. Maybe it should be kept in a bowl of water?

Quickly I handed the boys their "gold" from the mine. And they wanted to know did I really go in a mine. And Grant went to get his flashlight to look at it in a closet! And Stuart said it was probably pyrite.

There it was again. In the background Jane had said, "Hi, Mom-mee." I had heard it just after I stepped inside, but I hadn't heard it either. Then another very emphatic, "Hi, Mom-MEE," and she was leaning forward in her sit, almost off the table.

"Hi, Janey!" I gave her a big hug and kiss. And burst into tears. "Did you hear that, Bert?"

"Yes, she said it four times."

"Bert, that's the first time."

"I know."

The boys ran back in and saw me and asked what happened. I said, "Jane just called me 'Mommy.' And it made me happy. Remember, how you felt, Grant, last December?"

I gave Grant his Western bolo tie with the cowboy medallion slide.

"Hey, that's cool!"

And to Stuart the Indian beadwork pendant, a tie of sorts.

"Hey, that's cool. Where did you get it?"

I was caught off guard by the question. "From a chief I met."

Bert said, "What?"

"In the hotel. You know, there with a dance troupe." And I quickly brought out the jet pilot and stewardess' wings from TWA.

"Just what I wanted. I needed this too," and Grant started skipping back and forth.

"Did the chief have a headdress like mine? I bet he was Sioux————"

"Yes, I think he was, Stuart. Now it's Janey's turn."

I gave Jane her stewardess pin and the puzzle from the airplane, and all the Denver travel folders. Stuart did not want any of the extra wings and made an "ahg-g" sound.

"I do. I do." And Grant began pinning them on his shoulders and arms.

To Stuart I gave the TWA cards. He challenged Bert to the best four out of seven in 500 rummy.

The Rockies seemed a long way off. But coming back. Was that more of a thrill? I kept saying, "It's a good thing I went, Bert. I mean, her being motivated that way by my absence and my return, as if she's never had a chance to really *tell* me hello. You see, I've been here usually. Her volume is increasing too. You can hear her across the room now."

Then Dizzy was there. Came over to tell me what she saw Jane do. Outdoors. On the flagstone. In her outrigger. Just lay down and started patterning herself. Even the legs with the arms. Head. Everything in perfect rhythm.

"Really! What was she doing before?"

"She was lying there. Looked as if she might be going to sleep. It was very hot. And the flagstones were very cool, I guess. Then she patterned herself, two or three times. Then got up and crept away."

It called for a celebration. So I gave her a set of bracelets, even let her pick the colors.

"Nobody wears bracelets anymore," she kidded. "Only flowers. Haven't you heard?"

MAY 24, 1967. Boys went to bed tonight feeling Jane's fabric swatches, in the dark, trying to name them. Their idea.

Strange it should happen today. I was just chastising myself for talking so much about neurological organization to everyone. I'm getting sick of myself. And this program. My personnel methods from the old days are seeping back in: the false smile and graciousness when patterners drop out; the officious offerings of correction about child development (not enough crawling and creeping, yes, can make a poor reader), the little pats of praise, so the last two minutes of patterning will be as perfect as the first three; and the smile-laugh-smile, so no one will get serious when Jane's cute come-ons turn into breathless struggles to talk. I am so tired of bolstering, so tired of being so positive. The old simplistic personnel way. Am I just working at being unshockable? Am I unshockable now?

Maybe I will try to join Mother in her twice-in-a-lifetime trip to Europe, meet her for two weeks in Switzerland. Mountains we have here. To climb.

JUNE 9, 1967. Notes.

1. *Crawling* is too fast? Needs pants on for more friction, to slow her momentum; use more legs, less arms, they said. But it's so frustrating for her to crawl slow now. And too hot! I've got to make her wear the slacks, and just when she's beginning to do forty round trips a day without struggle. Maybe the top of the box needs to be lower? Her head is up too high?
2. *Creeping* is much less these days. The problem is not heads-up. But heads-down in *Geographics*. Three solid hours of page-turning on the floor yesterday afternoon. Eyes glued to each page. Whoever thought she could stay still so long? Is this healthy or unhealthy? "Lights off" bringing on nightly tantrum. Wants to sleep with the books. Books, no. Two fabrics, yes.

JUNE 12, 1967. Philadelphia. On the way to Philly Ed Goldstein, Stu's fifth grade teacher, talked about "the underachievers," education's new emphasis. It was a snail-pace beginning, but more teachers were looking at underachieving in a new light. Looking at the child, rather than at his amorphous "potential."

"When The Institutes named themselves 'for the Achievement of Human Potential,' " I said, "they must have had in mind the *process*." How can anyone really know what a kid's potential is, or will be? Fancy guesswork. Then some label, for the forms schools have to keep. How did that ever get started anyway?"

"How did the 'underachiever' label get started? That's a good question."

"Doman calls it a 'nicer name' to tell parents. So is 'mentally retarded,' for the more severe underachiever. Retarded, by definition, means 'held back.' When it comes right down to it, there's an understatement there somewhere."

He mentioned that more and more teachers are putting together reading problems, incoordination, and hyperactivity. That is a giant step.

Talking about Stuart's increase in I.Q. score—And how he's already completed the *sixth* grade reading curriculum—"We have kids with I.Q.'s even higher than Stuart's, but they are poor readers. Those are the ones I'm concerned about. They can't keep up, but they are too smart for a lower class. They make good drop-out material. One thing we need to find out: what is reading exactly?"

"That means taking a look at brain function——"

"It sure does."

A really intriguing question: does a sharp brain make a good reader? Or does a reader make a sharp brain? His I.Q. is high, his reading is poor. That seems to fuzzy-up the first question.

We talked about how to approach the reading game with his oldest son, age four. J. is turned off the whole thing right now. So I should be the last person he should ask.

And you couldn't very well ask Miss Eyeballs. She had her eyes on every truck on the turnpike, coming and going. After all this work, it would be a shame if she just twisted her head right off. Eye-head following was a good thing, up to a point.

IAHP: During Jane's re-programing, it was suggested we stop all dull reading words like *spoon* and *shirt* and give words like *eggbeater* or *lawn mower* to reawaken her interest. One a day is plenty. And do no testing since she's balking; just feed them in.

Ed Goldstein decided that's what he would do too, although he would borrow a few of our three-inch word cards for starters.

And we'd better get on the ball and make that tape. Since last fall we had been tapeless. Compared to what they wanted, Miss Jane had had "little intake" up the sound-discrimination circuits. Despite her experimentations on the floor with sandpaper from the boys' workbench and their boots and rubber galoshes. Making sounds everywhere, using the wildest combinations. The IAHP people were not impressed. She's beyond that— into listening for words. Get busy with six hundred to seven hundred nouns. Ones I would use for reading plus others. Now.

Bert said rather flippantly, "I made a list the other day to do this. I struggled to find three hundred and twenty-four!"

"Use the dictionary, take a walk through the Yellow Pages. We want this kid to hear stuff beyond her understanding!"

Ed could see what we meant about the staff. They love children and teach parents.

I forced myself to be honest during the "history." Her record had to be accurate. Graduate students from all over were invited to use their charts for research. "I have done the flashlight program, right-eye reinforcement, only a few times. I can't get any room dark enough in the daytime."

With all deliberate calm, the woman said she was sure we could darken a room somewhere.

With maskings I usually cheated, saying this time "about six a day."

How was Jane going to talk out on no breath? Long deep breathings must be made a reflex. Get one minute into each hour, from waking to sleeping. It wasn't the masking, it was the remembering I couldn't do.

Patterning: is not so perfect. We must keep her torso and head in line. We must brush hands and big toe *hard*. I whimpered about what to cover the table with. I'm sorry I asked. Try a variety of covers. Just change to a different tactile sensation every day or so. Some parents are having good success with this. Yes, it's those nuts I can't stand. Frustrated inventors or something.

Manual: Janey began right away to button the sweater the lady tossed her. The woman watched. Everything. J.'s hands, eyes, head, posture.

"Beautiful hand-assist! More tactile than visual. That's what we want to see. Hand should either assist or stay out of the picture, if not needed, while the other does the finer skill."

Snaps are still poor.

"But she's doing sewing cards and stringing beads easily at home."

"I should imagine so," was the woman's reply.

I brought out our surprise, the balloon drawing. Then the lady had Jane draw circles and put the best one in the chart! With a lot of fancy comments about eye-hands, head, posture, and stuff I never thought about before.

Language: I reported J.'s new blends: *qu* ("qu-ack"), *tw* ("tw-eet") and *tr* ("tr-ee"). But somehow poorer enunciation generally. She says-along our nursery rhymes during patterning. She asks for all the favorites, knows "titles." And in the last three weeks Jane has tried to say everything she sees. I know. We were interested in what she hears too. O.K. We discussed tape and masking already. And enunciating takes breath. O.K.! O.K.!

"She gets hung-up in speech like a stutterer. More like gagging. But she doesn't have a 'gag reflex.' "

The woman looked through the chart. "She does today. The doctor charted it today. First time."

It was time to impress them with something. The staff was always saying that they are more interested in increases on the sensory side of the Profile. I used a lot of superlatives about her *Geographic* interest and her ability to read those small words in her new wooden puzzles. (Last night I had Bert watch as I had her match the puzzle pieces that have the tiny words on them to the puzzle pieces that have the pictures [clothes, furniture]—all this on the table, not into the puzzle-ground at all. I had to be sure it wasn't the configuration of the pieces she had memorized, although that would have been impressive too.)

Then Bert told about Jane's seeing the orange roof across the turnpike and asking for "ham-mer-mer." Not only does she recognize Howard Johnson's in the distance, but never passes a Wetson's—anywhere—without twisting her neck close to off, to watch it fade away.

I was very disappointed when the vision gal did not write this down. Seems it is all expected or something. All they care about is "alternating convergent strabismus persists" and "horizontal following remains unsmooth"? Good grief. Everyone is so impressed with Jane with the *National Geographic* magazine that I mentioned it again. No response.

Auditory competence: Jane is showing some "earedness toward listening to whispers," we had noticed at home. No, she has no concept of today, yesterday, and tomorrow. "I don't use that with her, that I know of. She wouldn't understand."

I knew immediately after I had my mouth open, I had my foot in it.

Tactile: Jane chose fabrics from a bag without looking. Almost calmly. I asked to do the testing, I was so tired of how she acts down there on her "day off." J. knew the six I brought. I could have hugged her.

It was true. Jane received no further scoring increase in Visual competence. Neither reading small print nor seeing Howard Johnson's across the county is a milestone or anything on their Profile. Just "qualitative improvement," I guess.

But her manual competence went up twelve months. That did not surprise me. Something wonderful was happening to her hands and finger ability. I knew it all through the spring. They applaud very simply down there, "bimanual function now within normal limits." If you have that, you can do a lot of things. Like wash dishes for your mother, heh-heh. And button your own clothes from now on.

Dominance is hilarious. This time her eye is neither right nor left, but midline, like a baby's. Ear is "midline to right." I'm not sure whether we are standing still or moving. More like fluctuating.

Go back home with the same program, except for some new manual stuff:

1. Circles and other stuff with finger—try finger-paints in the bathtub! Outdoors in sand. Watercolors, etc.
2. Get plastic scissors; they cut better.

Ed said he had heard how cocky they were—they like what they are doing. Now he could see why.

In the back seat, saying, "I see the moon and the moon sees me—" to Jane, I asked them not to talk for awhile. The Whole Child was almost asleep.

JUNE 18, 1967. *Dr. Doolittle* was the best movie Grant had ever seen, it turned out. Besides *Mary Poppins.* Since he had seen only the two, for the first time I was batting 1,000 in the Mothers' League.

Did Dr. Doolittle really talk to the animals? Maybe he did, but they didn't really talk back to him. Why? Animals don't talk. Some do. Not really. We just suppose what they might say. Grant was adamant about it, some do. O.K. Have it your way.

On the train he was thinking. "Why can't animals talk?"

"Because they don't have a brain for talking. Like we do."

"What kind is that?"

"They just use the bottom part. A dog's top part isn't developed very much. We have a very developed top part called the cortex."

"Well, Smokey understands everything I say."

"Yes, dogs are very good at associating. You know, putting together the sound of your voice with what you are doing. Babies can do that too."

"Like Jane?"

"Janey is using the bottom *and* the top part of her brain now; she's talking and—she's not a baby anymore. Of course, she's still working on all the baby things she has not perfected yet, like creeping and associating——"

"Mostly she just likes to look at books."

"Yes, she's a real bookworm. Let's see, you've taught her how many words?"

"One hundred twenty-something."

"Boy, that's a lot——"

"Not really. I know probably five hundred. No, a thousand."

"Sure, you do. More than that, I bet."

"Why can't Jane talk very much?"

"That's an excellent question. First, she has to hear everything real sharp. Like you do. And she has to be able to breathe real big, you know, to put the words out——"

Grant took a deep breath and let it out.

"And a lot of other things go into talking. But she's doing a lot of other 'top' stuff, you know, reading and writing——"

"You mean drawing circles——"

"Yes, drawing. And then she'll start drawing letters and words."

"Mom, which do you think is smartest—Jane or Smokey?"

"Uh, in what way? They are very different——"

"In associationing?"

"Well, Smokey is such a smart little dog——"

"She's the smartest dog, I bet, in the world——"

"Well, she's not above wetting all over everything."

"Uuuts."

"Or eating blankets——"

His eyes twinkled. "And don't forget shoes and baseball gloves."

"How could I forget any of it?"

"Ma-um!" (Laughing uncontrollably) "Stop it."

"What Smokey needs is a teacher. She needs to *see* what you want her to do, and to *hear* the sound of your voice, whether it's sweet talk or scolding. She needs it a lot, every day, and she needs you to keep it up till she learns."

Hm-m. Intensity. Frequency. And duration. Smokey could sure use those three.

JULY 31, 1967. This really happened. Just like this.

"Ah wan dada tahk ona top."

What a long jumble! "What do you want to sleep with, Janey?" And I looked all around for a top of some kind. It would have to be something she can see from her bed. I was looking for boxes.

"Ah wan dada tahk ona TOP!"

It must be a fabric. But no, she was clutching the brocade, not handing it back.

She pushed the crib top back on its broken hinge and got to her knees. Oh, she wants the top back.

"TEP! Ah wan heah dada (pause) tahk ona TEP!"

"The tape! You want to hear Daddy talk on the tape!" I turned away, so she wouldn't see the tears. Oh, boy, it's here. It's here. She can put it together. A real sentence! "Good girl!" I was bursting, as I leaned over the crib with a dozen wet kisses.

She was trembling with delight. Just in ecstasy over my response. Just happy. About the tape, I guess.

I turned it on.

"Hello, Janey. This is Daddy. Are you listening? Canteloupe . . . canteloupe . . . canteloupe——"

Ran to tell Mother. This did it. The little imp must have known I was planning a trip away. I won't go.

We talked about it till Bert came in. Books say it's questionable when talking starts for big changes to take place in a child's life. You know, they tell you don't move, don't go to the hospital, all that stuff. Well, it could be traumatic if sentences are starting. You know, it was a struggle, but she put it together.

Mother understood. We had waited so long. I'd get to Europe someday. At least to Switzerland.

The travel man who had been so kind to grant all these special permissions to join Mother's "retired persons' tour" would think I was out of my mind. The first mother not to want to get away from the kids.

AUGUST 7, 1967. Took Jane to see her first farm animals yesterday. It was visitors' day at the 4-H camp. Stuart proudly got permission to show Jane a tractor. Grant wanted to be "taught" too, I gathered. When no one was looking, I showed her straw and [**straw**] . Then Stuart and Grant took turns interrupting each other to show her all those things she had learned about from her rubber animal set and from "Old MacDonald." I was so proud of them. My mother was smiling. And holding her breath?

"See, Janey, these are turkeys. What does the turkey say?"

"Ga-ob-le, ga-ob-ble."

"Oh, here are the cows, Janey. What does the——"

"Moo."

"That's *very* good."

And so on, over the hill and dale of the place. Jane was twisting around so in Bert's arms, he said, "She's probably looking for the 'e-i-e-i-o's.' "

"Hey, that's cool!" they chirped over and over, slapping him on the back, first Stuart then Grant.

Then Jane, leaning over his shoulder, did the same thing and said, "Coo-ool."

"Hey, did you hear that? Jane can say 'cool'!"

"She can repeat just about anything she hears. The problem is to pull her chain—the one that decides to say it tomorrow too. I guess it's such a struggle when you have to take another breath in the middle of most every syllable."

"Hey, Mom, don't you wish someone else had that problem—not talking so much?" Stuart murmured, moving his eyes in the direction of Grant.

"Stuart, whatever you're trying to start, I'm going to finish," Bert was saying.

"I don't wish that problem on anyone, Stuart. You just go around for a *half* day struggling——"

I dropped behind. "Have you noticed, boys? For the first time Janey is showing some frustration about having to talk. I think we'd better stop asking her for it. Just let her do it when she wants to."

"I noticed it!" Grant said.

"Grant, you don't even know what Mom is talking about!"

"Just ignore him, Grant. He's putting you down to make himself all puffed up inside. Stuart, stop the bossy bit. It's not becoming."

"I was only kidding."

"If that's an apology, tell Grant, not me."

"Sorry, Fatso."

"And don't call me Fatso. I'm not fat, am I Mom?"

"No, you're quite lean."

"We call everybody that here!"

"Ugh," I said. "I bet the counselors can hardly wait for Wednesday to come."

"They call everybody that too."

"Oh." A new kind of sensitivity training, this?

AUGUST 19, 1967. Something uncanny about Janey was her attention to hollow sounds: blowers, wooshing or booming things. How much of that stuff had tonality for Jane? Was that the reason her brain found it and hung onto it, producing a gaze—no, a daze. It bothered me. She lapsed into another world with those sounds, like she did with music. When Bert brought the boys in from the beach, I asked him about it—moving bedrooms again. It would not only get Jane away from the boiler but provide a change of creeping environment. Perhaps she would move more if the cabinets of toys were in another setting.

Bert agreed readily. Maybe it was summertime and he had forgotten how much noise that thing made. Maybe it was the difficulty J. was beginning to show with her speech. Maybe it was the reality that this is as good as she'll talk? We had been wondering why she never said any sentences except, "Ah want dada talk ona tep" and "I want hear tep." We were beginning to realize she had a long struggle ahead. We would do anything. Even move into that awful room ourselves.

Lucille—here from Tokyo—helped me and the boys move everything from room to room while Bert started supper on the outdoor grill. Had Janey done her crawl boxes? No (and thank you). So Bert started J. through the outdoor boxes, now moved from over the long sand pit we had made (before the record rains) to the middle of the yard, with grass as the floor. After a while Lu went out to give him a hand. An hour later J. had done her forty trips with the aid of split cherries and [**cherry**] the Winter girls had made.

At supper around the picnic table Lu was telling us how lucky Janey was to have these particular boys for brothers.

"Robin is luckier," Grant interrupted.

"Who is Robin?"

"You mean, Robin who is Jane's age, who can already walk and talk."

"Yeah, she's going to kindergarten when school starts."

Then Lucille, quick-thinking aunt, said, "From all those toys and books I just moved, I not only have a backache but a hunch that Jane will be getting a super-duper kindergarten course right here!"

Grant beamed, "That's exactly what Robin's mother said. Yesterday."

Stuart at bone-gnawing, "But Robin can't read. Jane can."

"Robin will though," I said. "No need to cover up what Jane can't do with what she can do, Stu. I mean that won't help Janey any. That's why we are working on the things she—the steps she must have before good walking and good talking."

Jane giggled.

"Mom, she knows everything you're saying!" Stu said in disgust.

"Yes, you're right. We must stop discussing her in front of her. She's understanding whole paragraphs now, I bet."

AUGUST 21, 1967. Dizzy got back today from her summer job at a New York camp for the "physically disabled." About two hundred children and adults, a mixture of "handicaps": muscular dystrophy, polio, arthritis, deafness or blindness or both, and a huge number of the "cerebral-palsied." She seemed terribly disheartened. I tried to cheer her up.

She corrected me, "I'm annoyed. That's it exactly. I'm annoyed." It was the children with "cerebral palsy." She wanted to grab them up and put them to work on this program. No one talked about "functions" there. There was no treatment, no one looking at them inclusively—at the whole child. The words *brain* or *brain-injured* were absent altogether. She never heard the brain mentioned once!

But Mary had warned her. She wouldn't be able to find a camp for children who were "patterned" and "programed." This was a "stay home and get well" philosophy. *Then* go to camp when you've made it. The IAHP group don't even like their kids getting together to do program! Even though some are doing it. Each kid's program is individual to his needs, his levels of functioning; his crawl box is *his* size, etc.

Mary had suggested writing to some of the organizations for a camp list. But not to mention a camp doing the Philadelphia program. Some CP centers are sending their directors to Philly for retraining. And some are wishing it would go away. New York therapists are among the latter, and seem to be getting together to wish. Better to work hard and help all you can.

Well, Dizzy did. She loved the kids, the adults, the staff, the whole run-down place. And she worked at getting everyone to meals, fed, the mess in the hall cleaned up afterwards, and everyone back to his cottage. But she was frustrated all the time.

It took her one hour to brace up a little eight-year-old girl, a "CP" she was called. She wore a back brace, a corset attached to that, and leg braces from hip to floor with knee hinges. During the day she sat in a wheelchair. "And that's about all she did, man." Even with her braces on, she did not weigh any more than Jane.

"Well, we don't know whether or not she could have developed a trunk and hips on this program."

"I know. But that's what was so annoying. She'll never know this way. I mean, someone put her into that thing for life, man. Without trying—— Everyone seems to accept it so—even the staff. You should see the CP's trying to button their clothes, those who try. It never dawned on anybody somehow to correct the hands. They button in some kind of compensating way. Someone taught them, like go inside the hole and pull it through. Their buttonholes have to be constantly repaired; they tug and jerk them through. Other CP's have been shown how to hold their clothes up and they get under and push the button up in a stab—oh, I wanted so much to tell them all about Janey's hands."

"Dizzy, they don't know what you and I know. You've seen J.'s hand brushed to death, padding over the world all day and picking up smaller and smaller stuff. For more than two years! Now that's even hard to imagine. Even Mary is impressed. She's downright shocked what crawling and creeping does for hands. And hands is her business, stuff like their flexors and extensors."

"I know. The only person at the camp who knew anything about this program was the speech therapist. Was looking into it, involved somewhere in one of those new perceptual programs, out West, I think. Oh, everyone had heard about it, but they didn't have any idea what it was except the family treats the kid like an animal."

"I've heard. That. And it breaks up the family. No, correction, it *could* break up the family, giving one child too much attention, *ahg,* as if getting the braces on and off and watching every buttonhole and spoonful wasn't an all-day job. Now I'm getting annoyed. Get out of here."

"First, I've got to ask you something. All the CP's, those who can walk, the adults even, all walk with their knees bent and turned in. You know, their knees knock together, kind of a tiptoe jumpy walk; their heels aren't down——"

"Yes, it's often called a 'spastic walk.' "

"I know. That's what I wanted to ask you. Isn't Jane a spastic?"

"You're wondering if she will walk like that?"

"Yeah, that's what I was wondering, if she didn't get any——"

"Well, you've got the picture. Every time I see a spastic walk I make new resolves, you know, work harder tomorrow."

"A lot of them have very slow halting speech too. Is Jane—are you worried about that too?"

"Dizzy, I'm worried about it all. I don't *stop* and worry. But I worry. Jane is O.K. down to here—now," and I pointed to my knees. "Mary says, it's as if Jane's spasticity is oozing out of her body down to the floor. So that means hips can separate now beautifully, so there goes your knee-knocking out the window. Score one. The pelvis can stay beautifully under the trunk, where it should. Score two. The trunk can sit under a strong neck, so there goes your slump. That's three. The slump in the sit is not all gone, you notice. But it's going. Four and five may be impossible. If you can't stand flat on the floor, off tiptoes, and you can't straighten your legs at the knee, you throw your fanny out back, like a Z, to maintain balance. Just try it. Up on your toes, knees bent, the hips hang out the back.

"Two big 'ifs' to go. Straight legs and feet flat in dorsi-flexion. We have her legs down to the table in patterning and trailing in creeping. We have ankle movement, left and right now. Now we've got to get the ankle to lift the foot up. Put all that stuff together and walk adds up to about four hundred muscles. We're going for them all. And the hardest job is from here on, where the spasticity was the greatest."

"What happens if—you know."

"Then we'll probably go the orthodox route—operations on the knee and

ankle tendons of the calf muscle. And do that again when they shorten
again. And in between, hold everything in place with a brace. Then we'll
start adjusting her to her difficulties, like everyone else. What will be different though is what she got from floor life. I expect she'll have the hearing
of a dog and the vision of a cat! Before she's finished. Remind me to tell
you about Puff—are you patterning Sunday?"

"Yeah, I'll be here. I'll probably be here forever just to see if it works!"

For the first time Dizzy was laughing and slinging sarcasm. "Well, my
frustration days are over. Guess I'll be forced to work with this one li'l kid,
when I could have saved the world." And she went over to let Jane ping
the rubber bands on her teeth.

"And I'll be forced to make all this time up, doing eye exercises at
midnight, if you don't get out of here."

"Well, I only wanted to give her a little socialization—you know, the
biggest thing we did there all day?"

"No, what?"

"Every afternoon, we hiked them all to a luncheonette, down the road
from the camp. The wheelchairs we pushed."

"To eat?"

"Yeah. Eating was the biggest thing there. And to go somewhere all
together."

SEPTEMBER 5, 1967. Back from a five-day weekend. I sat down with the
mail. A postcard fell out. It was from the kindergarten teacher at the boys'
school. Printed in even letters:

Dear Jane,
        I will be very happy to greet you when you come to school next week.
There will be new friends to meet and our classroom has many books and toys.
                                                            Your teacher,
                                                            Miss ———

That stab of pain again. Everybody looking forward to entering kindergarten tomorrow. I would call first thing to the principal that the teacher
has J.'s name on her list after all. He had been so kind about it last
February, when I returned the registration forms. Said kindergarten was
optional anyway. And it sounded as if J. is getting a kindergarten program
right at home. Yes, it wasn't the curriculum she would miss. It was the
date. Her peers were going. I would make the next year count. I put the
mail down. I could get an eye exercise in before supper.

Dizzy called about her day at the beach. "It's just this—Janey is like a
real person now, not a 'baby blob.' "

"Yes, I've noticed. It's self-identity———"

"She was so much fun to play with. I didn't even want to go swimming—she was just so much fun."

"For example?"

"It's hard to describe. For the first time she's a little someone, you can really have fun with her. She sizes up the whole situation. It's like she has a grasp of all her surroundings and herself in it."

"There's a name for what you are describing. It's called 'affect.' "

"Why do you have to spoil everything!"

Professional Evaluation

September 6, 1967. Trip to Philadelphia (J.'s revisit) and back lots of fun. Reading cards for the day were to be [**truck**] and [**restaurant**], but J. kept looking at the fancy water towers along the New Jersey Turnpike, esthetically shaped like balloons on a string. Not looking at [**tower**] card though. Bert teasing me, next trip he'll stop on the Verrazano Narrows Bridge for [**bridge**]. Upset though at my insistence to J. in Howard Johnson's to "use your fork." Bert saying, "Oh, not here, forchrissake," and the mother retorting, "But people don't eat half with fork and half with fingers on Fifth Avenue, remember?" and the waitress doing a double-take, and then all three of us giggling.

Trip through The Institutes another thing altogether. No place in "history" for what other people think about Jane, but I told them anyway.

Mary Lawrence keeps saying Jane has the best pair of hips and trunk she's seen in all her years of therapy.

During J.'s annual exam last month her pediatrician finally said (saw) something; he remarked about the change in her manipulative ability. (I had just asked, "Aren't you impressed with her sitting there like that, her legs over the table, sitting up to be examined, not lying back?") Assistant mentioned J. the strongest child she'd ever seen, both of us holding her down during blood-filling into the syringe for the thyroid check. Me adding something about kids getting this way who use torso-arms-hips in creeping. She asking how long did "they" expect J. to keep on creeping? Me: till she got it perfect.

Bert thinking they didn't even write my comments down for "history." Just the results of the doctor's PBI (thyroid) test and the current thyroid dosage.

Interested in this though: J. gets into sleep pattern (homolateral position) by herself 100 percent of the time. Also "rests" that way on the patterning table. Likes for me to caress her in that position, all along the extended side—down the arm and down the leg. Turns her head and extends other side—in a slow-motion patterning serialization—for equal fondlings! So cute.

Me with a question for IAHF: why do we still pattern, since she's got it?
Till she's doing everything we're patterning—arm-swing, toe-dig, the whole scene. (Several years more?) If it does take that long, we have failed. With patterning. (Is there something else?) A lot of things. Question is to find the best. Whatever works for Jane is best. (Oh.)

Visual: Big breath-holder. Would J. know the reading cards we'd brought, never before tested? Hoped for her higher interest with untested batch. I showed mine: lousy. Bert showed his, ones he'd introduced the five days we were away: she knew all but | **sparkler** | (wouldn't even look at it!). Bert beaming. Maybe I could sell insurance.

Most of it by pointing. Staff man said he knew before she pointed. Her eye hits the correct card and lingers there, then comes back to it quickly, then she points. Guessed | **tower** | and | **basketball** | were her favorites. (She's smart, don't you think?) Yes, she is smarter than we are. About the test. The reading is just a lot of good discrimination visually.

Auditory: All that great stuff about J. playing with Dizzy and role-playing with dolls, putting the right furniture into the right rooms of the playhouse Mimi gave her, all that is simply: "Comprehension expanding in terms of increased alertness and response." Something getting sharper in the ears-to-understanding system. That's all. (What about the eyes? Noticing what's going on?) Comprehending what is going on is the auditory system. (Have it your way.) You have to use it to get it. Vary the tape again. (For "headquarters." Jane's and theirs.)

Tactile: Good stereognosis. (But weren't they excited about J. seeing the fabric "brocade" covering the love-seat in the White House *National Geographic* article?) That's visual. Why am I not testing fabrics? (She knows *eleven!*) That's not the question. It's not the knowing, it's the using we want. It's the brain we want to use, not the fabrics. Determining this one from that one.

(She hates coins. Last year she was interested in *looking* at the two sides of a coin. But to *feel* the difference, heads from tails, that's impossible —I mean, at her age.) It is her age neurologically; she's up to that. (Oh.) The last tactile ability. (Well, that's good.) Good enough, let's say. A blind person develops a finer system. But Jane needn't. (I'll buy that.)

Mobility: (Told them I took J. out of the crawl box mornings so she would use her right leg, so we can get at it to "remind" her. Also box in backyard, too dirty to bring in.) Make a new box. Assist right leg, pinch it, but don't talk to her about it. Want right leg to move reflexively. Don't want her to think-and-do, that's cortical. (Yeah, we're working on a lower level.) Soon she'll be afraid of the pinch-to-come. That's association. Midbrain. (Not to mention a wee bit barbaric.)

Language: No comment. Just (a) feed into the auditory system, and

(b) mask for breath. And (c) forget it. Keep her on the floor *all the time,* get her mobility going. (I know. Do baby. You'll get baby.)

Manual: (There was nothing but rain this summer. But J. did a little writing in the sand, with us guiding her hand, numbers 1, 2, 3. Interested somewhat, but would rather do flip and dig motions with her index finger. No scissors tried till last week. No, no finger-paints till last week.) It would seem you've gotten busy lately.

Go home and do it all again. I would make a schedule first thing tomorrow. As soon as I get back from boys' school. Several teachers asking if I would tell their classes about the 4-H display I set up. Just this once.

7

From September 1967 to March 1968

SEPTEMBER 12, 1967. Bert and the boys made a new tape Sunday. This time I was upset over his choice of nouns. Supposed to be beyond her present level of understanding—but—words like *manager, touchdown, goal post,* and *home run* are just too much. He said it was fall, and that's what most of the conversation in the house would be about. I mentioned something about over my dead body.

So, guess what? Today—today is Tuesday—the kid came flying to me (the running-creep with head tossing, hair flying, outrigger along for the ride), saying, "I wanna hear uh tep."

Strange. The tape *was* on. I could hear *World Series* over and over in the background with the pauses in between. Then nothing. Complete silence. The tape was finished.

So Jane Napear knew that *World Series* signaled the end of the tape. Bert had left the last fourth of it bare. Whatta gal!

Or is it the next to the last word when she starts to anticipate. I played the tape. That would be *champion.* The words before that are *alphabet, lumber yard,* and *freezer.* All of them new to her.

I called Bert at the office. No, he had not played it at all on Sunday. And I played it at creeping time yesterday and today. And last night at bedtime. And half that time the other side was on. Could Janey really be that aware? Or is it memory, or what?

SEPTEMBER 29, 1967. Mother flew back from Switzerland today. The first thing Grant asked was did she have any more of that *Queen Mary* stationery? The poor airlines, for the first time in their lives, they are no longer Number 1.

We celebrated my birthday two days late.

The cake was lighted. I blew first. Then it was Jane's turn, so we lighted the candles again. Grant said he would help her and began to blow from his side.

"Wait!" Jane was blowing them, strongly and surely, blowing them out. Bert reached over to turn the cakestand around and around. He looked at me and I looked at him.

Stuart was saying, "Jane can blow them out! Good girl! Janey can really blow now."

Grant said, "Yeah, but not all of them. My turn."

I said, "Yes, she's got more breath in her whistles now too. And maybe more for words. Maybe that's why she's saying more couplets than one-words. It's so hard to tell. It's so gradual."

Janey had another birthday present for me. She's eating cake with her fork under the bite, instead of using the spearing motion. I had not noticed before. Was this the first day? Or had she been doing that for a week? It didn't make any difference, she was using her fork like we do.

And once more we sang "Happy Birthday" and "She's a Jolly Good Fellow" for Janey's sake. The next birthday was four months off. A long time between music. That's the best part. Watching her during the singing. She goes into a freeze, Stu calls it, a freeze-laugh caught in midair and a sort of tremble all over, with her body starch-stiff, and her eyes shifting slowly to each of us.

Birthday candles and cake are probably nowhere else so loved, so full of light and delight, as at our house. And over so quick. We always end the same. Who's birthday is next? The one I can't get excited about is Jane's. Hers is next.

OCTOBER 8, 1967. We returned from Homecoming at Union College. I feel that all I was has been drained away and in its place a nothing numbness. Very, very calmly and firmly I warned Bert. In the future, he is not to mention the program we do with Janey or introduce me to a single person who works with or has a brain-injured child. I cannot think about this twenty-four hours a day, especially when I am supposed to be away from it having fun.

Bert had asked me to speak to this couple—"He's dying to talk to you," and "He has a little girl like Janey." It seemed a simple thing.

I was halfway through the six areas that are evaluated and programed, each terribly interdependent on the others, giving appropriately Jane's breakthroughs, apologizing for their smallness and saying it's the smalls that add up to the big——

He knew all about it. And he had The Institutes' address. His daughter was in a state institution. He had been in touch with The Institutes to locate a place where he could send his daughter to do the program.

With side-glances at his beautiful wife, who had oohed and ahed as I talked, I went deep into this being a home program, no one was going to do it for you. Who else was going to put that much into making a child well? It took a lot of time, sure, but just look what may come from it. And I launched into the weird things we had done and the wonderful things we were getting. They would have to decide what their priorities were. Then I faced her directly. Something about how vain I was, if I can do this, anyone can.

What a dope. Bert had not known either. This was his date! Some years ago he and his wife were divorced. His little girl, at the age of four, had entered the institution after unsuccessful tries with housekeepers. She had a vocabulary of forty words when she entered. Six months later she had none. All her spontaneity and cuteness left years ago. He visits a little girl, now eight, dull and silent. The state pays sixty-seven cents a day for her three meals. Did I know what kind of food that would buy? She is living in a world of malnutrition and listlessness. The little girl he sent there was something. This one nothing. His one priority is getting her out of there and into this program.

He is a lawyer, assigned to the Joint Legislative Commission of the state, which is in charge of doing something about these children. There is a legislator—from Brooklyn—on that committee. I must tell him all about Jane. Senator Conklin would listen to me. He is a man interested in doing something about this . . . these children. He doesn't know anything first-hand about this program . . .

Just what was to be the outcome of any such meeting? The program cannot be done in groups, it's too individualized. The children would still be programed at home. It's the parents who are taught. It's the parents who can change the environment. All day long. I don't think anything less would work. Of course, life in an institution is just a step above solitary confinement. Solitary has *no* environment, no sights, no sounds, no touchings. Institutions have little, which to a brain-injured child is zero. Did he think the State of New York was about to switch their money from that to this? They are busy trying to improve the institutions. You know, they will have to exhaust that route first.

We moved out of the reception, yes, we must have dinner together to finish this. Bert organized the party, I don't remember the drive at all. He was saying I should think of the tens of thousands of children like his little girl.

I was saying I have to work at putting Jane first as it is, my phone rings several nights a week, someone always knows of someone who needs this program, and always they want me to talk to them, I could convince them. No, I must think of Jane, she's not going to make it with a half program. Other five-year-olds are moving every day. We have to beat that. To catch up.

He was saying I was thinking of only one. There were thousands I could help. And no, Bill Conklin probably would not come to my house. I would have to go to him. No, Bill Conklin would not go to Philadelphia, at least until he knew enough to interest him. And he was a terribly busy man on other matters. It was up to me.

The argument became so heated around the long table that several suggested we might talk about something else, we weren't getting anywhere, just making tension all around. And why couldn't I? The state was moving on this subject . . . just look at the BOCES program. And I said take a look at BOCES off paper. Cooperative Educational Services, my eye. More like the blind leading the blind.

I was glad when the boys, at the children's table, had run on ahead out the door. I felt I had been kicked in the heart. I had not eaten. Now I was getting near tears. Throughout the several hours, I was straight-faced and talking, inside I was promising to find out from The Institutes what's possible for those little girls, his especially.

I would continue with Jane. No Albany-Capitol business for me. No other projects. I would make that choice, no matter what all of Bert's friends thought of me.

On the way home. "Yes, you did right, Peggy. You can't be a missionary for this program. And do it at the same time. You know that. You tried that."

"But I was protesting then, Bert. Just screaming for all the world to hear. Still protesting from the wound. Of finally realizing, waking up to Jane. You see, Bert, all the time I was pregnant, all the time I was lying in the hospital for Jane to get out of the pediatric nursery—I was holding my breath that she was O.K., was born "healthy." What all women pray for. And fathers too. The reason I never put it all together for so long, was I never thought that would happen to us, to any of our children."

"I know——"

"I didn't want to know there was even a possibility of it."

"Besides the fact that no doctor ever put it together either."

"Now I'm holding my breath, that's what it is, just one long breath-holding, seizing on every eye movement and sound so I can relax a second, and take another breath."

"I know."

"I can't take on the State of New York. It would be like turning around on Janey. It wouldn't help with my breathing. Or hers. I don't feel like protesting anymore. The only wounds now are the little ones, under the great big one, the ones that come when she's plateauing, when I can't get my breath."

"I know. Did you talk to that other couple . . . what's their name? He's a doctor who spoke to you at the game."

"Did you send him over?"

"Yes, he wanted to talk to you later about his brother's—or sister's— child. They live in Westchester County. Thought maybe you might talk to the mother, what the program is like——"

Then I told Bert to stop it. About everybody's children. I don't care. And I can't.

OCTOBER 12, 1967. I had just started the second verse of "Twinkle, Twinkle, Little Star" that Jane Perlstein had taught me:

> When the glorious sun is set
> And the grass with dew is dry——

Janey giggled and said, "Wet."

"Oops. When the grass with dew is wet——"

Mimi just stopped patterning, "Would you change places with me? I want you to feel this."

I had been waiting for someone to confirm it. I hadn't said a word. "Tell me."

"Jane is doing the toe-dig herself, definitely, strongly!"

I had felt it under my hand when I did that leg Tuesday, two days ago. Or thought I felt it. It's all so gradual; I can never believe unless someone feels what I feel.

Everyone excited and talking at once. Muriel Dawson and Mary Unruh doing arms, saying they knew it was something good by Mimi's stopping utterly. But what?

"Got a toe-push on the left foot, that's what. We've been dorsi-flecting. Now the foot is."

We had been working together and talking about the "stupid ankles" for more than two years. (Later someone figured two years, seven months, and five days.) And we've been patterning the toe-dig since June a year ago. And here it was! Headquarters can send down a toe-dig message!

Arel saying, why don't we compliment her, she does the head!

Should we lighten up on the patterning to give her a chance to do more of it?

No, we still "put in." She'll "put out"—in the crawl box. Someday. Don't count on seeing it today. It may take weeks or months.

"Or years," Mimi mumbled.

Under my breath I mumbled something about the chaff one has to take with the wheat when you ask for volunteers. And we wound up silly as usual, Jane laughing and asking for "Mo juz."

Red-letter day. Remember this one.

OCTOBER 21, 1967. I told Mary Lawrence how awful it was, Janey creeping like an ape—really, just like a chimp, on the knuckles of the right hand and the upper thumb joint of the left hand, both hands in fists. She's now doing it about 90 percent of the time. How worried I was. How she holds her head up and looks so bizarre, going along on her knees that way. What could have happened to the hands getting flatter and "normaler?"

Mary thought it may be visual. Maybe that's it. She is suddenly interested in the stuff on tops of cabinets, the ones that are waist-high on me. Maybe. Did that happen in evolution too? Mary said they didn't have counters then, Silly.

And how all of a sudden Jane started crawling with her right knee turning in a lot, and the left one occasionally. It was the beginning of the zigzag-look, wasn't it? Yes, Mary thinks it is certainly. What did I think caused it? How will I ever know? But she's been resisting that knee-turning during patterning so much all last month and this . . . I think her brain just got aware it has knees, to turn, I mean. That motion. I guess she is aware now of that motion.

Mary asked me if we felt Jane digging her left toe into the patterning table. Oh, yes. I think the right one is starting some dorsi-flexion now. It's so gradual, just a little movement there, maybe a dig. Rightie is always behind leftie.

Mary said she couldn't believe anything that rightie does. She didn't even have good sensation in that leg, remember?

I remember it all. That's what keeps me going.

And Janey clicking nightly into her sleep pattern. I still turn her knee in, the one "in extension." Yes, it is still up in the air at night, from the knee down, not as much as when we started, of course. But enough to cause me to cover it specially.

What I don't understand is, the thing that Janey can do best, but never practices: knee-walking. She only does it on her day off—in Philly. How can knee-walking get so serialized, so speedy, without practice?

Mary says that proves what "they" have been saying for years. Better creeping makes a better walk. If J. gets straight knees and dorsi-flexion to the point of flat feet, she may only walk with a limp. Unless the right catches up to the left.

"Do you think we can get straight legs, Mary? Tell me."

"I don't know, Peggy. It's never been tried before without operations, then bracing. But she's gotten a lot of things I never have seen before—the hips, the trunk balance. I'd go with the staff at The Institutes till they give up. They won't until they are sure their program ideas aren't working."

"Mary, they do know what they are doing, don't they? It is the best——"

"Peg, there isn't anything else. That's what I say to all the nonbelievers in my business. 'What's your alternative?' "

NOVEMBER 8, 1967. Philadelphia. Yes! Jane has "active dorsi-flexion . . . evident at this evaluation." Just a "flicker" in the ankle, the foot lifting ever so slightly. But "seeable." Bert and I saying it wasn't much. Mary Lawrence with us, barely audible, "It will be interesting——"

What they are going to do about it? Jane is going to start Strumpels.

Jane may lie on her stomach or sit in chair. You will have her flex her knee, drawing her knee up to waist-height. And you, at the same time, *will prevent her* from doing just that. You will push against her pull up. The harder you go against each other, the more dorsi-flexion will occur.

Start with ten Strumpels, each leg; increase till she's doing several hundred a day.

"We will try it," was our answer. Did we understand? Ten Strumpels after each pattern each day, each leg. Then to the crawling box. Also more of them in the afternoon. Build to hundreds.

Another surprise: we would teach the concept of counting to J. during crawl boxes. How many does she do at one time? (Forty round trips.) O.K. We'll teach her that forty is a lot more than twenty. And twenty is more than nineteen. (I could tell the guy had done crawl boxes.) Trace her hand on the numbers; sand is good. Transfer a marble, a penny, etc., from one glass jar to another after each round trip. Be sure the jars are the same size. (I could have figured that out.) We want Jane to get the "concept" before the "numerals." A lot of kids can "count," but don't have the concept.

And remove all nursery rhymes, as well as music, from her environment. No matter how "talked," they are still singsong. (Sorry I asked.) (How will we get smooth patterning then?) Give her conversation over her head. Figuratively and literally. "Follows conversation to some degree. Difficult to accurately assess." But make the conversation clear and intermittent, to arouse listening.

There is "more attention in manual activities. Bimanual tests O.K." Stop pre-writing, stop fine-finger program, including scissors. Wait till she gets interested. When a kid gets interested, they like to use scissors to get into something, cut open a bag, etc. But Jane is not interested and would probably just tear it open.

After observing J. at, what Mary and I thought very difficult, free-form puzzles (no back board, no front-or-back difference), the woman commented, "She works it out in the air on the way down, see?" Then she said Jane was very smart. (I didn't even ask.) "The hyperactive kind usually are. You should be glad. It's the others who present a problem. This kid is self-motivating. She's a joy to watch."

"At puzzles? Those do seem awfully advanced."

"At everything. See how she's missing nothing in this room [J. now on knees]?"

Mary observing J. at puzzles, very quietly: "I wonder what the lady psychologist would say to this?"

Me: "Probably would be listening for Jane to say 'puzzle.' "

Another surprise: Have Janey start reading sentences. Just like that. Here's one: *The dog is running.* Teach J. *the* and *is.* (How?) Just use them. There are a hundred ways to take this next step. This is only one of them. Use nouns she already knows. The new thing here: verbs.

But first, train J. to read *pictures* left to right, drop down to the next row of them, left to right, etc. Judy Company See-Quees series good for this. In every picture-square, a different action; each sequencing to build a story. Go along, telling the story, placing the picture-squares into the frame left to right. Later let her place them in their proper story-telling order (a good way to test her comprehension).

When she is ready to read sentences left to right, drop down to the next line, etc., make a book for her. Several as she progresses. The dog doing this and that, so verbs are tested. Cat doing same things, for testing the noun. Pictures O.K., but *not* on sentence page.

Bert smiling as if he knew Janey could do all of it. I couldn't imagine any of it. Except the old program. Which was to be done also.

This guy surprised we were not doing visual-pursuit programs. (Maybe it has something to do with the hours in a day?) So he programed a whole range of those.

She received no scoring increase. Everything, even the dorsi-flexion beginning in the ankle, was some step in the big Profile blocks. Just a simple, "Jane continues to show progress."

NOVEMBER 14, 1967. There has never been such an interruption of a community meeting on education in this town. I am sorry. I probably set things back another fifty years. I am glad. I can at least live with myself. I stood up. I was counted.

This was the annual meeting, but the first on the subject of Children with Learning Problems. A film would be shown, *Why Billy Couldn't Learn,* produced for the California State Department of Education by the California Association for Neurologically Handicapped Children. Hallelujah!

Edith had given me publications from that progressive group. New York was at least looking far and wide. Maybe up. Certainly not in the sand anymore. Or at the teacher. Or her materials.

Auditory and visual perception were to be mentioned publicly for the first time here. The panel would be fascinating to watch. There were approach-differences represented there. Two were, it seemed to me, leaning away from "structuring" to "correcting." One was a reading consultant, the woman who had asked me that Montessori question two years ago. The local Board of Education publication had a picture of her last week teaching an in-service course. The caption under the picture read:

Mrs. ——— describes to teachers how perceptual problems in children can interfere with learning and how simple exercises, like creeping and crawling and other coordinated movements, can bring dramatic improvements.

That was the issue celebrating New York State's one hundredth anniversary of the public school system!

The guest speaker was famous for appearing on panels everywhere lately. He had a job to do. Most of his speeches dealt with the temptations abroad in the land. The Institutes for the Achievement for Human Potential was clearly the devil. The words *charlatan* and *fraud* were used in public now.

But other statements were coming in too. Rank-and-file doctors and certain cerebral palsy units were crying, "Our children are doing this program, count me out!" Was the establishment—itself no more than fifteen to twenty years old—having its death cry? Some on the pro side were warning Doman, Delacato, et al., they would be the establishment someday—note the lessons to be learned. Research would take us further. And someday— maybe—the Prevention people would have the last word.

For a while the speaker, a doctor, established himself, his history of his involvement in this subject, over the years. How the clinic he worked in would soon change over to a team approach for brain-injured children. No one needed to go anywhere else. We had all the services right here.

Aha, here it comes.

It did. The Institutes were never mentioned by name. It was the same script, down to "mothers being insecure" who run here and there to try anything. There was something to getting a qualified doctor's opinion and living with it. It would save time and money in the long run.

The only thing coming through new was this man's bias. It began to be apparent to the audience, several shifted in their seats to catch my eye. His hostility would hang him. Several people who had heard him before warned me, but I thought they were exaggerating. He was like Elmer Gantry. His face was one long smile, coating one long sneer. He was now on to press articles coming from everywhere (Philadelphia?), and don't be impressed with what a public relations department (Philadelphia?) can do.

How many people listening would know what he was talking about? Was it only those few, those many, who were now being tempted, he really wanted to save?

The film was a big disappointment to me. It dealt with recognizing perceptual difficulties, but not one word of changing them, just finding ways to teach *around* them. Of course, the brain wasn't mentioned. You would have thought that the school equipment had the learning problems. Change the scissors. Or don't ask the student to perform this activity. Because he has problems with his hands. Work together—teacher and psychologist—to determine his limits. We don't want to teach in ways he can't learn. That's cruel. We don't want Billy to feel bad about himself. The old Protestant ethic. If you work hard at having Billy feel good about himself, real hard, then you will succeed. At having Billy feel good about himself. Gee, whiz, Billy may have perceptual difficulties, but he is not blind. Brainwashing was O.K. to get something, not to cover something. It must be O.K. As a mother I use it all the time.

The discussion (I couldn't believe it) centered primarily on people who were programing children to *correct* these defects. The question was asked, Why didn't the school district get hold of these people to find out about that Delacato Method, or whatever you call it?

Apparently some children from this district *are* being referred by the administration to get that sort of evaluation.

The doctor turned around to the panel member who had made the quiet little announcement and said he wasn't sure the State Education Department would like that! If they were to hear about it! Visions of hell-fire.

The administrator said they were ruling out nothing. Their main concern was for whatever worked, might work, for these children. It was an infant field, people are just now recognizing difficulties that are perceptual.

Then someone broke it wide open with the question, "What do you have against the Delacato program?"

Oh, my, oh, my. Everything from what the parents are promised, to the lawsuits that result thereafter. If you know anyone who wants to practice law, send him to New Jersey, he can have a lucrative practice there, I tell you.

Everyone was laughing. Huge rolling laughs, this guy was all right.

I zinged to my feet. I apologized for breaking into his answer, I was a doctor's daughter, should know better. But what he was saying was not true, and he knew it. He had been corrected in public before. Why was he still saying the same things? He had been there for one day; it is Pennsylvania, not New Jersey. Maybe he should spend some time there and learn the program, as well as see all the doctors he says are not there, but most of all, see the children. I was probably the only one in the room that knew he was not qualified to answer the lady's question. He is biased and should say so—clearly there were now two Elmer Gantrys.

He remarked about how emotional I was about——

"That bit about the emotional mother doesn't get anywhere with me or anybody here. We are all emotional about our children's difficulties or we wouldn't be here tonight——"

The president of the PTA council who was standing near my aisle seat touched me and said, "That's enough, Peggy. Let him speak now."

There was something about not understanding the lady's question, wasn't sure she had one, and he had told what he thought about the people down there, and could we move on to something else?

There had never been one lawsuit against The Institutes. As of last June, when Bert told me that rumor was going around and checked it out. I was kicking myself for not correcting that point too. But what if there had been just *one* lawsuit since June, and the doctor knew of it? Oh, that's ridiculous.

The meeting had ended soon after. I walked quickly through the corridors, two people grabbing my arms, one praising me for "telling that guy off," the other saying she knew someone patterning Jane and to keep up the good work.

Barbara Barnhart was leaving fast too. As I went out the door, she was saying, "The strange thing about all this is no one ever heard of perceptual difficulties till the Philadelphia program fired them all to get busy on the subject."

"I really made a fool of myself tonight, didn't I?"

"Necessary, I'd say. In view of the circumstances."

"Thanks, Barbara."

NOVEMBER 15, 1967. Thought about telling the school district what it is they don't know. What it is the kid with "learning disabilities" doesn't know for sure. District knows he doesn't know his left from his right. Knows he has difficulty following "Simon Says" game. Knows he has a kind of orientation lack, where his body's at, that is. They've gotten that far.

Some teachers are even talking about body image now, trying to get a sense of balance, a better coordination via the kid-walking-the-walking-beam, over and over. The beam *is* a good test for it. Some kids move right across it, extending their arms for balancers, like perfectly working airplane wings. The lousy ones don't; they hug their bodies, neck, pockets, and anything of themselves they can grab onto and teeter across. Or fall off.

The teacher doesn't know that kids get all coordination *before* they ever walk. Or don't. The kid needs to know that he has two sides *before* he contends with that gravity up there. Needs to tell his brain all about it.

Thought about collecting notes on J. on the floor, back in 1965, when she was learning what two arms, two legs, two elbows, etc. *were*. How they are across from each other, my, my.

Then hit them with the now list, my notes on those wild shenanigans of the last two months.

Just to let them know what it is that Johnny doesn't know. That he needs to go back there to get it, not over the beam.

Thought about all this for about ten minutes. It's just too simple? Nothing you'd want to write in his school file? Don't think they are exhausted from all their other approaches to Johnny yet. Some just now beginning to use the doctors' catch-all term: dyslexia.

JANUARY 1, 1968. On New Year's Eve Bert and I used to sit before the living room fire with some champagne and informally review the past year. Last night we reminisced about those nights. But not about the past year. Too depressing, that 1967, to even think about. We simply dismissed the calendar change with the statement that 1968 would be better, because it could not be worse, and went on to bed.

The last year had begun with Jane's burns.

This one had started with Jane's hair shaved off to a stubby quarter-inch, just above the crusts of impetigo, which had formed there during three bedridden weeks. Bert had soaked her head in a pan of water and picked off the thick crusts morning and night until the medication began its healing. I had chopped her hair off that first night, blaming myself as I cut. Jane had only seemed congested and hoarse those three weeks. I was the one really sick. A bout of strep throat, we later learned. Perhaps Jane had it too, the doctor said. That's why the impetigo. Maybe that's why I left her bangs, a little touch of the old charm, around what now was another face, this one pale and thin, its glow all gone.

For the past six weeks Jane had stopped talking. We caught ourselves wondering if she really ever had. It was hard to remember even what her words had sounded like. Occasionally she might ask for juice, but it was almost unrecognizable. One day she had said "San Claus" looking at her Christmas cards.

The patterners had started returning the past week. To put a little cheer into an otherwise ugly picture, we decorated Jane's little tree with paper flowers, each named for a patterner, and leaned a sign against the stand, "Love and Flower Power from Janey."

We took a picture of Matt. Would it be our last? We were preparing the boys. Yes, Grandfather is getting worse. Not better.

Stuart got a picture of the giant tree before gifts were exchanged; it had come at the right time. We needed its grace and color; we needed to take our minds off our troubles. The boys had decorated it; this year they wanted flashing lights and lots of tinsel. And Grant had stayed on to add all the home-made paper Twelve-Days-of-Christmas ornaments we had packed away years ago.

I think that was the turning point of my depression. This wonderful child, Grant, oblivious to the blues with which his parents were eyeing Christmas, was up and down the ladder, tying this and that on with a delicate patience, and humming to himself a little tune:

> Five something THING-INGS-S.
> Four ha-ah-ha,
> Three Earl Morralls,
> Two Gary Woods,
> And one HO-mer JONES-S-S.

Besides some Judy See-Quees surprises from Santa, Jane was up to her eyeballs in Lotto picture-matching stuff of all sorts, and number and word games to rival the school district's Visual Aid Center.

The principal had arranged for me to send an order through elementary school channels to the Hammett Company for all the little things I could foresee during the coming year, floor surprises for Jane, all for learning. I had begun to realize that learning was Jane's favorite play. Deep visual involvement was her meat. I decided to feed her more of the same. But she also received a clown and a doll bed, just in case.

JANUARY 7, 1968. Called Philly to cancel Jane's January appointment. (No program, no re-evaluation, their rule.) And to ask approximately twenty questions.

I couldn't reach the man who programed J. last, but got one of the directors. Patiently he responded to each question, such as, "Where did you get the idea there is a bell she hits in Strumpels?" It was probably an analogy, oh. She'll get the idea soon enough. And, haven't we started Strumpels yet?

My last question was, "Has The Institutes had any lawsuits against it by parents?" I told him what was going around the New York area, I had heard two doctors mention it in public.

"No, there haven't been any lawsuits. Someone else mentioned that to me last month. But that is not your business. Jane is your business. Don't worry about what 'they' are saying. Just get busy with Jane."

"I know, I know. But has there been even one?"

"No. Not in the seven years I have been here. I would know if there had, I suppose. There are plenty of attacks against us. But not by the parents. Just concern yourself with Jane. You won't have time for the other."

JANUARY 22, 1968. With a dozen attempts J. blew out all six candles by herself. Everyone was silent. In fact, the whole party was one long breath-holding. She looked so waifish under the porcupine hairdo. Even the Swiss dress made her look pitiful and thin. All I could see beyond the white draw-string blouse was the bony chest and scarred arm. Robin looked more robust in the same dress a size smaller, her pink cheeks and blonde hair just right for the alpine touch. Running and jumping, squatting and twirl-ing, that's what makes a dress on a little girl.

The four teens all looked so pretty, their hair waist length. They all went along with their turn at the donkey. If they were embarrassed, they didn't show it. They laughed at their own attempts. Jane was watching as Laurie got the tail squarely on the nose. Jane confused about the concept. She would have none of the blindfold, and with a sigh she placed the tail on the end—from her seat in the chair drawn up close. Just do it. And let's get back to the candy cup.

Nothing too planned is ever fun.

Bert came home at four to take pictures. He too had forgotten about the hair-look, so took two and stopped.

I'm writing all this to remember. But really, Jane's birthdays I could do without. That dullness. Deep down. Time went faster this year. Even during that awful drag of 1967. I made the wish for her today. To myself. More breath. More speech. Soon. This next year she must be masked every single day. Every single hour. She will have seven to blow out next year.

FEBRUARY 9, 1968. Must stop and put this down. Saw into Grant's eight-year-old world tonight. I think the world just broke up under him and left him lying there.

All those days in school in tumult. All the questions from Mrs. Hefner to determine his turmoil. The backsliding, down the long road of reading, writing, 'rithmetic. All compositions reflecting "the grandfather." Even his "can't find" the Dr. Doolittle book, after his saying it was the best book in the whole world. Oh, how dumb I've been. We all are at thirty-eight about eight.

It was while I was talking about Jane to Bert . . . we must take the tape recorder back to the factory again. They must fix it right or give us a new one. *Anything* to help her talk. Bert saying it wasn't the only thing she's missing. Why wasn't she on the floor, and the crawl box just sitting there. And me just lying in bed. Did I know how dead I must appear to the children? Me saying I was just taking naps when he telephones. And if he were ever home, he'd see how busy I am. He reminding me what I said last year about Indian lore—and I, picking up the last of the afternoon's feather mess, getting ready with something clever about his seeing only the bits and pieces of the Whole Mother, just forming it—When . . .

Grant was saying something about Janey. "And she's not going to get any better anyway!"

Oh, my God. I put the box down, wandered into the living room, making believe I was tidying the newspapers. He was stretched out on the sofa, hugging the pillow on his chest.

"Do you mean Janey? Oh, she's coming along nicely——"

"No, she isn't. So I don't know why you say that all the time. You're always saying that."

"Well, she has a very long way to go before walking and talking and a lot of little things that come before th——"

"She's not ever going to talk. Or walk. You're always saying that."

"How do you know she won't?"

"Because she won't. She's just like Grandfather!"

"Like Grandfather?"

"Yeah, he's even worser. So is she. He can hardly talk. She's even worser. He can't walk either—now."

"My, you're very smart to notice. Yes, he's getting brain damage. More and more. Brain cells die in old people. There's a difference though. Janey's brain cells that don't work—whether there are a few or a lot, I don't know—well, they have always been dead. But there are a lot of others—billions—they have always been alive. She's making new doings now, right through those live ones. Just like a baby does. We're doing a lot of stimulation through her eyes and ears and body to start new pathways —— It's like trailblazing. The minute—the second—one of those cells stirs, then we've got a path to where 'he' is. We've got a connection. Babies get connections that way, make pathways for everything they do. But babies don't have to do such a strong program. But you never saw a baby get born and get right up and walk and talk, did you now?"

"Well, she can't, and she's no baby either!"

"That's right. Not in birthdays. But in walking and talking she is. She's got to hear the words—really good. And move about like the baby does— lots and lots. She's got to get good baby legs first. And she is, Grant. She's not going backwards. She's going forwards. You wait, she'll talk again. This is what they call a plateau. Like a long halt before she starts going again. She'll be trying the next part, soon, I bet; she always does after a halt."

"You always say the same thing, Mom."

"Well, I think it's true. That's why I say it. But Grandfather. Now that's a completely different matter. He's too weak and too old to start a program to make new pathways. Mary Lawrence has some patients, not so weak, who do it though. But I think Grandfather is going to die soon, Grant. I really do. It will make us cry. And we will miss him so. But that's the truth too. He has brain damage that is happening now, some each day perhaps.

Jane isn't having any more. Only what she's already got. Do you see the difference?"

"Well, she's not going to get any better, so no need to talk about it——" And he got up to leave.

"Well, I certainly remember the days she didn't say any words. So she's farther along than she used to be."

"All she can say now is 'juice!' "

"That's because she is taking a halt. A really long one this time. But I bet someday I'll have to remind you that you said this."

"If she talks anymore."

"That's right. If she talks anymore. In the meantime, what do you think we should do with Miss Nuisance—throw her in the garbage can?"

He laughed, "Mah-um, you are so silly sometimes. Anyway she can do other things. Like read. At least she can read the words in the books I made. I tested her last night. She even knows *New York City.*"

"You did? Well, in the future, don't. When she starts sentences, she'll need you for that. Just concentrate on your own reading, Buster. I found that Dr. Doolittle book yesterday. It was in your bottom drawer. Did you tuck it away there?"

"Yeah. I hate that book."

"Dr. Doolittle?"

"Yeah. It's fiction."

"Fiction? I didn't know you had learned 'fiction' and 'nonfiction.' Boy, you fellas really learn a lot in third grade. Don't you like fiction—good juicy adventure stories?"

"Sure. But Dr. Doolittle isn't even true. I asked. The library teacher said it wasn't."

"Not true? You mean none of that ever really happened, but you thought it did? But you liked it just the same——"

He ran out, tears in his eyes. "Nobody told me."

I moved after him. "Told you what, Grant?"

"Told me it wasn't true."

FEBRUARY 20, 1968. When I came back out to the living room today, I apologized to Louise, why didn't she wake me? It was 7:10. Bert's train must be late. She had started hamburgers, was that all right, and did I get a good rest?

I think Louise is becoming my closest friend. Else why would I have said so simply and so straight, "I'm sorry, Louise. I'm very depressed these days. All the plans to work with Jane four to seven while you're here are falling apart, as you can see. When she talks again, I'll be better. I know. It always works this way. What have the boys been doing?"

"They're fine. Playing that card game again."

I smiled. Five-hundred rummy.

"You know, I'm going to tell you again. Those boys are really nice boys. I told them you were resting. And they've been so good in there——"

"No fighting?"

"No, they started, but I told them to keep it a little quieter and let their mother rest."

"I bet Grant said something about that. It bothers him to see me in the bed in the afternoon."

"Well, I explained how busy you are——"

"But I'm not. I just peter out every afternoon when you arrive. The only thing that helps me— That— Well, Louise the way you let Jane follow you around as you clean, the way you teach her about what you're doing— You know, the way you talk to her— I think this is her favorite time of the day now. Just because she knows you like her so."

"I know. You know how I feel about that Janey. And you missed something! She said 'gloves' this afternoon. She did. She wanted my rubber gloves on the cabinet. I gave them to her. Is that all right?"

"Did she really? She never said 'gloves' before. Anything she says, she gets. Anything you do is all right, you know that."

Louise chuckled. "That Janey is going to talk, she is going to talk."

"She's taking a long halt this time. I just can't believe this is the end. Some children never get beyond this point. Something about Janey just *wants* to express. She notices things. She's keen to size up a situation— You know what I mean— She doesn't turn inward, she turns outward. To everything and everybody in this house. She's just made for expressing out— By the way, did she write anything, draw anything, while I was asleep?"

"No. Just played with the vacuum cleaner. Loves the vacuum, that child. I never saw anything like it. Most children are frightened. But not her. She gets right up to it, that head moving left and right, down on the ears, every time it's turned on. And she's plugging it in whether I'm using it or not."

"I know. She's got a thing with vacuum cleaners, echoes, and the music in the supermarket. Funny bunny."

"She's been singing herself, did you know that? Just singing along as she plays on the floor, like I do when I'm working. Not here, other places!" And she laughed.

"Don't be sarcastic. One of these days we'll all turn on with music in this stupid house. She started that back in November. You know, I wonder if that is interfering with the speech— You know, I never thought of that— But singing and speech are enemies in brain circles, from about the age of three to around six. Maybe two-and-a-half. In speech she's about a two-and-a-half—A three? I should have asked about that when I called Philly last month. But they don't jump to conclusions like I do; they don't even hint—but maybe that's it. Maybe the music is interfering with the speech function. And maybe the vacuum cleaner has something to do with it. Maybe it's very tonal. Louise, for awhile, don't do any vacuuming. I wish I could think of some reason for her lack of interest in writing."

FEBRUARY 22, 1968. No one would know she's brain-injured these times. Sitting beside me on the sofa, my arm around her in a hug, her eyes and ears into each new page as I read the good-night story. Then another one. And maybe a third. All the books she's looked at but never "heard." How she laughs at the right moments. And grows still to listen again. And reacts. And listens. How intense, this child before a book. How delighted. How eager for the parts she knows by heart.

After a few sentences, she's ready to turn the page. So I have to make it up from the pictures. And remember it that way again next time. Because she's got a better memory than Stu or Grant, I think. I'm holding her attention a little longer with each page each night. Who would ever have believed Miss Perpetual Motion-Machine would sit still for stories.

Then the "Birthday Story." Still her favorite! She plants the pictures in the board as I go. She sure knows the left-to-right-drop-down business. Filling egg cartons and candy-box compartments that way was a darn good idea. Wonder if the Smart People ever tell parents to do that?

Then "The Three Little Pigs" sequence board. How she loves the picture just after the wolf huffs and chuffs at the brick. Nothing happens. The house is still there. So cute, her giggles. Her gasps.

Then into the bed for lights-on time. To look at the books. No boards, dear. But maybe we'll have time to do them tomorrow night. (You lucky dog.) Which books do you want? This one? This one? So she can use her new word—*yes*. What a delicious word. After all these years.

FEBRUARY 27, 1968. Sunday we tried Strumpels—for the first time. Bert and I. Jane lying prone before us. After a couple of times of flicking the bottom of her foot, up, up and up, her knee came. When she stopped in the middle, Bert zinged her again, ever so slightly, he was shaking so. As he kept her foot moving away from his flick, I pulled back on her knee. And there we "stood" against one another: Jane, trying to push her knee past my hand to get away from Bert's flick; me, pulling, preventing it.

Later in the afternoon, I counted instead. Told her to move her leg, told her to push her knee against my hand, told her we would do ten. Told her we'd do ten on the other leg now.

She balked, whining, and said, "Cawl."

"You may crawl when we finish the Strumpels."

She was getting the idea. She didn't like it. But she didn't hate me. And

I cursed my timidity, my stupidity, for waiting since November to start this.

The right leg is much weaker. Not as much movement in the ankle there, when she's coming against my hand-pull.

This morning all the patterners were watching as Muriel tried the sets of ten after each patterning. They could see the slight flicker of movement in the ankles. "That's the beginning of dorsi-flexion," I was telling them. "If it works, the flicker will get stronger and her foot will begin to lift up at the instep. It needs to go all the way up to right-angle with the leg, ninety degrees dorsi-flexion they call it." They all knew it was a big "if."

"What makes her keep bringing her knee up as Muriel pulls back to prevent it?"

"If she stops, she knows I'll zing her one on the bottom of her foot to *make* that knee start forward!"

"Aren't you worried about the psychological part?"

"Not as much as I am about the neurological part. After she gets her brain organized correctly, we'll get her a psychiatrist. First things first."

"Yes. She's lucky she's got you for a mother."

She's making me that mother. So are the teen-agers. I'm learning free-wheeling from them. I remember how they used to hang their hair down between the slats of the crawl box just to get her to go a few of the eight feet to feel it. Then they would run to the end and lie down, and spread all that stuff out before them into the box! Because they figured out that hair-fun was her bag. That month. Their bodies, their voices, their contagious laughter, they used them all. She's touched and been touched all over her body. Many hours of each day. I think that's part of her security. The contact has been direct—with people, with this house, with that earth out there. And she's seeing it, hearing it, as well as feeling it, all the time. And I don't think it can help but get less confusing when a child knows it so directly.

And I'm loosening up. The way the teen-agers are to start with. I'm learning to climb way out—way out, as if on a crazy creative branch all the time—just to get her happy cooperation. And I found out something. That branch never breaks. It just gets longer. The teens say it doesn't break because she can't tell you how foolish you look, and she can't make a negative comment. Grant would. He often tells me how silly I sound or how crazy this or that looks. But Jane can't. And that's one of the advantages to Jane's silence. Well, it's the only one.

MARCH 5, 1968. Letter, the blue form. I guessed immediately. ". . . registration for kindergarten . . ." I skipped on down. There was nothing about *maximum* age. Next September was out. But the September after that? Would they let her go to kindergarten when she was seven? If they were sending the form again, they wanted her at six. But at seven?

Before I mailed it back, I looked at the form for the doctor to complete. How many years ago had this form been made up? They were asking about "orthopedic structural defect . . . posture . . . skin . . . feet . . . nervous system . . . speech . . . Has this pupil any defects, disability or allergy? . . . Is this child taking any medication on a regular basis? . . . Are there any problems relating to growth or development? . . ."

Didn't they know yet that most all that stuff was brain development, brain organization? But the word *brain* appeared nowhere on the form. Was it still a secret thing, to be kept from the parents, the principal—the nonmedical people? No, there was a good possibility the connection with *brain* had yet to be made by the pediatricians themselves! Otherwise how could they still be prescribing "medication," tranquilizers, for hyperactive children? There was no place, no line on the form, to explain that Jane's hyperactivity was going away as she becomes more sharply tuned in to the world. In fact, there was no place to mention her auditory system at all!

But then, pediatricians did not deal with the systems, the functions—just the eyes and ears. Just the hyperactivity that they see. And to calm the child down—for the mother's sake, the teacher's—they prescribe a tranquilizer. If it makes the child drowsy, that's still not as bad as having him out of his seat all the time.

How could I explain that Jane was neurologically a first-grader in both visual and tactile competence and somewhere near kindergarten level in auditory competence? The intake picture was looking good, perhaps a good deal better than that of some of her peers who had entered kindergarten last September. But the output picture, and that's the one they'd see, was painfully slow, albeit climbing upward. She was a kindergarten girl all right in manual competence, but she *wouldn't* write—not even with a ten-foot pole! And language made her look two-yearish rather than sixish. In fact, the world would never believe the "intake side of things" by the way she talked. At the moment, I wasn't sure we had talking. And in mobility she was neurologically complete only up to the level of a four-month-old. Functionally. But, of course, the world would say she is six but crippled. And she is. Now.

MARCH 19, 1968. Speech again. Finally. Three days now. Jane just lying there listening to the tape and trying to say each word as it speaks to the whole house—loudly, frequently, and most of the day long.

Bert caught it Sunday. He heard her as he entered the hall.

A huge balloon, this, picking us all up. Our little family twittering and running to eavesdrop, and rushing back to quote the latest. Grant has been hanging around her, just before he runs back to the school yard with his kite tail longer and heavier. He hasn't said anything, but neither have Bert and I yet, about what this is all about or how long might we expect it to last. If I notice it too well it will burst and blow away again, overnight. I can write it. But I can't say it. Yet. But I took another breath, Janey.

MARCH 21, 1968. So, all third-graders talk that way! Current put-down is no longer "Stupid Head" or "Stupid Ears," as in Stu's day. Now it's "retard." For everything uncooperative. Even an inanimate object.

Caught it several times during Grant's 4-H Club today, here for my copper-tooling stint. In their enthusiasm and competition, they bounced off comments such as, 'This tracing paper is a retard,' or 'Some retard's got my hammer.' "

Glad I didn't dig into that one with Grant last week, as I was tempted.

And at supper I referred to Janey's new *ts* sound practice. Words coming out with *ts* endings now. More as if J. were looking and finding them! (*Suits, pats, hits, sentence,* and just *ts!*)

Grant explained it to us, "That's because I taught her 'uuts,' like Curly [Three Stooges] says it."

"You taught Janey 'uuts?' "

"Yeah. Janey, say 'uuts.' "

"Uu-ts-s." Then chuckles all around.

"You know, Grant, she says it almost like you do. Remember, no one in Maine could say it like you did— I mean *exactly*——"

"Yeah. That's because I taught her."

Then Bert said we might be able to rent the Maine house for the whole summer.

And that broke it up. Grant went running to the center of the room to shoot an imaginary basket. Stuart said seriously, *if* we do, he would need a new rod and reel. Seriously, we would need a mother's helper. To pattern the other leg. Because this (pattern) takes several weeks for someone to get it smooth and correct. And definitely we'd need help with Strumpels. And turns with the afternoon crawl-box routine. And Bert asking did we want more of the supper he had gone to the trouble of cooking? And didn't we think it one of the best chuck steaks so far?

And I knew then (and writing it now): will breeze through April and May. Jane too, by golly. Just you wait and see, kid, what we get accomplished!

Professional Evaluation

March 26, 1968. Philadelphia. Ed Goldstein—on sabbatical from his fifth grade to get a doctorate in reading—with us to observe in the Reading Institute and catch J.'s revisit. Mary came in from Washington.

So what happened? Toward evening we got the same slavedriver for a programer! But extremely thorough. Looked back through J.'s chart during the day—now there's a book—to see when most speech occurred during any one period. Came up with, "Let's try something. Let's go back to homolateral patterning." During those days when Mary was programing, it was true, J. had started her first word-sounds, continued in a more consistent increase of vocabulary, right up to "bye-bye car." Perhaps with use of the pons—that homolateral (primarily) crawling period in a baby's life when he uses one side of the body then the other, when he uses one ear then the other—perhaps with a further workout of that old amphibian brain, we could make a sharper highway system for what The Institutes called early (baby) listening—sound discrimination. How tuned in to sound was she really? A little less than good is all it takes for poor performance.

What would the patterners say, after all that beautiful cross-pattern reptile stuff we had poured in? They even used the term midbrain occasionally! Would they think the staff here was stymied over Jane? Were they? Might Jane never talk? A lot of people had given up on her talking already. The patterners were often jittery, covering up lack of progress with talk about everything in the world, but not about her. I was going to cry. I had been on the verge of crying and barely breathing for some time. Till the last two weeks of speech-copying from the tape. Just don't look at Bert and I will be all right.

The man was saying something to Bert about, "Yes, you can pattern for more than five minutes at a time." He suggested seven, but not more. Seven minutes is a long time. Not for Jane. But for patterners to do it perfectly. Don't slop it up with a lot of aberrations. Tell the brain what we want it to feel. Just that.

Another thing we might try—(He was giving up?) They are doing some very interesting research at Princeton on the auditory system. It's called visual-tactile deprivation. Take everything out of the kid's world except auditory feed-in. Make a channel just for that. For listening. Make the brain concentrate on sound. Darken the room pitch black—well, then paint the white walls black. Cover her hands and feet with socks. Let her lie in her bed like that. Talk to her for ten minutes like that, twice a day. She is to see nothing, feel nothing. She's to *hear* only.

Oh, my God. They are giving up on Janey—or he wouldn't be so desperate, running out to try something from Princeton. Didn't The Institutes have an answer?

He corrected me. Most of the "programs" here to influence the brain had come from piecing together ideas from all over the world. Whatever is being researched, whatever might use the brain—that was the business

The Institutes was in. Don't knock it. They were in touch with whatever is being learned "out there." They made it their business long ago.

And we see thousands of children, more than all the hospitals around here put together, and we're learning from them, the children. Today we are learning from Jane. And you parents. And tomorrow we will learn some more. And we sit up nights putting it all together. We stop being medical doctors, physical therapists, speech people here. We become "functionalists." We become "cyberneticists." We think about getting to that little girl's computer there. Her computer has circuit breaks that no other child has. We are looking for circuit reinforcers for Janey.

We do not know whether this will help or not. But soon we will know whether to throw it out and try something else. There are hundreds, thousands, of things you can do to influence her auditory system. Time is short. We have to find the best. By the time you come back, we will know even more. Because we know a lot more than when you were here last time. About the auditory system and about Jane.

Now I knew we were going to try anything. Jane was not about to "catch up," by herself. Maturation, everybody called it. Whatever, neurologically she was going nowhere in speech. The world would treat her like an idiot without it. Unless she could say, "Don't talk to me like that. I understand you. I just have a speech problem." If only she could get to where she could just say those three sentences. Then she could go "out there." (Even if she couldn't walk well.) If she had to listen to everyone's baby talk back to her, she would become that baby, a dull drifting thing without a challenge, without a friend in this world. Except the compassionate ones. But without real companionship, real passion. Without someone to love her. How could you call it living, without that? She would dry up without speech, frustrated unto death.

She knee-walked the perimeter of the place, putting it all in order. Even the toes of the shoes—the funny ones used to keep walkers off their feet and on their stomachs—all were in a straight line as we rose to leave. The mobility man looked at me when I tossed it off with a respectful smile.

"Rigidity."

"What?"

"She's quite rigid. Rigidity is part of her picture."

"You mean it has something to do with brain injury?"

"Oh, yes."

"You mean it's unhealthy to be so neat?"

"You wouldn't want her to go through life that way, would you?"

"No, I suppose not. Perfectionism can be a pain to other people."

"And to herself."

"Is that some visual level she's on?"

"No, that's awareness, or the lack of it. A poor auditory system. She's tuned the rest of the world out—too completely."

I turned to Mary, "You once said, 'Jane has an attention span *too long* in some ways, she persists at an activity not at all appropriate for her age.' You caught this a long time ago."

Mary, quite solemn, said, "But I was glad to see her directed to any activity at one time. Remember back then?"

Jane has a damaged auditory system. I knew that. But I never thought about it. Really. Jane is not going to catch up. Perhaps never now. Maybe she will never tune in sharply to that world out there. *O God, let her perceive the world.* Let her take it in, even if she can't talk about it. Don't let her be content to straighten up the shelves all her life.

PART IV

Breakthrough

Output is that which you can *see*. Walking and talking, yes. Writing, yes. Reading, no; that's visual. Understanding, no; that's auditory. Tactile differentiation (heads from tails without looking), no.

You can't see reading. You can't see comprehension. You can't see the sensory coming in, only the motor going out. You can have Janey or Johnny check the correct answer to the questions at the end of the paragraph. But that takes writing—output. You can have reading aloud. But that takes speech—output. You can have it all acted out. But that takes mobility—output.

Brain-injured kids don't have (or have lousy) output. In speech we went through Jane's having "none" and then "lousy." Intellectually we were glad. Emotionally I think there were times we wished for "none" again. With "none" there is nothing to see to judge. The child looks quiet, studying everything in a book over there, happy.

When Janey talked . . . we . . . well . . . It's easier to show than to tell. Go into a room and close the door. (Yes, put the book down.) Now: hold your breath, don't exhale, and say "juice." While you're there, try "orange juice" for the fun of it. Do it again, but this time *really* hold your breath and listen to how it sounds. Now try a sentence. It'll leave you wrung out, but I'd honestly rather have you try that *one time* than read any of this diary.

Now you know why I suggested closing the door. It's nothing you'd want to share with anyone. It looks stupid as hell. To Jane it was probably a fighting hell, a fiery effort to exhale, a breathless brimstone void. One thing I know, she didn't try it much.

With lousy speech, though, we could *see* her respiration problem for the first time. And I could have kicked myself all around the globe for generally ignoring her masking program the last three years.

One good thing, it didn't look stupid to Janey. It helps to live through the days with the brain-injured, if your Jane or John has a poor auditory competence because they don't comprehend enough to compare "them" and me. They don't "know." Fortunately most of them are lousy at auditory —low on the ladder of listening, tuning in, getting it—a far cry below an 80-to-100 percent good comprehension of abstract concepts. As Doman had said, they don't have psychological problems about themselves because they are not up to abstract comparison yet; functionally, they are not a six-year-old. They don't even understand this abstract concept: stupid.

I said "most." But, remember, there are all degrees—from severe neurological loss to losses that are subtle, almost undetectable—in auditory dysfunction alone. One notable exception to "has a poor auditory competence" I have mentioned before—the drunken-looking-slob-of-a-guy coming toward you, weaving and jerking all around the sidewalk, saliva running down his chin, trying to tell you something in a flat, unintelligible monotone, out of a mouth drawing to one side: what the label-makers tagged "the athetoid" about twenty years ago. That guy flailing his arms all around at you, who's so offensive you're trying to avoid him, might very well be a college grad *summa cum.* So many of them are known to be more of a "physical case" than a "mental case," whatever that means. (The brain-split many therapists make here seems to boil down to smart and ugly vs. dumb but better-looking.) Anyway, he knows where it's at and he knows your disgust.

Others, such as the spastic Janes, by the way, are the ones you feel sorry for. They are hugging their elbows to their sides, thigh hugging thigh, tiny-stepping along from bent knees down in a daintier bounce. They are not all over the sidewalk. The spastic walk just looks pitiful— it doesn't scare you to death. They, too, like the rest of the population, may be very smart or very dumb or somewhere in between. But some, like Janey in 1968, are not with it enough to even sense your charity.

We started doing a 500 percent input program for the first time, just after that March 26, 1968 revisit to Philadelphia. We had seen Janey through new glasses: the tuned-out child. No longer would we brag about her attention span.

In fact, we stopped bragging about Janey altogether. Most of the time we were holding *our* breaths. And working.

And in the wake of our work, a very natural thing happened. We began to see Jane. See her do, that is. Output. The Big Three—walking, talking, and writing.

Output doesn't start with the Big Three. Walking has its beginnings with the involuntary movement of arms and legs—"fish" undulating on its belly. Speech starts with the birth cry. Writing starts with the grasp reflex. And there are dozens and hundreds of in-betweens. (In Philadelphia they will tell you they had a rough time deciding what to leave out in the blocks on the Doman-Delacato Developmental Profile, the first such profile on neurological development in the literature. Quite unconventionally their Profile does not deal in milestones. A milestone is an end in itself; sitting is an example of a milestone. The functions they profiled in developmental stages are *means* to ends.)* You, parents, may have caught moments of movement or sound I didn't in my notes. But if you look at what Janey achieved in Part III of this diary (you can recap it better in my lists in the Appendix) you will see some important steps to the Big Three—*sensory* steps to output, especially.

So, in and among the "downs" of those last eighteen months, Janey had arrived at some important "ups." She emerged a bit higher out of the animal, into the human. She began with output to be a child—not a pet or a project.

She would go on to become a kind of input to *us.* Programs were to get more bizarre, more difficult to execute, her program-day even longer, and her stamina—and ours—incredible, even to us. We began to admire her. A kind of respect emerged. We began to call her "Jane" almost exclusively.

We just stopped the nicknames altogether. Sometime along that way we stopped talking about her and gradually started talking *to* her. As a person.

These two chapters are the delicious beginnings of that output, the fun a diary should be—the diary of a child.

---

* For a discussion of how the Profile was devised to give the clinician a practical schema based on ontogenic, functional, developmental, and clinical considerations (including the assignment here to the functional midbrain the functions of other structures, such as the cerebellum, basal ganglia, etc.) see *Human Neurological Organization* by Edward B. Le Winn, M.D. (Springfield, Ill.: Charles C. Thomas, 1969).

8

From March 1968 to October 1968

APRIL 11, 1968. I had just stopped the car in the driveway, turned around to say, "Wait till I get a raincoat, and I'll carry you." But I never said it. She was at the side window, her index finger ever so cautiously tracing the little hieroglyphics through the fogginess. The back window was filling up again, but she had been there too. Probably at some red light on the way back from Louise's house. I could make out some circles, maybe a balloon or two and faces.

What a night, I had been thinking. How sorry I was feeling for myself, having to carry Jane back and forth to the car, the boys and Bert at a ball game and how she's too heavy to manage with an umbrella at the same time.

And I watched her, now at the back window again, drawing fluidly against the street light. And I was thanking the rain for coming. Just sitting there, trying to believe it. Janey *drawing* on the windows. Through the rearview mirror, just hoping this was the beginning of something.

APRIL 12, 1968. Each morning after the last patterner says "Good-bye, Janey" and waits for her to struggle through "Bye-bye," a stillness settles down onto J. and me (and the house!)—just us "three" there now—as I begin the last set of Strumpels I will do until tomorrow.

I force myself to do those twenty on the bad right leg first, while I whisper-count, then loud-count, then laugh-count, then high-count, then low-count my way through the teens into the magic twenty.

I could feel sorry for myself— She is struggling so through the mid-count, that awful eleven and twelve spot— She is the one who should gripe. And she doesn't. She looks back at me and smiles a little, as I say, "That was excellent. What a big gorgeous Strumpel!" And it was. The left foot is lifting higher today. Several times. And I'm pulling back a little harder. And she's taking it like a trouper. For some reason, I am proud of us both. I depend on her. She depends on me. You can do it, I can do it. We're getting in 120 a day now, Dear Heart. You keep getting more flicker there, I'll get more flicker here. My staying power is a thin thread. You make it stronger when you try so hard. You quit, I quit. Do you understand how I depend on you? On those ankles?

APRIL 16, 1968. Bert's father died yesterday. Quietly. He just didn't say anymore. After commenting upon Stuart's visit yesterday, saying what a fine young man he had turned out to be. And that was all.

I couldn't quite find the words for Bert. I sat with him on the sofa when he came home. Waited for him to settle back into this house, this life again. I had such urgent news myself. Mother's doctor in Chattanooga called. Mother was in the hospital with cardiac insufficiency. What did that mean? What could I do? I could change her life, that's what. I could move her out of the old three-floor homestead into an apartment where there would be an elevator and maintenance service. Mother's painting and papering days were over. I should do it while she's in the hospital.

He looked at me. "When are you leaving?"

"After the funeral. I've made the arrangements. Louise will come here. All day. The patterners and the teen-agers will cover the program. There's nothing for you to think about, really, Bert. Bert, the boys are waiting in the bedroom. It's midnight, I know. I know this seems strange, but it's your birthday, you know— But they thought it would cheer you up— Just a few little things they have for you——"

He smiled, "Sure, it's O.K. I'm O.K." I brought them in, each carrying a paper bag.

He glanced at the turtleneck, the tennis shorts—"Thank you, that's very thoughtful, fellas, very pretty."

And they said something about being sorry, he was very old and very sick, wasn't he? And Bert said yes, he was, and now Grandmother at his side all these months would have some time for herself, and maybe that was a good thing. And they said happy birthday and went on to bed.

APRIL 18, 1968. Chattanooga. Mother was dozing when I reached the hospital late in the morning. She hadn't known I was coming. She saw the big suitcase, and I explained I would be staying awhile. Doctor's orders were to find a place for her and move her in.

As soon as I had walked through the downstairs rooms, the telephone rang. Long distance from New York—

"Hey, Mom, this is Grant. You know Smokey?"

"Yes, Grant, I can hear you——"

"You know Smokey? Supposed to go to the vet?"

"Yes, dear, her appointment is for two-thirty. I told Dizzy. Her mom is going to drive you. Be sure to ask the vet the date— Or an approximate one— And what to do— Get a booklet if——"

"Mah-um. I'm trying to tell you. They're getting born today."

"No, dear, she's just going to the vet for a checkup——"

"Mah-um, will you listen! Smokey has two puppies. Right in my bed. One is black and——"

"Grant! Smokey gave birth since I left this morning? Do you mean it?"

"Yes, no— It's three now. Just a minute——"

"Grant— Grant— Hey!" and I started to whistle. I tapped on the phone.

"Hey, Mom, she's not finished. Dizzy thinks she's having another one——"

"Grant, just a minute. Just a minute. Tell Dizzy to come to the phone."

"She can't— She's— Just a minute——"

"Grant!" I waited. My heavens——

"Do I get extra pay for this? You call this baby-sitting?" It was Dizzy.

"Oh, my golly, Dizzy, how in the world did this happen? She didn't look that big. She was supposed to go to the vet today to find out——"

"I know all about it. But I called the vet and he told me what to do."

"What do you do?"

"Oh, don't worry— I got here at twelve and at twelve-ten she had the first one. Well, I almost walked right back out."

"Listen, Diz, you'd better not set one foot out of that house. Anyway think of all you're learning——"

"Just a minute——"

"Diz— Dizzy! Grant!"

"Hey, Mom, can I have first choice?"

"Stuart, is that you?"

"Yes, you said I could keep one— Dad said——"

"Heavens, Stuart, everything is happening so fast. Let's talk about it when I get back."

"Just a minute——"

"Stuart— Stu! Grant! Somebody!" I could hear them all in the background. Who was that squealing? Was that Jane?

"Hey, Mom, four so far. You should see them. They're all over everywhere. Two black and two some other color. Smokey is a nice little mother. Dizzy says she's giving them a bath first thing!"

"Grant, where is Smokey now? This very minute."

"On my bed— But Dizzy is trying to move her to a box. We're using the box with the Little League equipment."

"Grant! Did you take all the uniforms out?"

"Of course, you think we're retards?"

"Let me speak to Dizzy again."

"She's busy."

"I know. Look, go ahead and be very helpful. Leave the puppies alone.

Smokey will be very protective. And very jealous—and where is Janey right now?"

"We know all about it. Oh, oh, she's having another one— Well, bye!" And he hung up. Just like that.

The phone rang. Right in my hand. I knocked the lamp over. It was my brother, inviting me to his house up on the lake for the night. Lay plans for Mother. Maybe take a boat ride tomorrow.

"What about a drink? Do you have any liquor-stuff for a beat-out older sister? This afternoon?"

"Hey, when did you start all that afternoon stuff?"

"I'm starting today. I've been meaning to for a long time!"

MAY 1, 1968. I dragged into the house at 4:00 A.M.

Bert said, "Happy Anniversary."

I said could we celebrate this one later. And could he take me to the physical therapist in the morning? My back was one long spasm. And sitting on the plane hadn't helped. And standing in the airport parking lot all night waiting for the service car hadn't either.

Did I see the puppies?

"All I can see right now is stars, Bert. Tell me about Jane. Something good. Anything happening?"

"She's talking a lot. Just says everything you ask her to."

"That's what I wanted to hear. Good night, Bertie, I'm just going to lie here with my clothes on for a few hours. Did she miss me?"

"I don't think so. But she said your name a lot."

"Did she?"

"Yep. Grant told her you were in Chattanooga, Tennessee. That stopped it every time."

"I bet. I can hardly say that myself."

"How is old Chattanooga?"

"I don't know. I only saw its hospital and each of its apartments. I was really busy, Bert—you should see what we did in ten days!"

"Does your mother like it?"

"I guess so. It's perched out on the banks of the Tennessee with acres of birdcalls around it. Her balcony overlooks everything but a magnolia. And it reminds her of Lucerne. I didn't even leave a hammer in the place."

"That sounds nice."

"Boy, wouldn't that be great? How would you like to spend the next fourteen years in an apartment without a lawn mower? Or even a hammer? Or a dog? Someday, I hope we can do just that, Bertie. When this is all over——"

"All what?"

"All this busy-busy. Do you think we are busier than other people?"

"I don't know, Peggy. But I'd hate to get any busier."

"Me too. I don't think the program can get any busier, that's one thing. It just couldn't, could it?"

"No. It's lots busier than that time I kept her. Was that just last Labor Day?"

"Uh-huh. Let's see— Yes, that must have been last September. Seems far away though."

"G'night."

"G'night."

MAY 7, 1968. Well, now what do you do when you walk into your daughter's bedroom and find walls, built-ins, closet doors, and playhouse-front covered with scribble-scrabble? You beam, that's what.

Louise was ready to wash it off. "Let's leave it one day more. Maybe she'll add to it tomorrow." I went around, eyeing each pastel chalk stroke. There were continuous circles mostly, like that first lesson in penmanship the first grade teacher punishes you with! But there were a few half circles, no, curves, little curves. And some of it was in crayon. She must have been here twice then. Great.

"I think she's over the hump, Louise. Or out of the slump, as the boys would say.

"Hey, come over here. Look at this. I think she drew a crawl box. See the slats going this way between the two lines going that way? We used to do that, two summers ago, hoping she'd try it herself, vertical lines sitting between two parallel ones. Ah, and here's Daddy."

"Let me see Mr. Napear! Maybe we'd better not show him that!"

"Oh, he loves it. You know, every kid does this. I wonder what happens on That Day? To make them go to the walls and start? What triggers it? Funny, isn't it?"

The eye sees the big expanse? The hand moves with the eye? Or is it the other way around? I wonder what got the cave man up to the walls? Was it his vision changing to stereopsis, looking out and around instead of down and around on all fours? Did it happen when he started standing on his hind legs? Did he see the shadow-pictures from the fire? Or the dirt dusting off to leave its own faded picture? Did he see his own shadow and draw one like it? Did he have to go through circles and straight lines first? What sparked the very first time for each cave-dweller?

MAY 12, 1968. She is so sweet, such fun to please, I hate to pull away at night. Bedtime is the only time we have to drift, to take our time, to really look long at one another. She is so pretty again, her hair in its cute pixie shape, her eyes looking straight much of the time, her dimples so sly, so shifting, her smiles all so changing because of the dimples.

I've taken to stopping awhile at her bed. For a nursery rhyme or two. She's not going to be young much longer. It started that other night, when I leaned over to love her, rubbed her back, and she said, "Choo-choo" and I did "Down at the station . . . See the little choo-choos all in a row." When I had finished she murmured, "T-w-winkle, t-w-winkle," and I did, "little star." Then followed the requests for "Zipadeedoodah," "I See the Moon," "Fuzzy Wuzzy" "Fa-la-la" ("Deck the Halls"), "Deedle-Deedle" ("My Son John"), "Sing a Song of Sixpence," "Eensy Weensy"—all her favorites. What a memory this child has. And how she pushes those titles out, between breaths. That was the first time for nursery rhymes since November. I could have stayed all night just to hear those words in request after request. But I shouldn't. She needed her sleep. Tomorrow was another big day.

But how I love these cradling moments, the two of us in the dark, just her voice, then mine. I should really paint the walls black and put socks on her hands and feet, but I know I'll never do that Princeton auditory thing, since speech is slipping back. We simply don't have the time.

I like this better. No program. Just together. Rubbing her back. I know I am saying good-bye to the nursery years. For Jane's sake I should. There will be the grandmother years. Everybody says they are the best. I doubt that. How could a grandmother ever know a child this well? How could she ever love this well? Yes, Jane's babyhood—the first one, and this one we're doing again—has been love-filled, by so many darling people. But would her adulthood be? How loving she is—with people, with dolls, with all those people in the books— Oh, for her it must be. Now and on and on through marriage and memories with her own little ones.

MAY 30, 1968. Memorial Day for two of the Four. For Cathy Lovelock! Jane said her name for the first time!

She did not say "Marilyn." But she said "nine" as Marilyn traced J.'s finger over the hard glitter-surface of the red numeral on the ninth crawl-box trip. Marilyn said it was almost as good as saying her name. I'd say. Marilyn told me last time she was here—was it yesterday?—she thought J. stared at the 9 more than any other number. I agreed. Maybe because it's a circle and a line? Funny, I thought kids always got 9 and 6 the last thing, or mixed up.

Sweet kids. Almost wet-eyed when they told me. Cathy gets breathless, bubbly. Marilyn presses her lips together and nods her head up and down as I exclaim, ask questions, and generally try to picture what I missed.

"What is this girl's name, Janey?"

"Ca-ky."

As they did the last set of Strumpels I stood amazed. They do them every bit as well as I. In fact, Cathy does them stronger than I do, and still gets J. to the next one.

I watched Marilyn then do the other leg, holding her hand on J.'s knee, waiting so patiently for Jane to begin, and urging her with gentle praise and an unafraid firmness, mature beyond her years. There is a straight-from-the-shoulder truth about her way with Janey. She simply likes Jane and sees no need to pamper her. And Jane performs for her. It's almost as if she wouldn't want to let Marilyn down!

As they were leaving, we talked of her guts, this child. And our guts to stay with it. But you could tell it was working, stronger ankles you could see. And how cooperative she is.

Marilyn turned back and brought the card over to Janey, "What's the name of this number, Jane?"

"Ni-ine."

"Thank you for coming on your holiday. That means more than you know."

"Oh, it was worth it."

"Yeah, today was the greatest!"

"I hope you girls are happy about the right thing. Recognizing numbers isn't what's great. It's the speech—right? It's the volume. To be able to say 'nine.' "

"It's all of it, Mrs. Napear."

JUNE 5, 1968. In this awful nightmare could there be one tiny good thing? Maybe. For all the Robert Kennedys. For all the Janes. Over the network to millions of viewers the doctor was describing what will become of Robert Kennedy should he live. About injury to the midbrain. And what that means in dysfunctions. What the midbrain controls.

I hoped other doctors were listening. Several had told me no one knew the function of the midbrain. But this doctor does. And he was the expert they had called to interview. Yes, you can *tell by dysfunction* that you have a midbrain injury. He mentioned eye-tracking ability, but he did not go into the sordid picture of crossed eyes. And respiration, that ability to breathe long and beautifully through a sentence, or two, or three. And then he said it was now thought that certain movements which occur before walking are controlled there too. He did not say creeping on hands and knees, and I wasn't sure he knew.

In the midst of all my despair I heard these few minutes of hope. He was saying some things—truly important things—were not in the human cortex, the gray matter. Some were lower down. The midbrain is a mystery, but research is now discovering it plays a valuable part in human development. This man was not from The Institutes. He did not seem weird. And he was affiliated with a hospital, and that was always a good thing.

Oh, don't give up on Bobby Kennedy, I wanted to cry. His thoughts will still be racing through his head. Don't give up on midbrain injury. We need him so. Even if it takes years before we hear them again.

And I found myself crying out to myself. Don't ever give up on the brain. It's too much a mystery. Not what it can't do. But what it *can* do.

JUNE 9, 1968. Delicious moments: Jane said "Holly" today. Well, "Ha-ee" really. She can say *l*'s, but I think it's lost in the taking of the breath.

"She didn't say my name," Laurie said. Then she laughed. "My cousin always had trouble with that one too!"

Janey was eavesdropping again. In the middle of all this she looked over her *Life* magazine and said, "War-ee."

We all but hung on the living room rafters!

"Look, let me show you something." And I put J. down on the floor for a few crawls out of the box. "See those toes moving— Look at the left big toe. Quick, see that? That foot is beginning to point its toes out to the side. The beginning of the toe-dig, I bet a million dollars. It's not much," I told them. "But it's the start we've been looking for."

"That's simply great."

"Yep, she's getting into the right position for it. I think I'll put that in the term paper I'm doing——"

"I thought you finished that."

"This is another one about 'the program'—for social studies."

"You can also put in the fact that you two are as good as any physical therapist I could hire for Janey."

It was less a pep talk than a thank you and a prayer. Her heel cords are stretching. Her feet are moving. And maybe someday she will get off her toes and go down to heels. And walk.

JUNE 12, 1968. Called IAHP about the head shaking, so intense now, more frequent.

Jane has "involuntary head tremors with facial tic." Could be seizure equivalent. May be associated with speech spurt. Perhaps a good sign rather than bad. We're into something we haven't been into before—brain-wise? We're getting some electrical discharging through uncharted territory? Could also be related to sentence "concentration." Often higher visual ability produces this. Check it out on revisit—two weeks.

Just wait and see. Looks awful. People will think she's getting worse. But functionally she really is getting better.

JUNE 16, 1968. He didn't hear her the first time. The second time he did.

"Gwant."

He closed the refrigerator door. "What's my name?" as he walked ever so slowly to her table.

"Gwant. Juz."

"Janey wants juice? Janey wants Grant to get her juice?" And he skipped back.

"Just a quarter-inch, Grant."

"Hey, Mom, she said 'Grant.' "

"I know, I was listening in here. What you say, Monkey, is that your birthday present this year, do you expect?"

He came in wringing his hands, eyes like saucers in dramatic exaggeration, "Well, she's about two days early! But she sure knows it now."

"She's always known it, Honey. Saying it was the problem."

"Well, she doesn't know it's my birthday Tuesday. Now don't start telling me that she does."

"No, I wouldn't tell you that. But she knows you're going to be nine. That's her favorite number."

"It is?"

"Yes, want to see?"

"Yeah, what other numbers does she know?"

"You mean what other numbers can she say?"

"Yeah, that's what I mean."

"Nothing else yet."

"Hey, that's coo—tough. Only nine? Does she know how old Stuart is?"

"No. We were just talking about your candles today."

"That's what I figured, I didn't think she knew Stuart's age yet."

"Jane, what number is this?" And I held up the green nine.

"Ni-ine."

Grant almost touched her this time. Not a dig, but a touch. He leaned into her face and said, "Excellent." Then back into the playroom he followed me, where I was folding laundry. "She says that perfect. Exactly like we do."

"Yes, all her speech is getting clearer and clearer."

"I know. I told Mrs. Hefner."

"Oh, does Mrs. Hefner often ask about Janey?"

"Yeah. Everybody does."

"I can imagine why. Because this program is new and kind of special. And Janey's progress is special to a lot of people."

"You mean how she's talking the right way now."

"Yes, her enunciation is better, she has more breath now for the endings."

"I'm the best in my class in enun— That's why I get the plays. I'm the loudest from the stage." And he took a deep breath.

"Yes, everyone in the family has a loud speaking voice. Ugh."

He giggled and looked sideways at me. "Well, it's important."

"You bet it is. And we will go on with Jane, because it is so important. And this house will still have to have all the visitors, you know."

"I know. We have more visitors than anyone else."

"Yes. Which would you rather have? A lot of visitors? Or a few visitors like other houses?"

"I think I'd rather have in between. Like just have Mrs. Perlstein and a few others, and Mrs. Wallace and Mrs. Goldstein. And Dizzy's mother."

JUNE 26, 1968. Met Marilyn's mother and Cathy's mother tonight. After all these years! Here to talk about their daughters' help in Maine.

Jane had finished eating. And was listening. I explained I don't usually feed her supper on her patterning table, but I cut corners after taking the housekeeper home tonight. Wetson's hamburgers. "Jane, collect your garbage and put it on the hamburger papers, please."

Jane picked up the crumbs and then clenched the papers in a wad and handed them to me.

"Isn't that remarkable!"

"It's amazing, just unbelievable——"

Typical remarks.

As Mary wondered, will Jane have to run into the doctor's office and say hello and his name before he'll think she's improving? When we were there for the thyroid-level check yesterday, Jane must have looked the very same. And still on the floor in that wacky program when what the child needs is to get those tendons cut, the legs braced, and get on her feet? And don't expect too much, then you won't be hurt later? I wonder if he thinks like the rest? Or have I become terribly defensive, with those wild medical cautions about the program running rampant over the metropolitan area.

JUNE 28, 1968. Philadelphia. The copy of the report to Jane's local doctors and Mary Lawrence said it this way:

Mobility: Cross-pattern crawling and creeping. Very pleased to note increased ankle action even though she is still not using same for propulsion in crawling. Superb knee-walking.

Speech: Speech has reached a point of breakthrough in terms of increased vocabulary and combinations.

Manual: Continued improvement in dexterity, but not writing as yet. [Naturally she would draw nothing while in Philly!]

Vision: Alternate convergent strabismus persists . . . about the same. Mother is working on sentences and doing well.

Auditory: Improved comprehension, but restricted by the fact she will only work for her mother. [Down there, that is.]

Tactile: Good stereognosis.

Dominance: [Hand and ear midline to right this time. Everything else the
same.]

Seizures: Developed periods of shakiness and a facial tic during past period.
May be seizure equivalent.

Other: Periods of tic and shakiness bear watching. Orthopedic plans should
be deferred until later, awaiting further progress in comprehension and
speech.

In summary, I'm pleased with Jane's overall progress.

And then it was signed by one of the directors. Well, now everything but
vision was on the up and up, but no one was hollering. No scoring increase
again.

To get any further credit in speech she has to reach a Matterhorn of
sorts: consistent short sentences, combinations of three to five units. Good
grief.

To get any further credit in mobility she has to crawl perfectly (with toe
propulsion) and creep perfectly (with knees relaxed for consistent foot-
trailing.)

So, no one was hollering.

Again I was told, "Don't get bogged down in the minutiae, Mrs.
Napear." And again I said, "I'm not bogged down. I live on it."

But isn't there anything we can holler about?

Yes. Jane Napear is ready for a teacher. A fuller academic program.
Reading, writing, and arithmetic! One of the IAHP doctors will request our
school district to furnish a home-bound teacher.

But will they?

Their job is to furnish education to every child in their district. That is
the business they are in.

I looked at Bert. He was saying an old college buddy was moving to our
district to be the assistant superintendent of schools and maybe he could
help us. His wife patterns children where they live now.

Use pull if we like. But there shouldn't be any trouble. Jane should have
a teacher. At home. Because she has a lot of work to do all day. I was glad
the Philly folks were able to see the forest.

Spoke too soon. It looked as if they were going for broke this time. The
eye-following exercises were so numerous it was suggested they be done at
meals, using food as the pursuit object! God-help-us-all, Bert was thinking.
I knew that wide-eyed expression.

The crawl box was to be elevated gradually at one end to eighteen inches
off the floor. And widened. To allow possible toe-digs out to the side.

We would begin giving her dot cards for quick visual discrimination.
Don't worry, if kids see these enough, they can recognize them fast—up to
twenty dots and more and more. But just do up to ten now.

And sentences in story form. The books I would make. (I could have told you.) Go easy on the reading, just make interesting books and feed it in. Her teacher will take it from there.

It looked like a long day, anyway you scheduled it. And I wondered if Jane or I would see the lake at all this summer.

He was saying something important. Bert was writing it down. Jane may have only a regular elementary teacher. She may not have a teacher familiar with brain-injured children. This is no special ed request. The teacher should have no idea, no preconceived notions of what a brain-injured kid can and cannot do. We only want her to know Jane. If we get the right teacher, she will know Jane soon enough.

What if the district suggests she go to one of those special schools?

She can't. She's busy. Getting well so she won't ever have to go to one of those schools—or one of those classes—if we have anything to say about it.

I was thinking how I could get more program in each day. Bert was asking about those "special" classes in case she didn't.

We never want Jane in a group situation with other brain-injured kids.

We don't?

No. We want her to copy normal behavior, normal speech. Kids tend to mimic what they see around them. We want Jane's model to be the highest, the most enriched sensory environment we can provide. That's what this program is all about.

JULY 7, 1968. Maine. Arrived the Fourth of July. Bert helped us settle in before returning. Crazy trip here, the passing cars and the toll men definitely aware our two cars were "together": Bert's with two eight-foot crawl boxes stacked on top; my car, looking like the Winged-Witch-of-the-West with patterning table upside down on top, filled with suitcases, legs for anchors for two bikes, standing against the wind, flapping three orange life preservers from the handlebars. Bert carried third bike inside his car, along with Grant and his dog, who lay on J.'s crib mattress, her ears just brushing the ceiling, her nose just grabbing the inch of air left by windows closed against the packings inside. Good thing Stu was still at 4-H camp. Our car was just as crowded: Janey, Philippa, and me crammed together.

Philippa so different from her cousin Dizzy. Or maybe alike in different ways? Running commentary about boys, cars, and boys and cars. Eats anything, drinks "seven and seven." ("Is that like Seven-up?" "Yes, and Seagram's Seven.") Puts her fingers in her mouth and whistles to call Grant. Says "Cool it" to get rid of him. He adores it all. Paradoxically has most natural maternal warmth with Jane I ever saw. Did all maskings with J. on trip here without batting an eyelash. No reaction to my introduction to

J. of ⬜ **gas station** ⬜ and ⬜ **restaurant** ⬜ . Not curious about program or brain, as Diz was. Vacation for *my* brain.

Our living room here is a conversation piece around the lake, they say. New 44-inch-wide crawl box sections down the middle third of the room, shy just one yard of the double glass doors leading to the porch. Other end is solid against the back door, closed permanently for the summer.

BOYS' SCHEDULE IN MAINE

9:00–1:00	Jane's program, chores (personal and family), beach
1:00–5:00	free time
5:00–6:00	
or 7:00	"special adventures"
7:00	supper
till 9:00	quiet games, cards during J.'s program
9:00–9:30	Family story-time (*Huckleberry Finn*) at kitchen table.

Stu is doing Strumpels with Jane now. Grant very good with morning crawl-box routine, including visual pursuits. ("Jane, make believe this is an airplane . . .") They spend morning discussing plans for free time. Usually take a picnic and go fishing with kids around the lake.

JULY 13, 1968. Beach scene: Jane pouring from cup to cup with occasional pauses to mark in the sand. Telling Phil I must write this to her cousin (Dizzy). This she won't believe. We used to think up crazy ideas to get her to do both activities. Push and pull all the way.

"How many shovels of sand have you done, Grant?"

"Ten. That makes seventy for me. Can I do the other ten this afternoon?"

"No, twenty this morning."

"Boy, you can't even see where I put my ten. She keeps creeping over the pile."

"And that's exactly what we're doing it for. A few more days we'll be finished."

Philippa to me: "You know, I've written fourteen letters and haven't gotten a one."

"You will. Tomorrow we'll bike over to get the mail."

"Why don't you go today, and I'll do the program."

"Are you serious?"

"Sure. I don't mind."

"Don't you hate it?"

"Well, the Strumpels are rough sometimes."

"And the rest is so boring——"

"Yeah, but she's so wonderful about it all."

"Phil, you not only have horse sense about everything, you have a huge heart. That's to soften you up. Before the suggestion: What do you think about going to thirty Strumpels and thirty crawl boxes?"

"You mean thirty Strumpels each time in the afternoon? That's one hundred and twenty. Each leg? Each time?"

"Yes, and in the morning too. She could use the extra ones. That dorsiflexion is really coming now. When we started she had just a little flicker of movement there. Now look at it——"

She made a face. "Do you think she would do it?"

"I don't know. If it's presented right she'll do it. She loves the thirtycount with the flashlight bit in the closet."

"I know. She gets all excited when you get to about twenty-seven."

"Yes, she said 'hirty' yesterday after twenty-nine."

"Oh, yes, she did that with me this morning. I meant to tell you."

"I think she would. This whole program is like that little train. You know, the one that went over the mountain. For some reason, she does whatever she needs to do. It's the part of her I've never understood. It's like a secret she holds. The thing everybody remarks about. What makes her do all this— That's the part that surprises me every single day."

JULY 15, 1968. Lou Geyer's carriage-bolt idea had the two crawl boxes secured together for elevation, a long sixteen feet. Together with Chris and Billy Perrin and their friends, we raised the whole thing at one time, to elevate it eighteen inches at one end. They hung around to watch J. in it.

"Does she do this all day?"

"No, just two hours in the morning and about two and a half hours in the afternoon."

"Wow. She must be very strong."

"She is."

"Look, she likes it. She's kinda cute, isn't she?"

"Yeah, boy, does she always laugh? It must be fun. Wish I could try it out."

"Sure, Billy. She's very happy today to see so many nice boys."

"Does she like boys?"

"Yes."

"I don't like girls."

"Me neither."

"I like her O.K. Can we see her read this year?"

"I don't know— We're making her some new books——"

"Oh, can we see?"

"This one will be called 'The Beach.' "

"Hey, look, pictures of her— Did you take them here?"

"Yes. Here she's having lunch at the lake."

"What are the words going to say?"

"Well, this picture where the pan has floated away— This will say, 'Go get it.' "

"Can she say that?"

"Yes, that's her favorite sentence at the beach. But the other sentences will have new words. Ones she cannot say—yet."

"Mo grah-am crack-er."

"She just said, 'More graham cracker!' "

"Yes, isn't that beautiful? I hope it stays that clear. We got all excited about the gorgeous *marshmallow* word, but now she's calling it 'marsh-ow.' It's probably a shortcut from short breath."

"Hey, Mom, show them the masking!"

"O.K. It's about time anyway." You could have heard a pin drop while the plastic mask was over her nose and mouth, enlarging with each quick breath. Then the mask was off, and you could see her chest moving with the deep breathing.

"What makes that?"

"Oh, it's like when you run hard and pant. Then you stop—it's like removing the mask here—and you reflexively, automatically start taking deep breaths. She needs breath to talk out on. Just try it, boys. Try to hold your breath and talk."

Everybody tried it. Then they laughed. They sounded so stupid. They shuffled around with their heads down. "She's saying everything, now, isn't she?"

"Well, since she got to Maine, she's trying to copy just a whole lot. For her. And bringing it up out of storage and using it too."

"Do you think Maine did it?" Their eyes were wide with the thrill of it all.

"I don't know. Just one of those mysteries we go through with this program."

"But what could it be?"

"She says it's a mystery, Stupid."

"Hey, play the tape. Let 'em hear the new tape, Mom!"

"Not today, Grant. But some other time. It's closet time now. Time for her eye exercise."

"Can we watch her?"

"Not today. But some time during the summer, I'll see that each of you takes a turn in the closet with us. O.K.?"

"Oh, boy, me first."

"Don't worry. I'll get each of you. But don't spread the word around. Just you guys who helped. O.K.?"

"Yeah. Call us when you're ready to make it higher."

AUGUST 2, 1968. I read the "Roomful of Bones" chapter *twice* in Robert Ardrey's *African Genesis.* If it's true that ancient man-ape picked up an antelope bone for a weapon for food-prey or self-preservation, or whatever he did— If he went for a tool *before* he became ape-man— If man-ape-with-tool is the "missing link" before the human ape-man— If Dr. Raymond Dart is correct, if the skulls of *Australopithecus* he found in Africa did reflect a step in brain development—Then hand-use and the need to get up to wield the blow influenced that development. Made the brain something more. Something higher in evolution.

And does so in a baby today. Was the brain "human" before or after tool-use? In *Adventures with the Missing Link* Dr. Dart says *before.* Why? Man started the humanizing of himself when he began standing up. The getting-up mobility starts the cortex to function. Starts the flood of human functions: walking; hands freed for wielding tools, for gesturing and for hand-mouth sound-making of early speech; thumb-to-finger graspings into drawing and eventually writing; and the highest function of all in the sensory-motor system—reading of symbolic language.

And the $64,000 question: Did *Australopithecus* have a big brain and then stand up? (Dart thinks not.) Or did the gradual change, over thousands of years, up and up and up, with all that use, *make* a bigger brain, *make* that cortex the walking, talking, writing thing it is today? Dart thinks that's it.

And in 1960 The Institutes, having just published a two-year study on the treatment of the brain-injured, a treatment directed to the early mobility levels of the human in the *Journal of the American Medical Association,* received this handwritten note from Dart in Africa:

> I have just finished reading your AMA *Journal* article. I hope your method of treatment of brain-injured children is as good as it seems to be. But it is your scale of stages of the normal brain's development that intrigues me.

For, the thirteen levels of mobility that you use as a test of success are precisely the successive stages by which mankind rose, from four-footed animals, to become a unique, walking biped with hands freed to manipulate tools and a brain capable of inventing them. The development of the individual does indeed recapitulate the evolution of the species. More power to you and your work.

And when Glenn Doman and staff were studying the babies of the Kalahari Desert in 1966, they went to see Dr. Dart. And talked and talked about normal and brain-injured children, and the brain's dependence upon mobility levels to organize itself correctly.

And then the happy occasion later that year when Dr. Dart arrived in Philadelphia to head IAHP's new Institute Of Man. Dart joining them in finding ways to program the brain-injured. To recapitulate phylogeny in Philadelphia, even to the nasty business of putting the child down on its belly, that soft vulnerable-to-attack underside of him, which evolution had decided should be down, not up.

All other creatures had put their babies on their stomachs. And the bony vertebral structure on top for protection. It is only man who starts his babies on their backs.

AUGUST 6, 1968. This moment, the sweetest, the best. So far. I love those dear boys. And how they love their sister when she shines.

Phil and I had just moved the patterning table in order to open the windows to let the morning in. That delicious coolness from the pines. The first two patternings, the Strumpels, had left us all hot and exhausted. For a picker-upper we started doing a verb apiece, around the table—*cough, cry, laugh, hiccup.* Jane had loved it. I wondered if this time wouldn't be better spent listening for the nouns on tape. Most of Bert's new tape had stuff outside the home, like *post office, waitress, Wild Root Charlie.* Jane couldn't get enough of either side. And we were sick of it already. So we did the verbs. For us.

Now the sunbeams danced over the whole corner. We began to take our places with a little more bounce.

"Let's do verbs again. Just thought of a good one. W-h-i-s-t-l-e."

I stepped up to the table. "Great, Stu."

"Red . . . Blue . . . Wew-wo . . . Blue——"

She was naming them all. I inched a little closer, stiff as a statue, my new knit jumpsuit— Is this possible? She kept right on down the wide stripes, her finger touching each one.

"Blue . . . red . . . Blue . . . wew-wo—" She doesn't hear *yellow* correctly? How long had she known them?

Philippa edged in, "What color is this, Jane?"

"Gink."

"Yes, pink."

"What color is this, Janey?" I grabbed at Barbara Geyer's shorts and pulled her closer.

"White."

Stuart hoisted himself half onto the table, plunking his shoe against her side. "What color is this, Janey?"

"Black."

Golly, is she saying *bl?*

"Hey, Mom, she knows her col———"

"Sh-h. Don't stop."

Stuart was back with a life preserver. "What color is this, Janey?"

"Or-ge."

She had to breathe in the middle. Oh, my God, she knows the colors.

"What color is this, Janey?" Lou Geyer was pointing to his belt.

Nothing.

"Take it off! So she can see it!"

"That's O.K., Barbara—"

He had it off, holding onto his shorts.

"Belt."

"It's a belt. But what color is it?"

Nothing.

"Brown. This color is brown," Grant was saying as he swung around to our side of the table. He was whipping off his belt. "And do you know this interesting color, Janey?"

Oh, my, the dramatics were beginning. He was so cute, I could have hugged him.

"What color is the buckle, Janey?"

Nothing.

"She hasn't had that yet, Stupid!"

"Stuart, shut up. She's having it now. Silver. This is silver." And he ran out of the room.

"Hey, don't leave. We've got to start."

"Be back in a minute." And he dashed back, grabbing my arm, whispering, " 'g-o-l-d.' Be right back."

Stuart was in the bedroom. And back. With his long-sleeved knit shirt. "What's this color, Jane?"

"G-reen."

Was it *gr* or *gw?* So quiet, hard to tell.

"That's very good, Janey. Gr-r-ee-n. Gr-ee-n and white are Four-H colors."

Barbara, Lou, Phil, and I were like stone, quiet and trembly.

Philippa had the leather holder off her hair. "What color is this, Janey?"

"Ba-woun."

"Good girl!" We were practically all over her. And all at each other. Touching, hugging, exclaiming.

Grant was back.

"Hey, Grant, you just missed the best part!"

"Stuart, stop it."

"Hey, Jane, what color is this?" Grant held up the brass nutcracker we used for lobster nights. He had been to the toolshed.

Nothing.

"She wouldn't know that, Silly!"

"Stuart, cut that out. He's teaching her this very minute."

"Gold. Gold. This color is *gold*. Now, what is it?"

"Go-ld."

"Hey, man, she says 'gold!' "

AUGUST 10, 1968. Called Bert again.

"Now, listen, guess what she did— I had finished the sixteen— I told her the number as I 'sanded' it— As I reached for the next card, she said, 'Se-wan-ten,' like that."

"Wow, she's really going."

"Then she crept back to the water, saying 'eigh-ten' and 'nine-ten!' "

"Well, that's just wonderful—" Bert's voice full of emotion. "You know, that guy last time said the sluice gate was going to open on speech one of these days. And she'd start talking a lot— Do you think that's what has happened?"

"I don't know. It's the biggest speech spurt yet. And it's the most exciting thing I've ever lived through. Bert, she's not talking all the time, or anything. But it's just so much more sophisticated when she does. The verbs are coming now. About twenty of them. And 'in' and 'on'— Did I tell you? Oh, yeah, yesterday. And 'off' and 'away.' Yesterday morning she said, "Take off pink pajamas.""

"Yes, you told me——"

"But it's still a struggle. And so breathless! We're masking like crazy. And, Bert, don't expect too much. I mean, a lot of it is clear— She says the medial vowels right now——"

"What's 'medial vowels?' "

"The ones in the middle. She says short *e* and short *i* words correctly now— She hears them now, I guess. But she still says, 'I don't want e' instead of 'it!' But, Bert, I mean, don't be disappointed if you can't— It's clear, it's correct, a lot of it, but it's so *quiet*. You still have to be close to her——"

AUGUST 19, 1968. Telling Bert teens so unpredictable in their emotional swings.

So excited when they arrived about the Strumpels. What a difference after these Maine six weeks! Both girls keep saying, "Unbelievable!" "Look at this!" "This is even better than yesterday!" With 270 Strumpels for each foot by suppertime each day, we are betting squarely on their going to 90 degrees one of these days.

But when they saw the toe-digs in the crawl box, they just said, "Yes, we noticed it. Isn't that what's supposed to happen?"

"But aren't you excited?"

"Well, we've been working on it four years."

"Four years! Marilyn! You haven't been here that long! We haven't been doing crawling that long. It's two and a half."

"That's funny. I've been saying four years to everybody——"

"Me too. It seems longer," Cathy added.

"And all that time there wasn't much to see in Crawl Baby. But you stayed. And, now, look at this. It was never certain, believe you me. Not with brain injury. We can only try to get it. And if we don't we try harder——"

"Like Avis."

"Like Cathy and Marilyn."

AUGUST 22, 1968. The girls, sunning themselves on the pier, sat up as I shouted, "Now watch!"

And Jane started up the steps. With each terrace she lifted her right knee first. "See?"

"What does that mean?"

"I don't know. But Mary isn't going to believe it. Little Rightie flexing that high. And leading! Used to rub salt on Little Rightie there, just to wake 'er up to feel something."

Marilyn called, "Watching her come down is the greatest though. You'd think she would fall. But she gets that outrigger tail way up in the air and just backs down."

"You're right. I think it's the greatest too. That takes a lot of backward hip movement. Range of movement, the physical therapists call it. And creeping really brings it out. Remember, the hip-socket story? Crawling hollows the sockets sideways, creeping hollows them forwards and back-wards. Then they're ready for walking. That's what the Philly people mean when they say, 'Function determines structure,' not the other way around as some people would still have it. Of course, you're born with some struc-ture—at the hip, you've got the acetabular notch, but you have to hollow it out, finish it, make it a socket with function.

"She couldn't do that last year. This year she did it the first week. She's bigger too. That helps. Indirectly, that is. We can't carry her down here anymore!"

Bert, back from golf with the boys, called from the top, "Hi, Miss Swim-Girlus! Did you come all the way up from the beach by yourself? Such a big girl! Ready for lunch? Hey, you're so wet, getting pine needles all over Daddy——"

"Pi-ne nee-dles."

"Say, Miss Magpie, you're just the cutest, most wonderfulest— Let's get out of these messy panties— Hey, Peggy. Stay on down. Stu and I will give you gals a break——"

"You'll do the program?"

"Yep."

"It takes at least three hours now, you know. We put in another thirty, that's five sets of Strumpels——"

"O.K."

Cathy was saying, "I can't get over Janey, doing all this all day."

"You mean the program so full?"

"Exactly." Marilyn was up on her elbows. "We were talking about it last night. You know, when you work only in the afternoons for a couple of hours, you don't get any idea that she does this stuff *all* day."

"I thought you knew. You've patterned in the mornings——"

"But you don't live through it. You don't see the middle, or the night. She's so cute at night with those stories. You don't get to know Jane, like she really is——"

"That's it," Cathy interrupted, "You don't see how smart she is."

"She understands every single thing."

"But I thought you knew that——"

"But not like this. She's so smart, sometimes it makes me almost— It's all so different, living with her like this, that she does all this——"

"That's true. When you girls or the patterners are working with her, you're putting *in*. Not much chance for Janey to show you, unless you see her at meals, or free time. And, poor kid, even free time has an ulterior motive or two, like creeping."

"That's when she's the cutest, what she finds to do down there— She's so normal in the way she acts!"

"Yes, remember, when we first came, with the whole troop, to do the ramp—she was so, well, so—she wasn't interested in us. As people. She just liked the sounds we made. And she liked the lights. And she screamed a lot, and we had to distract her all the time. She was like a little animal. She was kind of scary. At first."

"I think she still may be to a lot of people," I said.

AUGUST 28, 1968. A clipping:

U.S. EDUCATION OFFICE TO STUDY READING PROCESS

Washington (AP). The U.S. Office of Education announced Wednesday a new research program to fill what it considers a basic knowledge gap: how people read.

In spite of massive research, testing and debate about how reading should be taught, the agency said nobody knows much about the actual processes by which people read.

And the office said such knowledge is needed to develop better methods and materials for teaching reading.

Officials said the gap exists because most research has focused on classroom methods.

The new research will try instead to find out precisely what takes place, when a person reads. It will analyze the complicated function of eyes, brain, chemical changes and even a person's mood when he reads.

Why don't they just call up Carl Delacato and ask him to send them his notes from the last twenty years?

AUGUST 30, 1968. The boys then stopped playing rummy. Like that. And swung around on the bed, legs dangling to the floor without a single sound. I had just asked Janey, "What shall we do now?" with a twinkle in my eye.

"Sto-ry."

I took the dirty clothes to the bag.

"Read a/sto/ry."

Golly, jeepers, I almost sat down. "And which story would you like to hear?"

"Ant/and Bee/Lived/ina/CUP!"

I couldn't say, "good girl" or anything. I walked away into the bedroom, to the pile of books. And brought it back. My knees were rubber, and everything was blurry before me.

Stuart was saying, "Hey, Janey, what story do you want?"

And Grant was saying, "Now that's what I call talking, man." He was standing with his hands on his hips, head forward, in mock surprise.

"I'll read it to her, Mom. Where should I sit?"

"Nice idea, Stu. I hold her in my lap in the chair. But maybe you'd better sit her next to you on your bed. Here, I'll carry her. Don't go through every p-a-g-e. It's too l-o-n-g. Just a few. When you're finished call me for the r-e-a-d-i-n-g."

"I'll do it. I know how. You just go through the sentences and see if her eye is following."

"You can't see her eyes. You have to watch her eyelids. Actually, you don't have to watch anything. Just don't go too s-l-o-w. She hates that."

"I know all about it."

Then he came back. "Hey, Mom, every single p-a-g-e from A to Z. No problem."

"That's great, Stuart. Have you finished?"

"Not yet. I'm letting Jane choose which book for you-know-what. She keeps changing her mind. She is so f-u-n-n-y."

(Jane in huge laughs.)

"Cool it, Jane. We're going to read this one. This is a *very interesting* book. The name of this book is *All About Girls*. Now the first sentence is *'Light the sparkler——'* "

"Stu, cool it a little. Not so much emphasis. She doesn't need that anymore."

SEPTEMBER 3, 1968. We all said good-bye to the lake, the paths, the parking area quiet—Marilyn, Cathy, and I, yes, Jane, most of all—and with a kind of mutual sadness followed Bert's car on out the long dirt road.

We were remembering last night, families gathered on the Perrins' beach for the Labor Day farewell. How directed was Jane's play this year! Directed to people. How we let her stay awhile for the campfire. How still she sat with Marilyn and Cathy. Indian-style, like the others. And how still, no rocking, as we *sang* all her favorite rhymes.

Then the girls said the best thing about Maine was living with Janey. And how no one can tell you. You have to see it for yourself. Then they were shaking their heads with wonder at her now. She was licking the cone, then her tongue would flash out to swipe her lips from left to right, way up over the top lip to catch the bit of ice cream there. Then another lick, then another "napkin."

Then we were home. And Maine was a long, long way behind us. Huge black carpenter ants had taken over the living room. The kitchen. You could see them in huge crawling clusters, running this way and that. The rug looked beige-and-black tweed, there were so many. There were thousands, it seemed, nesting under the papers on the white cabinet. I found them as I reached for the mail and headed back to the car to sleep. Bert took Jane to her room to undress her—none there. The boys to their rooms—none there. They didn't care, they were so tired. Bert shared their apathy. I felt nausea and dread. Bert would go to work, the boys to school, and Jane and I would be left to reach an exterminator first thing in the morning. The flashlight fell upon a letter from our school district. I opened it:

August 14, 1968

Dear Mr. and Mrs. Napear,

The information prepared by Dr. Wilkinson [from IAHP] has been for-warded to me by Dr. Schwartz [Bert's college friend in district administration].

Before responding to your request for home instruction, it will be necessary for the appropriate professionals in [this] District to review this information and conduct a personal evaluation of their own. The educational recommendations emanating from this evaluation will then be discussed with you.

Sometime during the early part of September, after the professional staff has reported to school, I will be in touch with you to make the necessary arrangements for the evaluation.

It is our intention to bring Jane whatever services are judged to be in her best interest. The evaluation will help us to make these judgments. If you have any questions regarding this communication, please feel free to call me at ————. I will be on vacation the week of August 19 and will return on August 26.

Sincerely,
PHILLIP ALLOPENNA, Director
Pupil Personnel Services

SEPTEMBER 4, 1968. My hand was on the phone when it rang. I jumped back. It was Mr. Allopenna's secretary calling. About setting up an ap-pointment for a school psychologist and a reading consultant to evaluate Jane— I was breathing hard. I could only find the words to say there were carpenter ants all over my house, right here on the phone too, and I was trying to locate an exterminator. But I wanted to talk to Mr. Allopenna himself. Before any of that process got underway. I would try to call him later today. And I thought it thrilling that Jane should be contacted this very first day of school. Her brothers would be so pleased.

The exterminator was really cute. His house the same. He just got back from vacation too. It's the dampness. It rained a lot here. Turn on the heat. Have a man here in a few hours to find out where they're coming from. Told him it's where they're going that's bothering me. He agreed, it's a frightening sight.

Jane and I spent the morning playing at puzzles and books in the car. Still loaded to the rafters. No, I did not want to read the Ant and Bee story. "You read it to yourself."

At lunch time Grant came home with the news he was in the "high fourth" with "all the guys" who had moved ahead of him from kinder-garten. I cautioned him a bit about having *then* to be in the middle groups; he would never catch them. They were probably six months ahead in reading, for levels were based on reading. I'm sorry I said anything. His thrill was simply that he could now have gym with the best athletes. "The real sports guys." Oh.

When Mr. Allopenna came on the phone, I was shaking so hard, I could hardly keep my voice going. He explained it all. The New York State process. He talked about "trainable" and "educable," and it was his duty to place Jane in one of these categories. For her sake. Had she ever had any evaluations, tests?

Yes, I said, "She is evaluated every two or three months. For intake. As well as output." I referred him to her Doman-Delacato Developmental Profile, which, I knew, had accompanied the letter of request.

It was his duty to provide the proper teacher, depending upon the psychologist's evaluation.

I described the proper teacher to him again. Somebody free. Who knew nothing about brain-injured children. After a few weeks, let *her* tell him all about Jane. How "educable" she was. For Jane there was no proper test or psychological evaluation available that I would submit her to, and label her with. Neurological, yes. Why didn't I send him a biography of her current doings? Or he might want to send someone to observe her for a few days, as she did her program. (Her stamina, perseverance, and personality you'd be impressed with.) Could someone stay here all day from 9:00 A.M. to a little after supper?

Silence. He would get back to me.

I hoped it would be soon. Jane was ready for the three R's. When they're ready, you don't like to wait too long. It's dulling. And Jane needed the most enriched environment we could provide. No child should have less than the best. New York State would one day discover that. Maybe here— right in this district—with Jane.

SEPTEMBER 5, 1968. The phone rang. I let it. We were in the bathroom. Doing number fourteen. I covered her left eye a little tighter with my palm, but so she could keep her eye open behind it. Yes, the eyelashes were tickling. The light flashed on. The pupil grew small. Fifteen. I flashed it off and waited. Then again. On and off. Sixteen. Seventeen.

I would start toilet training seriously now too. I could leave her about five minutes with a book. Then come back and do another basic vision. Maine had been no place for toilet training. Too far to carry her. That was the only thing wrong with it. And I began to picture the pines and the lake and the breeze.

Now Jane was counting. "T-wen-ty-se-wan, t-wen-ty-EIGHT, t-wen-ty-ni-ine, AND HIRTY!"

"Good girl. You're looking straight at the flashlight, and see how fast we are going today!"

The phone started ringing again. Jane laughed to the door. Then looked at me. "Now the left eye," and I placed my hand over the right one. "One— Oh, do you want to start? O.K."

Yes, there was the tremor again. Slight head shake. When I use the flashlight. Or is it with this fabulous speech spurt?

"Let the phone ring. I'll answer it later. Ten. Beautiful. You're looking at it." And I marveled at the eye. Must get new batteries again. The light is getting a little dim. The pupil gets small quickly after the dark. Zing. There it is. No smaller— Now. And I turned the flashlight off. And waited in the dark a few moments for the pupil to grow wide again. I love the stillness, and she does too. How can I love something this much? Little mole-baby sitting on the toilet.

Phone again. Bert's mother. Just trying to find out what Stuart's letter from Maine had meant. She read it to me: "Dear Sugar Plum . . . We picked two gallons of blueberries yesterday. I picked one gallon one quart by myself. We will make blueberry jam and whole-wheat bread. What is happening to Jane is fantastic. Sincerely yours . . . Stuart Napear."

I explained I hadn't known he had written her. Then I explained the rest.

SEPTEMBER 12, 1968. Losing so many patterners. But the transitions are easier with people like Jean Schwartz coming in. I praised her for wearing fuchsia slacks. How did she know? And I pointed to them and said, "Jane, this color is fuchsia. No, it isn't red. And it's not purple. It's *fuchsia.*"

The patterners were breathless as Jane named the tiny aqua flowers and chartreuse leaves in Ebie's shift.

"You should hear her say, 'Take off out-rig-ger' and 'Cawl in suit.' And last weekend she said her friend's name, Robin, for the first time." Lydia had said Robin still gets mixed up on her colors sometimes: when she saw her new uncle, a Negro, she asked him, 'Why is your face *green?*'"

Did the beginning of the toe-dig mean Janey would not have an operation on the heel cords? I explained that until her auditory system—and hopefully her speech, if we were right about causes—cleared up, she would remain in floor life, to further use the brainstem. It was difficult to get a child back to crawling and creeping after he knew about walking. And the lower functions were still not normal. Bert and I agreed to keep on working au naturel. It took us about five seconds to think it over. She had the rest of her life to walk. We wanted to give her the best feet and legs possible. Well, that's hardly it. We want to get her walking the way we do.

What about the knees? They'll have to operate there, won't they? I don't know. No one is hollering about anything but the ankles. I think we've got the left one almost to 90 degrees. And the right is only slightly behind. Then I showed them her occasional—10 percent of the time?—toe-push in the box. And said, it was the strangest thing. She's doing it more on the bad rightie.

SEPTEMBER 30, 1968. I wonder what October will bring? Her teacher, for one. She didn't say much on the phone. She has never taught a brain-injured child. Her name is Elizabeth Gross. Will come next week, after our Philly revisit. To meet Janey.

Yes, Mr. Allopenna does work fast. She said he's very interested in Jane's having a teacher. As he is with every child.

The visit "to see if Jane could benefit from instruction" from the school psychologist and Ed Goldstein (now a reading consultant rather than a fifth grade teacher) lasted about twelve minutes. Told us to go right on with what we were doing. So the women came back for the fourth pattern. And the two men watched. I tried to explain the dorsi-flexion we were after, and that's why the feet were patterned with that toe-brush. And then I lay down on the floor and tried to show them what a crawl was like with it, and how the baby works his heel cords that way.

The psychologist asked one question. He was looking at the "Jane Has Two Boats" book I had made. No, I never asked her to read it out loud because of the speech. But she knew all the words. He asked, "Do you mean she can read *boat* here?" Yes. And she can read sentences in which I substitute the noun or verb card, such as *Mommy is crying* or *Mommy is laughing.*

And they were gone. God bless a forward-looking school district. And a Mr. Allopenna, somewhere out there on that limb.

Professional Evaluation

October 1, 1968. Philadelphia. We rode the turnpikes on a cloud—Bert, Jane, and I—drifting in and out of conversation about the things you can "see" now—the speech, the dorsi-flexion in the ankles, the colors, the counting, the recognition of numerals, and the Indian-style sit. Would they be glad to see that! It added up to a lot.

Actually it added up to nothing. She had crossed into no new blocks on the Profile. The brain has its most explosive jumps functionally in the first year of life. Jane had passed through all that, except for perfect crawling and creeping. Then the onset of new functions slows down when you hit the two's and three's. And between three and six the pace is slower still. And that's where Jane was in all the other areas. At six you had the functional equipment you'd have for life. Not subject matter. But equipment. Either your computer was organized at six, or it wasn't. And if you wanted to oil up the rusty children after six, you'd have to go back to babyhood.

   Creeping: Poor cross-pattern with fair serialization. In testing, hand-base O.K. Hands flat 60 percent of time; 40 percent on knuckles of left hand, fingers of right hand. Knee base slightly narrow. Feet off floor and plantar flexed.

Knee-walks with facility in cross-pattern.

Crawling: Poor, unserialized cross pattern. Up on elbows. Hands pronate
poorly (especially right). Right hand partially supinates. Left hand
does not supinate. Knees flex to 80 degrees, generally with lower
leg in air. Occasionally foot is down on floor with some dorsi-flexion.
Pushes with knees. Legs never fully extend. Parents report at home,
is pushing with toes 10 percent of time in box.

In the margin to the left of the crawling report was the word IMPROVED.
I tried to tell them she crawls and creeps better than that. She's such a pill
in Philly, wanting to knee-walk only. You can hardly get her off her knees
to do anything. The point is: she does not zing right down into a beautiful
crawl. Or creep. The crawl is *improved,* yes, but we'd have to find a way
to get those feet to push. We'd elevate the box on up to twenty-four inches.
We'd put hills under the sponge rubber, with half-round molding. We'd find
ways to slow her down. We'd make the crawl boxes difficult. (And we'd
lose all our teen-agers right down the drain.) We'd find some place in the
schedule to start elephant-standing (on hands and feet). That takes dorsi-
flexion to do. And maybe mimicking her brothers to start it.

Strumpel dorsi-flexion is not 90 degrees, but it is 70! We would increase
the number per day. Unless, of course, her foot fell off.

Why not switch from numerals to dot cards for round-trip counting, to
spruce up her flagging interest.

In the language area, I was asked to what I attributed the summer
speech spurt. I ignored the students observing all this and burst out,
"Maine! I think motivation has a lot to do with speech. The spurt started
before we went, but I think somewhere it was motivation, the change of
scene, good for all of us. I truly think motivation has a lot to do with
speech!"

The lady said very quietly, "And don't you ever forget it."

Now we were finally to start speech therapy.

But, no, they call it a language program with some peripheral stimulation!

"I want you to rub cold peanut butter inside her top lip, way up, in
front of her teeth. She'll have to dig it out with her tongue and assist with
her top lip, like this—" and the woman began to squooch her top lip all
around. "Only do this with crawling, when she's moving everything at
once—neck, trunk, limbs, and now tongue. Four times a day. You can use
cold caramel if you wish." And follow this with sucking on an ice cube
in a washcloth.

"To quench her thirst?"

"And for the action that takes."

"Oh, I see, all that is just sensory stimulation for the brain to know it
has a top lip."

"Yes, everything here is just sensory stimulation so the brain knows it has everything." It was true. Everything was sensory intake to get motor output. For motor-output the program was simply: opportunity. The only thing complicated about it was the scheduling, I was beginning to understand.

Jane's gag reflex today. "O.K.—slightly delayed." No telling what a clump of hard, cold peanut butter could do for that!

Bert and I were delighted to watch Jane perform all the manual tasks. He was smiling big. She can spin a top smaller than a thimble, a deft well-coordinated finger-to-thumb side spin. She loved it, top spinning, spinning, over the table. Later we found that all the fine-finger tests, including filing her fingernail, were tests to determine handedness—right or left. And assistive perfection, when the other hand comes into use when it's needed and stays out of the picture when it's not.

Auditorially Jane was ready for abstract concepts, such as the days of the week and categories of all kinds. It is difficult to assess whether she yet knows fully the simple time concept of today, yesterday, and tomorrow. Just use it a lot.

Jane was so uncooperative in the tactile tests, thrashing out of her seat to get to the floor, raring back to avoid the bag, that she was excused. Which meant this lady gave up.

I thought of her new teacher. And a pain of dread lodged in the middle of me. Bert was quiet and watched her hard, began the pinching of his nose, and I looked away.

Then we were waiting for Jane to finish some tests for vision. And we talked with the student in the room. What in the world was he doing here, a graying physicist! He was interested in their work, that's all. Found the questions this place was asking to be possibly the best that were being asked about mankind this year. To be near the famous seventy-year-old Dr. Dart was a rare treat. He was lucky he had been accepted in this class for training. He was to be here for ten months.

And what was he going to do with all this? He didn't know. But he was not the same man he was before. Why did they make up the post-grad classes with people from a variety of professional backgrounds? They always balanced the classes. He saying maybe the idea was to drive doctors together with teachers and researchers.

When the visual gal came back with Jane, she smiled and said we must have been doing something in the last three months. Jane was so improved! She has a tendency to alternate convergent strabismus today, but much less.

"A tendency? You mean just a *tendency* to crossed eyes?"

"Yes."

"Then everybody is right. They all noticed it when we returned after two months in Maine. We hardly notice it anymore. Except when she's looking at you from across the room."

"Yes, at far-point. But she has very good control today. And her pursuits are good."

She used the word *good.* No one here ever uses that word loosely.

"So we don't have to do the visual pursuits anymore?"

"I'm only evaluating. Someone else will program you. Visually she's quite improved." And she marked "poor" in the Profile block "convergence of vision resulting in simple depth perception!"

Later, on the seat of the car, I found the books I had made for Janey, with a note by the woman who did Jane's reading today who had wanted to take a longer look at them. Inside the number book was "Number book— all books—beautifully done." That was better than her report on Jane: "Attentive to reading. Getting something. Did not respond to sentence in terms of recognition, but enjoys."

In a word, that's Jane at Philly. No response. Not one word of reading or writing. Copied the *c* of *c-a-t,* then plunked the pencil down.

Just like her to stop on a plateau somewhere the week she gets a teacher.

9

From November 1968 to July 1969

NOVEMBER 3, 1968. Mrs. Gross could teach in a one-room barn or high in an alpine meadow, using the wind and the stones around her. All she would need is the child.

I should have known, that first day. She hadn't expected such a cute little girl, so absorbed in a magazine. This she commented on three times. Fortunately the new *Geographic* had arrived just before Mrs. Gross. Jane hardly looked up, as we laid plans in the next room for Mrs. Gross to observe for a couple of weeks. Then Jane asked for a "Sears cat-tuh-logue." And then I gave her the new *Life,* and, as I did so, I realized I wanted to keep Jane occupied, not impress Mrs. Gross. It wasn't necessary. She was simply impressed with her span of attention. And I was toning her down, "For what *she* wants to do. Visually, that is."

And she said a few other things during those two and a half "observing" weeks. She understood every word. "It's very quiet, you have to catch it, but I understand her fine." As I ran Jane through the paces of her program, Mrs. Gross came at a different time each day, till she had caught it all. No, she wouldn't like to pattern. No, she wouldn't like to "play" with her. Or eat lunch here. She was not a patterner. Or a playmate. She was Jane's teacher. Now Jane would see that a teacher was someone different from all the others. What should Jane call her? Mrs. Gross. That's what school children call the teacher. Parents too. Mrs. Gross she would be.

All this with those eyes, serene, smiling. She could say anything and it would come out sound as a rock and warm and human. The thing Jane needed the most, she was telling me, was to *do,* to perform. She had had so much put in all day. In "school" she would give this child a chance to show us. And most of all—to communicate.

She would look at the materials J. used now and had used. And all the things in the closet still to be used. She saw the sentence I had propped on the sofa, after the last night's mishap left one corner of it resting on the rug. *The sofa fell down.* And I was glad it happened, so she could see how I could really get creative sometimes. And so she would know Jane's background had been enriched! And that was an understatement, she replied. We looked at each other. And we liked each other, from the very first.

And that last Friday, she decided she would start school Monday, using Jane's interest in colors. Perhaps painting. With our easel and brushes, our paints. She asked me how you do it, it had been so long since her sons had done that. And I said I'd set it up. Oh, let me do anything to really feel this, to really believe this, to see Jane start "school," I was telling myself. I would make the whole playroom into a schoolroom, whatever she wanted. No, just a table. And a chair. And perhaps one of these sliding-door closets for Jane's school closet.

And on that Monday, she grabbed some cardboards and scribbled *red, blue,* and *yellow* on them, as she went along with the child's cautious strokings. A couple she mixed and made *aqua* and *pink.* To get the red, Jane said the word. Because Mrs. Gross understood nothing less than language. And to put it back, you simply placed it with *red.* Mrs. Gross left with the comment that Jane's fastidiousness, her desire to avoid messes, could be a very good thing for school.

The next day they left the easel and went to the playroom table. And Mrs. Gross walked back to Jane's crawl-box program materials and brought the box of sand and glitter numerals into "school." Jane named the numerals she would like to see, and the color, and from the next room I could hear, "Black se-wan," and later, "Red t-wen-ty-se-wan." I almost cried.

Before you knew it, another day, the process was reversed, and then J. was making 27 with the 2 and 7 cards. And sorting things by categories: shapes in this pile, numerals here, and letters there. Because they were so messy, all dumped together in this box. And Jane likes everything to be neat.

Then they were putting them up, by squares and circles, by numerals, 14 and 15, and by letters, *m, o,* and *y.* And, you know, with all that you could make the word *mommy* if you had enough *m*'s. And then Jane was naming, and Mrs. Gross was putting up. Jane's eyes were on every item as they went. We really should ask Mommy to make us a lot of *m*'s. We need three.

And Mommy did. Three sets of lowercase ABC's with the patterners' help, lining each black one with light green paper, because you could get mixed up if you didn't know the front from the back. Mrs. Gross said J. didn't seem to be mixed up about anything—too bad I went to all that trouble. I laughed about "up till four o'clock and now you tell me!" And she said I "shouldn't underestimate this child." So I said The Institutes were always saying that too.

I asked what she was going to do tomorrow; she didn't know. Jane is so eager for numbers and has turned off words for the time being, it seems, she might start some "one-more concept" stuff. Simple equations. She'd think of something. Then that deep intelligent chuckle. All with a serenity, a firmness born of teaching and mothering, and an easy humor about playing it all by ear.

There is a picture that is Jane. Difficult for me to describe. But there are all the little facets, unique to Jane, not Grant, not Stuart, not Robin, or "girl." Together they make up this one child. Mrs. Gross already knows that picture as well as I. Her comments, whether light or thoughtful, tell me that. This woman is dealing with Jane as if she has been here for years.

JANE'S DAILY SCHEDULE

8:30   wake up; breakfast; mask.
        basic vision (thirty times, alternating each eye); toilet training.
        choose day-of-the-week poster, mother attaches it to wall:
           Monday–"Jane eats hot dogs for lunch."
           Tuesday–"Jane has a new bowl for cereal."
           Wednesday–"Jane takes a ride in the orange wagon."
           Thursday–"Jane takes a bath."
           Friday–"Jane wears the apron dress."
           Saturday–"Jane goes shopping with Daddy."
           Sunday–"Jane goes to New York City."

9:15 mask.
      homolateral patterning (seven minutes).
      Strumpels (thirty times each leg).
      elevated crawl box: five round trips; peanut butter followed by ice cube in
      cloth; visual pursuit of reward object—food (no sweets).
9:45   ”
10:15   ”
10:45   ”
11:15 basic vision (thirty times, alternating each eye); toilet training.
       elephant-standing on patterning table.
       dress for "school."
11:45 mask; juice; school with Mrs. Gross.
12:45 mask; lunch; basic vision (thirty times, alternating each eye); toilet training.
1:30 mask; tape recorder on.
      creep in romper suit and outrigger (free time).*
      basic vision (thirty times, alternating each eye); toilet training.
3:00 The following is done by teen team:
          alternate Strumpels (thirty each leg) with crawl box (five round trips) for
          120 Strumpels and thirty crawl-box trips.
          Note: Counting concepts (tactile numerals or dot cards).
          Note: Visual pursuits done at end of each round trip.
5:30 mask; basic vision (thirty times, alternating each eye); toilet training.
      practice standing (assisted and elephant).
      books and games (perceptual, etc.) on patterning table.
      talking records.
7:00 mask; supper; thyroid medicine with nonsweet dessert.
8:30 lights on, to bed with books; lights off, name fabrics in dark; tape recorder on.

* J.'s *only* creeping time. Cut to one and a half hours daily to reduce time foot spends in
plantar flexion (straight down from leg, as opposed to right-angle dorsi-flexion).

NOVEMBER 8, 1968. I wrote my name on Jane's attendance sheet, while
Mrs. Gross and I wished each other a pleasant weekend, at the same time
peering out at Jane, already busy with a book on the table.

"She certainly wastes no time getting back to it, does she?"

I smiled, "As you can see, she's only looking at the bottom of all the
pages. Her new hobby—page numbers. I bet she hasn't seen a picture this
week! Just the corners! By the way, why do I sign this attendance sheet
each week? So you can get paid?"

"State rule. Each child in school has to be accounted for."

"I know, but Jane isn't in school."

"She's enrolled."

"What do you mean?"

"She's enrolled at the school over there—the one Grant goes to—
What's the name?"

"Jane is enrolled in the elementary school?"

"Yes, her name is on the class list, but she's receiving home instruction."

"Janey's name is on the kindergarten list? Oh—"

"No, on the first grade list. She's in first grade——"

"She is? How could she be? She hasn't had kindergarten yet!"

"She's certainly beyond kindergarten, wouldn't you say? Sure, she's first grade. Let's say 'modified.' "

"But— She can't even draw yet! I mean, in writing she is certainly no first-grader. And she's so hung up on numbers, she's not interested in reading anything else but———"

"She will. And writing—she won't, but she could if I wanted to make a conflict over it. And I don't. With only an hour I don't see spending it in conflict. What we can do, is start writing sloppy. Both of us."

"Writing sloppy?"

"Yes. She knows that what she makes doesn't look like the real thing. So she doesn't try it. Because she is a perfectionist. Each letter, each numeral she's seen is perfect. The standard. She knows."

"Oh, yeah, in school a Jane can see that Tommy and Sally make sloppy numbers too. As beginners."

"Sure. Here she has only you and me. So start writing sloppy."

"Glad you told me. I was wondering about those messy words you made yesterday. Wondering how you became a teacher with printing like that. Every elementary teacher has perfect penmanship if nothing else."

She laughed. "It's a good thing I'm not an elementary teacher anyway. My handwriting would never pass the test."

"You're not an elementary teacher?"

"No. High school. Mostly math."

"You are? But how do you know all about this first grade stuff? I mean, how do you know what to do, and all?"

"I don't. I challenge Jane. She challenges me. It's like that!" And she went out of the front door laughing as usual, saying good-bye to Jane, she'd be back Monday.

I walked after her, across the yard. "But you two are busy every second— And you bring in so much—just off the top of your head that way? I mean, you always take her higher in everything, with such ease. You never taught first grade before?"

"No. But there's no stopping this kid. So there are a lot of ways we can go. Mostly where she wants to, right now. One of these days, I'll take over. Then we'll see how much she likes it!"

And now I was laughing. A joyful nervous laugh. This is all so much fun. Mrs. Gross is so much fun. You can tell she loves teaching. This marvelous woman who sees Janey the way I do. A child who loves to learn. But don't they all, really?

NOVEMBER 9, 1968. I called Lydia. Jane was enrolled as a first-grader. (Just like Robin.)

And how much had Robin covered already since September?

"Oh, I've got the whole thing here. The goals for this year. Robin's teacher read this to us the other night. You know, 'Meet the Teacher Night.' "

"One. One hundred-word sight vocabulary—*the, and,* plus nouns, etc. And Janey's done that already, and more, hasn't she?"

"Yes, she *knows* more than two hundred nouns, but you wouldn't know it by the way she's turned it all off. You know what that kid of mine is doing? Finding tens and elevens in words! Like *hello* and *balloon!* Everywhere she's finding tens and elevens—right in the letters."

Lydia giggled. "I'm not surprised, the way she bears down into a page. Here's the rest: Two. Phonics—you know, bring in a picture of something that starts with *f*."

"Yeah, I remember the boys doing that——"

"Three. Higher books, even though they don't know all the words. Four. Association with pictures——"

"Yeah, that's midbrain. Jane's had a lot of that stuff."

"Five. Writing—you know, lower-case alphabet, learn to structure all that on lines——"

"Jane'll get there by sixth grade if she hurries. Absolutely refuses to pick up a crayon, a marker, or anything that is messy."

"Six. Math—simple addition. You know, one plus one is the same as two——"

"Her teacher is starting that. But in the weirdest way. Boy, is she great! Started with the twenties, the way you hear them: twenty plus one equals twenty-one. Jane was so thrilled, filling in the answers, they went all the way through the thirties and forties that way. Then she had Jane putting in the signs for plus and equals. And finally saying the whole thing. I tell you, Lydia, school is great for speech. Mrs. Gross won't even accept 'blue book' from Jane anymore. Just asks her what is the *name* of the blue book. Everything is oral. Every question, even if only a one-word. Every answer. The teacher acts dumb and Jane has to speak. At least say part of it. Boy, what this kid could use right now is another mother. Another family. I'm trying to act dumb to encourage sentences. And she looks at me as if I'm missing some marbles, and she says the one or two words again. But louder! At least she's got the volume to emphasize now, and it's really cute."

DECEMBER 4, 1968. This is the beginning of something, I'm afraid. Or the middle? Deepening dull dread, it is surely not the end. For two and one-half hours Jane had continuous tremors. Severe—or decided—head shakings, eyes involved too in an awful darting jerkiness—all involuntary, all frightening.

Marilyn and Cathy were like two stoics as I came in the house. Frightened, but controlled.

"Mrs. Napear," Marilyn whispered while Jane was at the other end of the crawl box, "something is wrong with Jane. She's shaking, lots."

I watched. Jane turned around and headed back. Cathy was moving out the dot card—she was on the eighteenth trip. It wasn't a body tremor. Just the head. But all the time! No, little pauses. "Continue—I want to see—" I was trying to count the pauses, the seconds between. Boy, they were coming one right after the other— One and two and three. There it is again. One and two and three and four and five and six. There, again. One and two— Again!

Cathy was mouthing, "I don't think I can do the eye-following stuff, something's wrong with her eyes."

I got down on my knees and looked, "Give her a piece of Lorna Doone anyway. Just stop the eye stuff." One and two and three and four. "Did this just start?"

"It started about the fifth crawl trip. And it's never stopped. She's in a great mood. Even went through Strumpels easily. And I don't think she's n-o-t-i-c-e-d."

"All—jerking this bad?" I tried to whisper.

"Yes. Very bad."

"Yes, it's been over an hour now. I don't think we ought to do any more, Mrs. Napear, do you?"

"No—"

"Don't you think you'd better call the doctor?"

"Yes. I'll call a doctor at The Institutes. Someone who knows her neurological history and won't jump to conclusions. Like this program is too much for her."

"What do you think it is?"

"It's tremors all right, but more intense, more frequent than I could ever imagine. It might be connected with speech, except she's talking much less, no sentences much. It might have something to do with higher visual ability. Mrs. Gross has been noticing a few after deep concentration. When they're doing something new, something that takes real concentration, at the end of a time when Jane has been very absorbed. Well, if they think I should call a doctor here, I will."

It was six o'clock. I got one of the directors on the phone. The woman who programed Jane last revisit. All the doctors were gone. It wasn't a re-evaluation day, just my luck to hit a conference day. Just a minute——

Jane was asking for something. Yes, give her anything. And stay with her. But don't let her know you are watching.

Tremoring of all kinds is common. An interesting phenomenon. Perhaps it is associated with the higher concepts—visually—in school. That's good, if it is. Electrical discharging in the brain where there is activity for the first time. It can tell us a lot. Observe it. Call tomorrow morning to speak to one of the doctors if it is still occurring. Doubt it. No, if she hasn't gone into a full seizure by now, she won't, undoubtedly. There is nothing to indicate Jane ever will.

But you should see it. Her head has been jerking spasmodically for an hour and a half. You're probably right. It looks like "static" in the brain, the way it's so uncontrollable.

It might get worse. It might involve her body too. Or it can stop as fast as it came. But all in all, it's probably a good sign we're influencing something in that brain.

Another thing. I read some articles against this program in *Children Limited*—the newspaper of the National Association for Retarded Children—telling about parents who took their kids off the program because of this shaking that occurred after the program was underway. They called it "battle fatigue."

Yes, some children have gone off the program just when they needed to smooth out the static areas—with using the brain. Did I think Jane is suffering from battle fatigue?

No. That's the interesting thing. She's so happy, busy like this all the time. You know how energetic she is, eager for the whole bit each day. All the people she sees.

Let's not call it battle fatigue or anything else, until we know what's causing it. Call in the morning if it is still continuing.

At six-thirty it stopped. Abruptly. Just like that. Nothing during dinner. Or the story. And no more since. Not even slight ones.

But, if this can happen once, can it happen again?

I don't care if it's a good sign or a bad sign. I just want her to be able to talk her problems out. Even if it's to say, "I hate you."

PROGRESS REPORT—JANE NAPEAR
by Elizabeth Gross
for December 12, 1968 revisit

The stress has been on work with numbers and colors.

She names and recognizes all colors.

She names all numbers to 40, also 50, 60, 70, 80, 90.

She will arrange any number in this range that is called for with cut-out numerals.

She counts up to 40.

She knows the concept of "what comes after."

She arranges objects in categories, such as, animals, numbers, letters, shapes.

She recognizes seven letters.
She arranges the different pictures in a simple story sequence, in the right order,
    after considerable exposure to the material.
The stress has been on finding the beginning, the middle, and the end.
With considerable difficulty she will pick out the one picture in a set that has a
    detail different from the rest.
She recognizes and names various shapes, such as triangle, heart, star, square,
    etc.
She shows no interest in handling a writing tool of any sort, and after some
    initial enthusiasm for painting has lost interest in that also.
She feels most comfortable if the hour of instruction is structured the same every
    day. Starting with numbers and then going to work with letters, etc. Her
    attention span has been about forty-five minutes and can only be main-
    tained if she is physically involved in the program.
Any suggestion on future goals and procedures will be much appreciated.

DECEMBER 12, 1968. Philadelphia. Two teen-girls with me today instead
of Bert. On the way down in the car, I kept watching J. in the rear-view
mirror. Was I a fool to keep the appointment after her fall last night? But it
was the place I wanted to be if Jane had suffered any further—had she
fallen on her head? It wasn't likely, bursting through the crib's wire-side
that way— When I picked her up, I knew something was hurt— Maybe
only breath——

We got lost and arrived in Philly at noon instead of at eleven. J., still in
her pajamas, whimpering as I carried her in. I put her on the floor. And she
lay there. Trying to cry a little. And there she was examined. And, yes, you
could tell, she was protecting one side. Her leg, probably the hip they said.
X rays would tell. We should take her straight home, where her doctor can
follow her.

Before we left I asked for some ideas for encouraging Jane's reading
(something besides numbers) and writing. We don't have sentences in
speech— They just faded away— Maybe reading. For sentences. For
speech.

The woman I asked, like Mrs. Gross, could probably teach a stone fence
how to dance. She knew tricks. I sat there, intrigued by the quickness of
her suggestions, and left with a couple of pages of notes.

It was eleven when I called Mrs. Gross and told her not to come
tomorrow. Jane has a torn ligament—probably—in her hip. X rays all
negative. Rest tomorrow.

Then I read her my notes to spark J.'s two R's. She would look into the
typewriter idea, but she thought it an escape avenue. She would order the
programed reading (Sullivan book) that was suggested. The rest? She was
doing the directions-on-cards bit. But she thought we should avoid gim-

micks. Jane didn't need them. She should go into reading the way first-graders do it. She thought she'd begin phonics for the eventual pleasure Jane would have in sounding out, figuring out for herself a new word. Don't worry. Her best friend is a book.

"I think her best friend now is a set of numbers. Did you know that there are numbers on a package of Wrigley's gum? I think it's the patent number. Look sometime. Jane found them today. It led to a whole bunch of papers picked off the floor of the car, everything small we could find!"

Indeed, that's how we managed the trip home.

DECEMBER 18, 1968. Jeannie knew how to make a 4. She had just learned this week. Wonderful, let me see. I glanced. At Jane. Janey was glued to the drawing tablet as Jeannie hesitated, made the right angle backwards, hesitated, then crossed it.

"Is that right?"

"No. It goes the other way. Let me show you." And slowly and sloppily I wavered a primitive 4 onto the chalkboard. Jane giggled. And dug into the chalk box for a pink. Then *she* started to do it. A huge sweeping right angle, the size of the board. "Now cross it." And she did. I did not say excellent or anything. I turned to Jeannie, who was making several 4's in the lower corner that was left. "I bet you could make a forty-four, Jeannie."

"How?"

"Like this." And I erased the board and slopped out a 4 and another 4, large and uneven, and kind of thin. "—And cross it."

"I never made any big numbers——"

I ignored Jane, turned my back on her and concentrated on teaching Jeannie 77 and 47. Jane was digging into the box for a lavender. She slapped out two huge 7's side by side. "Se-wan-ty-se-wan!" (I could have said a sentence in that span, I reflected.)

"Now, Jane's turn to make a forty-seven." I should have kicked myself all around the block. Jane stacked the chalk box onto the chalkboard and handed me the whole package without a word. Tune out.

Jeannie and I went to ask her mother if she could come over one afternoon a week to "learn some more." And Jane could watch. And maybe learn from Jeannie. Wouldn't that be fun? Tuesday afternoons to start.

Just before I put Jane down for creeping, I made a funny wavy 7 on one of the chalkboards, and positioned the box and the eraser at its base. Later I went in nonchalantly, putting the clothes away. Yep. I'm really smart. There beside it was another 7. And below it a 17!

This was the first day I had not lain beside the chalkboards "messing around" and "making mistakes" and "trying" to write down what Jane was "dictating." I had guided her hand a few times, in a slow slapdash way. But

Mrs. Gross suggested getting rid of the crutch before it was built. So, I took the tack of doing a couple, then running off, because I had so much cleaning to do. Challenge her, but get off her back. Get to where you don't care, and she won't either. But leave the new chalks there.

DECEMBER 20, 1968. This, of all the moments, was the loveliest we had ever spent together, Jane and I. For an hour she never moved her eyes from the TV screen. For an hour. She gasped with the leaps of the "ballerina queens," she giggled with the Russian dance, she tilted her head slightly whenever the Nutcracker appeared in the arms of the girl. She sighed. She smiled, long and fixed, at the fantasy of the Snowdrops, dancing and twirling and gliding in a daydream world. She did not once break her attention to look at me. Except with loud chuckles—then gasps, then chuckles—then looked to see if I was laughing at the jugglers, the Oriental pair, and the lady with the skirt-house.

At times she was propped onto her elbow, her hand cupping her cheek, and every single movement reflected in her changing eyes. All the times I had seen "The Nutcracker" ballet, this was like the first. No, this was better. I watched her face, from the corner of my eye, and I marveled again at her rapt attention. When she looks, she lives.

And I promised. Someday she will have the whole thing again, but with the sound on. The first day she can have music back in her life, I will look up "The Nutcracker" ballet and take her there. That is how we will celebrate.

CHRISTMAS EVE, 1968. This is the best Christmas so far—I knew it shopping with Lydia. This is the first year Jane's gifts will be peer level! Lydia and I were together going the same route—pathway games, jigsaw puzzles, the reading-numbers-counting biz. She was getting ideas from *me*. Not one under-age thing this year. Thanks to Mrs. Gross. She laughed when I asked about some more perceptual stuff, more tactile or visual or anything. She said why not give her role-playing stuff like she likes—villages, doll-in-a-stroller for sure, families, houses, the things all little first-graders go for. Oh, and one baby thing—paint with water. And with hope.

JANUARY 13, 1969. Morning: We are now seeing a few tears from the patterners, the first ones after four years of gritting and grinning. She is saying their names.

"What is her name, Jane?"

"Edna."

And Edna weeps a little, and mumbles something about "so clear." In November it had been "En-da."

. The mornings are all on high like that, things they can see now. Jane had learned the ABC's in three weeks! Millie cried as she watched Jane name the letters. (In the fall I had seen Millie moved to tears with number-recognition and so said this day, "Want to cry a little?")

Noon: "Today is Monday. What do you do on Monday?"

"Eat hot dogs!"

"And how many would you like today?"

Giggles all over the place. "Eight!"

"Oh, Janey, you are so silly! How many?"

"T-wen-ty-three!" And the child almost falls off the table with the excitement.

"Twenty-*three!* Nobody can eat twenty-three hot dogs! Not even Daddy! How many hot dogs can little girls eat?"

"Two!"

"Exactly." And you are adorable. I can see it now. And so can everyone else.

And now have a ball creeping. Literally. Here is your bucket of balls. There is the Big Fun this month. J. throwing little rubber balls ahead of her to creep after. Her idea. For the fun of lifting up at the waist against the outrigger, balancing there to decide, and tossing this one over to the fireplace.

And night: Supper, a series of announcements, interruptions, put-downs and buildups for each of us.

And to the nightly cook, "It was a very good supper, Bert." And, "Take your dishes to the kitchen as you go," while Jane and I are converting the table to fun time, for girls who don't have to go to bed just yet. And Stu is bringing in the little cup of water, and the chalkboard is ready, and if you've never tried it, brushing watery 7's and 10's on a chalkboard is the best fun of all. For there is nothing static about it; it starts fading a second later. It's magic. And there is nothing as disgusting as a chalkboard now with nothing on it. And she's thinking, put-something-else-quick, it's so blank that way.

I come back to the table with the psychedelic paints and the drawing pads, and let's do whatever you wish, Jane. It turns out to be chartreuse we want, and big *U*'s from one border of the paper, down—bump—and up to the top again. And another page, please, because I want to make another big *U,* but hot pink this time. And some royal 2's. And then scribble-scrabble, because I didn't start that one right. And then complete disgust.

I think I might let you use some green glitter paint for the first time. Because I am becoming an expert at *motivation*. And there we go again—see? *M*'s are the most fun of all. Otherwise, why would she be making six of them before looking up.

And now to bed: "Would you like to hear Carl Sandburg talking?"

"Ben."

"Who do you want to hear?"

"Ben talk."

"And what is the little girl's name?"

"MY-ra."

"Oh, yes, let's listen to the John Ciardi family. *You Read to Me, I'll Read to You* is the title. I like that record too." It's a good thing we like them both, I am thinking. Since they are the only two without music—any music—in the whole wide metropolitan area.

JANUARY 17, 1969. "Eight-ten!" and then a banging noise, another— She was cutting up again in school. I moved toward the playroom a bit. What a Pill.

"We haven't finished page seventeen. We finish each page. Then we will go on to page eighteen. Each day we do one page. Today we are doing seventeen. Now which picture shall I cross out? 'B-all,' 'b-aby,' 'd-og,' 'b-utton,' 'b-ike——' "

Mrs. Gross' voice, always even, deliberate and kind, patient with discipline, continues:

"Listen once more. Does this picture start with a *ba* sound? Yes. Does this— No! No throwing in school. Don't ever throw a pencil in school. Pencils are to write with. It isn't funny. I don't think you are at all funny. Turn around here. We will finish this page. Today. If we don't finish page seventeen today, we will have to finish it tomorrow. Now, look at the pictures— Quick now, you can do it. You may not like to do it, but you can do it— Look at the page. How are you going to see the picture if you don't look at it— That's not nice. Open the book. We will just sit here until you stop the noise. No. We aren't going to do this page until you stop the noise. That's all right. We will sit. Until you are ready. We will sit here until school is finished."

"Bye-bye."

"School is not finished. We are sitting. Waiting for you to be quiet."

"Num-ber *book!*"

"No. We will finish page seventeen in this book before we have the number book. School is finished for today. When I come back on Monday, we will finish page seventeen first. Then we will do the number book."

I had tears in my eyes, I guess. I could hardly see the attendance sheet. "That's three days now," I whispered. "How long do you think?"

"I don't know. As long as it takes. She's getting the point. See you Monday."

"Good-bye, Mrs. Gross. See you next Monday. Have a nice weekend. O.K., Jane, take off your apron dress. I'll get your lunch." I could hardly see the pan through the blur. Well, Mrs. Gross, is doing the right thing. I'm sure she is. I suppose there is no other way. When you go to school, you have to do what the teacher says. Even if you are bored. Even if you don't like the stupid page. That book is stupid anyway. Ten or twelve lines of stuff to do. Why don't they have short pages? Drill work! It's boring to a child. But that's not the point. Society is the point. That's Mrs. Gross' point. She couldn't care less about the *b*'s and *d*'s either.

JANUARY 20, 1969. Today school lasted exactly twenty-two minutes. Most of it in silence. Waiting. To finish page seventeen. I couldn't stand any of it, the way she carries on with those eerie out-of-this-world ghost sounds, I'd call them, tuned out so completely she won't even look at Mrs. Gross. Or banging her hands down on the open workbook, like some wild thing. And laughing and carrying on till she realizes Mrs. Gross isn't even looking—or listening. And all the while inching the book away from her up the table, till she is lying on her arms full out, her fingertips still on the book!

Mrs. Gross left, saying they were still on page seventeen. And when they finish that page, they will get onto the other books. And it is a shame Jane is taking such a long time with page seventeen. All this to Jane. Not to me. To me she shrugged her shoulders and smiled a broad smile. I shrugged my shoulders, but my smile was more of a question.

"See you tomorrow. Good-bye, Janey."

"Bye-bye." She didn't look up from the magazine of course.

JANUARY 21, 1969. "You know the answer. I know you do. Let's not take all school time on this one silly page today. We have so many more things to do when we finish this page— No. We don't turn the page till we have finished page seventeen. Don't be so loud. You're not funny."

I had no more silent suggestions of my own, listening at the door. Mrs. Gross had tried them all and more, ignoring the clamor and proceeding to ask her which picture should "we cross out" and once again naming each picture: "ball," "baby," "dog," "button," and "bike."

Jane was off again into the wild blue yonder, this time just squealing and breaking it off into a chortle. Then with face up to the ceiling, raring back in the chair, she screamed, "DOG-G-G-G!"

Almost in a whisper, Mrs. Gross said, "Yes, the answer is 'dog.' I can hear you. You don't have to be so loud. Now the next page is number— what?"

"Eight-TEN."

"The first picture is what?"

"Nilk."

"It starts with an *m*. M-ilk."

"Milk."

"Yes, that is correct. What other *m* words do you see?"

"Mouse!"

"Yes, and?"

"Mit-tens."

"Yes, and that's right, cross that one out. Very good. House does not start with the *m* sound. It starts with *huh,* so we cross that out. And write the *h* beside it. Do we cross out *monkey? . . .* Should I cross out *monkey?"*

"Nope."

"No, we don't. *Monkey* is an *m* sound also. We're going fast today. When we finish this page, we will have time for the number book because we are going so fast today. What's this picture?"

"Dog."

"It starts with a——?"

"Dee-e!"

"Yes, now let's find the other *d* pictures . . ."

JANUARY 28, 1969. "Hi, Janey, what's my name?"

"Mi-mi."

"Good girl!"

I took a wild stab in the dark, "Jane, what letter does *Mimi* start with? *Mimi."*

"M!"

Mimi backed off and just looked at me. I acted as if it was nothing. And said, "Let's see, what does *nine* start with?"

She waited. *"N!"*

"Excellent!"

"And what letter does *Debby* start with?" Debby Wiggins leaned in.

Turn around, tune out. She had found a book with pages of magic. Three numbers instead of two. She began to point and smile, "Wa hun-ded an' WAR!"

I explained that she just said "one hundred and four."

When Mrs. Gross came in, I slipped over to her and said, "She knows the *m* sound. And the *n.*" And I told her about *Mimi* and *nine.* "And that's not in her workbook, so that couldn't be just memory."

"She knows all of them. Except *v.*"

"She knows all of them? You mean, all the sounds, I mean, with the letters? With the words? Just by hearing it?"

"Sure. I thought you knew that."

"You didn't tell me. How could I know? I clean now during school, you know. From now on, tell me these things!"

"Phonics seem pretty easy for her."

"Well, I know she is terribly interested. She knew the names of those four paper dolls the first night, I think. By their first letters, I bet. She really looks down at the name and goes, 'N-an,' like that. Isn't that marvelous?"

"Don't underestimate her so. If she wants to do it, she can."

"But you don't understand! That's very refined. She's discriminating sounds on her peer level! I mean, she was like a baby in auditory competence when we started!"

"She's doing very nicely. I am going to start the programed reading next week, I think. We'll see what she does with that."

"Oh, she'll love it. I saw it in the cabinet. It's all about an ant. She loves ants. Or did last summer. But it does look awfully slow, very structured."

"Yes, you can't go too slow with her. We'll see. By the way, did you get more pictures of those letters? She's so interested in letters right now. That's the problem. She's off words. And on letters. Right now."

"And numbers over a hundred!"

She laughed. "Not anymore. In school. Only letters and sounds. She's definitely off numbers."

"What are you going to do about it?"

"Oh, I'll think of something. Probably start reading. And then she'll get interested in numbers again!"

FEBRUARY 11, 1969. Jane singling out parts of a word to emphasize now. And that takes breath! Ro*se,* fi*ve,* honeyco*mb.* (*Honeycomb* she can say with only breathing once in the middle.)

Very lip-minded, pooches her top lip up and looks down on it. The weirdo look of the year! Does that when people are here, of course. Couldn't do it in the privacy of her bed. The patterners say she looks like her troll-pencil when she does that. All we have to do is dye her hair lavender, and we've got Miss Troll.

I'm doing peanut butter and maskings (every half-hour). Mrs. Gross is doing phonetic endings now. So heaven knows, we must be doing something right.

And Jane Napear is saying something finally besides colors, proper names, numbers, and letters! Things like, "Turn on tape" and "Crawl in suit"—all that is back again. And a lot of new adjective-plus-noun couplets. And Mrs. Gross is even getting sentences now and then.

FEBRUARY 17, 1969.

"Janey, tomorrow we are going to Philadelphia."

She trembled and giggled all over in anticipation. Or was it simply that we were *going* somewhere?

"Yes, and Daddy invited some friends to go with us too—Don and Monica Gutstein."

She smiled as I tucked her in and gave her a patty-pat on the fanny. "See you in the morning. Yep. Tomorrow we go to Philadelphia. Good night."

I walked in to where Bert was and handed him Mrs. Gross' report for tomorrow. "See? Now you believe?"

PROGRESS REPORT—JANE NAPEAR
by Elizabeth Gross, Home-bound Instructor
February 1969

Colors: Can name all colors and shades and match the written word to the right color for red and blue.

Numbers: Counts in sequence up to 100.

Counts objects to 20.

Recognizes written numbers up to 100 and can "write them" with pre-cut numerals.

Starting to write numerals 1, 2, 4, 5, 7, 9, 10.

Starting basic addition equations using plus and equal signs.

Reading: Is on the suggested programed reading. This program was only started a short time ago, so that evaluation is difficult. (Programed Primer 1 and 2, Sullivan)

Has a good concept of beginning sounds of words—is associating the sound with the correct letter. Book: *We Learn to Listen* (Stern).

Recognizes all letters.

Is verbalizing much more.

Attention: The daily lesson is about forty-five-minutes. It is difficult to discipline her to attend to material she does not like or finds hard. She has, however, improved in the last weeks.

FEBRUARY 18, 1969. Philadelphia. On the way down in the car, friend Donald Gutstein (who is a chiropractor incidentally) wanted to know why The Institutes had ignored Jane's periphery—the legs and the feet. The structure there was pitiful. The calf muscle was atrophied.

The truth is it never had developed. The legs and the feet were like that before Mary saw her, but they hadn't gotten any worse. They had gotten better. We had movement there now!

He thought from what Bert had told him and what he'd read himself that the program was great. But in addition to it, you could give electrical stimulation to that calf, and some passive exercise. And you could have her move her ankle up and down. And more—about her back, her neck—And blood supply—And the only thing I could think to say was, "But when? She's free after nine o'clock at night."

He was wondering why they don't let her walk more, to get that calf muscle going. And he should ask them. But I knew you needed a cross-pattern gait, a serialization of movement, and a lot of other stuff that comes from crawling and creeping. It's taken time to get all that, and it still wasn't perfect. But we had the ankles going now. And I trusted they would get to the tight knees at some point. Was patterning and crawling all they knew to produce leg extension?

He was saying he'd like to start some stretching of the knees too. And he should ask about that today.

He did. He queried all three doctors and others who saw her today. Such things as why was she not on vitamin E—for increased oxygenation to the brain. And calcium for muscles, whose supply is taken from the bones and is often depleted. In fact, why was she not on the new megavitamin program?

His questions were given serious attention, all this over Jane's clamor and rebelliousness. They were quite interested in vitamin E and in the possible benefits of large doses of vitamins to the brain-injured. Some of their patients were already on them, and they were watching. And we were welcomed to try.

But as for electrical stimulation to the calf muscle, Robert Doman, M.D. (physical medicine and rehabilitation), was quite brusque. In nineteen years as chief of a department of physical medicine at a medical center, he had never seen one child walk from electrical stimulation to the muscles or from passive exercise. Walk correctly, without braces, crutches, etc. In fact, I am sure he would have added, before this program there was no hope for normal walking for the "spastic" category of brain-injured child. Mary had told me all about that. She had never seen one either. Neither had any of her colleagues in the business.

But Don wanted to try it with Jane, and some other things.

Everyone said the same thing, "Go ahead if you wish. But don't drop any of this program to do it."

Then the surprise. We saw Carl Delacato for the first time since Stu's evaluation there. He was the same—great with kids, listening and watching. That's all he did. Just watched Jane. You had the feeling he was looking at it all for the first time. A telescopic look, a microscopic look, both at the same time. That is the impression I got. So did our friends with us, they said later. Even when we were talking and questioning, he was looking at Jane.

At 9:00 P.M. Jane was knee-walking her way to exhaustion. Or winding up to blow. It was hard to tell. Going through a ghostly "nan-nin-nine-none" practice with a strange gaze—haze?—on her face. I had the impression if you said boo to her, she would have screamed. She had done a lot of that already. So we left her alone.

Delacato asked about her school behavior, and I told him Mrs. Gross' big concern. She did not want to say, "Be quiet" to Jane because she learns a lot from her when she is yelling like that. Like the day she wanted Jane to read (orally, of course) the word *stands*. And after a terrible scene, Jane yelled, "Not tens." And Mrs. Gross agreed it was "not tens," but, yes, it did sound a lot alike. Now that she has more volume in her voice, she can yell. I wasn't sure I didn't like the sweet nontalker we had before a lot better! I gave a nervous giggle.

"Hey, Dad, get Jane in your lap. Whisper in her ear. Over and over. Up close. Hot, blowing breath."

"Wha— What shall I whisper?" Bert was picking her up and she was struggling to get back down. And Bert was saying, "Let's sit in Daddy's lap. How's my big girl?" and stuff like that. And Jane was squirming still.

"Hold her there, Dad. Now whisper 'Daddy.' Till I say stop."

You could have heard a pin drop. He was right up against her ear, his lips in her hair. Jane was jerking away everytime he started the word. Breaking out of his reach, coming back to nestle in his arms and holding still for him to start, then moving away out of earshot. And then Bert was holding on to her head.

"O.K. Jane, hit the floor. Tell you what I think, Napears. I think this kid is living in a frightening world. I think her auditory problem is responsible for the random behaviors, the random mouthings. And the poor speech. Mother, if you could have one problem of Jane's cleared up, which one would you choose?"

"Speech. Oh, speech, of course. That unbearable frustration that goes with it. I think she knows now she talks differently. I really think a lot about the psychological problems now. She's running out of time."

"Right. What's the second thing?"

"Walking, of course."

"Right. And we're going for all of it. We're going for the whole package. We are going to zero in on these two areas. Later we'll have to come back to basic vision. I don't care about reading and writing. I do care about her auditory problem. The most. Here's what you will do. Get a stethoscope—" and he tossed a stethoscope across the table to me.

"I have an old one the kids played doctor with. It's pretty beat up, but it belonged to my father, so it is a real one—would that be O.K.?"

"If it works, it is a stethoscope. I want this kid to have for the next few weeks whisperings into both her ears—equally—twenty-four hours a day. Hot, blowing breath. Up close. One sentence. Every time you pass by her, whisper. Keep the house quiet. No more tapes, no more talking records. Hold her head and whisper to her. After three or four weeks, when she will let you whisper into her ears—not until—I want you to have her talk into the stethoscope the other twenty-four hours a day!" Then he smiled.

"O.K. How do you do that?"

"Put the stethoscope in her ears and encourage her to talk into it. Touch it right to her lips. If she screams and yells into it, that's fine too. She'll get a pretty good idea of a scream into a stethoscope. Let her hear it."

Everyone laughed. And there was a lot of seat shifting.

"All her waking hours. We are going to channel sound into that brain. One magnified. The other barely audible. Stethoscope and whispering. I want all tonality out of this kid's life otherwise."

"But if she's busy doing the program, I could only get this in here and there between other progams."

"You've got the idea."

"Thank you." And I meant it.

It was 11.00 P.M. as we left. Another mother saw the sketch I was holding and began shaking her head as she went out.

"Do you have to make that overhead ladder thing too?" I burst.

"Yes. You too?"

"Yep. And I'm wondering how we'll do it. My husband was reared in a New York apartment and is not the best in the world with a hammer."

"Mine too. This is going to take a lot more than a hammer. I'll have to figure it out."

"Me too. Wish we lived close to each other. Where are you from?"

"Canada. A rural area of Canada. Nobody lives close to me." She flung open the door with her knee, dragging her bag of diapers and the day's mess behind her.

Holding the door, she said quite seriously, "But you know, that is a darn good idea, and it just might work."

"What?"

"A brain-injured kid walking—the ape-to-man way. With brachiation-assist."

I would ask them all about it next time. It was too late to think.

FEBRUARY 26, 1969. Jane and I bumped smack up against society today. I'm hurt. But I'm learning what to expect.

Ophthalmologist's office. Crowded. Lifted J. from her new wheelchair (she loves it!) to sofa with this absolute, "No, you may not crawl. This is a waiting room. We do not crawl in a waiting room." That was my first mistake. At Dr. Donald Gutstein's office last Friday night she did. At Philly she does. Here she doesn't. So don't worry. Just discipline her.

We were waiting for the eye doctor in the examining room. "That looks like a spoon, but the doctor uses it on the eye. Isn't that cute?" She moved her hand toward the box of lenses. "No, we don't touch the little glasses. The doctor touches those. Maybe the doctor will let you wear one while we are here." And we waited. I didn't mention the eye chart because J. is best when something is "new." She bores easily, I suppose.

The doctor took the "spoon" from Jane and asked her not to "touch my things, please." From then on Jane would have *none* of it. Anyway.

"Just tell her what you want her to do, just explain it as you go. She understands." I was pleading and I was scared to death.

The glasses were tried and quickly retrieved. "No! Keep your hands down," the doctor said. And some other things. And Jane began to cry. And the doctor leaned back in the chair. Just looking. I was wiping with quick jabs of the Kleenex and saying, "Now the crying is all finished."

And Jane saying, "Cawl" and the doctor asking what is the matter. And I'm saying she wants on the floor. The doctor is asking if I prepared her for this. I said no. The doctor said you certainly should have. Maybe I should, but she does what I tell her to—when I get to a place—so I'm not so sure visits like this need to be softened. And Jane is now into a full-blown tantrum and stretched out on the floor. The worst I had seen since that day in the elementary school, unless it was in Philly last week.

I am getting my examination, deciding to ignore her. Because whatever I am saying or doing is not working. The doctor has already said an examination of her is impossible. Let's go ahead with my eye checkup.

The rest I don't remember too clearly. The doctor was asking me what I intended to do with her. What plans was I making for this child? What is the question? She's still on the Philadelphia program. And the doctor is pushing on. My husband and I would have to think about that. It's difficult. But Bert and I would have to start thinking about it soon. Not to wait too long. And I remember saying I was very pleased with her program. I did not say "progress." I think I said "program." And Jane even louder now, I was noticing. And occasionally the doctor throws a glance to the wild thing on the floor. I'm getting angry and telling her to stop that this minute! Just cut that out! And the doctor very patiently is telling me that "these children" do that, and that they get worse as time goes on. That is why I will have to think of my other children. And it would be a lot better if my husband and I could come to some decision now.

My neck is on fire. I don't know what is wrong with my neck. And my face is burning up. I'm mumbling something under the glasses about how her teacher thinks she is doing very well. And something about reading and writing. I really would like to have her eyes tested, to see if she's inherited nearsightedness from all of us. And the doctor saying to the secretary who has come in about "this child going on and on," that in the future she should give double appointments in a case like this. Didn't I, the mother, realize that? Like some far-out fool I was saying I didn't know Jane would be like this. And during the exam I am half-listening, I am so busy pushing the tears back in. How much longer did I expect to work with "this child?" I am saying weakly, but I am saying it, "Till she is well." I am saying that bending over her, wiping her face that's contorted into one long red blur of mucous.

And out into the cold I was pushing her wheel chair, furious at myself for not bringing a blanket. Everyone in New York City was looking at us. It was snowing now. People on Lexington Avenue staring now. At this child, the wind whipping at those awfully thin exposed legs, below a frilly dress of all things. And I wanted to shout, "The raincoat has a warm lining in it." Her face is beet-red and terribly shiny, and her mother bringing her out into weather like this. I hated them all. Everybody who wanted to sweep "them" off the streets into the institutions. So they wouldn't bother the other children in the family, so we wouldn't have to look at them. The way they are so uncontrollable. You'd think the mother would do something about her. If she cared about her other children at all. And I was starting now to shake it off. I was bending over her, smiling and drawing her bunny-hood tighter, so everyone looking would know that *I* liked her, that I was glad she was here, that I was delighted she was mine. And the "other children" you all are so concerned about can *walk* and *talk*. So what are you worrying about them for? They are so lucky, you wouldn't believe it. And they better know it too. If they have a psychological problem over this, then go tell it to the psychiatrist. And while you're at it, be aware as hell that you can *tell*. Because what is worse than any old psychological problem is not being able to talk about it—*at all*.

I know what it is, Peggy. You are scared. I know. I know. And that's a good thing. I didn't use to be scared enough. And I didn't work hard for her, because I wasn't scared enough. Just thinking it would all turn to rose-color someday.

The hardest thing about being a parent of a brain-injured kid is deciding what you are going to do. Not about the kid, but about yourself. Not how you are going to live with the child, but how you are going to live with yourself. On Lexington Avenue you can get a pretty clear picture of it. Because there are no blankets to crawl under and no one to run to. Just you and the child. You can see the child, clear as a bell. Right through the tears.

Chiropractor's office. At night we went back to the city. Because Don Gutstein could not see her on Friday this week. And he talked to her—as he would to me. And he required. No, he was not going to start until she was on the table. He would just wait. She knee-walked through all the rooms one more time, and with head held high in a "don-dan-din-done" practice, she sashayed right past him and boosted herself up to the table.

Once she kicked him. And he slapped her hard. Right back. That's why it was only once. And he talked to her. Eyeball to eyeball. When he was finished, she "may work the buttons under the table." A sequence was involved. It was the timer that was messing her up. I got up to straighten her out. "Sit down, let's see. There's only one way to get everything going together. Let's see how long it takes for her to figure it out. Ah, that's it. She did it. Now let's see——"

"Oh, oh, she forgot the timer again," I was whispering.

"Yep, but she's studying it now. She's checking what's on and what's off. There she goes."

And from then on Jane was home free.

"This kid's really smart. And she's terrific with her hands. That's remarkable. Her hands are great."

"You should have seen them when we started. She's come a long way."

"You don't have time to think about where she has come from. The fact of the matter today is that she is spoiled rotten."

He went on to tell me she has me pegged on everything. When she held the cup out, why did I get her water? Can she say "water?"

I said, "Yes, she says 'mo wa,' like that."

"And you get her water when she says that?"

I could see what he meant. He was about the best "daddy" with a patient I ever saw. Jane knew it before I did. I left not knowing a thing about the vertebrae that were tight, or much about the neck movement which is needed for good blood supply to the brain—one-fourth of the body's blood goes to the brain! But I understood I was taking home a spoiled child. And that I intended to change.

When she asked for "huice," as she has done in the past year, I said, "The word is 'juice.' It starts with a *j*."

"Juice," she repeated. And smiled.

MARCH 19, 1969. Uprightness for the first time. I've been standing in the kitchen, making believe I'm drying dishes, but all the time watching. And counting out loud Jane's hand-holds (easier than the irregular steps), up to 200. She goes along under the overhead ladder, back and forth, without hesitating, if she thinks I am not looking. But all the time I am drinking in the picture.

From where I stand the crawl box—elevated at one end to thirty inches and stretching sixteen feet across the room—blocks my view of her legs. And I see only a child walking (from hips up) swinging along like anyone else with hands above her head. The contracted knees and the gait on toes I can't see. It is the first time I have ever thought of how Jane would look—walking.

Yesterday I went over to her during walking time, to see where she comes up to me. I have never thought of her tallness, only her length. She is almost to my shoulders! Standing back-to-back with the boys was always a proud moment. But with Jane, I shudder at her tallness and wish she could have been a "shortie." For her sake. For the sake of leg bones, which are growing on. For the shortened muscles which must be made longer if Jane is to ever walk correctly. And I am watching daily to see if she puts her heels to the floor. She doesn't. Still on toes.

MARCH 20, 1969. Mrs. Gross and Jane making a memory. Me listening outside the school door.

"Let's look at our box of pictures today. Maybe you would like to choose which letter we'll talk about. Would you? Which pictures shall I look for?"

"*K*."

"All right, let's see what pictures we have for *K*. Oh, oh, we don't have much, I see——"

I was now into the kitchen, trying to get her attention to tell her, write a sign—Don't do *k*—we only have three pictures for *k*: king, kitchen, kettle. But she didn't see me. They were going on.

I listened.

"Why, of course, the kettle goes on the stove. Good idea, Jane."

I perked up my ears.

"Oh, yes, and the king is cooking. Oh, he's walking to the refrigerator, I see. Now walking back to the stove. What is he cooking?"

"Suppah." I must tell Bert this!

"And what will he eat for supper?"

"Roast beef!"

"Good. Let's make a supper list. What else?"

"Em!"

"Em?"

"I-ce ca-ream!"

"I-c-e c-r-e-a-m, ice cream. And what kind of vegetables will he cook?"

"Gr-een beans!"

"G-r-e-e-n, that's one word, and b-e-a-n-s. And another kind of vegetable?"

"Corn."

"What color is corn?"

"Wew-wo."

"Wew-wo?"

"Yel-low."

"Y-e-l-l-o-w. Oh, this is going to be a pretty and tasty supper, c-o-r-n. Oh, oh, there's the siren. What time is it?"

"Ta-welve o'-clock!"

"Yes, and the king is going to eat supper tonight. What time does he eat supper? I wonder what time he eats supper!"

Nothing.

"I bet you eat supper when your daddy comes home. What time does your daddy come home? We'll have to ask your mother. How about bread——"

"Toast!"

"All right. T-o-a-s-t. What will the king drink for supper?"

"Nulk."

"Nulk?"

"Milk!"

"M-i-l-k. That's a very good supper list. Let's put that on the wall for today."

Wondering all afternoon, where did she learn what a kettle is? Probably saw it in a book somewhere.

APRIL 2, 1969. Until now I had not even started thinking about Jane's character, or her future opinions or ideas. Someday we would have to pour in the subject matter after we got the "equipment" oiled up.

I suppose the process is pretty much the same. Bombard the brain with all the ideas, especially the opposing ones. All the grays with the black and white. All the shades for finer discrimination.

I began thinking of a plan to start subject matter with Jane. Why wait? Why limit it to one hour of school a day? We would combine "encyclopedia" with stethoscope. Now she was begging for the "stethoscope toy," after the initial introductions with the two newspaper pictures I had shown her: one, a girl playing doctor with her doll; the other, a boy at some sort of science fair. I pasted them on a poster, and occasionally let her look at them for a few moments and wear the toy in her ears. That's all for now. Maybe we'll have time tonight. It had taken four weeks longer for the left ear to get used to whisperings. We were now ready to go. She didn't like the idea of freely talking into it. But naming pictures she would do. Especially if they were new. And things she has probably looked at but never known the names of. Like the page of girdles in the Sears catalogue. For some reason she liked all those different styles on one page. To me a girdle was a girdle. Yes, it was time to think of expanding her vocabulary. While we were magnifying it in the stethoscope.

APRIL 6–9, 1969. Washington, D.C. Mary and I waiting for Grant, climbing the Washington Monument, towering above us. She is showing me the in's and out's of a spastic walk. How walks look after tendon-cutting for hamstring and heel-cord lengthening. And how the operation is then repeated—and again. Because the brain cannot do its extension function, and so the muscle again becomes shortened, atrophied, with that disuse. How in between operations the limb is braced. The child can stand straight up, stiff. A "spastic" never has a walk as good as ours because that rubber-band jerkiness is still there. Even if you lengthen the tendon at the knee and at the heel in an operating room.

What seems to be happening in Jane's case is so remarkable you hate to mention it. Yet. Her spasticity is less and less. And Mary is still wondering if it is possible to get rid of it altogether at the knees. Since we seem to have none at the ankles left, or so little it's hard to detect. And it all went from the arms and hips a long time ago.

Now she is showing me a walk on the outside of the foot, when the eversion muscle is weaker than its opposing inversion muscle. To walk flat, you must have a good balance of both. You must have a *true* dorsi-flexion. And that is why we are pouring it in—the exact correct way—in patterning and in Strumpels. To use those muscles equally. If not, she will stand on the side of her foot; the outside is the more common error with "spastics." We don't want a messy dorsi-flexion, we want a perfect balanced lift of the foot.

Mary wishes she could see Jane's heel-cord function, since it sounds as if we are over the hump there. You can always do an operation there. It's the last resort. Which most people take first.

That's what Don Gutstein had said. She could be operated on at age twenty for that. And why give up, when you're out in front?

JANE'S DAILY SCHEDULE
APRIL 1969

Note: whisper into J.'s ears all day.
Wake up, practice stands in crib.
  8:30   mask; breakfast; stethoscope.
  9:00   mask; begin morning mobility program (two and a quarter hours).
          homolateral patterning (seven minutes, including foot-brush and knee-feel).
          Strumpels (twenty left, forty right).
          16-foot crawl box (elevated thirty inches) and peanut butter, followed by ice cube in cloth (five round trips).
  9:35   ”
 10:10   ”
 10:45   ”
 11:15   mask; toilet (twenty minutes): basic vision, once; stethoscope.
 11:40   school with teacher.
 12:30   teacher leaves; mask.
          overhead-ladder program: (200–300 steps) with play-break one minute after each round trip (fifteen steps) (thirty minutes).
  1:00   mask; toilet (twenty minutes): basic vision, twice; stethoscope.
          lunch on tray on patterning table.
  1:30   creep (free time): backyard (one and a half hours).

3:00   begin afternoon mobility program (two teen-agers):
          mask (every half-hour).
          Strumpels (twenty left, forty right) for four sessions for a total of eighty
              left, one hundred and sixty right.
          16-foot crawl box done twenty-six round trips (with sand-alphabet cards),
              peanut butter and ice cube in cloth.
          "silent treatment" except for naming ABC's and for vocal encouragements.
          Note: Numerals and counters discontinued, since she's writing numerals
              now and knows counting concept.
5:00   mask.
          overhead-ladder program: (200–300 steps) with play-break one minute after
              each round trip (fifteen steps) (thirty minutes).
5:30   mask; toilet: basic vision twice (stays on toilet).
6:00   mask; stethoscope.
          Gutstein program: rotation (inversion, eversion) of ankles; dorsi-flexion on
              command; Achilles tendon-stretching (twenty minutes).
6:30   ride in car to take Louise home. (Works from 3:30 to 6:30 four days.)
7:00   mask; supper.
7:30   overhead-ladder program: (200–300 steps) with play-break one minute after
              each fifteen steps (thirty minutes).
8:00   Gutstein program (Bert does usually): hot bath, rotation of ankles, dorsi-
              flexion on command and Achilles tendon-stretching (thirty to forty min-
              utes).
8:45   mask; stethoscope; to bed with books.
9:00   lights out; sleep pattern: alternate homolateral.

APRIL 15, 1969. Bear with us, Child.

"Uh 'ing is hu'ting."

"What did she say?"

"I think she said, 'The king is hunting.' Probably some more Mrs. Gross
stuff. I tell you, that lady is beautiful! She just threw out the reading books
for awhile and started putting all the king sentences on white paper with a
picture. I think the two of them are writing their own book. One sentence
is, get this, 'The king drives a brown car!' Another one is 'The king eats
bread' with that big bread loaf picture on it. And you remember that plate
of toast we didn't know what to do about? Well, that's 'The king eats
toast.' "

Jane was saying the same thing, "Uh 'ing is hu'ting."

"The king is hunting, Janey? Is that one of your sentences in school?
Janey has such interesting papers for her king book!" And as an aside, I
mouthed, "Probably used the gun picture that way."

The seven minutes was up and Debby Wiggins next to me said, "Oh,
no!"

"Sure, did you think it was more like seventeen?"

"Look here! She's been telling us too! Her fingers are hurting!"

Jane's knuckles were all bleeding. Barely—but bleeding. Skinned off.

From Debby's push against the top of J.'s hand with the heel of her own, a way I had shown her just seven minutes ago, as we discussed how to keep J.'s palm flat when she tries to "fist it."

"Oh, Janey!" Debby cried, hugging her. "I'm sorry! Fingers hurting. Of course they are."

And Janey smiling up at Debby, smiling with her whole body that way, a little tremble, whenever the communication gap is closed.

APRIL 16, 1969. Bert's birthday. Jane's gift:

"Bert, for your birthday gift, Jane didn't make anything—the way the boys did——"

"She can't anyway!" That was Grant.

"Grant, be quiet!" That was Stuart.

"—because she is going to make it now—while you watch her." And I brought the little slate and a box of chalk to the table. "Let's see, Janey, what is the first number?"

She started with 1, and right away it was erased and a 2 stood in its place. Then 3 with dispatch. Jane was dashing them off—manually and vocally.

"War."

"War?"

"*Four.*"

Some of them were rather wavy and sloppy to behold. And I was hoping that if a comment about that was forthcoming from the little group looking on, that it would be positive, not negative. You know, what a *wonderful* sloppy writer!

Through the teens there was breath-holding all around. And somewhere someone whispered, "She says '-teen' now."

And Jane was stepping off into the twenties now, each number ending in a flourish down at the bottom there. She was using the same piece of chalk, resting it on the table during the erasings. Her left hand holding the slate firmly to the table. Just the way you would.

"T-wen-ty-*four.*" There was no movement on the bench by the wall until Stuart got on his knees to see better. Grant, resting on his elbows, was doing a lot with his eyes and lips—mostly to me after each performance. And you knew with 28, if you can make an 8 that way, you are pretty much a little schoolgirl. So 29 and 30 were actually anticlimactic.

When she finished, while Bert was finding some words, Grant skipped to the center of the room and threw an imaginary basket. Then Stuart did a half-twist from the corner and hooked one over his shoulder. Then Grant copied that.

Now Bert was opening another present and saying, "That's really something, isn't it?"

"The writing or the interest?"

"Both."

The writing I expected. The interest I never did.

APRIL 28, 1969. After-supper scene:

Jane handing her empty plate to me.

I'm sitting stoic, looking straight ahead as the spaghetti sauce sticks to the hairs on my arm.

Stuart: "She wants you to take her dish, Ma!"

"I understand everything that is going on. If Jane wants something, she can tell me."

Jane is pushing the dish against my chest now and saying "Dish."

I'm not moving an inch, except my head toward her to say, "Dish? What about the dish?"

And Jane saying, "Dish" and lifting it higher up near my eyes.

Stuart is leaving the table, furious.

"What do you want me to do about the dish, Jane?"

Nothing.

Stuart, standing at the head of the table, is bursting, "I know what you're doing. But you're wrong. It's not fair. You always took it before!" He is going to cry.

"I know. And from now on I won't. Without the words."

"But how does she know that?"

"So, that makes tonight a difficult one. I agree. And if I were you, I'd not watch the rest. It doesn't have to be difficult for you. Just for ner. And me."

He turned and left and said, "It still isn't fair."

"Would it be any fairer if she's still handing her dish out to me when she's twenty? She's ready now, Stu. She has the ability. I wouldn't ask it of her if she didn't. Now, Janey. Put your dish down and tell me in words what you want. I'm listening."

"Dish." This with a squinched-up face, the one that says, I-am-beginning-to cry, can-you-see? But her eyes were dry as bones.

"You could say, 'Take the dish.' Or you might want to say, 'I'm finished.' What would you like to say?"

"Take uh dish."

I took it without a word. Into the kitchen. And brought her dessert, thyroid, vitamin E, and calcium back. Then I went in to Stuart. "You know, Stuart, yesterday——"

"I know what you are going to say." Disgust.

"I've never said this before. Yesterday you were happy when your birth-day card from Aunt Lucille read *Mister* instead of *Master*. You even figured it out: Does that mean at thirteen you are no longer a 'Master?'

And we didn't know if Lu did it on purpose or not. Probably she did. But the point is, you were proud. There is something in each of us that wants to grow up."

"I know what you mean. I want to read this now."

MAY 5, 1969. Mrs. Gross gave me the report of Jane's progress to take to Philly. Copy went to the school district.

PROGRESS REPORT—JANE NAPEAR
by Elizabeth Gross—Teacher
May 1969

Writing: The biggest advance in the last three months has been Jane's writing ability. She is able to make circles and lines that are confined to prescribed lines and is getting progressively smaller in number and letter formations.

She is now able to write all numbers and also many letters.

She is starting to write simple words using the letters at her command.

Reading: It is very difficult to get a realistic evaluation of Jane's reading ability. Because of my insistence on getting *verbal* responses, progress is probably slowed down.

On the other hand it has produced a great deal of speech, almost all related to the reading program.

It is interesting that Jane will spell words correctly in writing practice that she refuses to read.

Attention: In the last month the lesson has become much more structured, and it has been a real battle to get Jane to adhere to the program. I feel that real progress has been made in this area, although much work needs to be done.

MAY 6, 1969. I was growing in the job, as they say. I only had questions for them tomorrow about language. There were those things I was doing instinctively, that I felt were right, but I needed support or correction. And I was dying to know, what is Jane's speech problem exactly?

1. J. does the following: for the first day (first week), she articulates *new* word or words very well. (Like we talk.) Then she gets "sloppy" in articulation to point of becoming almost "guttural."

    Why? (I think it's largely due to breath problem. Too much trouble to try.)

2. Am I doing this right?

    a. Since February I have not answered (just ignored her) the old sounds (words said in 1965) in order to encourage correct pronunciation; for example, *deedle* for *cookie*.

    Results: She pronounces them correctly now.

    b. I went further: I started requiring several words to encourage sentences eventually. (I ignored one-word requests.) For example, "Water" was ignored; "Drink of water" or "Water in a cup" was accepted—I would get it.

    Results: I ignored the whining, tears, frustration, and kept to it consistently. I praised her with comments such as, "You can talk now," or "Let's hear some pretty words." If she whines, I don't hear her. Since she can make combinations, I thought I should now require it. She's got the idea.

3. Stethoscope used last month only because J. was still sensitive in her left ear till then. (Right ear O.K. after first two or three weeks.)

    a. Whisperings and quiet house: How about going completely (as possible) into silence (in the home) during summer when boys are at camp?

    b. We are having about five two- to five-minute sessions with stethoscope daily. You said all day though. Cannot integrate it into the other programs.

    Note: I have integrated it into toilet training, the time she also does basic vision exercises! Help!

4. Straighten me out on the following:

    a. How would you explain where Jane's speech damage is? Or do you know yet? Are we working cortically; i.e., has midbrain creeping (fusion of sound—stereophonics) done all it will do for speech? For the auditory system, I mean?

    b. Since February Jane has stuttered about a dozen times. The real hang-up kind, difficult start of a word. Like Stu used to do. Teacher noticed this too. Do you expect Jane to go through stuttering now?

Postscript: Delacato was not there this revisit (5/7/69). My questions were inserted in J.'s chart, so we could refer to them when we saw him next.

MAY 12, 1969. Received copy of letter to J.'s local doctors today from IAHP revisit May 7. How anyone could know what she is doing from this—or how she is doing—is beyond me.

Dear Dr. ———,

    Today we saw, for the thirteenth time, your patient Jane Napear, whose status we are reporting at this writing.

As a result of the evaluation, we found that once again Jane has had no measurable gains on the Profile, and this does concern us, inasmuch as Jane has had no measurable gains on the Profile since June 1967.

In light of the functional picture, we have thoroughly reviewed things with the family and have outlined a program which represents a substantial change, compared to the previous report. Hopefully, this work will set Jane moving again.

We shall then, with your permission, continue along these lines of work and plan to see Jane here for her next recheck in approximately three months. Thanks for the opportunity of seeing her once again today.

Sincerely,

I suppose that is all they could say. You couldn't very well tell her pediatric group that you were going to begin to make a monkey out of the patient.

The gains may not be "measurable," but Mary took one look at Jane in the back seat and gasped, "Peggy, five hundred percent better! Wow! The gaze? The alertness? Awareness? Something. Hard to put your finger on it. It's in the face though!" The last time Mary had seen Jane was in March of '68. And Mary doesn't lie or give false encouragement.

On the way to Philadelphia we talked about the assortment of professionals now jumping on the bandwagon apparently. Mary said a couple of New York giants in the field of rehabilitation have been asking about the program on the sly, according to several colleagues. And she related one such probe. Then she said, "I think what they would like to do is *kill* it first. Then start the same program under their own name!" She added, "But they are impressed. They never got that kind of child out of passive exercises and personality development, I tell you."

Then Bert asked what was wrong with passive exercise.

Mary said often you come out with more tightness. "I would not touch passive exercise to Jane with a ten-foot pole." How she had done passive exercise to the muscles of the brain-injured type of child, years of it, and had gotten nowhere with it. Any physical therapist could tell you the same story.

Bert was saying you could feel the muscle relaxing when you worked it.

And Mary said, "And when you come back two hours later—or minutes later—it's tight again, right?"

Bert said something about IAHP did not say no when Don Gutstein suggested it.

Mary wondered why they didn't. It is so alien to their philosophy: function determines structure. "Brain," they are thinking in Philadelphia.

I thought they were about to suggest an operation on the knees, if not the heel cords. Because she is growing so fast. They don't seem to be paying much attention to the knee-tightness that is left. I thought they were giving up on her knees. "You felt that way too, didn't you, Bert?"

"I sure did. She's seven now." And he didn't say much the rest of the way.

MAY 24, 1969. Notes about new program:

In Philadelphia:

1. When they start on knees, they start on knees! She was standing under their overhead ladder, but could hardly reach the floor with her toes, it was so high. Only her fingertips were around the rungs. I ran over to say it was too high, ours was at fifty inches. "She can barely reach it!"

"That's the idea. Leave the walking to us, Mom. Write this down. [Bert borrowing paper from a student observer.] Put your ladder at fifty-eight inches at home."

"How?"

"Isn't your ladder adjustable?"

"Heavens, no. We were doing well to nail it across two tall sawhorses!"

"Well, make it adjustable. [Discussion of how here.] Take her up gradually if you wish, but get her up to fifty-eight inches as soon as you can." All this over his shoulder, as he's encouraging Jane.

"But she'll have to walk all stretched out!"

"You've got the idea. You will raise the ladder another inch when she is able. And another. And so on."

"How will I know if she's able?" I am hugging Jane now.

"You will raise it. If she can reach it and still have her toes on the floor, she is able."

Note: Mary smiling, thinks this an ingenious idea for knee-stretch functionally—without full weight-bearing. The muscles get a rest periodically, but it is an all-day workout. They said something about its importance to the *chest?*

2. Creeping looks great except for foot-trail. Right hand completely flat and slapping the floor. But most of the time ape-like. Note the knuckles are now spread *open* even! "Is that some evolutionary higher step?"

Bert laughing at me.

Till this. If Jane has had no toe-digs with thirty-inch elevation in the box, she won't. Her arms can get her where she wants to go and fast without developing one. And you could hardly elevate the box higher for fear of losing the patient. Anyway they had other ideas for Jane. We would discontinue crawling and creeping.

We would what?

3. It clearly looked as if we were going for the ape stage. Jane would hang from a gym bar in the doorway for one minute. Twenty times a day.

"Wha——?"

We would work up to a minute. But no more. For we had other things to do.

4. Like gravity work. Bert was writing it down. I was getting Jane "water in a cup." Something about hanging her from her heels. Two people. And swinging her between them. And turning. And moving back and forth. Then by an arm and a leg. And then the other arm and leg. The man was flipping a little red doll around in a number of ways. Bert was saying, "Like I played with Grant and Stuart when they were little." And the man said, "Exactly." The phrase "Monkey see, monkey do" kept running through my mind. The man was saying something about kids hanging from trees, spinning, twirling, hanging upside down. They use their vestibular system that way. And if we wanted Jane to use her vestibular system, we would have to do it for her in the living room. Twenty times a day.

"But my husband isn't home during the day."

Mary was asking, "The vestibular system is responsible for balance, right?"

"Yes, a kid gets his body-sense-in-space with all that tree-fun stuff. He learns to operate in negative gravity (upside-downness) and in positive gravity (spinning, twirling, and so forth). We want Jane to do both."

"But don't you think Jane's balance is excellent? She's got the best trunkal balance in knee-walking I ever hope to see!" That was Mary.

"Yes, she does. But the vestibular system is tied in with the auditory system. Besides the inner ear, there is the auditory nerve and certain auditory tracts to the brain involved. The point here is Jane has never used her vestibular system this way. A child develops his vestibular system by using it."

5. Do twenty sequences a day of the programs as outlined.

6. And continue patterning and Strumpels.

You're kidding. But Bert was writing it down, so the man must mean it.

As many Strumpels a day as we could get in. The sequence of programs does not take all the thirty minutes. Between sequences give Jane a rest. Five minutes should do it. Kids love all this stuff.

At home:

1. Grant heard Bert and me discussing the purchase of a gym bar.

"Don't tell me that's going to be in the living room!" And he ran out of the room. Crying?

"Grant, it is a gym bar. You know, like kids have. Come here, see, it's going to be right here in the doorway to the kitchen. For her to hang from. You know, kids chin themselves on it in school——"

"Oh-h, is that what it is?"

"Yep, just a gym bar."

"Hey, tough, can I use it?"

"Sure. She only uses it every half hour. You can have it the rest of the time. And any of your friends who want to try it. They might want to swing on her overhead ladder too. For her it is for program, but for visitors it is for play."

2. Afternoon girls gathered here to learn about the new program.

"Crawl and creep is out, for awhile. And——"

Chris Sleeper tilted her head and asked with a twinkle, "Strumpels? Out?"

"Strumpels are in. Sorry."

A great "ugh" went out in unison.

3. By May 12 the gym bar was in place. Motivation gimmicks complete:

negative gravity—call it "butterfly" for Jane

positive gravity—call it "airplane"

With "airplane": up, up and away; then say, "Twinkle, twinkle little star" if needed; then down, down for the landing.

With gym bar—call it "monkey."

With "monkey" say, "What a good monkey girl to hold on till I say 'pop.' " Then say "All around the cobbler's bench, the monkey chased the weasel. The monkey thought 'twas all in fun, POP goes the weasel." Drop on "Pop." Verse fast or slow depending on need. Goal—sixty seconds. Good if you can get three to start with.

JUNE 4, 1969. Copy of Year-End Progress Report to school district by E. Gross:

PROGRESS REPORT—JANE NAPEAR
by Elizabeth Gross—Teacher
June 1969

Looking at Jane's progress during the school year I feel very gratified. She has come a long way in many areas.

Behavior:

In October she had to be physically involved every minute of her school time. It was impossible to keep her attention unless she herself was handling concrete material. She spoke very little and her words were often hard to understand. She lapsed into random mouthings and movements as soon as she got tired or bored. She insisted on having the hour structured the same every day.

By June she has become a small schoolgirl. The random mouthings and movements have almost disappeared. She communicates in words and follows verbal instructions. She accepts whatever program is demanded from her, in whatever sequence. Her attention span is still only forty-five minutes, as it has been from the beginning, but her concentration is quite intense at times.

Numbers:

She has progressed from counting to basic concepts of "more" and "less" and the beginning of addition facts. She is starting to tell time.

Oral Reading and Speech:

It would be premature to say that Jane is reading, because her performance is so erratic; it is, however, quite evident that she is very close to reading. She has a good concept of beginning sounds and word structure. From a child who could say a few words, she has now progressed to the point of being able to interpret a picture and tell a simple story about it. Although she still has a most limited vocabulary, she can make her point understood.

Writing:

Her letter and number formation is very crude, but recognizable. Rather than doing penmanship exercises she has been writing the key word in notes to various people.

I think that the greatest thing that has happened to Jane this year is that she has become a communicating person. Where before she made her wishes known through gestures and combinations of sounds that had meaning to those who know her well, she is now able to tell her thoughts, as well as wants, and even to write them. She still speaks poorly, but anyone can understand her. Her writing is crude but legible to all.

With modification she is on a first grade curriculum.

It has been a pleasure to work with this delightful child.

JUNE 6, 1969. Today Mrs. Gross is teaching the teens how to teach Jane this summer.

If you have a book and Jane, don't worry about a thing. Always start at the beginning. You need not do a whole basic reader, but always go beyond. If she is talking about "the dog chasing the ball," ask her on the next page, "Where is the ball now?" If she says "under the chair," say, "Yes, but the kitten is not under the chair. Where is the kitten?" She knows almost all directions—under, on top, around. Take her into the ones she doesn't know. Adjectives—short, fat, tall, thin—think of some she doesn't know. Expand her vocabulary. Higher concepts. Count the balls in the picture. Combine arithmetic, reading, speech as you go. Don't compartmentalize.

The job here is to compare, to correlate, to communicate. You have a highly motivated child to start with. The Jane-Dick-and-Spot books were made with her in mind: she loves families. She laughs with them, she cries with them. She is a dog with Spot, that's how involved she gets.

Then take her from the picture down to the words at the bottom. Let's *read* what this page says. Does it say, "The dog is chasing the ball"? No. It says something else. Use phonetic hints to sound out the words. If you've gotten a few pages of looking and relating and reading, then put that book away. You will know when it is about time to change to something else. But keep reinforcing the three R's as you go. Writing you can stay away from pretty much. She's going to have that in her program all day.

Most of all, let her tell you. Ask a quick question. Let her tell you *more*. And so on.

You can use anything from this cabinet, and here are the new materials we borrowed from the first grade teacher.

No one said boo to me. I listened from the living room. If they have questions, they call Mrs. Gross. I know nothing about Jane's schooling. That will be their job.

That's the problem. I don't know what the teacher is doing. So when Jane handed me this note today:

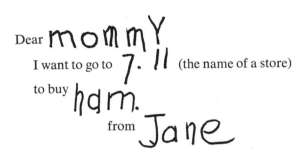

Dear mommy
I want to go to 7.11 (the name of a store)
to buy harm.
from Jane

I raced after Mrs. Gross, up the street, till her car stopped. Panting, "That's all very well and good, but could you lend me some money!"

JUNE 17, 1969. This morning went something like this:

Bonnie, who is moving away, spent her last Thursday morning here. A gift for Jane. A tiny mod doll in a rain outfit, part of the "Flatsy" series. You could dress and undress—see the hot-pink raincoat and hat, and little red boots! And you could attach her to a shadow picture frame and just look at her if you wanted.

"What is the dolly's name, Jane? I think Bonnie is a pretty name. Why don't we call this doll Bonnie?"

"Nope. Kay."

"She has *blonde* hair. Just like Bonnie's! Don't you think Bonnie would be a good name for——"

"Dolly is *Kay!*"

"Hey, Peggy, here it is. They all have a name. Let's see, it should be on the frame. Oh, yes, her name is Dewie."

"You're kidding. Dewie? Jane's favorite teen programer these days is Kay Dewey!"

Janey was chuckling to the doll and saying, "Kay Dewey."

It's all right. I don't believe this either.

Or, this, in the afternoon:

The doctor was seeing the boys and Jane for their annual checkup. For the first time in years he made two remarks about her. And not about her thyroid level or her psychological testing.

Again I mentioned beforehand he should tell her what he wants her to do. (She understands. Just talk to her.) When she stuck her tongue out and said, "Ah" on command, he burst, "Hey, that's the way!" and smiled broadly.

His second remark was "Her legs are looser."

Jane only cried a little when he extracted a syringe of blood from her arm. He commented on her good-girlness.

I hopped in. Jane has been understanding instructions for four years now. Actually she is up to abstract concepts now. Days of the week, time, that sort of thing. Actually she is in first grade now. She has a regular teacher, sent by the school district.

He looked at me with his warm smile. Then he asked if I would have the teacher call him.

"May I ask why?"

"I would just like to get an objective opinion about Jane."

He didn't know it, but he was talking to the most objective person in this world about Jane Napear. Her mother. I know what Jane can do. And I know what she can't do. I could never exaggerate any of it. I know it too well.

Postscript: Mrs. Gross called him. "I mentioned offhand something about her going to school in the future and he asked me did I anticipate that—her going to school someday. I said I didn't see why not. For some reason it seemed he didn't realize Jane is 'in school' now, so I explained she was already—curriculum-wise."

I told her about the psychological test, that Jane was considered only trainable.

"This child? Why, you know that's silly— Why do you let that bother you? You know she's not."

"But who listens to parents?"

"Well, all they have to do is look at Jane."

"That's the point. For an hour the psychologist looked at her——"

"Well, I wouldn't give it a second thought. Any teacher with this child would discount it anyway."

"But that's the point. If I hadn't kept that test under wraps, kept Jane under wraps, she wouldn't have *had* a teacher. She would have been given another psychological test, labeled trainable, and sent down that road. She would never have made first base. Never have had you. Only me. The overprotective parent of a brain-injured child who won't face the facts."

JUNE 19, 1969. It's a terribly happy week. Teens observing Mrs. Gross, amazed at Jane's sentences in school. Does she talk like that every day in school? Well, it's picked up considerably in the last two weeks. Mrs. Gross is completely cock-eyed over it. (J. laughing, "The boy is hiding!")

And something else. Jane isn't taking a breath in the middle of words anymore. In fact, as near as we can figure, J. is saying two or three syllables without taking a single breath. (Everybody's counting as she talks!) We know she's saying *cereal, Melanie* (new gal coming with Debbie Collins), and *patterning* without a break. Oh, yes, and *Kay Dewey*. The pronunciation is perfect.

JUNE 20, 1969. Atlanta airport. Grant sitting with new-found friend when I returned to the waiting room: a nine-year-old boy, traveling alone from a visit with his grandmother in Houston. Going to Chattanooga also.

He showed each of us the gift he had purchased with his own money in Houston. "This is for my little sister!" Then giggle, giggle, giggle. It was a diaper-bag-kit with a thousand and one colorful plastic items. To carry around for the pleasure, I suppose, of carrying around.

"How old is your little sister?" I asked.

"Five." Then looking at Grant and giggling, he asked, "Do you have a little sister?"

Grant: "Yeah, I have a little sister. But—well—but——"

Me: Racing in with the words tumbling, I somehow said, "Sure, Grant has a little sister. She's really adorable too."

Grant: "Yes, but—well——"

Me: "She's seven, and she'd love that diaper-bag-kit too!"

Grant: Under his breath, "She's a retard."

Boy: "Yeah, all sisters are retards . . . (giggle, giggle) . . . they got crazy brains." (Lots of giggling.)

JUNE 21, 1969. Chattanooga. At night we went to the airport for Stuart, arriving after his ball game. (Grant had foregone his last game of the season to ride the Delta Super-8 to Atlanta.) While we were waiting I noticed the posters in the lobby. Children at the Siskin Rehabilitation Center. A boy "walking" between two parallel bars at waist-height. He had braces on and something on his foot to hold it in dorsi-flexion. And he wore a football helmet. His eyes were crossed and he was smiling. The poster was asking

people to join the 365 Club, a penny for every day of the year. I was
wondering how many such requests you saw in airports and lobbies
throughout the country. And you gave. It was the least you could do.

JUNE 27, 1969. Chattanooga. Friend Frank was plying me with questions about Janey's program. He had watched a kid who goes to his church
over a period of time. He saw how much he had changed, how completely
different he looked, after doing this program, and he isn't finished yet. He
used to be carried in to a pew up front for communion. And now how he
walks from the back to the altar rail by himself. Without support of any
kind. But the biggest mystery of all was what happened to his face. His
"look." He had lost that "look" he had had.

"How would you describe it, Frank? I know what you mean. But what
adjectives would you use? To me, that's the hardest thing in the world to
describe——"

"Let me think about it—kind of a dancing, shifting look . . . amorphous . . . a face that's a fluctuating fluid-bag, as if there's no bone structure . . . his features shifted, or something . . . his nose changed
shape? No, something like that . . . I really don't know how to say it. But
he looks great now. All that's gone."

I was thinking about it too. It's the gaze of a person. If that gaze, that
look on the face, is clear and sharp, you have a totally different appearance
about you. If you have even a *little* less than perfect, you have a messy
look on your hands. It was this I had heard the parents at The Institutes
exclaim over more than any other single thing. The face literally changes
with the eyes. As Doman had said to us back in 1965 in that auditorium,
he had never seen a brain-injured child without a visual problem. It's the
most delicate expression of brain injury.

JULY 1, 1969. Chattanooga. Mother's friend called to invite me to visit
Siskin Rehabilitation Center for a morning and to lunch afterward.

Of all things, the director was my old childhood recreation-playground
director. Before I knew it I had dropped the information to her that my
daughter was brain-injured but not going the orthodox route through
physical therapy, speech therapy, occupational therapy, and all that. Instead we were redoing her babyhood and beyond, brain-wise. Yes, she
seemed to have heard of it somewhere, as we got deeper and deeper into
Doman-Delacato. And I must talk to the physical therapist, tell him all this.
And some other people in Speech and Hearing.

I found the staff spirit unbelievably open to whatever I said about Jane.
Then it was suggested by a couple of the teachers that the staff could be
assembled if Mrs. Napear will speak to us. And I was begging off. I was
not qualified, they really should send a team to Philadelphia to get the

whole picture of the whole child. I might pique their interest, but it wouldn't help the kids any. And the physical therapist said he had heard of the program and he was impressed with the progress I was describing of Janey up there in New York. He had also read the con statements by some physical therapists, the whole process of such a statement being made by a few he fully understood, they never poll the members on those things. That's what Mary had said. What you had now was a split among physical therapists. Those who did the old, those who did the new. The old guard was, of course, the statement-makers. And he had to go, he had stayed to talk with me, and wished I weren't returning to New York tomorrow. But his wife was waiting. They were to get their adopted baby this morning! And I was fairly screaming, "What are you waiting for?" And "Be sure to keep the baby on the floor!" And he was turning on the stairs and asking, "What?" "You know, don't get a playpen—the floor—for crawling, you know!" And he was saying, "Oh, I intend to. Know what you mean."

And in one of the viewing rooms—with one-way glass—I made the mistake of making a long-distance diagnosis of sorts. They were discussing one of the new children, somewhere in that age range three to six, wherein lay all the children in this quite special early learning center. (After three years here their deposition to special school, public school special class or home would be decided.) They weren't sure what this boy's problem was. And he was almost six and wouldn't be allowed to stay beyond September. And that was bothering them so.

"I think he has a feedback delay—auditory system." I had been thinking this as I heard the hesitating cadence of his speech. And here I was saying it out loud. So I went on, as if I had meant to. "He probably has a feedback delay, you know, he isn't hearing his words as he says them, the very split-second synchronization. You can tell by the way he talks, each of his words is probably being heard a few hundredths of a second later. That's why he slows down. A speaker does the same in an auditorium when the mike is bouncing his speech around a second later. He hates the acoustics in the place, but he keeps going. He slows down though. A child would do the same, if each word he says is heard a little later. It's like you're living in an echo world all the time, I think. You delay your speech to hear your speech."

The two Speech and Hearing women who were sitting in the room observing, said as I was leaving with the director, "Excuse me, we were listening to what you were saying. What do you call that again?"

"Oh, the feedback delay?"

"Yes, what do you do for it?"

"You have the child talk into a stethoscope, one thing I know. There may be other things you could do. But the time it takes for a word to go from the microphone piece of the stethoscope to the ears—up that rubber tube—well, that helps to reduce the delay. Gets the synchronization the brain needs to know about. The research on this is quite new, the mid-fifties, I think. It was found that speech was accelerated with this sort of stethoscope use."

"That's fascinating. How do you know so much about it? Are you Speech and Hearing?"

"No, my daughter is one of the guinea pigs on the new stethoscope program. She might very well have this problem." I told them about Dr. Edward Le Winn's book, which discusses this,* and, "I'll try to get you some more information on it."

"Oh, please do. And you think that little boy there has this problem?"

"He gives some indications of it. The speech plus what you were saying about his not being able to sit still in class. He's probably living in a pretty buzz-filled world."

All that had been quite enough. But I had yet to meet Marjorie Lander. And that I shall never be able to forget.

Marjorie Lander was still pretty, but she must have been a beauty queen at one time. She was secretary to the something-something director. And worked in the front office at Siskin. And at home or at work her heart was with fourteen-year-old Bobby Lander. A beautiful child, she said, who stands at the window now sifting sunbeams through his fingers. All day long. No speech, but there was some up until he was four. The last ten years had been one long road leading nowhere. From Florida to Chicago and to the offices of psychologists, speech and hearing specialists, a famous out-of-state psychiatrist, and another, and another. Ten thousand dollars had been spent on two years in Florida. The only thing Bobby got from that was a tan.

But did they say he was brain-injured? What did they say?

Marjorie Lander told me in exact quotes what this one and that one had said. "He had suffered innocent rejection, but rejection just the same." "Take him home and love him. Believe me, that is what I would do if he were mine." "Send him to the state institution for kids (and adults) like himself. If he stays home with you, you run the risk of ruining your family." And everywhere, always, "There is nothing we can do. There is nothing anyone can do." She had heard of the Doman-Delacato program, but thought somehow it was for younger children.

"Well, I suppose you've been through everything there is to go through, Mrs. Lander. I wouldn't blame you if you didn't want to keep on looking——"

"I feel just the opposite. If you'll send me some information to show my

* See *Human Neurological Organization,* by Edward B. Le Winn, M.D. Charles C. Thomas, 1969, Springfield, Illinois.

husband, to start the application process, I'll somehow get Bobby an evaluation."

"You mean, you aren't all washed-up—all cleaned out spiritually over ten years of this sort of search— This program also could be a dead end, but I wouldn't pass Delacato by if I had a child with a speech problem. If I were you. But you would go on?"

"Mrs. Napear——"

"Call me Peggy."

"Peggy— You call me Marjorie too— I know this sounds—well—you know— But I would go out there now and throw myself in front of a truck if I thought Bobby would benefit——"

"I know. I know. I know just what you mean. It's as if you'd give up your future for his——"

"I've had a ball. I wish he could."

I embraced her. And did not feel strange. That's what hurt the most. You couldn't bear seeing them not have a ball.

July 5, 1969

Dear Janey,

I often say to myself these "letters" when I'm doing dishes. When I'm wondering—in a fearsome way. Fingers crossed and breath caught up. But this letter I'm writing down. To remember. You see, now I'm wondering in that other direction. Because you're turning around, My Little One. We all know it.

Our return from Chattanooga brought a new report from Chris and Kay. You have been very silly in school. Very playful. And you seem to be planning it! Each naughtiness is much more directed. Each testing-of-the-establishment is much more sophisticated. (Have you been reading the daily papers, My Little One?) School, at best, has lasted twenty minutes with the teens, you are so silly. And I am crushed. And I am glad. You are very difficult these times, but are more aware. I ran to Mrs. Gross' house that first night home and asked her to come back for the two weeks before her vacation trip. And she will, her son will switch his swimming lessons to allow it. Maybe teacher and mother leaving at the same time was not a good thing?

The next day Laurie Watson taught you school for fifty minutes. Nonstop. And could have gone on longer. But couldn't believe it herself, so just stopped. Her buddy Holly and I sat down afterward at the school table to see what books, what workbooks, what materials they had covered in so priceless a session. You are saying words like *through* and *inside,* directionals more sophisticated than *under* and *on.* Laurie can tell when you are hearing something new. It's in your eyes, your posture, the special little head tilt. How easy it is to know when you are "getting it."

Your tremors are back again. Head only. But quite frequent and intense at times. I'm beginning to see a pattern and not panic. They ride the breakers of both higher speech and higher vision, and as impossible as it may sound, your tremors *are* a good sign. They arrive without warning, but they go as quickly. And we don't see them for weeks or months. But they signal another turn in the road, I bet.

I hate to write it down, so fragile a hope, but you are talking, Child. Like we do. Clear and loud. Phrases are coming fast. Your speech has developed a voice and a clarity unheard up to now. All of a sudden. The last month. And we're all standing around to hear you say, "All right, all right" and "O.K. O.K." and "Oh! No!" The word *and* is coming into every possible spot it can. "Chris and Kay" you say when you first awake and as you go to sleep. Is it that you want to see them that much? (They *are* funny and silly, aren't they?) Or do you love the alliteration? All three syllables on one breath. And all spoken as distinctly as we say them ourselves.

You are very smart. Or you are very aware. Or you have an excellent memory. Or something. After you said "tree and tree" and Marilyn said "trees," you quickly caught the idea of plurals, and plural-consciousness became your bag. Happiness is finding pictures for plurals when you've just caught on: boys, girls, and boys *and* girls, that's a fun one.

All the hundreds—thousands?—of pictures you are naming daily into the stethoscope, for four minutes now every half hour. Everyone is amazed at the weekly change in your stethoscope-speech and your picture-knowledge! One team almost flipped as you named "desk" and then went on to say "ink bottle" and "blotter." They hardly saw them themselves. I suppose your noun-knowledge is way into the thousands now. All this with beautiful diction.

And there is another turnaround, Janey, that leaves us hoping. Silently. Your knees. They are losing that rubberband resistance, that spasticity, that tightness in those muscles. We're all noticing it in patterning. And you're standing taller. The ladder has been raised, an inch at a time, from fifty-eight to sixty-one inches. Surely you have not grown three inches in two months! Much of that is in the knees? Sixteen times a day as you stretch-walk your way—toes to finger-tips—under the eight-foot overhead ladder, someone is watching those knees. Yes, they are straighter than a year ago. The pediatrician is right. Your knees are looser.

And feet? Function determines structure—it must be so. You are using your foot. And so, it is developing into a foot. A little girl foot. See? The eversion muscle is showing on the bottom.

And ankles! The hollow shows there beside the heel cords when your foot is lifting up. Dear Jane, doing 480 Strumpels a day on your right ankle. And 240 on your left. You can do it: we can do it.

The picture of you hanging onto the gym bar for a full minute and adjusting your hold to stay there—is that the most exciting picture of all to watch? What is it exactly that brings on the smile, that special eagerness when you are lifted there, again and again sixteen times a day, seven days a week, for two months now?

Does it all have something to do with your writing? Does that fine-finger grasp on the bar—the way you hold by the ends of your fingers to the last moment before you readjust—does that account for your very, very fine-finger aptitude these days?

Your writing strokes are heavier too, surer, more precise. All your geometric figures are closed solid and angles and corners are sharp. You can't bear to start the first stroke of a *k* the least bit on the diagonal! Since last December you went through all the years from three to six in pre-writing and writing. Three years in half a year?

Walking, talking, writing—we're seeing them, Janey. Close enough to say it now.

JULY 11, 1969. Jane has started stuttering. Just this week. A gagging, long, hang-up when she commences to say anything. A complete inability to elicit the first sound at all. Only a tonal hum can be heard. And all this with both hands making involuntary slapping motions at her sides. When thirteen-year-old Valerie worked with her this afternoon, she was to look Jane in the eyeballs and wait. As if to say, "I'm not alarmed, Janey, so why should you be?"

"And, Valerie, it will tear your heart out, to see her like this. But go right ahead with the sequences. You can cry when you get home. After all, it might be part of the normal route of speech."

"I won't cry."

"You might. It's the worst I've ever lived through with her myself."

JULY 16–20, 1969. Boston. Bert and I sitting at breakfast in Boston with friend Frank Opton. Frank mentioning offhand how his daughter Barbara is interested in baby development too. And how wonderful if we could get together. She is here in Boston at the Center for Cognitive Studies at Harvard with psychologist Jerome Brunner. Had I ever heard of it? I would find it quite interesting. I should go there.

I almost fell out of the chair, saying yes and no, as he insisted on calling her about it.

And then I was crossing the Harvard campus, wondering what I would find. The first person I met in the center was Barbara.

I saw three "babies" (eighteen, twenty, and twenty-four-months old), an hour apart, at Barbara's "toy," a specially constructed device she designed, as tall as the child and several feet long, with multiple things that could happen. If the baby made them happen. Babies in age groups two months apart had been doing this "toy" for four or five months now. Later she would decide what to really look for. Then she would attack one aspect. That was the best thing about what Harvard was doing. Keeping wide open. The word *intelligence* was not even permitted in this center!

I was of course watching the babies' bilateral handedness at this age, and the other postural cues of the two-year-old. A baby's coordination rather than his cognition processes. I was wondering if babies under one year, under cortical life, would be put to this "toy." Probably not, because they don't think? Cognition comes with cortex use?

Other psychologists were doing head-eye movement studies with babies. An object was moved horizontally, with and without a screen, and then lighted in a darkened room. As I watched I crossed my fingers that this group and The Institutes would pool their research someday on head-eye movement. These babies were seated or propped, looking out and around. I hoped they were also doing stomach-positioning, so the babies could look down and around, as they naturally do at this age. They had already seen that the head and eyes parallel each other, as the baby follows the object. I was wondering myself about what age does the child begin to move eyes independently of head, trying to remember when the switch occurred in Jane, thinking how some kids in first grade are still baby head turners with their viewing.

In another room I saw the ingenious system of lock boxes, devised by another psychologist. A series to work, a continuum. You couldn't start in the middle, that's for sure. And how old is a child who can do all this correctly? The young lady said usually a five-year-old can. But they had had a three-year-old "genius" who did it. I was wondering if his fine-finger ability, his visual perception, his eye-hand smoothness would not also be as interesting a study as his cognitive powers. And why *are* some smarter than others?

What is Brunner interested in?

How skills (along the way) are modularized, the models involved in children's learning processes (imitation, etc.). And she mentioned Brunner is interested in the relationship of tool use and language.

"Really? Great! He really should get together with the Philadelphia folks!"

Turning it all over in my mind, they seem to talk a different language here. Brunner, it seemed to me, was investigating what The Institutes would call the natural evolutionary triggering—from one step to the next. What causes it? The Philadelphians would say use. Number of times. This level well done will trigger the next level.

The best hope was that the two centers had the same subject under the microscope. The baby.

Waiting for a taxi, I asked Barbara, "Look, what would *you* say to mothers?"

She thought a minute and said, "Listen and look!"

Finally we were on the same wavelength. She was worried about the Cambridge mothers she sees, intellectuals, who want to know exactly what to do to make a bright child. What they really ought to do is get to know their children.

JULY 21, 1969. Marvelous homecoming. I guess I was running; almost fell on the tiled playroom floor, my sneaker turned. "Hey, listen! Jane is talking so clearly—without breathing—four words! She just said, 'No, I am not' as clear as I say it. She sounded completely normal—like a seven-year-old—saying, 'No, I am not.' "

"Sh-h! They're walking on the moon———"

Grant, staring straight ahead at the TV picture, was saying, "She's been doing that all week. When you were in Boston."

"Will you all, please, stop talking!" and Bert got up to turn up the volume.

"Grant," I was whispering now, "she said what all week?"

" 'No, I am not' real clear like that."

"Look, if you all are going to talk, please, go in the other room."

"She's saying a lot of things like that," Grant added, and then, "I'm watching the men walk on the moon right now, Mom. But she's talking real good, that's real good, isn't it?"

I skittered over to his chair, "Yep. What's good is the longer breath," I whispered in his ear. Then half-sat on the footstool to watch the great moment in history. Figured I'd catch it on the late news, and went in to stand outside her bedroom door. Finally I brought a stool into the hallway and listened, my ears straining to catch mid-breathings as she "talked" to the book pages. It is quite true. In one week Jane's volume has increased. That exhale breath for talking is at least one syllable longer. All of it is louder.

Professional Evaluation

July 23, 1969. Philadelphia. We felt especially good heading for this revisit. Bert and I both had worked hard, a nearly 100 percent program this time. And more! I had added many program extras and sensory surprises, filling each thirty-minute sequence with the richest intake (and chances for output) she had known:

1. Clothing, of all fabrics, for her to dress up in, a different texture from each teen who came to work with her. (They worked hard to find something they had at home which was not denim!)
2. Other tactile-manual joys, like play dough, clay, scissors, and path-way-board games like Chutes and Ladders, Candyland, etc.
3. ABC's, numerals and geometric figures, both *in*put (felt, sand, plastic, cardboard, rubber, wood) and *out*put (most recently onto one-inch ruled paper with pencil).
4. All maskings were with Jane supine, as we found her chest could rise higher that way.

5. The knee-stretch feel was added to every pause in the Strumpel sets when the leg was in extension.
6. An all-day quiet environment as an encouragement to Jane's voice to fill the void. (A Philly program which we did above and beyond, taking advantage of our vacation and Grant's being away from the house at camp.)
7. Whisper-times, to create an effect opposite of stethoscope magnification, despite the limitations it put upon our heavy discussions at supper. (Stu and I had a whisper argument one evening that left us weak and trembling. And laughing.) Jane was drawn to these conversations like some eavesdropping-magnet-of-a-child. She listened harder, so we did it more.

We had literally run a Head Start program all day. While watching J.'s reaction—to catch boredom or "pressure" before, not after. And still she had her free times and floor frolics a few minutes before the start of the next sequence. We were consistent as well as creative, and she trusted us.

Still her program was four short of the twenty sequences. Sixteen half-hours had been all we could manage. But those we had done well, every single day since May 7th. She had had *no* crawl or creep and little knee-walk opportunity. And the transition had been smooth. Except for the first few weeks of kooky eyes with the gravity swings and turns, I could find no negative reaction to the change in her life-style. The only answer to their question, "Do you see anything worse about Jane?" I could think of was that week of stuttering.

I could only exclaim how her output was on the move. Things you can *see* now.

But it was the input side they took a look at first. Tactile, auditory, and visual competence. And it was traumatic. For Bert especially. (Stu and Grant were giggling, I noticed.) A new room, a new man, and the same Jane. Up to a point.

"Knock it off!" He was yelling at her. "Don't try that with me!"

Jane eyed the man squarely. And she did not cry.

Again, "Stop testing me! I said get the *s* out of the bag. No! I only want the *s*. Thank you. Now the *p*. I want only the *p* from the bag. No looking. Just put the *p* on the table. That's right. Now the *a*—I'm not finished. Knock it off!"

Jane, with a face of squinched eyes and set lips, turned her head to the wall and rummaged around in the bag for the *a*. You could have heard a pin drop. And she plopped the plastic piece on the table and banged back in the chair with an air of finality.

"Now, Jane, which of these is the tallest?" And he held a flashlight and a dowel upright on the table. Apparently, a new auditory (understanding) test for Jane. Good sign. "Hands off! Just the tallest. I'll hold them. Which is the tallest? That's right," he said, as she flicked a reluctant finger at the stick and looked my way.

Then some more tallest and shortest stuff. I was leaning back in my chair for the first time. No, now this last stuff was "fattest" apparently.

"Knock it off, Jane. I asked you which is the fattest?"

Jane had stopped the squirming and dead-set shenanigans of I'm-here-but-I'm-not-here-so-there and sat bolt upright on the edge of the seat and yelled, "Be quiet!" It was the loudest I had ever heard from her, and it was long and drawn out. On one breath. From wing to wing of this building. Did the man realize?

"Excuse me," I was speaking very low, "but did you notice that new volume?"

"Oh, yes, that's what I'm writing down now."

I liked the way these guys worked. When it came time for reading, I took over with a vehemence. Despite tears. She could do it, so I required it of her. Just three lines about "Oh, Dick" and "Oh, Jane" and "Jump ——." Bert was excusing the boys to play football-catch in the drive, I noticed. He too would have liked to dig himself a hole throughout this scene.

It was all half-cry, half-whimper. And all fake. When that was done, I suggested another book and another page. So Jane would not feel she had won any rounds. The man agreed. Testing we were both experts on.

Afterward I told Bert, Mrs. Gross would have done the same thing. This was the way to handle her. This was the game she played. And she wanted to be its loser. That way the ending was not a mystery. She knew that I was the mother and she was the child. She was finding out who she was every single rebellion.

Perhaps it was fitting that on this day we should find Glenn Doman sitting down beside us in the waiting room. The first time we had seen him since his orientation-day-night almost four years ago. He asked to see her file as we began to talk.

"Oh, I can help you with this one." He was referring to one of her current problems: J. was wetting herself in some sort of urinary "explosion," Chris and Kay labeled it. The doctor had suggested a specimen of her urine, which we still had not been able to collect.

"You know about that? I mean, is it a urinary infection?" I asked.

"Very simple to explain. The bladder gets used to pressure this way, when a child is on all fours. And when the child comes upright, the bladder has to get used to pressure this way." He was demonstrating with his hands as he talked. "Time will take care of that. The bladder will get used to her new uprightness."

"Thank you. Do you mind if I make a suggestion to this program? Something we discovered at home."

"What you got?"

"When a child is masked, the lungs can blow up bigger if she's lying down. Bigger than if she's sitting, don't you think? You could tell parents to try it that way."

"You're right. Of course, now we know a better way. So masking isn't as important anymore. Last year masking was the best thing we knew for breath. This year we know a lot more."

"You do? What is it?"

"Isn't your kid on the new program?"

"She's always on a 'new program,' " and I laughed. "Now she's hanging from a gym bar and—" Someone was steering him away. Darn it.

"That's it," he called back. "That's what we learned from the astronauts."

Well, that's where it's at. Since May 7 Jane has been one of the first to go home and try what The Institutes had learned from the Navy's program for the aero-space men. That and a whole lot they had put together themselves. It was toward evening when we found out just what The Institutes *had* been researching these last months.

Jane was to do forty sequences a day from now till November.

She was?

We were to drop everything else. Including patterning and school. But don't get rid of the patterners. We would need them for this.

No school?

No school.

But she talks to her teacher. More sentences than to us!

Now she's going to work for more speech to everyone.

But she's doing so well in school. And she loves it. It's her favorite thing. At least give her school!

"If we could give Jane one gift, do you know what we would give her? To her and to all the other brain-injured kids?"

"No, what?"

"A large chest." The man (the same "Knock-it-off" guy) was bubbling over with surprises. "That is the greatest gift we can give to a brain-injured child. Room for those two lungs to blow up big in there. To send oxygen to that brain. To make the breath to talk out on. Now we've got the answer. Now we know how to give a large chest to a Janey."

Bert was on the edge of his seat, taking notes. I was lost in space, thinking up an explanation for Mrs. Gross. And the school district.

"—and the Navy gave them some checkers to play with," he was explaining. "And bit by bit, bite by bite, they removed the oxygen from the room where the checker-players were. And you can imagine what happened."

"What?"

"They began to fumble the checkers during play. Thumb-to-finger grasp got sloppy——"

"Oh, I see——"

"And the speech began to slur. Sloppy speech, we call it. And their vision began to blur——"

"Uh-huh."

"And their walking began to get a slight stagger— And they took another bite of oxygen out of the room."

"And all their functions got a little bit worse?"

"That's right. And if they had continued, they could have taken the men all the way down to coma that way. And then to death. And if you want to watch all areas improve," and he slapped the arm of his chair, "you do the opposite."

"So give some more oxygen," I was saying.

"A lot more," he was saying.

"And that's what we're going to do with Janey?"

"That's what you *have* been doing with Jane. The last two months. That's what they did for space-flight preparedness. They worked to give themselves larger chests. They hung from gym bars and——"

"All that brachiation-assist, arms stretched up to the overhead ladder, that's it too, isn't it?"

"Yes, that's what we came up with, and, at first, we weren't sure; but now you're going to do a lot more of it. Because now we know it works. Every kid coming back here has increased volume like Jane!"

"It's so true. Her speech is so clear now. And she's got four syllables without breathing, that I know of."

"We're going to expand her chest more than has ever been thought possible. In a few months. When she comes back, we don't want to see it micrometers larger, we want it centimeters larger."

"What is a centimeter? In inches. I've forgotten."

"An inch is two point five centimeters."

"Golly, that's a whole dress-size chest-wise."

"A large chest. And straight knees. That's what we want for Jane. Now. If she does this program all day, she will not be the same child she was come November. You can count on that."

Did we notice the way the men were walking on the moon? Toddler walk, arms at shoulder-height, more on the toes, moving around in an early cortical walk, as the baby does in its first encounter with gravity here on earth.

"Well, I didn't notice the moon walk that much."

"I know what you mean," Bert was saying.

"The astronaut has to learn to walk in one-sixth gravity up there. A brain-injured kid has to learn to walk in this gravity. Balance is ninety percent of the problem with these kids. He has the same difficulty as the astronaut on the moon, just maintaining his balance on this earth. We want to give him the best vestibular system he can get."

"But Jane has excellent balance——"

"Maybe we will see it get even better. Delacato wants this program for her for auditory reasons. The vestibular system is tied directly with the auditory one. They are probably more interdependent than anyone realizes."

"And school is definitely out till next revisit?"

"School is not the biggest thing she needs. Oxygen is. Then we should see all functions improve."

PART V

Function Determines Structure

To get some strong types—to work in teams of two to swing Jane upside-down between them in "negative gravity" and by an arm and a leg for "positive gravity," it was suggested by teens Marilyn and Laurie to put some posters around summer school:

Get a partner (if possible)
Volunteer three hours a week
"FLIPPED-OUT PROGRAM"
for Janey (seven years old)

1. Negative Gravity
2. "Hanging"
3. Masking
4. Positive Gravity
5. Strumpels

6. "The Rack"
7. Somersaults
8. Elephant Walk
9. Stethoscope
10. Free Time

This sequence (with two volunteers) is done every fifteen minutes twelve times, for a total of three hours. Watch it happen and make up your mind.
Open House: at Janey's ————

From then on it became "The Flipped-out Program." And with the ten-foot overhead ladder (on tall sawhorses) labeled "the rack," the living room sounded pretty much like a torture chamber to those who didn't work here.

J. had a five-minute free time between the fifteen-minute sequences, forty of them a day. All her houses and families, costumes and books, surrounded the patterning table, the label outlasting its old function. When it was time to start the next sequence, Jane was picked up fore and aft and someone murmured she could finish playing at the end of the sequence.

If you had dropped in during those days, you would have thought, this is silly (for a brain-injured kid to be doing) or this is barbaric (for the same reason). The latter was *said,* we were told.

Actually it was not barbaric, but it was primitive. Jane was literally between animal crawl and creep and human walking. She was somewhere into early uprightness—with brachiation assist, arms above the head. Somewhere in the stage between ape and man: chest expanding with the brachiation; fingers holding onto the "tree branches" of the overhead ladder; feet for the first time touching earth; legs for the first time stretching out. She was somewhere millions of years ago.

It was easier for the primate to contend with gravity if he held onto branches, for the first steps anyway (a few thousand years?). It is easier for the baby-toddler if he holds his arms at shoulder-or-above height. It is easier for the astronaut on the moon if he holds his arms in the same position.

Contending with gravity here—or one-sixth gravity on the moon—takes a lot of practice. You're pretty much a toe-walker, your heels aren't down yet (note the footprints on the moon), your knees buckle, your stance is insecure, and you tend to thrust head and shoulders forward. It is not easy to center down. You can see the same primate posture in the toddler, in the astronaut—and in the brain-injured.

We had decided to go the operation/bracing route only as a last resort— to try first Nature's way up the no-detour to development. For normal walking you need the brain to operate about four hundred muscles head to toe. You need a cross-pattern gait. And you need a serialization of all that together. Regardless, about 90 percent of walking is balance—contending with earth's gravity. Vestibular, and partly visual too.

It's okay, if you want to swing baby up to the rafters, turn him inside out, etc. The baby will add a sense of body-in-space to that sense of body-against-ground (no gravity) he got in crawling. When he's older it's not a bad thing to encourage him to head for the trees.

The day that Glenn Doman and staff got around to what is baby doing just before he pulls to stand, the day they pictured baby sitting there extending his arms above his head, that reflexive-like arm extension *then* finding the furniture, the world (the mother) above him to clutch and stand on—that day, with Dr. Dart talking, I would imagine, about early man doing the same thing, keeping to the trees for refuge from the open threat, reaching up to those branches, learning to stand—that day they saw once again the prehistoric leftover in the baby—that day, the day they discovered the *missing link* in mobility, brachiation—that must have been a great day.

They not only put uprightness into clearer focus, but they also found the way to give a child a large chest for oxygen to nourish and activate the live brain cells. The brain-injured kid has that undeveloped, sunken-in chest. Midbrain injury causes shallow respiration; sitting around all his life prevents his lungs from developing. Now they knew a quicker way to get deeper breathing.

Jane's new program had three goals: (a) a better vestibular system; (b) more oxygenation from a larger chest; and (c) the stretch at knees.

It sounded good. All you needed was someone to program it. We found it in Art Sandler, a new breed of physical therapist like Glenn Doman.

To do a program like this in a living room is another matter. There are no trees to stretch up to or down from, no side branches to graduate to later. You have to make all that as you go. Fortunately we had friends and programers who knew how to make ladders, splice ropes, tie knots.

I learned about board lumber, doweling, and galvanized pipe in the process. Made the first dozen visits of my life to marine stores. Was *there* when wooden ladders became extinct. Bert went after the hard items, charging many a luncheon conversation with questions like, "Does anyone here know where to get quarter-inch elastic parachute shock cord?"

Once again it was a small corps of people we needed more than anything. We began to pay teens a dollar an hour, then one-fifty to come more than once in a week. We settled back to this after a while: first time here each week—volunteer; second and third time here in a week—pay. This worked for *us.*

To pay for this we said good-bye to Louise Ames, our twice-a-week (at the time) housekeeper. I would miss her dreadfully. I needed the adult talk as we worked together. And she was Jane's fun, Jane's freedom —more than the boys, more than her daddy. Louise talked *to* Jane. Told her in detail about everything she was doing. Asked Jane questions, whether she "was talking" or not.

It was not until Louise had left that I learned this. She had actually done more for Jane neurologically than socially all that time. Not once did she send Jane packing or get angry with the repetitious behavior: Jane turning the vacuum cleaner on and off, turning the faucets to full force, and constantly flushing the toilet. All that stage went with Louise. A new stage of listening pleasure came with the stethoscope. The vacuum cleaner would never hold such a fascination again.

10

JULY 26, 1969. Mary Lawrence here. We slumped on the sofa and discussed how much had been learned—by "them" and by us—since we started all this.

Actually there were more programs than the day had hours in it, if you wanted to influence the live stuff of the brain-injured person. The problem now was what to leave out. And each child was different. There were no two brain-injured people who had the same set of symptoms in the same degree.

Mary interrupting, "Peggy, do you know what I'm aware of? This minute? How calm she is, sitting on the table-edge like that, listening to our every word— I've never seen her like this, so calm."

"Yes, Mary, I don't want to say it yet, but I think her hyperactivity is going—all away."

"Peggy, I think it's gone. Look there. How long has she been sitting like that? Hands in lap. Just listening to us."

"The random mouthings, the random movements, I guess, they *are* all gone."

"You know, this is the longest calm I've ever seen in a 'hyperactive' brain-injured child!"

AUGUST 5, 1969. All week, now and then, Jane is saying six syllables without breathing: "Oh, God, oh, Grant, oh, crap." That's right: "Oh, God, oh, Grant, oh, crap." Stu and Grant have never been so happy with her.

Today during the "open house" for new teen help, I was hoping it would not be one of her six-syllable days! Instead, she said "goddam" two times! A first, of sorts.

I was explaining "the flipped-out program"—what the poster was all about. That the gym-bar hanging, followed by masking (when the child is huffing and chuffing from the gym-bar workout), and the walk "under the rack" were for a large chest. Brachiation. At the end of every day Jane would have spent two hours on expanding her chest.

With negative gravity (swing by the heels) and positive gravity (swing by arm and leg, both sides equally each day) and somersaults, her brain's vestibular system would get used. Someone was trying to figure how much a child gets in gym class.

"I don't think we had *any* of that," a new girl was saying.

"Oh, you did some somersaults, probably some upside-down stuff on a rope, skin the cat, spin in a tub-thing———"

Then I lifted my foot up and down to show dorsi-flexion (up) and plantar flexion (down) and said for dorsi-flexion use, Jane would be doing one minute of Strumpels forty times a day and a half-minute of elephant walk (on hands and feet) forty times a day. The push-off of the toes in somersaults and the give-away floor under "the rack" would be that much more stimulation to the heel cords (Achilles tendon system).

For straighter knees the forty minutes a day walking with overhead ladder assist on the give-away floor was the main thing. But if you looked close enough, you would see a certain knee-stretch involved in the gravity work. And look at the elephant walk too, when she learns to do that by herself. "When Jane does a half-minute of elephant walk forty times a day for a week, she's done more for her heel cords and vestibular system than most babies would do in a month, I expect."

"What makes her do all this— I mean, she looks so happy—Doesn't she mind it? I mean, how do you get her to do all this?" Everyone nodding heads, as the girl went on.

"We're always asked that. And I don't know. Habit? Doing 'a program' is her day? Children go to school without thinking whether to or not—consistency? All of you coming in, like a little girl's private three-ring circus every day? I really don't know.

"One thing you will find out. She's probably the *strongest*—physically strongest—child this age you've seen. She has a tremendous torso-arm-neck strength. Her legs too are getting that way with all this exercise. Which reminds me—sometimes with a new person in Strumpels, she'll kick back at you. Her kick is powerful. Great hips from years of creeping, I think. The first time she does that, you are to hit her hard—like this, see my hand is back all the way—right on her fanny. Just once. If you hit her hard enough, that will be the end of it."*

"I think she's adorable-looking. She has dimples, doesn't she?" That was Diana.

"Yep. And she'll be a lot cuter with walking and talking, let's remember."

Then I told them to never skip a picture with the materials for stetho-

---

* Other than the situation mentioned here we never had occasion to spank Jane; we worked at knowing the levels of her understanding and tried to match discipline, teaching, to those levels.

scope-talk. She knows and says everything—like *rocket, satellite, launching pad,* and——

"She knows all that?" (One of the boys).

"Yes. Not the concepts, of course. But pictures are her favorite things, you will discover." And I showed them the lotto sets we had turned to in desperation, to perk up the stethoscope bit every fifteen minutes. Categories of fish, birds, animals, community workers, village landmarks, weather, etc. "They may look far-out, but she will enjoy distinguishing the finer ones."

We did not get forty high schoolers. We got six. Each *volunteered* two afternoon sessions a week. Their idea.

AUGUST 12, 1969. Spent the hot, sticky day in New York City looking unsuccessfully for a saucer sled. (For positive gravity, what else?) Called Marilyn to see how everything's going.

"Guess what?"

"Just tell me."

"I was doing the sequences by myself, you know, eleven to noon, till Laurie got here—well, I was pretty tired, after the morning ones with Chris, and kind of disgusted, well, I was feeling a bit lazy or something, so went to get a drink of water. I said to her, 'O.K., Jane, do your somersaults by yourself, I'll be along in a minute.' I looked back and she was doing them! Pushing off her toes. Her ankles move too."

"Marilyn!"

"That's not all. I said, 'O.K., Jane, do your elephant walk.' "

"She didn't!"

"She did!"

"Marilyn! You are completely incredible!"

"So when Laurie came, we did the same thing. Now all you need is one person to push her fanny over sometimes in the somersaults. She's tucking her own head under. She does about four pushes with her toes, then goes over. All she needs now in elephant walk is for one person to hold her fanny up. Her ankles are moving, weight is on the toes. Really!"

AUGUST 20, 1969. This occurred just after Bert and I settled Jane into the back seat, after her joyous bout with Don Gutstein. We had watched her hang and rehang her sweater on a wire coat hanger, and then stand in the closet doorway, hand on the doorknob for support, and do it again. Her knees are straighter. And her running knee-walk back and forth across the waiting room is quite unbelievable. We all got down to try it. She actually lifts her knees in "high steps" while racing in this fashion. Her new love: run as fast as you can on your knees; stop abruptly; change direction and head back, fast. Then do some somersaults because everybody is watching.

As the car started up, I waylaid Jane's thirst by accidentally starting a "conversation"—Jane's first:

ME: Two Debbies are coming to our house tomorrow! Debbie Collins and Debby Grant. And Marilyn will be there too.

JANE: I don't want her. (*Bert behind the wheel, jerking his head around, catching my surprise with his: her first "her"—and clear as a bell!*)

ME. I know [I didn't] you don't want her. But Marilyn is coming anyway. Because tomorrow is Thursday. Marilyn comes on Thursdays. (*As well as a bunch of other days.*)

JANE: Bye-bye Mar-i-wyn. (*Five syllables without breathing.*)

Me, exhilarated, half-laughing to myself. It was like that in my house too. The fellows my parents liked, I didn't want.

Bert dropped me off where I was spending the night—and tomorrow—in the city. I watched them go, Jane in the back, Daddy up front. Her chauffeur. Her footman-in-waiting. About now she was asking for "ice cream, please." And about now he was saying, "Would you like a Dixie Cup—" and letting her know he would find a delicatessen and stop the car, very soon now.

He was also her escort. To a friend's swimming pool each and every evening after her program.

He was her nursemaid. He carried her to the bath and bathed her. He would buy first one kind of bubblebath for her, then another. These days he was pretty excited over the Tinkerbell brand. He held her against the sink and taught her to brush her teeth, and talked about the different toothpaste tastes to her. And he brought her new clothes from the city, from clown pajamas when she was a baby, to gingham nighties now that she was a big girl.

Each Saturday he had done the grocery shopping. And there he had entertained her weekly with what's in the bookstand today, as well as what's new on the shelves this week. Unpacking the groceries upon their arrival home, there would be a doughnut missing out of the box and the usual banana peel, a new brand of cereal of the high-nutrition variety, and two new books.

The apple of her eye, the pal and playmate was Daddy. You could count on him to take you for a ride at eight in the evening. Or to the beach at eight in the morning, even if it were just for an hour. Jane in the back seat with her books clutched to her chest, watching Daddy drive up front.

AUGUST 21, 1969. Marilyn said when she went to pick Jane out of her crib this morning, J. said, "Bye-bye, Marilyn!" Bert had told her, before he caught his train, about last night's conversation. "She really *didn't* want to see me today."

"You know why, Marilyn. You're doing the program correctly. You're keeping the play out. The giggling. The talking to others working there. You're giving her the quietness which Delacato suggested. And she can't stand it. She's filling that void with her own language, believe me, and that's all that's important."

"I know, Mrs. Napear."

"We don't want Jane to be a listener, a watcher, a mimic. We want Jane to be a talker. You give her no show to watch. And you're about the best we've got. And Marilyn, she likes the way you make the requirement. She can't make up her mind. She likes to giggle at the others too. And show off. Her new self-identity is showing. Her new awareness of her achievements too. I think she likes both feelings."

"I know. But I really do want to play with her. Like we used to. I miss it too."

"I know. But we're not in the sentimental business."

SEPTEMBER 12, 1969. The first day of school* Mrs. Gross said she had heard J. say more in one hour than all of last year put together!

And today her announcement that she saw no more need for review. J. simply remembered everything. *Including what page what sentence is on. In each book!* J. had quickly turned to one of the old "struggle" sentences, and rattled off, "Nip naps on the mat," as if to say, "See, I can do it now." The problem would be to turn her on to new material, Mrs. Gross was thinking.

I was thinking Jane was probably bored with those old books anyway.

And Mrs. Gross was correcting me. Jane likes to master a thing. Her tendency is to perfect, not to leave undone. She likes to perform her very best. Like other children do. And she is thrilled to go back now, with her new breathing ability and dispatch those sentences. "You can just see her pleasure. Her pride. She almost trembles with each successful recitation! But we must go on. She still will not discuss with me her out-of-school life. I want to see her relate school—the book families—to her own family, their situations to hers. But I can't get her to do that. I want to see her find these same words elsewhere. She's so ready for it. But she won't make the transfer."

We decided to put those words into a box to be shuffled into other sentences, for stethoscope work. Would like to get off the one-word label-ing of nouns and verbs anyway. Now perhaps we could combine out-of-

* Despite the "no school" orders at the last IAHP revisit, we decided to continue with Mrs. Gross' one hour of home instruction daily, with the promise to ourselves that we would get into the day the entire number of sequences as programed, even if that meant working later into the evening, and as long as Jane seemed capable of such a longer day. At the next revisit we would report what we had done. Telling after, as anyone knows, is better than asking before.

school reading with stethoscope-talking. I'd try. Some simple ones, like, "Jump down, Smokey" or "Grant is chasing Brownie." You weren't really a first-grader till you started finding words you could read just everywhere. We've got to get her out of first grade.

"Jane is now in second grade." And Mrs. Gross turned at the door.

"She is? But she couldn't be. She's still doing first grade stuff. A lot of it——"

"Oh, you look at any second grade class. Some of the children are still doing first grade work. Let's say 'second grade modified.' "

"Oh, let's."

SEPTEMBER 27, 1969. Every part of Jane seems to be moving. Every combination of her moving parts! There are progressions in somersaults, right up to a beautifully coordinated roll with the hands stopping—zing—into a balance role at the shoulders, right onto a well-balanced Indian-style sit!

And is somersault-confidence grounded in early body-image (my arm here, my leg there), and all that's new is a brain-sense of "going over" in space? And what does this have to do with orienting (me) to everything (them)? What does comprehending yourself have to do with comprehending "that?" What does my body's knowing about edges, angles, distance, up, down, and around—and left and right—have to do with my brain's knowing about "what those people are doing in that story there?"

More and more educators are getting on the bandwagon of body-image, to floor activities like crawling and creeping, to even earlier pivotal movements, in their kindergartens. It doesn't sound so crazy anymore.

Mrs. Gross told me that crawling and creeping was done in several kindergartens in this district. One school had incorporated it into the kindergarten program three years ago! The principal still thought the gym program was the big key to remedial reading, and the place where reading problems could be largely prevented. All he had to do, I suppose, was to get the psychologists on his side.

Something new is happening to Jane's lower back. Hip region? Beautiful to watch, that arch like a swan-diver or a trapezist, head and shoulders up, when she's swung by the heels. Doesn't give in to it anymore, with her head down, but places her body in this beautiful curve, to look all around.

Same thing spinning in the saucer sled, head up now, as if to say, "I've conquered the feeling." IAHP didn't mention it, but I bet this is good for vision: J. trying to see as she's spun clockwise, then counterclockwise, gets set with her head and eyes before the reverse.

When she's not busy, often we find her lying on her back, lifting those hips and banging them down. Or on her stomach, to see how it feels that way. Don Gutstein agrees, her back is more mobile and stronger. That's the incredible part. Muscle imbalance is supposed to be synonymous with brain injury.

I almost forgot. Her new sit. There really are progressions of sitting. Hadn't realized there was anything after Indian-style. There is. Side-sitting. The way I sit on the floor. On one hip, with legs tucked around to the right or the left. Jane has been practicing this, ever so silently. And occasionally smiling to herself.

OCTOBER 17, 1969. Weekend with Mary Lawrence.

Out of the blue, Jane is stuttering now. So severe. Can get *no* word out. Just a kind of long hum with the first letter. For a week. How you want to run out screaming, "Not now! When she's beginning sentences!" But you don't. You just observe her, wondering how long it will last. Like that one week in July? Is it bothering *her?* She can't talk to tell you about it. And you just warn everybody and go ahead with her program, all the time hoping this is the last day of it. Each morning again, you pick her up, and she is trying to speak and can't.

Mary listening, then smiling, "So is Adam. A little. He just started——"

"Really? Lydia's little Amy is too. For a while now. She had been watching for it, a little eager expectation to see if the Philly people knew what they were talking about with respect to the bilateral two-year-old. God, I wish I had been expecting it——"

As Mary was showing me to my room, I said, "Mary, if Jane got rid of all the spasticity in her knees—I mean, if Jane did not have any more spasticity left in her body, what would we call her—what would 'they' call her?"

"I don't know."

"I mean, she wouldn't properly be a 'spastic,' would she?"

"I think they would just shout. That's not supposed to be possible, you know."

"I know, Mary. But I think that is happening."

"One thing. And I've thought about it before. We're going to have to get a whole new vocabulary because of this program."

OCTOBER 27, 1969.

Week of October 11 to 14: Severe stuttering. Inability to get any word out. Hung-up on a humlike start of a word.

October 17 (afternoon): Programers reported "some" stuttering. No response to stethoscope, wouldn't attempt! They thought she was bored with Lotto-card incentives (knows them all).

October 18 (morning): Programers reported no stuttering at all. (I was at Mary Lawrence's.)

October 19 (morning): Stuttering.

October 20 (morning): Stuttering.

October 20 (afternoon): Robin and Betsy (2:30 to 4:30) reported stuttering so bad, took five minutes to do five Lotto pictures in stethoscope program. I stopped stethoscope program last three sequences.

Claudia and Patti (4:30 to 7:30) did stethoscope all sequences. (I said to wait for her response.) They reported good speech—not as bad as on October 12. It was really bad then.

October 21 (morning): J. counted stripes on Mimi's skirt during mask-ing—"fist, second, fird, fourpf"—into the teens! Mimi and Debby very impressed. Didn't know J. knew ordinal numerals. Debby did all the stethoscope work. Said no visual material, just talk into it. J. talking about Buddy (Wechsler) all the time. Mimi and Debby said she's talking more than ever.

October 22 (morning): Pat Chapman said it's the first time she's ever heard J.'s speech struggle. (She was not here that week in July and J. didn't stutter last Wednesday at all.)

October 23 to 26: So severe! No words out at all!

October 27—today: J. spanked herself, so frustrated. Could she know yet she is different? Mrs. Gross: "She knows she *did* talk, and now is having difficulty. That's enough to make her spank herself, as if to say, 'Come on, Janey, what's wrong with you, falling back that way?' "

I was reading over the "chart" I had hastily put together, waiting for Delacato to come in over long-distance. Thinking of that last awful Friday, was it the twenty-fourth?

Now I was telling Carl Delacato how bad it was. How that Friday night my husband quite seriously had asked me, "Do you think someone might have dropped her on her head—and not told us?" That's just how quick all this had started. *Counting* is all she can do without a hangup. She's even started to count backward, just starts in the twenties somewhere and counts on back to one. Just to talk without stuttering? Does she know it? Before all this started she was whistling a lot. And all through the month of September some crazy involuntary throat-clearing, which began in imita-tion of one of the teens and was copied to the point of doing it all the time, without knowing it, I think. But everything else in speech has been so normal, so beautiful. Even sentences now! Lots. For her.

Delacato was asking about her revisit date. A week from tomorrow. But I couldn't wait. It's so awful.

Then he was asking me to take a look at what she was doing when all this started. Did he mean psychologically or neurologically or what? He meant everything.

That's what I had been doing. You couldn't see a pattern anywhere.

OCTOBER 31, 1969. Halloween for Jane. First good opportunity for calendar concept, and Jane drew an X across the calendar block (for the thirty-first) and turned the page. Aha! Tomorrow we would start the month of November. An opportunity in school to use the hand stapler again, and Jane made mashed flowers of orange and black crepe paper and place cards for tonight's supper.

There was no need in today's school for J. to talk. But with six (grandmother coming for dinner) pretty objects, there was a lot you could learn. Combinations of 5 + 1, and 4 + 2, and still you had 6.

And Mrs. Gross had dozens of things one might do, when talking was such a difficulty, that all added up to school.

You could go out this year house-to-house (as a witch), and not sit at the door in some stupid clown's costume like last year. Because now you are much older, and know exactly what is going on about Halloween. In fact, you remembered from last year. The *first* day of school this year, you mentioned Halloween and pumpkins to Mrs. Gross, because that was one of the first things just after school starts. Mrs. Gross was very impressed. Mostly about how much you remember that we don't know you know till you talk it. That day you were really talking!

NOVEMBER 3, 1969. I read Mrs. Gross' report while she was teaching Jane:

PROGRESS REPORT—JANE NAPEAR
by Elizabeth Gross, Home-bound Instructor
November 3, 1969

At the resumption of school in September, it was clear that Jane had made great strides in speech over the summer. She was able to repeat any word spoken to her and had started to communicate in short pertinent sentences. This situation has changed radically in the last few weeks, so that at this time I neither demand nor get verbal responses from her.

At the end of last school year I had felt that Jane was very close to reading. I had hoped that she would maintain the momentum and the interest she showed in word patterns and letter groupings. At this time however reading "leaves her cold" and consequently her attention span in this area is very short.

On the other hand she has become very interested in coloring, drawing, and writing, most especially numerals. Consequently the emphasis in these first weeks has been on number concepts, simple addition equations, ordered sequences—first, second, etc.—groupings, elementary concepts of sets as a group of similar things.

Since she gets great pleasure in drawing recognizable shapes and objects, she is willing to label them and so is getting some experience in spelling as well as letter formation, although in a most unstructured way. She is anxious to color pictures but as yet unable to stay in the lines.

I found her retention over the summer good and so she is able to recognize beginning sounds and words that were familiar to her even though she has made no further progress in reading.

But according to yesterday and today's performance in school, Mrs. Gross was dealing with a "talker" again. For two days now, no stuttering. All gone, the hum with it, the difficulty (to the point of gagging) just vanished. Jane at this moment was reading orally for Mrs. Gross. Or running her eyes and mouth along a previously-memorized sentence? So hard to tell, since she seems to have some kind of photographic memory.

I was dying to ask The Institutes staff about the dominance picture. She had been doing so many little "practices" with that right leg. In her free time she was often found lying on her left side, moving her *right* leg forward and back, then doing foot circling with her *right* foot. Before these days, she had gone through a lot of zigzag practice, I called it. Getting first into the homolateral pattern, facing left. Then moving into it facing right, the arms and legs making the appropriate changes in organization. Really she was patterning herself in a slow, deliberate, conscious fashion. But now she was practicing the right-stuff, not alternating, like lying on her stomach and moving her right leg or her right foot, and watching it.

All her mobility was increasing. She put on her shoes and socks with a more-decided dorsi-flexion of the feet these days. She was doing huge pumping-swings on the gym bar, and her feet were showing dorsi-flexion while doing this, for the first time. And everyone marveled at a seven-year-old kid doing all that for a minute, thirty-seven times a day, and never falling or fearing! And for a brain-injured kid to be doing this, well, that *was* news. She was now attempting backward rolls, having mastered them the other way. In fact, she was terribly aware of what her body was all about, against surfaces, in space, upside down, and sideways. She seemed quite thrilled with it, and quite busy trying something else she hadn't tried before.

NOVEMBER 9, 1969. Philadelphia. The letter (re: the revisit) to Jane's local pediatricians had been another exercise in brevity, according to the copy we received:

. . . Although Jane's neurological age has not advanced this past period of time, there are several functional changes that we find significantly better.

There appears to be a definite improvement in knee extension. Jane is able to walk on her toes, with an overhead ladder, with knees in approximately twenty-five to thirty degrees of flexion.* Basic language function shows good improve-

---

* According to Mary Lawrence, RPT, Jane lacked seventy-five to eighty degrees of knee extension at the outset of this diary. Consequently this report represents an improvement of fifty degrees.

ment. Jane has better breath control and seems to be more spontaneous with speech usage. Basic convergence still is poor, but ability to control her eyes has improved. A marked difference was noted in today's evaluation in that attention and cooperation were markedly improved over previous visits here at The Institutes.

We have basically kept Jane on the same neurological program as before, with some minor revisions.

We plan to see the Napears in three months for re-evaluation and shall certainly keep you informed of all revisits here . . .

It was to Art Sandler, the "knock-it-off" guy, that Jane was sent first. She went right to the chair beside his desk, right through whatever he wished to learn about her via functional tests for auditory and visual competence, all this, as if she had decided to turn over a new leaf at The Institutes.

At some point I found the courage to say a very quiet, "Excuse me, but you know what I'm impressed with? How she sits there so calmly today."

He looked first at me, then at Bert, and said proudly, "I just wrote that down. Almost in those words."

Later Carl Delacato said Jane's auditory problem could be one of these three, he thought:

1. Hyper—when *all* noise feeds in, no channel to one thing. For example, the distractable child who hears in school the kid behind him turn the page, the teacher put her pencil on the desk, the principal talking across the hall, the class at the end of the hall taking recess.

2. Hypo—when you have "less than" tuning in. He gave a whistle through his fingers, the loudest I had ever heard. Jane came running to his side. She reached over, at his knee, and put his hand back up to his mouth. Yep, he was going to do it again. Bert said, "Excuse me" and left the room. I ducked down and covered my ears; they were still hurting from the first blast, as if pierced through. He did the second whistle, every bit as loud as the first, if not shriller. Jane looked up at him and smiled, ear to ear.

3. Or you could have "buzz within the system"—delayed feedback, echoing, that sort of thing.

He thinks Jane "probably is *hypo*-auditory." The cause doesn't really have to be settled here and now. We are doing a program with her that would attack all three causes at once. That way we don't waste time singling one out for months, then another. But we are doing something right. "We have a cooler, calmer child here today," he added. Then he said some children are so hypo they are almost deaf. They are often labeled deaf. "Those kids are extremely difficult to evaluate. Even for me. And it's my theory!"

"So what do you do if you don't know if they are deaf or not?"

"We program them for a while, to get their listening started, if we can. Sometimes we can evaluate them better after they've been on program for awhile."

Then I told him about how Jane's favorite toy used to be the vacuum cleaner. And how she doesn't react anymore. Just takes its noise in stride. How her favorite pastime used to be echoes, only a year ago. Whenever I took her to Don Gutstein's office she would do a do-re-me both up and down the scale, perfect in its notes, except she did *o*'s in scalelike noises. She did this each time between the elevator and his office door, along the echoey corridor. She seemed to thrive on echoey things. Wouldn't that be "buzz within the system?" Or is it that she can take more of those weirdo sounds because she's taking them in softer than we do?

Whatever, we are attacking all three at once. For calmness, and for our speech to feed into that brain clearly, and for her speech to be thus copied correctly.

Bert had something to get off his chest. About Jane's life: no fun, no friends, no way to get out there and see some of this world, the poor kid was so busy all day.

Several times I tried to say all that didn't matter if she could *someday*.

Sandler and Delacato were asking me to let him go on. Then they were *telling* me to shut up. My turn would come next.

Bert was telling them what going swimming each evening had meant to Jane this summer. He thought *that* was responsible for an easier, calmer child to manage. She was happy— Just how long would we ask her to go on doing a full day's program? Mentioning studies about "diminishing returns" if you overworked someone. And what Jane is doing all day is unbelievable, even to us. When are we going to give some play and some friends to Jane? And get out of this house some? Just how much could she take of this? It's getting us all down.

I waited for him to finish. He seemed to have drained it out to the last drop.

"May I say something about this now?"

"And we've been doing this for, let's see, four, five years——"

"But, Bert, she's going to live for seventy more!"

"Will you shut up and let this guy finish?" Sandler had still not said, "Knock it off" to me, but I sensed it was just around the corner. Wouldn't Janey love that! She was over in the corner, sitting with her stethoscope in her ears, saying little one-words into it, looking at a book, apparently oblivious to the fact her mommy and daddy were about to have a fight.

"That's about all I wanted to say."

"O.K., Mother, what do *you* have to say about all this?"

"Well, first, about seeing the world— Jane knows so much—from books! She already knows a lot about that world out there——"

Delacato jumped forward in his seat. "Don't you believe it. Don't - you - believe - that - for - a - second!"

"Well, I didn't mean I accepted books as a substitute for getting out there, I just mean she's not dumb!" And I leaned forward in *my* seat.

"He's right! There is where we want her!" and Delacato extended his arm for emphasis, finger jabbing at the "world" out there.

"But I think seven years of her life or even more to do this program is nothing compared to what's ahead of her. She's got to talk *good* when she gets out there. Anything less looks idiotlike. I'd do anything, for as long as it takes, to keep her moving up and up to *really* well. Because I couldn't stand for them to treat her like that. She's so smart! Sure it's rough. But the other side of the street is rougher. And Bert knows it. And I can't figure out what you are suggesting. Stopping this work with Janey? Just what in the world are you talking about anyway?"

"I'm not suggesting we give up the program. Just that we lighten it a little, so she can do some other things. My God, she works till seven-thirty at night!"

"And she likes it, Bert. Not a single person who works with her has said anything but what a happy kid she is, *while* she's doing it. Simply gets a thrill out of somersaults, the overhead ladder, loves the whole bit. The gravity swinging sends her into tickles just to know that's next! So where's all the unhappiness you're seeing?"

"I didn't say she's unhappy. She just loved going swimming so much, at the end of the day like that. I just want to stop the program earlier, that's all."

Result. We would go from forty to thirty sequences a day. Actually from thirty-six or thirty-seven, the most we had gotten in the past period. Was everybody satisfied? I was. No more Strumpels or elephant walk—her dorsi-flexion was so good. Instead of the give-away floor we would have her walking on the carpet again, but with the overhead ladder from low to high (not exactly parallel to the floor), so as to extend the knees a little each single walk.

In high-top sneakers! To be put on while her feet were in dorsi-flexion, and tied snugly. Like a dope, I forgot to ask if she had to wear the sneakers throughout the sequence. I figured not. Those feet digging into sneakers before each walk with the ladder (now *two* times within a sequence) would be excellent use of the heel cords. At least I had decided to go the sneakers-on-and-off bit, and Jane's friends were all willing to go along with it. In fact, since we returned, that has been the funniest bit of all, checking who's good at lacing sneakers fast. And beating your partner!

At the last minute I spouted my two cents to Art Sandler who was programing all this mobility stuff. I thought Jane might be getting a dominant left hemisphere. And I asked him a few questions about the stuttering, which was all gone, I know—

"Look, forget all that about the brain. No one is about to think dominance with Jane. She's got a long way to go before that. Just let whatever is happening happen. Just be her mother, O.K.?"

DECEMBER 1, 1969. Jane's ten-day vacation from the program *was* probably what she needed. Today in school Mrs. Gross found her eager to list verbally the details of our Thanksgiving in a restaurant, including "New York City," "gold velvet dress" and "gold tights," who was there plus "grandmother." And the entire menu from "apple cider" through "vegetables."

We would probably never know what lay behind J.'s struggle for words the past month. It hadn't seemed to be a reoccurrence of what I had labeled stuttering, before our November 4 revisit. No, this was more of an *inability* to talk at all. Her mouth would open, but nothing would come out. In fact, I had called The Institutes on November 21 because it seemed that *all* of Jane's school abilities were lying dormant under a bog of some kind. As if she were searching to do even the simplest tasks, such as groupings of ten in arithmetic plus two more. Worse still, and let's face it, she was not performing in numbers or letters or in the most elementary beginnings of anything visual. And she was trying. There were no random behaviors, no restlessness, no testings of the teacher. Her attention was good. "It's as if she *can't* or something. Has nothing to do with *won't.*" Mrs. Gross felt terribly sorry for her. She was delighted with The Institutes' prescription: give her opportunity to do absolutely nothing, just let her play, and leave her alone to do it her way.

So, we let Janey alone. She often produced through the cloud of word-search the request, clear as a bell, "Go to bed." In the middle of the day she would say, "Turn light off" and would one-by-one list the items she wanted in her crib, apparently the bigger the better: her doll crib and the big brown plastic doll, the springs and mattress of the little bed forming a shelf over all that, the little bulletin board next, and then the huge box of play dishes on top. That stack of toys was joined on the other side with a similar tower of big stuff, including a toy chair. All this in the crib cage, with Jane Indian-style in the middle. Before I was out the door she would be urging me on, with "Bye-bye" or "Bye now."

At other times she was out in the living room on the patterning table or on the floor. But with it all went the pink blanket over her head and the mirror.

The bed scene she labeled "playhouse" after the second day. And there she would set tables, rearrange the furniture, and quite often snuggle down to a book in the midst of it. For ten days that was her favorite play. She liked dressing herself in funny flowing robes: a shirt of Stu's, a kimono or two from Aunt Lucille, an oversized shift from the Goldsteins. Or she put her clothes, whatever she was taking off, onto the huge Negro doll. Then she'd look at books for a while or get on with the housework.

If she wanted to stay there, I would bring her lunch to the "playhouse" on a tray. I was having a ball myself, cleaning my own house for a change. I called everyone and told them to stay home. I sat back on the refreshing turn of events, knowing for a week I would be free of schedulings.

DECEMBER 20, 1969. I headed off the mailman as he came in to deliver a box to Jane. Didn't want him to see her like this. I wouldn't have time to explain it to him, to tell him it must *mean* something—maybe some secret neurological reason for all this.

All this week I had warned everyone beforehand the instant they stepped in the door, drawing them aside, saying right off, "Now don't worry about it, but Jane has developed this awful thing. Her face contorts all over to her right side, and her head jerks over to the right when she's trying to talk. It looks just awful. But it happens with every single word, just before she gets it out. You may have to watch that sort of thing right through a combination of words. I want you just to wait for her to finish the 'sentence' or whatever. Just try not to let it bother you too much."

They had all been wonderful. For some unknown reason fifteen-year-old Beth Goldstein didn't get the warning. She was alone with Jane, did the program, and ran home afterward in fright to her mother, about you-should-see-Jane-today, and it is the most horrible thing. And it is.

All week Bert and I have been stopping to chat more. Mostly about her being like this. But under an umbrella, a question mark: is Jane going to look like this? Is it permanent? He has not asked me if someone might have dropped her on her head, but he has reminded me of what Doman said to the parents during our orientation about the group of brain-injured known as "the athetoids"—those with constant jerking of head and body, how all those "athetoids" begin up that road from what looks like a normal baby. Was Janey one of those? Was Jane in the old vocabulary both "athetoid" *and* "spastic?"

I had asked a pediatrician, what would you call a spastic child who lost all her spasticity? What "category" of brain-injured?

He was thinking. He was saying, quietly, "You could call it 'beautiful.' "

And I smiled, and laughed. He was right. It would be so remarkable, there was no name for it.

And now this. Janey had never looked ugly. Brain-injured-looking, yes. But not ugly brain-injured. She was always one of the prettiest in the waiting rooms at Philadelphia, we thought. (Did the other parents, from years of knowing each little movement, feel the same about theirs?) But Jane in the last years had gotten prettier and prettier as her eyes continued to straighten and her gaze clear. Her increased awareness, especially the higher and higher auditory competence seen recently, would place her face in the category with her peer group, or at least close to it. Now, out of the blue, we were dealing with a mouth drawn to the right side and down to a neck, itself jerking to the right and taking the out-of-control head with it. Her eyeballs were moving all around, pupils somewhere up and out of sight, with most of this nodding, jerking hell.

I somehow didn't want to have to explain it to Mr. Pohl, the mailman who was so eager to see Janey "better."

His back was to her, handing me the receipt forms for the packages; that was good, he was on his way. Before Jane could go into her "face" and her utterances, mostly expletives of a new breed, loud now with the increasing volume. Something of feeling rather than thought, easier for the brain to get out. Like "Goddam it" or "Aw, heck!" or "I'm sorry, never mind!" or "Stop it, O.K.!" The cute ones, like "Well, I'll be darned" and "O.K., good-bye now" I wouldn't have minded at all—they even sound like someone talking—but you never knew ahead of time which one would come out at the end of the struggle.

The packages (from my mother) I did not put under the Christmas tree. I let her open them. It was what she needed. Jane went into the unwrapping with full expectancy, fingering and patting each costume out of the boxes. First a full veil on a gold crown, decorated with colored stick-on stars. Elastic at the back, as she pulls it on, ducking in a chin-down sweep from side to side. And picks up the mirror; smiles at herself. Duck a little. And smile again. Then the yellow apron to match, of organdy. But first, a turquoise skirt of ruffled net, round and round she turns it, looking at the pink bows here and there nestled in with a dot of silver sequin, oh, my.

Now swishing and swaying and patting her sides. And back to the box for the cape. It matches. She ties a flip sort of knot and bends low now to the mirror. A ruffle of a hat to match. You are a princess. You're adorable again. Because you are too busy to talk now. Your shaking comes only with speech.

In the windows she sees herself, dark now out there; she's lifting the skirts up one by one, and smoothing them down one by one, turning to see the profile.

CHRISTMAS DAY, 1969. On airplane to Chattanooga.

This morning I put the finishing touches on Snow Village, my gift to Jane.

Finished instructions to sitter-programers. Terribly revved up these days over her breath increase, more and more, week by week. You can hear her even from outdoors now. "Goddam it" more than anything else. How beautifully loud and clear she can say that now. Even with the face-head contortions.

Reminded them all to continue the stethoscope program regardless. She doesn't mind. Just follow the stethoscope to her mouth, wherever it goes. Be sure she gets the whole word, or words, into it. Following the jerkiness is rough, but everybody is a wonderful sport, doing it correctly all the time. Say they love to hear the expletives, roaring sergeantlike out on the breath they are making!

All month what fun to see J. increase her vocabulary, her knowledge even further. Women (and teens) gasp over what she knows for her age now.

Jane had looked at nothing, opened nothing, heard nothing, since the Barbie doll from Aunt Lucille appeared this morning. She hadn't even eavesdropped, it seemed, till Daddy began the countdown, so we wouldn't be late to the airport. I had *never* seen her so occupied. The four sets of clothes, shoes, purses, hats, had already been on and off Barbie and the hot-pink velvet slack suit back on. That had truly shocked me. The closures— whether tiny snaps or buttons or zippers—were simply no problem for J.'s fingers. Only a challenge. And off she went. And on. The loops on the peignoir set *were* impossible. I could not open the teensy elastic myself. I was glad J. was seeing that Mommy can't even do it.

Had clutched Barbie through the late morning, the Christmas dinner Bert had managed, including turkey and trimmings, through the afternoon and into the car. Kept stroking Barbie's long brown hair and cooing and purring. The other little doll from Bert's mother was along for the ride too.

"Jane, what are your doll's names?"

"Bar/bie /an'/ Dol/ly."

"Where are they going?"

"To / the / ci/ty."

"Which city?"

"New / *York."*

That had taken an awfully long time. For between each word there was all that preparation or whatever, a severe facial and head tic, but who was going to care what it was— It simply made you want to turn and run. But she was persevering right through it to communicate. And what she was saying was coming loud and clear.

JANUARY 20, 1970. Another annual community meeting on education. Another panel: "Motivation for Failure." My notes:

> What is failure? What is normal?
> First—check out his innate ability. Set those standards first.

What then if he fails to make the standards we set?

We (educators) might not (punish) but family and community probably would.

What about the child who is a successful human being but not at school work?

I almost said "Yipes" from the audience. But someone on the panel was saying it:

As a general rule, how can one say that, when school is such a big part of his life?

At least some panel members agreed the problem could affect your life. Forever. And they seemed to be asking questions, that was good.

Why are there more boys than girls who have this problem (learning disability)?

The psychologist thought he knew. Too many women in a boy's life. (The room was in a gentle buzz, as if the mothers were making a collective decision of some sort.) I turned to Barbara Barnhart next to me and whispered, "I can think of a dozen developmental reasons for that one."

"I can too. Like what?"

"Not allowing him to be a baby. We are so eager to see him *standing* tall and strong and being a world-mover. Girls you don't mind leaving down and dumpy for a while, playing with sissy things, like sights and sounds and swatches of cloth!"

That, and you're not so afraid of what a girl will do if you take her out of the playpen. Everyone knows boys are made of puppy-dog tails. Too many women in his life? Only one, sir, to wreck the Grand Plan.

For the last thirty years we've seen the new math, we've seen science programs beefed up. But very little innovative techniques in public schools. We had hoped special ed would be *temporary*!

A cry for help! From a district administrator. That took guts.

The pediatric neurologist was going to straighten it out for us and listed the categories of children we were talking about:

1. severe emotional disorder
2. organic learning disorder
3. mentally retarded
4. physical disability—tremors in hands, for example
5. culturally deprived

I wondered after making the five-way split each day, how the doctor slept that night. Poor kids in Harlem always get number five, so goes the current literature. Take another look. Fourteen kids on a bed while four mothers are at work. The woman who is keeping them cannot afford a playpen, but she's got a double bed for all of them, babies and pre-schoolers, right in front of the TV. All morning. Then lunch or not lunch. Then the afternoon. There are all kinds of programs to watch. But they have one thing in common. Continuous, unbroken, one-pitch sound to the ears. And you can't get Johnny to listen to a "word I say." Try it over TV. That's his channel. At least he has a pathway for the TV sound, if not for the TV words. Johnny does not listen. You are right. He has never used his auditory system to catch this or that. He has never had the great boon of silence indoors if the TV's been on all day all his baby-sitting life. And with that buzz that permeates Manhattan shore to shore all day, all night, it may be that he's found no silence outdoors either. Silence, this sound, silence, that sound—that's how baby John learns to listen. Bang some pans around, whisper sweet nothings, play some sound effects records (or make the sounds yourself), as he crawls on his belly, where he can use first one ear then the other. Start him out like an animal, yes, if you want him human. And feed him lunch. One-quarter of his body's blood, river-way for the barge traffic of oxygen, goes to his brain. But for heaven's sake, don't label him anything. (Stop arguing about whether he's "culturally deprived" or "culturally different" if he listens and talks poorly; listening and talking are brain functions, whether the brain is in Harlem or not.) And don't color him either. (Percentage-wise, there are more white readers in Manhattan with a poor comprehension score—listening to what you read to yourself. And white suburbia, like black Harlem, has all the failures it can handle and, apparently, according to tonight's panel, all those it cannot.)

Someone from the county's Association for Children with Learning Disabilities was coming into the discussion. I was eager to hear what she would add. She had guts. Pediatricians, in her opinion, don't tell the parents the child is neurologically impaired because they might lose a patient.

The pediatric neurologist was not finished either. The parent *should* go to the family doctor first. He can say to "kooky overprotective" moms to "take the pressure off, let up on him." You had to be careful. There were all sorts of ridiculous get-well-quick schemes abroad. "There are people down in Philadelphia preying on parents—making millions of dollars——"

Barbara looked around at me, as if to say, "Here it comes."

I leaned over, "That's a new one. I thought doctors objected to it because it was so *in*expensive!*

---

* To date, including Jane's intitial evaluation at IAHP in October, 1965, we had spent $1,160 on her program (fees to IAHP), not including monies to programers (tax deductible as medical fees) or monies for program materials, which were not recorded, and which should not be considered insignificant, considering the cost of hardware, books, records, etc.

Barbara and I left before the question-and-answer-period. As far as I could see, no one yet thought to find out how the normal kids got normal. Did they think the "innate ability" depended upon the star you were born under? Or you got the lucky (unlucky) gene at birth? Then why bother with education?

JANUARY 22, 1970. Come to the "breathe-in." It was Marilyn's idea to call it that. And they nearly all came to entertain Jane on her eighth birthday. Doing *her* program. Without her! That was her gift: four hours of a kind of Doman-Delacato do-it-ourselves.

And Janey very quiet with a sigh or two, as if to say, "Anybody can stand on his head [one of her programs for negative gravity], let's get on with the birthday party."

Then the place broke wide open. My ribcage still feels the exercise. I think that is the hardest I have laughed in years and years. And Bert shaking so, the movies are sure to be ruined. It was the knee-walking race. One at a time. Start in front of the sofa, circle "the rack" on all sides, and back to the finish. Fastest one gets a dollar. Everybody trying to beat the nine-second record. And screaming the whole run, "It's killing my knees. Even through jeans! How*ever* does Jane *do* this?" (Callouses and charm, of course.) Around and around each one went, clunking and tripping, and falling across the finish, onto whoever was still there laughing from the last race. And Holly up, and pandemonium. "Take her picture. Take her picture. Don't miss this. You are out of your mind, Holly!" And she was collapsed on the hearth, holding her knees and crying dry tears, and so were we, holding our sides and saying she deserves more than any dollar. Seven seconds. Janey edging off the table now. In hysterics, like the whole scene. "Let her do it. Let her do it." Janey was at the sofa spot. Off and running. And everybody was screaming, "Clock her. Clock it. She's faster. She's the fastest. You can tell. Look at her go!" She tripped on her skirt hem once and never stopped, knees up in a real high-stepping run, all the way around. And they grabbed her when she came across the finish, and of course I didn't clock it because I am lying here on top of somebody, too weak to sit up. Tears were rolling down Bert's cheeks as he leaned against the wall, trying to get the welcome scene into the camera. And all of us lying in a muddle on the floor, grabbing at our sides. She *is* the fastest, can you imagine?

JANUARY 29, 1970. Yesterday one of the doctors at The Institutes threw a new puzzle piece into the ring. Or fit something together, perhaps.

The doctor had just said to Jane, "Let's see if you are a working girl. Yep!" (It was J.'s brown, calloused hand pads that were being examined!) So I launched right into how we had done the program every single day, except for Christmas and New Year's, and the ten-day vacation at Thanks-giving. And I had never called back because after that *one good day* of school when Jane listed everything about Thanksgiving to Mrs. Gross—it was the Monday after Thanksgiving—there was never another good one. Until yesterday. And Bert and I described the awful facial tic, the shaki-ness all over to the right, then sort of chin-down center, and gradually less and less. And it just disappeared overnight two days ago. You wouldn't believe it was Janey, she looked like someone else. And, of all things, now she is talking again. Better than before! Please, explain it to us.

"It's probably emotional."

"But isn't it a seizure equivalent? Aren't all tics seizure equivalents?"

"*I* don't think so. There is a staff difference about it. We're split about half and half on the subject. Something we're investigating though."

"What do you mean, 'emotional?' "

"Perhaps it was like a long, dark tunnel she had to go through and come out of. To a higher, more sophisticated speech."

And we talked about Jane's awareness. She was so aware, in fact, that for the first time in all our visits there, I handed in my notes so she wouldn't hear her difficulties being discussed. These days nothing we were saying was going over her head. And all our comings and goings were her major interest. Everything I had reported under "auditory competence" was new:

Increased awareness of all preparatory sounds of mother leaving the house. Generally more aware of all such "doing" sounds in and out of the house.

Knows schedule of teen-age volunteers, who follows whom, and on which days.

Originates jokes (usually substitution of name); for example, in naming who is coming next to work with her, she will say, "Claudia and Grant." (Grant *never* does sequences.) Huge laughs.

Much role-playing with houses, people, families, furniture, villages, and vehicles. Constant companions are two dolls: Barbie and Dolly.

Probably knows "yesterday, today, tomorrow." Seem to get all this without confusion. Never used in speech though.

Eavesdropping continuously. Knows whenever we are talking about her, even though her name is not used. Laughs at other people's jokes. (J. can have her head down in a book, all the while she is listening to us!)

Seems to get most of "high comprehension" stuff people whisper into her ears two times each sequence. (I suggested they use this opportunity to feed in new stuff about *their* lives, not hers: "I'm going to the bank to cash a check" or "I have a lot of math homework to do tonight."). She gets this sort of sentence sixty times a day, loves the whisperings.

Loves stethoscope stuff. Often role-plays after day's program with stethoscope in her ears, naming pictures in Richard Scarry's *Best Word Book Ever.*

New interest in making noises to listen to: she pitches objects onto cabinet tops or behind her in car, to hear them drop. Slams glove-compartment door and other doors while looking away from the sound.

No longer shakes her head in rhythmic left-to-right motion with the vacuum cleaner. It doesn't seem to produce any reaction anymore.

I was telling Mrs. Gross, they said yesterday in Philly she might have many more such struggles; this might be Jane's way as she tried to talk like the rest of us. As she attempts to correlate her output with the input she is now so aware of.

Mrs. Gross agreeing. The picture fits her so well. The perfectionist. Why not in speech also? And with a day like today, you can see for yourself that her only interest is in sentences and in stories with sentences. About each of her family, especially Daddy and what he does. Today in her new-found clarity she was thrilled to go back to some of the earlier stories and read them aloud. Or repeat from memory? How could you ever tell when a child wants to go non-stop that way?

"I saw Mr. Allopenna yesterday while you were in Philadelphia. I told him I wasn't going to give him my report this time. How everything had changed overnight! How her school day on Tuesday had made the whole report obsolete!"

We reread her report, laughing at each of the worries, and that day before the Philly trip, when Jane talked like she had never talked before. This was the report she didn't turn in to the school district:

It is very difficult to evaluate Jane at this time since she is encountering tremendous difficulties in speech and in many other areas that had been relatively easy for her last school year. Specifically she has trouble writing letters and numerals, although this *last week* this has improved. Since her reading has always been tied to speech, I find that with her lack of verbalization has come a complete lack of interest in reading.

She seems to look forward to her school time and her attention span has increased to one hour without any trouble. We have worked a lot with puzzles and drawings and have cut out both letters and words which were used in sentences and labels.

Although her interest in most activities is high, she is much more an observer than a participator. This is quite the opposite of her pattern of last year. She follows directions well and very often tries to do the task requested of her, only to give up with some frustration.

So I gave it to IAHP with this whimsy, "This report is obsolete as of yesterday!"

"Did they laugh?"

"They smiled, as if they had heard it all before, and then asked me how you used that hour of school each day during the speech struggle. I showed them one of your stupid sentences, with the words cut out and pasted on lined paper, with the huge black dot at the end, 'The king is eating hot dogs on rolls.' I said you made these things to teach sentence structure. I showed them the daily weather papers. And the calendar concepts. I told them that you kept on going higher and higher with her, whether she was talking or not. And Jane sits there for an hour, pretty well glued to your every word. Jane drew a picture of a cat—with hat, buttons, and I don't-know-what-all. It looked like a thing you might see on a bad trip. But she was saying 'hat' and 'buttons' as she drew them, so she must have seen a different picture. Then she wrote *c a t* under it. Lousy, but you could read it. And we all breathed a sigh of relief. She seemed to think she knew what she was doing!"

"What suggestions did they have for school?"

"They said you were on the ball. Just feed-in and forget about her output. But they say that to everything. She'll read and write when she needs to. Right now, apparently she needs to find out what's going on in the world. And she's making it her number one hobby." Not so much "nosey," as "earsy."

JANUARY 30, 1970. Laughing with Bert today about what to call the crazy new way to do "negative gravity." Cathy and Marilyn, who had traveled to Philly with us Wednesday, had thought of "Bat Girl," but then we had all agreed it sounded too much like "bad girl," and that's all the neighbors would need to hear. Bert showing me the letter he had written to his sister, saying, "That is *the* weirdest thing to try and describe."

Dear Lu,

I really haven't forgotten how to write, but the truth is that I just haven't been in the mood to do so.

We went through a very rugged period with Jane. She seemed to be making tremendous progress in speech over the summer—in fact, for the first time I really believed she might talk like anyone else—when all of a sudden it stopped. For the past three months she's had a tic and was virtually unable to get a word out without going through facial contortions. However—we went to Philadelphia on Wednesday—as if by some miracle, much of the problem disappeared. She performed better and with more attention than ever before. Everyone was pretty much pleased with progress in everything but mobility. Her knees are very tight and she is nowhere near walking.

We are starting on a form of therapy that will probably cause us to be hauled before the humane society. Jane, fifteen times a day, will hang by her heels from the rafters for a period of thirty seconds that will build up to four minutes (one hour per day). We are rigging up a pulley system so she can be yanked up pretty much like a side of beef. A friend of mine and I are going to a boat yard tomorrow to get a block and pulley so we can rig it up in the living room. Peggy doesn't quite know how to approach the shoemaker about making an anklet (two) for Jane that will be sturdy enough for her to hang by. . . .

BERT

FEBRUARY 4, 1970. Another plateau is ended. She is talking again. A glorious week of it. Talking in strings of things. Originating little two-part dialogues while she's role-playing. Devising little scripts, for a conversation between this person and that. Jotted this one down from my kitchen listening-post. (The slash means a pause, not necessarily breathings.)

SOMEONE: "No, no water now/ Jane-ee."
SOMEONE ELSE: "No water now/ Bar-bee-ee."
SOMEONE: "Daddy is in the city/ coming home soon."
SOMEONE ELSE: "No! Not now! (*Drops something.*) Oops. Whoops-s."
SOMEONE: "Daddy coming home/ seven o'clock/ supper/ with Jane-ee. Oops."
SOMEONE ELSE: (*voice high*): "I'm sorry."
SOMEONE (*voice low*): "Never mind."
SOMEONE ELSE: (*voice high*): "All righty."

Now I am wondering at the higher, more sophisticated level of each new spurt after the long, dry spells. As if she listens—for months—planning to copy it, planning to use it, but getting it terribly pat first. Or too busy listening to try any of it yet? And this week's effortless speech, all day, on and off, mostly on, rapping with Barbie.

Wondering about the speech-troubled children who arrive at nine on a Tuesday morning to take a test, a psychological test. Or even a battery over a period of days. This week Jane just might pass. Last week she wouldn't have.

This week she started listing all the days of the week while driving from Diana's house after dark: "Wednesday morning, Wednesday afternoon, Wednesday night, Thursday morning," and so on. Because Diana had just mentioned not coming Wednesday? Who knows why! How can you tell what she's aware of, till she says it? Mrs. Gross and I both agree, talk to her as if she does. You'll know whether she's listening or not, that's for sure. Knowing whether Jane is tuned in or tuned out is never the problem to us who know her.

Mrs. Gross could write a book about it. How you wish you had not required verbal answers, oral reading, etc., when the plateau hits. How you walk into school day after day all set to do feed-in stuff. And, lo and behold, she fills in the words this time. She's talking again. And Mrs. Gross brings out the readers this day, the workbooks, the everything. Today you can find out what she's learned in the last four months. A test of sorts. For a teacher's knowing. Until the next plateau, to which, I find, I am looking ahead already.

Telling women this morning: This child, who had made sixteen trips to The Institutes, finally had a good one last week. Short simple sentences anyone could understand. Because she had enough breath, for one thing.

Credit for higher language? No. She would have to talk all the time in three- to five-unit sentences to get full credit for the block on the Profile, "2,000 Words of Language and Short Sentences." No one-words. No couplet talk. Sentence talk, pure and simple.

"What about the chest?"

"It increased four times the normal rate—for her age—since November fourth——"

"Wow. What about the legs?"

"Better extension at the knees, both of them, they wrote down. The kid boosted herself to a treatment table down there, and the left knee went straighter to do it. Oh, yes, guess what? For the first time in her life she stood with her heels about one inch off the floor instead of on her toes. And another thing, the kid has a toe-dig on the left foot in crawling—can you imagine?"

"You mean they still check up on crawling?"

"Oh, yeah, crawl and creep and the whole bit she's not perfect in yet. I figure they'll check crawling and creeping till they are perfect—the toe-dig, the straight legs—everything has got to appear in the baby-stuff as well as walking, I'd bet on it."

"You think she's got more crawling and creeping to do *after* straight legs and her feet are flat on the floor?"

"I bet. They don't deal in detours, that's why."

"Ugh."

"Right. Here's the mobility report I turned in."

People commenting on her supine position (while masking). Now legs are together and more fully extended, closer to floor. She used to lie with her legs in a horseshoe position, knees flexed and out. This is noticeably different.

Overhead ladder: wide steps now of hands and feet. Bigger strides.

Gym bar: easily one minute. Good hand-adjusting. Swings on it with her legs extended in front of her into the air, as far as they can extend! Pumps herself, etc.

Gravity swings: during the positive-gravity swing by arm and leg, J. holds onto opposite shoulder with her free hand. For negative gravity she arches her back (both forward and back in "experiments"), head up and looking, like in a swan dive. Is this a higher body image? And is she crossing mid-line now (for the first time), finding that opposite shoulder "over there"?

Feet in dorsi-flexion to enter sneakers. Pushes down hard with her heels, harder though with her right foot than the better left one. Weird?

Gorgeous, finished, balanced somersaults. Arms used in balance-roll at waist-height as she comes to full sit.

She is allowed floor activity thirty minutes before supper because of her verbal request during speech struggle, and contrary to IAHP wishes. Knee-*runs* or creep-*runs*. Tries assisted standing occasionally, looks improved to family: better balance, more secure, perhaps a little straighter in the knees, hard to say.

In all of J.'s activities, I think her right foot is getting to be the preferred one. During masking, she draws circles on the floor with her right heel, also crosses her right foot over the left in some sort of secret practice. She never uses the left foot for any of this. Don't you think this is interesting—that Jane is crossing midline with her lousy right leg? ("Stop thinking dominance with Jane, Mrs. Napear.")

In last week's scene in Philadelphia, she may not have appeared as any sort of exciting case to them, but to us she looked like a raving beauty. We stumbled into the waiting room, over and around children, big and little, lying still or sitting or sprawled prone at toys and food on the floor. There were twenty-four back for revisits, three times the normal number. Something about Glenn Doman away next month. Reschedulings each day this month. I saw it all immediately through Cathy's and Marilyn's eyes, tear-filled from the moment we stepped inside. Shock. Your heart falling out to see so many this way at one time.

There was four-year-old Billy, a tiny towhead. His mother, cute and blonde and from the Midwest, was holding her hands over his on a piece of wooden dowel, occasionally lifting him off the floor to hang a second, as she chatted with us. He was developing a hand-grasp or something. I figured she had spent the day doing this at home, and, out of habit, just continued doing it in Philadelphia while waiting for the next staff person. He was all smiles whenever she lifted him up, and she didn't seem to mind either. And Marilyn and Cathy and I sat there in total awe.

Billy had never crawled forward, after one and a half years of patterning. "We just about patterned his pants off too. Perhaps he was *too* young neurologically." Too vegetablelike. Anyway, they had put him on the new UED. Her husband had made it. And now he was moving forward, under his own steam.

"The new what?"

"The UED machine. It's got a motor under a carpeted floor that undulates. Like this." And she made waves with her hand. "It sends the body forward in the undulating motion, like babies first do. Boy, that's the greatest. A guy down here figured it out. A physicist who came down here for training and stayed to invent a machine to get fishlike movement for a nonmovable kid like Billy. It's the greatest idea they ever had. You can just see it happening, each day they move the tiniest bit by themselves. He's graduated from it now, from fish to amphibian. After four years, Ole Bill's amoving. Aren't you, fella?"

"That's lovely. But what does UED mean?"

"Uterine Extension Device. That's what they named it. Because that's what it is. All that undulating movement starts in the womb. Missing block they filled in, or something. For the nonmovables. Better than the slide-idea for him. Just in time for Billy here. A little more of patterning and we would probably have quit on him."

For the nonmovables. A lovely name. "Vegetable" was going out of style, like so much of the vocabulary of yesteryear. No one said "village idiot" anymore either. The kids coming after Jane would be luckier still. The world might even get interested in the nutrition of the mother during pregnancy, the important weeks when the baby's brain and nervous system are emerging and getting oxygen from the mother. We're so much smarter than we used to be. We say words like *handicapped* instead of *crazy*. We have a reverence for life now, don't we? Sure, it's 1970. At least in Philadelphia.

"He's doing it! Look at that!" Billy was hanging from her fingers. Holding onto her fingers. I was counting, four—five——

Her husband came rushing across the mass of kids on the floor. "Would you look at that!" Billy had started up again, his mother lifting him off the floor, as he clutched her fingers with his hands, and bubbled up at her, his head thrown back. "Hey, Billy, you can do it. See? What a big boy!" And she almost drowned him in kisses all over his head and neck. "After all these months, would you believe?"

"You mean this is the first time?"

"Yes. You just caught a first. Right here in this God-forsaken waiting room. Will wonders never cease!"

Marilyn and Cathy and I got up to get coffee, or whatever, stumbling along in one big wet blur. Billy was about the cutest blond "animal" I had ever seen at The Institutes. After two and a half years on the program, you couldn't say Billy was a failure. Because he was just beginning. He had movement forward, and today a grasp. The beginnings of manual competence.

We talked to the Californians and the Minnesotans. I saw the first wheelchair there in all these years, a twelve-year-old who had come by plane. And an eight-year-old boy, only slightly pigeon-toed, about to finish and "get outta here" with Delacato's blessing. Or maybe he would continue to perfect walking. Like the girl last time, all finished except for a limp.

Nine years old, the highest student and best reader in her fourth grade class. On the program seven years. Her mother, I remembered, talked to no one, just read a magazine, as if she was finished talking about it too.

And there was Karen, from the Bahamas with her Daddy this time. About six or seven. Half of those years she had been one Karen, now she was another. He said she had taken ill. Epiglottitis—inflammation of the epiglottis. For a time she couldn't breathe, and the lack of oxygen to the brain brought with it the Karen leaning against my knee. Her eyes had been a tremendous problem. But visual competence was one of the earliest of all areas to show change on this program. Here's a kid I would give anything to see a year later.

In the late afternoon we found out that two of the very severely hurt children belonged to the same mother. Sitting opposite us most of the time. Two of them, each on a program, in the same home, the same hell. This mother was not bouncy. In fact, she was quite cool. Works till 12:30 on program. Each day. And that is all.

"You mean, they only have half-day programs?"

"No. That's just all the time I spend on it."

"Why is that?" I could have bitten my tongue off.

"What do you mean? I have other things to do, that's why."

"Oh. Yes." And Marilyn and Cathy and I tried to figure it out. Perhaps The Institutes allowed them to stay on the program on that basis, because they had a heart here, as well as a head. Maybe she had a houseful of other children at home. Perhaps we don't have any business discussing it. What is it like to be kicked twice? Hard. In the heart? To be doing this program with a six-year-old child when you're pregnant. To be giving birth then to another one. Philly is a good place to go some days to feel lucky. On a clear day, when she's talking and playing like that, when you can look around you . . .

February 12, 1970

Dear Lucille,

. . . Barbie is the best thing that ever happened to Jane. We have a big speech breakthrough! How much is due to Barbie you can guess. We have heard the following sentences in the last month:

Barbie doll dropped on the floor.
Get down on the floor with Barbie. (J. wants)
Sit on the couch with Barbie. (This is after Barbie is pitched there.)
Daddy is in the city and coming back soon.
Barbie doll is in the city and . . . (same as above or "coming home seven o'clock.")
Barbie doll is sick in the bed, has a bad cold.
Barbie doll go to Wetson's, hamburger and Coke with ice.

I want Barbie doll right now.
(Where is Barbie doll going?) To the bedroom. (Also "village" and "city.")
Give Valentine candy to Barbie.
Wake up, Barbie. Go to sleep, Barbie. (Etc.)
House with Barbie sleeping. (J. wants)
House with people. (J. wants another house.)
Take Barbie doll bye-bye in the car.
Take her (teen working here) home with Barbie doll.

In short, The Kid is getting by with murder, because if Barbie gets to do all this, you-know-who goes too. You can be sure we follow-up every single request, when Barbie's "mother" talks them out this beautifully! . . .

MARCH 23, 1970. So shocked to hear, "When is Mommy coming home?" It *sounds* like a little girl.

And her hanging there *with one hand* from the monkey bar, every sequence like that.

So cute! Finding excuses to use only that right hand. With the left very "busy" pulling her shirt down, turning on and off the kitchen light, etc. And when she gets bored with that, she "walks" her hands side to side over the bar.

And swinging like that upside-down from the rafter. Did you notice how she can arch her back—to the front and to the back, *both* ways now— while she's hanging there? Now there is a beautiful bunch of muscle power!

And those somersaults. Better than a lot of children, don't you think?

Continuous forward rolls. Over and over, maintaining the balance, arms and legs, head all in the right spot over the carpet. I'm impressed too. You know what she does after that program all day? Lies there, attempting *backward* somersaults. During her free time, the thirty minutes or so of "floor" we give her before supper. Whoever is walking by gives her a little boost, over. Twice she's done it by herself, lands sideways, and tries it again. Stu is so eager for her to accomplish it, always running in to help her. Grant saying, "Watch me," and doing a bunch himself. All this is unheard of for a Janey who couldn't sit up five years ago.

"Mrs. Napear, I think she's *better* than a lot of children. I mean, hanging for a minute like that from that bar, that's something a lot of them can't do, wouldn't you think?"

"Yep, I think a gym teacher would be impressed. I know the local cerebral palsy center would be. Janey, how about a kiss for Louise? Oh, Louise, it's so good to have you back—even for a day as a sitter! And the house was a mess, and look how you've put it together again!"

Taking Louise home and telling her what I could barely admit to myself. "At least we know she can form a sentence from scratch and put in the pronouns and prepositions and everything in the right place. Brain-wise, I think she's going to talk O.K., I really do. Emotionally, I don't know what we are headed for."

MARCH 29, 1970. Easter Sunday. Jane is catching up. To candy! (And water to quench the thirst.) And music, of all things! As Grant brings his guitar to the sofa and strums, "Home on the Range." And then the "other one," "Skip to My Lou." And Jane is at his knee, bending over this magnificent music maker she has never seen. Nor heard, if we could help it. In some sort of frozen pose, only the smile flickering a sign of life.

"She's not supposed to, you know, so we'll have to cut it short," I was mouthing to Bert's mother.

And Grandmother is saying what you might expect, "Oh, let her. She loves it so. It's the cutest thing! She's just fascinated!"

We are all singing along with Grant. Janey too. Going up and down with the rest of us, and with her eyebrows, would you look at that?

"She is so adorable. When did she learn to sing?"

Rue the day. About a month ago. When the speech stopped, the singing began. Real singing with a beautiful breath-filled voice. All of which we had ignored. But for every *word,* we had beamed and praised. And it was more *singing* we were getting. With high notes and low. Not the monotone it used to be. Quite pretty, but she'd be the last to know.

And today it was tug all the way. Crying on the inside and letting her listen. Then a change of heart and stopping the music altogether. What you don't know, you don't want. And what you don't want, won't hurt you not to have. That was the secret. All the tomorrows we would go the work route. And make that a lot of fun. And think about her future. Get ready to say, "They may have, you may not have." Because the time was surely coming when she would learn her day was a different one. When her auditory competence reached that level of making the concrete comparison about "them" (walking) and "me" (in a wheelchair), than the abstract conclusion about not "doing so well." Already she was entering that world with Mrs. Gross once a week. They had been to the Easter display of animals-you-may-feed on the mall of the shopping center, but it was the people Jane was watching. She had turned off the animal bit immediately and tuned in to the department store whirl. And Mrs. Gross said to me, "Let's face it. She's tuned in to people and what they are doing. And that's that."

APRIL 24, 1970. Mrs. Gross was back with Jane from their weekly trip. Carried her to the patterning table. And quickly ushered me into the kitchen.

"Guess what?"

"What?"

"We got in the car out here, and when I started the ignition, I realized the radio was on. So I reached over to turn the music off. And she said, 'Leave it on, please.' Just like that. As beautiful as this: 'Leave it on, please.' "

"And you did."

"And I did. All the way to the library."

Mrs. Gross, fairy godmother, know's where it's at.

And I do too. I figured it out this week. I wonder if Glenn Doman and Carl Delacato didn't years ago come to the same conclusion.

> *To get speech for a brain-injured kid you need:*
> 6 tbsp. breath
> 6 tbsp. auditory competence
> 4 tbsp. motivation
> _____
> the whole cup

It is *not* the speech center of the cortex that is damaged? It is the midbrain, which controls early sound reception and the early mobility that gets the breathing going? And I'm not sure that motivation is not a sub-thing under auditory competence. Motivation is wanting it, needing it. And you have to be aware of it to want it. So maybe it's this recipe:

> 8 tbsp. breath
> 8 tbsp. auditory stuff

And most of these kids, who from *birth* have had the problem, are hurt in the midbrain, the most vulnerable part of the brain during the early wombdays. That The Institutes has been saying all along. That's why they don't care about the output. It's that input that makes the change. It's also the large chest.

And for the first time since we started, I feel like shouting. Because, I think, we licked the speech problem. Basically. Neurologically. J. can talk now. Emotionally maybe she's not ready to sail out there as a full-blown talker. Much of the time speech is on "hold" or "off". But she's "able," I know it.

When I am not shouting, I'm crying. Because I hope I'm right, about them—the silent, speechless brain-injured children the world over—and about her.

APRIL 29, 1970. Mrs. Gross brought her report for us to take to Philadelphia tomorrow.

Because of the severe word search that Jane has been plagued with most of the year, her academic program—as we had pursued it last year—has come to a halt.

My report would be the same as the one I submitted the end of January except for the following observations.

Once a week Jane goes on a field trip outside the house. This has stimulated great enthusiasm and participation.

She is very attentive and well behaved, and the erratic behavior we noted last year has disappeared.

After school Mrs. Gross said, "But I think Jane's pulling one of her before Philadelphia turnarounds. So this may be obsolete next week!"

Yes, the speech was back. Especially in school. The feedback from the field trips was "worth all the other school days put together," she had said.

And as usual, after the long struggle (this time with head-facial tic and a stiff-neck look about it), the speech is higher and more sophisticated. And perhaps this *will* be J.'s pattern of moving up and up. Perhaps the struggle hinges on being more aware and feeling more inadequate to copy or to originate it. I say perhaps. It's delicate ground to do unearthings in. And I really don't care. I can live through the long dark tunnels if the light is going to be brighter each time at the end. I can get used to patterns.

"You know, Mrs. Gross, this report is true. As far as it goes. But I don't understand why you didn't mention the other things you do. Is this all you are going to say?"

"What else do you suggest?"

"Well, the speech is output. What about all the increased awareness? Affect. Input. You keep saying she's 'getting it.' That would be very important to them. And to the school district."

"Didn't we put all that in the last report?" She read both of them again. And chuckled. "You know, it's a funny thing, all that understanding—that comprehension, well, I guess I just take it for granted now."

"Well, that's a good sign."

"Yes, you forget fast how she used to be."

And so she added this to her report:

In spite of the lack of measurable program, I strongly feel that Jane's comprehension has improved markedly. Our school time involves stories and talk (on my part) that is *not* reinforced by pictures, and which deal with some abstract concepts.

She is drawing elementary figures with some detail and starting to cut on prescribed lines.

E. Gross
Home Instructor

"How's that?"

"Fine. If you mean it."

"I wouldn't put it down if I didn't."

You would never want to exaggerate Jane. That we agreed on. And yet, I don't think we ever mentioned it to each other.

Went to library to get J.'s library card. Thinking about the field trips. The language from it. About motivation. How right Bert has been. She needs to get out more. To have more to talk about. How difficult, when you have to direct your speech from center stage all the time, sitting in the middle of the patterning table. How much easier it comes offhand to Barbie or to Mrs. Gross when you're not so conscious of the talking, you're so busy with the scene.

And I am wondering how long, how long. And how to beat the emotional overlay before it gets full-blown in and around her. Before she's finished the program. That old pain always there, deep inside, wanting her to know the happinesses I have had. Wanting her not to be hurt. Wanting to trade places with her. Thinking I could stand it. Thinking she could not. It's so rough out there. They'll tear her down.

Professional Evaluation

April 30, 1970. Philadelphia. On the Pennsylvania Turnpike Bert added this to the notes I was preparing, "Well, I think she's worse than a year ago!"

"You what?"

"I sure do. She looks ten times worse."

"You mean that awful tic with the speech?"

"How do you know *what* it is? How does anybody know? And a year ago she was talking a lot more than she is now."

"Last fall."

"O.K. last fall. And she didn't look like that when she was talking."

"You mean like Helen Keller throwing herself around in *The Miracle Worker?*"

"That's about it."

"Don't you think she's more frustrated because she's more *aware* now?"

"I don't know what she is. And I don't think they know either. She just looks worse."

"You mean when she's *in* that struggle."

"Well, she's in it all the time!"

"The last couple of days it's gone away."

"O.K., so she's had two good days."

"You forgot that one month—all her sentences about Barbie I wrote to Lucille about." I read him my notes on Jane since the last revisit. And then, "So you see, she has traveled upward. But you don't see it. You don't see her. Because you are waiting to see walking and talking."

"That's right."

It had always been that way with Bert. Don Gutstein had known it too, and suggested Bert do the exercises to leg and ankle he had suggested last year. But that extra work hadn't lasted long. We had entered the forty sequences a day soon after and rarely did Bert have to do the program when he was home on weekends. And even if he programed her every day, it probably wouldn't have changed anything. Don had said, "Bert wants to see Jane walk and talk. And he's not interested in all the other stuff. He's like everybody else out there. When Bert is happy with Jane's progress, you can be sure, she's made the grade."

Jane needed one of us to know the little things about her. And one of us to remember the big. The Philadelphians thought it was good to have one of us not bogged down in the minutiae, I was sure.

And when we *left* Philly, I wasn't sure he did not deep down feel the same. All of it would be minutiae to Bert.

This: 90-degree dorsi-flexion in both ankles.

And this: knees straighter since last time. ("Marked reduction in knee-flexion contractions.")

And this: no operation indicated.

There were two good reasons why operations on tendons at knee (and ankle) should be a last resort. One, you could so easily destroy the delicate balance which exists between the calf muscle and associated muscles. And you would come out of the operation with a too-relaxed thing— "back knee"—more the rule than the exception in this sort of surgery. The best surgeon in the world knows it's a gamble, and there's very little winning. That's why, after the casting and convalescent period, the child goes to the brace man. To fit a brace up the leg, to hold the droopy knee into a straight line. And possibly crutches to help the stiffened brace-gait along.

Two (the biggest reason to them) is what it does to the child. It creates a personality change. It destroys the child's trust in you who dealt him the excruciating pain that accompanies this healing. His trust is never the same again. He never figures out emotionally why they did this to him. And, if that were not enough, the hospital staff, more often than not, treats the brain-injured child as if he has *no* brains. Ask their mothers.

I had invited Mary to join us in Philadelphia, knowing this would be discussed. She'd either be impressed with the knee change since last July or she wouldn't. But she couldn't get away. She suggested that we take pictures of Jane hanging from the rafters. With no clothes on, in case they needed to see the hip alignment.

So Bert had taken a roll of them, from all angles. To show the staff how straight J.'s knees *can* get. The staff passed them all around and laughed with us about what the film developers must have thought: a nude child upside-down from the rafters of a living room? Or was it some other kind of room? You could see the overhead ladder in the background.

The pictures were impressive. And something else too. The overhead ladder had been raised three inches, as the knees would allow it. And she had not grown three inches taller since January 28.

But she had grown! This too was medical news. Unless they wanted to toss it off as some "growth spurt due to maturation." They might want to, but this was "extreme" by either medical or anthropological norms. We listened to Jane's "accomplishments," as the usual letter was dictated from The Institutes to her doctors back home:

. . . She has shown an extreme accelerated growth this past period of time. Her height in the last nine months has changed ten centimeters [4 inches], which is almost three times faster than normal. Her chest circumference in this period of time has grown 5.4 centimeters [2 inches plus], which is four and one-half times normal . . .

We devised some techniques so as to assist us in helping the knees get straighter and to eliminate toe-walking . . .

The last was an understatement. Art Sandler used his imagination to come up with this:

To get a heels-down functional walk, which will incorporate the new 90-degree ability of the foot, she would walk on a floor of four-inch poly-foam under the overhead ladder and wear an orthopedic high-top shoe with a steel shank (steel inner sole) the whole length of the shoe. It would give Jane two choices in how she stepped along: (a) she could walk on the tips of her toes over the foam; or (b) she could walk flat-footed. One thing, she'd never bend that shoe to walk on the balls of her feet.

The bottom of the shoe would have a thin crepe sole glued on. (He borrowed this idea from the old physical therapy bag of tricks to prevent a poor walker from sliding on the floor.) As J. came out of the foam-step each time, she would have to step out with her toe leading, because with crepe on foam rubber she could neither slide nor shuffle. In fact, her foot would have to go into a higher dorsi-flexion "to get out," higher than 90 degrees. See? We have more. We bent our feet up, to see the skin wrinkle across the front there.

That wasn't all. As she got the flat-foot walk with the ladder at the present height, we would raise it an inch higher. Get the same walk there. And so on. Gradually we could also go to three-inch, to two-inch, to one-inch foam. The calf muscle would continue to be stretched functionally both at the knee and at the heel. All this without full weight-bearing with the overhead ladder assist.

Nothing you would find in a book. Because he was figuring it out. For this child. At this time. This is where she's at.

We are going for walking, period. All day.

The rest of her program was dropped. Temporarily. (For months? Years?)

Are they also a bit psychic down there? Because finally they were on Bert's wavelength. Get walking. If she could get off her fanny, no doubt her frustration would be lowered. That should make a clear world for speech. At the same time her chest will continue to increase on this brachiation program. Volume she can always use.

No, she is not allowed to knee-walk or do any other kind of walk. She will do *this* kind of walk all day. No, Mr. Napear, she may not have a free time on the floor before supper. Why undo what she's been doing all day? We want the brain to feel straight knees and heels down. That's all we want it to feel.

"If you're telling the brain about this kind of walk, you don't want to tell it about the old bent one at the same time."

I was thinking you could call the whole program "patterning" and be correct—oh, oh, he was giving in to Bert, "O.K., fifteen minutes, if you feel you have to. But no more!"

Bert was looking up a little? No, he had another complaint. He was looking ahead. How we're losing people because of lifting her. She weighs 65½ pounds, and she's *too* tall. And you're asking us to lift her to the overhead ladder all day long now? Concern for his wife's back, how rough it is on her now, and there'll come a day very soon when she will no longer be able to carry Jane.

Dr. Raymond Dart was sitting in the room. Observing. Over seventy, I knew, but eyes clear and sharp, face young and tanned. And I was wondering if he goes back and forth to South Africa (or is he in Philadelphia all the time?) when he spoke up for the first time.

"Think wheels."

"Excuse me, sir?"

"In the United States I would have you think 'wheels.' "

"Oh, I know what you mean. Somehow put her table on wheels? To get back and forth to the overhead ladder?"

And Bert saying you wouldn't have to go back and forth. Just leave it there, till you had to do "her hangup" thirty minutes later. Then both of us explaining how a teen-aged boy named the upside-down hanging "her hangup."

I was bursting. We could extend the ladder slightly over the table, and she could swing down to the floor of foam. And when she returned from the round trip, we could boost her back up to the table.

There were altogether about six or seven people in the room observing, all of them passive, listening along with Dr. Dart, to Bert and me "thinking wheels."

Now Bert was onto the important business. Summer was coming. And it's a crying shame, keeping her inside that way till supper time. Couldn't this little girl get out for a swim, say at five o'clock? What could a few more walks matter, and something about diminishing returns anyway, and there were a lot of people who think water therapy would be a good thing for her. But mostly she needs some fun.

"I order it." That was Carl Delacato.

"Excuse me?" That was Bert.

"I order you to take this kid swimming every day at five."

"You do? Thanks."

"Don't mention it. I think you're right, that's all. She needs the fun."

Whether Janey understood the plan of the future was a mystery. But understanding she had. Final credit for the sixth level of auditory competence: understanding two thousand words and simple sentences. "She could have had that long ago," Delacato said. It was true. She was higher than that actually. But they wanted a certain amount of speech to prove it.

As far as they were concerned J. was not at all yet into the sixth language level: two thousand words and simple sentences.

It was late. Delacato was leaving for home too. So I did not ask him if breath plus auditory competence equals speech. A lot, I gathered, would depend upon walking. And we were going for walking, come hell or high water.

11

From April 1970 to March 1971

MAY 1, 1970. Left this note for Chris and Kay:

> We are going to phase out the present program and start a new one. Starting today—with you—we shall phase out one thing. You may choose what that will be. (The thing you hate the most!) You may *not* choose "her hangup" or "the rack. Those are the only two things that are going to remain in her program.
>
> When you have decided, keep it out till I return (3:30). J. has to go to the doctor at 4:00.
>
> MRS. N.

J's appetite down. Seems rather lethargic. Or is she just so calm now? Asked doctor to check thyroxin level.

Barbie and Dolly stayed in the car. Girls and boys go to the doctor's office, dolls don't. She laughs, and reaches for me to pick her up on my leg, then high on my shoulder.

Informed the secretary-assistant Jane is able to go into the treatment room by herself now. I will wait out here. Just let her get onto the table by herself; she may need a boost. Tell her what to take off. Doctor should tell her what he's going to do. Then let her get dressed by herself and come out to the waiting room. Just as her brothers do.

Me, reading a magazine with one ear cocked and breath at "hold." Lady was hovering around J. anyway. I moved fast. Beckoned her to the hall. "I asked you not to help her. She can manage alone."

"I'm not helping her. I'm just afraid she might fall off the table."

"Jane can do gymnastics on a table like that! She's on one at home a great deal."

"Well, how was I supposed to know that?"

"I wouldn't have told you to leave her alone if she couldn't handle it. I know she won't touch anything either."

Went back to my magazine, without any sort of softening statement. Burning. Wondering if this were another example of the myth I would eternally have to buck: that parents overestimate their brain-injured child. (The *reverse* is more the problem—underestimation—with parents and professionals alike.) Only wanted to prove one thing. You do what you are told in a doctor's office. Later you can go out to tell Mom what you thought about it.

"She's getting dressed now. She'll be right out."

"Is she finished? Is that hers?" I stared at the huge blood-filled syringe.

"Yes. Only took a minute this time."

"But I didn't hear her cry!"

"She was very good today. Just stuck her arm out and that was that."

"Didn't she make a fuss?"

"Not much."

Glory be! And later this: the doctor asked, "Did she put all that on?" (Calico dress with long back zipper, white tights, and Mary Jane shoes.)

The lady: "Well, I certainly didn't."

I wandered to the corridor to receive J. With a frozen smile I said, "Jane has been dressing herself for years. The back zipper is the only new bit. And the calmness."

MAY 2, 1970. Hot May Saturday. Bert and I driving through the crowds of shoppers with Jane. Search led at length to an orthopedic shoe expert: "If anybody can do it, he can."

The guy would try. He had never seen a prescription like this one: steel shank, full-sole length. "Half-shank you can get."

"We know. Everybody we've been to today said that. Why do they make only half-shanks in these orthopedic shoes? Why not full; what are half-shanks for anyway?"

"Drop foot. All these kids have drop foot." And he showed us a picture in the catalogue, how the steel piece, long and narrow, runs from the heel forward, about halfway to the toe. Between the soles, inner and outer.

"Because they have been operated on to make the Achilles tendon—the heel cords—longer," I was musing to Bert. "Then the foot is *too* relaxed at the ankle. Remember? Like the 'back knee' Mary Lawrence and Art Sandler told us about."

He had J.'s shoes off and was measuring; then he looked at the size inside the Mary Janes, "I don't see how she wears these. Too small."

"She rarely has them on——"

"You know, she has ninety-degree dorsi-flexion!"

"Yes, she just accomplished that."

"She sure does. Don't ever see that."

"I don't suppose you would. I mean, they wouldn't need orthopedic shoes."

"Well, I don't suppose there are many around that haven't been operated on. That's the thing." He's standing and looking at us, "What is she going to do with these shoes exactly?"

I explained the details of the foam floor. And the overhead ladder assist. And the crepe sole on the bottom of the leather one. How we were going "to pattern" the heel-down *feeling* into her walk. I ended in a nervous laugh, I-know-it-sounds-weird-but——

He broke in, looked at Bert and then me, and said, "You know, nobody in New York knows anything about any of this." And he looked at the prescription form again, at the letterhead. "That's the place. Only people doing any of this. I have a nephew on that program."

"He goes to Philadelphia?"

"Yes. You know, nobody in New York has thought of *any* of this."

"Well, the Philly people are just *trying* it with her."

"It's a great idea. It'll take time. But it should work. She's got the dorsi-flexion."

"How about a new pair of shoes for Janey, Bert? Pretty ones."

"Good idea. Can hardly get these on. What is her size?"

"Thirteen and a half B."

"Are you *sure?* First of February we bought sneakers—for her program. I think they were eleven's."

It's true. In three months J.'s foot has grown two and a half sizes larger. From walking on it? "Function determining structure?"

MAY 4, 1970. Monday. Reported to Mrs. Gross J.'s re-evaluation last Thursday at IAHP.

"They think J. may have 'almost total recall!' They think it may have something to do with her thyroid level having been maintained above any sort of state of lethargy, the fact she never napped. Never spent a large part of her life asleep. (Does our culture require too much sleep of babies?) They don't know. They have another kid—also born without a thyroid gland—he's the same way. One of the doctors, interested in all this, asked us about Jane's memory. I almost burst. I always thought it was photographic or something, the way she remembers everything."

Mrs. Gross: "She does. She has good retention. Could be."

"I told them I think she memorizes the sentences so fast—through her ears—that we can never be sure she's reading or not. You know, when you fill in a word on old material, and she runs on with the rest of it. Perhaps her recall *is* that good."

"It's hard to tell, all right."

"Oh, guess what! That woman down there you talked on the phone to when you started with Jane—she's one of their educational researchers or something—she checked Jane out this time in the sensory areas. Could probably make a piece of wood come alive for testing. Tickled Jane with all sorts of silliness, 'Jeepers, creepers, where'd ya get those peepers?' as she's evaluating visual accommodation, and all. Jane loved it. One time she said, 'I like you. Now you tell me!' And Jane said, 'I like me.'

She turned around at one point and said to us, "I see all the difference in the world in this Jane and the one I saw in October of 'sixty-eight!"

Bert had been so impressed. "See how easy it is to test her, when someone like this does it?"

Mrs. Gross doesn't pamper. And still she gets performance. Wished he could observe school sometime. He'd love it.

Mrs. Gross said, "Now would be a good time. She's talking more again. Especially when it's offhand. Or off-the-cuff."

"Yep, that's the secret now, I think. Speech before she realizes she's *going* to talk."

"I find that when I start a sentence, drift off, you know, in a halfhearted way, she'll finish it automatically. I'm getting a lot of speech that way. Or if we're 'concentrating' on writing a story verbally, the speech comes, as if she's forgotten 'talking' to me, she's so busy 'telling' the paper!"

"Exactly! Down there Thursday she wouldn't name the colors in the wall-hanging. Then I started naming them incorrectly, and she couldn't wait to correct each one. Just rattled off their names, right behind me."

"Yes, the negative approach is always useful!"

"By the way, she still gets no credit for writing down there. It's got to be spontaneous writing on her part. She wrote a large messy *Jane* for them, but I suggested it."

"Same with me. She needs a real elementary school teacher. Someone who knows the ways and the byways to encourage writing. Someone to do the same with reading. I've been talking to Mr. Allopenna about getting her a first-rate elementary teacher for next year. She should have a different teacher every year. Like the other children. She's ready too. Her behavior is school quality. But I want to leave her with a good one."

I had known it was coming. I just didn't want to talk about it.

MAY 8, 1970. Last night for one and a half hours Jane talked. In strings of things, to herself.

"You hear that?" Grant's subdued phrase, repeated every few minutes. Pasted each paper and picture onto his 4-H Record Book pages, as if in slow-motion, looking up at me and saying, "She's really talking."

Quiet as two mice we heard every word, every word-ending, every syllable coming from the living room.

SOMEONE: Stop it right now. And sit down. And be quiet. Barbie. Right now!
SOMEONE ELSE: I'm sorry, never mind. Too noisy.
SOMEONE (*with lots of giggles*): *Too noisy,* Barbie. And Dolly. And Jane.
SOMEONE ELSE: Stop it, Stuart!
SOMEONE (*laughter*): Stop it, Grant, right now. Too noisy, girls.
SOMEONE ELSE: Now stop that banging and sit down and be quiet. Right now.
    And I mean it.
SOMEONE: I'm sorry.

Then out of dialogue into long experiments with one idea.

Daddy is in the city. No. The girls in the city and coming back soon. Going home on the twain. The twain. The t-w-wain. The tr-r-rain. Go to bed, Barbie. In the city. No. Go to bed in the bedroom. Jane goes to bed in the bedroom. With Barbie and Dolly. Go to bed, Barbie. Go to sleep. Read a story. Daddy read a story. No. Daddy in the city and coming home soon.

Today Chris and Kay sat spellbound on the sofa between sequences, listening to two hours of this. I felt there was a huge mirror up to the parents somewhere, as most of it sounded terribly autocratic.

She made me a Mothers' Day card in school today. A face in a flower, with a variety of colored petals all around (to practice staying in the lines, I guess). And inside she wrote *mommy, love, Jane*—with Mrs. Gross supplying *to* and *with all my,* and *from.* She needn't have. The last twenty-four hours had been Mother's Day.

MAY 23, 1970. Called Bert's mother. J. wanted to speak to her.

"Did you say 'Janey'?"

"Yes, your Lady Jane."

Jane was on her knees at the bedside table, having knee-run all the way from doll-play in the hall. "H'wo." Then nothing.

"Excuse me, Selma, she wants to sit on the bed the way I do. Just a minute." I moved. And Jane hoisted herself easily into the mother-role.

"H'wo." Nothing. Still nothing.

"Go ahead. Tell her to come see us."

"H'wo. Come to our house." A pause. "Bye now."

I almost fell over. She knows *our*. That about winds up the pronouns. Except *you, your, we, us, they,* and *them*. Well, there are more pronouns than I realized!

Grandmother was barely coherent. Very quietly she said, "Peggy, she's talking. I heard every word. She sounds so—well, it was just like a child talking. That's the first time I really heard her talk that distinctly."

"Didn't she talk that day you took her for a walk in the city?"

"Not much. She was too busy with that Barbie doll. I tell you, that was the cutest thing. The way she leaned over in that wheelchair to walk Barbie on the sidewalk."

It *is* cute. Also frightening. I think Jane wants to walk. Now. All role-play is now about walking. She has noticed. Everybody does it. On sidewalks it's very noticeable. As people's legs swing by you. When you're sitting, you get to be quite an observer.

JUNE 10, 1970. Picked up Jane's orthopedic shoes today.

About six Stu came in, right to J.'s table, put the lacrosse stick down and stroked her shoes. (Primed? No. That would never do. Boys better at freewheeling than I am.) "Oh, are these Janey's new shoes? They are like *boots!*" he purred.

"They look like *desert* boots." (That came from Grant in the playroom.)

"They are very pretty, Janey." And on to the next room to straighten Grant out. *Desert* boots are suede, for one thing. And another thing, they are not tight around here. And they don't lace up at all!

"I know, Stupid! I'm the one who has them, remember? I just told her that. Before you even got here."

Bless this house. And all who are in it.

JUNE 19, 1970. Grant, licking icing off beaters, paused, looked out across the kitchen, and made this announcement: "Well. I'm kinda surprised we survived this week."

I wanted to say a whole lot of things: how perceptive, you felt it too all this time, how many other weeks have you felt the same way, or is this the first— But all I said was, "I'm kinda surprised too. Boy, what a week!"

My purse was bulging with the *notes* alone.

Monday, the 15th: Mrs. Gross and J. "wrote a story" about what they had seen on Friday's field trip. Fireman Ed, the guide. His office, his phones, red and black. Each item of fire truck and equipment discussed and colored. J. talked; Mrs. Gross wrote.

After school J. asked for "Choo-Choo Cars Book," a Christmas gift from Stuart. Hadn't seen it since January, but turned immediately to the section about fire engines. The man *does* look like Ed! (That child's memory!)

Bert not here to read *The Little Engine That Could,* their evening ritual these days. So I suggested *she* read Barbie a story. J. asked for " 'Choo Choo Cars,' no, 'Train Book,' " and I sat Barbie against the end of the bed. J. scooted up, turned around, and nestled in against Barbie, the way Daddy does when he reads to Jane. I listened in the hallway:

Ed goes to the off-sis in the firehouse. Off-sis. No. Ossfis. No. Off-sis. Offsis. Ossfis. Oss-FIS. No. OFF-sis——

About seven or eight times? I started counting the trials. Twenty-one, twenty-two— Finally!

—OFF-ice. Office. Ed goes to the office in the firehouse. Ed and Daddy go to the office in the choo-choo train book, no, in the choo-choo train. Ed goes to the office in the firehouse. Daddy goes to the office in the city——

Tuesday, the 16th: Ordered table on wheels (operating room type gurney table) from drugstore. Everybody leaving program for summer. Must shift to one-person program on wheels. Now! Teens graduating from high school. Women headed for vacations.

Annual pediatric checkups for camp. And Jane 3:15 P.M. (J. no program: Marilyn and Cathy studying for exams.) Stu in first. J. on her knees ran away from me and screamed when I said, "Your turn now." I said it again, complete-announcement tone. She went.

J. did not cry at all or fuss with blood-taking today! Assistant said, "Very good today. Even better than last time."

Doctor said, "She's older now."

Yes, her auditory competence is. Her understanding is, that is.

I did sequences from 4:30 to 6:30 with Chris. Her last time here. Ever. I didn't cry. I didn't even say good-bye. Enjoy New Hampshire. Enjoy Minnesota. "See you around, Chris." I closed the door. And then I cried.

Wednesday, the 17th: I watched school again through the almost-closed Dutch door between the playroom and me. To place these last few days with Mrs. Gross in my memory forever. To live on if the new teacher next fall is not a Mrs. Gross.

Marion here at sequences with Jane when the two men from drugstore arrived with the gurney table. The last day of the patterning table; everything is changing. I'll set it in the playroom for a while until I can get used to throwing it out after all these years. There were so many firsts on that table, so many personality breakthroughs, too, as Jane began emerging. A baby grew up on that table to girlhood.

Kay here without Chris. This girl also would be here one more time, on Friday. Wheeled the table under the pulley, hoisted Jane up. Ah, as we thought, J.'s chest was still in contact, as we fastened the rope to the wall hook. Push the table out of range, she's fully hanging now. It works. A one-person deal. I hung around anyway. To enjoy the last of Kay.

Thursday, the 18th: To village at nine, for metal straps and nails. Peg Wallace and I screwed metal straps onto the joint of the newly extended overhead ladder, hammered the separating piece to the base to spread the sawhorses an even twenty-four inches apart, laid the foam floor, and got in one sequence. On the third of the ten round-trip walks, Jane swung *herself* down to the foam from the new table. Peg had predicted she'd do just that before the end of the day. I was glad J. did something grand; Peg had come even though her son and daughter-in-law were in New York overnight and were leaving just after "Jane" this morning.

J. made Grant a birthday card in school. She wrote *happy* and Mrs. Gross wrote *birthday* because there was so much to do, all about coloring a boy and a baseball picture, and the words *Grant* and *Jane*. The whole thing was a foot tall on the wall when he arrived for lunch. He gave a perfunctory nod and asked, "Did she do all of this?" Everything except *birthday*. "That's what I thought. You can tell Mrs. Gross' writing. It's not as sloppy."

Marilyn and Cathy here. Their last day.

I raced to the nearest Macy's store. Found some psychedelic-looking shorts Grant might like, a golf meter for his wrist, and a bicycle pump I'd wrap all funny ways. If he guessed it, he'd get his bike fixed free by his parents again.

Picked up Diana on the way back for the 4:30 to 6:30 spot. The new cake mix, orange-something, had turned out beautifully, thanks to Marilyn. The laundry was all done, thanks to Cathy. Each had worked alone with J.

It was time to tell them good-bye. I broke into sobs. I couldn't think of anything to say. Cathy was the one I always felt the urge to put my arms around. I just loved that girl. Because she was so loving, I suppose. A long, quiet loving of my child, that's what Cathy meant to me. And so I just hung onto her. And cried. And then I grabbed Marilyn. Somehow she was like my mother. Both of them—the most capable teens I had ever known. I was telling Diana that in all the years, they had only rarely not filled their scheduled turn with Jane. A turn that was more often than not every other day. Or two days in a row. And all the summers! These two—you could mark off Jane's dorsi-flexion to them. They, with Laurie and Holly, poured thousands and thousands of Strumpels and crawl boxes into that child. I wondered might she shrivel to a plateau somewhere when they left.

And Stuart was coming in the patio door, crying. "Ma, Brownie is dead."

I was looking for the Kleenex box. "What's the matter?"

"Brownie is dead."

"Our dog? Brownie?"

"She's just lying out there, dead. The flies are all over her."

"Honey? Your Brownie?" And I covered the distance through the yard. Diana was there too. Brownie lying there, in rigor mortis, her foot caught under the wire fence of the pen, and blood and flies. She must have bled to death during the night, but she didn't whimper. Daddy or I would have heard her. Maybe an artery and quick.

Grant was explaining it all. He had just come out into the yard to let the dogs have a romp. And Brownie didn't come. She just lay there. And how he had walked over. And run as fast as he could past the house, over to the school yard where Stu was playing ball. To tell him his dog was dead.

Bert was coming in the door, to manage Grant's Little League game. And Stuart was selecting the spot to dig a grave. And I was finding my old college suitcase in the shed to bury her in. Bert was crying now with the rest of us. As we passed each other we cried aloud. With Daddy here it was worse. Because he loved that dog, and that dog loved him. He was telling Stuart he could have another little puppy to raise. As soon as they could find one.

Diana was doing sequences with Jane in the living room. By herself. And the gurney table. Jane was boosting herself up to the table once in awhile. It wouldn't be long before we wouldn't help her with that either. Thank you, Diana. It was the first time I had stopped crying in almost two hours.

On the way to Diana's house, we discussed J.'s increased awareness, her new "world view," which is noticeable today again to Diana. "She's so different from when I first came here. Or is it that I realize how much she understands?" Both. But the affect is so much higher in the last few weeks; I'd say now there's no stopping it. And I told Diana about Jane listening for her own correct speech too. Like the office-bit the other night. Twenty-three times till she got it right.

"She's really great, this kid. Really sticks to it; she's like that. She's just like that. I don't know what you call it, but this is one child that never gives up."

True. Part of it is the perfectionist. But part of it is a secret. She's just like that.

The three "men" returned from the game in a cloudburst, and Stu strode quickly out to the backyard in the rain.

"Supper-party's ready."

"Leave him alone," Bert said. "He wants to check the grave."

Smokey would spend the night inside tonight. She was so lonesome. It would take her a while to get over it. Grant had figured what each eye glance and ear twitch had meant since "it happened."

Our eyes were burning bright and wet as we sang "Happy Birthday to You." Jane, I noticed, was very different with this singing. Calmer? Quieter? Just looked at Grant intently, with her head cocked a little to the left. None of that frenzy tonight with the start of the song. In April we had noticed it too. (And we hadn't been looking for a change.)

As soon as it was over, J. without looking left or right, swung her plate over to me, as if in pantomime with a hat and cane. Everybody saw it at once and laughed. "Grant is going to open his presents now. We'll have cake after supper." No howl. What do you know?

JULY 1, 1970. To everyone these new instructions: IAHP says to say to Jane "Put your whole shoe down" or "That heel was down. That one was not." For the first time we are asking Jane "to do." Heretofore, we have simply changed the environment (this hour will be spent in the crawl-box), to get the performance we want to see. But now the cortical approach is O.K. ("Think-and-do-this.") Walking is a cortical function anyway. Praise her like crazy when she does it.

And for the first time in this child's program—no, in her awareness— Jane is trying.

I got her cue. Yesterday, after the sixth walk in the ten, I said, "You are doing it, Janey. I knew you could do it. You're putting your whole foot down. Just like all the people who walk on the sidewalk! And it looks very pretty today." And she listened and smiled. And for a second hid her eyes behind her hands, peeking out. She has become self-conscious. Just when it started is hard to say. Perhaps with the tic-bit last winter? When speech fell below its previous level? She has developed a shyness at times, as any child does with the directness of such a remark.

JULY 15, 1970. Grant and I picked up Stuart at the camp bus.

"Well, how was the last week?"

"Fine."

"You didn't put your shirts somewhere again and forget where you put them, did you?"

"Nope."

"See any of those kids you worked on the farm with last winter?"

"Yep."

"Hey, Stu, pass your intermediate swim test?"

"Nope."

"Did you get any sleep last night?"

"Yep."

"Look, Grant and I would like to hear about some of your experiences, and we would like for you to hear some of ours. So could you just share one or two things with us?"

"What would you like to hear?"

"A different attitude, for one thing."

"Well, let's see. Here's one thing. I won the Sportsmanship Award."

"Really? For what sport?"

"I give up."

"Don't give up. You've hardly started. Just explain it to me."

"It's not for a sport."

"I'm listening."

"It's just an award. You know, sportsmanship."

"It means the best camper, Mom. They have it every year." That was Grant.

"How's Janey doing?"

"Oh, she's entering the 'terrible two's' again, we think. Very frustrated. Wanting to walk, it seems. Have to watch her. She's been trying to walk, standing up on her gurney table! When we're not looking, of course. She's quite self-conscious, hiding behind her hands in a sudden burst of shy-ness——"

"She started that before I left."

"Well, it's more often now. She's terribly frustrated. I think she's begin-ning to know, if not already, that her walking and talking leave something to be desired. Once in awhile she throws herself down and around uncon-trollably, as if in a complete give-up or something."

"She's always done that."

"When was the last time you saw that, think?"

"Oh, last year, the year before——"

"That's what I mean. She hasn't for a long time. This is not to get attention, I don't think. It's like she's saying, well, like 'I give up.' Just terribly frustrated. People get like that when they start *wanting*. And she wants to walk and talk. She's never shown that before."

"How's the walking coming?"

"Left heel down a lot. Right heel lousy. Both a lot better since you left."

"Does she like it?"

"Oh, loves it. Wouldn't do it, if she didn't, I guess."

JULY 16, 1970. I was driving Diana home. All I said was, "Well, how's your other three days? At the cerebral palsy camp?"

"I don't go there anymore."

I hesitated and then, "What happened?"

"I went there three times and I couldn't take anymore of it."

"You mean they look so bad?" Immediately I saw the insult of my remark. Diana, if anyone, could stand the way they looked, she knew so much about the brain and what it did to appearances. "Excuse me, Diana, I shouldn't have said that to you, of all people."

"That's O.K. No, it wasn't that. It's the nothingness, the waste. I couldn't bear to see the waste. The first boy I had, that first day, couldn't walk. And that's all he wanted to do. I was to push him from activity to activity in his wheelchair, 'to get him involved,' as a spectator, you know, watch the others and get interested in their activities. He was all the time trying to leave the chair and asking to walk, wanting me to take his braces off. He couldn't even stand up, they told me. I asked for someone else for the next time because I didn't know how to handle it."

"That's rough."

"Well, the awful thing, he wasn't the only one. So many kept this up all the time. Other volunteer girls were having the same problem. We were told to treat the children as if they were normal. To distract them, just ignore it, and try to get them involved in what the other kids were doing.

"There was this little girl. She was the same age as Jane but half her size. Very thin and undeveloped-looking. Her head drooped down on her chest, like so many of them there. She cried the whole day. There was only one way to stop her and make her smile—by saying 'chocolate pudding,' and that's what we did. So I took her, and like the rest, tried to encourage her and to get her involved. I wheeled her from activity to activity, holding her head up because, Mrs. Napear, I don't think she could see with her head drooping that way. But even at the edge of the pool I couldn't get her to attend to any of it. There wasn't one solitary thing there she could do. And I just couldn't take the make-believe. It's such a waste, her spending her day there."

"But was it a waste for everybody?"

"Definitely. They've got all these normal things to do, but nobody can do them. I thought about it. I think the parents feel it's probably the only thing to do, to get them out of the house and let them enjoy themselves."

"What other things did you do?"

"Well, we were told to get them involved. That means get Bobby to draw a picture. And you can see that Bobby can't pick up the crayon. Or anything! So you either guide his hand or draw the picture yourself, adding this or that, a face, some hair— And at the end you say, 'Very good, Bobby!' And that just killed me. And I felt it was an insult to him to make-believe he did it."

"Didn't the other volunteers think it an insult?"

"I can't understand it. They are told to do that. And they just do it. And I think it might have been different for me, but not after working with Jane. I'm really helping her. I can see her change. I don't care how much work it takes— There's just all the difference in the world, her program, the way we treat her, just everything about it is different. I didn't feel I was helping them."

"Well, at least you were a baby-sitter of sorts."

"You don't really mean that. The thing that broke my heart were the teen-agers, the brain-injured ones, not the volunteers. They've got awful psychological problems about the way they look, knowing they are not as popular as the younger, better-looking ones. And it's true. They wander around all day, knocking what the younger ones are doing—in crafts, on the swings— They are bitter. That's what got to me, contributing to that make-believe, that waste— We were told to 'Cheer them up,' 'Make them feel better about themselves.' And that's what the job was all about."

Thinking what Mary Lawrence called it: "do-gooders at bureaucratic baby-sitting."

JULY 24, 1970. When Marilyn left the message that she was available a few weeks to work with Jane again, I couldn't believe it. And it was to her I first showed my new system. Walk along *with* J. and mention every single step, count the good ones, encourage the not-so-good rightie, but let's get those heels down. Do all of this without bugging the child. It is possible.

And Marilyn had taken up the torch and with less fervor and quieter cheering than I, simply had required of Jane that she put every single heel down. I still couldn't believe it. Today I watched her again. Fourteen consecutive heels-down steps that child took, with Marilyn barely batting an eyelash to get it.

All week I had paid her to come in and show the other girls. So they would know it is possible, first of all. And to show them, this is now the requirement. When we find Jane *can* do a new thing, we then *require* it of her. Otherwise we will never get to first base with walking.

The next base is to move this child on to an increase in ladder height, and still get her heels down. But we've got to get a heels-down walk at this height first. And if we raise the ladder when she is asleep some night, then how is she to know what her knees will have to do on the morrow!

AUGUST 5, 1970. Fran and Emily not only take J. to the pool at five o'clock, but they have been teaching her to swim! Took the life preserver off and have her swimming (human stroke, you know, dog paddle) from one girl to the other. About ten feet. No fear at all. She's having a ball trying it. Something we could say about the full cycle. Astrologically. Earth, air, and water child?

Also, someone figured the distance Jane walks each day:

10 feet × 2 × 15 walks a sequence × 16 sequences = 4,800 feet.

AUGUST 6, 1970. Took Jane to the library to choose two new books. And who did we run into at the entrance but Mrs. Gross! Immediately the backs of J.'s hands went up to her eyes. Gradually she moved them aside, to peek, then back again, as Mrs. Gross spoke to her. From the moment she spotted Mrs. Gross she had started an ear-to-ear smile, and that ecstatic trembling. And I said something about there being happy self-consciousness as well as the negative.

Mrs. Gross talked about Mr. Allopenna's eagerness to find a good elementary teacher for Jane. I couldn't shake off the feeling. What would the teacher see first thing? Decidedly the frustration level was increasing. And Jane at times was resembling Helen Keller in the first act of *The Miracle Worker*. The speech hangup was back. We hardly heard anything but our names said over and over and over.

"Mom——"

"Yes, Jane?"

"Mom——"

Standing and waiting.

"Mom——"

"What is it?"

"WHAT!" (This said at the top of her voice. Accompanied with thrashings of arms.) Then, "Mom——"

"I'm listening. Finish the sentence."

"LISTEN!" (Or some word repeated from what I had just said.) And more waiting. And more struggle. Till some one-word request was squeezed out.

And with bitter projection I wondered what lay ahead, what I would learn about the psychological side of things, as I had learned of the neurological. And the urgency of this day.

SEPTEMBER 9, 1970. Called Mrs. Gross about The Institutes' no-no yesterday. Jane needs a free person for a teacher, not a technician to put her through "the skills." That's what she needs now. She will write, she will read, she will develop all the skills when she *needs* to. Children break apart words to analyze them at some point anyway. "Do you see that little boy who was just in here. Talk to his mother about it. Last month she called, all upset over his reading. He was finding all the *b* words and sounding them out; then he went through all the others doing the same. Wasn't interested in the story at all, just busy at word analyzing, like he'd found a new game." I remembered Jane finding 10's and 11's in all the words with *o* and *l* together or two *l*s. That's when she hit the number-kick for the first time.

Jane has the manual competence, the visual perception, and whatever it takes neurologically. But remember, she is a "lone" student. She is not under the value-systems that the teacher sets up to overlay classroom work. "On this wall I shall keep a list of those who master the addition facts first. Over here we will hang the best penmanship papers. When you finish the questions on page forty-four, you may get up and choose a book from the library shelf." A classroom teacher does not wait for the time when a child *needs*. Competition takes care of starting and stopping.

What then for Jane's teacher? Do: feed in ever higher and higher concepts. Feed her increasing auditory awareness—that's her bag right now. Feed her visual interest. Skills she can always get later. Don't ruin them for her now. When she wants to write a letter or a note to someone, she will fling herself headlong to the task. Writing should be kept in its "communication drawer" anyway. Keep the teacher you have, if she is as free as you say. Let her take Jane higher into this world, keeping in mind always its wholeness.

Coincidence from all corners. Mrs. Gross reported she had been asked to stay on with Jane anyway. She was coming back Monday.

SEPTEMBER 15, 1970. Mrs. Gross brought in a pet for Jane to feed and care for. (A good way to learn about death, we decided) A turtle, which Jane named "Buddy," after a series of girls' names wouldn't do.

Mrs. Gross still could see no behavior problems, no Act One Helen Keller.

You know what we did? We instituted a rule: you are not allowed to scream or shriek. It works. Just as Carl Delacato suggested, nay, programed, last week. "We shall allow her more frustration, as we would for a stroke patient, but we will cut out the loudness. That seems to be what is bothering you Napears the most. The embarrassment, the humiliation should disappear with the screaming and shrieking, don't you think? The new volume we love to see, but can't stand, right?" I had my second heart-to-heart talk with her. (The first one was about learning to walk.) About big girls not doing babyish screaming and shrieking. It was simply too noisy. Girls get a new bed and a new room. Babies don't, of course.

"Where is her new room?"

"The boys' room, here, behind the playroom."

"Where are they moving?"

"To our room."

"Where are you going?"

"To Jane's room."

"What brought all this on?"

"Oh, everything. We used to move about twice a year to give Jane a new floor show, you know. But this time it's for us, a change so the boys can have a bigger room, with study areas other than this playroom table. Each will have a half, with a desk-divider up to the ceiling, between their new beds. We were just too busy the last two years to do it. Jane should have been out of the crib-cage when she was allowed to go upright."

"I've been thinking of a new school setup for her. I wonder if we could use her new room. Get a swivel chair she could propel herself around in. Have a science table, an audio-visual corner, a chalkboard, maps, a place to hang her papers, you know, all that a real schoolroom has."

"Great!"

"Perhaps this will cut out some of the speech requirement and let it come off-the-cuff as it accompanies what we are doing. She's even too heavy to carry to the window to see the weather now. So she just stays in that one spot for an hour, at the table, having to direct all speech from center stage as she does in the living room. I think she's ready, been ready, to do everything herself anyway. Learn to get out and put away all school material——"

"Oh, she'll make 'A' in that, the perfectionist."

"She needs to find there is learning in a lot of things besides books. Buddy is the first in that direction!"

"Great!" We were now in what was to be Jane's new room.

Before Mrs. Gross left, she had offered a nine-foot Formica counter to go across one end of the room under the window, her son David's old desk. And I agreed to cut the boys' old dressers down to support the counter. And color-code the drawers—perhaps in white, blue, red, and yellow. And throw color and Con-Tact paper, ginghams, florals, stripes, on the various shelves of the four bookcases. Some shelves we would paint. Others we would burlap.

"Fine. We can't have too much color." A room you could fall in love with.

SEPTEMBER 18, 1970. It's a small, small planet all around. Last weekend took Grant fishing at our church camp. Annual fall family-thing something else again. As usual it was quite difficult to escape the subject of Jane and the Brain.

Don Gutstein there.

Jane missed Don and often role-played and talked about "going to New York City / on Wednesday / at nighttime / to Don's office / and play on the floor." It was her favorite sentence for a while. We had stopped taking her months ago, her program was so full. Don agreed he had nothing to supplement all that.

Everywhere this weekend I was to give reports on Jane, especially to friends who were educators and psychologists. We discussed the put-down of Doman-Delacato by the professionals. The warning flags were out to parents in such journals as the quarterly *Academic Therapy:* don't look for miracle cures where the child is subjected to retraining from his wake-up time to his bedtime. Often this was followed by a whole series of warnings: it's a fact these children are even patterned while they are asleep. Beware of a program therapy that allows no time to develop interests or to make friends. (It will make him wonder what is wrong with him, his parents give him so much therapy: "Aren't they happy with me the way I am?") And this one: parents, for shame! You should have more resistence to these sources of help! What's wrong with you, not accepting him as he is? Then the biggest warning (visions of lightning and fire) about getting "trapped" by the Philadelphians, snared "by your guilt feelings if you don't go down there [Philadelphia]."

How it is the social skills which will gain him a place in life, after the academic years are over anyway. Who cares if he stumbles over figuring a 15 percent gratuity. Nobody's going to hold that against him. One article went so far as to suggest it's a rather engaging trait to demonstrate such a lapse.

Sitting beside the lake at night, thinking it all out. In the denials, in the protests, I had the feeling some of the readers of those articles must be crying on the inside of that adjustment, at least some in that audience who still wished with all their hearts "just so it's healthy." Me wondering how it must be, having a child not working (like mad) to get well, listening to speeches about accepting "it" and "her" like this and this and this and never that. Would she accept herself as she is, even if I "talked her into it"? That's what I couldn't have been sure about, sitting in that audience of readers. What would 'she' have to say about it all? She was me, and I wouldn't like it one bit.

Doesn't "socializing" her as the articles suggested, having a friend over to spend the night, getting into this or that special Scout group, finding a friend "a little younger" (five years?) to have over for tea, teaching how to comb hair, brush teeth, eat neatly with a set of poor hands (fingers you can forget)—doesn't that take all day for a parent too? And is it anybody's business to save parents? Are they such a blur of a category, these parents of brain-injured children? The pitiful creatures, the Janes, we know are still in a category. Am I too? Bert and I?

And then this: some people are way out in front. Doing the impossible. Friends at the camp invited me to a private screening of a twenty-minute film about Neal Miller's research at the Rockefeller University in Physiological Psychology, reported in last year's *Science*. Miller and his associates had found out in the last five years that the autonomic nervous system can learn. The film bears this out beautifully. I saw rats, mice, *and* men doing the impossible with this supposedly involuntary system! Learning to raise or lower their heart rate and blood pressure; influencing brain waves absolutely; regulating kidney function; even controlling the flow of blood to specific organs. (I saw a rat regulating the flow of blood to one ear only.) How? Through the reward-punishment system: learning.

And today! What should come in the mail but the autumn issue of *Human Potential,* the journal-forum published by IAHP for "presentation and discussion of issues related to all aspects of human progress and development." And the lead essay, of all things, is by Lawrence Lessing of *Fortune* magazine. His essay for *Human Potential* is all about Neal Miller's research! About its far-reaching effect on learning theories for one thing, the study of neurological organization, and the treatment of some cardiovascular and gastrointestinal disorders. The door is open to a new therapy for psychosomatic disorders; man could now unlearn what he learned in the first place!

But Lessing has other things on his mind. He discusses how Miller's research is "a cautionary tale on the evils of authoritarianism in science." How when Plato split the "mind" from the "body," as Norman Douglas puts it, "this set of notions . . . tainted the well-springs of honest research for two thousand years." How the " 'invidious dichotomy' tended to block all rational investigation and development of human learning for centuries."

And Lessing throws out a new ball. "Only the anthropocentric fixation that denies the *physical basis* of the *brain, mind,* and *intelligence* stands in the way of developing the human potential in its oneness and fullness with all life."

I think someday words like *mind* and *mental* and *psyche* will drop out of the vocabulary entirely.

SEPTEMBER 29, 1970. The orientation for new girls from four-thirty to six lasted till seven!

They came all right. Some were in Health class and learned of our request from the teacher. Some heard about it from friends. Nine altogether!

I explained that Jane was at this point in time "on a silent plateau somewhere." Not talking. Had been that way since July, for the most part. But, please, talk to her as you would to me. Believe me, I wouldn't dare exaggerate her to you.

They came, and they saw. Gave them a Glenn Doman-type talk with a

Mary Lawrence seriousness. Demonstrated what she used to look like, if you could call it walking: the old scissor-legs up on toes, knees bent. Two girls weren't listening, just whispering to each other. So I asked what was the matter.

"We can't get over it. At the cerebral palsy day-camp, they had kids with legs crossed over like that and— *She* used to be like that?"

"Yeah— I wouldn't make it up——"

"Oh, I know, but— But——"

"Go ahead."

"Well, she looks so different— You mean, she's got cerebral palsy?"

"To use your term and theirs, yes. It's more accurate, I think, to say she's midbrain-injured."

"What's the midbrain?" Another girl asking the third question so far.

"Tell you in a minute. I'd like to hear how she looks different— After all, we are in our sixth year of this stuff— Why don't you think she's cerebral palsied?"

"Well, the thing that's the most shocking is what she can do. Just everything about her— She's not small— She's developed-looking——"

"And her hands, my God— She's buckling that thing on? I've been noticing her hands ever since we got here—" Jane was putting on her leather anklets for "her hangup" (upside-downness).

"Yes, her hands are finished now."

"I really don't understand. I had this one girl at camp who had hands— Well, they kept telling me to encourage her to draw. Well, I felt really sorry for her. She couldn't— She couldn't hold the crayon— So one day I was in the room where they had all the equipment, you know. And somebody said that girl used to wear this, so try it. It was a thing she wore on her forehead; you strap it on and put the pencil or whatever in it— That's how she draws. With her head. She was very happy with her pictures that way. She couldn't talk, but you could tell— You know?"

"Yeah, but they aren't working, like here, to get the hands better, like that handpull against the floor you said, to open them up, I mean, that girl's not using them. Her hands are just staying like that——"

I hoisted Jane upside-down up to the rafter, pulling on the rope. "It's all perfectly safe, and she loves it," I said, as I rolled the gurney table away. "Four minutes. No more. Look at her legs get a tiny bit straighter at the knees with what I'm doing: I'm holding her here in the waist where there's nothing but flesh, and pushing down to the floor with all my weight. If you do it right, it will kill your wrists, arms, shoulders—one full minute, that's all, rest half a minute, again, one full minute I'm putting weight on her body now— But it's a pretty good isometric exercise for the bosom, so the gals tell me."

"Her legs look straight to me."

"Yeah."

"I can't believe any of this. If she started with her legs like you said." (That girl again.)

"One of them is just about straight, but one is not quite as much."

"That's right, you're very perceptive. The right one. What we have now is the makings of a limp. We're giving that right leg some extra work, beginning tomorrow. But let's take her down now." Jane brought her head up, her body up at the waist to table height, and hand-walked onto the table as I rolled it under her. "That is beautiful arching, isn't it?"

"It's all unbelievable. There is not one thing I've seen her do that any of them could do. To me, she doesn't look like she has the same problem. She just looks developed, like any little girl."

"My sister couldn't do that bending up to the table, I bet."

"This is the cheerleading part. Let's make each step a beauty. Use any adjective that comes to mind—*fantastic, superb, excellent, outtasight*— every time she sets each heel down. She loves the praise. If she's tuning out your cheerleading, vary your voice, go to whispering, go to a louder-rah-rah-rah. I don't care how you get it, but don't waste her time.

"When she's getting all heels-down steps under this ladder height, we raise the ladder some night when she's asleep. Get the same thing at that height. And so on. You won't have to wonder if it's working. You can watch the ladder go up. And the steps stay down. Someday we'll decrease the thickness of the foam, all the way back to carpet."

I showed them the new ten-foot wooden ladder that will go up tomorrow. "My husband will attach it to that rafter. Good thing we have a cathedral ceiling."

"Does she know how to climb a ladder?"

"We don't know. Tomorrow we will know. After she can move up and down it like a cat, we're going to take out every other rung. To make her stretch the twenty-four inches. You know the feeling, stretching back for a rung. Back-of-the-knee feel. We're going to take one-third off her walking time under the overhead ladder and put it into this. Until the day the overhead ladder is high enough to do the job. If she can't reach the twenty-four inches, we'll make our own ladder and build up to this one. If she can stretch *more* than that, we'll throw this one away and still make our own. And if it's not getting what we want, we'll throw the whole idea out."

"I bet she can do it."

Jane asked to "Crawl on the floor, p'ease," and headed for the sofa in a running knee-walk. Wedged herself between Carol and Sue and began to practice hair-styling! Jane first gathered all the long dark-brown stuff at the nape of the neck in her right hand, bringing a couple of strays from the face with the other hand, checking it again, oops, one more stray on the other side. Then plop. Up it went on top, pushed forward now to create a bun effect, now a ponytail. Carol getting edgy.

"Please, let her. I've never seen her do this except on Barbie. This is very good for her. She's getting to know you."

"She does already if you ask me!" Sure enough, Jane was finished dividing Carol's hair into halves and making pom-poms above the ears. Then grouping it all under the chin and smoothing it down on her chest. Leaning now across Carol to peer at the long red hair next door.

"Oh, she's found me!" All of them laughing at Jane staring at Barbara. Sure enough, she knee-walked around Carol's feet and wedged in between them.

On the way home more questions, like what is "mentally retarded?" "They used 'retarded' more than 'cerebral palsied' at the camp, but Jane isn't mentally retarded."

"Give me an example."

"You know, she's smart."

Told Bert and the boys gathered around the new ladder, "Think of a name we can call it."

"Call it 'ladder,' why don't we? We never had just 'ladder' before." That was Grant.

"I heard a nice compliment about our living room from one of the new girls tonight. Lisa said it had purpose. She said in most living rooms you can't do anything but look. Isn't that sweet, Bert?"

"Yeah," said Grant, moving his hands out from his body for emphasis. "Most living rooms they have these fancy chair-r-r-s—Like— Like for President Nixon."

It's true. We have one sofa, propped up by a stack of books at one end, and one piece of yard furniture—a folding yacht chair. Impressive to a Lisa, but I'm not sure it really is to a Grant.

NOVEMBER 26, 1970. A friend passed this along to me:

Dear ————,

I'm fairly sure that the "program" to which you refer is the Doman-Delacato program which Matthew was on for four years and in which your friend and her daughter are presently involved. On the off chance that I am right, I'll make a few comments which you can pass along to her.

Matthew stayed on the program so long as he continued to made steady progress on all counts. Eventually, his neurological age almost matched his chronological age—in fact, it did except for his eye difficulties. . . . i.e., he is a swift and efficient one-eyed reader—he clicks off his left eye for near work because he sees double, then clicks it back on again for distance. All other systems were go, and that was the important thing. By that time, of course, his behavior was exemplary in comparison to his past compulsive, perseverative behavior patterns, and he was learning just as fast as we could expose him to academics. It was with the full agreement and sanction of the Doman-Delacato people in San Antonio that we withdrew him from their program.

I admire your friend more than I can say for sticking to a program that is time-consuming, arduous, and continually under fire from the medical profession. I know we had to take our lumps here from the doctors, many of whom still say that the miracle of Matthew is merely normal developmental maturation—or some such balderdash! Here was Matthew still drooling, still unable to make himself understood at age six, a program is begun—and within six months he is speaking clearly and the drooling has ceased—and this is normal maturation?

And it is also true that while people are maligning the D-D people, they are also using many of their methods—under another name—multisensory or some such thing. So I say to your friend gung ho—and good luck.

I would say that the only weakness in the Doman-Delacato program is that they still do not know why it works for some kids but not for all. I have seen many kids spurt on the program and others, alas, stand still. Of course, the program has many ingredients which are difficult to assess, not the least of which is how well the work is being carried on at the home front. My guess is that on the average we accomplished about 95 percent of the daily program over the years—and I stayed awake nights worrying about that 5 percent that we just couldn't seem to jam into the schedule . . .

The question of why the program helps some kids but not all was one that The Philadelphians continually debated among themselves. (This was true before the "brachiation"—oxygen—knowledge; I am not sure that that didn't clean up a lot of it.) They did not think it was the parents. Most of them became astoundingly innovative, went the further mile—beyond program—to provide an enriched neurological environment. No, it must be the brain.

It was to Glenn Doman that the "failures," as well as the children neurologically younger than Jane, went on revisits. And I knew from the look he had surveyed Jane with, that he studied them hard. I had heard reports (second-hand) about "the people in Philadelphia told the parents not to try it anymore." It seemed so unlike the man to give up on "kid here." It would be more like him to go for "finding answers next year," because they had surely learned so much this year.

Recently they had become biochemists and nutritionists, as well as cybernetic developmentalists. They began to aim at the nutritional quality of the brain cells they were trying to influence from the outside. They began to look beyond the high-protein, fluid-restricted diet they had programed.

Don Gutstein, the chiropractor who had accompanied us there, had really laced into them about that. Why aren't the children on massive doses of Vitamins B, C, and E? And calcium? Why are they serving sandwiches of cold cuts in the waiting room at lunch and supper? The place looked as if they knew nothing about nutrition: Were they trying to influence the brain on these trash foods?

It was mentioned in every room, and they all said, "You're right."

For that internal environment—proper chemical balance inside that brain, to insure there was no internal biochemical disorder where synapse must take place between one cell and another, and to build a healthy cellular foundation all around—they increasingly moved the children into a daily megavitamin program as well. (Jane had started it all, with Don's help, in February 1969, the day after we returned from that visit. The only thing I could be sure about: it had not hurt her any. It might have contributed a long way to that "calm" Mary Lawrence had seen in the once-hyperactive child the following summer. It is supposed to.)

DECEMBER 4, 1970. I suppose I can chart it now (fingers crossed): On November 15 J. ended a six-month speech plateau. This one all in silence—90 percent of the time. The 10 percent was more like an abyss than a plateau: one-words, accompanied by a struggle I'd label the worst. And the 10 percent reached its nadir just in time for the new girls to see it in September! A weird worst, interspersed with perfect counting, much singing, and a kind of jargon sing-along.

Back on June 29, I had written this down:

CLAUDIA: I just heard her talking. Like those sentences you've been talking about, but I had never heard. And I can't believe it. And Betsy can't either. And my last day here. It's like she knew!
JANE: Crawl on the floor when Daddy comes home.
CLAUDIA: You ask Daddy when he comes home. Where did Daddy go?
JANE: Daddy went [*past tense!*] to the city.
AND THIS: Daddy is coming home from [!] the city for [!] supper.

Six (really five) months later she climbed up out of the abyss on or about November 15, into a speech spurt I'd label the best. Higher, more sophisticated. Vocalizing all day long.

1. Contractions: "Daddy, it's hot in here." "Lisa, I can't climb." "Let's go to Wetson's / dark." "Don't do that, it's not nice."
2. Past tense: "Lisa went outside." "And the girl talked."
3. Last names of people spontaneously. (New girl interest?)
4. Mom-Dad or Stuart-Grant dialogues "talking to herself" (uses their exact tone, but creates new words).
5. Telephone role-play, more sophisticated.

6. Labeling everything in sight and correcting her own pronunciation: "lan shade, lamp shade, laMP SHade."
7. Uses jargon "in the middle" for expediency, as if she wants to hurry to the end for the "practice" she wants to try, especially "telephoning": "(blither-blabber) Perlstein, (blither-blabber) Wednesday morning, no, Thursday morning, (blither-blabber) fine, yes, fine. Bye, now." (The "bye nows" are the most fun, done in a flourish of inflection, bang goes the receiver down.)
8. Fun of using *for:* Daddy is coming home for hamburgers for supper for Jane, and for Grant, and for . . ."
9. Time concept interest expressed in new ways: "Daddy is not coming soon [pause] on the late train [pause] late at night [pause] not seven o'clock [pause] late train [pause] asleep."
10. Enlarged vocabulary to the point of my not stopping to list it—every day many more.
11. Mrs. Gross says full sentences are at least 50 percent of her talk.

Funny thing. The new talk gets the sentences. The old talk gets the one- or two-words: "Juice." (How about a sentence?) "I want orange juice, please."

DECEMBER 10, 1970. Delacato's "three priorities" for Jane in yesterday's revisit to Philly, in this order ("Forget everything else about this kid"):

1. *Walk.* Telling the morning women and the afternoon teens:

"You just accomplished the best job—the most improvement that's ever been done on a kid in the shortest time, I bet anything. In fact, her legs are so much straighter, we are going to skip going to three-inch foam to two-inch to one-inch and to the floor. We're going to the floor *now.* And we're going to get down on our hands and knees behind her heels and program all the steps—slapping the whole foot down, pressing the heel all the way too—for five laps under that overhead ladder. And then we're going to get up and require her to walk a sixth lap just like we just gave her to feel those five programed laps. And when we get her doing it consistently over that ten-foot span, we're going to raise the ladder some night when she's asleep; and get it at an increased height with her further stretched out. And we're going to do two sessions of that stuff every half hour, plus four minutes of 'her hangup' from the rafters, with three minutes of it in 'weighting down.' And some of you may not be able to do it. You may not be strong enough. We may have to go to boys, whose hands are larger and stronger, so, please, start looking for boyfriends——"

The women—who had been there a long, long time, most of them—said nothing. The new teens beamed. One thing, it was no news to any of us. During the foam program the overhead ladder was gradually raised six inches without Jane's knowledge.

She had not grown six inches taller, but she had since the last revisit in September amassed this data:

MEASUREMENTS*	PREVIOUS	PRESENT	CHANGE	AVERAGE	RATE OF CHANGE
Height	130.9	135.2	4.3	1.4	300%
Sitting height	70.8	71.5	.7	.5	140%
Chest	65.5	66.5	1.0	.5	200%
Head	50.8	51.1	.3	.1	300%

* In centimeters. This table represents about one-fourth the number of measurements taken of Jane each revisit and their comparison to the normal range (10th to 90th percentile), according to *Nelson's Textbook of Pediatrics*.

Months ago Art Sandler, the physical therapist, speaking of these anthropological measurements (done on every child every visit by the same trained person) had said, "We're going to literally stretch her bones too. They'll tell you that's not possible. We're going to show that it is."

Why anybody would want to "stretch bones" in someone whose calf muscle was already too short for the shank bone it attended was beyond me.

But, indeed, we proceeded to stretch her bones. (The long explanation here boils down to "a lot of use.") The underdeveloped lower legs, before our eyes (everybody mentioning it), got longer and longer and began to catch up to the rest of her body.

2. *Basic Vision.* That was Delacato's second priority for Jane. A new idea they had. Borrowed from some doctors in Switzerland, modified a bit for IAHP purposes, to line up crossed eyes without the use of vision at all. To attempt to line up the macula in each of Jane's eyes, the center of vision we all have, that bump on the back of the retina. In a cross-eyed person, it's not centered on the retina the way it should be. The program: a flashlight (with a black dot of opaque paper the size of a half-dollar glued to the center of the glass) shining on Jane's closed lids, making "dots" on those lids for twelve seconds, alternated with the old basic vision exercise involving sight.

3. *True Reading.* Telling Mrs. Gross about Delacato calling in the woman who had evaluated J.'s sensory side that morning. He banged his hand down for emphasis, "I want to see true reading when this kid comes back!"

I gave Mrs. Gross the gal's handwritten notes, goals, and suggestions to get Jane off her duff by next March 9. (And bring at least one book she can read with us.)

And Mrs. Gross saying, "Thank you . . . good suggestions . . . but mastering one book like that would bore her . . . but I think I'll go along with what we started two days ago. She doesn't want to do anything but talk right now—and spell."

"Yes, but they want true reading—performance reading—by March!"

"I do too. That's why she's telling me word after word, that I am writing down at her request. She wants to see how talking looks on the page."

And yesterday the kid had received a scoring increase in language, the first such increase on their Profile in four years. In October 1966 she had finally conquered their fifth level: "Ten to twenty-five-words of language and two-word couplets." That had taken a year at The Institutes.

Yesterday she got half-credit for Level VI: "Two thousand words of language and short sentences." Simply, it had to be apparent to people outside the home. Now anybody could see she talked in three-to-five word sentences—50 percent of her vocalizatons. (When she talked!) To conquer that block fully, she would have to talk like a normal three-year-old.*

There were some other gifts: J. can have music, but no more than one hour a day of it. And this: Delacato said, "I want you to put something under Jane's Christmas tree from me," and he wrote across a piece of paper and handed it to me, "a walkie-talkie set."

JANUARY 22, 1971. The school door flying open, Mrs. Gross running to me across the playroom, tears welling up in her eyes, "More of that yellow oaktag paper, please. She just started writing by herself, a sentence! Quickly, more of that yellow paper. She wants to write another one— Anything will do, cardboard, anything— A shirt cardboard is fine—" and running back into the schoolroom, and in a few minutes back again, "Mrs. Napear, we would like to invite you into the schoolroom today, to see something Jane has made—" And aside to me, "She just decided to write! *Sentences!*"

Standing up in the molding tray (the place for sentence-building) where the desk top meets the wall:

And now Jane was taking *Jane* down and substituting *Mom* (on shirt cardboard, a rectangle cut out hastily by herself) and saying, "Now it says, 'Mom likes P.J.' " (P.J. is her new teen-age doll.)

* This scoring increase was later retracted when The Institutes changed the time-frame ages on their Profile.

Now the yellow card *Jane* was taking its turn, "Now it says, 'Jane likes P.J.' "

Mrs. Gross had been busy getting set, checking all the jigsaw parts of a Raggedy Ann puzzle, and Jane, waiting, had decided to "start school." With a felt marker, she wrote the sentence on a long one-inch wide strip of oaktag that was lying around, cut the strip into words, and began the teaching.

Today, you can make a note, Jane began spontaneous writing. (I pick up the pencil, I decide what to write, I write. Nobody suggests it.)

Also today is her birthday. She is nine years old. Neurologically she is younger, but older than she was yesterday.

JANUARY 26, 1971. The year is new. The problem is the same: the child isn't walking and talking. A Christmas "thank you" from a girlfriend:

. . . Your supper party [here] . . . was a much-remembered occasion, to see Janey getting about [knee-walking] without being carried pleased us a great deal, also the way she dressed herself, and the way she enjoyed the Christmas carols.

Her husband after the occasion (J. as blah as I've ever seen her, not about to say a word) was moved to send us a long account of a village for the mentally retarded, with many acres, and cottages with a set of normal "parents" in each, its own main street and other beauties, wherein the attitude, the requirements, the encouragement, the trainability for "the retardates" is much the way you might want it to be outside the village. The fact that "the retardates" are dealt with from a standpoint of human respect was mentioned often. Across the margin he had written, ". . . We rejoiced to find the boys well and Janie dressing herself."

FEBRUARY 28, 1971. Now J. is interested in the spelling of words and not in sentences at all. Interested in only one book: *Science, Safety and Health,* so she and Mrs. Gross went through the magnet unit, the seed unit, the thermometer unit, and the water unit.

Not long ago it was railroad "tiny stuff": signals, cargo, tracks, switches, flashing, blinking or sustained lights, or crossbars only. So all reading materials dealt with trains.

Then she hit the big time: churches, steeples (tall and green or fat and black), crosses, weathervanes, cupolas, and domes. And Mrs. Gross would draw a picture only *after* Jane read the sentence.

And with an interest in steeples, cupolas, domes, you can somehow add to the reading vocabulary such words as *climbing, falling,* and *ladder.* You can even test the weather: "The sun was shining. It was hot on the roof of the steeple."

"What should we write next, Jane, forty degrees?"

And Jane says, choking with laughter, "Sev/enty degrees/no, no/ not *for*/ty degrees / not *cold.*"

Mrs. Gross erasing 40° and writing 70°, "Yes, that *would* be silly." And Jane never knowing she was in a test or what grade she just made.

And the steeple story continues: the firemen rescue Sam from the top of the steeple with a what? Jane reading, "a brown wooden ladder." And Mrs. Gross draws an action picture.

And that night I put this same story onto white poster paper, drawing in the pictures (green steeple), leaving afterwards the same size blank rectangle for the appropriate word-card: | **green steeple** | . But I do two such boards because we want to check out | **black steeple** | , as well as every noun, verb, and adjective.

And the next day J. takes one look at that whole story-board, finds it very difficult (extreme frustration the likes of which Mrs. Gross has not seen since the "random behavior" days), and refuses to do it. Mrs. Gross says we will take our time to match it all. And they do—forty-five minutes.

And the next day, what does Jane ask for? Yesterday's "toughie!" And runs through it, plunking the rectangular word-cards on the empty spaces just as fast as she can. And there's time left to draw up a word list from the story. Jane loves it. She knows twenty-two of the thirty words, and her "very good" paper is pinned to the wall, where we can see it.

And for a week there are no stories, only word lists. You can see them on the wall. In the drawer is one list with "lousy" dashed across the top.

PROGRESS REPORT—JANE NAPEAR
March 5, 1971
E. Gross

With the lessening of Jane's speech difficulties in December we entered into a period of good progress in school work. She became interested in word-formation and spelling, and from there went into spontaneous sentence writing. The sentences are very simple (three words), and she uses words that are both easy to spell and write. To do this original work always is a great effort for her. It is exciting to see Jane initiate a process that entails spelling, reading, writing, and speech. She is well acquainted with the vocabulary in two homemade books and in addition lists the days of the week, the months, colors, seasons, and holidays. She insists on the same order, however, and so is depending on her memory rather than reading ability.

Her attention span is good for the whole hour of instruction. Since her word-recognition has improved, she is interested in books and pages that have no pictures and will follow the story line and even ideas of an abstract nature. She is very much interested in the ethics of characters and the "good" and "bad" aspects of behavior. She demands punishment in the stories for the wrong-doings, although reward for good deeds is not always necessary. She is very interested in expressing ideas in short sentences rather than in the single words she previously used.

We covered units describing family, holidays, birthdays, seasons, and weather. It becomes increasingly apparent that Jane has a truly astounding memory and it is often hard to judge what she memorizes and what she reads. Her writing is crude but legible. During the last week I have noticed some speech difficulty again. It is, however, not nearly as severe as it was in the fall.

Professional Evaluation

March 9, 1971. Philadelphia. An eight-hour day at The Institutes today. Teens Diana and Holly came along. At one point before our 7:00 P.M. dismissal I considered the possibility of leaving Jane there. "Here, you all straighten her out!" Diana was moved to remark, "What's wrong with Jane today? I've never seen her like this!" And Bert saying he wished they could hear Diana's remark; they always see her at her worst.

Me bragging in the morning to the woman taking the history, telling her about Jane's auditory competence, her new interest in ethics.

"What do you mean 'ethics?' "

"You know, good and bad." During her three-week writing period a lot of her little sentences were about her dolls—"P.J. (or Barbie) is good (or bad)"—and how Jane's daydreaming is accompanied with fantasy conversations reflecting people at their best or worst. "You know, she's just much higher in her awareness of how people act. That's quite advanced."

"That's not very advanced. Four-year-olds do it all the time."

By the end of the day, I wasn't so sure Jane knew anything but "bad." Into some kind of orbit, like a wild thing let out of the cage, whining, whimpering, not still for a second, she raced in a knee-walk to the door and out of each evaluation room.

With a variety of antics and flanking maneuvers, the reading woman attempted some new material with same-level vocabulary, watching Jane's eyes peruse the several sentences. Then she proceeded to ask comprehension questions of Jane. Jane was given the opportunity to point to the correct word or sentence for her answer. And this to us: "Don't underestimate the brain's ability to go that fast. It's like a sponge—a fast visual sponge. Jane doesn't have the speech to let you know, but I know. They are all that way."

Carl Delacato: "Sit down and behave yourself!" That was to Jane.

I had just brought up the subject of schizophrenia. Jane now sat still, eyeing Delacato from her chair, and so I continued. "And if a child begins to set up another world because the one she's in is so boring— Doing the same program every day while we are doing the things she's fantasizing about in that talk-talk-talk eerie daydream of hers— Well, then, why is that different from the teen-ager who can't hack it, comes home after school and builds a lovelier world in daydream in his own room— And a few years later really *lives* two worlds, really is schizophrenic———" I stopped.

Delacato turned to Art Sandler, "What do you think? Is Jane a schizophrenic?"

Sandler shook his head no.

Delacato: "I don't think so either." Then studying the girls Diana and Holly. "What do you have to say about all this?"

I interrupted with, "A new girl started on the program and said it was too bad Jane wasn't 'with it,' she was———"

"Don't answer!" That was to me.

No one saying anything.

"I want to hear it from them. You [Diana], what do you think of Jane's behavior?"

"It's true. She *is* tuned out. Most of the time. It started last month, didn't it? You can get her to pay attention to what she's doing. But you have to really keep at it, break into all that daydreaming."

And Bert coming on, about when is this child going to get some free time in her life, how much can you expect of her—a little girl—spending every day doing these same sequences over and over— "My God, do you know what is the biggest thrill she has? Once a week going to the diner with me on Sunday mornings at eight to eat pancakes!"

Me finding my way out of the room, looking for Jane through a blur, up and down the halls.

Returned to find Bert still talking to Delacato, saying he wasn't suggesting we stop the program, but just give her some time off. "I think she should *go* somewhere, *do* something, for several hours! That's what she *wants* to do. That's the problem. It's like everything out there is what she wants to talk about, daydream about. What we do, where we go— That's all she talks about, me going to the city, me coming home, me cooking supper— My God, this kid is bored to death!"

And Delacato saying it all sounds reasonable, and something about time. And J. was to be given two half-days off per week.

The new hanging-upside-down program Art Sandler ordered was hysterical. Jane hanging upside-down from a loop in a figure-eight around her ankle-instep—by one foot—and he is turning her, twisting her. Then giving a turn to her waist, her hips—whatever he can grab—he starts the unwind. Jane, spiraling, spiraling, gasping for breath, screaming, "Mo—m, mo-mm-mm-ee-ee—" And fighting it like crazy, arms grabbing at the air, legs stiffening against—against—against.

And that's why. Fighting it, she would use muscles she doesn't normally use.

"How long do you expect her to do this?"

"Until we don't need it anymore."

"I mean, screaming and crying like that?"

"I expect the screaming and crying will be much subdued the second time. But I want the knees to go on fighting it."

"How do you get them to do that, go on after she's calmed down?"

"They will do it automatically, reflexively."

I asked a question about the inclined ladder climb, something about weight-bearing.

"Lord only knows." Or was it, "How the heck should I know?"

One thing he does know: he got Jane's legs straight for the first time. He evaluated her as she lay on the floor. He looked up at me, at Bert, at the girls, and said, "For the first time her legs are all the way down." Supine. The back of her knee touched the floor.

"Art, you mean they're all the way down? The right one too?"

"Yes, it's not easy. But I got them down. For the first time——"

"Oh, Art——"

To Jane's doctors back home:

. . . During the past period of time, Jane's legs continue to straighten at the knee and she is continually walking more flat-footed. This is evidenced by her physical growth and by pictures. In the past nineteen months of the program, Jane has grown 15.3 cms. [six inches plus] as compared to average growth of 7.7 cms. for the same period of time. Her sitting height has increased 5.2 cms—an average child [her age], 3.0 cms. Her chest 4.9 cms., compared to average of 2.7 cms., and her head circumference 1.6 as compared to average of 1.4* These are quite fantastic growth measurements for a child who has always grown slower than average in all respects . . .

No one was shouting—yet. But the camera must have—I just know the feeling—taking down the evidence.

* Should read .4.

April, 1970

December, 1970

March, 1971

RIGHT LEG   LEFT LEG

PART VI

Function Determines Behavior

Most brain-injured *babies* do not look brain-injured. As they grow into little girls or little boys, they *get* crippled. As they get older, they get more crippled. The bones get taller, the muscles stay short. Some of the muscles. The ones the "control center"—the brain—is not controlling. With Jane it was the extensors, the adductors. But she could flex, bend—fingers, wrists, elbows, knees—almost everything except her ankles; she did not have dorsi-flexion. Her thumb was so flexed, so unable to extend, it was inside her fist, against the palm.

The muscle imbalance, because of brain injury, can work in reverse, with everything in extension, nothing flexing.

When muscles are not used, they go nowhere. The three-year-old is easier on the eyes than the seven-year-old. Both are less crippled than the seventeen-year-old.

The normal little girl, on the other hand, has a normal little girl's leg. Maybe she begins ballet lessons. But the ballerina she becomes has a bulging calf muscle. It gets more than normal use.

Yes, function determines structure.

You can go down the list of everything the brain controls—eyes crossed (muscle imbalance), mouth open (muscle imbalance), sit slumped (muscle imbalance)—whatever you want to pick out to look at, and it's the same story. Everything gets worse. The brain-injured child grown up is looking uglier and uglier—with disuse.

And mom is working harder to keep her looking clean and neat, to buy the prettiest shoes, the newest eyeglass frames. Other girls can go around in blue jeans and flannel shirts flapping in the wind. When a girl's gaze is sharp—normal sharp—she's a beauty, no matter what she wears.

When her gaze is not perfectly sharp, when her mouth is hanging open, she looks stupid. Maybe she is. Maybe she isn't.

It matters more sometimes than at other times what society thinks. The dental society is an example. Maybe she has the auditory competence—the understanding level—to begin routine dentistry. Maybe she doesn't. But if she does, the dentist will never believe it. As a matter of course, the "stupid" nonverbal (or practically nonverbal) brain-injured children like Jane are put under general anesthesia for all dental needs, including

cleaning, usually at a hospital annex, in an assembly line of "incompe-
tents," where dental students need the experience, where the cost is less.
Jane's one hour under general anesthesia in a *private* office cost $700. We
further learned that it is almost impossible to find a dentist who will attempt
routine dentistry in the chair, even if you tell him she is able. Finally we
found one: $150 for a series of three "training" sessions. (In one of these
sessions she brushes his fingernail, he brushes hers, she has a front tooth
brushed in like manner, and she's back in the waiting room four and a half
minutes later. The dentist reports she has "experienced four tools: the
mirror, the suction thing—")

A sizable number of people have now heard about "patterning." And
at least some of those are close to a child on this program and know something beyond the picture of the village idiot or the cerebral palsy poster
child.

But the mother of the brain-injured child still must see her child in the
old perspective as well as the new. A double take of sorts everytime a
mother looks at her Jane: (a) the way society sees her; and (b) as if from
a center within the child herself.

That gulf in perspective, incidentally, is not so very wide. It is more a
thin line. It is drawn imperceptibly during the months a normal baby or a
brain-injured child crosses over neurologically from a grunting, gesturing
being on the floor into the human: walking and talking. Without walking
and talking he or she is "half-human," "animal-like." If only the world could
accept the truth in those labels: get to where it can look at the animal
likeness, learn from it, diagnose from it, treat from it. Otherwise, it will
stay where it is: standing the child up "anyhow" and calling it walking;
working with lips, tongue, and breathing and calling it talking.

A parent of a brain-injured child doing this IAHP program tries not to
think about the future. But it's there all the time. What if she doesn't get
any better? What it will be like to her the first time a toy is grabbed away—
or a necklace or a purse, now that she's older. Thank goodness our Jane
can say, and does, "Don't do that. That's not nice." On the other hand, will
she be pampered to death, or completely ignored? Maybe it's better to be
knocked down: at least you can say she was noticed today.

Fortunately we have been honest with Jane about "her." Since the staff
at The Institutes asked, "Why don't you think Jane should hear all this?"
(her history since the last revisit: regarding her speech hangups, facial
tic, etc.), nothing about her has been hidden from her. She has already
heard, "You are being a pest"—from Carl Delacato, no less. Stuart: "If
you are going to act babyish, I am not going to do your program with you."
Grant, when she is a pain in the neck, calls her Jane, the Pain. As yet no
one has called her crazy—seriously. As yet.

The parent even finds himself thinking about what will happen if she *does* get well. How can she come onto the scene later? And how can you come that innocent, that affectionate, that "socially immature"—without the early school years to show you the first-hand experience of hostility, of defense. Thinking we all have to unlearn a lot of childhood terror along the way—when you were a pill, a pest, unpopular; when you were inadequate, insecure, incapable; when they ganged up on you. Wondering if you could just skip altogether what you'll have to change about yourself later? Sometime later, just come as you are—loving, open, knowing that people are great; they always come around to fill your day, help you out. Maybe she could circumvent it for awhile with a full-time tutor, make up all the curriculum she's missed, get involved with an extracurricular swim group, maybe— Then drop into the scene at school?

A lot of people have asked, "Doesn't it bother you to see her at home all the time, not out there with children?" (Yes.) "Doesn't it bother you that she is missing all that fun of childhood?" (Yes.) "Well, then, why don't you—" (Here a host of suggestions which boil down to recreation programs for the handicapped.) The answer is simply this:

> And men ought to know that from nothing else but from the brain come joys, delights, laughter and sports, and sorrows, griefs, despondency and lamentations. And by the brain in a special manner we acquire wisdom and knowledge, and see and hear, and know what are foul and what are fair, what are bad and what are good, what are sweet and what unsavory . . .
> —Hippocrates

There is a kind of Hippocratic oath I would want my friends, if not my doctors, to take in case I get hit in the head by a car tomorrow (or get Parkinson's disease or have a stroke): I promise I will not come to entertain you. I promise I will come to work you—like a baby.

We are doing for Jane what we would have someone do for us.

At one time, if I can see it clearly, wanting Jane well was more for ourselves than for her. "Just so it's healthy." (Just so we can cope.)

It is an evolution of another sort, what happens, when you are thrown into the ring together by The Philadelphians, breath to breath. You get to *know* your Jane. And somewhere you arrive at love—the kind you can put your finger on.

Now I am sure. That is why we do all this: for her. So *she* can cope. I am sure now, too, it would be her choice. If we had ever thought about it in those earlier days, no doubt, we would have come to the same conclusion. But we were reeling back then—into ourselves. It was awhile before we started reeling forward—to get our balance, to get hers.

One thing about choices when you are faced with a brain-injured child (whether it is your own child for life or somebody else's child for an hour or a day), when you are deciding what to do "with her" or "for her": it *is* possible to do the right thing. But first you have to know her—where *she* is—functionally. For program, of course, but also for her play. Take the kid to the circus? When Jane finally saw her first circus (in the spring of 1971), what did she see? What did she react to with *oh*'s and *ah*'s, sighs and screams, and long giggling glee? She saw people climbing ladders to the ceiling, walking in quite pronounced steps across tightropes, hanging from bars by their hands, somersaults galore, and teen-age girls hanging first by one ankle then the other, winding, unwinding, spinning dizzily. Everything vestibular an IAHP child could identify with. Elephants and tigers and clowns? Baby stuff. (Or adult stuff?) As Grant said, "Wouldn't you bet this is her all-time happiest so far?" This is really recreation (not a do-good trip), because the ability to work eyes in concert, see at a distance, and enjoy (comprehend) what's there, is functional. What pleasant dreams are made of. If you had asked her that night what she wanted to be when she grows up, I am sure she would have said, "A circus!"

And don't look to Jane—or any other IAHP kid—for program tips to treat your child. Each is unlike any other. For example, from Jane's birth to the advent of patterning—that is, for the first three years of her life— she did not crawl. During the last six months of that period she was creeping all day (in the outrigger-harness-line arrangement), but she still made no attempt to crawl. Later, when crawl box (and leg use) opportunity was prescribed by Mary Lawrence, I tended to ignore her instructions. The result of that situation is a child who becomes more developed from the hips up than from the hips down. (A child in a wheelchair gets some opportunity for waist-up movement, and often shows the same upper versus lower inequity in body structure when first seen at The Institutes.) Therapy to such a pronounced inequity as resulted from Jane's year of creeping (before IAHP saw her) is, at best, difficult to devise. Her developed upper body became a liability, adding years to treatment, I am convinced.

Jane, by the way, is a success in only one way: she is not getting worse. To The Institutes' staff Jane is not even one of their case histories they mention, much less brag about. (At this point in her therapy.)

But what Jane has achieved up to now, she *has*. Her "credits" on the Profile are not half-baked. It's more the opposite: the staff demands true function. Their forty-two blocks on that Profile are arduous, if not completely impossible, for a brain-injured child. The normal baby, however, goes through *half of them in the first year of life before he walks*. So far, Jane has conquered thirty-six blocks, with six of those considered "functional" but not yet "perfect."

Yes, you can do some shouting about Jane if you want:

1. She is not "spastic" anymore. That's impossible, I know. ("Brain damage causes that.") But it's true.
2. She is not crippled anymore. Even her legs are straight, heretofore an

impossibility without lengthening the tendons surgically. But they are, and she has had no operation.

Note: In the summer coming up—1971—she will have her legs placed in long leg casts in a straight-out position, as a short cut to therapy to get the last tightness out of cartilage-ligament system. The recovery period will be prolonged by an injury of some kind to the right leg. And in the long run, it is probably not a shortcut. What we were doing might have finished those knees faster.

3. With her glasses for nearsightedness (June 1971) she is cosmetically not cross-eyed (degree of strabismus is 6 degrees). Neither has she had an operation to correct "the muscle imbalance" there.

4. Jane can talk in sentence language.

5. Jane is moving well academically despite the fact that she had "an I.Q. of 40" her first four and a half years of life and is, "therefore, trainable" rather than "educable."

6. Jane is not underdeveloped-looking. (The shanks of her legs, not used yet in full weight-bearing, are an exception to that statement.)

After Jane gets walking, the plan is for her to go back and pick up the rest—programs aimed at other deficits, such as the strabismus (depth perception) that is left, all the programs that were temporarily at "hold" since 1970. Once again she will be in Carl Delacato's office as much as she has been in Art Sandler's. I, for one, can hardly wait to see what's new!

You remember in 1969 he said Jane could be (a) hypo-auditory (doesn't hear enough); (b) hyper-auditory (hears too much); or could have (c) white noise within the system (bring every sound in the restaurant together, feed that in, and you'll understand). She was probably hypo-auditory. She was not distractible enough. That *was* Jane before stethoscope-talking alternating with ear-whisperings and silence were introduced into her program, before she began to sit still in the waiting room at The Institutes.

It was *after* the change in Jane's behavior that I was able to look back and see it clearly: with a hypo-auditory child the greatest listening pleasures in the world—besides vacuum cleaners, air conditioners, machines, music and echoes—are water flushing, water gushing, water sloshing. Leave one of these children in the bathroom, she's flushing the toilet over and over, turning on the faucets full force, and trying to get the bath started. In Philadelphia she was always leaving the room of people in search of the repetitive noise of toilets or typewriters.

It was after we'd left Delacato's office (to get walking before we returned) that I began to understand what had taken place there. That is where Delacato sees, hears, touches, gets close to the children. And where he sits back and watches them some more. What is he looking at? He's watching what a child is feeding in to himself, watching *a child treating himself neurologically:* with vestibular turning round and round, rocking, swaying, upside-downness; auditory sounding, sounds like *nin-nine-none* or *ooh-e-i-o-ooh* or *yang-yang-yang-yang*. Whatever brain channel the child needs to use, to open up, as it were, through the buzz. It takes a certain kind of listening and watching. And it helps, I suppose, if you've seen thousands.

Yes, function determines behavior. (Dysfunction determines weird behavior.)

There was the time when hypo-auditory Jane could not get enough of booming, banging, drum-beating, shrieking, shrilly, siren noises. She couldn't wait for Delacato's fingers-in-the-mouth whistle. In Maine she probably loved Philippa for her whistle alone, as she, likewise, crept after the cleaning woman (the vacuum cleaner, the water sloshings) wherever Louise went about the house.

On the other hand, the *hyper*-auditory kid hears too well. He almost breaks his neck and yours getting away from that terribly frightening toilet. School buses and lunchrooms are terror-filled. Delacato says watch his frenzy there, throwing books, dishes, himself around. In the classroom his secret wish might be something like, "If only they weren't so noisy putting their pencils down, so I could concentrate." His secret desire is probably to dig a hole somewhere to get away from it all. And many have.

In the institutions where "school" is not required, you will find him in the shower room, vacant during the day (faucets off), against the wall in the farthest corner "digging in." Others may be climbing the walls to get away. Apparently, according to Delacato, there are even children diagnosed as "deaf" who "hear" if you whisper to them! One thing about them all: children with a hyper-auditory system have a different look to them—white, pasty-faced. Why? It's one of the things Doman and Delacato have not figured out yet.

Parents in orientation at The Institutes these days get the benefit of such news as this: kids can also be hypo or hyper in other senses as well. Some children are so hyper in smell, they can't take people—everybody smells. Some are so hyper-tactile, they cannot stand to be touched. In today's affluent madness, where babies are even fed propped up in crib and carriage, even carried around without their parents' touch—in that cute seat or this new container—is it possible that they are becoming more and more hyper-tactile? (Don't touch me, I'm not *used* to it?)

These same children are labeled "autistic" by therapists and teachers who are as yet unfamiliar with the functional deficits which underlie such repetitious behaviors. They think something went wrong emotionally, since autism is characterized by "withdrawal into oneself." (The judgment is that the child "wishes" to be alone.) Some are so withdrawn, it is said, they have no contact with reality (the world as we know it); they set up fantasy worlds, so goes the thinking, as a protection against the destruction of themselves which they fear. (That, incidentally, presupposes a high level of auditory competence, more on the understanding level of the therapist who figures it out, I would think.) Others maintain some contact with reality, although withdrawn; but they are very negative. All of them react strongly to a change in schedule or activity or from whatever it is they want to engage themselves in—wander aimlessly, stare at bright lights, move objects up and down in front of eyes, spin around and around, rock back and forth, bang head (or body) against surfaces, scratch or tap-tap-tap on tables or walls, tap repeatedly or cover the ears or eyes, bite arms and hands or fail to meet one's gaze, etc., etc. (Name it, they do it.) Some are so withdrawn they are "non-verbal." All of this is discussed. The level of auditory competence which produces the tuned-out child is not discussed and is probably not known.

Have you ever seen one of these so-called autistic children? Book after book has been written about them. Would you like to see one of these children up close? Go back and read the first pages about Jane—yes, Jane—and the development of (her) auditory competence in the Appendix. Change "sociable" to "hyperactive" wherever it appears in those early years. (While you are at it, you might as well change "hyperactive" to "auditory problem," etc.) Not only was she a perpetual-motion machine, she also had a perpetual smile on her face. You can wipe that off. It's not "sociable" either; it's part of the brain-injured picture. Jane was never sociable at the outset of this diary; she made no contact with people. She went toward the noise, not toward the people. She responded to *it,* but not to *us.* You might say Jane "wished to be alone"—with noise. At the age of three years, she knew only sweet talk from scolding. Perhaps she loved the scolding more because it was noisier. If you follow the notes of her increasing auditory competence, you will be able to see the gradual fading of her autism—a rare success, if not a first, in the literature about these children.

There are many sub-symptoms of autism which have been classified and labeled. The vocabulary is endless, as is all vocabulary based upon bizarre behavior. As an example of how fine you can get when you start labeling *symptoms,* here's one you'll remember in Jane: "Jane, do you want some orange juice?" Her answer was not "Yes," it was "Orange juice." They call that "echolalia." An abnormality. If you didn't know better, or if you were intent on trying "to understand the behavior there," you might think the child who echoes whatever you say is downright negative, uncooperative, defensive, "disturbed." If you know better, you know that the sensory-motor of hearing-and-saying "yes" falls in the normal hierarchy of vocabulary increases somewhere after "no" (which, the child, no doubt, hears more of). These "autistic" children are also said to have trouble grasping the concept of "you" from "I," evidenced in their speech; and this, too, is clouded over by some psychological judgment, such as their lack of self-image (ego maturation is low, etc.). He may be eight years old with what is labeled "echolalia" or "inadequate self-concept," but to Doman and Delacato he's at the level of an auditory baby—functionally.

Since the 1940's this child with the withdrawn behavior has been labeled at most places this way: "childhood schizophrenia: autistic type." Whether the cause is innate or environmental has comprised a great deal of literature. Most often his history is judged to be one of parental deficits (the mother is mentioned as overprotective, oversolicitous, aggressive, or too mechanistic toward the baby's needs, or too ambivalent about the child, that sort of thing). The child's prognosis is dim. He's spending the day in a center for emotionally disturbed children, if he's one of the "lucky" ones to get in. There his day is planned (away from his usual bizarre behavior) to more constructive and purposeful behavior, since he is not able to plan for himself. (Other therapy is of the opinion one should not intervene in the usual behavior to get healthier attitudes and mannerisms; the child should be allowed to regress further into his behavior to feel the survival feeling he so desperately needs and so that he may teach the therapist by his behavior how he views himself.)

The state institutions are full of these children. They are usually the first ones admitted, as Delacato will tell you, and more often than not, having never made "human contact," they grow old there, unless they can master the goals of that custodial care, the Activities of Daily Living: "feeding, dressing and grooming" themselves. If they do, they can graduate —to a halfway house.

In 1965 one of the teens who worked with Jane brought up the subject of brain injury at a center for emotionally disturbed children ("They certainly look brain-injured to me, Mrs. Napear," and here endless descriptions of the poor coordination seen there in each child) and got a gentle chastisement for mentioning such a thing. Today that same center admits that those children *are* brain-injured, but it prefers not to bandy such a term around. "Autistic," let's face it, is prettier (and more remote) than "brain-anything." (Brain-stuff is scary, crazy, fixed, permanent, hopeless.) Even the chart is "nice" about it nowadays: "childhood schizophrenia, autistic type, with accompanying retardation and neurological dysfunction." But the treatment is still psychological. Behavior—not brain—is the byword. Even the diagnoses of "maturational lag" or "maturational immaturity" are seen in terms of the social development that is lacking, but never in terms of the functional steps that are missing. The question must be asked: Do they know as much even as a parent at The Institutes knows? By the developmental histories taken at such a center, it would seem they do not. Perhaps the published work of Delacato (see Recommended Reading List, page 433) will throw more light on the subject. Perhaps the day is here when the so-called autistic child need never again climb the walls or withdraw into a corner of "his mind."

I would like to believe that there is more overall hope for the brain-injured (the crippled in mobility, as well as the crippled in auditory, visual, and tactile competence) in 1972 than there was the year Jane was born—1962. The chances for an early diagnosis of *brain injury* are better. Babies like Jane, whose birth reflexes are absent or abnormal, who have kernic-terus (jaundice, i.e., yellow skin), hyaline membrane disease, and other ripening deficits, are now labeled high-risk babies and watched. The lack of a thyroid gland—cretinism—is rare but is detectable in those early days. (It always was.) Depressed tendon reflexes as late as four and one-half months—even with a cretin who didn't grow at all till then—are today certainly a sign of brain injury, I should hope. And by now, perhaps everybody has read about the importance of the last two weeks in the womb to the central nervous system. This above all: if the doctor doesn't know, let the parent tell him. *It's high time the parents became responsible for the child's birth and development.*

In 1972 the orientation for parents at IAHP, Philadelphia, takes two and one-half days longer than it did in 1962. The wait for an appointment is less than a year. There are more and better programs, more departments (institutes) and staff consultants, such as Adelle Davis in nutrition. The vitamin therapy is no less important than crawling and creeping. Brachia-tion is heard in the halls as much as patterning ever was. In the waiting room parents mention programs I never heard of.

Certainly 1972 is a long way from 1952 when *Karen* (and "cerebral palsy") was published.

The world out there for the Janes has changed. The world in here, in our home, has changed drastically. "The rack" has been replaced: the over-head ladder to get Jane's straight-legged, flat-footed walk is now sus-pended by a bright orange metal bracket affair attached to the rafters (conveniently eight feet apart as needed!) The instructions to and schedules for programers that are pinned to the wall change, change, change. All manner of things suggesting life and growth are brought in by the pro-gramers and affixed to the walls.

Five of the original women who started with patterning in 1965 are still with Jane. Unless you have been through all this, you could never know what that means. Five people who lived it all, who sweated it with you.

Ninety percent of the teens go into preparation for careers with the "handicapped." Many work with the Janes at other places: the cerebral palsy centers, the day-care centers for the retarded, the centers for the emotionally disturbed, the state schools connected with the institutions—

to learn and to compare. The college students write in about once every couple of months for information about this program for some project or other they are doing.

The current afternoon programers are straight out of Stuart's classes at the high school. I've never discussed it with him, but I think he's proud of their coming. To Stuart, Jane is still pretty much "my sister." That's about it.

Grant at twelve is quite grown up. In the summer of 1971 he will push Jane's wheelchair through most of Switzerland and half of Austria, into and off of trains and cable cars, and he will become her best friend in the process.

He will encourage her up the ten-foot ladder leaning against our chalet to make thirty round trips, three sessions a day. Just after I have finished her walk on a Swiss-made overhead ladder arrangement in the yard.

And when we are on a sidetrip, overnights too, he will keep watch over her in the swimming pools (his idea), coming back whether she needs him or not, flicking flies off her back or whatever. And help her into and out of churches for a walk between the high-backed pews, a kind of brachiation assist they have in Europe without knowing it. At the top of a castle he will lean out of a turret and call, "There's a ladder you have to climb to the top floor. Bring her up. She'll love it, Mom, believe me. It's perfect for her program. And she can sit inside a steeple when she gets here!"

The three of us having a real vacation, six weeks, for a change.

But I am getting ahead of the story.

12

What *is* the story exactly? Is it the diary? Or is it the non-diary chapter that even the teens could write—once they decided to find out? Is Jane lucky? What are the alternatives, the choices we might have made? If Mary Lawrence, on July 23, 1964, had not been preparing for "the next brain-injured child who comes into this department," had not put Jane on the floor "until I find out what else to do," had not, on her own, taken up the challenge of finding out, had not followed Jane's development to learn some more—what might have been the story? How might Jane have been diagnosed and treated?* What would Jane be doing now? What *is* Jane doing now? And which is higher?

It depends a lot on who is doing the looking, what there is to see. With today's new eye a physical therapist (or even a teen-ager) can see all the child at once. A yesterday eye can only see the child-piece he's trained to find. The doctor looks at structure—that's his business. The psychologist looks at behavior—that's his business.

Let's suppose it is 1964 again. Jane is two and a half. She clearly looked crippled when she attempted to walk; and a friend, a pediatrician, let's suppose drops in for a visit. Watching that cruising along our sofa, he would say *cerebral-palsied* or *spastic,* or both. (If he had seen her after she talked, he might have added something about athetoid speech—flat, monotone, hesitant.)

He is saying all this to himself. To me he makes the usual suggestion: an excellent cerebral palsy center or a department in the hospital, to get her some physical help, some physical therapy (for the spastic state of the muscles), to "keep ahead of the growing bones" and "whatever else they might suggest to aid her learning to walk."

* As it was, according to information received in the course of this book's preparation, no diagnostic work-up could have been more meager than her original evaluation and program:

"July 17, 1964
Diagnosis and Disability: Cretinism. On four grains thyroid extract daily. Tightness of hamstrings and gastroc bilaterally, less marked at external rotators of hips and elbow flexors. Weakness of neck flexors.
Orders: Stretching of hamstrings, gastroc, external hip rotators and elbow flexors bilaterally.
   Active assistive exercises: neck flexors.
Instruct mother in exercises to be done three times a day."

A psychologist, on the other hand, let's suppose drops by when Jane is neither standing nor cruising with furniture support. He sees an active— hyperactive—compulsive machine-type of child circling the perimeters of the room, all rooms. She's in a walker with a high-backed canvas sling-chair, jabbing a bunch of keys at the windows and woodwork. (She is jabbing because she cannot extend her elbows fully, but no one has seen that yet.) The child is in a "world of her own," the smile ever constant. Her language is limited to explosive shrieks and an occasional guttural sound. (The "ma-ma—more "a" than "ma"—is not directed to the mother.) She is clearly *autistic*. Especially when he learns this child exhibits this repetitious behavior throughout the entire day. And is awake half the night.

He is very interested in how I have dealt with her up to now and might I like some help— And he makes a suggestion: an excellent center for the emotionally disturbed child "to take a look at her" and see if I indeed have "been given" an autistic child (or perhaps she "got" this way, so many of them do, through no intended fault of mine, of course). The finest in psychological testing and medical work-ups— Where the staff will do all in its power to reach her through her autistic state—that world she lives in.

We now have two pieces of Jane (as well as the original cretin): the Jane from the waist up, the behavior that strikes the psychologist at first glance; and the other one from the waist down, the structure that is automatically apparent to the doctor when she attempts to walk. So far we have seen retardation in behavior and retardation in structure. And we know of two places to go. (More honestly, the child who is crippled, cross-eyed, and structurally a mess, is found in the center for the "cerebral palsied." The one who is only incoordinate rather than crippled is seen in the center for the "emotionally disturbed.")

So far, no one has mentioned she is "mentally retarded." She is a little young. It is hard to get a definite assessment of I.Q. at this age: it is 1964, and there is more sophistication about all that now. I mean, we will *give* her the test, but let's keep open about it, not jump to conclusions this early. For the child's sake. (And for the parents' sake.)

It is 1970. Jane is eight. Let's imagine she has been given periodic psychological tests and "her I.Q. has remained at around 40" all that time.

Her lack of coordination is all that's left of a six-year miracle of leg-and-arm straightening, let's suppose, by the physical therapists. And her autistic half has been to the center for emotionally disturbed children.

The center is very pleased. (We are still supposing.) She is an altogether different child. You can "relate to her" if you do "this" and "this." You can stop this repetitious behavior if you are consistent. You can "get her to respond." Now we know how "to reach Jane." And she is beginning to live in our world—what we hoped to accomplish. And we did.

Oh, yes, she can talk now. ("She is no longer nonverbal.") Let's suppose she not only has speech, but that she has language. (That is, she says "lamp shade" for any lamp shade she's likely to see.)

She is not noticeably autistic (she attends to this world). She is not crippled. You can see that she is not. But she is definitely *mentally retarded:* the third piece of Jane.

Her I.Q. tests show she is still a "40." So suppose we send her to an excellent school (or center) for the help of retarded children. She rides a school bus back and forth each day—just like normal children do. It's full of children like Jane. Friends. (We parents get together to discuss our children, our common problems, our adjustment to the situation as it is. We get the kids together too—after school and on weekends.)

And? Yes, we still have a lot of hope for Janey. Yesterday she showed us how she has learned to button her coat. By herself! Didn't even want me to help her. The teachers there are wonderful. They care about each and every child. Jane's behavior is just as much their concern as ours. Her incoordination is their concern too—techniques to improve her walking (walks across walking beam, etc.), her throwing, as well as her buttoning. And there are a lot of things "she can be trained to learn." Yes, even with a "40 I.Q." That's what the world doesn't understand about these marvelous children. With dedication and persistence, there's a lot they can be taught. (And so on, and so forth. . . .)

I'll show you. Better still, let a high school student's paper on the subject show you.

Although the psychologist wanted to set me up in one of the higher functioning classes, I requested one a bit lower in function, and consequently more characteristic of the center as a whole. I was placed into a class of approximately eight and nine-year-olds with an average I.Q. of about 40. I was allotted one hour of class time . . .

The most immediately striking impression was that every child had poor coordination—some walked with arms bent at the elbows, some dragged one of their legs, and some walked with what appeared to be a drunken gait. And no child had good speech. They all had articulation problems, and their vocabulary and understanding of word meanings was particularly low. Some children had *no* speech (less of this kind than at the center for emotionally disturbed), and some chose a few phrases or syllables to repeat over and over again.

The teacher was in the midst of herding all the children—a total of fourteen —to the bathroom . . .

One child sat on the floor the entire time and rocked. One finger from each hand was plugged into his ears. The only deviation from this pattern was occasionally he took his fingers out of his ears and tapped his head. Another child seemed fascinated with shoes and roamed around feeling everyone's shoes and occasionally stepped on them. The latter was abruptly stopped because it is not socially acceptable to step on someone else's feet.

A few of the children could not be kept from the faucets—always on high— and the rest retreated, moaning. One girl alternated hopping from foot to foot with flapping her arms. Another child sat on the floor and bit her arms. One little boy was watching his fingers with rapt attention; another child began to creep on hands and knees and was told to get up because he was not a baby. . . .

All the children were aware of my presence (in contrast to the center for "emotionally disturbed" in which half of them took no notice).

The episode in the bathroom lasted about fifteen or twenty minutes, and upon completion, the children were instructed to go back to the classroom. One little girl tried to hold my hand, but the teacher discouraged this, stressing the babyishness of it.

Once back in the classroom, the teacher formed a horizontal line of desks in front of the blackboard and began her lesson dealing in colors. The children were required to point to the color she would name and then select the correct word from the box. Rewards were given out for correct responses, but contingent on their being *said*. (The reward method is used in many other institutions, including ——— State, to serve as motivation in learning.)* There were certain children who always responded correctly, although their speech was less than perfect, and always got rewards; the rest of the children never responded correctly, try as they might, and never got rewards. The lack of success was often attributed to no speech, although the teacher tried hard to show these children how to say the right word. All the kids seemed eager to please.

The last activity was snack time. Any child who was misbehaving (not paying attention, stepping on people's feet, being excessively loud) did not get a snack. Furthermore, no child was permitted to dunk his cookie in the juice because such behavior is babyish.

As the psychologist explained later, the emphasis in dealing with these children was on socially acceptable behavior and cooperation. The children had to learn how to conduct themselves maturely in preparation for their later lives.

Here the "Some Subjective Observations" of a student's paper ends.

Should we jump to conclusions about something we've only seen for one hour? Let's just ask some questions.

First, take a look at Janey in the bathroom there. (Isn't each some "piece" of brain-injured Jane?)

In 1964 she would have been that rocking child, treating himself to constant motion.

In 1966 and 1967 she would not only be checking out everybody's shoes

---

* The author does not say what is the reward here, but at the state institution's school she refers to, it is in the form of colored discs—like poker chips—which are "cashed in" at the end of class for candy.

in the room, but would be trying to get them off, so she could creep with them on her hands, "stepping" them on the slate and across the tiled playroom, and especially on the bare floors in Maine. If the doors were opened from the rug areas, she would creep in and out—to the noise, back to the not-so-noisy rug—back and forth. Rubber galoshes, sneakers, high heels, loafers—she tried them all. For two years the most fascinating thing about people to her was their shoes. Maybe it had nothing to do with people? Maybe the intent is auditory learning? Perhaps the child is programing himself—neurologically—right inside that school for the mentally retarded? Stomping on them to make them move, go? Make noise? (He's hypo-auditory?) Stepping on them to make them stop, be quiet? (He's hyper-auditory?) Or maybe it's tactile learning? Who knows?

And might the child biting her arms be doing the same thing, telling herself "something" tactilely—I can feel it—there's an arm there? I never saw Jane bite her arms; maybe she did as a baby. The sensation there was "normal" (Levels II and III of the Profile—both vital [pinch] and gnostic [pleasant] sensation) when Mary first evaluated her. But in those 1965 floor pictures, we saw her rubbing her *hands* fiercely over the carpet, the screen, the slate, the brick—both the palm and the back. And, that same year she "inspected her fingers" and pinched the back of each, in what is termed "repetitious behavior." Possibly she did not bite her hands because she was allowed to see if they were "there" in floor ways?

If Jane, too, had not been allowed to creep, she would probably have checked out each foot (here's one, here's the other) in some weird hop, her arms flapping (balancing?).

And the children making that wondrous waterfall noise at the sinks, that's hypo-auditory Jane up to 1969? The ones retreating are hyper-auditory?

Are we not, indeed, viewing a bunch of neurological babies? Are not the fourteen trying somehow to change that one environment in the bathroom into fourteen individual environments that each one specifically needs? Are they perhaps programing themselves neurologically there in the midst of the teacher's programing? Is not the teacher trying in one class to "deal with" Jane in 1965 and Jane in 1967 and all the other years of Jane?

What might the teacher do with fourteen *brain-injured* children, no two of them alike? It's a key question.

What do I think? I think fourteen separate rooms in even a center for neurological organization for these fourteen children would never be as good as fourteen homes. Maybe someone will prove me wrong.

Maybe I am wrong about some other things. You know as much as I do now; ask your own questions. Like, "Do all the fourteen have at least outline perception?" That's an easy one. They all noticed the visitor. Perception of the "details within" that person there? Depth perception? We don't know because even if you saw someone across the room, it would be babyish behavior to start picking at his buttons. Remember, you are eight and nine years old. Act like it.

Is Jane lucky? Let's ask a question a student asked after returning from visits to a center for emotionally disturbed children, "What do they mean when they say 'the autistic child' is more interested in things than in people?"

Remember when Jane was "autistic?" At two and a half she made no response to us—to food, yes, to the bunch of keys, yes. After she was put down in her outrigger, it was metal waste baskets and spoons against them all day. All day—if you'd let her.

When she started school in 1968 Mrs. Gross said she had to be involved in concrete material—sorting this, handling that—the whole forty-five-minutes to an hour of instruction. Then gradually the percentages changed; she only had to be physically involved a part of the hour.

Later she reported Jane no longer needed pictures, props of any kind, for reading. Look at the first-graders, and look back to pre-school stuff—a different scene entirely.

The normal child—or the brain-injured child with proper programing—moves up the normal hierarchy, from the autistic world of things to "this world" of people.

It seems to me, these "autistic" children whether they are in a center for "emotionally disturbed" children or in a center for "mentally retarded" children—are stuck on a low neurological level. And they are staying there, somewhere below the age of one. So often those histories say, "Baby was fine in the first year of life . . . didn't show aberrant behavior till second year." Couldn't it be simply a matter of arrested neurological development? I mean, even if you are emotionally "rejected," the parent is a lousy one, and all that, wouldn't it just follow that your neurological day would be a lousy one, as well as your psychological one? When you "reject," do you usually pitch the child to the floor to crawl around, or do you pen him up somewhere? Do you give him more environment to learn from or less?

A functional evaluation of the child's development according to The Institutes' Profile—what auditory level the "baby" is on, for example—is not only nice to have, but necessary. It clears up how you can best "relate to him." To the child who's inspecting everyone's shoes in the class, you will, as a teacher of the "mentally retarded," no longer need to stomp on his foot and shout, "How would *you* like it if someone stepped on your foot?"

To the "emotionally disturbed" child who spends his day in a world of his own, draping himself upside-down (negative gravity) or who spins crazily around in clockwise circles (part of positive gravity), you will not have to say a single psychological word. For example, you can spin the latter child *counterclockwise* (the other part of positive gravity) and truly help him "to find himself" (as they say). Delacato tells of doing just that when a child in one of these centers was interrupting his lecture with such repetitious clockwise spinnings!

Instead of thinking these kids do what they have to do, behaviorally (to protect themselves from the destruction they fear), think this way: kids do what they have to do, neurologically (to learn more, to feed their brains).

You have to ask yourself, "What does this child spinning around and around want to know about, now, this level?" Is it this, as the psychologist would have us believe: myself in relation to people? Or is it: myself in relation to gravity? (The vestibular of it all?) And where do you learn about gravity for the first time? When you go up—off the earth—on your hands and knees and begin to creep!

What does the "autistic" child, or the "mentally retarded" child, or the "cerebral palsied" child who is staring at bright lights wanting to know? Is he not trying to tell his brain something about vision he's missing, basic vision, baby vision?

A functional evaluation at The Institutes will eliminate the guesswork. Especially if the mid-brain functions right across that Profile are all either non-functional or functionally poor, as you might suspect.

The first thing first: to get a child to be a normal baby. And that, of course, means a hassle with the psychologist, the parent, with everybody who's working to get him to stop acting babyish.

Let's not forget this picture of what Jane's story might have been—this one in a rehabilitation center (or a cerebral palsy center, if we had not decided to go back to the hospital) with a team approach, where all the "pieces" can be treated by a physical therapist, a psychologist, and a speech and hearing person:

. . . Down the hall is a group of little Negro children, mostly spastics or youngsters whose limbs are unbalanced from cerebral palsy; they struggle, grotesquely but gallantly, to move through the music-timed paces of a kindergarten game. One of them, Kathy, aged four, a chocolate-colored Dresden doll in starched pink frock, ruffled panties, and spotless white shoes, was born so badly deformed that she cannot lift her arms and is forced to sit with her legs straight in front of her. Kathy, with help, makes it to her feet when the other children "dance" and follows them in a stiff-legged gait in which she manages, almost imperceptibly, to move her toes. When you see her strain to keep time to the music by hunching her shoulders and even by manipulating her eyebrows, you cannot help choking up . . .*

After the choking subsides, take another look at Kathy there. Contrary to the reporter's understanding of it, she was *not* born deformed, any more than the normal newborn, whose legs are flexed at the knees and hips and are pressed against his buttocks. (If you've ever diapered a baby, you have the picture.) She was born with frank brain damage, more than likely, and it prevented her from developing. She was not able on her own to provide herself with the environment she needed to develop; she couldn't move around the way the normal child moves to develop the body's musculature, to use the brain that moves the muscles. With inactivity she got more and more of whatever she has in crippling. Her legs are in extension, cannot flex. (She's the opposite of spastic Jane in 1964.) More than likely she's stiff-legged because she's in braces. One thing for sure, when she's a bit older, she will not be a "Dresden doll." One thing about the four-year-olds: they grab you. The teen-age Jane will not grab you if she has been left neurologically disorganized. She will offend you. You will not see her on a poster.

On the outside, they look pretty much alike, with a little different arm or leg there, and eyes that are either kooky, kookier, or kookiest. And they come in all colors. But inside, they are *very* much alike: *live* brain cells under a microscope look like brain cells.

What about the child with Down's Syndrome? If Jane had been a mongoloid baby, would we have attempted this program of neurological organization with her? Yes—if The Institutes in 1965 would have accepted her. And I'll tell you why. The only mongoloid child I know personally who did this program was, long ago, in Stuart's nursery school class, age four. At that time none of us had heard of Doman or Delacato. The parents of that child had simply set out to give him the best neurological environment possible without knowing it—a whole babyhood of sensory stimulation. And he did not take juice and cookies at snack time like the others; something about "diet" they had learned. Otherwise, he did the whole nursery school bit, outdoors and indoors. Later he was given this program of neurological organization; he was programed toward a better coordination with more crawling and creeping—locally by someone trained in Philadelphia. The last thing I heard about him he was reading well on his grade level in public school—junior high. So, yes, if I had a mongoloid child, I would work hard to be like that mother who gave her child with the "possibly deficient brain" an environment I would call superbly enriched even for a normal child. I mean, you really don't know how far he will go

* From a 1960 *Saturday Evening Post* article about a rehabilitation center.

till you make the 500 percent input attempt. I saw one! That is usually enough for me.

Now perhaps you can see why there's a hot and heavy reaction to what we've been about with Jane from people who went to the top in rehabilitation—structural and behavioral—these last twenty-five years. When you have worked around the clock to find bracing ways to get the child outdoors into the sunshine, the world; when you have worked your heart out to find techniques to "reach him," to socialize him, to civilize him so his life won't be one long tease, so there will be fun in it, some productivity with it; you just cannot believe (dead brain cells are dead) that anybody would attempt total wellness without some profit scheme attached.

So the professional graybeards issue their warning. And the reporter picks it up. And it becomes a "definite thing".* The doctors—think, *the doctors*—don't approve of this program! (If the doctors, the healers, don't approve, that means the program could hurt the child.) The fact that the doctors are picking your brains at the next cocktail party to find out what it *is* you are doing and "what's she like now" is not reported in the press. (Is she toilet trained? Yes. That's exceptional! Not really; it goes with the mobility increases. What size is the crawl box? Depends on the size of the child. And the favorite question: But does she have dorsi-flexion on command? Of course, I just told you. She's using it in walking. I mean, can she move her foot up and down, like this? Yes, she can move her foot from plantar flexion to dorsi-flexion and back to plantar flexion if you ask her to; but she's higher than that. She's walking with it alternately that way, like we do. Really? Yes, really. How did you get her to do that? Well, first we told her brain she had an ankle———)

Somewhere along the way we began to think for ourselves—Bert and I. Nobody could "lead" us—not even a Mary Lawrence. Maybe it was when we began to see we knew more than the doctors we might seek advice from. Maybe it was that we began to see Jane as a person, someone you would want to try for the top with. But we did come to look at it hard and cold, even with an eye to acupuncture treatment. We still look at it, and we still make our own decisions.

It has been my experience that parents of a brain-injured child (who have admitted that brain injury) after awhile cannot be led, cannot be fooled. It is also true that they do not take no for an answer, do not give up on their child, and do not mind the word *brain* at all. In fact, they are happiest when someone is looking at the brain of the brain-injured. Also they could not care less about professional opinion, who says it, for what reason, and from what standpoint. Their attitude is more utilitarian, like, "If it works, I'll use it."

* See *New York Times,* May 7, 1968, and *Time,* May 31, 1968.

Doctors, as well as parents, will have to liberate themselves. From the likes of the American Medical Association *Handbook on Mental Retardation* (1965), for one thing:

The nature of impairment varies with the age of the individual. Below school age it is a lag in self-help, locomotion, eating and communication skills; in school, disability in learning; and at the adult level, inability to remain independent or to meet employment requirements. . . . Seen in terms of intellectual potential, the "mildly" retarded child is generally defined within an intelligence quotient range of 50 to 70; the "moderately" retarded, 35 to 50; the "severely" retarded, 20 to 35; and the "profoundly" retarded, below 20.

The doctor will have to see for himself. He will have to involve himself with the "brain child," both the normal and the brain-injured—from one he will know the other. He will have to learn neurological *function* and its hierarchy of development, for it is responsible for the structure or the lack of structure (or the "muscle imbalance") on the table before him.

Right now he depends upon the EEG—the electroencephalogram— brain-wave measurement—to nail down a diagnosis of brain-injury to confirm what he suspects before him. And that's where the doctor fouls up. He's measuring the brain waves in the *cortex,* when the problem is, 90 percent of the time (according to records at The Institutes), in the midbrain. Oops, the EEG looks O.K. (The child is not brain-injured.)

The eight needles on the eight areas of the cortex can only show three possibilities: (a) an area is not working at all; or (b) an area is working badly (a wild seizure pattern or some such); or (c) the brain-wave pattern from the two sides of the brain do not match. It will never show brainstem incoordination or any of the other steps missing from that first year of life.

. . . From the time of Hughlings Jackson on, all investigators of the brain's functions are in accord with the statement that the cortex cannot be viewed independently of subcortical influences and vice versa. In other words, the hierarchical development of the brain is well established. Cortical control of functions depends on the integrity of subcortical structures . . . (p. 101).*

And since the EEG does not show the doctor that the child has brain dysfunction, the child is usually seen next in the psychologist's office.

This situation is not likely to change for the better, regardless of how ably the need is presented, until the medical profession approaches the problem as a whole from a perspective that seeks to diagnose and treat the neurological dysfunctions of children as dysfunctions of a developing brain (pp. 76–77).†

PHYSICAL THERAPIST: Yes, the hanging upside-down is great. No spasticity with it, as they say. Great for the kids with eye problems too (some-

* Evan W. Thomas, M.D., *Brain-Injured Children* (Springfield, Ill.: Charles C. Thomas, Publisher, 1969).
† Thomas, *op. cit.*

thing about "postural reflex" here), a really great idea—reduces hyperactivity—

ME: But basically it's for vestibular problems, balance, right?

THERAPIST: Basically it's for a lot of good reasons.

ME: They've even named it now: SIR—suspended inverted rotation!
Isn't that a scream? They just haven't figured out why yet.

THERAPIST: I think I may have. When a person is on his stomach,
everything is in flexion—all the flexors are stimulated by that position.
When a person is on his back, everything is in extension. Hanging by the
heels cancels both. It's just too simple, something we physical therapists
would never think about, it's so simple.

Another thing, they've located in the developing brain just about all the
stages phylogenetically: fish, amphibian, reptile, ape, man-ape, ape-man.
But not *bird* yet. I think the upside-downness may be the step they've
overlooked: bats—and possums.

ME: Bats and possums? That's wild! Maybe you just fit a puzzle piece
in!

THERAPIST: I think they just did, some stage we all go through perhaps,
just a little while as we are growing up. I may be wrong, but—

ME: Well, it's an idea— Makes you want to go study up on bats and
possums. What is it they do? What level are they on? Hey, maybe the bat is
treating himself neurologically! He's got lousy vision, that's for sure.
Maybe he's "cooling himself down," his hyperactivity, with hanging upside-
down, so he can go to sleep. He sleeps that way daytimes, you know. One
thing, he's got about the best auditory system there is—sonar or something.
This is crazy— Seriously, every kid just loves that pick-me-up-by-my-heels-
stuff when daddy comes home. They actually beg for it.

In fact, all persons involved in the evaluation, diagnosis and treatment of human functions and their disturbances, and all who are interested in the achievement of human potential, should have a role in the study and development of
human neurological organization (p. 17).

Those words appeared in the 1969 publication of Dr. Edward B. Le
Winn's book, *Human Neurological Organization,* at about the time it became increasingly evident that doctor and teacher, therapist and parent,
were in the same field, whether they wanted the role or not. Parents were
often the leaders, in calls for time-out for community meetings, but everyone was running hard to catch up. The fuss was all about the new kid at
school.

Let's suppose (again) that the center for the mentally retarded has
worked a miracle, and Jane is going to move into public school. She's not
disorganized enough to be considered "mentally retarded" (just a slow
learner) or "emotionally disturbed" (just hyperactive) or "cerebral

palsied" (just clumsy). She is now labeled *learning disabled* (in the 1970's).* It's news, as the world finds out there is this child—*the fourth piece of Jane*—right in the schools. If you knew how to read it, you could see the revelation coming:

Dr. James Allen, former United States Commissioner of Education, made the following speech on September 23, 1969:

The Right to Read—Target for the 70's

. . . From a variety of statistical information accumulated by the Office of Education regarding reading deficiencies throughout the country these shocking facts stand out:

—One of every four students nationwide has significant reading deficiencies.

—In large city school systems up to half of the students read below expectation.

—There are more than three million illiterates in our adult population.

—About half of the unemployed youth, ages 16-21, are functionally illiterate.

—Three-quarters of the juvenile offenders in New York City are two or more years retarded in reading.

—In a recent U.S. Armed Forces program called Project 100,000 68.2 percent of the young men fell below Grade Seven in reading and academic ability.†

As 1970 arrived (March 11) the New York *Post* carried Pete Hamill's article, "The White High Schools," which confirms that it is not true that the problem "belongs" to the blacks, the poor:

The figures for the 9th grade as of February, 1969 (the only grade scores available), show that of the 13 schools only two were reading at grade level (minimum grade level is 9.6) . . .

This is the English language, the language that these people have used since they learned to talk . . .

Obviously something is going terribly wrong here. Something is terribly wrong with the elementary and junior high schools when 9th grade students can't even pass examinations in their own languages . . .

Out in Omaha they have the problem too. By June 29, 1970 (New York *Post*) the doctors have taken care of it, with a supporting leap by the teachers, it appears: "Omaha Tries Peppy Pupil Pills" behavior modification drugs for the hyperactive).

And of course it is here: One of the teens working at a local elementary school's "special class" said:

You know, I told you about that little boy we have— So hyperactive, always in trouble— That they were trying to do something about him— Well, he's been

---

* Formerly the terms were "PH" (perceptual handicap), "dyslexia," and a host of other names. Only the child is the same.

† Quoted in C. H. Delacato, *A New Start for the Child with Reading Problems* . . . (New York: David McKay Co., 1970), pp. ix–x.

given tranquilizers now— He brought his pills in, first day, and he really broke my heart— He said, "Now I won't be a bad boy anymore."

Except for the teen-ager's alarm, I hear none at the elementary schools. The action is all at the high school, where pills are appearing—amphetamines, "ups" and "downs," the new vocabulary.

But who will sound the alarm over the pills in the elementary school? The teachers? The parents of the child? Even the little boy feels good about being one less trouble maker. As the article about Omaha said:

After the pediatricians began spreading the word in December of 1968, more and more teachers began identifying students they felt could benefit from the drugs . . .

By November 17, 1970 *The Wall Street Journal* sees the problem and spreads the news. You hope the doctor reads *The Wall Street Journal,* especially the paragraph about "medical aspects of the condition," how massive doses of vitamins B_2, B_3, B_6, C, and E, along with high-protein diets have the same "calming results [that] have been obtained by giving hyperactive children large amounts of tranquilizers or amphetamines (which, though stimulants for adults, have a calming affect on small children)." A truer prescription for the brain's chemistry. For the child, not the teacher.

By February 13, 1972 *The New York Times* is devoting six columns of a page to it; "Experts Now Link a Learning Disorder to Delinquency," by Jane E. Brody. And you read, appalled at their confusion at the fourth annual convention of the "learning disabilities" people, that the Office of Education is spending $1.5 million to build centers to train teachers to help children with "learning problems."

Help! So now it is a "tiny physiological defect somewhere in the brain" that's causing all this discussion, this expenditure. And again the answer is more buildings, more places.

It is 1972 and all the children now in school will have graduated or dropped out by the time the professionals figure it out. And it is not likely that they will have Carl Delacato's experience:

The constant search for the answer to an important problem made these exciting days. I had three jobs. My work at Chestnut Hill Academy suffered. During the afternoons I worked with both brain-injured children and with reading problems at the center. Periodically, a disturbing error occurred. I would be working with a mildly brain-injured child and would confuse him with one of the children with reading problems . . .*

Perhaps the professional does not want to have the experience. He wants scientific evidence? The only *true* way to prove whether *this* program influ-

---

* Delacato, *op. cit.,* pp. 16–17.

enced Jane's brain at any point would be to open up her skull, lay back the cortical layer of the cerebrum, delve deeper to the midbrain, and proceed to plumb the depths of the pons. And watch the brain at work. I thought I'd never live to see the day that the "old" brainstem would be open to such an examination. But it's here already. If you know how to read it.

If you want to do it professionally you can start by reading the sources (most of them since 1960, interestingly enough) listed in the bibliographies of the books listed in my Recommended Reading List. Those sources include, among other research, what the Russians have been learning about brain function, and it's impressive.

Or you can find it in magazines. Take *Life*'s glorious four-part series on "The Brain," begun October 1971, for example. This gem appeared in Part II, October 22, 1971, "In Search of the Mind's Eye" by Rick Gore:

. . . since most of the information we glean from our surroundings is concerned with edges and contours and corners, they call these basic sets of cells "the building blocks of perception.". . .

This strongly suggests that in order to perceive an object properly we may have to establish some kind of *pattern of movement* [italics mine] in relation to it. . . .

There seems to be an intimate interaction between patterns of sensing and patterns of *eye movement* [italics mine], whether it is the eyes, the rest of our bodies or the outside world that does the moving.

To perceive this world properly our brains must take our own movements into account [italics mine] . . . *the act of moving our muscles ourselves seems to be essential to proper perception* [italics mine].

Movement of all sorts so affects our perception that many scientists are beginning to think we have a separate visual system devoted to it—centered in two little mounds, the superior colliculi, buried deeply in an *old* [italics mine] part of the brain. . . .

Sir Charles Sherrington called the brain the "great raveled knot." He knew the answers lay hidden in all its tortuous pathways that feed into each other. The disentangling will be slow and arduous, but it has begun.

What *Life* apparently did not know in the fall of 1971 about brainstem movement (*some kind* of pattern of movement), *Newsweek* told us February 21, 1972, albeit inadvertently. The brainstem (pons and midbrain) is terribly interesting if not downright important: it moves us—even better than the motor area of the cortex.

The Electric Brain

. . . In a series of experiments in which slender wire electrodes were implanted in the brains of monkeys, the Stanford researchers mapped 200 sites in the *brain stem* [italics mine] that, when electrically stimulated, produced such elementary movements as the flexion of wrists, elbows, shoulders, knees or hips, the opening and closing of the mouth, rolling of the eyes, wagging of the tongue. Indeed, the movements were even more precise when governed by the *brain stem* [italics mine] than they would have been if the motor cortex itself had been similarly stimulated. . . .

And how do you get those "elementary movements" that the brainstem elicits? Let's not guess. Let's see. I happened to have recorded (in those notes for Mary Lawrence) the whole range, it seems. I agree with Dr. Thomas in his book *Brain-Injured Children:*

These children provide a wealth of potentially valuable information that may well be of greater value than investigations designed to study the results of injuring the brains of animals experimentally. (p. 33)

My Notes on Body Image

Since no one till now has had such a list to publish; since it is only in the slow-motion of a Jane that one might ever catch this explosive development, I submit this evidence from my notes as a separate entity with this word of caution: the brain is complex and its functions are interdependent. At the same time that the baby is discovering his body parts and their relationship to one another—the schema of halves, opposites, cross-patterns—he is at the same time building a visual spatial orientation to everything he bumps into and an auditory conception about what and where he just touched. He's learning distance and direction, the smooth and the scratchy, the straight and the curve—"the building blocks of perception" as *Life* has it.

I believe it is this knowledge of the body schema that is lacking in the millions of school children who are said to have a learning disability— the hyperactive, incoordinate poor reader (Delacato's Syndrome). It is this orientation, developed out of that first year on the floor and the months beyond that makes one pre-schooler "smarter" in Simon Says, one more "coordinate" on the walking beam, and gives us the child who *does* "know his left from his right."

It is hard to know input from output here. It depends upon when you observe it. The beginning moment is rarely seen and is most probably an accident. Or maybe the child is just fulfilling some long-ago plan. One thing is sure, opportunity starts it: a blueberry bush or a woolly bedspread or a change in the carpet.

Given that floor opportunity, the "brain child" goes something like this as his brain learns about the parts of his body and vice versa:

Moving **lips, tongue, jaws** in silent chopping motions.
On **back of hand:** raspberry and Indian warwhoop sounds.
Finger blitherings on **lips.**
Tongue extended in tasks.

Very interested in **tongue, lips** with play mirror.

Very interested in occluding **ears** (alternately) against hair.

Reacts to differences in floor surfaces (rug, wood, slate, tile, concrete), stops, looks, or lies down and brushes **hand** across while resting.

Alternates **left and right arms, legs** in touchings and rubbings on wall surfaces (brick, sheetrock, pegboard).

Alternates **left and right elbows** in touching and tapping wall surfaces of all kinds.

Alternates **left and right feet** (lateral side) in touching wool bedspreads.

Alternates **left and right sides (shoulder to hip)** in touching and rubbing wool bedspread and pegboard walls. Watches herself turn around to get into position for **other side.**

Alternates lying **prone** with balancing on a **side;** involves both left and right **sides** with this.

Rubs **back** against brick wall and door frames.

Awareness of **thumbs** against rims; *i.e.,* thumbs inside of rim, fingers outside.

Awareness of **backs of fingers:** pinches each in sequence, first one hand, then the other.

Hand-brushing motions.

Brushes **hand** alone or holding toy alongside body, prone; lies on **side** slightly to watch this.

Makes "dots" with **fingernail** scratch.

Looking at **fingers** through clear, opaque, and screen material; later through colored cellophane.

Index-finger pointing, but not at anything.

Tosses objects, as if interested in **wrist** flip.

Pushes **thumbs** against rims.

Fascinated with **finger** combinations she can make: first and second, first and third, etc.

Stirring motions of **arm.**

Throwing balls, **arm** extension (shoulder?).

Arm extension to **back of head** now for hair-brushing practice.

Prehensile **grasp** changing to cortical opposition of **thumb to finger** (flat).

Blinking of **eyes,** squinching of **face.**

Practicing **eye-head** movements horizontally and vertically (head moves, eyes don't, and vice versa).

Eye-following practices involving toys rolling, brushing.

Covers **ears** with **hands** or with **inside upper arms.**

Former **forearm-pull** in crawl now changed to **hand-pull,** but still under chest.

Crawling **homolaterally** now with weak push involving **thigh-knee.**

Creeping changing from **homologous** to **cross-pattern, feet** just beginning to trail.

Sitting on knees with **trunk** erect; **hip-**wiggles to scoot highchair.

Prone, rubs **heels, big toes, medial sides of feet** together (like a fly!).

Supine, taps **bottom of one foot** for a while, then the other; **knees** up for this.

Inner knee area now involved in crawl push.
Tops of feet now involved in creep.
Moving **ankles!**
Moving **toes!**
Much **arm** extension, up and above and out (slaps walls, etc.).
Creeping now totally **cross-pattern—opposite hand and knee.**
Reaches, throws with **right hand.**
Pronation and supination of **wrists;** both hands simultaneously practice this.
Crosses **eyes** voluntarily.
Lots of mirror play with **eyes.**
With **tongue and teeth** together, makes *ts-ts-ts* sound.

Knows the moment **hand** touches something new (root, etc.); stops, examines.
Spanks **right leg with right hand,** looks back over **right shoulder,** then moves
   right leg; turns to **other side** and does the same.
Lifts **hips** when pants are put on (supine).
Much **toe** movement.
Arms outstretched when passing anything; to see if can reach?
Using **thumb** to turn flashlight on and off.
Knocking motions with **closed fist: knuckles.**
"Practices" cortical opposition of **thumb to finger.**
Hand-pull in crawl now reaching ahead of face, no longer under chest.
Crawl now involving **insteps of feet** for push.
Crawl changed from homolateral to **cross-pattern,** faster!
Beginning to walk on knees, **trunk** erect, arms swinging with knees in cross-
   pattern.
Makes **eyes, faces;** plays peekaboo.
Examining **inside of mouth** and **eye movements** in mirror play.

Uses **index finger** (without looking) to turn page.
Hands slapping against surface in creep, a "practice" for noise-making?
Tops of feet trailing more consistently in creep.
Pronation and supination of **wrists** improved: turns knobs, twists open medi-
   cine-size bottles, opens car doors.
Cortical opposition of **thumb to finger** improved: undoes diaper pins.
"Socks" another person (**fist**).
Spreads **fingers** and looks through them.
Voluntary **eye-crossing** a lot (noticing **nose?**).
Much interest in **tongue.**
Improved **knee flexion** and push with **legs** in crawl.

Using **index finger** to point (with purpose) and to feel fabrics, etc.
Cortical opposition **thumb to finger** now normal—tip to tip.
Rubbing **bottom of foot** on rug while sitting or kneeling on other **knee** (alter-
   nates to "practice" both sides).
Arm extension to use **hand** at **back waist** to dress herself in pants.
Eye-head movement with following of shadows from blinking lights.

Now occludes **ears,** as well as shakes head, when vacuum cleaner is on.
Change in sit: sitting on one knee (one **buttock** on shank of leg) with other
leg forward and curved in front of her.

Can now get into **homolateral** sleep-position involving head with **arms, one
flexed and one extended with head facing the flexed one;** does not involve
lower extremities yet.
Change from hand-pull in crawl to **finger-pull** not involving palm; fingers used
as one (not rotating thumb to little finger yet).
Crawl-pull now has **arm** in extension above head; no longer under face to
start. (See finger-pull above.)

Note: The normal child who is allowed to develop on the floor will use
his lower extremities at the same pace as his upper limbs, unlike Jane; will
eventually include a big-toe dig as his crawl-push; will have a smooth
reaching pull, one that "runs through" all the fingers from thumb to little
finger; will have a serialization of movement that involves neck and limbs,
a zigzag look about it as legs learn to rotate inward and completely for
faster locomotion. And his crawl will precede his creep, whether that crawl
is homologous or homolateral to begin with. The cross-pattern ability seen
eventually at its best in creeping will be the highest form of arms plus legs
he will ever attain, as it is seen in walking also.

Further Notes on Body Image

When the child is neurologically older (Jane in 1967–69) it is this sort
of body practice he can be seen entertaining himself with (or teaching
himself about?):

Body image practices on knees: (a) Moving **right arm forward and back,**
stopping it abruptly at side; eyes watching all this. Looking at **left arm** and
doing same maneuver. (b) Swinging **both arms** simultaneously—fast; same
thing—slow. Checking **distance forward** (tries different degrees of swing);
checking **distance backward.** Looks out of corner of eyes with head facing
forward or over first one shoulder, then the other, to observe all this.
Body image practice in creep-stance: Lifts **right leg high** in air, looks over
right shoulder; tries **different heights.** Same with **left leg,** looking over left
shoulder.

Practices on knees on table: (a) Started checking out **opposite arms,** one
hand crossing midline to hold onto **opposite forearm, opposite upper arm.**
(b) Did **opposite shoulder,** left and right, once each, that I saw. Does all
this with quiet smiling intermittent with outright laughter.

Some more practicing of body **homolaterally.** I started offhand labelling "left"
and "right" as she does this.
Prone and supine, practicing banging **hips** down, up, down (**lower back**).

Supine, crossing **right leg over left,** back to floor, repeat, over and over. Also circling motions with **right foot.**

Lies on side, moves **right leg forward and back;** prone, moves **right leg up and down.** (Checking distance here?)

Practicing **leg extension,** both together, supine and from sit.

Note: For notes on body image in *space* (with opportunity for gravitational changes), see Development of Mobility from May 7, 1969, Appendix.

Yes, children can provide the scientific evidence. An athletic coach was intrigued by the differences in performance between the Hopi and the Navajo children before him, especially since the Hopi, whose coordination is better, are geographically surrounded by the Navajo. He set about to find out why, and before he "was aware of views about the concepts of neurological organization and the possible significance of mobility in early childhood." What did he learn? That the Hopis (higher in I.Q. scoring, as well) are floor babies; the Navajos are cradleboard babies.*

The schoolroom is not the answer. Nor are the additional classes (to teach around the child's handicap). Nor a building program for centers. The brain is the answer. Use it.

Therefore, the teacher's role, it would seem, is like the therapist's: get them to be normal babies. First thing first. Just call it "floor physical fitness," or think of another name a child might like, if crawling and creeping sound babyish.

Perhaps you have heard of "the Robbins report"†—and it turned you off Doman-Delacato? It turned me off too. *Is* he giving the school children a Doman-Delacato program of neurological organization?

Reading through it the first time I had the feeling only: something's missing.

That is impossible. The fellow has left out crawling!

For some unknown reason, it appears he set out to "do creeping" and "laterality" (dominance). That's like leaving out the first months of life!

What about getting the two good sides first (that you want to coordinate together in creeping)? What about the two good eyes and ears (that you want to work in concert, fuse, in creeping)? No homolateral crawling, no movement on the belly? And he hopes to go to dominance without it? How can one cortical hemisphere become the controlling one without the foundation to make two good halves? How are the students who may have a suppressed eye, amblyopia, etc., going to work *both* eyes in concert when

* "The Significance of Mobility in Early Childhood," by William D. Misner. *Human Potential,* Vol. 2, No. 1 (1969), pp. 15–20.

† Melvyn P. Robbins, "Test of the Doman-Delacato Rationale with Retarded Readers," *Journal of the American Medical Association* (October 30, 1967), pp. 389–393.

one is not even being used? And how can you get two eyes to "get used?" The answer: homolateral crawling (whether in place or moving forward), where one side of the body (left) works, then the other side (right) works.

Does he think the "homolateral sleep-position" is the same thing? If he does, it's incredible that he would set out on such a study with such fuzzy knowledge.

And incredible, too, that the *Journal of the American Medical Association* might publish such a paper without first checking with Doman and Delacato to ask, *"Is* this your program?" (I can only guess that such a check was not made; otherwise, why would the *Journal* publish it?)

I have never discussed "the Robbins report" with anybody at The Institutes, but I would think they either cried or laughed out loud. It was discussed though, and quoted as "proof against," "scientific evidence against" The Institutes' program by teachers, for one, and by the "Official Statement" of April 1968,* for another.

I would hope a teacher or psychologist or whoever is planning to set up a "Doman-Delacato Program"—whether it is for a paper or for a child— would take the moment, if not the courtesy, to ask the authors of the program, "Is this your program?"

One extra thought: to hope to see significant changes in reading scores in a group of children from a two-hour-a-day, five-day-a-week program in *six weeks* (even if that program included crawling)—that in itself is a rather irresponsible hope. The first year of life is a heavier scene than that; it is not a six-week bit of floss, believe me.

It is important to distinguish what is and what is not Doman-Delacato in what you read, if you want to understand the subject of "neurological organization." For example, techniques that are employed to teach around the child's neurological deficits—that, of course, is not neurological organization. No, it's straighter than that: to get the Janes in school to be as perceptually organized as the normal child who sits in the next seat.

In our schoolroom here at home we have something of an oddity: a brain-injured child who is not having and has never had "reading disability." Except for a less-than-perfect ability in visual accommodation—using vision at desk here to chalk blackboard there and back to desk here again, which she needn't do with a tutor at her side—the only "can't read" symptoms Jane showed at any time were (a) small words of the two-letter variety, *in, on, it;* and (b) a lack of stop control when she started writing verticals on a line, *1, 7, 11*.

* American Academy for Cerebral Palsy *et al.,* "Official Statement: The Doman-Delacato Treatment of Neurologically Handicapped Children," *Archives of Physical Medicine and Rehabilitation,* published by the American Congress of Rehabilitation Medicine (April 1968), Vol. 49, No. 4.

Jane never had a problem in school with hearing, reading, or writing *b*'s and *d*'s or any other reversals of words or numbers; no trouble following a series of directions; no horizontal or vertical spacing disability in writing; no lack of closure or cornering in geometric figures; no inability in crossing the midline of a figure (going left to right all the way through), as in + and ×; and none of the other standard problems.

The Institutes said in 1968, when Jane was six, that she was "perceptually ready" for school. She had the brain functions of the first year of life down pat: early sound discrimination for phonics, if the teacher taught reading that way; outline perception (the whole of a configuration) needed for look-say, if the teacher taught that way; the ability to see details within a configuration (while still seeing the whole), if the teacher wanted to break apart or put together a word; and left-to-right horizontal eye-following for sentences across the page (and right to left to get back to the margin a shade lower for the next line).

Most of all, she had the body knowledge born on the floor to help her comprehend a story: its talk about people "coming *out of* a building, going *around* the corner, *down* a street, and *across to* a park" never lost Jane for a second. The picture would show you a park if you had never seen one, but it couldn't show you the direction, the time, the space, the distance of "out of." You had to feel that yourself as you traveled with the people in the story. You needed to have some knowledge of "out of" yourself, long before you were ready to deal with the language process, even before the *hearing* of the word-symbol *out of*. You can learn a lot more about "out of" when you are a baby on all fours than you can on your two feet when you are older, I would think. Let's say the former gives you more tactile reinforcement. And early, when the brain is processing that sort of stuff for the first time.

In school work Jane was never confused by anything visual, and gradually not by the auditory either, in case the teacher wanted to just teach it talking. She was never a "slow learner" or a "learning disabled" student. Yes, perceptually she was ready when she "went to school."

Yes, the normal baby is perceptually ready for reading when he stands up to walk. Or he is not.

Somebody is having a baby. What kind of Jane will this one be? Sure, who the grandfather was—the genetics of the thing—is important. But does anybody ever reach the full height of the genetic picture? What are the facts? What is that genetic potential?

There are 10 to 13 *billion* brain cells in a human brain it is estimated.
Therefore, there are twice as many brain cells in each human head as there have been people forever.

There are 60,000 synaptic (connection) possibilities for each brain cell.

Each day some brain cells die, beginning with the day you are born. Brain cells do not regenerate. Yes, we are walking around and talking around our dead brain cells this very minute.

Cancel out more live brain cells—a hundred? a thousand?—if:

    you've ever had temperature over 104 degrees;

    you've ever been hit hard on the head (attention, police officers and parents);

    you are over thirty-five (take away 100,000 daily).

It is estimated that each of us uses only 10 to 12 percent of our brain cells anyway.

It's not the number of live cells that's important, it's how well insulated the neuronal pathways are.

How does a pathway get insulated? Use. It's called myelination, the process of building a myelin sheath. This happens with use. *Life* refers to the "sticky glial cells" attaching themselves to the whole circuit of a pathway, in and out. Pathway insulation keeps the interference out, the buzz out, what's happening in the pathway "next door" in the brain—it makes for smooth performance, input and output.

Yes, it is difficult to separate potential from function. Simply, the brain seems to have been made to be used. Or is it the other way round?

Advice to parents can be a bore. Probably because it's always been so conflicting. Also it's usually about how to manipulate your child—after he walks and talks, of course—so you can understand him. Up to the time he walks and talks, there's nothing much to do, it's a drag. And the void is filled mostly with the Activities of Daily Living: "feeding, dressing, and grooming."

I think it's high time advice was simplified. Just manipulate one thing: his neurological environment. Think about the baby more than his layette; his learnings more than his lotions; his gaze more than his smile; his floor activities more than his walking; and his "gets it" more than his "says it."

He will use three of his four "brains" that first year—spinal cord (and medulla), pons, and midbrain. When he starts to walk after the end of that year, he's more a product than a beginning. The beginnings were long ago in his life. He has already been through evolution once in the womb and through most of it again at one. It's so explosive, that first year of brain organization, you might want to stay at home to share it with him.

The current emphasis of the child developmentalists is turning from the three- to six-year-olds and going straight for the beginnings: from the importance of a nutritionally sound mother at the time of conception and throughout womb life, on to a natural birth when the baby is ripe, and into life out here, this room, this "school" with his "new teacher"—the person who brings out the opportunities rather than the guidance.

Of course, there are the endless advertisements that fill the press and screen, where technology is all-important. Perhaps parents will come around to boycotting that technology which could be harmful to the baby's neurological organization, just as they've always kept a watch for open safety pins. That would include everything from convenient labor-induction and nerve-blocking anesthesia to "the motherless electric baby stroller."

Opportunity: that's the parents' role if you want, as I know you do, your baby to become a child successful in his communicative skills—reading, writing, talking. Limitation of opportunity can slow, impede, or stop altogether the development and organization of a child's nervous system. The Philadelphians can prove it.

After trips to England, France, and Italy to test children, to gather information, to see if they too had "our American reading problems" (yes), and to see if they too were the result of neurological disorganization (yes), Doman and Delacato decided to take a look at opportunity. They went to look at cultures in which any floor (ground, actually) activity was not allowed, either because the insects were so harmful or because of custom. (It took five years just to make four expeditions into the Stone Age cultures of Indian tribes south of the Amazon River.) They went to test their theory away from European-American life, and they went to test children's abilities in each of Doman's and Delacato's four successive stages of brain development. What did they find?

The Xingu Indians in the interior of Brazil Centrale and the Bushmen of the Kalahari Desert had the same problem: they were seriously lacking in nervous system development, including their ability to deal with abstract symbols, which, of course, is written language. It would be impossible to teach them to read or write.

What are the "four successive brain stages of development" a parent should be aware of, so he can "do what's right" for the human being in his care?*

1. From Birth to Six Months

The three "in" channels (visual, auditory, tactile) and the three "out" channels (mobility, language, manual) must be used together. Delacato writes:

Vision without hearing and mobility is incomplete; mobility without vision and hearing is incomplete; hearing without mobility and vision is incom-

* The following stages can be read in further detail in Delacato's book, *A New Start for the Child with Reading Problems.*

plete. . . . The opportunity to do all of them simultaneously is the first goal of this stage, which in turn sets up *differentiation* of function . . . the process makes itself visible in his use of one side of the body at a time.*

Here the parent sees the infant crawl one-sided—left side, right side—homolaterally.

Here the parent sees the baby's head turning toward the forward or active hand. That feat introduces the use of eye and ear *alternately,* separately.

The baby is learning to see, learning to hear, learning about his arms and legs and hands—all at the same time. Head, neck, trunk, appendages—even his tongue!—are adding up to brain development.

He's already learning about his two "sides." Later he'll hear them called left and right, but now it's more like "this" and "that." And to work two sides in concert (the next stage), you need to know (your brain does) you have some sides.

2. Between Six Months and One Year

He's a very different baby.

He learns to use parts of both sides of his body together.

The parent sees the cross-pattern: the opposite hand and knee have found each other. Yes, he is creeping, off his belly.

He learns to use both eyes (and ears) together:

He no longer takes in the world one eye at a time. His brain now begins to develop the ability to take in two separate visual sensations at one time and to convert them into a single perception. This requires a more complex brain circuitry and is the basis for depth perception (p. 66).

All he needs is opportunity to do just that.

At this time not only do the eyes begin to work together, but the hands and eyes begin to operate in unison. The baby needs to do much exploring; visual activity accompanied by sound and touch should be encouraged. Mother should talk whenever moving about the room to help the infant to discover the third dimension of both sound and sight. . . . (pp. 66–67).

The parent sees the child looking "here," listening "here", because the parent is moving "here," talking "here." The parent knows to do "there" also. And "over here."

Without opportunity to creep about, which gives a baby's eyes and ears at this distance, at that distance, the brain development of this stage, what happens? As with the skipping of any stage of the four stages:

* *Ibid.* p. 64.

The result will be a somewhat "unfinished" human being, which is another way of describing a reading problem (p. 61).

3. Between One Year and Eighteen Months

At about fifteen months he begins to walk. The parent sees he is beginning to walk. The parent allows it. The parent does not teach it. Creeping in cross-pattern (in the stage before) taught it.

He begins by pulling himself up onto his feet while holding onto furniture . . . a whole new world in which the balance requirements are quite different; his hand use is different, and even the world he hears is different . . . (p. 67).

Without seeing and hearing perfect balance is impossible, and without balance perfect seeing and hearing are impossible. As balance improves, the development of the eye-brain and ear-brain channels changes. Being in an upright position allows the child to see a world at greater distance, and depth becomes more important in vision. To see in depth the child's brain must fuse the two pictures, coming from the two eyes, into one image and must make sense out of it. Since he is now walking and moving from side to side his brain must begin to fuse the pictures coming from each eye at a *very rapid rate* (p. 68).

The parent allows the child to walk. Not sit more than walk. Not ride more than walk. The opportunity is for walking.

Here often opportunity to hear outweighs his opportunity to see, as parents allow him to listen and decode verbal abstractions (our words) but not read them. Happily, television, Delacato says, is filling that visual void, and fewer children each year are suffering from this lack of visual experience. (They are reading the brand-names they see repeatedly, at least.) The opportunity for ear-brain and eye-brain relationships would be in even better balance if parents would provide the opportunity to read in the manner of Glenn Doman's *How to Teach Your Baby to Read,* as we did with Jane.

The baby has progressed from using very low brain levels up to and including the cortex, the outer portion of his brain.

And he is saying a word or two. The parent of course now hears, as well as sees, his baby's development.

4. Between Eighteen Months or Two Years and Six or Seven Years

Baby has become quite *human.*

His brain has too, resulting in one-sidedness with this final stage, and the ability to read, write, talk, as no primate brain below it can do. It will during this stage organize itself, so that one-half its outer cortex, one hemisphere, will become the language-controlling one.

Here is where reading, writing, talking and the learning of language are controlled. Here is where reading and the decoding of speech take place, as well as the storage of language. *If one of the halves does not become dominant, then the brain is not completely developed and a problem with reading usually results* (p. 70).

The parent should allow this to happen, allow the child to *use* the side of his body (his hand most notably) that he is tending toward.

As their handedness becomes more established, their eyedness usually follows and they then are able to deal with smaller perceptions and more sophisticated differentiations; because, as the perception goes into the dominant eye, it is controlled in the dominant cortical hemisphere (p. 71).

To not allow is to give him toys, play equipment, and activity where one hand cannot be chosen; because "this toy" needs two hands to pick it up, throw it, stack, it, pull it, or ride it.

Note: Don't confuse the bilateral (two-sided) nature of a toy (child) with the bimanual four-year-old who uses one hand "to do" and the other hand "to assist" (hold, steady, stay)—the child at Level VI of the Profile who can work a zipper, button, and crayon. (See Appendix, p. 504)

Reading from the bottom up, everything in that Profile through the fifth level is the bilateral child: two hands, two feet, two sides, and includes walking (the previous stage).

Now—during this final stage—he is becoming, and finally does become unilateral.

The parent sees his one-arm throw, his one-foot kick, his one-hand pickup. The parent sees he doesn't throw a ball with two hands anymore. Activities are simple to figure out because the parent can see it. The parent will provide opportunities for unilateral activity. Swimming? Bilateral. Hopscotch? Unilateral with some bilateral mix in there with the feet. Wrestling? Bilateral. Darts? Unilateral.

When this happens—the transition from your old bilateral baby to your new unilateral child—you don't have to run out and change all his toys within the hour of course. It will probably hit you more like, "He's not hugging his teddy bear anymore." No, because he's dragging it around by one ear! So when you get the point that he's using that one hand for the rest of his day too, you will be a different parent in the toy store next time. No more huge cumbersome things that need two hands to move. Just figure it out: large cardboard blocks are bilateral, small wooden blocks are unilateral; cars and wagons and bikes to sit in and on and "drive" are bilateral, cars and trucks to push on the floor or table and "drive" are unilateral; the playstove is bilateral if you want to play rearrange-the-room, but unilateral if you want to cook on it. So if you want it to be unilateral, you will buy some pans and pots with it. In the store at some point, you will probably be playing with it, picturing yourself seated, lying down, standing, *using* it. And there's your answer.

When the child is five you (parents and kindergarten teachers) will want to decrease gradually the amount of music in the environment to allow the language hemisphere to become dominant. (An abundance of music before five? Sure, why not?) "Musical skills in the form of listening to it, as well as singing, begin to move into the other, or subdominant hemisphere," Delacato writes.* And, of course, the parent will provide the opportunity for that to happen.

The child who has been allowed the organization of the previous stages even starts and stops stuttering so you can see it. He starts as he reaches the height of his bilateral days—two equal hemispheres both wanting to do language. And he stops as he moves into his unilateral life. Parents who know are really quite fascinated. Instead of, "Oh, he's stuttering," they say, "Ah-ha, he's stuttering." Sometime after he stops, they say, as with everything, "Hm-m, when did that happen?" and are sorry they missed the moment, the day, the week they forgot to notice. You see, he is so fascinating today.

When he finally is "organized" at about the age of six he will close his mouth, and his parent will sometime later say, "Hm-m, he doesn't go around with his mouth open anymore."

But his first year is his enrichment year, as well as the all-important organizing one. That's where he starts off as a wide-awake organism or a sluggish one. That's the true head-start place. For an excellent source of home ideas for those beginnings, I suggest the article by Glenn Doman and Carl Delacato, "Train Your Baby to Be a Genius" (*McCalls,* March 1965).†

And if the word *genius* bothers you, I would like to change your "mind" about that. In Lewis Terman's studies of genius‡ he found two conditions were universal: (a) early reading, and (b) early sensory stimulation. (One of the loveliest parent-guides-without-knowing-it is found in the early pages of *Genius in Residence,* by Audrey Grost, listed in my Recommended Reading List.)

Interesting the degree of opportunity a child can *take.* The picture of the baby I get from both the Doman-Delacato article and from Audrey Grost's book is: sponge.

* "Research has been carried out at the Montreal Neurological Institute indicating that the subdominant hemisphere is usually the seat of tonal activity. For an excellent review of this and other research on brain function, see *Cognitive Processes and the Brain* by Milner and Glickman, Van Nostrand, 1965" (p. 75).

† Available for 25¢ at The Institutes for the Achievement of Human Potential, 8801 Stenton Avenue, Philadelphia, Pa. 19118.

‡ Lewis M. Terman, *The Intelligence of School Children* (Cambridge, Mass., Houghton Mifflin Company, 1919).

You are saying that's all fine and good, but what do you do when everybody else on the block gets bikes, bikes, bikes? Well, you can get a bike for your child too, if you think you can manage his not being on it most of the time from age three to six. Or buy an exciting unilateral something and start a neighborhood fad. Meet the competition, as Mary Lawrence would say, and, "I am sure you can think of some game way to get this over. . . ." (You get better and better at it.) And if that doesn't work, you will just have to be one of the new-fashioned parents. With a human being for a child.

(A couple of paragraphs you learned in school but somehow never connected to anybody you knew at the time. Perhaps you will want to make that connection now.)

Fact: Twelve days after conception the human fetus has a brain and a spinal cord. In twelve more days there is a heart—beating. At nine months weight has reached seven pounds. That rate of growth, if maintained throughout life, would catapult that weight into the twelve-million-ton range! But the rate of growth every day is less than yesterday, and the process is over altogether at the age of twenty.

Fact: The human brain, in contrast to the body, has a development three times as fast. In the normal child its development is *over* after eight years, and each year before eight sees *less* development than the year before. He will learn more those beginning six-to-eight years, fact for fact, than he will learn in the rest of his life. We learned this from Glenn Doman's orientation of parents at The Institutes. Having observed Jane's fact-finding about the details of her surroundings, I am inclined to believe he's right.

And Jane is a fact. Not for another child, but for herself. And for the theory of neurological organization.

Perhaps you want to believe it is not the program but the person doing it—there were 193 of us altogether; or you may have the opinion that her progress could be the result of natural maturation. In any case, you would have to explain further what you mean. Because, it seems to me, *that* discussion might take us right back to programing.

The truth that you can *see* is that every child has a daily environment, every child is being programed every minute of it (with or without people). Unless he is in solitary confinement (some prison or institution or silent dark corner of his room—or "mind"), he has some environment, some programing anyway. So it's really *what* program the brain-injured person gets that matters to his brain, just as it is with the normal baby.

Jerome Kagan, professor of psychology at Harvard, has apparently been researching what The Philadelphians have known and have been programing for years. In the special Saturday Review series of articles on the subject, "The Child" in *SR/Research: Science and Humanity* (December 7, 1968), in an article entitled, "His Struggle for Identity" he writes:

Lights that blink on and off are more likely to capture his attention than is a steady light source. Intermittent tones of sound are more attention-getting than continuous ones. . . .

He explains that by measuring the child's heart rate and the duration of his gaze, it can be seen that the "earliest" thing that gets an infant's attention is the "high rate of change" of the stimulus.

Visual events with high black-and-white contour contrast possess more power to recruit sustained attention than stimuli with minimal contour contrast . . . They elicit attention without prior learning. These factors dominate the attention during the first twelve weeks. . . .

Remember what I told Mary about Glenn Doman's orientation concerning the three mythical mothers on the block, the sun going down and coming up, and how mothers can speed up a child's programing simply by turning on and off the lights in the nursery, and some other things? Remember the ghetto children, whose mothers are away at work, watching (and hearing) TV all day?

We certainly do not wish to reject the idea totally, but we prefer to balance it with the possibility that lower-class children are not so much deprived of parental vocalization as they are deprived of distinctive vocalization. . . .

That's why it just seemed to be a better idea at the time (to The Philadelphians) to run the word-tapes for Jane with the five-second intervals of silence between the words to "wake up the listening" than to, say, turn the TV on. "On and off," you see, is better than "on" for auditory, visual, *and* tactile. Kagan continues:

This research generates implications for pre-school enrichment programs for lower-class children. There is a zealous attempt to bombard the lower-class child with pictures, crayons, books, speech, and typewriters, as if an intellectual deficit was akin to hunger and the proper therapy required filling of his cerebral gulleys with stuff.

I would like to argue for a more paced strategy, a self-conscious attempt to intervene when the intrusion [I would hope he means words after silence or loud after soft or soft after loud, etc.] is likely to be maximally distinctive.

You not only need the specific intermittent stimulus Kagan speaks of, at a time "maximally distinctive," but you need it directed to a specific Jane, since various levels of visual and auditory competence are represented in the one classroom Kagan mentions.

The only way we can see if Jane's program is helping Jane is to see Jane. Is Jane looking more like the normal child? Is she looking less like the brain-injured child? Can we see where the brain-injured child and the normal child meet, where one melds into the other? Are there moments, glimpses, that Jane can give us to prove these "two children" are indeed, let's say, the younger and older sisters of the same brain child?

Who is Jane in 1972? First let's tick off a couple of items in 1971, since I got ahead of the story. One, Mrs. Gross' June 1971 Progress Report, for the sake of consistency:

Jane has made big strides in reading comprehension and associated speech in the last three months. She has progressed from word-recognition and the reading of familiar stories to reading sentences as they are written before her. The vocabulary used is familiar to her, but she is now able to fill in a word that she does not know by using the beginning letter and general content of the sentence.

She is most interested in all types of "games" that use reading as a basis for success, and in stories that are spontaneously made up, dealing with characters she knows, often in absurd situations.

During this spring she has planted seeds and is interested in the growth and care of the seedlings. She has learned to read the thermometer and associates temperature with weather and season. She has experimented with magnets and grasped the difference between metal and nonmetal.

Because the emphasis has been on oral reading, Jane has been talking in longer and more complex sentences as her reading skill has improved to that level.

On the whole, she has been a very enthusiastic and responsive student, eager to learn and with good attention for the hour of her instruction.

And two, the following notes with respect to legs:*

JUNE 10, 1971. Orthopedic surgeon's office:

DOCTOR: Hips? Hips are very good. Really very good. Ankles are fine. You've done quite a job, yes. The knees: no problem. Loose enough to extend the legs for casting without pain. Yes, I agree with their recommendation [at The Institutes]. Probably can get them fully extended with the initial casting. Depends on how relaxed she is. If she is not relaxed enough to put them into full extension the first time, I'll do a wedging procedure with the casts, take them out a little more a second time, or a third. We want to cast with as much relaxation of her knees as possible. August nineteenth when you get back from Switzerland is fine. Even if they are somewhat tighter when you return, no problem. No, you don't have to do a program. Have a good trip.

* Mary Lawrence, during a Memorial Day weekend visit in 1971 to see Jane, was so impressed with the straightness of her legs, she suggested we ask IAHP about casting J's legs as a possible shortcut to any tightness that remained (now as opposed to fall when Sandler said "We'll take a look at it"). June 2, 1971: IAHP staff doctors and Art Sandler agreed to recommend it to an orthopedic surgeon they would suggest in the city of Philadelphia.

An hour later. Phone call to IAHP:

ART SANDLER: Over my dead body. Sit in a wheelchair all day in Europe? Are you kidding? Immobility brings muscle atrophy. She's going to get plenty of that during casting.

Program in Europe: one hour a day, preferably in twenty-minute periods: (a) walk stretched-out with overhead-ladder assist, press heels down five laps or less, and she has to do the sixth lap or more by herself the same way; (b) climbing inclined ladder for weight-bearing; against outside of chalet is fine.

You understand, we are not asking for progress those two months. Just maintain what we got. Just don't bring her back here "tighter," you understand?

OCTOBER 14, 1971. Orthopedic surgeon's office. (Cast removal after third wedging procedure; legs in cast eight weeks altogether):

DOCTOR: Looks good. [J.'s legs straight as two thin swords, lying out in front of her.] Often they spring right up to the chin and stay there after the casts are removed, spasmodic reaction. Looks better than I expected, but you might see that drawing up of the legs later, or partially so. Don't worry—exercise. Push down on her kneecap, all the way to the table, like this, release, do it again, release—get long-leg night splints to hold her knees in full extension while she's sleeping. Bring them with you, one week.

An hour later. Phone call to IAHP:

ART SANDLER: No exercises for flexion?

OCTOBER 21, 1971. Orthopedic surgeon's office.

[J. in excruciating pain if she moves an inch. Left leg locked uncontrollably in full-extension. Right leg locked uncontrollably in flexion. Legs thin as bones from loss of function in casts; looks completely devoid of any muscle. Skin cannot bear to have even air touch it. Wants blanket over her legs all the time.]

DOCTOR: Leave her alone. Allow her to get up, walk around, holding onto furniture, whatever, when she's ready to. Use leg splints at night. Gradually increase slight pressure at knee to take flexed right leg into full extension, more and more, hopefully by a week from now.

One hour later. Revisit to IAHP. Quick examination of J. in back of station wagon in parking lot of The Institutes.

ART SANDLER: Am I happy? I'm not happy about it at all. We've got to get that left leg to flex. Just because it's straight doesn't make me excited— movement, function, that determines structure.

This program is to be started immediately:

Attach feet to pulley, gradually till tailbone is off the table, fifteen seconds five times a day. Increase each session by fifteen seconds a day and increase by one session every other day till you reach fifteen sequences a day and five minutes of full hanging each sequence. Allow a half-hour between sequences; do no more than three an hour. I prefer two an hour.

One week from today, have her stand in place under the ladder before hanging or after, if function is better that way, or alternate (one to three minutes, fifteen times a day). The height of the overhead ladder according to her longer leg. Allow her to walk under the overhead ladder gradually, working up to it. Break bones? Breaking her bones is the least of Jane's worries right now, and yours too.

Three baths—twenty minutes each—pinch or tickle leg to get her legs to move.

Get her out of the bed except at night. Have her lie on her stomach on the floor [and do her crying]. Yes, have school down there too.

Sleep any way she wants to. Night splints over my dead body. We want function, any kind of function, not immobility. Call in one week. Aspirin (and hanging upside-down) for pain.

NOVEMBER 11, 1971. IAHP. J. walking stretched out under overhead ladder, very flat feet even during turning.

ART SANDLER: If we're not careful, she may walk right out of here.

One hour later. Orthopedic surgeon's office. J. began whimpering the moment he walked in. During examination on the table she went into a death-struggle like we had never seen, lying prone trying to get up, while the doctor held her down, trying unsuccessfully to pull her legs down into extension. Crying, screaming, clutching her father as we talked.

DOCTOR: I should have been able to overcome her resistance if they are straight like you say.

ME: She's very strong. And so frightened. She was just resisting, really——

NOVEMBER 15, 1971. Long-distance call to IAHP:

ME: Art, something's wrong with Janey. She won't bear any weight on her right foot, will hardly step on it. Since we were down there in Philadelphia. The next morning she wouldn't step on it. And I did such a stupid thing. To show her what I was talking about I pushed down on it just a little, above the knee, and she screamed bloody murder. It hurts or something.

ART SANDLER: Sounds like a pulled muscle. Drop back on the amount of the program . . . wet heat between sequences now and then. Call me . . . That's the one that was locked into flexion, right? Don't ever apply pressure to a knee like that. It's a good way to make a spasm a worse spasm.

ME: Art, Bert and I have been talking about that. That's why you didn't want us to use the night splints, wasn't it?

ART SANDLER: Yes, and because it's not natural to stretch a leg out and hold it immobile that way. We want function for recovery. And we want function for straightness.

13

JANUARY 1, 1972. Propped in the sentence builder on Jane's desk I find, now and then, a little surprise, a kind of thought for the day:

P. J. cries white tears.

Who knows what her other thoughts are—the ones too complex to write, to say. I wouldn't want to guess. Even if I knew, I wouldn't want to draw the picture. Outlines are no good drawn around children.

She is quite unique and has her own special personality. But then, none of us is a category.

The loveliest thing of all, she is finally expressing herself. She's finally able to tell us who she is, what she likes, what she doesn't like. Actually, it just serves to deepen the mystery.

JANUARY 13, 1972. Noting, then sitting back to wonder:

J. covering mouth when coughing now.

Puts P.J. doll—lying in a leather anklet, buckled securely around her—through the entire specifics of "her hangup," even to making the two figure-eights on the wall to stay the rope, even to checking that the rest of the rope is over to the wall, so no one will trip passing by while hanging-upside-down is in progress, even to the timing of each hang—a secret three-minute timer in J.?

Folding everything in sight (that usually requires it); ruffling fabrics, including the deft, sophisticated way for a girl to layer-up the back of a dress or slip before putting it on.

Thinking of all that Jane has picked up with no teaching on our part. Thinking what observers sitting people become! This child, who can put up groceries better than her father, knows this house—where things are kept—better than any of us. Knows the "finer knowings" we all miss in our dash and drift. And, heaven knows, has remembered closet-holdings, drawer-containings, all these years after crawling and creeping, down to where she put the purple hair of the troll-topped pencil four years ago.

ME: Purple hair?
J.: (laughing): My pencil hair.
ME: Where is it?
J.: In the cabinet / in the playroom.
ME: I can't find it yet. I think we lost that purple hair a long time ago, honey——
J.: (in frustration): HON / EY!
ME: Now don't get angry. Tell me where you put it.
J.: Boys' games / cabinet.
ME: With the boys' games? You mean those spin-the-spinner——
J.: (showing excitement, all over body tremble)
ME: There are so many games. Where should I look?
J.: T-t-d-dy WINKS house.

To make a long struggle short, the purple hair was stuffed into the ceramic mushroom target for tiddlywinks—in 1968.

January 25, 1972

Dear Mary,

   . . . For Christmas Jane got music too for the first time, a Swiss-chalet music box, two nightgowns, boots, a study lamp, a slip, two books, and perfumes and lotions. I think that all speaks something "new" about Jane, don't you? Mrs. Gross said she didn't need more concrete learning materials, she's beyond all that now, so I avoided Creative Playthings for the first time in fifteen years, and thumbed my nose at Childcraft, as well.

   Everyone except Stuart had the Asian flu, on and off since January 1, and Jane missed a whole week of program and at about half-mast since. And too, terribly disorganized (only good word here) lately, for some reason: using left hand 100 percent of the time, including with scissors and paper clips! Even when the material is over to her right.

   Her awareness is so much higher since, let's say, before our trip last summer. Mrs. Gross is just pouring in the reading—things like quotations, questions and answers, etc., and J. is reflecting all this in speech. How that kid moves when you add the visual!

   Jane is beginning to make conversation for the first time, probably from seeing its setup on paper. Heretofore all speech has been from wanting either objects or information.

   We still have leg straightness, maintaining it with her upside-down hanging, while we work at walking (with overhead ladder assist, of course).

   New programs: walking backward with overhead ladder assist; walking, holding onto elastic parachute cord. . . .

PROGRESS REPORT
by Elizabeth Gross, Teacher
March 1972

   . . . Jane found herself for the first time on straight legs, long leg casts supporting her, and she was, therefore, able to walk about, holding onto furniture and walls. This unprecedented freedom of upright movement in the house was very stimulating and generated more awareness and speech. . . .

   When casts were removed mid-October, a very rough time followed for Jane. Her legs were extremely painful and sensitive, and for the first time in the years I have taught her I saw her in acute physical discomfort. But even more than the pain, there was her complete incomprehension that the people she loved and trusted would knowingly put her through this ordeal.

   Because Jane has always responded better to written material over spoken words, we made a book describing in some detail the procedure she had undergone and tried to explain, in simple language, the goals she might achieve with her new straight legs; for example, "walk out of the house." This book went a long way in comforting her and she referred to it as the next step of progress was reached (next page, etc.). Curiously, she always stopped reading at the exact point she was in and did not go on to the "happy ending." . . .

The episode left her weak; and it has taken months for her to get her strength back. . . .

Now her energy is back to normal, and I am, therefore, able again to demand greater effort from her.

I will write down short episodes, as she slowly unfolds the plot, using short sentences. She is reading beginner's books, having less difficulty than before in differentiating between various two-letter words (*in, is, it,* for example), although she still has some.

She can match pictures to words, or the other way around, in a puzzle situation.

Since her trip to Switzerland last summer, she realizes that English is not the only language; and I have built a whole unit on differences between Switzerland and the United States.

I have stressed the seasons and holidays, and although she still is unable to stay in the lines when coloring, she has made creditable birthday and Valentine cards.

At this time these are the concepts and activities Jane is working on:

Putting the right word under a picture (noun or verb).

Putting simple sentences next to a picture depicting a situation; for example, "A boy has no shirt on." (The descriptive sentence is her interpretation of the situation. I put the words individually on cardboard and cut them out. The words for about five sentences are mixed up and she chooses the right ones for the sentence she is working on. She often needs to hear the word she is searching for repeated for her, but she is quite successful in this task.)

She is reading books of the Ladybird series with good results.

It is the first time that Jane is holding what amounts to a conversation with me. A verbal exchange that has nothing to do with any book she is reading, but rather with experiences or ideas she has had.

After quite a struggle, she is able to apply the concept of "more" and "less" to mathematical problems and so is doing simple additions more consistently correct.

Every day we discuss the date and weather and spend time on any holiday that comes along.

Her attention span holds up for about forty-five minutes on difficult material, and the last fifteen minutes of her school hour is spent on easy or fun projects.

She is a well-disciplined student who is eager to learn.

APRIL 6, 1972. Conversations during Philadelphia revisit.

ME: I thought you were impressed with her walk.

ART SANDLER: It stinks. She's walking with an overhead ladder assist. Anything less than the way you and I walk is lousy.

ME: Stand in linoleum?

ART SANDLER: Yes, linoleum. Make a tube for her to stand in.

Get about ten feet of it. Roll it tight, tight against her hips, so she'll have to work to shimmy into it. Top end about two to three inches under her armpits, bottom end on the floor. Pad it slightly at the top, not too much, so she'll feel uncomfortable with that digging into her armpits, so she'll want to rise above it, so she'll stand straight-kneed above it. In every half hour she's to stand in it fifteen minutes. Part of that time play "hot potato" with her in it, sideways, back and forth, six to eight inches between you and someone else, or alone just bat her back and forth into a corner——

ME: Excuse me, did you say fifteen minutes of every half hour, just have her stand in this— What do you call it?

ART SANDLER: I call it a tube of linoleum. Yes, fifteen minutes, and we need some longer periods. What does she do after supper?

ME: Have a reading time, story or whatever, and go to bed.

ART SANDLER: What does she do before supper?

ME: She finishes her last sequence at six. Then usually she plays alone, strings her dolls upside down on the pulley—you know, puts her dolls through "the program." Then she plays at the sink while her daddy is cooking supper. It's about an hour before supper.

ART SANDLER: Good. Let's have her stand in the tube that hour— watching TV or whatever. With the prolonged periods, I know she'll have to bear weight on that right foot; she can't stand on the left one for that amount of time. She'll have to shift weight. Also have her eat all meals in the tube, if you can manage that. What would the teacher say to having her do school standing up in the tube?

ME: I don't think she'll believe any of this.

ANOTHER MOTHER (*in the waiting room*): I remembered *you,* we talked, about three years ago, I think— But she is so completely different, I wouldn't have known it was the same child. I remember your husband— And you— That's the only way I know it's your child.

ME: It's apparent, huh?

SHE: It's incredible. She's a completely different child. I wouldn't have mentioned it— But——

ME: I know how you feel— That happened to us once, just once have we seen the same child, that I know of. It was exactly one year after we started here. We saw a little boy from Canada. He had been in that initial three-day evaluation, rocking endlessly in the middle of the floor, convulsions around the clock— My husband had tripped over him on the floor that first day. A year later he was sitting in a chair, looking at a book. Not only had the rocking ceased altogether, his convulsions had too. He could say ten words, all from his reading program. I remember running down the hall to get my husband, to show him—he would be so thrilled. I only had that experience once, but I know what you mean.

SAME MOTHER (*showing her eight-year-old daughter the samples of Jane's writing that I had given her*): Isn't this wonderful! Jane is beginning to write, like you are . . . (*To me*) My little girl knows ninety-nine dots on a card, knows one hundred dots on a card—just with a glance. And she can do mental arithmetic—it's fantastic——

ME: What do you mean?

SAME MOTHER: Down here they ask her problems like: 482 minus n plus 10 equals 478, and immediately she answers 14. She's better than that; I just can't think of some of the more difficult ones they've thrown at her.

(*Child trying to tell mother through a gagging speech hang-up, facial tic, etc., she wants to go to the bathroom.*)

ME: Is this a new thing with her?

SAME MOTHER: Yes, how did you know?

ME: I've been through all that myself. It'll drive you crazy, but if she keeps on going, she'll get out of it someday, into a higher speech——

SAME MOTHER: Let's hope she gets where Jane is.

ME: Let's hope they both go further.

ME: I thought both of her legs were straight.

ART SANDLER: The right one is not quite perfect. I have to exert a bit more pressure on the knee than I should, to take it to full extension. A slight difference, but a difference.

ME: (*reading from notes just taken*): "While she's upside-down, we will be stretching ligaments that hold the joint capsule together—at the knee. We won't be dealing with muscles because they are taken care of in the stretch that comes with upside-downness." Then you said, "Even spasticity goes away with upside-downness." You mean in everybody? What do you mean?

ART SANDLER (*telling how he found that out*): This boy, thirteen and a half, still couldn't walk. Before he came here, he had had physical therapy, surgery, braces—the works. After two years of our patterning, crawl and creep, his knees were still very contracted, but he could duck walk in cross-pattern three or four steps. After six months of brachiation, using the overhead ladder assist, he walked like a higher-legged duck, knees not as contracted, but a duck, nevertheless. Even with the best test positioning, the most any of us had gotten his legs into extension was to forty-five degrees.

Wanted to program upside-downness for gravitational aspects—for vision. But he had this ninety-pound, sixty-year-old mother . . . a sparrow of a mother . . . Thought maybe she could hold him against the wall somehow upside-down. . . . I noticed his legs went to twenty-degree contraction. I thought his pants were caught at his ankles somehow—and made it look that way. So I had him roll his pants up. . . . Stood him upside-down against the wall again. . . . Called Glenn in, "What do you make of that?" Glenn said what he usually says, "I don't know, but keep it up here," tapping his temple. . . . To make a long story short, it happened with every kid we put against the wall, contractions were drastically reduced, completely in some children.

So we did what we always do, the staff hanging upside-down by the ankles, cardiograms taken, blood pressure monitored, the whole bit. We almost lost one guy on the staff, we thought he was fifty, he turned out to be seventy. We started with thirty seconds, increasing ten seconds every other day. . . . We worked up to four minutes. . . . A real euphoria there . . . No, not like yoga. You're dealing with muscles in yoga. Hanging by your ankles requires no muscles at all. . . . More like the feeling in the middle of a dive, we decided. . . . For some reason, all the spasticity goes away. You can get stretch without dealing with muscles, spastic ones, at that . . .

Dr. Robert Doman had just said something about—most creative people do not have cortical hemispheric dominance.

ME: I think you are right. Do you know why?

ROBERT DOMAN: I have some ideas about it, nothing conclusive. Do you have an idea?

ME: It might be another cultural impediment. The child with cortical hemispheric dominance becomes the star performer in academics, the star performer on the field—you know, the quarterback, the baseball pitcher, the center at basketball, the hit-the-target fellow. He's so outstanding as the skilled classmate, he becomes emmeshed in that. He's known for knowing the right answers, and more and more, I think, he becomes more the formula thinker, the answer man, the goal-maker inside and outside the classroom. That's what he uses the most, that's what he's encouraged to use. More and more. He's looked-to for that. His time is filled with that. And it doesn't leave much time for wandering, observing, stretching out, this way or that way. He's too busy performing, measuring up, and going beyond his last achievement. I think the school promotes that, without even knowing it. It needs a winner, so it pushes the winners to win some more. Do you think that could be part of it? Use? Time?

ROBERT DOMAN: I think you are right. Of course, there is no way to prove it. It seems to be especially true in the U.S.A. You can reach cortical hemispheric dominance and be one of the least interesting people to spend a day with.

ME: How many people, do you estimate, have cortical hemispheric dominance?

ROBERT DOMAN: Fifty percent.

ME: Do you think really it is that high?

ROBERT DOMAN: Yes, we do. What do you think?

ME: I have no idea. But only ten percent of the students in our school district are in the top "track" in English, so I suppose they have cortical hemispheric dominance, since they are the best readers.

ROBERT DOMAN: Oh, you can have cortical hemispheric dominance and still be somewhere below the top track level. The difference is the difference between a neurologically enriched environment and one that was "enough."

ME: And whatever genetic endowment you started with——

ROBERT DOMAN: Yes, there is all that chemistry to consider, but none of us has realized all that yet. I don't think we have any idea of potential yet—true potential.

APRIL 7, 1972. Asking friend Sallie (married, twenty-seven, no children, perceptive and honest) to describe Jane exactly the way she sees her, now that she has spent a day with her (Philadelphia revisit yesterday):

"Like what?"

"Like everything. Just describe her. First thing you probably see is the open mouth."

"Yes, open mouth . . . person not all together. Sitting there, let's see, general posture, I'd say 'slovenly.' The limbs seem disconnected. You see a hand, arm, leg, but no smooth flowing of body, no flowing smoothness of appendages. You can see her limbs O.K., but they don't seem to be part of a central whole, they seem 'limp' or something.

"It's very difficult to tell what Jane is clued into, what she is thinking. You can usually tell by a person's eyes, posture, movement, or talking. There is a 'knowing' look, an eye-look, a moving-look in people that tells you, and she doesn't have that.

"She does make a response to an absolute, pointed question (you can tell she got the question). Sometimes Jane initiates the talk, I mean, you can tell ahead of time she's going to say something, she starts agitating——

"There is very little facial expression. By the age of ten a child usually has many expressions. How would you say it? You are aware of cheekbones more in the usual ten-year-old—brows more, nostrils more, eyelashes, the whole bit. They seem to use them even while listening; they certainly use them with talking. With Jane, you see glasses on, long hair coming down, but her face doesn't have that 'angular' look—that's the only word I can think of."

"Yes, you're actually describing a less than perfect gaze."

"Gaze? What's 'gaze?' "

"Go ahead, I'll tell you later———"

"I was just about to say it's the same with her body. If people don't have 'lines,' 'body lines—' that's all I can think of to call it—the person looks slovenly. But she, no, doesn't look at all 'underdeveloped'—perfect body size, a little tall maybe. From the knees down, her legs hang over the seat, well, like polio? Smaller than the rest of the body.

"Speech: she blurts—sporadic spurts when she says anything . . . no free conversation on her own. In response to questions, you almost can't hear her sometimes, her voice is so soft. Sometimes it's loud, suddenly. An explosive vent . . . volcano . . . eruption. Both ways I would call 'abnormal.' I noticed you and Bert—or other people in command of the situation—get a more favorable response from her than I do. I asked her if she were cold, and she didn't answer. I asked another time if she were hungry and she said, 'No-o-o-o,' as if to say, 'Dummy, I just ate,' or some such disgust. She doesn't know, hasn't learned—culturally?—how to carry on chitchat. I am not a teacher or a requirer, and apparently she feels no need to give a command performance for me—it's an informal, off-the-wall encounter. To you and Bert, I noticed, she gives a clear, audible statement with much more inflection, tone, and directness."

APRIL 26, 1972. A quite subdued Mrs. Gross after today's school:

"Do you know what your child did today? It's amazing—how much she does know—reads—I told you she didn't want to read anymore, after a year of wanting to do nothing but! How this whole month she's wanted to spend the hour talking. Talking about everything 'out there'—the high school, girls in the high school, especially two named Lori and Amy, about everything she can think of to talk about, and that's all she wants to do. Well, today, she kept saying this word, and I didn't get it—you know, she's talking about so many things, and I don't always know what context we are in. So, after saying it over and over, she got disgusted with me. And guess what she did? She got out a box of reading words and went through them all till she found the word. To show me! It was 'cherry!' It sounded exactly like 'cherry' too. I just couldn't imagine she would be saying 'cherry.' And the rest— I still don't believe that."

JUNE 4, 1972. Thinking about the stage she's reached, the level she's on, the whatever you call it. How she loves to be asked about favorite anything and how quickly she will tell you, and how her preferences are showing a full-blown interest in people: white lace blouses and blue jeans like the teens wear, soap operas over other programs on TV, eating inside at a drive-in where the tables (and people) are, standing in her "steeple house" (tube of linoleum) and playing with us—mother-baby, teacher-child. Wondering just when it all started.

Remembering Glenn Doman's orientation talk to us, about a kid's coming into likes and dislikes, about a child's ability to discriminate, those precious years between three and six. A normal three-year-old is curious about everything, and asks the same questions the thirty-year-old scientist is asking: "What holds the stars in the sky?" "What makes grass green?"

Children are not dehydrated adults, as we think of them. It is not true that children want play and games ("play and games" equal "happy children"). They want to learn. They choose "to play" whatever "teaches" them more. And they throw it away when it has no further learning value. Learning is what they wake to. Learning is their survival, the way they look at "survival," the way they feel survival. A three-year-old wants to learn about everything.

A normal four-year-old has no discrimination. Buys anything. Appreciates all his input, all he was programed today. Will accept great art with the same impartiality that he accepts junk. His questions deserve at least a try on our part at truth. But we often give him fairy-tale answers. He'll buy them. The level of his auditory perception is into abstract concepts, but he is not yet to the point of making judgments about them. He is not discriminating.

On the other hand, the normal six-year-old will simply tell you, "I don't like that picture." (Or "Marie draws better than I do." Or "I am the fastest ———— in my class." Or "I am one of the lousy ones.")

Jane, now expressing favorites and dislikes, is beyond the normal four and not yet to normal six in her auditory understanding, I would guess. She's "socially" (they call it) like the dull kindergartener, the child who hasn't been around much. In "skills" (they call it) she's more the elementary school girl. Her perseverance and stamina would place her with the adults.

You could present her with all the toys in the world right now, and they would stay on the shelves—unless there is a person in the wrappings! She is far beyond the fireman-policeman-community-helper "unit," beyond the "my family" unit, and somewhere into "your family" (specifically, tell me), "your house" (and its people), "your city" (and its people). Remembering Switzerland last summer, the murals she drew, the maps she made (our chalet to the village, the village layout—a three-week project, and from Saanen to Gstaad via highway, river, and rail), the book she made ("A List About Switzerland"), where she saw and heard the new vocabulary we call "social studies." She enjoyed (did not refuse!) the "outputs" she did with felt marker, watercolor, tracing paper, scissors and paste, but it was nothing but a drag compared to sitting in a busy railroad station. A cable car is nice, but if you've done one, you've done them all. But the people inside the car! Anyway, why do it (on paper) when you've just done it? Let's get on to tomorrow.

So why did we do it? Because no one would ever believe she knows "Switzerland" or "beans" if she can't talk it, write, it, walk it out. Output is what schools seem to be about. That's as it should be.

A child's first six years are what input is all about. And, of course, he had that at home. Because he's more curious at three than he is at six—about everything. When he becomes discriminating, he increasingly limits his own input from then on—limits its variety, its intensity, its frequency, reduces the raw data to his own brain. He now has hobbies, "decides" to be a jet pilot (not copied, not forced into giving an answer to what-do-you-want-to-be). He looks at all the airplane pictures he can find. And if he can't find any, he'll draw them.

Right now if you asked Jane what-do-you-want-to-be (do), I think she would answer, though not in these exact words, "A person." That's what the current learning is all about.

They are so cute when they begin to want people. When they want to see them *all*. And after you've seen them all, don't you then come back to yourself, just you, at sixish, and ask, "Well, then, who am *I?*"

JUNE 18, 1972.

Dear Grant,
You like baseball
I like you.
      Happy
   Birthday
      Jane

JUNE 23, 1972. "Why, Jane Emerson Napear! That is beautiful!"

Jane, with one hand grasping a rung of the overhead ladder, is standing on her right leg with her left foot poised against the standing knee, her free hand on the angle that it makes. Like this:

And the other side:

She has been "practicing" all this now and then for a week. She may be doing nothing more than checking out straight knees and pointy knees, but it looks like a slow ballet. And the right leg bearing weight that way is really incredible.

I hasten to encourage it. "Oh, let me get Louise to see this."

(Louise Ames is back this summer for cleaning once a week. That exciting event is probably the reason for the following floor show.)

Louise, not quite sure what to exclaim over, arrives just as Jane has finished the overhead ladder rungs and has shifted her hand to the elastic parachute cord "rungs"—strung between the wooden ones—for the next program. She turns at the end, heads back, stops—center stage—facing Louise and me, the audience.

First, an oldie (week before last's "show"): Stand on left leg, cross this right foot over left's ankle, smile; assume original two-foot position. Now do the "other side." Stand on right leg, cross this left foot over right's ankle, smile, go into the next routine.

The mother in the audience freezes. Her daughter is beginning the new stuff with only a hand assist on elastic cord. Her eyes get wet because the daughter is doing it all, in a perfectly serialized routine, without buckling at the right knee. And down goes the free hand to rest on the kneecap on the flexed knee. The whole thing looks like a salute to Art Sandler, the mother is thinking, as Jane stands and stands and stands on her right leg. "Jane Emerson Napear! Wait till Art Sandler sees that! Oh, Louise, it's the first time she ever did that. With elastic cord the only hold."

Louise, too, is blurry-eyed. And Jane with such a wide grin (Look, Ma, one hand, one leg!) decides to do it all again.

"Oh, Jane, what can I say? What will Art say about those lovely ballet dance steps?"

Jane, in a mimicking high voice, the way you might wake Goldilocks, "Why, Jane Emerson Napear——"

Let's see, she got her right leg looking strong like her left one with the help of that ridiculous tube of linoleum in—ten weeks! (Five hours a day altogether.)

And if that's a new idea of Sandler's to get someone to stand on the weaker leg, and if Jane is one of the first guinea pigs (as I suspect), then after her revisit day July 13, there are going to be "steeple houses" all over this world!

JANE'S DAILY SCHEDULE, JULY 13 to SEPTEMBER 20

8:45– 9:00   breakfast (plus vitamin B complex, extra panothenic acid, calcium); standing in the steeple house

9:00–12:30   six program sequences* (and more breakfast with next steeple house)

* A program sequence:
1. Alternate A and B with every other sequence:
   A. hang by the heels
        both legs—one minute
        left leg—three minutes
        right leg—three minutes
   B. stand in steeple house seven minutes. (J. may have TV.)
2. Walk with overhead ladder assist four laps (two round trips), alternating walking backward.
3. Walk forward with overhead elastic shock-cord assist (one-fourth-inch diameter "rungs"), encouraging feet to keep flat on turns, as well.
4. Stand "alone" with heels two to four inches from wall. No hand assist. Goal: two minutes eventually. (May give her assistance to get positioned straight at knees. When knees buckle, give positioning assistance again. Try for longer ability each day.)
5. Walk with overhead series of vertical rope assists ten minutes (new overhead deal), allowing thirty-second chair breaks when necessary, i.e., if she shows any sign of fatigue.
   Note: May wash off with cold washcloth if it's a hot day, give drink, toilet this point if Jane asks. But start next sequence without a rest period.

12:30– 1:30   stand in steeple house, including lunch period (and tablets listed above with breakfast)

1:30– 2:00   school†

† Summer school: Privately we paid Mrs. Gross to teach Jane one-half hour daily during the district's vacation, for the purpose of J.'s daily pleasure.

2:00– 6:00   six program sequences (and dessert with first steeple house)
          Note: Swimming for one hour at William R. Grant's pool to break this period if it's a hot day. Afternoon snack at 4:00.

6:00– 7:00	stand in steeple house
7:00– 8:30	some special adventure out of the house including supper; dessert (plus thyroid, vitamin E, and calcium) at home
8:30– 9:00	to bed for thirty minutes, lights on to read, play alone
	Note: Vitamin C is administered four or five times throughout day. Food-intake is given in five or six smaller "meals" instead of three main meals—for purposes of increased nutrition to the brain.

JULY 31, 1972. I am in the kitchen watching Jane myself. Grant sitting on the sofa watching Jane, hoping she will "forget the ropes" while he is there. (She occasionally takes a couple of independent steps—left-right, without knowing it—to grab one of the vertical ropes farther up the line. When she does, she keeps a perfectly upright posture and we all but die watching it.)

About thirty-five minutes later she does it, and Grant, lying on elbow, gasps, and says barely, "Jane, I bet you're going to be walking— Walking all by yourself— By— By— By your birthday [January]. Jane, how would you like that for a present, huh? Don't you think that would be about the best birthday present you could get?"

(No response, nor was there any expected, I think, and he continues to muse aloud, and Jane continues to walk a lap, turn around, walk a lap, turn around, and so on.)

"You know, Jane, you're going to be able to walk over to Mrs. Frohnhoefer's house [programer here from the beginning to the end]. Instead of Mrs. Frohnhoefer coming here to visit you, you can go there to visit her. Wouldn't that be nice? [Beginning to chuckle all over himself.] Hey, how would you like that? You could just walk right across the street to Mrs. Frohnhoefer's house, ring her bell, and watch her faint! Boy, oh, boy, is Mrs. Frohnhoefer going to love that!"

AUGUST 15, 1972. Stuart, looking up from his bed and this book, "Ma, I always knew Jane was smart, but— It's this way: I knew she was very smart, but I didn't know she was so *advanced.* I've been talking to her like she's not very advanced. I didn't realize she did all this school stuff— I am going to talk to her very differently from now on."

"Yes, we all should. She could use a new family—for that. Jane is more sophisticated with Mrs. Gross than anybody, because Mrs. Gross requires it."

"Has Mrs. Gross read this?"

"Yes."

"What did she say?"

"She said it's accurate; she wouldn't change a word. But I should add the fact that Jane always loved school—from the very first—even during times of struggle. She thought the reader should know that about Jane."

"Well, I had no idea Jane has all this stuff in school. I've been talking to her like she's not very advanced, or not this advanced."

The next day he goes to Jane, who is sitting on the gurney table, un-buckling the leather anklets she hangs upside-down by, about to start a walk session:
"Hello, Jane, how are you this morning?"
(No response.)
"I asked you a question."
"Fine."
(Hops up on the table next to her.) "Let's see, how's everything? Uh, I hope you have a nice day today. Uh, I'm getting ready to have a nice day too. I'm going out to play football now. At the school yard. You know where the school yard is—not the high school, the elementary school—well, that's where I'm going now, but I'll be back. In about an hour. And twenty minutes. I am going to play with Bill. He's a friend of mine. You've seen Bill. He's been here. Uh, you know Bill! You could see him only one time, and, I bet, you'd remember him, wouldn't you? We might shoot a few baskets. Uh, while we're there we might play a little basketball too. Later I've got to do some running. Then I'm planning to lift some weights. I'm doing a program to get in shape for football. To make my legs stronger. And, uh, to build up my breath. Like this. (Inhales and lets it out.) Your friends are coming to do your program. Which friends are coming today?"
(No response.)
"What is your answer?"
"Diana and June!"
"Very nice. That's right. Diana and Ju— Well, have a very nice day. And I'll be back. To do the rest of *my* program. As I said, in about an hour and twenty minutes. Well— When I come back I'll show you the leather things I wear around my ankles. They've got weights in them. The weights are made out of metal. It's very heavy metal. That's why they are called 'weights'—of course. Well, I'll see you later, Jane. First, let me see that beautiful walking this morning."

AUGUST 20, 1972. Sitting here, thinking about the future. Jane is ten now. Puberty? Menstruation? That's not far off, but it has only crossed my mind. Jane is used to Band-Aids for bleedings. A sanitary napkin will probably hit her about the same way. (She has never, for example, asked why a cut bleeds. Her inspections of everything show she may be asking a lot of whys, but her language doesn't.) With a higher auditory level she can learn all about menstruation the way her peers are doing in school these days.
There is really only one hope and one fear that counts. I feel it every time

I think of her. Every time I cross the room she's in. Every time I am in a moment of silence beside her. It's the one thing that breaks me up and leaves me sobbing or causes me to plant too many kisses on her cheek. It's what I told Mimi Goldstein.

MIMI: Did you know that Diana was holding Jane under the arms and walking her to the toilet last week when you all were away?

ME: Yes, she told me. I thanked her—and then I gently chewed her out about that. Diana was supposed to tell Jane when she asked to go, sorry, there's no one here to help me carry you, or Mrs. Gross will be here soon to help me carry you, or whatever. I distinctly told her to explain it to Jane and to wash off urine on the legs, because, if you remember, it stings. I went into the whole thing with her. What I didn't tell her—what she didn't understand—is that Jane is not allowed to walk in any kind of incorrect way, my mistake——

MIMI: Well, I can surely understand Diana doing it— Going to the bathroom— Let's face it— That's the ultimate in human dignity!

ME: It is not! That's your grandmother talking. That's the press reporter talking about the institutional "pits" where the "snakes" are, where the bodies but not the brains are. Let me tell you, Mimi, the ultimate in human dignity or anything else is walking and talking. Communication. That's what she needs—the most. I don't care if she wets all over herself. She's not to spend one minute in that kind of walk. When she can walk the way I can walk, when she can talk the way I talk—then she can spend her day in the bathroom, for all I care.

To the reporter who comes away from the visit to the institution and writes about the stench there, and to all his readers who are lost, as well, in that business of clean up the institutions, I say this: Cleaning up people is a low goal. So is training the inmate in "feeding, dressing, and grooming" himself. All of that follows as the brain organizes itself. Neurological organization—that should be the goal. An enriched neurological environment—that should be the program. It is up to the reader to determine his own hope, his own fear, where those children are concerned. (You can forget Jane; we are doing her.)

And to the therapist who's reading this and saying I didn't know anything could be done about brain injury, I can only say: You should have thought of the live brain cells that are left. Because you had the live body before you. How could that body be alive, if its brain is a concrete block of do-nothing?

Where do you start? Put them all on the floor, face down. Tomorrow morning. In the urine and the feces down there? That will be more tactile stimulation, more eye workout, more brain use, than they are getting huddled in the corner, or strapped into a clean chair, or wheeled down the road to the luncheonette. Teach the brain first that it has legs, has eyes, has skin, "down there somewhere." Teach the brain about its animal self. Say "animal" enough, it still sounds like "animal," nothing worse.

Follow the route to normalcy. Jane's development is recapped for you in the Appendix. No other way to get there. If you want normal, you have to use normal, step by step. The important steps are on the Doman-Delacato Developmental Profile. No detours. No pieces, please. You simply can't take one program here and another program there and put them together—and expect to help Johnny that way—it's been tried and it doesn't work.

Of *course* it's possible to close down the institutions, the dulling day-care centers too. To the parents and readers who sent their injured children there, I leave this word: Get the kid a functional evaluation for the first time in his life. Start programing him where the normal development stopped. So he's sixteen and has adjusted to the institution? Talk to yourself about it. I can't help you and your brain-injured child further.

Well, maybe this: If the parents won't take him back, maybe another family would, a community of families? I have been told that in Boston there's a warehouse full of all sizes of patterning tables, crawl boxes, etc.—a store of paraphernalia I once envisioned! (Under the sponsorship of the local Association for Brain-Injured Children, I believe.) Whether it's true or not, that's the spirit: people getting together can do most anything. It's a lot more fun growing a person than paying money to attend the fashion shows and charity balls to help the poor slob in the center, believe me.

To parent-readers who are in a quandary about all this and want some advice, I leave this suggestion: Forget what the doctor who doesn't know says about it. Forget that the nursery school director doesn't know what you are talking about. Take a look at your own child. Do you want to check him out? If you promise not to read out of context, I would suggest Delacato's book, *A New Start for the Child With Reading Problems: A Manual for Parents* (McKay, 1971). Forget the title if your child is normal or not yet reading. The tests for checking are all there. So are the programs if your child is missing some developmental steps.

Get emotional about your child. How can you help if you stay "detached," "objective," or "adjusted" to the situation as it is? Tell the doctor what *you* know about your child. Tell the nursery school director too. Who knows, maybe next year they both will be among the most interested in "neurological functioning."

And to everyone who really cares: Stop the pity and the pennies. Stop the millions that go for adjusting the child to his "affliction," that go for programs to help him "live with his difficulties." Go take a new look at these children. Then—help them to get well.

Epilogue

On September 13, 1972 Jane walked off her vertical ropes and out of the room. Along the walls and tables, not for support, but rather like a blind person who wants to know about confidence. Yes, legs straight, feet flat and with full weight-bearing.

Mary Lawrence (over long distance) said, "One more time. Go through it one more time—what you said."

Stuart (home from high school football practice) said, "I know. She's been doing that all week. When you weren't here."

Bert said, "I saw it two weeks ago—at the Feiwell's pool. She got out of the water and walked up the stairs to their back door and right into their kitchen, straight like that, in flat bare feet! You were so upset when we came home; remember how mad you were I kept her there so long, she missed the rest of her sequences, remember that day?"*

In the first hour Jane treated herself to the wonders of a new world. It was something like "picturing myself," I think:

Cruising fast past the living room counter, turn the corner, look over my shoulder, down at the one foot I'm standing on now (all by myself), on to the playroom door, past the toy cabinets (forgetting to hold on), turn on the "big" TV, turn it off, walk-walk-walk through the living room again, pause, jump once with both feet together (muffled giggle), look down, jump again a little higher (outright laugh), take a shortcut (four independent steps), walk into the kitchen.

Get two cans of soup out and make an announcement: "Let's all have chicken vegetable soup. Just a bit of soup, please. Smokey (laughing) cannot have soup. Dogs don't eat soup. Ay (they) eat ere (their) dog food. Babies don't eat soup. Babies don't *even* eat! (*Mimicking high voice*) 'I want my bottle.' And babies can't *even* walk. Ay (they) just cry." (*Make-believe crying.*)

And I forgot, walk-walk-walk, go get an apron . . .

---

* Stuart and Bert had the same initial reaction I did: she's doing something not part of the program. Should I ignore it or what? My call to Art Sandler ("What should I do about it; I didn't know whether to call you or not, since our revisit is next week") got this reply: ". . . all sorts of nutty reasons over the years, but you didn't know whether you should call about *this*?"

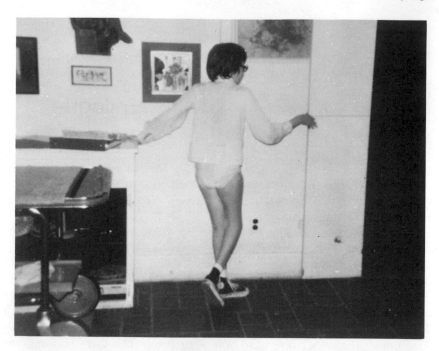

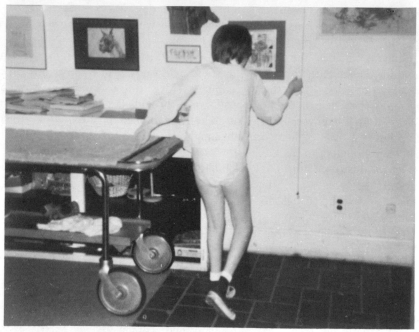

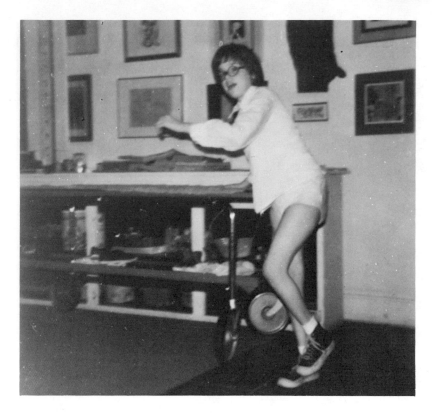

Carl Delacato said (in the waiting room, IAHP, September 20): "I want you to get that walking smooth—and soon—Jane, because I can hardly wait to get my clutches into you again!"

Art Sandler said something about it being only a case now of weak quadriceps but there was still a lot of hard work ahead. "Take a copy of this [Statement of Goals]. You understand, these are my goals for mobility only. Delacato—when I give her back to him—will discuss with you her goals for graduation from here."

Here is what he dictated:

One: November 1972—walk across the room. Two: let's see, February, 1973 —functional walking in the house; begin walking outside. That means on uneven surfaces. Three: (pause) May 1973—walking in cross-pattern and complete functional walk. Like we do, yes, arms down and swinging, the whole bit. Uh, four: (long pause) August 1973—begin running. Five: November 1973 (short pause)—begin ballet.

Laughter and shrieks among family and observers in room.

SANDLER: "Why not? She has already done what they will tell you is impossible. Why not ballet?"

It's a good place to stop. What Jane wants to do with her walking, where she wants to go with it—that's her business.

Recommended Reading List

Delacato, Carl H., Ed.D. *A New Start for the Child with Reading Problems: A Manual for Parents.* New York. McKay, 1970: A no-guesswork guide to the parent who wants to learn whether or not his child's reading problem is, indeed, neurologically based. Step-by-step evaluations and programs are outlined with interesting commentary on what the parent is observing. Part I is the fascinating story of the up-and-down search and findings of the author and his colleagues over the last thirty years.

Delacato, Carl H., Ed.D. *The Autistic Child.* To be published in 1974 by Doubleday. A new look at the "autistic" child from the author's vast experience with such children at The Institutes for the Achievement of Human Potential and around the world, their causes and cases, and what to do to get them well.

Doman, Glenn J., *How to Teach Your Baby to Read.* New York. Random House, 1964: For the parent who wants to add to his baby's development brain-wise and who can do this kind of "play" with baby without getting uptight about its results with respect to "school." Especially for the parent who already "knows" and "enjoys" his baby's development.

Doman, Glenn J., *What to Do About Your Brain-Injured Child.* To be published in 1974 by Doubleday, New York: Recommended sight unseen, since it is *the* story and *the* hope for brain-injured children, the book the author has finally found time to finish after a ten-year-ago start. If it reads with the same magnetism that holds his audiences around the world, it will, no doubt, become the best seller his first book proved to be.

Grost, Audrey. *Genius in Residence.* Englewood Cliffs, N.J. Prentice-Hall, 1970: The true story of what is termed "a child prodigy" (in some genetic sense, I take it), but in my opinion the result of a highly neurological, enriched babyhood. His mother has offered us (without knowing it?) one of the best guides to parents of newborns in the literature. I deeply regret that my volume could not contain Audrey Grost's pages 19 through 23 at least. Consider them the icing on my cake when you are next in the library.

*Le Winn, Edward B., M.D. *Human Neurological Organization.* Springfield, Illinois. Charles C. Thomas, 1969: A readily accessible and collated grouping of facts relevant to the development, clinical characteristics and

---

* Contains a world of further reading in the author's references to sources throughout, together with listed bibliography, extremely up to date regarding international research on the subject of brain function. Further material, including Carl Delacato's four books on his findings between the years 1959 and 1967 (Charles C. Thomas, Springfield, Ill.), is listed in the official Order List available at The Institutes for the Achievement of Human Potential, 8801 Stenton Avenue, Philadelphia, Pa. 19118.

unique features of human neurological organization. Written with clarity and directness stemming from the author's broad experience as clinician, researcher, and medical educator. For the attention of professionals, including those who work in most fields of medicine, who want a colleague to put it all together for them.

Melton, David. *Todd.* Englewood Cliffs, N.J. Prentice-Hall, 1968: The true story of the author's son from a world of "special" education and continually discouraging medical reports to his entrance into a regular school class, and the years in between at "this program." Unlike Jane, he is one of the many who are mildly brain-injured and present untold confusion to the teacher and the doctor. Soon to be a major motion picture for which the author wrote the screenplay.

Melton, David. *When Children Need Help.* New York. Crowell, 1972: A comprehensive view of the run-around by parent and professional alike to "get a diagnosis." The absence of "to get treatment to get well" is one of the themes here, and the author records that scene "out there" with a clear logic, a supporting cast of cases and personal experiences, and a desire to increase the level of involvement by both parent and professional. A likable gift to the parent in that "swim," so, at least, he can figure out just where in the process he is at this moment. A very up-to-date guide.

*Thomas, Evan W., M.D. *Brain-Injured Children.* Springfield, Ill. Charles C. Thomas, 1969: It's all there: an interesting survey of the problem as it *has been* presented in the medical literature with such symptomatic diagnoses as cerebral palsy, mental retardation, epilepsy, behavioral disorders and dyslexia; together with the *new* perspective in the management of children with non-progressive brain injury. A most readable book for parent and professional alike.

Watson, George, Ph.D. *Nutrition and Your Mind.* New York. Harper & Row, 1972: The result of twenty years of research by the author on the interrelation between nutrition and behavior. A best seller and a best reading for the entire world, which seems to have one foot in the seventeenth century and one foot in the grave on this important subject. His cases will grab you and leave you looking at your neighbor, if not your own family.

I also urge the reader to grab a copy of a long-delayed paperback now on the stands: Adelle Davis' *Let's Eat Right to Keep Fit,* newly revised and updated. It may be the most necessary reading you will ever do for your brain-injured child, especially the child whose behavior is a bit bizarre—and that's all you can detect in the reading of my account. It is suggested reading for all parents at The Institutes in Philadelphia. It should be "required" reading for all of us.

Also, do not be put off by the length of the Appendix to this volume. Its breadth is worth it. Here is the real story of Jane, more "child" than "brain," much of it new to the reader, especially the last five years. A helpful record, I would hope, for in-service study for teachers and therapists who want to follow "the neurological child." Take your time and enjoy it.

* *Ibid.*

Author's Notes on Jane's Development and Professional Profile

These developmental lists together with professional evaluations and The Doman-Delacato Developmental Profile which follow and to which the notes refer, offer the reader the fuller story here and serve as an index to the diary. Working by date, referral can be made to the corresponding dates which head the right-side pages throughout the diary text.

Development of Mobility

Note: Before Jane's evaluation at The New York Hospital for the purpose of determining functional levels (according to the Doman-Delacato Developmental Profile),* Mary Lawrence, RPT, Supervisor of Therapy Programs of that hospital's Department of Physical Medicine and Rehabilitation suggested an interim program involving (a) play and rest on the floor (or ground) all day, except for feeding, diapering, loving; (b) attaching a harness (outrigger) and harness line (heel-to-tail-to-heel), to prevent Jane's rolling over to back and standing, cruising, walking; and (c) providing sensory opportunities on the floor. The following notes represent changes seen in her mobility during that six-month interim period.

From July 30, 1964 to September 25, 1964:

With outrigger and harness line: onset of cross-pattern creeping to about one-third of time; otherwise, homologous "hop."

Without outrigger, etc.: does only homologous "hop."

Improved sitting balance, hips to back of chair, head more erect, back straighter; but holds on to chair arms or pushes down with hands against seat to maintain sit balance. (No longer needs baby car seat.)

Can get onto and off sofa or bed now.

Heels and knees a bit looser maybe. (Shank of legs still high off floor and scissored in creeping though.)

Arms so strong, can pull herself up to anything!

Pulling to stands in crib or car more; cruising along side of crib more. (On toes, knees flexed, legs scissored, two-hand support.)

Learned to scoot from one end to other of long seat, using hip-wiggle.

See language changes this period.

From September 25, 1964 to January 25, 1965:

Sits on piano stool, knees supported under keyboard, back slumped.

Does some cross-pattern creeping (an occasional step or two) without outrigger now.

---

* In 1970 IAHP changed its vocabulary from "out," "poor," "perfect" when scoring Profile functions to "nonfunctional," "functional," "perfect."

Can free one hand in four-point creep stance for use (i.e., improved creep balance).

See language changes this period.

January 25, 1965 initial evaluation: The New York Hospital (by Mary Lawrence, RPT): Doman-Delacato Developmental Profile Level: III marked "poor"; with II "out."

. . . [Jane] moves all her extremities, with some limited ROM [range of movement] in lowers. . . . She has demonstrable spasticity in all extremities, especially lowers. . . . Does not crawl and mother does not think she ever did (or did so very poorly for a very short period at age seven months). . . . She creeps homologously; very seldom in a cross-pattern (without outrigger and harness line attached). . . . She cruises on her toes with poor balance and two-hand support.

(With the harness line to her heels, she creeps only in a cross-pattern, although the harness does not prohibit homologous creeping.)

From February 14, 1965 to May 1, 1965:

Patterning: homolateral, four times a day begun; no difficulties after two weeks.

Crawling (homolaterally) now with assist to right lower extremity only. This occurred in the following progressions this period:

a. Reflexive crawls on the floor after patterning, until she began to develop use of legs in a push (thigh and knee-area in contact with floor only); to

b. Assistive crawls after push was established, involving placement of my hand at bottom of her foot for her to push off from; to

c. Her present crawl.
   Note: In April she changed from a forearm pull to a hand pull, but still under her chest.

d. Crawl-box crawling begun in April, but not done much because only uses her left side, except for a slight right-hand pull.*

Creeping (cross-pattern 100 percent of time with outrigger; cross pattern 50 percent of time without outrigger—otherwise, homologous); feet not trailing consistently, but not up all the time now—occasionally foot touches floor; knee base too broad; hands not flat to surface, i.e., fingers still curved; good hand-knee relationship and good serialization finally.

Other:

a. Floor play: moves head and arms together in patterning serialization (no legs involved); pivoting "practice"; balancing on side "practice"; sitting against wall (without hand support on floor).
   See Tactile Competence this period.

b. Moves about house or yard in steady creep, stopping occasionally to investigate cabinet, or closet, or bush, or ground surprises.

---

* Until Jane's initial evaluation at IAHP 10/25/65, her crawl-box program was rarely carried out by me. Inadvertently this mistake allowed her upper body to get stronger and more skilled than its lower half.

   c. Hangs from patterning table, grasping opposite edge. (See Visual Competence this period.)

   d. New sit: sits back on haunches (buttocks sitting on shanks of legs) in middle of patterning table and in highchair (moves around till she accomplishes this). Also can scoot highchair to counter top and get out onto counter.

May 1, 1965 re-evaluation by Mary Lawrence: Profile Level: same. III marked "poor," with II now marked "poor."

. . . In mobility she is able to crawl, which she does in a homolateral pattern, but she does not use her right leg unless manually encouraged to do so. Her cross-pattern creep has improved and with her outrigger she does a very good cross-pattern creep; knees and hands strike together and her feet are beginning to trail. She curls her fingers somewhat. Without the outrigger she does about 50 percent homologous creeping. In range of motion I could find no limitation in the upper extremities, improvement in the lowers, especially the hip adductors, but moderate tightness in the hamstrings and heel cords. . . .

From May 1, 1965 to June 22, 1965:

No program for two to three weeks (mother's illness).

Crawling (homolateral pattern) now without assist, but push is weaker and not always consistent on right side (knee). No push yet with feet in crawling, although occasionally see a push off of instep, especially the left one.

Creeping in cross-pattern 100 percent of time without outrigger; homologous "hop" not seen anymore. Almost runs in cross-pattern creep: knees closer together, hands (fingers) in fuller extension against surface; hand-knee relationship very good; lower legs down considerably, feet trailing a lot.

Other:

   a. Moving ankles.

   b. Moving toes.

   c. When leg is flexed in patterning, patterners sometimes now feel Jane's foot pushing against their hand.

   d. Knees looser.

   e. Much arm extension, up and above and out: reaches to slap walls, etc. when crawling or being carried past.

June 22, 1965 re-evaluation by Mary Lawrence: Profile Level: same.

. . . Her crawling has improved in that she uses her right leg spontaneously in a good pattern and would appear to be going into cross-pattern crawling. Use of arms has also improved. Creeping is now entirely cross-pattern even without cords on shoes (not used at all anymore) and outrigger is still used to keep her from standing. Her hands are now almost flat on the floor, knees are closer together, hand and knee relationship is very good, feet trail nicely and lower legs are almost entirely on the floor. . . .

From June 22, 1965 to September 2, 1965:

> Crawling in cross-pattern. Faster crawl, but sometimes does not get good push off right foot (instep).
>
> Creeping—almost dances with head bouncing and hair flying in this running cross-pattern creep. Always serialized, but feet rather kick up behind her when trailing; knee base looking almost normal, although takes smaller step forward with right knee, so moves her in slight diagonal forward.
>
> Other:
>
> a. Patterning: full legs and toes touching table now (knees looser).
> b. Lifts hips when I slide pants on (supine).
> c. Much toe movement.
> d. Pats foot up and down while lying supine (knees-up position).
> e. Creeps up and down three steps.
> f. Can sit on edge of chair seat, no hand support, back not as slumped.
> g. Walking on knees, trunk and head erect, right arm swinging in exaggerated motion (Miss Struts).
> h. Passes by everything with arms outstretched.
>
> *Note:* During this period, patterning pattern was changed from homolateral to cross-pattern.

September 2, 1965 re-evaluation by Mary Lawrence: Profile Level: same.

> . . . In mobility she cross-pattern creeps and crawls (neither perfectly, but *very* well) and the RLE [right lower extremity] activity has improved a great deal. In patterning her legs are almost flat (left 95 percent so, right somewhat less) and I wonder if her reflexes are not less active than a few months ago. . . .

October 25, 1965 initial evaluation IAHP: Profile Level: same. III "poor," with II "poor."

> Dominance [foot]: not observable.

From October 28, 1965 to February 8, 1966:

> Very little program this period, with exception of patterning.
>
> Running creep in cross-pattern: knee base better, I think; hands slapping (flat) against surface (a kind of "practice"); feet trailing more consistently (dirtier).
>
> Pulling to stands indoors (no harness line to prevent it) with outrigger attached to her back (arms and torso so strong).

February 8, 1966 re-evaluation IAHP: Profile Level: same.

> Qualitative improvement seen in crawling and creeping.
> Dominance [foot]: not observable.

From February 8, 1966 to June 1, 1966:

> See Tactile Competence for patterning modifications this period.
> Change in sit ability: from buttocks sitting back on shanks of both legs to

buttocks on shank of one leg, with other one in front of her. Sits this way on table for book-looking, etc.

Sits independently on side of patterning table, no hand assist for balance, back straighter.

Beautiful hip movement with pulling on her own pants (supine).

Ankles resist foot-brush in patterning, showing slight ability to evert her foot (first use of eversion muscles).

Ramp program: pushes getting stronger, higher knee flexion (right weaker—less high—than left).

Interested in rubbing bottom of feet on rug while sitting or kneeling on one knee.

June 1, 1966 re-evaluation IAHP: Profile Level: same.

Crawling—improved knee flexion and push with legs. Creeping—qualitative improvements.
Dominance [foot]: not observable.

From June 1, 1966 to October 18, 1966:

See Tactile Competence for patterning modification this period.

Crawling: right foot (instep) pushes off consistently now. (No toe-push either foot yet.)

Creeping: with shoes on hands. (See Auditory Competence this period.)

Patterning seven days a week during five weeks in Maine; five days a week other three months (problem with patterners for weekends).

Ramp program: forty times daily, consistently.

Crawl-box program: made double-long (sixteen feet) new one and added floor mat of Rubatex. No program for five weeks in Maine.

Sleep pattern (homolateral, alternate each time position her). Can now get into sleep pattern by herself from waist up, but does not involve her legs by herself (i.e., has head and arms flicking into position with serialization).

Prefers to sit on side of patterning table instead of in middle (with one leg forward, one leg back). (See previous period.) Excellent balance with this, although still slumped.

October 18, 1966 re-evaluation IAHP: Profile Level: same.

Crawling—marked improvement in use of arms. Leg flexion also improved.
Creeping—improved.
Dominance [foot]: not observable.

From October 18, 1966 to January 3, 1967:

Crawling: hand-pull no longer involving palm; now finger-pull. (See Manual Competence this period.)

Crawling: saw toe out to side, slight push, a couple of times in crawling box, left foot only. Getting in forty rather than sixty round trips per day this period.

Notice J.'s legs look more spastic, more scissored when first taken out of bed in morning than at other times during day.

Outrigger not keeping Jane down as well as before, pulling up to cabinets and tables (outrigger attached; one foot-holder of harness line "lost" under leaves outdoors).

January 3, 1967 re-evaluation IAHP: Profile Level: same.

Continued improvement in crawling and creeping. Parents report that Jane is pulling to stands more than before.

Staff feels Jane's tight leg and ankle problems "peripheral" now, no longer "central." Will wait six months to discuss possible orthopedic procedure (surgical).

Dominance [foot]: not observable.

From January 3, 1967 to June 12, 1967:

No program for three months from 1/7/67 to 3/30/67: convalescence from burn injury.

See Tactile for patterning modification this period.

Patterning: Jane resisting strongly ankle turn, knee turn; much movement of ankles and toes during session. Therefore, now able to counter our inversion of her foot with her own eversion of it! Also same "sensing" of knees as well as ankles now?

Less actual creeping this period, because into book-looking on floor every chance she gets. Constructed playhouse at base of crib to encourage creeping in and out, wide Roman doorways for outrigger.

Crawl-box program: fifteen minutes between patternings for one hour in the mornings; forty round trips in the afternoon for two hours. Goes very fast (hand-pull stronger than foot-push). Should "ceiling" be lowered? (No, put long pants on to slow her down.)

June 12, 1967 re-evaluation IAHP: Profile Level: same.

Continued qualitative progress noted in crawling and creeping.

Dominance [foot]: not observable.

From June 12, 1967 to September 6, 1967:

See Tactile for patterning do's this period.

Crawling: does not use right foot-push in crawl box; began "free crawls" out of box after patternings (used right leg then)—O.K.? (No.)

Creeping: built twenty-five-foot-long crawl box with four-inch sand base outdoors, but too much rain to use it much. Creeping indoors most of this period, but have to hide most of the toys and books to keep her moving.

Sleep pattern (homolateral, alternated each time we position her). Gets into serialized pattern by herself, including legs, but does not turn inwards the knee of her extended leg. Likes to do this (alternately facing left and right) as I caress her extended leg, often during day on patterning table between "programs" (a game we made up).

Much better trunk balance with sit, straighter back.

September 6, 1967 re-evaluation IAHP: Profile Level: same.

No appreciable change in crawling and creeping. Parents report improvement in sitting balance as noted at home.

Dominance [foot]: not observable.

From September 6, 1967 to November 8, 1967:

Crawling: in new indoor sixteen-foot crawl box; no use of right leg. Splint the left one? (No, use finger-flick to foot bottom as a "reminder.") In free crawl out of box: improvement in knees turning in—right very much, left some, for a zigzag motion coming (Marines under barbed wire).

Patterning: pushing off with left big toe for some time now; pushing off with right big toe now a few times. (Does this under our hand, can feel it.)

Creeping: on left fist (upper thumb joint), right knuckles—90 percent of time. Because of new visual interest about what's on *tops* of counters, tables?

November 8, 1967 re-evaluation IAHP: Profile Level: same.

Quality of crawling has improved—serialization is good. Active dorsi-flexion was evident at this evaluation. Knee-walks in cross-pattern."

Dominance [foot]: not observable.

From November 8, 1967 to March 26, 1968 (*Note:* 1/16/68 appointment cancelled.)

No program from 11/15/67 to 12/26/67. (Impetigo from possible strep infection.)

Patterning: six days a week until February; five days a week since. Jane can pattern herself involving legs with head and arms in perfect serialization.

Crawling: does not use right leg in crawl box unless we give stimulation as a reminder (rub our foot on nylon carpet as we touch her for "friction"; when she sees our hand coming to right leg, she pushes). Free crawl out of box ten minutes after Strumpels, more lift of foot (dorsi-flexion) and arching of feet.

Creeping: On left fist (upper thumb joint), right knuckles. Last two weeks creeping on backs of hands to hold object or just "practice."

Strumpels: twenty after each patterning in morning, for eighty on each side; twenty or forty in afternoon on each side. More dorsi-flexion in one month. (Did not begin Strumpel program until a month ago, including ten days out for knee-boil.)

Sleep pattern (homolateral): Do not have to do any positioning of Jane for this now. Gets into it by herself, including knee turn-in!

Doing a lot of right-side, left-side "practices," involving arms, legs, hands. Not crossing midline with these "self-exercises" though.

March 26, 1968 re-evaluation IAHP: Profile Level: same.

Crawling—cross-pattern—dorsi-flexion is improved. Creeping—cross-pattern with previous aberrations persisting. Walking—stands, holding on to objects. Walks on knees in good cross pattern.
Dominance [foot]: not observable.

From March 26, 1968 to June 28, 1968:

Crawling: crawl box (two hours daily); turns head side to side more consistently now, but keeps right foot up (not contacting surface), pushing with thigh and knee only. Free crawl out of box; much movement of toes, left big toe especially; seems to be getting left big toe into position for toe-dig push.

Creeping: on side of left fist (as before), on right knuckles (as before); but occasionally is seen on back of hands, usually for purpose of carrying object. Distance of "step" less on right knee (less hip flexion).

Strumpels: better flexion in ankles (left better than right).

Sleep pattern (homolateral): "clicks" into it (with verbal request), but extended arm moves into place a little late.

Note: Patterning was changed at March 26, 1968 re-evaluation from cross-pattern to homolateral and increased to seven minutes (from five) each session.

June 28, 1968 re-evaluation IAHP: Profile Level: same.

Cross-pattern crawling and creeping. Very pleased to note increased ankle action, even though she is still not using same for propulsion in crawling. Superb knee-walking.
Other: . . . Orthopedic plans should be deferred until later, awaiting further progress in comprehension and speech.
Dominance [foot]: not observable.

From June 28, 1968 to October 1, 1968:

Crawling: sixteen-foot crawl box elevated at one end to eighteen inches, (fifty round trips daily). Got toe-push in August. Not much propulsion forward with toe-dig (weak). Seen 10 percent of time. Better on right. (See Visual for slowdown incentives in box.)

Creeping: Still on thumb joint left hand, knuckles right hand; but outdoors this summer on flat of hands. Only gets in about three hours a day now. Leads with right knee with creep up and down stairs. But right still less skilled (less "step" distance).

Strumpels: Thirty times for eight sessions a day, each leg, 240 Strumpels each leg a day. Right foot dorsi-flexion as good as left now? I think they are up to ninety degrees. (IAHP says seventy degrees dorsi-flexion.)

New sit: Indian-style, legs crossed in front of her, nice balance; started August one day.

Some more practicing of body homolaterally, not crossing midline. Sometimes when she's doing this, I label vocally "left" and "right."

October 1, 1968 re-evaluation IAHP: Profile Level: same.

Walking: No credit. Pulls to stand. Knees flexed and narrow. On toes with toes rotated in.

Creeping: Poor cross-pattern with fair serialization. In testing, hand base O.K. Hands flat 60 percent of time; 40 percent on knuckles of left hand and fingers of right hand. Knee base slightly narrow. Feet off floor and plantar flexed.

Crawling: Poor, unserialized cross-pattern. Up on elbows. Hands pronate poorly (especially right). Right hand partially supinates. Left hand doesn't supinate. Knees flex to eighty degrees, generally with lower leg in air. Occasionally foot is down on floor with some dorsi-flexion. Pushes with knees. Legs never fully extend. Parents report at home, is pushing with toes 10 percent of time in box. Improved.

Dominance [foot]: not observable.

From October 1, 1968 to February 18, 1969 (12/12/68 evaluation not done because of hip injury in fall the night before). See Tactile for Patterning.

Patterning: Toe-pushes—seen all the time during patternings.

Crawling: sixteen-foot crawl box elevated at one end to twenty inches, including new half-round molding on floor under Rubatex mat to make "hills" to push against: toe-pushes left foot from fifty to ninety percent of time; right not at all until middle of December. Then all toe-pushes stopped, except those seen in patterning. January started asking patterners to brush foot harder; have been lax about this with "patterning conversation," getting more emphasis than the patterning! Now see a few toe-pushes, especially after Strumpels during crawl-box program.

Creeping: Opportunity reduced to one and a half hours daily this period to limit time foot spends in plantar flexion.

Strumpels: Much improved dorsi-flexion. Left to ninety degrees, I think (see little hollow in ankle next to heel cords). Right not quite as much dorsi-flexion.

Last report to referring doctor said "stands with toes in"; that is incorrect, she stands with toes "out."

Cruises (two-hand support) from chair to chair after supper—O.K.? (IAHP says "No.")

February 18, 1969 re-evaluation IAHP: Profile Level: same.

An IAHP physician: This seven-year-old girl can't walk and her speech is very limited. When I first examined her [October 1965], the right side was more involved than the left. This is no longer apparent in examination. She also has less scissoring, but she has flexion contractures of both knees. I was unable to extend her legs. When held upright she stands with knees flexed. Her patella reflexes are hyperactive, but it is difficult to obtain reliable tests on this girl because she resists all examinations. It might be well to have the opinion of Dr. ——— [orthopedic surgeon in Philadelphia, not on staff] with respect to her contractures.

An IAHP physiatrist [M.D. of Physical Medicine and Rehabilitation]: This seven-year-old girl has been on program for three and one half years with some improvement, but very little on the output side. When I first saw her at onset of program she had bilateral heel cord and hamstring contractions. At this time the child prefers to knee-walk and therefore has her knees frequently bent.* She is extremely hyperactive and rebellious. When pressure is applied to her legs with hips and knees flexed, the flexors begin to relax, following which the knees passively can be nearly fully extended. In the same fashion the heel cords can passively be stretched to ninety degrees.

Recommendations: (1) Walking with overhead ladder assistance, building to fifteen minutes, two times a day; (2) Supportive shoes [for this walk]; (3) If the above do not help, I would recommend an orthopedic consultation. (I have no objection to their friend with them today trying electrotherapy to her legs.)

From February 18, 1969 to May 7, 1969:

Crawling: No toe-pushes with thirty-inch elevation of box at one end.
Creeping: Right hand flat and slapping surface (as if "knows" hand is completely flat now). Most of time still creeps on right knuckles, now spread, and thumb joint of left hand. Both feet arching when creeping.
Patterning: See both feet arching in patterning, left one more than right.
Strumpels: Changed program from thirty each foot per session to twenty left and forty right, to give extra effort to poorer right. Left dorsi-flexion looks strong, pure ninety degrees (inversion and eversion ability equal, producing a balanced lift of foot); right has slight inversion in dorsi-flexion.
Walk with overhead ladder assist: doing very well—toes and knees pointed forward, not out as at first. Still on toes; knees still bent. Ladder fifty inches above floor. Barefoot; decided (per IAHP staff) not to use orthopedic shoes yet. (See 2/18/69 re-evaluation.)

May 7, 1969 re-evaluation IAHP: Profile Level: same.
From May 7, 1969 to July 23, 1969:

Note: Crawling and creeping programs discontinued temporarily.
Walk with overhead ladder assist: J. walking stretched out, fingertip grasp to toe tip. Ladder put at fifty-eight inches above floor at start of this period; increased to sixty-one inches by end of this period. Does sixteen sessions a day, each session one minute; barefoot.
Strumpels: left—240 per day; right—480 per day; left still better dorsi-flexion.

* Doctor apparently mistook Jane's incessant knee-walking at IAHP as a sign she "frequently" has her knees bent. Home program allows no knee walking.

Feet: developing now; can see eversion muscle showing on bottom of feet; also arching continues to strengthen.

Knees: better than a year ago; can now *see* a difference: (a) standing a little taller; (b) Strumpels show higher flexion and straighter extension; (c) patterners mention knees have no spastic reactions (no rubber-band tightness, no bounciness in joint). Used to be able to pull leg into extension (stretch modification of patterning since October 1, 1968) only every second or third serialization (whenever relaxed enough to do so), but can now do smooth leg extension every time leg moves into extension—both sides, but left better.

July 23, 1969 re-evaluation IAHP: Profile Level: same.

. . . There has been marginal gain in the tightness of the legs, but do not feel that this is significant at this time. . . .

From July 23, 1969 to November 4, 1969:

Note: Patterning dropped from program in favor of brachiation emphasis to expand chest size, use of vestibular system, and programs aimed at walking with feet flat (dorsi-flexion) and legs straight: forty sequences a day, each sequence is fifteen minutes.

Strumpels: left leg "half-hearted" about whole business now, and right-leg more energetic, more cooperative, "tries" harder. Reverse of former state of affairs. Is right foot possibly becoming "preferred?" (IAHP: too early to talk about that.)

Walk with overhead ladder assist and give-away floor: much improvement in knee extension (everybody mentioning it).

Gym bar hang-by-hands: while hanging the minute, J. draws knees up, pumps herself in a "swinging," extends legs to reach back. Last week started dorsi-flexion involvement with this.

Elephant walk (plantigrade): no assist after September 15. Leads with right foot a lot (strange, since that's her less skilled one), hands are flat and fingers are pointed out to side now, rather than forward as originally.

Somersaults: progressions of improvement to present roll: finishes in Indian-style sit with hands in balance role at shoulders.

Attempts backward rolls.

November 4, 1969 re-evaluation IAHP: Profile Level: same.

. . . There are several functional changes that we find significantly better. There appears to be a definite improvement in knee extension. Jane is able to walk on her toes, with an overhead ladder, with knees in approximately twenty-five to thirty degrees of flexion.* . . .

From November 4, 1969 to January 28, 1970:

Walk with overhead ladder assist (in high-top sneakers, laced with foot in dorsi-flexion): wider steps of feet and hands.

---

* This represents a fifty-degree improvement in knee-extension since the outset of this record. See text footnote p. 307.

Gym bar hang-by-hands: good hand adjusting. No assist needed. Swings in this position with legs in extension (as far as they will) for both forward and backward "pumpings."

Positive gravity: while she is being swung by arm and leg, Jane holds on to her opposite shoulder with her free hand, instead of swinging it free. First body touching I've seen which involves crossing midline.

All gravity work shows improved body image in space: arched back with head up and looking—really beautiful sense of being "in charge" rather than former "giving in to it" picture.

Getting sneakers on, Jane uses dorsi-flexion (good at pushing her heel down too), so we put sneakers on and off with every walk of every sequence, sixty times a day. This allows bare feet for everything else.

In supine position (while masking) legs are together and more fully extended, closer to floor. (Used to lie with legs flexed and knees out). Also crosses right leg over left, back to floor, repeat, a kind of "practice" she's doing— crossing midline?

January 28, 1970 re-evaluation IAHP: Profile Level: same.

. . . Jane's chest has shown increase of four times the normal rate during these past two and a half months of time. She is able to manipulate herself, using an overhead ladder. . . . There is better extension at both knees. . . .

From January 28, 1970 to April 30, 1970:

Three weeks ago J. started leg-extension "practices." Does this while supine or sitting on edge of patterning table. Has sense of "boosting" at knees to reach wall telephone, to get up on table after therapy walks, etc.

Has stopped using prone position for tasks, play, etc.—whether on patterning table, floor, or bed-for-play. Now prefers Indian-style sit 100 percent of time.

During thirty to forty-five minute free time on floor before supper, she practices stands a lot (involving one-hand rather than two-hand support). Stands better with derriere in and under, knees straighter and more parallel. Still on toes, knees flexed.

Practices cruise with one hand; also cruising backwards, hand holding on to counter top—beautiful balance!

Does continuous forward-rolls in cross-legged position.

Arches back (both ways) while hanging from heels in her "hangup" (pulley system from rafter). Beautiful sense of body in space, as reported before when swung manually by the heels.

Overhead ladder at 68¾ inches at one end, 67½ at other (finger-grasp to toe). This is increase of three inches since last revisit.

April 30, 1970 re-evaluation IAHP: Profile Level: same.

. . . She has shown an extreme accelerated growth this past period of time. Her height in the last nine months has changed 10 cms., which is almost three times faster than normal. Her chest circumference in this period of time has grown 5.4 cms., which is four and one-half times normal. She has shown a marked reduction in knee-flexion contractures. She is able to walk, using an overhead ladder, with legs much straighter, still up on toes.

From April 30, 1970 to September 8, 1970:

Heels are down in walk program; the left is more consistently down than the right.

Knees look straighter.

Walks about a mile a day in program! Can hear her deep breathings as she walks (with overhead ladder assist) in brachiating position.

September 8, 1970 re-evaluation IAHP: Profile Level: same.

. . . During the past period of time, Jane has shown continued straightening of both lower extremities. Her ability to walk, using an overhead ladder, has improved. She is now able to get her heels down fairly consistently. . . . Our major emphasis is on mobility and Jane continues to make progress in these terms. . . .

From September 8, 1970 to December 9, 1970:

Pictures show knee extension and lower leg developing.

Walk with overhead ladder assist on four-inch foam (polyester): walking flat-footed, heels really down. Ladder up either six or eight inches (lost count). (I think ladder at same height all the way across is better for Jane, rather than one end higher than other.)

Vertical ladder with alternate rungs removed: don't think this twenty-four inch distance is as far as she could stretch in climb down. Much breathing with this. Leads with right foot both up and down.

An emphasis on right foot last two weeks in walks—becoming the preferred one? (IAHP: forget "dominance"; get walking first.)

December 9, 1970 re-evaluation IAHP: Profile Level: same.

. . . She has made marked physical developmental changes from 140 percent to 300 percent of average of growth changes for a child of the same age in the same period of time. She is now able to put her feet flat on command when using the overhead ladder. Her lower extremities are much straighter. . . .

From December 9, 1970 to March 9, 1971:

Walk on floor with overhead ladder assist:

    a. Programed walk (five laps): brought teen boys into program for a really strong setting down of her heels last six weeks (hands are bigger). Interesting that right foot seems to be cooperating more than rather lackadaisical left last three weeks; can feel this difference under our hands. Preferring right foot? Or the rather resistant left one? (See Manual Competence this period, for left-handedness.) Feel weight-bearing more and more under our hands.

b. Self-walk (one lap): heels down with overhead ladder one inch higher than it was last revisit (increased half inch twice).

Inclined ladder climb and down (normal rungs): twenty-five degree angle. Jane standing tall (sense of stretch) as she touches her head to cathedral ceiling; occasionally she pauses up or down to "stretch." Weight-bearing noticeably more.

Attempting "jumps" (both feet off floor, down, repeated) as she returns to table for breaks—two-hand support.

Pictures look great.

March 9, 1971 re-evaluation IAHP: Profile Level: same.

. . . During the past period of time, Jane's legs continue to straighten at the knee and she is continually walking more flat-footed. This is evidenced by her physical growth and by pictures. In the past nineteen months of program, Jane has grown 15.3 cms., as compared to average growth of 7.7 cms. for the same period of time. Her sitting height has increased 5.2 cms.—an average child, 3.0 cms. Her chest 4.9 cms., compared to average of 2.7 cms. and her head circumference 1.6 as compared to average of 1.4.* These are quite fantastic growth measurements for a child who has always grown slower than average in all respects. . . . She does well using an inclined ladder, climbing and coming down . . .

From March 9, 1971 to June 2, 1971:

Hanging by heels, winding and unwinding: J. loved this, but discontinued May 1 because webbing was breaking.

Note: Mary Lawrence saw Jane do program for a day. Thinks Jane's legs look beautiful. So straight on inclined ladder when she "stretches." Asks: why not cast? Sure they can be fully extended without pain. With legs this straight she wonders if final cartilage-ligament tightness might be obliterated quicker with a casting period. Why wait till fall (Sandler's suggestion to "look at it then")?

June 2, 1971 re-evaluation IAHP: Profile Level: same.

From June 2, 1971 to April 6, 1972 (No full re-evaluations this period. Mobility programs in period following cast removal 10/15/71 were ʻituted almost week by week via telephone according to parents' report, and ı. .its to IAHP were limited to discussion designed to bring Jane along to the following):

Walk (forward) with overhead ladder assist: straight-legged, flat-footed 100 percent of time. Ladder at seventy-inch height. Bearing less weight on right foot. Is that right hip or whatever was hurting her after 11/11/71 all right now?

Walk (backwards) with overhead ladder assist: does it well. Weight-bearing on right foot as good as left.

*Should read .4.

Inclined ladder climb and down: right leg weaker in weight-bearing, both up and down, but alternates feet nicely. Think recently Jane began to use arms to pull herself up more than legs to push up.

Hanging upside-down by heels (together and separately): continues to maintain legs straight, but more back of the knee dimple in right, if you want to get into minutiae.

Walk with parachute shock-cord assist: started only five weeks ago. Left knee in perfect extension with this, then flexes, then straightens—beautiful. Right poorer in first sequence or two in morning, but warms up with proper requirement; has never straightened its knee *functionally* to full extension, as left can do, but getting better and stronger daily.

Swim pool: kicks to top of water, supine: one hour a day done only about twenty days. Kicks stronger. Left stronger than right, but both look great. (Have to remind her occasionally to keep right one extended during kick; wants to flex it slightly when it gets tired.)

April 6, 1972 re-evaluation IAHP: Profile Level: same.

. . . Jane has shown good progress in overall ability walking under the ladder, but the right lower extremity still presents a problem; it is not straight yet, and weight-bearing is incomplete . . . All efforts again are being made to increase weight-bearing and use of the lower extremities in preparation for walking.

Development of Language

Note: During the six months of floor activity (see Note to Development of Mobility), prior to Jane's evaluation by Mary Lawrence, The New York Hospital, the following changes were observed in her language development:

From July 30, 1964 to September 25, 1964:

New sounds: *wah, ah, ya, yo, nam-nam.*
Jargon all day now.

From September 25, 1964 to January 25, 1965:

More repetitive throat sounds in jargon.

January 25, 1965 initial evaluation: The New York Hospital (by Mary Lawrence, RPT): Doman-Delacato Developmental Profile Level: II.

. . . She verbalizes a great deal . . . no sounds involving lips or tongue . . . does not create meaningful sounds. . . .

From February 14, 1965 to May 1, 1965:

Raspberry and Indian war whoop sounds on back of hand (encouraged).
Moving lips, tongue, jaws in silent chopping motions, etc.
With mirror (for floor fun): Indian war whoop and finger "blitherings" on lips.
First sound used meaningfully 4/22: *ba* for *ball.*
Other sounds used meaningfully:
  eh-o – hello (4/27).
  bye-bye (sounds more like *ba-ba*).
  mo ha – more water.
  mo or *mo ma* – food.
  deedle-deedle along with "My Son John" song.
  oh-ah along with "How I" part of "How I wonder what you are" in "Twinkle Little Star."
  ba-a – bath (only four times).
  combining *p* sound with *ch* sound—more a "practice?"
  li – light and *tuh* – tongue—maybe.
Tongue is extended with tasks; also very interested in tongue now, looks in play mirror at it.

Moments between idea and speech—thinking?
Jargon all day now.

May 1, 1965 re-evaluation by Mary Lawrence: Profile Level: IV.

. . . Her language has improved and she is able to make throat, lip, and tongue sounds, and she uses at least five words spontaneously and meaningfully. . . .

From May 1, 1965 to June 22, 1965:

No program for two to three weeks (mother's illness).
Words heard many times:
> *mo wa* – water.
> *h'wo* – hello.
> *bye-bye* and waves (usually *after* door is closed, person gone).
> *li* – light.
> *ma-ma* when needs help, but not really for mother or to mother.
> *yum-yum* – command for food.

Words heard one or two times:
> *day* – Daisy request for "Bicycle Built for Two" song.
> *I'll ini* – request for "Ten Little Indians" song.
> *bah* – bottle; repeats (like *bye-bye*); means wants bottle (hungry), but never used with object.
> *ni-ni* – nite-nite.

New sounds: *da, de, di*–lots of *d* sounds; *ts-ts-ts* practice with tongue and teeth together.
Sings along whole song (short song)—tune, not words.
Whispers now.

June 22, 1965 re-evaluation by Mary Lawrence: Profile Level: same.

. . . Since her last evaluation, her mother was unable to carry out the full program (especially mobility) due to an acute back strain. It is interesting to note that during this period of little floor activity Jane verbalized much less . . .

From June 22, 1965 to September 2, 1965 (*Note:* C is for words used in command, wants):

> *h'wo* – hello with play telephone and people.
> C *bye-bye.*
> *ba-a-ll* – ball, occasionally repeated like *bye-bye* and *ba-ba* (bottle).
> C *mo wa* – more water.
> C *li* – light.
> C *lock* – block.
> C *soo* – shoe.
> *sa* (was just *s*) – sock.

C   *ba* (repeats like *bye-bye*) – bottle.
    cah – car.
    zull – puzzle.

C   *ga* – glasses (sunglasses).

C   *cahg* or *deedledee* or *deedle-deedle* – cookie; got this confused with "dee-
      dle-deedle" going along with "My Son John" song the same week.
    gum – gum.
    eh-eh – banana.
    wow-wow – dog, if she sees one.

C   *wow-wow* – wants Yale "Bulldog" song.

C   *yum-yum* or *nam-nam* – eat.

C   *pen* – open.
    sh – push.
    p sound only – pants.

C   *coll* – crawl (creep actually).
    mama – calls for help.

C   *mo gum* – more gum (may be a repeat rather than a spontaneous couplet).
    no no (shakes head) – no.
    paper and *tongue* each attempted once.
    ba-a – bath.
    kitty – tries to say this, always comes out different.
    Looks into people's eyes now and says full "sentence" of jargon.
    Note: Her voice is very thin, almost inaudible, have to go right up to her
        to hear any of this.

September 2, 1965 re-evaluation by Mary Lawrence: Profile Level: V "poor."

. . . She has twenty-five words of meaningful speech. . . .

October 25, 1965 initial evaluation IAHP: Profile Level: same. (V "poor").
From October 28, 1965 to February 8, 1966:

"Nothing" period November, December, most of January! Could be "nothing"
    program? (Except for patterning this was a lousy period of programing.)
Attempted couplet on one occasion "bye-bye car" (may be one-word).
More inflection in jargon now.
Much interest in tongue.
Saw birthday cake January 22 and said "ahp bir ay" (happy birthday).
Most language sounds the same (says only first part of word).
Calls for mother now; screams if mother takes too long.

February 8, 1966 re-evaluation IAHP: Profile Level: same.

More tonality in speech. Child attempted a couplet on one occasion.

From February 8, 1966 to June 1, 1966:

Asks for dolly and teddy bear.
Likes to try to say what we ask her to.
Sings "Ring Around the Rosy" partially, no lyrics.

Body words from reading program, says: *eye, no* (nose), *tee* (teeth), *yin-yin* (chinny-chin-chin), *arm*.

Other words, such as the following:

da-da – daddy	*seer* – cereal
la-la – doll (also *dah*)	*ka* – kitty-cat
te be – teddy bear	*ap* – apple
pee – peaches (baby dessert)	*ya* – pants
juz – juice	*sa* – sweater

June 1, 1966 re-evaluation IAHP: Profile Level: same.

More sounds—better tonality. Obvious attempts to communicate vocally.

From June 1, 1966 to October 18, 1966:

See Visual this period regarding reading program; begun in earnest in Maine 8/1.

Fifty-plus new words—more like words than sounds now—even endings.

Reading contributing 90 to 95 percent of language. (Mary was right, should have done this last summer here in Maine.)

Volume better.

Whistles.

Says "click-clack"; loves "words" like this.

Talks to animals.

Tries to say what you ask her to say.

Couplets:

Bye-bye car eat (Go to village to eat).

Don' wan' ee (Don't want it).

Don' wan' nite-nite.

Says "bye-bye car" when sees car picture, so not a couplet?

Language list (partial):

dress	truck	ear	grapes
book	tree	hair	lollipop
sweater	boat	foot	johnny
puzzle	airplane	eggs	house
cake	bath	hamburger	record
Stuart	arm	toast	balloon
Grant (?)	nose	soup	table
kitty-cat	belly	apple	window

Note: This is not the way Jane says these, but close enough to understand. Doesn't talk very loud though, little *wee* voice.

October 18, 1966 re-evaluation IAHP: Profile Level: V O.K. now.

Fifty new words: two to four-word sentences.

From October 18, 1966 to January 3, 1967:

Sentences: "I want"—"I don't want." Asks for most things this way now.

Says all new reading words (nouns).

Uses language only for "I want" and with reading or picture-looking.

qu sound: *quack,* not *kak* anymore.

f, v, z sounds now.

Repeats *everything,* especially new stuff, but doesn't use latter spontaneously (doesn't intitiate this stuff herself).

Likes to hear, "Can you say"; says it, then laughs (like a game?)

Still says stuff learned last year with incorrect pronunciation (*ba-a* for *bath,* not even *baf*); but new stuff says pretty good.

Might have said *Grant* one day.

January 3, 1967 re-evaluation IAHP: Profile Level: same.

Increased repetition and able to say all reading words. Articulation improved.

From January 3, 1967 to June 12, 1967:

No program for three months from 1/7/67 to 3/30/67; convalescence from burn injury.

Poorer enunciation (volume).

Gets hung up in speech like a stutterer—gagging?

qu–, tw–, tr– beginnings: *quack, tweet, tree.*

Is trying to "sing along."

ymh "word" – pants wet?

Last three weeks, tries to say everything she sees.

June 12, 1967 re-evaluation IAHP: Profile Level: same.

Increased vocalization—blends and phonemes—but inconsistencies persist.

From June 12, 1967 to September 6, 1967:

Think our asking her to say everything too much pressure, so stopped it. Now testing reading without talk (choice method), unless good mood to talk.

No sentences except "I want ———." Desperate "want" produced this:

I want dada talk on tep [tape].

I want hear dada talk on tep.

I want hear tep.

September 6, 1967 re-evaluation IAHP: Profile Level: same.

From September 6, 1967 to November 8, 1967:

On the one hand, says part of word (e.g., *ken* for *blanket*); on the other hand, lots of couplets, saying two words when could get by with one (adjective and noun instead of noun only).

No new verbs, so all combinations are with "want" only.

When alone, "practices" saying, "Twinkle, twinkle" and "Zippidee-doodah."

Says *today* and *tinkle* (toilet word) reversed: *dotay, kintle.* (Speech is so inaudible, hard to tell.)

Blows candles and whistles with greater ease (volume better?).

"Talks" almost all day long, but nonsensical.

Gestures (like disgust) with difficult starts. Knows she's having trouble, it looks like.

O.K. to make believe I don't know what she's pointing at? (Yes, if can carry it off.)

O.K. to ask her to repeat language when I know she can do better? (No.)

November 8, 1967 re-evaluation IAHP: Profile Level: same.

Some vocabulary increase. More gestures with speech. Articulation is improved. More couplets.

From November 8, 1967 to March 26, 1968 (*Note:* 1/16/68 appointment cancelled.):

No program from 11/15/67 to 12/26/67.

Awful "nothing" period mid-November to almost mid-March. During winter plateau, one new word (*Santa Claus*). Reason? Maybe because only reading last six weeks and very little tape input also? Desperate kind of motivation illicits some words; e.g., wanted housekeeper's rubber gloves so badly, so said "gloves." Singing a lot after mid-November.

Showed real difficulty getting anything out, covers eyes these times (in knowledge of inadequacy?); I stopped any pressure to talk.

Last week spent whole days repeating words from tape, trying each one. (Till then, tape recorder not working most of time.)

ts practice: endings.

Says yes occasionally to answers, instead of repeating a word for the answer (key-word in question).

March 26, 1968 re-evaluation IAHP: Profile Level: same.

Pronunciation is improved. Several new words. Now puts endings on words.

From March 26, 1968 to June 28, 1968:

Note: The following "speech spurt" may be due to change in patterning (back to prior homolateral pattern—basic mobility of pons level of brain) or because we started working "harder" with Jane, or for some other reason altogether, but "speech spurt" it is:

a. Old "I want" sentences back again plus many new words.

b. Will copy (repeat after us) immediately; likes it. No worries about pressure because she wants to try it.

c. Our emphasis on enlarging her vocabulary: "What kind?"

[Cookies]: Oreos, chip (chocolate chip), vanilla wafer, Lorna Doone.

[Juice]: orange, grape, Coke, appleberry (Mott's A.M.).

[Soup]: chicken, noodle, beef.

[Meat]: chicken, ham, baloney, liverwurst, bacon, steak, hamburger, roast beef.

[Story]: "mouse," "kittens."

d. Uses *more* a lot now.

e. Names: Stuart, Grant (first time?), Daddy—lots more use; also "Mama," Marilyn, Cathy, Jeannie.
f. All old nursery rhymes by name—tries to say first lines.
g. New sentences (desperate motivation):
    I want go Wetson's ham*burger*.
    I want light, no, this light.
h. Says *nine*.

June 28, 1968 re-evaluation IAHP: Profile Level: same.

Speech has reached a point of breakthrough in terms of increased vocabulary and combinations.

From June 28, 1968 to October 1, 1968:

Biggest speech spurt yet!
Proper names.
Prepositions: *in, on, up, down*.
Adjectives: all colors, *hot, cold*.
Adverbs: *away, off*.
Verbs: besides *want*, about twenty others.
Nouns: trying to say all nouns, especially new ones from tape.
Asking for story at night by title: *Raggedy Ann, Surprise, One-Two, Buckle My Shoe*, etc.
Sentences: not complete, but lots of three- and four-unit combinations (partial list):
    Go get ee (it).
    Go away.
    Take off pink pajamas.
    Take off shirt.
    Take off pants.
    Take off outrigger.
    Get up.
    Get down.
    I don't want ee (it).
    Cold ice water.
Also says "nope" and "yep" appropriately.
Desperate need brings forth beautifully enunciated requests such as, "Piggyback ride" (to Philippa, teen helper).
Still talks from motivation and need, except for colors and a few numbers labeled spontaneously for the fun of naming them.
Quality: first time she says it—good pronunciation and volume; after a few times—poor, half-said. Probably due to breath control? Medial vowels good, even short *e* and short *i*.
Loves to talk—great pleasure when she is understood (usually shakes with delight).

Very interested in defining food, story, objects, wants—as if she loves the idea of "making the choice," asking for the specific.

October 1, 1968 re-evaluation IAHP: Profile Level: same.

Increased vocabulary including many couplets and three- to five-word sentences—articulation poor but improving.
Gag [reflex]—O.K.—very slightly delayed.

From October 1, 1968 to February 18, 1969 (12/12/68 evaluation not done because of hip injury in fall the night before):

See School Reports by home-instructor 12/12/68 and 2/69 (pp. 248, 257).
Says patterner's names (they cry!).
Shades of colors: *chartreuse, aqua, fuchsia, royal blue, navy, light blue, turquoise,* etc.
ABC's.
Verbs: *crying, laughing, coughing,* etc. (See Auditory for patterning "talk-in's.")
Names of rooms in house. (See Auditory regarding "Wednesday" concept: wagon-ride through house.)
Numbers to 100: very articulate, except no *f* (*warty-war* is 44, 50 is *v-e* or *ee-i*, 7 is *sewan*,—teen is *ten*); seven*ty* and eigh*ty*, etc. is beautiful, also *eleven, twelve, twenty.*
Not O.K.: *f, j, p, v, y*—*f* is *v, j* is *h, p* is *g* (*gink,* not *pink*), *y* is *w* (*yellow*).
Improved pronunciation (volume?) last two weeks: ro*se,* fi*ve,* honey*comb.*
Did the peanut-butter "routine" at least six times daily since December 1 (I didn't realize instructions at first—wipe mouth out, refrigerate peanut butter); notice pooching lips up to look at them. Any connection with peanut-butter (lip) program?
Vocabulary limited completely (until two weeks ago) to colors, numbers, ABC's. Now more verbalizing. No sentences, only combinations involving phrases: "Turn on tape," "Crawl in suit"; lots of adjectives plus nouns, and old "I want ———."
Teacher says Jane verbalizing in school, and school is conducted that way. Teacher doesn't understand, says so, and Jane must then "speak better." What J. needs is a new family, who doesn't understand "old speech," old ways to get something.
Volume. Started masking every thirty minutes instead of every hour December 15 approximately all day. Improved much; everyone commenting about this.

February 18, 1969 re-evaluation IAHP: Profile Level: same.
From February 18, 1969 to May 7, 1969:

See School Report this period (p. 270).
Says *p;* continue peanut-butter program?
Verbalizing a lot in school.

May 7, 1969 re-evaluation IAHP: Profile Level: same.
From May 7, 1969 to July 23, 1969:

> Enunciation—unbelievable! Like she's been in a diction class. Had started slightly before May 7, then occurred fast. Definitely three and four syllables without breathing in between now: *cereal, Melanie, patterning, Valerie, Chris-and-Kay,* etc. Volume, right?
>
> Auditory must be better too: can correct her own mispronunciations with our questionings. (*Gink?* She laughs and says, *"Pink."*)
>
> Quantity: talking more, especially where required by teacher.
>
> a. More combinations.
> b. Telling story about picture, what each is doing, etc. Says this in sentences often.
> c. Likes to "practice" names of people with connective *and.*
> d. "I want" sentences are back, as if desires to say full sentence rather than key adjective and noun for wants.
> e. Plurals—*s* on most plurals with looking at pictures during stethoscope-talking program, actually finding all the pictures she can do this with as a "practice."
> f. Expletives: "All right, all right!" "O.K., O.K.!" "Oh, no!"
> g. July 21: "No, I am not!"
>
> Stuttering: started Monday July 7, ended July 12; very bad, gagging, really long hang-up with struggle to elicit first sound. Accompanied with bilateral hand movements—slapping. (Last fall some of this with right hand slapping few times.)

July 23, 1969 re-evaluation IAHP: Profile Level: same.
From July 23, 1969 to November 4, 1969:

> Biggest speech spurt yet! Even thinking she will talk someday O.K.; so good cannot possibly plateau now.
>
> Volume. From one syllable in May to seven and eight from August on. Maybe nine syllables now without breathing in between! Beautiful pronunciation.
>
> Vocabulary.
>
> a. Expletives: "No, I'm not!" "All righty!" "Goddam!" "Oh, God, oh, Grant, oh, crap!"
> b. To patterners: "Go away [where?] waiting room [playroom]."
> c. Yes, no.
> d. "Close the door," "I don't want it," etc.—surprises.
> e. "Please," "Thank you," "You're welcome."
> f. September: repeats (immediate recall) any sentence beautifully; sometimes not full sentence, but would change it quickly, easily, with joy if asked to.
> g. Engaging in "conversation" we "stretch" (September); lots of surprises with this.
>
>> J.: Take her home.
>> Me: Take who home?

J.: Go to Debbie's house.

Me: What color is Debbie's house?

J.: White and green.

Me: What do you want to wear?

J.: Red plaid [pink-striped, etc.] dress [etc.].

h. Pronouns: *her, him, I.*

i. Stethoscope-talking incentives, says everything in the following:

object lotto: with desk picture says *blotter, ink bottle, clock.*

zoo lotto: farm, jungle, birds, fish.

lotto (categories): weather, family, community workers, pets, neighborhood.

pictionary book: satellite, launching pad, rocket, etc.

phonetic books from school cabinet.

shapes, including lesser-known ones.

reading words and sentences—tried this with her a little.

j. Counting backwards from 20 or somewhere in 20's.

k. Ordinal numerals to twent*ieth* (says *twentiepf*).

Whistling! A lot since September.

Throat-clearing—involuntary now? Started mimicking one of the teens one day, been doing this ever since.

Teacher said she talked more the first day of school than all last year put together.

Can hear Jane's speech in the next room, so much louder now.

Stuttering: October 11 to 14 so severe could get no sound out at all. On and off since, but not so severe. This often alternating with talking more than usual.

November 4, 1969 re-evaluation IAHP: Profile Level: same.

. . . Basic language function shows good improvement. Jane has better breath control and seems to be more spontaneous with speech usage. . . .

From November 4, 1969 to January 28, 1970:

Horrors! Awful speech hangup started approximately December 1 and continues. Accompanied soon after (approximately December 15) with facial and head tic, everything in face drawn to the right: head turned to right, jaw and tongue to right, eyes all out of control but looking to right at same time.

Speech so difficult, but eventually comes out. For *every* word the tic first, and so on through combinations. Tic gradually subsided to slight tremoring only, with all speech.

During the time the tic was subsiding these progressions were noted (is this important?): jerking to right side, head and face involved but not tongue; jerking of head centered (not to right), down on chest, eyes involved but not tongue; jerking of head centered but head involved less and less.

Took ten-day vacation from program to let Jane "play." Monday after

Thanksgiving teacher returned and found Jane eager to make Thanksgiving list, etc. That was the last time Jane talked without difficulty until week of revisit.

Last two weeks more combinations than all combinations heretofore added together! Partial list:

Get down on the floor.
Crawl in [sic] the floor.
Sit on the couch.
Water with ice cubes in it.
House with people. (Command.)
House with Barbie sleeping. (Command for another house.)
When going home? (To programers!)
Dropped on the floor. Dropped it.
Wake up. (Commands of this kind to dolls and "families.")
Daddy is coming home. When coming home?

Uses possessive correctly: Barbie's (etc.)

New interest in "practices" involving in, on and with.

New pronouns: my, it.

Most language before January involved huge expansion of expletives (said in frustration?).

Most language after January involved with role-playing with Barbie doll.

Pronunciation just perfect at times except blends: gr, gl, br, bl, th, etc.; I think with stethoscope-talking even blends are perfect, except th. (Favorite play on floor—thirty minutes before supper— is naming pictures into the stethoscope!)

January 28, 1970 re-evaluation IAHP: Profile Level: same.

. . . Jane's chest has shown increase of four times the normal rate during these past two and a half months of time . . . and there is a definite improvement in responsiveness and language. . . .

From January 28, 1970 to April 30, 1970:

Another speech spurt after a period of difficulty. (See last period.) "Practices" strings of things:

When is Daddy (Mommy) coming home? Daddy's coming home 7 o'clock. Daddy is in the city and coming back soon. The girls in the city. Barbie doll is in the city.

Much dialogue practice—two or three people asking and answering; Jane varying voices for this.

February 6: "Mary [Brower] is home sick in bed, has a bad cold." Programer P. Wallace here, said, "I think I am going to cry, that was so beautiful."

Adds "right now" and "please" to former short commands, such as "orange juice."

Very interested in "practices" involving to: "Go bye-bye in the car to Mary's house." ". . . to New York City." (Where are you going, Jane?) "to the bedroom." "Give Valentine candy to Barbie doll."

Talks to herself: "No, no water, Jane."

Endless combinations with role-playing with Barbie doll, together with little talks to "Jane."

Last names of people: Buddy Wechsler, the first one; new auditory interest in families who have three members working with her—the Perlsteins, the Sleepers.

Jane dictating daily "story" for her teacher to write down; use for reading later, etc. (Ideas suggested, but Jane forms the sentences.)

End of February till revisit:

Another awful speech hangup, accompanied by torso as well as head movement, perhaps stiff neck and a bending backwards a more accurate description. Head tremor is same as reported last period.

Dropped stethoscope-talking program, and all requests to talk, about March 6, except for occasional "test" to see if she still had a speech hangup.

Occasionally this clears. Week before revisit, coming in driveway in car, she said, "Going home now, Barbie." Also said, "Go bye-bye to the field and play in the car. No, go in the car."

When Jane is having difficulties she usually says "one-words" for requests. Otherwise prefers to say a "string of things," more like "practices," often in bed before sleep, making substitutions for nouns in the same sentence, trying this and that.

Volume just great. Very understandable. Can shout and emphasize now—cute! Can blow candles out without having to turn birthday-cake plate around for edge candles. Can hear her puffing and huffing during sequences; *huge* breaths in mask.

April 30, 1970 re-evaluation IAHP: Profile Level: same.

From April 30, 1970 to September 8, 1970:

May: calls me "Mom," an address at beginning or end of sentence. Varying inflections with this! Same with teacher, "Gross" (not "Mrs. Gross"). Also in phone role-play, "Grandmother, come to our house."

Also in May: hours of "strings of things" with role-play or without, just "practicing" talking, trying out this and that. Also can ask her these days to "Put that into a sentence"; e.g., "Leave" will come back as "Go out the door."

Talking for two months with complete sentence structure and with much increase in vocabulary, and, all of a sudden it stopped. Entered period of extreme frustration (tantrums), hiding behind hands, etc., when attempting to speak. Facial tic recurred. (Otherwise, very happy, outgoing behavior.)

See Auditory Competence this period: increases in awareness.

September 8, 1970 re-evaluation IAHP: Profile Level: same.

From September 8, 1970 to December 8, 1970:

Worst speech hang-up until November 15:

No speech 90 percent of time; otherwise one-words with struggle.

Counting instead; no problem.

Much singing and jargon singsong.
Followed by huge speech spurt:
More sophisticated level of speech.
Vocalizing all day long.
New:
  a. Contractions: *it's, can't, let's,* etc.
  b. Past tense.
  c. Last names spontaneously (new teens "interest" here?).
  d. Days of week listed, including *morning, afternoon, night.*
  e. Enlarged vocabulary to point of my not stopping to list it—just every-
     thing she can think of to say. Labeling everything in sight for perfect
     articulation, corrections, etc.
  f. Mom-Dad dialogues, Dad-brother, etc.—mimicking these overheard the
     night before, etc.
  g. Interest in using *for* in every sentence that will take it.
Teacher says Jane speaks in full sentences *at least* 50 percent of the time,
  including past tense. ("And the girl talk*ed*.")
I think Jane is saying everything "new" in sentences; the "old" gets one or
  two words. ("Daddy is not coming soon/ on the late train.")

December 8, 1970 re-evaluation IAHP: Profile Level: VI marked "poor."*

. . . She has shown two months of neurological growth in this past period
of time. She has made marked physical developmental changes, from 140
percent to 300 percent of average growth changes for a child of the same age
in the same period of time (chest, head, etc.). . . . She has shown an
infinite increase in verbal abilities. [Language increase of twelve months since
October 18, 1966, divided by six functional areas on the Profile, gives average
of two months "neurological growth" this period.]

From December 8, 1970 to March 9, 1971:

Vocabulary increasing fast. Sophisticated: *delicatessen, terrible,* etc.
Pronouns: *I'm, my, mine.*
All-day vocalizing in daydreaming, fantasy, role-playing situations involving
  people, behavior, discipline, punishments, etc. This done in two or three
  voices, a drama script of sorts. All in sentences, also listings—days of week,
  months of year, counting forwards and backwards, etc.
Speech otherwise (communication): objects, food, information wants are
  expanded to full sentence-asking as we "wait," or with our encouragement.
Seems to have stopped initiating sentences without our requirement.
Quality: volume increased greatly. Beautiful enunciation. But mistakes in
  blends no better.
No speech hang-up or tic or tremoring through December, January, most of
  February. Last two or three weeks have seen speech hang-up resume

* This scoring increase was later retracted when The Institutes changed the time-
frame ages on their Profile. It represents the only such retraction in her case as Profile
Levels go in this Appendix.

slightly and infrequently. Spitting with sibilants (Elmer Fudd) or outright facial tic with no sound for a few seconds.

March 9, 1971 re-evaluation IAHP: Profile Level: same.

. . . These are quite fantastic growth measurements for a child who has always grown slower than average in all respects.

There is more verbalization on Janey's part. She is doing well in academic studies with her teacher. . . .

From March 9, 1971 to June 2, 1971:

Uses full sentences (if you don't answer one-words) for wants and reading only. How do you get her to use speech spontaneously—for comment, for conversation, etc.? (Delacato: What you have is a dull child.)

I taught her to say "Fine" after people ask, "How are you, Jane?" One day I didn't get there in time to remind her, and she answered Mrs. Perlstein's inquiry with, "I am happy."

June 2, 1971 re-evaluation IAHP: Profile Level: same.
From June 2, 1971 to April 6, 1972 (No full evaluations this period. See Mobility this period.):

Sentences 100 percent of time (*when* she talks).

More directed verbalization; almost no fantasy, except directed role-play talk, telephone play, etc.

Quality: halting; monotone generally, but not as much as formerly—inflection surprises now and then of a more sophisticated nature. Does Jane have what they call "athetoid speech?" (IAHP: Tonality increases with auditory competence and volume, a matter of development.)

Only less than a dozen moments have any of us seen speech hang-up involving gagging or tic or stuttering of any sort since June; no tremoring.

History of new stuff:

a. Last summer on trip to Europe applied cortical think-and-do efforts to get Jane to answer questions: "Don't say 'ginger ale' when I ask 'Do you want ginger ale.' Say, 'Yes, I do' or 'No, I don't.' " It worked.

b. After trip, began to talk to her about "You are learning English," as separate from languages she heard in Europe, including my struggle and Grant's over German (feeling of inadequacy, hesitation like Jane's). Began to spend suppertime saying a sentence in three languages and commenting that Stuart is learning French, Grant is learning German, "You are learning English" (so, therefore you are experiencing the difficulties attending that sort of learning, frustration, etc.) Just showed this by example, and it really lowered her feeling of frustration somewhat. "Practicing" language became an O.K. in the house. Began to hear this sort of communication from Jane:

(In bed, during recovery period after casting): "Shut up / no / that's not nice / sorry, Mom / and go away / and don't bovver me/ and leave / and close the door / pease. (Me: Pease?) Pul-leese/ I want some Fresca soda / and oatmeal cookies / pease / pul-leese / and some books / five books / all right." (Me: All right.)

To teacher: "I want you to call my mommy / no, not my mommy / my muvver / now. I am tired / no / so tired."

c. We started praising her, "What a beautiful English sentence!"
d. School involved in the fall much reading of quotations, and during that period Jane very interested in questions and answers. Answering in a more sophisticated way became a kind of practice with her. "Yes, I do want it now." "No, Mom, that's baby*ish*." "Yes, I want to go to the (va) johnny right now."
e. Now current interest (can you believe?) is having a conversation, sit-down and talk together—on side of bed at night, in school, etc. Jane initiates this, tries to string it out herself.
f. Jane doing full-sentence dictation with ease in school:
   This (vis) door is red with (wif) a gold doorknob.
   Dear Mom / no / Muvver,
      Please, give me a ham sandwich with a pickle, and a glass of Fresca. For dessert, chocolate ice cream.

   Love (Wuv),
Jane

g. Big motivation (newness) brings this kind of sophisticated speech:
   (Jane fussing with new pages I just finished an hour before for her new album.)
   Teacher: Before we start, do you want to show me something?
   Jane: Before we start, I want show you my new pictures./ Me and Grant in Switzerland / chalet/ in bed./ *laughing!* / Laugh*TER!* / not asleep!

April 6, 1972 re-evaluation IAHP: Profile Level: same.

Development of Manual Competence

January 25, 1965 initial evaluation: The New York Hospital (by Mary Lawrence, RPT): Doman-Delacato Developmental Profile Level: III.

. . . She has demonstrable spasticity in all extremities. . . . She has a good prehensile grasp but poor cortical opposition in either hand. She is using her thumb in crude cortical efforts. . . .

From February 14, 1965 to May 11, 1965:

Hand-brushing motions in floor play (copying patterning "brushing?").

Brushes hands (or holds toy and brushes that) alongside body, while lying prone on floor; lies on side slightly to "watch this."

Scribble marks with pencil, very faint and wavy.

Makes dots with fingernail.

Index finger pointing but not at anything (just practices this).

Clenches fist to prevent flat hand-brush in patterning.

Drops objects into containers. (See Visual, and Tactile Competence, appreciation of "depth," this period.)

Tosses checkers across the floor to make them roll, watches.

Pushes thumbs against rims of everything while sitting (usually waiting for meal in highchair).

Fascinated with finger combinations she makes: first and second, first and third, etc. Does this repeatedly, watches.

Stirring motions.

Throwing balls.

Arm extension to back of head now for hair-brushing practice.

Beginning to use left hand to assist the right one (becoming bimanual).

Dressing and undressing interest seems to be beginning, pulls shirt over head.

Looks to me as if she has that new grasp: thumb to finger for picking up things. Not prehensile anymore?

May 1, 1965 re-evaluation by Mary Lawrence: Profile Level: IV marked "poor."

. . . Her manual skills have improved and she is now bimanual and beginning to use the right hand as a dominant hand even though it is less skilled than the left. Her cortical opposition has improved, but she uses the finger-to-thumb in a flat rather than tip-to-tip position. . . . In range of motion, I could find no limitation in the upper extremities. . . .

May 1, 1965 to June 22, 1965:

Full arm extension, up and out: reaches up and out, slaps walls while crawling on floor or being carried. Loves pulling shirt on and off.

Holds cup with right hand after letting go with left.

Can use spoon quite well without spilling, but holds it in prehensile grasp.

Reaches for everything with right hand.

Throws ball with right hand.

Pronation and supination of hands now.

June 22, 1965 re-evaluation by Mary Lawrence: Profile Level: VI marked "poor."

. . . Manual competence continues to show progress. Hand skills are good, thumb-to-finger opposition is tip to tip and the right hand is definitely now dominant. . . .

June 22, 1965 to September 2, 1965:

Seems to do everything with right hand, including eating with spoon.

Can alternate pouring motions, but sometimes misses the mark (supination is poor in hand holding the container).

Can untwist, but cannot twist (i.e., twists open, but not closed).

Using thumb to turn flashlight off and on.

Bimanual function using hammer to pegs (right hammers, left holds).

Knocking motions with closed fist.

Opposition of thumb to finger still not perfect tip-to-tip?

Nests blocks but more by accident than senses sizes larger and smaller.

Constructs tower of fourteen blocks with edges kept perfect the whole way. (See Visual and Tactile this period.)

Makes row of choo-choo blocks on command.

Loves puzzles (nursery school wooden, five single-object type—four or five in one puzzle—quite easy now; needs help with large wooden jigsaw type). (See Visual Competence and Tactile this period.)

Practices cortical opposition of thumb-to-finger in the air, for the fun of it.

September 2, 1965 re-evaluation by Mary Lawrence: Profile Level: VI O.K.

. . . There is no demonstrable spasticity in her arms. . . . Manually she puts nursery-school age puzzles together; identifies by tactile only, and enjoys all forms of activitiy. . . . She is very adept at using her hands, but her cortical opposition is not yet perfect. Her manual skills are still somewhat impeded in these activities which require new intellectual functions, but ultimately she is able to learn new skills. . . .

October 25, 1965 initial evaluation IAHP: Profile Level: VI "poor"; with Level V "out" (no credit) and Level IV noted "flat."

Dominance [hand]: right.

October 28, 1965 to February 8, 1966:

> No spoon or other feeding implements allowed; thus, finger-feeding this entire period.
>
> Picks up crumb-size pieces, pennies; right hand better tip-to-tip and faster in simultaneous pickup, I think.
>
> Opens car doors from inside.
>
> Turns doorknobs.
>
> Twists open medicine-size (small) bottles.
>
> Undoes diaper pins.
>
> Fits shapes into shape-sorting box—seems very easy for her. (See Visual Competence this period).
>
> Very good at puzzles (still one-picture, one-hole type).
>
> "Socks" another person.
>
> Spreads fingers and looks through them.
>
> Slapping hands flat on ground while creeping—some new practice of hers.

February 8, 1966 re-evaluation IAHP: Profile Level: same (VI "poor"); with V now "poor."

> Cortical opposition bilaterally and simultaneously has improved from *out* to *poor*. Bimanual function has improved but remains *poor*.
>
> Dominance [hand]: right. Preference for dextrality probably influenced by pathology.

February 8, 1966 to June 1, 1966:

> Puts own pants on, including back pull at waist.
>
> Uses index finger to point to doll parts.
>
> Picks up tiniest crumbs with ease.
>
> Works wooden jigsaw puzzles—eight pieces, approximately.

June 1, 1966 re-evaluation IAHP: Profile Level: same. Level VI "poor"; with Level V O.K. now.

> Cortical opposition bilaterally and simultaneously now normal.
>
> Dominance [hand]: right.

June 1, 1966 to October 18, 1966:

> Seems to have poor cortical opposition in left hand sometimes, a bit flat; also brings third finger in to help oppose, instead of index finger only. Right always looks perfect.
>
> Has learned to point (with purpose).
>
> Now interested in buttons, zippers.
>
> Pours good. (I think.)
>
> Unscrews better than screws.
>
> Pop-it beads; pegs in pegboards: should have had earlier, really too easy for her to spend much time at; no interest in designs or filling up the board, or making *long* strings of beads.
>
> Loves wooden jigsaw puzzles; three or four simple cardboard puzzles also.

October 18, 1966 re-evaluation IAHP: Profile Level: same.

> No change. Basic function good.
> Dominance [hand]: same.

From October 18, 1966 to January 3, 1967:

> Works zipper well; buttons well, but looks like beginner; unsnaps; snaps—gives up too easily; no ties yet—not interested.
> Pre-writing: no circle yet separately; can do vertical line but looks thin and wavy (poor control).
> In all tasks right hand is skilled hand, left hand assists—holds fabric, paper, etc.—automatically.

January 3, 1967 re-evaluation IAHP: Profile Level: same.

> Marked improvement in bimanual function.

From January 3, 1967 to June 12, 1967:

> No program for three months from 1/7/67 to 3/30/67: convalescence from burn injury (including upper right arm).
> Very good manual program after convalescence.
> Buttons good, including small sweater buttons of patterners; snaps poor except "doggie," whose ears, etc. have heavy-duty larger snaps, easier to see. J. snaps "visually" but buttons more tactilely than visually now.
> Sewing through Masonite sewing cards, but doesn't finish design.
> Stringing beads with great pleasure, with ease (if there is a good lace with long pointed end, otherwise gives up after one or two beads).
> Loves Creative Playthings' "auto" puzzle with small knobs for each of small autos. (See Visual Competence this period.)
> Works every purse clasp and lock-idea in sight, including Creative Playthings' lockboard (a cinch).
> Pre-writing: will draw balloons with closed circle and good strong vertical line attached. Also apples with stems interest her.

June 12, 1967 re-evaluation IAHP: Profile Level: VI O.K. now.

> Bimanual function now within normal limits.
> Dominance [hand]: mixed—strongly right.

From June 12, 1967 to September 6, 1967:

> Writing: did some writing in sand, finger-pictures in sand, using circles and lines (circle around my face, face within my circle, clocks likewise, etc.); started numbers. Mostly guiding her hand, because if not she wants to do finger "flip" and "dot punch" in sand instead.
> Scissors: no interest for this.
> Favorite play fun: arranging small furniture in rooms of playhouses, moving rubber and wooden people into all positions—a great deal of this is fine finger work (loves the small lamps, etc. the best).

September 6, 1967 re-evaluation IAHP: Profile Level: same.

Substantial improvement noted in gross hand-eye coordination and general dexterity.
Dominance [hand]: strongly right.

From September 6, 1967 to November 8, 1967:

How do you teach scissors? J. really not interested.
Writing—ugh! Went back to free circles, lost interest. Have someone else do it? Teach numbers? What is the motivation?
Fork: changed from spearing motion to underneath scoop motion; looks just like *we* eat.
Do writing every day?
Where do you get jigsaw puzzles—good, well-fitting ones (not lousy cardboard type)—more than fifteen pieces?

November 8, 1967 re-evaluation IAHP: Profile Level: same.

More attention in manual activities. Bimanual tests are O.K.

From November 8, 1967 to March 26, 1968 (*Note:* 1/16/68 appointment cancelled.):

No program 11/15/67 to 12/26/67. (Impetigo from possible strep infection.)
Eats with fork beautifully, including lunch on tray on floor.
Sewing cards and bead-stringing again—likes it.
Writing is continuous scribble circles, for the purpose of holding up to light to see writing from blank side.
Left chalk and chalkboard on floor, as well as Magic Marker and pad: rarely touches any of it.

March 26, 1968 re-evaluation IAHP: Profile Level: same.

Uses hands together well—dislikes using pencil.

From March 28, 1968 to June 28, 1968:

Circles, straight lines, and faces on foggy car windows.
All this and some other drawings on woodwork, walls, and furniture of her bedroom, using colored chalks and crayons.

June 28, 1968 re-evaluation IAHP: Profile Level: same.

Continued improvement in dexterity, but not writing as yet.
Dominance [hand]: mixed—right.

From June 28, 1968 to October 1, 1968:

A little drawing on smoked windows and sand and paper; scribbles continuous circles and individual straight lines. (No program, just spontaneous).
Did lots of pouring this summer.
Where do you get good puzzles like IAHP has?

Can button and buckle very well. (Does not wear shoes, so I have not attempted ties yet.)

October 1, 1968 re-evaluation IAHP: Profile Level: same (VI).

Tests for Level VII:

Writes	R	Threads	—
Eats	R	Files	R
Screws	R	Combs	R
Unscrews	R	Cuts	R
Throws	—	Pencil Grasp	R
Spins	R		

Makes circles and lines. Some attention span for writing. (Jane attempted to copy *c a t.*)
Level VI:
   Buttons well—assist with right hand today.
   Screws and unscrews well.
Dominance [hand]: right.

From October 1, 1968 to February 18, 1969 (12/12/68 evaluation not done because of hip injury in fall night before):

Hallelujah. She's writing and is interested! Went through these progressions since December, after teacher's 12/12/68 School Report. Teacher gave job of writing to me.
   a. Circles: much better eye-following of hand.
   b. Swings of circular motion from one side of blackboard or paper to right corner. Also reverse (from bottom of board to upper left corner). Also *u*'s touching top and bottom edges. This with water on brush, then paints (psychedelic great), then pencil. Also this period got her started with Platt-Munk books—colors in pictures come forth when water is brushed on.
   c. Quick small lines: straight and circular—in start-and-stop motions.
   d. Numbers 1, 11, 7, 4 (for 4's, I have to say "cross it").
   e. 2, 5, 9.
Winds wristwatch each day.
Does cortical opposition practice each day with crawl-box counting routine, transferring marbles, pennies, discs, shells, pegs, etc.
See School Report 2/69 (p. 257) regarding writing numbers in school.

February 18, 1969 re-evaluation IAHP: Profile Level: same.
From February 18, 1969 to May 7, 1969:

Biggest spurt in writing. (See School Report this period, p. 270.)
Closes circles well. Stays on lines. (See Visual this period.)
Afternoon teens guiding her hand during crawl-box "breaks": letters on slate. Also have her feel letters on glitter cards. Jane loves all this.

May 7, 1969 re-evaluation IAHP: Profile Level: same.
From May 7, 1969 to July 23, 1969:

Gym bar program: Can now do fine fingertip grasp (ledge grasp); also can readjust hold before she slips completely.

Writing: coming now, but still no spontaneous "words."

    a. Geometric shapes (square, circle, rectangle, triangle) and vertical lines and curves of all kinds on slate. (J. very perfectionist about closing top of triangle, corners, etc., almost too much so (goes back and draws over a micrometer of space between.)

    b. All ABC's first on blackboard, then went to lines, but not much drilling, leave it up to J. Leave the lined paper nearby, etc. Loves to practice favorite letters, like *k,* over and over; if gets any part of it wrong as to perfect vertical or slant or connect; erases immediately and starts again.

    c. Has these errors:

        makes three loops in *m.*

        b—not lo (but *b*)—jumping ahead.

        f — l, − , ⌐

        p and *q* mixed up.

        s—starts too low in space provided and gets frustrated.

        x—vertical plus a diagonal.

        all verticals too long, no stop control.

    d. See "Writing" in School Report this period (p. 275).

July 23, 1969 re-evaluation IAHP: Profile Level: same.
From July 23, 1969 to November 4, 1969:

Program:

    a. Hands extremely strong; can maintain grasp and re-graspings for at least one minute on gym bar (likes to swing body).

    b. Hands very calloused from wooden overhead ladder assist.

    c. Hands flat and pointed out for good stance in elephant walk (plantigrade locomotion).

    d. Hands flat beside face for somersault push.

School: since October 1 (approximately) finer workout for right hand:

    a. Crayons—for the first time (interest). Also colored pencils. Cannot stay within the lines. Need lots of use? No time in day for practice.

    b. Writing—mostly numbers.

    c. Workbooks: checking, circling, underlining, numbers, etc.

    d. Scissors, glue—just a little. (Teacher: How do you teach scissors?)

    e. Hand stapler—paper chains, etc.

    f. Better pencil control.

November 4, 1969 re-evaluation IAHP: Profile Level: same.
From November 4, 1969 to January 28, 1970:

Finer abilities in right hand:

    a. Zips up back of her dresses; good left-hand assist.

    b. Small snaps, buttons, and loops on Barbie doll clothes.

    c. Small buckles on Mary Jane shoes (new).

    d. School: hand stapler interest and ability.

No writing! Won't perform in drawing very much either; teacher says interested but "can't or something." (See School Report this period (p. 319)—obsolete by re-evaluation day.)

January 28, 1970 re-evaluation IAHP: Profile Level: same.
From January 28, 1970 to April 30, 1970:

Wants no help with any part of getting dressed, including changing wet pants and holding her coat for her. (Has been dressing herself for years, since she became bimanual, but would let you assist her for speed reasons.) Even wants to comb her own hair now.

Finds excuses to hang from gym bar by right hand only (switches on kitchen light around the corner, pulls her shirt down, etc.)

Cutting paper on prescribed lines in school.

Some writing, drawing in school the last month. (Before, J. most interested in stories she dictated to teacher about herself, her environment; so school's emphasis was those readings—self-made book, etc. Now speech hang-up prevents all that. See School Report this period (p. 328)—obsolete before the coming re-evaluation.)

April 30, 1970 re-evaluation IAHP: Profile Level: same.
From April 30, 1970 to September 8, 1970:

Can lace new orthopedic "boots" correctly (from observation of our lacings), but no such attempt at ties yet.

Occasionally writes her name spontaneously.

September 8, 1970 re-evaluation IAHP: Profile Level: same.
From September 8, 1970 to December 9, 1970:

No spontaneous writing, no interest yet. Teacher and I are saying now, "You are *learning* to write," so now J. tries writing without so much frustration. Script: large and uneven, but good spacing and line sense.

Drawing: more interest.

Painted her own Christmas tree decorations (Creative Playthings kit: wooden stamp-outs) and hung them on her tree (for programers). At my suggestion, painted caps, mittens, buttons, stripes, etc. on figures. Loved this.

Finger-counting interest spontaneously.

"Discovered" inside of nose and ears, abdomen under pants: "checking this out" all the time. Also started twirling her hair between index and third finger, right hand.

December 9, 1970 re-evaluation IAHP: Profile Level: same.
From December 9, 1970 to March 9, 1971:

Spontaneous writing! Sentences, of all things! "Jane likes P.J." (new doll). Wrote on oaktag strip, then cut apart and placed into sentence-builder molding strip across back of desk (as the teacher does). Then wrote "Mom" and substituted for "Jane." "Now it says, 'Mom likes P.J.' "

For three weeks much interest in writing her own simple sentences; interest waning now. (See School Report this period, p. 361.) Discovered with this that J. knew how to spell a lot of words. Just before "writing" commenced, J. had taken a great interest in word formation, the teacher's emphasis the month before the January 22 first sentence. Problem: J.'s writing output is not up to "thoughts" in sentences, so when teacher asks for this original output, J. writes the easiest sentence possible: "P.J. is O.K.," "Barbie is bad," "A pan is not a pot," which she can spell easily. Can spell by sound though: *blond*, etc.

Handedness: Left hand used a lot for first time in J.'s "preference" last two to three weeks. Also seen in puzzles, scissoring. With new or very fine-fingered stuff, left may start but transfer is made to right hand, as finer need is realized. Holding fork with right hand, but finger-feeding out of dish with left hand. All this is on and off. One week in school she used left hand only. Teacher has been discussing "left and right," so maybe this is a kind of cortical think-and-do tryout of all that.

March 9, 1971 re-evaluation IAHP: Profile Level: same.
From March 9, 1971 to June 2, 1971:

Almost no writing in school except special occasion, because teacher spending all time on reading.

Teacher said last week I should put crayons and coloring books at J.'s disposal; noticed she's coloring better (stronger, within lines better, etc.).

Using left hand a lot. Reaches with left across to right side to pick up words to be placed on "game" boards for reading. I suggested, as a test, teacher place some words on left, some on right of board. She did. The next move J. made was to use right hand to reach across to left side! Often eats for awhile with left hand, then changes to right as before. Before, she has always been right-handed.

June 2, 1971 re-evaluation IAHP: Profile Level: same.
From June 2, 1971 to April 6, 1972 (No full re-evaluations this period; see Mobility this period):

Will do writing willingly, but not any kind of main interest: short pieces, sentences, cards, occasions. Enjoyed signing and addressing and writing "thanks" or "thank you" on cards with Thanksgiving fruit baskets she filled for programers.

Occasionally we find on her school desk some spontaneous thing, sentence or part sentence or simple drawing she does before getting into bed.

Continuous left-hand use for about three weeks in January. Teacher noted in school during that period her left hand was used for all fine-motor: scissoring, paper clips (new), thumbtacks (new), page-turning, all puzzle pieces, etc. Just before that three-week period Jane, especially with crayoning, was switching hands in studied confusion, as if thoughtfully seeing which would give better performance; but would "decide" right. For example, cutting a heart out: much ambivalence with distinct pauses, then going to right. I noticed too she was reaching and eating with her left hand. Teacher says on certain days now, J. is more left than right; never knows when, just comes and goes. (Could this be (a) her extremely bilateral program; or (b) teacher's talking about "left" and "right" in concepts this school year; or (c) our talking a lot about her left and right feet and legs in program? That Jane is now checking all this out with cortical think-and-do?)

April 6, 1972 re-evaluation IAHP: Profile Level: same.

When asked to write today, Jane wrote "I love Jane," but staff person dictated these words to her, since she seemed to want (need) a suggestion.

Development of Visual Competence

January 25, 1965 initial evaluation: The New York Hospital (by Mary Lawrence, RPT): Doman-Delacato Developmental Profile Level: III marked "poor."

. . . She has a good light reflex and beginning depth perception. She has an alternating strabismus which she controls on attention to a convergence of two inches. . . . [She] cannot differentiate similar but unlike simple objects.

From February 14, 1965 to May 1, 1965:

Blinking of eyes, squinching of face.

Practicing eye-head movements horizontally and vertically (head moves, eyes don't, and vice versa).

Eye-following "practices": rolling checkers, etc.; hand-brushing or toy-brushing alongside of body while prone, watching.

Looking at fingers through clear, opaque, and screen material.

Looking at light through colored cellophane.

Looks at mom's mouth for language during auditory program (objects behind mom's back).

Knows edges of patterning table, no fright now on table.

Notices lights outside car at night.

Seeing depth—third dimension: light switch, doorknob, glasses on faces, lifts up dresses, opens blouses on people, white button on white blouse.

Shows attention now—really looks and watches.

May 1, 1965 re-evaluation by Mary Lawrence: Profile Level: V marked "poor"; with IV "out" (strabismus).

Visually she uses her eyes together much better but still has difficulty in the lateral gaze. She has an alternating convergent strabismus but much less pronounced than in the original examination.

From May 1, 1965 to June 22, 1965:

No program for two to three weeks (mother's illness).

More alert look.

Strabismus less frequent?

Crosses eyes voluntarily (new eye practice).

Lots of mirror-play with eyes.

New interest in walls, doors, trees she passes.

Attends to pictures (same size as object, outline only).
Selects pictures on command (five).

June 22, 1965 re-evaluation by Mary Lawrence: Profile Level: V is still "poor"; with IV from "out" to "poor."

Her visual-symbol identification is poor; strabismus continues to improve.

From June 22, 1965 to September 2, 1965:

Looking at picture books and family photographs.
Makes edges flush in block tower and choo-choo train of blocks.
Noticing small pictures on side of blocks.
Increased attention span!
Makes "eyes," faces; plays peekaboo. More awareness of brothers, their fun, etc. (See Auditory Competence this period.)
Lots of mirror-play on floor; examining inside of mouth and eye movements.

September 2, 1965 re-evaluation by Mary Lawrence: Profile Level: V O.K. now; with IV still at "poor."

Her eyes seem to focus together over 50 percent of the time and I hope the problem is one of left internal strabismus and that there is no suppression of vision in that eye. She is able to optically pursue into all visual areas.

October 25, 1965 initial evaluation IAHP: Profile Level: V (as reported above); with IV "out" (strabismus is more than 50 percent of the time).

Left convergent strabismus.
Dominance [eye]: not observable [none].

From October 28, 1965 to February 8, 1966:

Very little program this period.
Gaze still improving.
Better control of fusion.
Voluntary eye-crossing a lot (noticing own nose?).
Examines two sides of a penny, new interest.
Reads eight words but disinterested (or my disinterest!).

February 8, 1966 re-evaluation IAHP: Profile Level: VI (Reading); with IV from "out" to "poor" (strabismus is less than 50 percent of the time).

Mild left convergent strabismus persists but control has improved. Child is reading for the first time.
Dominance [eye]: midline to right.

From February 8, 1966 to June 1, 1966:

Distinguishing people (recognizes patterners).
Looks out of car windows now.
Gaze still improving.

Eye-head movement with following the shadows from blinking Christmas tree lights.

Distinguishes doll parts.

Differentiates shapes before slotting into sorting box.

June 1, 1966 re-evaluation IAHP: Profile Level: VII marked "poor"; with IV still at "poor."

Convergence continues to improve as does visual attention and appreciation.

Reading—progressing well.

Dominance [eye]: right.

From June 1, 1966 to October 18, 1966:

Reading seventy-plus words, one per day, could do more; gets *car* and *ear, nose* and *house* confused.

Crossed eye is *right* one now, as well as left? Eyes look worse somehow (something is changed).

October 18, 1966 re-evaluation IAHP: Profile Level: same.

Mild right convergent strabismus. Reading progressing well.

Dominance: same [right].

From October 18, 1966 to January 3, 1967:

Reading three new words a day—loves it.

Reading over one hundred words (says all, easier to test now).

Loves books, catalogues, calendars.

Visit to ophthalmologist: (a) 20/60 both eyes at least (no check each eye); (b) alternating strabismus; (c) saw Jane fuse, said will never get beyond first fusion—"something missing at birth"; (d) "very impressed with this young lady."

January 3, 1967 re-evaluation IAHP: Profile Level: same.

Visual convergence remains poor. Reading going very well . . . over one hundred words now.

Dominance: mixed to left.

From January 3, 1967 to June 12, 1967:

No program for three months from 1/7/67 to 3/30/67: convalescence from burn injury.

All day during convalescence looked at *National Geographic, Natural History,* catalogues, sometimes eight continuous hours; wanted no other toys, etc. in bed! (Incredible, but had favorite *Geographics* she wished to keep awhile longer, the others were O.K. to put back. Could determine which simply by flicking through the pages, and in a second or two either keep or give back. Seemed to know them intimately after one run-through. Some of them

so loved she preferred to keep them beside her bed even while sleeping at
night!)

Reviewed reading words at end of program hiatus—excellent retention; missed
less than ten out of one hundred!

Now making reading cards with two-inch red letters, down from three-inch.

Visual distance and/or association: sees orange roof of Howard Johnson's a
mile away and says "hamburger"; sees other orange roof and says
"Wetson's."

Wooden picture-and-reading puzzles from Creative Playthings: reads all
words in "Boy," "Girl," and "Bedroom" ones—one-quarter inch print!

June 12, 1967 re-evaluation IAHP: Profile Level: same.

Mild alternating convergent strabismus persists. Horizontal following remains unsmooth. Reading going well—learning a word a day.
Dominance: mixed.

From June 12, 1967 to September 6, 1967:

Reading 150 words.

100% Retention	No. of Nouns
Body words	11
Names	8
Toys	8
Tools	2
Clothing, accessories	16
Animals	6
Vehicles and buildings	9
Bathroom	6
Food	27
Furniture	11
Nature and yard	9
Dishes, utensils	5
Fabrics	5
	123

Eyes: kooky with fatigue; kooky with swing.

Distance: Jane looks outside the car. Watches lines change on highway.

Books—favorite "hobby."

Loves *National Geographic* magazine.

Still likes catalogues—busiest pages with lots of small pictures.

Saw East Room's brocade love seat in "White House" article in *Geographic*
magazine and said, "Bo-cade!"

September 6, 1967 re-evaluation IAHP: Profile Level: same.

Convergence remains graded poor—parents note that eyes cosmetically better
for longer periods. Reads approximately 150 words.
Dominance: near point, left; far point, right.

From September 6, 1967 to November 8, 1967:

Reading 170 for sure, forty new words.

Placing new word with object on floor where she will see it now; no auditory feed-in necessary.

Still likes books, especially Sears catalogues, for free-time play.

Can go to one-inch letters now? (No, tends to myopia.)

November 8, 1967 re-evaluation IAHP: Profile Level: same.

Alternate convergent strabismus at six to eight inches. Good control to far point. Movements are smoother. Refused reading test.

Dominance: right.

From November 8, 1967 to March 26, 1968: (*Note:* 1/16/68 appointment cancelled.)

No program from 11/15/67 to 12/26/67. (Impetigo from possible strep infection.)

Reading sentences one-inch letters; no "test" yet, but very interested; take away quickly homemade book with new page each day (J. not allowed to play with it in between); use cover card as she proceeds from left to right.

No attention to one-inch black words on floor (with object).

Left-to-right-drop-down-to-next-line practice going nicely with Judy Company's See-Quees sequence boards: "Birthday Party" and "Three Little Pigs."

Also am giving her opportunity to fill left-to-right candy boxes, egg cartons, etc.; also give her cookie pieces and snacks in left-to-right "line."

Catalogues, *National Geographic* interest still strong, but now wanting "action" books, pictures with people in situations.

March 26, 1968 re-evaluation IAHP: Profile Level: same.

Strabismus persists. Pursuits are improved. Does well with attention. Reads several short sentences.

Dominance: near point, right; far point, left.

From March 26, 1968 to June 28, 1968:

Very little visual program this period.

Eyes still a problem (crossing) when looking at a distance.

June 28, 1968 re-evaluation IAHP: Profile Level: same.

Alternate convergent strabismus persists . . . about the same. Mother is working on sentences and doing well.

Dominance: same.

From June 28, 1968 to October 1, 1968:

Did full visual program every day.

    a. Basic vision (dilation and contraction of pupil): fifteen times per eye, six sessions a day.

    b. Pons (visual pursuit of object with alternate occlusion of eyes): ten times per eye, two sessions a day.

    c. Midbrain (visual pursuit of object with eyes working in concert): five times, two sessions a day.

    d. Same as above, with mother guiding hand (J. holds object).

Strabismus is better; never see one eye go toward nose for near point; still crossed to see across room.

"Reading along" with sentences, otherwise no "reading program"; homemade books with pictures on separate pages (eight to twelve sentences in each book): "A Book About Jane"; "Jane Has Two Boats"; "Pail and Shovel"; "Bye-Bye Butterfly"; "The Beach"; "Number Book"; two books about colors.

I think eye-hand coordination is better.

October 1, 1968 re-evaluation IAHP: Profile Level: same.

Has a tendency for alternate convergent strabismus, but less. Very good control. Good pursuits.

From October 1, 1968 to February 18, 1969 (12/12/68 evaluation not done because of hip injury in fall the night before):

See School Reports by home-instructor 12/12/68 (p. 248) and 2/69 (p. 257).

Strabismus worse (distance), I think. Does the fact that creeping program was reduced to one and one-half hours a day bear on this?

Reading every number she can find, especially loves to find ones in *very* tiny print: chewing-gum wrappers, page numbers in tiny books of Cracker-Jacks box variety!

Anticipates visual pursuits.

Tremors with flashlight with basic-vision exercise.

Doing eye-hand visual pursuits poorly even with hand guided.

Eye-hand (See Manual Competence, writing).

Reads numbers and letters outside car now.

With bad tremors November and December, she'd try to copy shaky eye movements after involuntary movements stopped. (Likes it? or trying to reconfirm it?)

Teacher sees tremors sometimes toward end of intense visual concentration (end of school session).

February 18, 1969 re-evaluation IAHP: Profile Level: same.
From February 18, 1969 to May 7, 1969:

See School Report by home-instructor May 1969 (p. 270).

Strabismus at far point looks worse?

Starting to tell time. (See Auditory Competence, "abstract concepts" this period.)

Starting to read full sentences *orally* (teacher's requirement).

Good visual attention with writing.

May 7, 1969 re-evaluation IAHP: Profile Level: same.
From May 7, 1969 to July 23, 1969:

No visual program; no creeping.

With first days of new program, eyes very kooky as if in dizziness; called
IAHP. Said would clear in two or three weeks, result of gravity work most
likely. It did.

See School Report by home-instruction 6/4/69 (p. 275).

July 23, 1969 re-evaluation IAHP: Profile Level: same.
From July 23, 1969 to November 4, 1969:

New sequence program involves no specific visual programs.

See School Report by home-instructor 11/3/69 (p. 306).

Reading: very little except some review by teacher and some use with
stethoscope-talking. Seems to have an excellent retention visually; at beginning of school, turned immediately to particular pages of old books to
read orally the sentences she had struggled over to speak.

Strabismus at far point during August and September, the worst eyes *ever*
looked. (Eye turned in longer time, more definitely "there.") In October
teacher said hasn't seen crossed eyes in school for weeks. Last Tuesday
programer (here since beginning) said eyes prettiest, clearest, most alert
ever saw them. They are!

November 4, 1969 re-evaluation IAHP: Profile Level: same.
From November 4, 1969 to January 28, 1970:

Getting nearsighted? (Since both her parents are, I bet!) Squints to see across
the room when looking for particular object. Squints other times.

Some dizziness returned with spinning in saucer sled.

Picture-reading in stethoscope-talking program excellent. Knows everything
in "pictionary books." Now using Scarry's *Best Word Book Ever* (and it
is!). Everyone amazed at J.'s "visual knowledge." Sometimes looks at word
when isn't sure of picture. With new pictures, we give phonetic hint and
point to word.

Until this week (See Language hang-ups this period; See School Report this
period (p. 319)—obsolete by re-evaluation day) J. not able to perform in
three R's, but attention the best it has ever been! Called IAHP 11/21/69:
gave Jane week-to-ten-day "vacation," but problems persisted. Therefore,
school mostly auditory feed-in by teacher; no visual requirements.

January 28, 1970 re-evaluation IAHP: Profile Level: same.
From January 28, 1970 to April 30, 1970:

Strabismus more pronounced, more frequent than when on crawl-creep program, everyone commenting. Sometimes the clearest! (Maybe near point
versus far point good and bad.)

Reading: word-interest rather than picture-interest in school now. (This may
be auditory, because J.'s still not measurable for reading except orally—
this teacher's requirement since the beginning.)

See School Report this period (p. 328)—obsolete by re-evaluation day.
Hiding eyes behind hands or closing eyes a little after hanging by heels at
   two and a half-minute mark and higher.

April 30, 1970 re-evaluation IAHP: Profile Level: same.
From April 30, 1970 to September 8, 1970:

Never see eyes crossed except with extreme fatigue once in a while.

September 8, 1970 re-evaluation IAHP: Profile Level: same.
From September 8, 1970 to December 9, 1970:

Nearsighted? Head back, looking down cheeks to watch Macy's Thanksgiving
   Parade on TV.
Eyes crossed again, not as good as they were last summer.
Problem keeping in lines in coloring. (Not much practice; should do a lot
   to get good?)
No School Report this period (teacher on vacation week before re-evaluation
   day).
Does simple addition and subtraction facts. (See Auditory, "concepts" this
   period.)
Eye-hand use in spinner-type pathway games.

December 9, 1970 re-evaluation IAHP: Profile Level: same.
From December 9, 1970 to March 9, 1971:

True Reading: See School Report this period (p. 361).
Sentence-writing shows good spacing horizontally between words and words
   centered well in middle of paper strip or on line. (No spatial orientation
   aberrations apparently.)
No reversals in writing; spelling accurate for simple words she uses.
Strabismus no better. Think far-point difficulties are influenced by nearsightedness; will make appointment for eye checkup—finally.
More discrimination out of windows: steeples, bell towers, flags, poles, roof
   lines, churches, schoolhouses, etc. Reflected in picture-finding of all this.
Jane's visual (auditory too?) memory so superior, teacher cannot use same
   written materials (workbooks, lists, matching boards, reading puzzles)
   after a couple of times. Will have pages memorized by page numbers, so
   must use homemade books (e.g., "Jane Likes Christmas Trees," "Jane
   Likes Birthday Cakes," "Presents," "Spring," "Jane Is Learning to Walk,"
   etc.). Can know one key word on page and read off the sentence(s) without
   looking. This makes all written material practically useless immediately.
Started homework assignments after supper for word review and other
   "dull" reinforcement, since teacher does not like to spend school time
   having J. finish this book, then that book, etc. Uses homemade books in
   holistic way—for total communication—e.g., birthday concepts, lists for
   your party, address your own invitations. With same words reappearing,
   J. learns to read those. So J. does vocabulary and sentence review, math

workbook "pages" at night occasionally, when needed. (J. started keeping English and math notebooks first of this school year.)

March 9, 1971 re-evaluation IAHP: Profile Level: same.
From March 9, 1971 to June 2, 1971:

Appointment made for June 11, to have J.'s eyes checked for nearsightedness. (Wants to wear mother's prescription glasses at Little League ball games— looks all around to see trees, etc.)
Very little visual program this period—my error.
See School Report this period (p. 408).

June 2, 1971 re-evaluation IAHP: Profile Level: same.
From June 2, 1971 to April 6, 1972 (No full re-evaluations this period. See Mobility this period.):

See School Report this period (p. 413).
J.'s nearsightedness corrected with glasses from 20/400 to 20/40, June 11, 1971. (Her eyes are same as mine without glasses.)
Degree of strabismus with glasses: six degrees.
Degree of strabismus without glasses: twenty-two degrees.
With glasses, J. does not look crossed-eyed most of the time; still see strabismus occasionally; shows in flash-bulb photos.
Gaze still not "perfect," even without strabismus showing.
Wears glasses all day since the day she got them, happy as a lark with everything in sight. (Should have had them long before.)

April 6, 1972 re-evaluation IAHP: (First full re-evaluation since June 2, 1971); Profile Level: same.

Development of Auditory Competence

January 25, 1965 initial evaluation: The New York Hospital (by Mary Lawrence, RPT): Doman-Delacato Developmental Profile Level: III.

. . . She has no startle reflex; responds to her mother's and father's voices; knows the difference between sweet talk and scolding. She does not understand spoken words or follow directions . . . extremely hyperactive . . . three-year-old . . . involved in nothing constructive or meaningful. . . .

From February 14, 1965 to May 1, 1965:

Covers ears with hands or with insides of upper arms (especially during auditory program).

She really "listens" for word now in auditory program.

Reacts to music with swaying and covering of ears.

Hears and shows great interest in echoes.

Reacts to family arguments, crying.

Listens to sound differences in floor-play: things tapped or banged on wood, slate, brick, metal, screen, rug (none!), etc.

Attends to front door opening now.

Listens for "z-z-z-," "woof-woof," "fee-fie-fo," and rhyme sounds; reacts pleasurably.

Knows word-substitutions in songs now (likes the idea and gets it).

Understands functions of these objects: hat, brush, shoe, sock, purse, book, paper, pencil, cup, eye glasses, spoon, telephone, ball.

Understands at least twenty-five words of speech now (chooses objects correctly in Auditory Program).

Understands teasing, "controlling" the situation, doing "wrong."

Decrease in fearfulness.

May 1, 1965 re-evaluation by Mary Lawrence: Profile Level: V marked "poor."

. . . She understands over twenty-five words of speech and is beginning to comprehend two-word couplets. . . . Her attention span has increased significantly as well as attempts to communicate her wishes.

From May 1, 1965 to June 22, 1965:

No program for two to three weeks (mother's illness).

Understands words for all objects and toys in day's routine.

Understands other words: *bath, eat, bottle, water, bye-bye, game, puzzle, cookie, no-no, Daddy, tongue, nose, ear, finger.*
Associates picture with fruit-puzzle names: *orange, apple, berry, banana, grapes.*
Understands couplet and follows this command: "Get the ball."
Responds to discipline of no-no variety.

June 22, 1965 re-evaluation by Mary Lawrence: Profile Level: same.

. . . Word understanding is slightly better but certainly not outstanding. . . .

From June 22, 1965 to September 2, 1965:

Tests us now by cutting up.
Understands function of language!
Knows "echo" in playroom.
Seems to hear words better.
Understands these body words now maybe: *arm, foot, hand, hair.*
Understands these furniture words now maybe: *chair, table, door, floor.*
Understands these commands and follows these simple directions:
    Go get it—Lie down—Sit down—Turn over—Turn it—Push it—Twist it—
    Open the door—Close the door—Give the ——— to Mommy—Brush
    (kitty or dog picture)—Pat—Kiss—Give yum-yum to (feed kitty or dog
    picture).
Understands more than fifty new words, including "Ma-ma" and "Jane."
Makes "eyes," faces; plays peekaboo.
More awareness of brothers, their fun, etc.

September 2, 1965 re-evaluation by Mary Lawrence: Profile Level: V O.K. now.

. . . She seems to understand well commands which are spoken to her in a conversational tone and without repetition. Her attention span increases constantly . . . enjoys puzzle work . . . she asks for what she wants with much less erratic hyperactivity; I am encouraged with her gains.

October 25, 1965 initial evaluation IAHP: Profile Level: V, with I marked "persists mildly."

Startle reflex persists mildly.
Dominance [ear]: not observable.

From October 28, 1965 to February 8, 1966:

Misses music? Hums "Ring Around the Rosy" a lot.
Moves head frantically left to right with sound-effects records, vacuum
    cleaner, machines.
Responds to sounds in next room (anticipates patterners coming from play-
    room to living room, much pleasure this gives).
"Listens" to her own jargon, repeats the same inflection again.

Understands so much more now.

Beginning to understand "deal" concept (make a bargain): you do this now, then we'll do that later; when you finish this . . .

Beginning some role-playing with doll and teddy bear, plays with them.

Feelings get hurt very easily if said no to or talked harshly to (Sarah Heartburn act).

Loves to slam doors; would do it all day if allowed.

February 8, 1966 re-evaluation IAHP: Profile Level: VI marked "poor"; with I still marked "mild."

Comprehension has improved. . . . Affect: more aware of her environment. . . . Dominance [ear]: not observable.

From February 8, 1966 to June 1, 1966:

Attends to people and their fun more, plays with programers.

Attends to repetitious spots in nursery rhymes and talking record.

Attends to sounds outside house: airplanes, trucks.

Covers ears alternately against floor and shakes head when vacuum cleaner is on, looks weird, but wants it *on* not off.

Very *involved* reaction to family arguments, crying: she begins to cry too.

June 1, 1966 re-evaluation IAHP: Profile Level: same.

[Auditory competence] continues to increase. Poor time concept. Mild startle reflex (persists).

Dominance [ear]: not observable.

From June 1, 1966 to October 18, 1966:

Very interested in tape of nouns (same as reading nouns to be covered), says some words while listening.

Understands most everything in experience.

Never misses airplane, train in distance.

Can make a deal: understands "When finished, then you may have (do) ———."

Sings (with intense interest) a little of "Ring Around the Rosy" (no lyrics).

Goes wild if hears this song (a second or two of it); otherwise, has no music in life.

Continuously makes *ooh-e-i-o-ooh* sounds and "ha, ha, ho, ho." (Boredom? Don't think so, since does this during free [creep] time when so busy having fun.)

Spent rainy-day creep time in Maine going in and out of banging screen door to porch; loves noise like this, also creeping with loafers on hands on bare wooden floor (for tap-tap sounds, I think.)

October 18, 1966 re-evaluation IAHP: Profile Level: same.

Increasing understanding. Startle reflex normal today.

Dominance [ear]: not observable.

. . . good progress. I feel she is capable of doing better, however, if more discipline were exerted. [More requirements.]

From October 18, 1966 to January 3, 1967:

No tape (broken), but listens to sound-effects records a lot.
Using nursery rhymes instead of music during patterning: J. loves.
Is fascinated with new kitty's *purr-r-r-r*.

January 3, 1967 re-evaluation IAHP: Profile Level: same.

Auditory comprehension improved in attention and response.
Dominance [ear]: right.

From January 3, 1967 to June 12, 1967:

No program for three months from 1/7/67 to 3/30/67: convalescence from burn injury.
No tape program (broken).
Poor auditory program (little intake) this period.
Shows "earedness" for first time, to catch whispers, I think.
Understands everything; I don't think very much about "how" I'm going to say it.
No concept of yesterday, today, and tomorrow yet.
Making faces; lost in space—vocalizing.

June 12, 1967 re-evaluation IAHP: Profile Level: same.

Comprehension improving in terms of basic concepts and reasoning.
Dominance [ear]: mixed to right.

From June 12, 1967 to September 6, 1967:

Played tape every day—loves it. (Hates the intermittent silence, wants it played again immediately, but understands "waiting period" now.) Reacts by laughing at times to its words.
Understanding—just everything! Talk to her very normally.
I started varying language on purpose so as to "feed in" higher verbs, enlarged vocabulary all around, etc.
Affect: lots of self-identity within increased grasp of surroundings; sizes up situation. More like a person to play with, not a baby blob any longer, says Dizzy.
Role-playing with furniture and houses (has three different kinds); puts furniture into appropriate room, likes wooden or rubber families to add to all this, especially tiny baby doll who can sit on furniture, lie in bed, bath, etc.

September 6, 1967 re-evaluation IAHP: Profile Level: same.

Comprehension expanding in terms of increased alertness and response.
Dominance [ear]: same.

From September 6, 1967 to November 8, 1967:

> *Loves* tape. Second day of new tape, knew "World Series" signaled end of it. Asking for it to be replayed *before* it stops.
>
> We vary words in nursery rhymes during patterning, and she "catches" it. Door-banging stage—again.
>
> Understanding is better and better.

November 8, 1967 re-evaluation IAHP: Profile Level: same.

> Follows conversation to some degree. Difficult to accurately assess.

From November 8, 1967 to March 26, 1968 (*Note:* 1/16/68 appointment cancelled):

> No program from 11/15/67 to 12/26/67: Impetigo (from possible strep infection).
>
> Understands some of conversation of patterners—perhaps is able to follow all of some conversations (at least is trying).
>
> Understands "counting" concept.
>
> Understands "tomorrow" (like "later" to her?), maybe "today," but not "yesterday" for sure.
>
> Swings head left and right during vacuum cleaning in a weird sort of fascination; positions herself directly over it, or lies down beside it and covers first one ear and then the other against the carpet.
>
> Listens to two or three Golden Book-size twenty-nine-cent stories at a sitting.
>
> No nursery rhymes (see program) during patterning, but likes our counting loud and soft; also our "very soft"—whispering; also silence *then* talk.
>
> Listens some to patterners' conversation.
>
> No music, except at supermarket, doctor's office, etc.
>
> For the first time follows more than one command in a series: "Why don't you get your blocks (large cardboard) and go find your doll and baby blanket and make a bed and put your dolly to sleep?"

March 26, 1968 re-evaluation IAHP: Profile Level: same.

> Understanding of some conversation . . . many requests . . . deals, etc. . . . colors.
>
> Dominance [ear]: right.
>
> . . . Attention span continues to be the main problem. [Too long!] Quality of understanding appears much improved.

From March 26, 1968 to June 28, 1968:

> Patterning was changed at March 26, 1968 re-evaluation from cross pattern to homolateral (from midbrain back to pons function).
>
> Level of understanding is higher!
>
> May understand "tomorrow" and "today." No response to "yesterday."
>
> Able to follow series of "Bring me—" or "Go do—" commands; have been doing this with her for practice, for the fun of it.

June 28, 1968 re-evaluation IAHP: Profile Level: same.

Improved comprehension, but restricted by the fact that she will only work for mother.

Dominance [ear]: mixed to right.

From June 28, 1968 to October 1, 1968:

Even better! Now she's hearing stuff she's not supposed to hear; wants to do things she has overheard, so have to spell a lot. Eavesdrops on adults' conversation.

Likes tapes very, very much; listens as intently to new ones as to old ones, more maybe, because she's asking for new ones (says words).

During patterning, started feeding-in verbs in game-ways; loves this.

Knows colors, shades of colors (learning now).

Interested in counting, numbers.

Short *e* and short *i* vowels are said better.

Less hyperactive. Activity is more directed.

October 1, 1968 re-evaluation IAHP: Profile Level: same.

Has sense of time but not sure that she has concept of today, tomorrow, or yesterday . . . Colors okay . . . Categories: animal but not vegetable or fruit . . . Recognizes 1, 2, 3. Maybe some after . . . No response to groups . . . Right and left—no . . . Startle reflex: mild.

From October 1, 1968 to February 18, 1969 (12/12/68 evaluation not done because of hip injury in fall the night before):

See School Reports by home-instructor 12/12/68 and 2/69 (pp. 248, 257).

Teacher is now in charge. J. follows day's plan, etc., but there's a discipline problem with this. Teacher's ambivalent regarding this, because J.'s random speech and carryings-on tell her some stuff she didn't know, e.g., in trying to get J. to read the word *stands* in a sentence, J. screamed, "Not tens."

Found two talking records without music background: Carl Sandburg's "Poems for Children" and John Ciardi's "You Read to Me, I'll Read to You." Jane loves both.

Reintroduced "Talking Record for Girls"; J. answers questions about colors, but likes Sandburg and Ciardi records better.

Still do tapes too, but J. not as wild as before about them, prefers talking records, maybe because newer idea or newer people.

See School Report (p. 257) regarding phonetic beginning sounds. Since J. so interested in, knows all but *v*, so easy for her. Isn't this a good sign of much better auditory competence?

Last week, began better ending enunciation; practiced it over and over—ro*se*, fi*ve*, honeyco*mb*.

Using patterning time to change words (make "mistakes") in our conversation, etc.—J. loves all this. Also "teaching" informally *loud, soft, fast, slow,* etc. during this time—J. loves.

Abstract concepts:

> May know yesterday, today, tomorrow. Tested her with Christmas, Valentine's Day, two January birthdays (hers, peer), Philadelphia revisit.
>
> Days of the week: knows Sunday, Thursday, Monday, Saturday "associations" we set up: tomorrow is Sunday, what do you do? (She answers "New York City.") Monday—eat hot dogs, etc.
>
> One more concept? Not sure.
>
> What-comes-after in counting—knows beyond 100.
>
> Left-and-right labeling: feet maybe (I haven't done much with this).
>
> Categories: working on animals, fruits, vegetables, etc. (Lotto games helpful too.)
>
> When "test" J. at IAHP revisit next time "Which is more?" make less abstract? I suggest asking "five cookies or two cookies?" instead of "five or two."

February 18, 1969 re-evaluation IAHP: Profile Level: same.
From February 18, 1969 to May 7, 1969:

> See School Report by home-instructor May 1969 (p. 270).
>
> Allows whispers in both ears now; left ear took four weeks longer to accomplish.
>
> Loves talking into stethoscope.
>
> Overhears patterners' conversations in next room; becoming a real eavesdropper.
>
> No days-of-the-week program since February, but sure she knows Saturday, Sunday, Monday, Wednesday (orange wagon-ride night).
>
> Starting to understand telling time.
>
> Does J. have feedback delay problem? Is that why the stethoscope? Or does she use stethoscope for magnification of sound? Or both reasons?
>
> Are we doing whispering versus stethoscope to create big high-low differences (soft versus loud to make her attend more)?
>
> Stopped all nursery rhymes, poetry, everything possibly tonal; she accepted it all readily because she's so fond of stethoscope "toy."

May 7, 1969 re-evaluation IAHP: Profile Level: same.
From May 7, 1969 to July 23, 1969:

> See School Report by home-instructor 6/4/69 (p. 275).
>
> Stethoscope-talking program sixteen times a day—from one minute each sequence to four minutes now.
>
> Lots of drumming, tapping (bilaterally: two hands, two feet, etc.).
>
> Whispering "environment" tried about June 1, then done seriously two weeks later and throughout this period, including whispering even during supper.
>
> Keeping very quiet house; patterners keeping silence.
>
> Phonetics: beginning and medial sounds during stethoscope program (June 15 to now), match-and-check wheels. *Pictionary, Listen to Learn* book, words in lists, etc.—all as material for stethoscope incentives. Jane going through all this very fast.

Behavior: very silly; "testing" authorities a lot; very playful, more planning of naughtiness, more directed with more perseverance. We are countering with higher requirements, ignoring "idiot behaviors," responding to "higher" behaviors only.

July 23, 1969 re-evaluation IAHP: Profile Level: same.
From July 23, 1969 to November 4, 1969:

See School Report by home-instructor 11/4/69 (p. 306).

Great push for consistent discipline by all who work the program.

Ignored idiot behavior, silliness; we watch our behavior for mimicking prevention.

Silent treatment very consistent until school started, have been lax in this since September.

Abstract concepts:

Opposites.

"Month" concept begun with October, changing to November, with red-letter Halloween day.

Talk about telling time occasionally, informally.

Ordinal numerals—*pf* for *th* at end of words, e.g., *twentiepf*.

Stethoscope forty times a day—one minute each sequence—till last ten days (called Delacato about this).

Speech clearer during stethoscope-talking program. Everyone commenting.

Muffles right ear during car rides (noise bothers her? maybe she's checking the on-and-off sound of car by covering that ear on and off, to confirm it?)

November 4, 1969 re-evaluation IAHP: Profile Level: same.

A marked difference was noted in today's evaluation in that attention and cooperation were markedly improved over previous visits here at The Institutes.

From November 4, 1969 to January 28, 1970:

See School Report this period (p. 319)—obsolete by re-evaluation day.

New interest in rhythmic, repeated banging: toy metal dish against wood, slamming glove-compartment door in car, pitching objects onto cabinet tops; intentionally "not looking," just "listening." Does all this with right ear toward sound (head to left). Still opens and closes doors *of all kinds* for banging effect, but this represents a "finer" banging of a sort for the first time.

No longer shakes head in rhythmic left-to-right head-turnings with vacuum cleaner. Vacuum cleaner doesn't seem to produce *any* reaction anymore.

Increased awareness of all preparatory sounds of mother leaving house, more generally aware of everybody's comings and goings—new where-ness concept, I call it.

Knows schedule of teen-age volunteers, who follows whom and on which days; also who works with whom (two in teams): when-ness?

Originates jokes in speech, substitution of number or name; huge laughs with these jokes. Who is coming next? J. answers: "Claudia and Grant." (Grant is not a programer.)

Much role-playing with houses, people, families, furniture.

Eavesdropping continues; laughs at jokes appropriately rather than old mimicking ways. Knows whenever we are talking about her, even though her name is "out." (For this reason, I wrote all notes down for re-evaluation, so Jane won't hear us talking about her. IAHP: Jane's the patient, *should* know we are talking about her.)

"Yesterday, today, and tomorrow": seems to get all this without confusion. Has never said those words though.

Likes whispering in her ear now. Good opportunity to feed in more sophisticated stuff by a lot of people: "I am going to the bank to cash a check." "I have a lot of math homework to do tonight." We do this two times each sequence for a total of sixty times a day.

Now takes stethoscope out of ears during the two minutes of program. Verbal reminder takes care of discipline here. Why? Has always loved stethoscope program.

January 28, 1970 re-evaluation: Profile Level: same.

. . . a definite improvement in responsiveness and language. . . .

From January 28, 1970 to April 30, 1970:

See School Report this period (p. 328)—obsolete by re-evaluation day.

Affect continues to increase. Role-play "favorite fun."

School field trips each Friday with teacher, one to two hours, involves village stores, community workers, money exchange, cash register, etc. J. is more eager to see the world than take the ride or eat out. J. hated first trip to a children's playground; wanted busier place such as department stores.

Uses concept of "today" in speech now. Said into wall phone (role-playing) "Coming here tomorrow," referring to grandmother's impending visit, but may be a repeat of our conversation.

Understands calendar concepts, knows Easter comes in March; might answer "April" re: Dad and brother's birthdays. Would correct you if said she took field trips on Tuesday.

Started singing (no lyrics) whole songs (nothing recognizable) since last revisit, involving highs and lows. This started end of February when speech hang-up started. (We ignore it.)

Voice practice: two weeks ago started wee voice and low, deep voice jargon.

More frustration regarding speech, wants, and permissions not granted. More mature (aware), less possibility of leading her. All of this is increased awareness, I suppose.

Might go into a tantrum with someone whom she thinks she can influence that way.

No misbehavior with teacher or mother or during sequences with programers who know her. Same with trips outside home, waiting rooms, etc. Depends on whom she's with, more than where.

April 30, 1970 re-evaluation IAHP: Profile Level: VI O.K. now.

Delacato: Jane could have finished Level VI auditory competence before now, but we wanted the speech to prove it.

From April 30, 1970 to September 8, 1970:

Abstract concepts:
days of the week—O.K.
months of the year—fair.
associates time with events, but not yet "telling time."

Awareness increasing by leaps and bounds, especially with regard to "self," as if she has a sense of self-*desire* with respect to walking, talking, keeping dry throughout day, what to wear, etc. Wants to wear hair long like teenagers and Barbie doll, I think.

Self-consciousness showing in frustration over speech, I think. Also when she's too much noticed, when she's very "center stage" in a situation.

Hyperactivity just about gone. Wondering if she, in fact, is no longer hypoauditory. Seems very tuned in to conversation. Gets a lot of talk we pitch "over her head" on purpose; it's increasingly difficult to keep anything from her. Wondering if she does not, in fact, understand *everything* she hears, including teen talk to teen, adult to adult.

Wants daddy for whole evening routine, including good-night story. Adores his rendition of *The Little Engine That Could.*

From September 8, 1970 to December 9, 1970:

No School Report this period (teacher on vacation the week before re-evaluation day).

Tremendous increase in affect—outside home, people interest.

Speech shows taking in everything.

Teacher says understanding great: calendar, time, tell about the story: J. often asks for "story," rather than "book" now, i.e., by plot instead of title.

Much interest in perfecting articulation (except blends, *th,* etc.).

Role-plays everything she hears (conversation night before, telephoning, etc.).

Now possible to discuss behavior, goals of program, etc. with her; responds well to the "higher requirement"—older girl behavior versus babyish behavior. No screaming or shrieking.

Interested in finer details of trains, etc.: tracks, signals, switches, function of cars, etc. (All this from car windows and books, as she has never ridden a train yet.)

December 9, 1970 re-evaluation IAHP: Profile Level: same.

From December 9, 1970 to March 9, 1971:

See School Report this period (p. 361).

Increased awareness, especially with regard to personal relationships: behavior, ethics, "theirs" and "mine." Results in role-playing all this with

dolls, with situations more sophisticated than before, especially involving
nuances of discipline and punishments. All is springboard for endless
fantasy and vocalizing during most of day. (This daydreaming was heretofore occasional; now it is all day.) All fantasy involves "groupness," three
or four voices in discussion or argument.

In school, did the above only one day and for most of the hour. Otherwise
never.

Likes bedtime stories of this level: *Wizard of Oz, Martin and Judy* series.
Raggedy Ann interest for a while, but waning now. Loves poetry; read
John Ciardi's to her because it makes more sense than rhyme (singsong).
Can attend to stories of full-page length without a single picture. Actually
will listen to anything with full attention the first time; but will tell you
no next time you suggest it if not a favorite; e.g., does not like animal
stories.

No undue interest in echoes, vacuum cleaners, etc. for full year now.

Seems to have an outstanding auditory memory, as well as a visual one.
Gets and retains new concepts without need for review, so teacher is now
able to talk in higher and higher concepts without as much visual reinforcement.

J. more like "all ears" these days instead of heretofore "all eyes". Very interested in what, where, when about people. See no "why" interest yet
though, no onset of "comparison" sense.

Developing quite a sense of humor, especially with respect to herself and
others in situations. (This is more sophisticated than earlier silliness, more
of the chuckle than laugh variety.)

Enjoys other people's mistakes, messes. Beginning to tolerate own mistakes.
Beginning to be messy herself; not so perfectionist anymore; e.g., doesn't
have to stack books she's finished, or put away and put up and straighten
what she just played with: dolls often dumped in naked heaps with their
suitcases of clothes in complete dishevelment (before, located precisely on
hangers). This reflected too in school work.

Allows others to choose clothes for the day without a fuss. Before, very
definite about which dress, etc. she wants today, often the same one for
several days' running. Has current favorites but accepts laundry facts,
substitute suggestions, etc.

March 9, 1971 re-evaluation IAHP: Profile Level: same.
From March 9, 1971 to June 2, 1971:

See School Report this period regarding concepts, etc. (p. 408).

Awareness continues to increase with respect to the outside world's doings.

Fantasy drastically reduced, almost nil. Role-play with teen-age dolls only
occasionally now, as if "forgets" them most of the day, remembers only
when going to bed. New interest in block-buildings especially with steeples,
turrets, tunnels, etc. Tremendous re-interest in set of Matchbox cars with
favorites accompanying her on half-day "trips" and into bed. Back to

book "hobby" again, especially "old" school books. (May be silently read-ing some of this?)

Teacher impressed with J.'s sense of humor, especially "love of the absurd."

Very emphatic pronunciation of everything, such as *it* (with desire to make the *t* heard). From reading and from teacher's requirement, I think, as well as interest in auditory practice?

Started correcting her own mispronunciations. If *peaches* comes out sloppy, slurred, J. says, "No, pea*ches*."

In school, J. needs context of reading material set up for her ahead of time (for better performance): This is a story (list) about . . . seasons or spring or seeds or (category). She seems to be at a loss visually until these auditory clues are given.

June 2, 1971 re-evaluation IAHP: Profile Level: VII marked "poor."
From June 2, 1971 to April 6,, 1972 (No full IAHP re-evaluations this period. See Mobility this period.):

See School Report (p. 413) this school year regarding concepts, etc.

Trip to Switzerland, northern Italy, Austria reinforced old concepts, such as weather and temperature and introduced elementary social studies: ways of other peoples, languages, maps and map-making, transportation, geog-raphy, country versus city, mountain versus valley, river versus lake, etc., as well as other elementary comparisons with respect to food, shelter, clothing—as much, I think, as any third-grader in our school district has in a unit on "Switzerland" and preparatory concepts to that. Reinforced this travel with an hour of "school" most days during the six-weeks' trip, involving her drawings: wall murals, walking map of village, one village to another via road and rail, and homemade book "About Switzerland." Has no concept of crossing huge ocean in airplane, or couldn't care less? No concept of boundaries of countries, but readily grasps fact that in warmer places (southern Switzerland and Italy)—the flora and fauna and houses—look different from those in colder Swiss mountain areas.

An emphasis, albeit informal, was placed on "time" with purchase of her own alarm clock, setting it and referring to it with respect to travel, trains, getting up, going to bed, etc.

Entire six-weeks' trip the best time of her life. Particularly thrilled with churches, the rows and rows of pews to walk between, the stained-glass windows, bell towers (another "time" reinforcement), bathrooms of all kinds, first rides on trains, boats, airplanes, etc. And loved the children who were learning to talk English, a tack we began to take with her (see Language this period) to lower frustration: You are learning to talk English, Grant and I are learning to talk German.

Noticed this trip and thereafter, J. prefers to be with people—home or out—to anything else, including solitary book interest, playing with dolls (interest just about gone). Would rather be in a busy train station or restaurant than on the train (after awhile) or in a quiet tearoom having sweets. (May be a noise need, but did not react in old ways, more a matter of "all the people," I think.)

Hyperactivity, as far as *I* know, including random behavior, is gone.

Proper behavior, when it is required, is no problem in or out of the home. Current interest in "playing baby" (things babyish) needs to be controlled when out (embarrasses *us,* not her): "Play baby at home. High school pool is for older boys and girls, not babies." She laughs and stops "baby" (crying, talking about bottles, milk, doing her leg-kicks wrong and saying "babyish").

Has this one leftover random behavior, looks "stupid": looks at stiffened hand when excited. Also when excited. very happy, goes back to earlier baby reflex: arms flexed, clutched to sides, trembles all over. It's as if she gets so excited (self-consciousness too with this) she will blow her mind unless she settles down, gets back to the real (my hand, my body). As she *does* more and more (experience) she will probably have this kind of postural reflex only for the very big moments as we do?

Music in car (not to exceed one hour a day): might prefer rock station, but acquiesces to mom's decision easily: sweet, classical, country-western.

Interest in telephoning, real and role-playing.

New interest in babies and "babyish" probably from huge interest in ten-year album of pictures of herself, received for birthday 1/22/72. Sentences throughout reflect concepts involving growth, learnings, her program, as well as time and place, etc.

Now wants "laughter," as well as "crying," wants us to role-play with her— everybody cry (tears), everybody laugh. Interest in laughter from album picture in Swiss chalet with J. in bed, next to Grant in bed (not sleeping— laughing—many a night, drawing reprimands from me).

Has "picked up" covering mouth when coughing and other niceties, but does not understand concept of "Excuse me" to interrupt (just interrupts).

Role-plays "school" and "teacher" a lot before she goes to sleep at night with appropriate vocalization, but reflecting nothing regarding behaviors, rather about "doing next" and "learning."

Prefers conversation to bedtime stories, beginning after she received the birthday album, but loves *Heidi* and books about school.

April 6, 1972 re-evaluation IAHP (First full re-evaluation since June 2, 1971): Profile Level: same.

. . . She continues to show sophistication in articulation and speech, and is doing well in basic academic studies. Her general responsiveness continually improves, tantrums appear to be less, and hyperactivity has reduced. . . .

Development of Tactile Competence

January 25, 1965 initial evaluation: The New York Hospital (by Mary Lawrence, RPT): Doman-Delacato Developmental Profile Level: IV marked "poor"; with II and III noted "lower right."

. . . Responds to pain stimulus well in all extremities except right lower. Same for nice sensation of tickling. . . . Has the tactile understanding of third dimension in objects which appear to be flat . . . [Also "Babinski on the left."]

From February 14, 1965 to May 1, 1965:

Notices what she creeps over (if new or different, stops and examines).

Very interested in occluding ears (alternately) against hair. (See Auditory this period.)

Reacts to differences in floor surfaces (rug, wood, slate, tile, concrete); stops, looks, or lies down and brushes hand across while "resting."

Wipes cornstarch in quick back-forth and circular swishes on patterning table; does same with wetness when washed. (Think this is more a "tactile fun" than visual copying of mother's wipes.)

Much zip after salt-glo bath to body; notices salt, alcohol sting on raw places.

Knows outdoors from indoors now (breeze difference?).

Gives herself hot-water bottle and tuning-fork program during floor play.

Alternates left and right arms, legs touching and rubbing wall surfaces: brick, sheetrock, pegboard (floor play).

Alternates left and right elbows touching and tapping wall surfaces (floor play).

Alternates left and right feet touching wool bedspreads (floor play).

Alternates left and right sides (shoulder to hip) touching and rubbing wool bedspreads while in creep stance. Feels and rubs against pegboard wall the same way, alternating both sides.

Alternates lying prone with balancing on a side; involves both sides with this. ("Practices" this when outrigger is off, during breaks between crawls.) Also rubs back against brick and door frames in sit!

"Practices" pivoting on rug, slate, concrete floors.

Awareness of thumbs against rims (highchair, plastic table shelf, feeding dish, etc.): i.e., thumb inside or rim, fingers on outer side; "practices" a lot.

Awareness of backs of fingers: pinches each in sequence, first one hand, then the other.

Feels inside of objects to see if empty (or just to feel inside?): purse, containers. Puts hat on head with more precision than in December when she started this with Stuart's ball cap (maybe arm reach is better).

May 1, 1965 re-evaluation by Mary Lawrence: Profile Level: IV O.K. now.

. . . She has good vital and gnostic sensation on all extremities with a slight slowness in response in the right lower extremity. She has good tactile understanding of the third dimension. . . .

From May 1, 1965 to June 22, 1965:

No program for two to three weeks (mother's illness).

In prone position, rubs heels, big toes, medial sides of feet together (like a fly!).

New interest in tapping bottom of right foot while lying supine, knees up.

Rug burn more on left leg than right at inner knee area (uses left knee more in crawl push).

Tops of both feet are dirty, so feet must be trailing more in creeping.

Much tactile play in backyard.

New interest in edges of puzzle pieces.

Stereognosis: identifies pencil from pencil flashlight and spoon from fork by touch alone (bag game).

June 22, 1965 re-evaluation by Mary Lawrence: Profile Level: same.

. . . The tactile identification program is slow with some inconsistency, which makes it difficult to evaluate.

From June 22, 1965 to September 2, 1965:

Felt mosquito bite on right leg and scratched it. Is that leg completely equal to other one in sensation now?

Much play on sand, pine needles, against blueberry bushes; knows the moment her hand touches root, stops, examines.

Stereognosis: identifies by touch alone (objects in bag) medium-size objects (ABC block, from large wooden dice with beveled corners, from wooden barrel, etc.), right hand better than left.

More of that body-discovery stuff? Spanks *right* leg with *right* hand. Looks back over shoulder, then moves *right* leg. Turns to other side: spanks left, thinks (left?), looks *left,* moves *left* leg. Mostly outdoors does this.

Lifts foot up and down, knees up, lying on back. (See Mobility this period.)

September 2, 1965 re-evaluation by Mary Lawrence: Profile Level: V marked "poor."

. . . She has shown improvement in tactile differentiation and hand skills generally . . .

October 25, 1965 initial evaluation IAHP: Profile Level: IV left, V right.

Dominance [tactile]: right.

From October 28, 1965 to February 8, 1966:

> Very little program this period.
>
> Can turn pages without looking (index finger midway down page).
>
> Stereognosis: identifies medium-size objects without looking; both hands good now.

February 8, 1966 re-evaluation IAHP: Profile Level: VI (both hands).

> Bilateral improvement seen in stereognosis.
>
> Dominance [tactile]: right.

From February 8, 1966 to June 1, 1966:

> Patterning modified (a) to be done on rug surface; (b) foot to be inverted to brush *bottom*.
>
> Using index finger only to feel fabrics.
>
> Interested in rubbing bottom of foot on rug while sitting or kneeling on one knee (alternates to "practice" both).

June 1, 1966 re-evaluation IAHP: Profile Level: same.

> Stereognosis—identification faster, although not more refined.
>
> Dominance [tactile]: right.

From June 1, 1966 to October 18, 1966:

> Patterning modified to include inverting foot, brushing big toe.
>
> Stereognosis: very good at this—usually four in bag of similar but unlike small size objects, including a supply of charms from dentist-friend. Can distinguish charm-size skillet from clock (painted face) from record (painted label), all same metal material. Brothers amazed, think "it's hard." Children come by to play this game with J.'s materials. Also adding discs from games to charm-size record, J. doing. But she wants things she can "do with" afterwards, like jack for spinning. Therefore, very uninterested in coin differentiation even with my attempts at spinning quarter or penny or whatever she got right.
>
> Magnificent weeks in Maine with its superb outdoor tactile stuff.

October 18, 1966 re-evaluation IAHP: Profile Level: VII marked "poor."

> Stereognosis improved.
>
> Dominance [tactile]: same.

From October 18, 1966 to January 3, 1967:

> Stereognosis: can differentiate fur, wool, velvet; could do more (my error, lousy program this period).
>
> Started feeling fabrics on her own (floor play); brushes index finger over bedspreads, etc., then feels carpet, then back to bedspread.

January 3, 1967 re-evaluation IAHP: Profile Level: same.

> Stereognosis improved.

From January 3, 1967 to June 12, 1967:

No program for three months from 1/7/67 to 3/30/67; convalescence from burn injury.

Patterning modified to swing arm way out (full extension in recovery phase).

Looked at so many books this convalescence period; began to turn pages adult-fashion—top right corner, hand slides down as page is flipped. Also started this period to turn pages in a perusing way, flipping pages using thumb (in a holding way to allow only one page to turn)—fast and perfect, by touch alone. Also good stop control in thumb with this. (See Manual Competence this period.)

Will now let me play "This Little Piggy Went to Market" with her toes.

Stereognosis: differentiates by touch alone fur, wool, velvet, net, dotted swiss. Am now working on jersey, cotton, corduroy, cheesecloth.

Feeling all fabrics with thumb opposed to index finger, rubbing between, like thrifty housewife in bargain basement.

June 12, 1967 re-evaluation IAHP: Profile Level: same.

Stereognosis better—still room for improvements.

From June 12, 1967 to September 6, 1967:

Patterning do's: brush hands and feet harder; keep torso and head in line.

Very interested in fabrics, started holding them in bed in dark, asks for two or three favorites at bedtime. Jersey the big favorite.

Saw East Room's brocade love seat in "White House" article in *Geographic* magazine and said, "Bo-cade"! (See Visual Competence this period.)

Stereognosis: Differentiates eleven fabrics by touch alone. No coin program —not interested in "man" (heads) or "house" (tails); how do you do it? Has sense of "bumpy" brocade, but coin bumpiness not interesting to her.

September 6, 1967 re-evaluation IAHP: Profile Level: same.

Good stereognosis.

September 6, 1967 to November 8, 1967:

Hates coins program for stereognosis, but interested in feeling "scratchy" side (tails) in dark; soon throws out of bed and asks for jersey, favorite fabric still.

November 8, 1967 re-evaluation IAHP: Profile Level: same.

Stereognosis is fairly good.

From November 8, 1967 to March 26, 1968: (*Note:* 1/16/68 appointment cancelled):

No program from 11/15/67 to 12/26/67. Impetigo from possible strep infection.

No tactile notes this period.

March 26, 1968 re-evaluation IAHP: Profile Level: same.

Stereognosis was fair . . . dislikes final test here. [Coins.]

From March 26, 1968 to June 28, 1968:

> Stereognosis: no coins program yet; no fabric program in six to nine months, but now feels clothes, especially visitors' a lot.
>
> Likes tracing finger on glitter-rough numbers ("counting" concept with crawl-box round trips).

June 28, 1968 re-evaluation IAHP: Profile Level: same.

> Good stereognosis.

From June 28, 1968 to October 1, 1968:

> Stereognosis: coins a few times, but very uninterested. Painted half-dollar eagle with nail polish, also Kennedy "head"; showed pictures of eagles; just not interested even in looking. What did IAHP say about getting a coin machine?

October 1, 1968 re-evaluation IAHP: Profile Level: same.

> Parents report stimulation with coins (occasional program). Jane much too distracted today, uncooperative. Suggest program change.

From October 1, 1968 to February 18, 1969 (12/12/68 evaluation not done because of hip injury in fall the night before):

> Patterning modified to include feeling of stretch (extension) at knee when leg is relaxed enough to allow it.
>
> No stereognosis program, but made a book of fabrics she is quite uninterested in.
>
> Started school year with painting, but hates messy hands or any paint dribbles anywhere; very perfectionist about "messes."
>
> In school, using ABC's in sand, felt, plastic, cardboard, paper; using numbers in these tactile ways too.
>
> Now likes to paint with water, but prefers brush to finger.
>
> Playdough and clay occasionally.

February 18, 1969 re-evaluation IAHP: Profile Level: same.
February 18, 1969 to May 7, 1969:

> No program except art media, sand and glitter letters, etc.
>
> Tactile *letters* now instead of numbers to denote crawl-box round trips, since J. writes all numbers now.

May 7, 1969 re-evaluation IAHP: Profile Level: same.
From May 7, 1969 to July 23, 1969:

> Likes dressing up in costumes, other people's clothes: reinforced fabric interest between sequences with things of velvet, corduroy, satin, lace, dotted swiss, wool, silk, denim, net, taffeta, and cheesecloth.
>
> Playdough, clay a little. (Sequence schedule too tight for extras.)

July 23, 1969 re-evaluation IAHP: Profile Level: VII O.K. now.

> . . . There has been a definite tactile improvement . . .

Note: Since Jane now "normal" in tactile competence, no notes follow this date.

THE DOMAN-DELACATO DEVELOPMENTAL PROFILE, by Glenn J. Doman, Carl H. Delacato, Ed. D., Robert J. Doman, M.D.

	Brain Stage	Time Frame	Visual Competence	Auditory Competence	Tactile Competence	Mobility	Language	Manual Competence
VII	Sophisticated Cortex	Superior 36 Mon. Average 72 Mon. Slow 108 Mon.	Reading words using a dominant eye consistent with the dominant hemisphere	Understanding of complete vocabulary and proper sentences with proper ear	Tactile identification of objects using a hand consistent with hemispheric dominance	Using a leg in a skilled role which is consistent with the dominant hemisphere	Complete vocabulary and proper sentence structure	Using a hand to write which is consistent with the dominant hemisphere
VI	Primitive Cortex	Superior 22 Mon. Average 36 Mon. Slow 70 Mon.	Identification of visual symbols and letters within experience	Understanding of 2000 words and simple sentences	Description of objects by tactile means	Walking and running in complete cross pattern	2000 words of language and short sentences	Bimanual function with one hand in a dominant role
V	Early Cortex	Superior 13 Mon. Average 18 Mon. Slow 36 Mon.	Differentiation of similar but unlike simple visual symbols	Understanding of 10 to 25 words and two word couplets	Tactile differentiation of similar but unlike objects	Walking with arms freed from the primary balance role	10 to 25 words of language and two word couplets	Cortical opposition bilaterally and simultaneously
IV	Initial Cortex	Superior 8 Mon. Average 12 Mon. Slow 22 Mon.	Convergence of vision resulting in simple depth perception	Understanding of two words of speech	Tactile understanding of the third dimension in objects which appear to be flat	Walking with arms used in a primary balance role most frequently at or above shoulder height	Two words of speech used spontaneously and meaningfully	Cortical opposition in either hand

III	Midbrain	Superior 4 Mon. Average 7 Mon. Slow 12 Mon.	Appreciation of detail within a configuration	Appreciation of meaningful sounds	Appreciation of gnostic sensation	Creeping on hands and knees, culminating in cross pattern creeping	Creation of meaningful sounds	Prehensile grasp
II	Pons	Superior 1 Mon. Average 2.5 Mon. Slow 4 Mon.	Outline perception	Vital response to threatening sounds	Perception of vital sensation	Crawling in the prone position culminating in cross pattern crawling	Vital crying in response to threats to life	Vital release
I	Medulla and Cord	Superior Birth to .5 Average Birth to 1.0 Slow Birth to 1.5	Light reflex	Startle reflex	Babinski reflex	Movement of arms and legs without bodily movement	Birth cry and crying	Grasp reflex